CAMBRIDGE LATIN AMERICAN STUDIES

54

THE MEXICAN REVOLUTION

VOLUME I

THE MEXICAN REVOLUTION

VOLUME 1

Porfirians, Liberals and Peasants

ALAN KNIGHT

Department of History, University of Essex

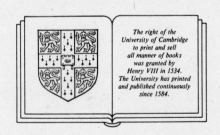

The right of the
University of Cambridge
to print and sell
all manner of books
was granted by
Henry VIII in 1534.
The University has printed
and published continuously
since 1584.

CAMBRIDGE UNIVERSITY PRESS

Cambridge

London   New York   New Rochelle

Melbourne   Sydney

Published by the Press Syndicate of the University of Cambridge
The Pitt Building, Trumpington Street, Cambridge CB2 1RP
32 East 57th Street, New York, NY 10022, USA
10 Stamford Road, Oakleigh, Melbourne 3166, Australia

First published 1986
Reprinted 1987

Printed in Great Britain at the University Press, Cambridge

British Library cataloguing in publication data

Knight, Alan
The Mexican revolution. – (Cambridge Latin American studies; 54)
Vol. 1: Porfirians, liberal and peasants.
1. Revolutions – Mexico – History – 19th century
2. Mexico – Politics and government – 1810–1821
I. Title
972'.03   F1232

Library of Congress cataloguing in publication data

Knight, Alan, 1946–
The Mexican Revolution.
(Cambridge Latin American studies; 54–55)
Bibliography: p.
Includes index.
Contents: v. 1. Porfirians, liberals, and peasants.
1. Mexico – History – Revolution, 1910–1920.
I. Title. II. Series.
F1234.K65 1986   972.08   85–12798

ISBN 0 521 24475 7 (volume 1)
ISBN 0 521 26651 3 (volume 2)

To Alex, Henry, Katy and Lidia

Tezcatlipoca: he was considered a true god, whose abode was everywhere – in the land of the dead, on earth [and] in heaven. When he walked on the earth he quickened vice and sin. He introduced anguish and affliction. He brought discord among people, wherefore he was called 'the enemy on both sides'. He created, he brought down all things. He cast his shadow on one, he visited one with all the evils which befall men; he mocked, he ridiculed men. But he sometimes bestowed riches – wealth, heroism, valour, position of dignity, rulership, nobility, honour.

Bernardo Sahagún, Florentine Codex, Book 1.

Contents

Preface

Like its subject, the Mexican Revolution, this book developed in a way that was unforeseen and unplanned. Indeed, it is unlikely that it would have been written at all had the conventional criteria which govern the production of academic history been followed. It is unfashionably long, ambitious in scope and, perhaps, narrative in form. It began with a commitment made years ago in days of post-graduate *naïveté* and financial constraint, when the proposed result was a succinct history of the Mexican Revolution, based on secondary sources. Already, however, my doctoral research (which focussed on the role of foreign interests in the Revolution) was generating a wealth of surplus material and prompting broader questions concerning the nature of the Revolution. In consequence, the book grew and grew; its 'data-base', primary and secondary, expanded; its objectives became more ambitious. Ultimately, I sought to write a history of the Revolution, during its armed phase, which, while it could not be called definitive (few if any histories are) was at least comprehensive, national, original and, perhaps, the closest to a definitive, unitary (i.e., single author) history that we have. Whether these aims have been achieved others must judge; but I would plead that the aims justified the considerable length of the work.

This undertaking required a combination of analysis and narrative, of primary and secondary sources. As regards the first, what Hexter terms the 'rhetoric of history' – I see no intrinsic superiority of one form over another. It all depends on the job in hand. I have therefore shifted from narrative to analysis and back again; I have made brief excursions into 'theory'; and I have ventured global comparisons with other revolutions and rebellions. In doing so, I have probably pleased no-one entirely, and offended everybody some-what. The aggressively numerate, in particular, may regret the relative absence of statistical material. This is deliberate: I share Chevalier's scepticism about much of the statistical evidence for this period, and E. P. Thompson's belief that, especially as regards popular radicalism, the usefulness of statistical evidence is easily exaggerated. Cliometricians may therefore come away disappointed. So, too, may Mexican or Latin American historiographical nationalists (those, fortunately few in number, who believe that Mexican and Latin American history is best avoided by foreigners working from foreign sources). For the reader will soon appreciate that, while abundant Mexican primary sources have been used (especially national collections: Gobernación, Trabajo, the Madero, Robles Domínguez and Carranza Archives etc.), these are probably outweighed by foreign sources: the French Archives des Affaires Etrangères, the British Foreign Office and, above all, the American State Department. In part, this derives from the unplanned pattern of research: my doctoral work introduced me to consular reports which, it became clear, were a magnificent source not just for the history of foreign interests in Mexico, but also for the history of the Revolution in all its facets. Accomplished local historians, like Falcón and Ankerson, have shown how consular reports – especially American consular reports – can provide a stream of valuable historical information. I have used the same sources (still relatively unexploited) to build up a national picture. Of course, this source, like all sources, involves bias and must be used judiciously. But in many respects the bias of foreign observers (especially those based in the provinces, far from the high politics of Mexico City) is clearer, hence less distorting, than that of Mexican observers and participants who, of course, were rarely in the business of filing regular reports to some external agency. Similarly, I found the *Mexican Herald* to be, for all its rank editorial prejudice, more useful than the shackled Huertista press for the years 1913–14. If unplanned, therefore, my reliance on foreign sources is not regretted. Furthermore, the picture these sources reveal is corroborated, not negated, by the extensive Mexican archives I have also used. The two are complementary, not antithetical.

These primary sources form the basis for much of this study. But in addition, I have tried to incorporate much, if not all, the published work on the Revolution, which has recently proliferated, and which makes the study of modern Mexican history so profoundly stimulating. The memoirs of old participants, the solid narratives of an earlier generation of historians (neither of which should be disdained as sources), have given way to highly scholarly monographs, many of them devoted to regional, local and 'micro' history. These have been immensely valuable and without their contribution (which I have all too briefly and partially recognised in the acknowledgements) this study would not have been possible. Yet, when all is said and done, the Revolution was a *national* phenomenon; it stretched from Tijuana to Tapachula, from the Río Grande to the Río Hondo; it touched the lives of all Mexicans. It therefore deserves a *national* history. And, without a national history, it is impossible to gauge whether local studies are typical or aberrant.

My basic aim, therefore, has been to write a national history which both takes into account local and regional variations, and also delves below the level of high politics and diplomacy. The latter cannot be neglected, but nor can they be understood *in vacuo*. There can be no high politics without a good deal of low politics. This is particularly true since, I believe, the Revolution was a genuinely popular movement and thus an example of those relatively rare episodes in history when the mass of the people profoundly influenced events. At such times, national politics are only explicable in terms of local and popular pressures. By a strange irony, this view seems to have become increasingly unfashionable, particularly in those recent monographs on which I have heavily relied. True, Marxist historians (of abstract bent) still assert the central role of the masses in the Revolution, but they often assert more than they illustrate. Many recent historians of the Revolution, on the other hand, have deployed their considerable research and learning to show that the Revolution was less an autonomous, agrarian and popular revolution than a series of chaotic, careerist episodes, in which popular forces were, at best, the instruments of manipulative caciques, of aspiring bourgeois or petty bourgeois leaders. For these historians, the Revolution is not the great and heroic popular movement typified by Zapata and described by Tannenbaum, but the more sordid vehicle of class and individual ambition driven by Calles and sketched by Jean Meyer. In all this, I am an unashamed conservative, or anti-revisionist. That is, I believe that Tannenbaum and his generation grasped the basic character of the 1910 Revolution as a popular, agrarian movement – the precursor, the necessary precursor, of the *étatiste* 'revolution' of post-1920. Of course, such interpretations are not entirely antithetical, they hinge upon questions of emphasis and degree; yet questions of degree which are not amenable to precise, positivist measurement. We cannot do a head count of 'agrarian' rebels, nor is it clear how many 'agrarian' rebels must be found before the Revolution counts as 'agrarian'. By way of defending my view of the 1910 Revolution as fundamentally popular and agrarian, I can only point to the evidence presented in these pages (itself a sample drawn from a larger stock of evidence) and hope that it convinces.

In presenting this view (and others) I have sometimes taken issue with other historians working in the field. Such arguments, I stress, are never *ad hominem*, and are designed solely to clarify my position *vis-à-vis* that of others. To the extent that particular authorities are 'interrogated', it is precisely because they present cogent arguments which demand serious attention. Vapid accounts can be more easily ignored. And, though I may convince myself that my arguments and evidence are superior, there will no doubt be many who disagree, many who, in turn, cap my arguments and evidence with their own. For, necessarily, I have had to skate over some topics (the diplomacy of the revolution, perhaps) and, in places, hazard conclusions which are tentative or downright risky. If these are seized upon and corrected, so much the better. A few hostages may be given, so long as the whole campaign is not thereby lost. As for the campaign itself, it remains to be seen whether subsequent history will absolve me.

Alella, Spain, July 1984 ALAN KNIGHT

Acknowledgements

The origins of this book date back many years, and its final publication now affords an opportunity to thank those institutions and individuals who have helped me in its conception and completion (without, of course, incurring any responsibility for its errors and defects, which are mine alone).

Professor Michael Cherniavsky first encouraged my interest in history, which was the initial step down the road, and the late Professor Jack Gallagher, while teaching me British imperial history in his inimitable fashion, pointed out the attractions and opportunities of the path I eventually took, that of Latin American history. That path taken, I undertook my doctoral thesis and did much of the preliminary research for this book at Nuffield College, Oxford, where I was a graduate student and research fellow. I therefore owe a large debt to the Warden and Fellows of Nuffield, especially the late Philip Williams and Lawrence Whitehead, who took a lively, constructive interest in my early Mexican studies. My second, major, institutional debt is to the History Department of the University of Essex, which gave me research time and resources to continue and complete the work; in addition, the Nuffield Foundation, the Twenty-One Foundation, and the British–Mexican Society generously gave me grants for travel and research in Mexico and the USA. Thirdly, I must thank the Cambridge University Press which accepted and carried through the publication of this unfashionably *magnum opus*. In particular, I would like to thank Malcolm Deas, under whose editorship the manuscript was first considered, read and accepted; his successor and my colleague, Simon Collier, who was a scrupulous and sensitive editor at the final stage; and Elizabeth Wetton and her staff, especially Sheila McEnery, who were unfailingly helpful and efficient.

Many individual debts have also accumulated. Over many years I have derived great benefit from both reading Professor Friedrich Katz's work on Mexico and, when possible, discussing our mutual research interests. Since our initial meeting over tea in Sanborns in 1970, these discussions, though infrequent, have been extremely valuable and remarkably unaffected by differences in our respective statuses or interpretations. I have also benefited greatly from the research, opinions and encouragement of many fellow-students of Mexican history: Leif Adelsen, Tom Benjamin, Romana Falcón, Javier Garciadiego Dantón, Linda Hall, Gil Joseph, Eugenia Meyer, Bill Meyers, Segundo Portilla and Asgar Simonsen. And I would particularly wish to acknowledge the support of the small but select group which has sustained the study of Mexican history in Britain in recent years: David Brading, Brian Hamnett, Tony Morgan, Simon Miller, Guy Thompson, and, above all, Barry Carr, whose help dates back to the beginning, and Ian Jacobs and Dudley Ankerson, whose sure grasp of local history has been invaluable. I have also, on my travels, benefited from the help and hospitality of the Grant-Suttie and Cherniavsky families of Washington DC; of the Granel and Portilla families, Enrique Márquez, Francisco Suárez, and Laura Salinas of Mexico City; and, last but by no means least, Juan and Lidia Lozano Martín of Alella, Spain, who allowed me unstinting use of their house, *bodega* and study, where most of the final version of this book was written up. Finally, I wish to thank those to whom the book is dedicated who − though they did not exactly speed its completion − certainly gave me valuable insights into what one author has called the 'revolutionary personality'.

Glossary

acasillado	resident peon
acomodado	privileged resident peon
adicto	unconditional supporter (of regime, faction)
administrador	estate manager
agrarismo	agrarian reform movement or ideology
alcabala	internal tariff
alcalde	mayor
Anti-Re-eleccionismo	see *Re-elección*
arriero	muleteer
atropello	outrage, abuse, arbitrary act (especially political)
ayuntamiento	town council
baldío	of land: lacking private title
barranca	gorge
barrio	quarter (of town, village)
boleta	(voting) slip
borracho	drunk
bracero	labourer; especially migrant labourer to the US
bronco	wild, untamed; hence, of the Yaquis, independent
burro	mule
cabecera	'head town'; seat of local government
cabecilla	local revolutionary leader
cacicazgo	example of cacique rule
cacique	local political boss
caciquismo	boss system of politics
cafetal	coffee plantation
campesino/campesinado	peasant/peasantry; rural labourer
canario	native of the Canary Islands
cantina/cantinero	saloon/saloon-keeper
capitación	head tax
capitalino	native of Mexico City
caporal	estate foreman (especially on cattle ranch)

cargadilla	addition made to a (peon's) debt
casco	main buildings of an estate
catrín	dandy, smart dresser, hence 'city slicker'
caudillo	political leader based on armed clientele
cerrado	dour, taciturn (usually pejorative)
charro	of dress, appearance: relating to the typical cowboy of central Mexico
chegomista	adherent of the Juchiteco cacique, 'Che' Gómez
chilapeño	straw hat
chilero	native of sierra, especially Sinaloa/Durango
chusma	horde, rabble, gang
Científico	adherent and apologist of Positivism and Porfirismo; hence, a minion of the old regime
cofradía	confraternity; local, religious association of laymen
Coloso del Norte	'Colossus of the North'; the United States
comerciante	merchant, businessman
compadre (compadrazgo)	God-parent; hence, friend, crony (relationship of)
compañero	friend, ally
congregación	small rural community; hamlet
Convencionista	supporter of the Aguascalientes Convention, 1914–15
Cristiada	Catholic revolt against the state, 1926–9
cuadrilla	work gang (of peons)
cuartel	barracks
cuartelazo	barracks revolt
Cuerpo Rural	rural corps: mounted police
cura	parish priest
curro	smart (gentleman); cf. *catrín*
Defensa Social	community self-defence force
disponible	available; 'up for grabs'
ejido	land corporately owned by community; hence land conferred under the agrarian reform programme
enganchado	worker hired, maybe held, by *enganche* system
enganchador	labour contractor
enganche	'hook': advance payment made to secure worker
entreguismo	handing over; hence, 'selling out' (of Mexico to foreigners)
extranjero	foreigner
finca (finquero)	rural property (owner), especially Chiapas
fundo legal	town or village site
gachupín	Spaniard (pejorative)
gallinero	chicken run; hence, backyard

gavilla	gang (of bandits, rebels)
gente	people, followers, rank-and-file
gente decente	respectable folk, middle and upper class
gente de razón	whites/mestizos, townspeople
gira (electoral)	(political campaign) tour
Gobernación	Ministry of the Interior
gobernador	state governor
gobiernista	supporter of the government
gringo	North American
guanajuatense	native of Guanajuato
guayule (guayulero)	rubber-producing shrub (collector of)
guerrillero	(military) irregular
hacienda (*hacendado*)	rural estate (owner of)
Hacienda	Ministry of Finance
hidrocálido	native of Aguascalientes
hijo (del país)	son (of the locality)
huaraches	sandals; peasant footwear
indigenismo	movement/philosophy advocating the protection of the Indian and Indian culture
interinato	interim regime (of de la Barra, 1911)
jarabe	popular dance (especially western Mexico)
jefe	boss, leader
jefe político (jefatura)	political boss, prefect (prefecture)
juez (de paz)	justice (of the peace)
ladino	white/mestizo (as against indian)
latifundio (latifundista)	great estate (owner)
lechuguilla	fibrous plant, especially cultivated in San Luis
leva	press-gang
licenciado	roughly, graduate
machetazo	machete blow
macho	aggressively 'masculine', violent, generally unpleasant
maestro	schoolteacher
manco	one-armed
manso	'tame', docile; of Yaquis, integrated into the mestizo state and economy (cf. *bronco*)
mapache	lit., racoon, a Chiapas rebel
máquina loca	'mad' locomotive: driverless locomotive, mined and used as offensive weapon
mayordomo	hacienda foreman
mesón	lodging house

mestizo	'half-caste', of mixed Spanish–Indian ancestry (but see Chapter 1, People)
milpa	corn plot
mordida	bribe
Morelense	native of Morelos
muchachito	young lad
muera . . .	death to . . .
mujeriego	womanising
norteño	northerner
novio(-a)	fiancé(e)
obrero(-a)	(female) worker
oficial mayor	lieutenant-governor
ojo parado	wall-eye
paseo	walk, Sunday evening promenade
patria chica	'little fatherland'; i.e., local region eliciting quasi-patriotic allegiance
patrón	boss, patron
pelado	'skint', hence, plebeian, uneducated
peon	rural labourer, sometimes endebted
peonaje	rural labourers (collectively); or the labour system, often associated with debt
poblano	native of Puebla
político	politician
Porfirian/Porfirista	adherent of Porfirio Díaz
Porfiriato	the regime of Porfirio Díaz, hence the period 1876–1911
Porra	large stick, club; hence gang of political thugs
porteño	port-dweller (e.g., inhabitant of Guaymas)
Potosino	native of San Luis Potosí
presidente municipal	municipal president; mayor
pronunciamiento	(military) rebellion
propietario	property-owner; or incumbent, usually of elected office (e.g., deputy; cf. *suplente*)
pueblo	village; or 'the people'
pulque	alcoholic drink obtained from maguey plant
ranchero	owner/tenant of *rancho*; smallholder
rancho	farm, sometimes implies homestead, but can also constitute a small hacienda
realeño	privileged peon (Morelos)
Re-elección	practice of repeated political re-election, hence *immobilisme*, associated with the Porfiriato (cf. *Anti-Re-eleccionismo*)

reivindicación	restorative demand, claim, act (usually agrarian)
reparto (de tierras)	distribution, share-out (of land)
rural(es)	member(s) of *Cuerpos Rurales*
sarape	heavy shawl, blanket
señorito	young gentleman (often derogatory)
serrano	mountain-dweller, highlander; adherent of local autonomist movement (see Chapter 3, The sierra).
sierra	mountain range
sinverguencista	shameless person; rebel lacking political credibility
sufragio efectivo	'effective suffrage', i.e., a real vote
suplente	stand-in for (usually elected) office-holder (cf. *propietario*)
suriano	southerner; specifically, adherent of Zapatismo
tapatío	native of Jalisco
temporal	rain-fed agricultural land (non-irrigated)
tequila	liquor distilled from maguey juice
terrenos baldíos	see *baldío*
tienda de raya	company or hacienda store
tierra caliente	hot country; tropical lowlands
tierra fría	cold country; high plateau and mountains
tierra templada	temperate, sub-tropical country, especially the valleys of central Mexico
tinterillo	'ink-pot', hence, village intellectual/scribe/lawyer
torero	bullfighter
transacción	deal, compromise
vale	token, chit, issued by hacienda or company
vaquero	cowboy
vecino	'neighbour'; member of local community
vendepatria	one who 'sells his country'
yori	Yaqui term for whites/mestizos
zacatón	fodder grass; also used for brooms, brushes
zafra	sugar cane harvest
zócalo	main square, especially Mexico City

Abbreviations

GEOGRAPHICAL

Ags.	Aguascalientes
Baja Calif.	Baja California
Camp.	Campeche
Chih.	Chihuahua
Coa.	Coahuila
Col.	Colima
CPD	Ciudad Porfirio Díaz
Dgo	Durango
Gro	Guerrero
Gto	Guanajuato
Hgo	Hidalgo
Jal.	Jalisco
Mex.	Mexico State
Mich.	Michoacán
Mor.	Morelos
Oax.	Oaxaca
Pue.	Puebla
Qro	Querétaro
Sin.	Sinaloa
SLP	San Luis Potosí
Sra	Sonora
Tab.	Tabasco
Tamps.	Tamaulipas
Ver.	Veracruz
Yuc.	Yucatán
Zac.	Zacatecas

POLITICAL

CROM	Confederación Regional Obrera Mexicana
PCN	Partido Católico Nacional

PCP   Partido Constitucional Progresista
PLC   Partido Liberal Constitucionalista
PLM   Partido Liberal Mexicano

ARCHIVAL

AAE   Archives du Ministère des Affaires Etrangères
AARD   Archivo Alfredo Robles Domínguez
AFM   Archivo Francisco I. Madero
AG   Archivo de Gobernación
AJD   Archivo Jorge Denegri
ALB   Archivo León de la Barra
ARC   Archivo Ramón Corral
ARE   Archivo de Relaciones Exteriores
AVC   Archivo Venustiano Carranza
AZ   Archivo Zongólica
CRCFM   Convención Revolucionaria y Correspondencia con Francisco I. Madero
DDCC   *Diario de los debates del congreso constituyente* (see bibliography)
DEAS   Departamento de Etnología y Antropología Social
DHRM   *Documentos Históricos de la Revolución Mexicana* (see bibliography under Fabela)
FO   Foreign Office
MCETA   Mexican Cotton Estates of Tlahualilo Archive
PHO   Programa de Historia Oral, Museo de Antropología e Historia
SD   State Department
SGIA   Samuel Guy Inman Archive
SRE   Secretaría de Relaciones Exteriores
SS   Serie Sonora
STA   Silvestre Terrazas Archive
WWP   Woodrow Wilson Papers

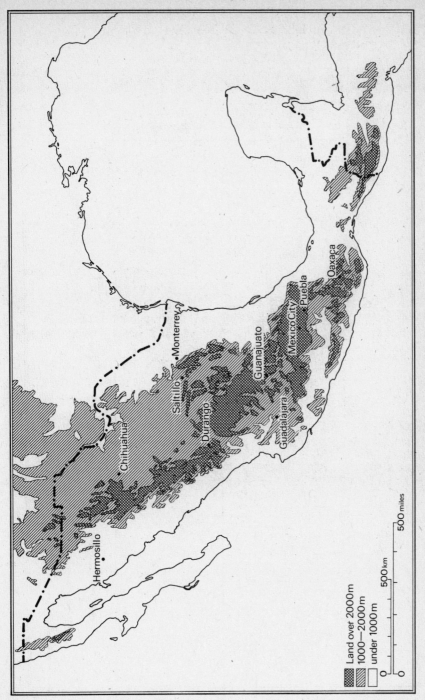

Land over 2000m
1000—2000m
under 1000m

500 miles

500 km

0

Map I Mexico: relief

Hermosillo

Chihuahua

Durango

Saltillo

Monterrey

Guadalajara

Guanajuato

Mexico City

Puebla

Oaxaca

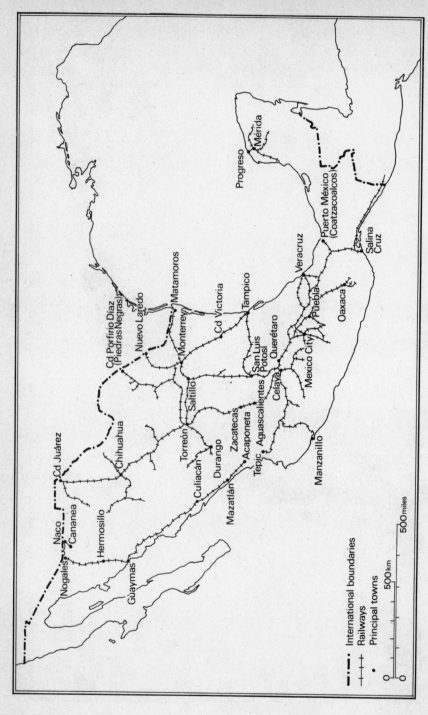

Map 2 Mexico: towns and railways (1910)

Progreso

Mérida

Puerto México
(Coatzacoalcos)

Salina
Cruz

Matamoros

Cd Porfirio Díaz
(Piedras Negras)

Nuevo Laredo

Monterrey

Cd Victoria

Tampico

Veracruz

Puebla

Oaxaca

San Luis
Potosí

Querétaro

Saltillo

Mexico City

Torreón

Zacatecas

Celaya

Aguascalientes

Acaponeta

Culiacán

Durango

Tepic

Manzanillo

Chihuahua

Mazatlán

Cd Juárez

Naco

Cananea

Hermosillo

Nogales

Güaymas

International boundaries

Railways

Principal towns

500 km

500 miles

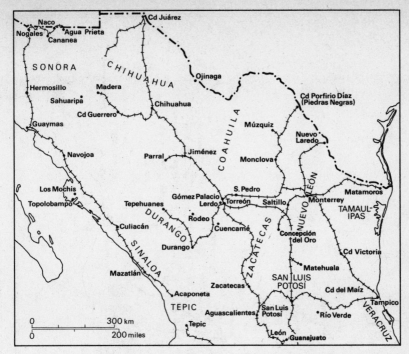

Map 3 Northern Mexico: towns and railways

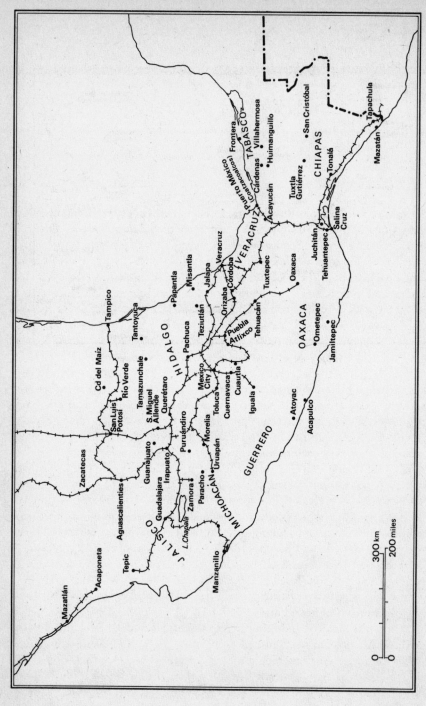

Map 4 Central Mexico: towns and railways

1

𐂷𐂷𐂷𐂷𐂷𐂷𐂷𐂷𐂷𐂷𐂷𐂷𐂷𐂷𐂷𐂷𐂷𐂷𐂷𐂷𐂷𐂷𐂷𐂷𐂷𐂷𐂷𐂷𐂷𐂷𐂷𐂷𐂷𐂷𐂷𐂷𐂷𐂷𐂷

Porfirian Mexico

Histories of the Mexican Revolution traditionally begin with the Centennial celebrations of 1910, the great bonanza laid on to commemorate Mexico's initial rebellion against Spanish rule, an event which happily coincided with Porfirio Díaz's seventh re-election to the presidency. So far, then, this is traditional history. But the Centennial was, above all, a Mexico City affair: the parades and processions, the banquets, the unveiling of monuments and mental asylums were designed to impress Mexico City high society, the press, the diplomatic corps and, perhaps, the fickle Mexico City populace – 'this capital', as an army general put it, 'always full of amusement . . . this people born to amuse itself'.[1] And, by all accounts, they were impressed.[2]

In all this, provincialism had no part, even if the provinces made their gastronomic contribution (a hundred sea-turtles from the Guaymas fisheries, a thousand Río Lerma trout, which formed part of one of the master-chef Sylvain's lavish banquets).[3] Overt provincialism, however, was frowned upon at such cosmopolitan occasions, and strenuous efforts were made to ensure that Indians in their baggy white shirts and drawers were kept off the streets of the capital. Outside Mexico City, it is true, there were attempts to make this, the hundredth anniversary of the Grito de Dolores, something special, and thereby to foster the tender plant of patriotism: the Indian children of Morelos were got up in clean white blouses and had patriotic recitations drummed into them; in Chihuahua and Durango the authorities did their best to combine patriotic enthusiasm and public order during three days of torrential rain.[4] But, probably more typical of most Mexicans' experience in the summer of 1910 was that of San José de Gracia (Mich.), where the Centennial was ignored, and where two years of drought and the appearance of Halley's comet attracted more concern and attention.[5]

Yet the real Mexico, and in particular the Mexico of the Revolution, was provincial Mexico. In some histories the story begins and the metropolitan angle is fixed with the Centennial; from this angle we focus on the comings and goings of revolutionary leaders – boorish, provincial interlopers – in Mexico City, and on the intermittent paranoia of the diplomatic corps, fearful of a repeat of the Peking siege. But the Revolution cannot be comprehended in these terms; unlike its Russian counterpart, it arose in the provinces, established itself in the countryside, and finally conquered an alien and sullen capital.[6] And, unlike its Chinese counterpart, it failed to produce either a vanguard party or a coherent ideology. Rather, in its provincial origins, the Revolution displayed kaleidoscopic variations; often it seemed less a Revolution than a multitude of disparate revolts, some endowed with national aspirations, many purely provincial, but all reflecting local conditions and concerns. The forces thrown up by these revolts concluded regional deals, adopted national political labels, and entered grand, ephemeral coalitions; but, beneath these spreading ramifications, it was the local roots which gave the Revolution its sustenance. And, even as revolt gave way to reconstruction in the years after 1915, the chief problem of the revolutionary victors – newly but precariously installed in Mexico City – was that of imposing their authority on the recalcitrant provinces, whether by conquest or diplomacy. It was a problem which had exercised Porfirio Díaz throughout his long regime.

Thus, to understand the Revolution, it is necessary to look beyond the capital and beneath the major, national leaders; to comprehend something of the diversity of the provinces (the Mexico City saying 'fuera de México, todo es Cuautitlán' – 'outside Mexico City, it's all Cuautitlán' – says more about the *capitalino* mentality than the sameness of the despised provinces).[7] For the Mexico of 1910 was, borrowing Lesley Simpson's phrase, 'many Mexicos', less a nation than a geographical expression, a mosaic of regions and communities, introverted and jealous, ethnically and physically fragmented, and lacking common national sentiments; these sentiments came after the Revolution and were (notwithstanding some theories to the contrary) its offspring rather than its parents. The Porfiriato, it is true, saw trends working towards a more centralised state and national economy (and these trends, though halted in 1910, reasserted themselves after 1915); nevertheless, Mexico on the eve of the Revolution still retained much of its nineteenth-century character as 'a semi-fictitious political entity', a character which the Revolution revealed to an alarming extent.[8] The initial task, therefore, is to depict, in broad strokes, the 'many Mexicos' of 1910, the Mexico beyond Cuautitlán, the human and physical backdrop for the great upheaval which began in that year.

PEOPLE

'Many Mexicos' implied many allegiances. Mexicans, it may be suggested, displayed five kinds of primary allegiance which, taken together, in various combinations, and with no single allegiance necessarily prevailing over all others (even 'in the last analysis'), determined their political conduct during the years of revolution. These were: ethnic, regional, ideological, class and clientelist. Ideological allegiance will figure prominently in chapter two, class in chapter three; the importance of clientelist relations will become apparent at many points. This first chapter concerns itself with two allegiances which were the most visually obvious, if not necessarily the most important: those of ethnicity and region.

Following the conquest, the Spaniards imposed a colonial and clerical hierarchy on the sedentary Indian population, whose members continued to plant corn and beans under new masters, and whose old gods were subsumed into a hybrid Catholicism. Miscegenation between Indian and Spaniard created a spectrum of racial types which the regime sought to classify with bureaucratic precision, creating a colonial 'pigmentocracy'.[9] Though, after Independence, these distinctions became juridically irrelevant, they remained of great social consequence throughout the nineteenth century and beyond.[10] As of 1910, at least a third of the Mexican population was reckoned to be Indian, and a little over a half mestizo. But, not only are Mexican statistics for this period notoriously unreliable; in this case the constituencies they seek to measure are fluid and uncertain. As in the rest of Indo-America, ethnic categories of this sort were socio-cultural, rather than biological; they related to perceived characteristics – language, dress, income, food, literacy and domicile. Such characteristics, and the ethnic status they implied, were subjective and mutable. Pedro Martínez passed for an Indian in Yautepec, but was called a *ladino* (mestizo) in his native Azteca: the uncertainty stemmed partly from perspective, partly from the individual's transitional status.[11]

Individuals could – through the murky process of 'acculturation' – shed Indian attributes and acquire mestizo status; some made great strides down the available – albeit narrow – paths of advancement offered by the army, the Church, and the law. Some, remaining in or returning to their native villages, performed important roles as organisers and propagandists; they became the 'village lawyers', the 'pen-pushers' (*tinterillos*) who acted as intellectual captains of popular revolt.[12] Others broke away from the *patria chica* and rose high in state and national politics: Próspero Cahuantzi, the fat, somnolent Governor of Tlaxcala, seemed a 'delightful Aztec gentleman'; Manuel Alarcón, four times Governor of Morelos, was an Indian 'of plain beginnings'; Policarpo Valenzuela, 'an Indian who was at one time a timber hewer' in the forests of Tabasco, rose not only to govern but also to own a large slice of the same state.[13]

Indian ancestry was no bar to the presidency. Juárez, the liberal hero of the Reform, was a Zapotec (a group known for their enterprising traders and teachers); while Porfirio Díaz, the son of a Mixtec mother, could remember from his childhood the chill fogs which blanketed the mountain villages of the Mixteca Alta, on the summit of the continental divide in Oaxaca.[14] But progress to the presidency wrought necessary changes; with 'acculturation' Indian characteristics were, where possible, removed and, where the characteristics were physical, politely ignored; the Indian was 'whitened'. As an

American of twenty-four years residence in Mexico put it, Porfirio Díaz gave Mexico the strong 'white man's government' which, as an Indian country, it required, therefore – he rationalised – Díaz 'of supposed only one-eighth [sic] Indian' was in fact 'probably all white'.[15]

Yet more important than this process of individual acculturation was the collective, corporate form: the transition – made, for example, by Huatusco (Ver.) in the nineteenth century – from Indian to mestizo status.[16] Acculturation was gradual, it was not unilinear, it was capable of halts and reverses. Yet some consideration of the degree of acculturation experienced by Indian communities is essential in explaining the character – even the very fact – of revolutionary commitment. Some commentators, on hearing the word 'acculturation' reach for their revolvers – the same they have used to pepper old, dualistic scenarios in which 'civilisation', radiating from dynamic, modern, poles, penetrates and 'modernises' the inert, traditional countryside. We may be well rid of such scenarios, but it must be recognised (as even some fervent 'monists' recognise, *sub rosa*) that there were variant forms and degrees of Indian acculturation, which had important historical consequences.

Some communities, while retaining Indian language and mores, were firmly integrated into colonial – later national – society as labourers, taxpayers and subjects; indeed, there may be no contradiction here, for the maintenance of the Indian community was in many cases functional to the survival and prosperity of the hacienda – the two lived in a stable though 'unequal symbiosis'.[17] The villages of Morelos, for example, had co-existed with the sugar plantations since the sixteenth century; travellers, used to the suspicious and taciturn Indians they encountered elsewhere in Mexico, found the people of Morelos more forthcoming, 'distinguished by their obliging manners'.[18] Towns like Tepoztlán – outside the immediate sugar zone, but 'in the heart of Zapatista country' – were key points in the state's network of trade and administration and played an important role in local politics.[19] The Zapotecs of the Isthmus of Tehuantepec, though similarly integrated into the mestizo state and economy, had a record of resistance stretching back through colonial times; they were also reckoned to be 'freer, prouder, more enterprising and vivacious' than other Indian groups.[20]

Elsewhere in Oaxaca the case was different. Few villages had escaped the impact of colonial authority and colonial market relations. But, after the collapse of the cochineal trade in the late eighteenth century, Oaxaca lapsed into subsistence farming and barter trade, and even the opening of the Mexican Southern Railway in 1892 provided only a slow, tortuous and costly means of access from the north. While the regime of the hacienda was established in a few fertile valleys – Cuicatlán, Zaachila, Oaxaca itself – the bulk of the Indian population enjoyed an economic and political independence in proportion to the inaccessibility of their villages and the undesirability of their lands. Many, in fact, possessed abundant land, and agrarian conflicts pitted village against village rather than village against hacienda; groups like the Mije remained 'rabid isolationists' well into the twentieth century.[21]

In such regions political authority was wielded by local caciques whose rule was tolerated and sometimes utilised by a distant central government. The *finqueros* of Chiapas assumed the role of paternalist protectors of Indian lands and communities – thus perpetuating the 'colonial' symbiosis well into the twentieth century; mestizo caciques ruled in the Sierra Juárez of Oaxaca; the old Indian cacique Juan Francisco Lucas travelled by sedan chair through the Puebla sierra around Teziutlán, where he held sway throughout the Porfiriato and where, a member of the Chamber of Deputies pointed out, the Indians had managed to retain a form of vigorous self-government.[22] If such fiefs lay within the interstices of the mestizo state, enjoying a conditional, partial independence, there were other Indian groups who retained a fuller, 'quasi-tribal' freedom, fending off the embrace of the state and the commercial economy. They stood at one end – and a diminishing end – of the spectrum of acculturation, and they had usually parted company with at least a section of the 'tribe' which had succumbed to the embrace. The Chamulas and Lacandones of Chiapas, though being drawn into the Soconusco coffee economy, lived in their scattered highland settlements, where mestizo control was often tenuous and census officials needed an Indian escort if they were to avoid attack.[23] The Huicholes maintained a similar independence, entertaining 'a profound hatred for the mestizos' in the wild country of Tepic; nearby, the Cora Indians of the mountains contrasted with their more 'acculturated' cousins of the lowlands; the Tarahumara of western Chihuahua were similarly divided.[24]

But the best example of this pattern of development was the Yaqui tribe of Sonora, whose resistance to the incursions of whites and mestizos (collectively the *yori* in the Yaqui tongue) gave rise to the protracted Yaqui wars of the Porfiriato. Part of the Yaqui 'nation', dispossessed of its fertile valley lands, became hacienda labourers or urban workers (the American consul at Hermosillo had a Yaqui washerwoman); these were the *manso* (pacified) Yaqui, who had taken the first reluctant steps towards 'acculturation' and *mestizaje*.[25] Another part of the tribe, however, labelled *broncos* or *bravos*, maintained a fierce resistance in the mountains. Both groups played a major part in revolutionary events after 1910, displaying an evident degree of ethnic cohesion, and continuing their ancient struggle under new, political labels, whether in shaky alliance with mestizo forces, or in outright opposition to the *yori* in general.

Over time, however, such ethnic allegiances tended to give way to others – class, ideological, regional and clientelist. As inexorable external pressures compelled tighter integration within the nation and national economy, so the Indian mass merged into the ethnically indeterminate *campesinado*; Mayan Indians became Yucatecan peons; caste identity was supplanted by class identity.[26] For this reason (we might interject at this point) there is little point in attempting analyses of 'mestizo' society, paralleling those of Indian society. For, while the latter has a certain socio-ethnic validity, the former is a chimera. There has been no definable mestizo society – or social personality – only mestizo *campesinos*, mestizo workers, mestizo priests, politics and businessmen, their shared *mestizaje* relevant only in that it collectively differentiated them from the Indian. Hence, the thumbnail portrait of the mestizo penned by Eric Wolf and taken up by others – the rootless, *macho*, power-hungry mestizo, 'relegated to the edges of society . . . belong(ing) to a social shadow world', prone to drink, fantasy and gambling – is at best a crude national stereotype, of dubious validity.[27] At the same time, the diametrically opposite image of the mestizo propagated by Molina Enríquez (the mestizo as the higher racial synthesis, the quintessential Mexican, the carrier of the country's destiny) is of interest as a theme in Porfirian and revolutionary thought, linked to other integrative, nationalist myths, but it has no validity as a concept for historical inquiry.[28]

In 1910 the transition from ethnic to alternative allegiances was very far from complete; hence ethnicity figured as an important factor in the Revolution, sometimes complementing these allegiances, sometimes competing with them; and in doing so, it helped determine revolutionary commitments. The Zapatista and Yaqui rebellions, for example, obeyed common agrarian causes, yet they assumed different modes of expression – the first steeped in liberal, patriotic tradition, politically articulate, and nationally aware (if not nationally effective),the second, fundamentally atavistic and anti-national. Similar distinctions may be noted among those rebel movements which I shall categorise as *serrano*. If, later in this book, it is the common causes of such rebellions which are stressed, it is worth noting at the outset the different degrees and modes of acculturation which characterised, say, the Zapatistas and Yaquis, and which in turn determined the manner of their revolutionary commitment.

Indian social organisation displayed certain recurrent features. It exalted the *patria chica* above the national state which, for most Indian groups, was at best a remote figment, at worst an arbitrary oppressor. Hence Indian movements were fiercely parochial: many – like the Chontal/Mixtec pueblo of San Bartolo (Oax.) – 'seemed to have their municipality on the brain', outsiders found them *cerrado* (locked up, introverted) and their social organisation 'very clannish'.[29] This exclusivism extended to other Indian tribes (there was no Pan-Indianism), even to neighbouring communities of common ethnic origin. Hans Gadow arrived at Huilotepec, a Zapotec village in Oaxaca, riding a Huavi ox-cart, accompanied by a Mexicano guide; but 'the Zapotecs did not care for the Huavi, would not even allow them into the house, and . . . the Mexicano hated the Zapotecs'.[30] Hence tribes could be pitted against each other: Pima against Yaqui, Zapotec against Mexicano.[31] Inter-village disputes were endemic: among the people of Morelos, the Maya of Yucatán, the highland communities of Oaxaca. Sometimes land was at issue, sometimes (as in the conflict between Chan Kom and Ebtun) political authority; some feuds had been going on for so long that their original rationale seemed lost in the mists of time, even though the feud still prospered.[32] There were also cases of intra-village conflict between rival *barrios*. When the Revolution came, factional allegiances tended to follow these ancient fault lines.[33]

Within Indian communities religion – a syncretic blend of Catholic and pre-Columbian beliefs and practices – was pervasive; there was no clear differentiation between sacred and secular. Political authority – when it emerged from within and was not imposed from without – mingled with religious, creating intertwined civil–religious hierarchies which served to integrate the community and to provide, where permitted, a vigorous form of self-government, resistant to external pressures. In addition, while Indian communities were by no means egalitarian, nevertheless internal stratification was kept in check by mechanisms of redistribution, such as feasts and other religious expenses.[34] Thus, like the atom, the 'closed corporate community' remained bonded together, defying the fissiparous forces which threatened its dissolution from within and without; like the atom, too, when dissolution occurred, it released violent energies.

Not that Indian communities had a monopoly of these defensive and integrative characteristics. They may be discerned, too, in some rural mestizo communities like Tomóchic, in the Chihuahua sierra, or Arandas, in the Altos de Jalisco.[35] Nor are they confined to Mexico: 'inward-oriented villages', complete with 'community survival mechanisms', have been noted throughout the world, wherever peasantries exist on the margin of subsistence, facing the combined threats of government, landlord, and the elements.[36] The peasant's alleged conservatism, hostility to innovation, and 'sheer unadulterated cussedness and pigheaded stupidity'[37] were traits induced by the subordinate and precarious position of peasant communities; they were social responses, to given social conditions, not products of Indian culture *per se*. It was rather the case that Indian communities – almost by definition – had developed these traits to a greater extent, over a longer period of time, and had maintained them more fully intact in the face of outside pressures.

These supposed characteristics influenced outsiders' opinions of the Indian. Though the Porfiriato saw stirrings of interest in and concern for the plight of the Indian – anticipations of the full-blown *indigenismo* of the twentieth century – the prevailing view among the political nation, when it went beyond indifference, was at best paternalistic, at worst domineering and racist.[38] The well-to-do prized their creole ancestry, 'Quelle horreur!', exclaimed the wife of a Mexican diplomat in Tokyo when it was suggested to her that she shared a common, Asiatic racial heritage with the Japanese; as the choice of idiom implied, her kind (especially the Catholic creoles of central Mexico) looked to Europe, and particularly to France, for their cultural inspiration.[39] Pablo Escandón, briefly Governor of Morelos, was 'more at home in Europe than in Mexico'; to a Lieutenant Colonel of the Zouaves he seemed 'le plus Parisien des Mexicains'.[40] Landa y Escandón, speaking perfect English as he took tea in Cuernavaca (he had been educated at Stonyhurst), 'look[ed] like an Englishman and is proud of it'.[41]

In their eyes, the Indian represented a drag on Mexico's 'progress' (a concept to which constant appeal was made), and white immigration, on Argentine lines, was the preferred – though unattainable – solution.[42] Meanwhile, the stereotypes of the 'lazy native', familiar in colonial contexts, were invoked to justify low wages, land seizures and forced labour. 'The Indian', as the Yucatecan proverb went, 'hears through his backside'; without the discipline of hard work on their henequen estates, the planters of the peninsula maintained, the Maya would live on 'sunlight and a patch of beans'; and similar arguments were heard in Morelos.[43] Attitudes of this kind were confined neither to conservative Porfirians, nor to members of the landed elite. Revolutionaries – especially those from the progressive, mestizo north – subscribed to the racist and Social Darwinist ideas which passed for scientific thinking in those times; they inveighed against Chinese immigrants, and they saw the Indian population of central and southern Mexico as alcoholic degenerates, ready for a rough redemption.[44]

Racist practice was, of course, anterior to pseudo-scientific racist thinking (which, for a literate minority, merely rationalised existing attitudes); and it was particularly significant where it underpinned a local, political hierarchy. Indian communities were frequently dominated by a handful of *ladino* (mestizo) caciques, who monopolised land, commerce and political power. Azteca was controlled by a few such caciques who 'had money and rode fine horses and were always the officials'; at Tepoztlán the caciques lived in the best *barrio*, owned most of the private land, controlled the communal fields, and enjoyed political contacts in the capital.[45] Mestizo caciques were not necessarily despots; or, at least, they could be enlightened despots. Vicente Mendoza of Tepoztlán was one such; so, too, was the cacique of Huixquilucán (Mex.), 'an old mestizo of rather forbidding manners but kindly spirit', under whose regime the village seemed to prosper.[46] More typical, perhaps, was Don Guillermo Murcio, blacksmith and cacique of the Triqui pueblo of Chicahuastla (Oax.), where 'he has gained almost unbounded influence among the simple natives. His word is law and the town government trembles before his gaze'; the traveller Lumholtz encountered another blacksmith/liquor dealer/cacique at Yoquivo, in the Chihuahua sierra.[47]

Mestizo caciques, like their landlord betters, justified their exercise of power and their commercial sharp practice in terms of the Indians' sloth and fecklessness (even mestizo priests, condemned to the Indian backwoods, were inclined to agree).[48] Indian degeneracy invited contempt and exploitation. 'What these people needed', declared a mestizo schoolmaster at Huancito (Mich.), who reportedly 'despises the Indians within his charge', 'was a second Cortez [for] . . . they had never been properly conquered'.[49] For the high-minded, of both 'conservative' and 'revolutionary' persuasion, a second conquest was required to eliminate Indian vice, filth, superstition and alcoholism, and to inculcate values of hygiene, hard work and patriotism.[50] Some communities were polarised by this socio-ethnic division. At Naranja (Mich.) dispossessed Indian villagers clashed with mestizo hacienda workers; at Acayucán (Ver.), where such conflicts had produced a minor 'caste war', 'the whites and mestizos live in the centre of a large Indian community, but the separation between them . . . is as great as if they lived leagues apart . . . (and) between the two a conflict over land has gone on for centuries'.[51] Other 'bi-ethnic' communities of this kind – such as Tantoyuca in the Huasteca, and Jamiltepec on the coast of Oaxaca – figured significantly in the Revolution after 1910.

But mestizo control could also operate at a distance. Frequently, a mestizo town acted as metropolis for outlying Indian satellites which, though they might retain land, still languished in the grip of mestizo merchants and officials.[52] Tlacuiltepec (Hgo) was a mestizo pueblo which 'has charge of several Indian villages'; Chilcota, head town of the Once Pueblos in Michoacán, was mestizo, while dependencies like Huancito (home of the *maestro* of conquistador mentality) were 'primitive and purely Indian'; Izúcar de Matamoros, in Puebla, had fourteen such satellites.[53] On a grander scale, the commercial tentacles of the city of Oaxaca embraced the surrounding sierra, while the merchants of Acapulco dominated the hinterland of the Costa Chica.[54] In some cases this dependency involved the direct transfer of resources – land and water rights – from Indian satellites to mestizo metropolis; when this occurred (as it did at Ometepec and Jamiltepec, communities lying athwart the Guerrero–Oaxaca state line) agrarian rebellion could assume the guise of a localised caste war. Indeed, it is likely that some of the ubiquitous inter-community conflicts of the revolutionary period derived from such unequal political and economic relationships, as yet uninvestigated.

Certainly the landlord and merchant victims saw Indian rebellion in terms of caste war (there had been enough nineteenth-century precedents, and not simply in Yucatán).[55] Where the social historian discerns agrarian rebellion, contemporaries often saw something akin to Carleton Beals' 'feather-shanked aggressions, disorganised seizures of ancient patrimonies'.[56] Zapata's agrarian revolt was soon construed as a 'caste war', in which members of an 'inferior race' were captained by a 'modern Attila'; the creole planter Pablo Escandón came to fear the rise of a 'true Niggerdom' in Mexico – terms which came readily to the lips of some British and American observers too.[57] Agrarian revolt revealed the other side of the lazy Indian: the bloodthirsty, atavistic savage, 'half devil and half child'. Urban readers were titillated by stories, mostly apocryphal, of refined brutalities, while those responsible for combating 'Indian' rebellion not only used similar methods as colonial governors, but also evinced similar attitudes. 'Hunting for Zapatistas', according to the version of the aristocratic Alfonso Rincón Gallardo, 'seems to be the biggest kind of "big-game" shooting'.[58] As for the troublesome Yaquis, the leading Catholic paper *El País* was prepared to advocate the genocide of a tribe 'unworthy of membership of the great human family'; while revolutionaries justified repression (and the traffic in Yaqui prisoners-of-war) on the grounds of the Indian's 'instinct for pillage and evil-doing'.[59] To the *gente decente* of town and countryside this sudden volte-face of the Indian – from deferential peon to belligerent savage – necessitated tough measures, just as it smacked of treachery and threatened a reversion to barbarism.

PLACES

The ethnic face of Mexico corresponded to its physical face: the Indian population was to be found – along with pine-trees, pulque and pneumonia – in the high country; and Mexico's ubiquitous mountains, slicing the country into distinct regions and discrete valleys, shaped not only patterns of settlement but also modes of government, of economic development, and, after 1910, of revolutionary conflict. The mountains march south in two mighty parallel chains: the Western Sierra Madre continuing the line of the Rockies, the Eastern Sierra Madre rising among the hills of Nuevo León in the north east and sidling towards the Gulf coast in its progress south. These, which with the lesser sierras cover a quarter of the country's area, harboured a distinctive, *serrano* population: Indians, hardy pioneers, independent villagers, remote mining and lumber camps, bandit lairs.[60] In the north, between the arms of the mountains, lies a broad expanse of high plain, at its broadest and most inhospitable in the deserts, dunes, and trapped rivers of Chihuahua, Mexico's largest state. Chihuahua, which has the strongest claim to the disputed title of 'cradle of the Revolution', was a land of sprawling cattle ranges, dotted with isolated haciendas, settlements, cities and mining camps, populated by few men but thousands of cattle, dependent on the rivers flowing eastwards out of the mountains into landlocked lakes, or via the Conchos down to the Río Grande.[61] These northern plains were the theatre of the keenest fighting in 1911 and again in 1913–14, but many of the revolutionary protagonists were men of the sierra who had ridden down from the mountains to oppose first Díaz, then Huerta. In Chihuahua, as elsewhere, the Revolution took on the character of a conflict between highland and lowland, matching the conflicts between villager and landlord, Indian and mestizo, 'sandal and shoe'.

Water, not land, was the scarce resource in the north. Men jostled for access to the irrigated valleys of the north west, especially that of the Yaqui River. Further east, on the Durango/Coahuila borderlands, the River Nazas wound its way down to the cotton country of the Laguna which, thanks to its seasonal waters, appeared in summer 'toute blanche . . . sous sa neige de coton'.[62] The Laguna was a region of dynamic growth: Torreón, the main town, 'misbegotten on an arid site for no better reason than that of the intersection of the railway lines', became a bustling, Americanised metropolis; and the waters of the Nazas became a bone of bitter contention.[63] After 1910 the Laguna (like the Yaqui valley) was a hotbed of revolt; and Torreón, with its strategic railway junction, was the site of the bloodiest siege of the Revolution.

This northern region had been patchily settled in the colonial period, chiefly in response to the silver boom; the Indians of the Gran Chichimec were wild, nomadic and less numerous than those under Aztec dominion to the south and, since they could supply neither tribute nor a docile labour force, they were annihilated or pushed into the mountains (a process that was long, bloody, and barely complete in the 1900s). Northern society, mestizo rather than Indian, was shaped by the operations of mine and hacienda, both of which prospered and expanded with the advent of the railway in the 1880s. This was a pattern of development dependent on local initiative and self-sufficiency − virtues displayed in the struggle against Apache and Yaqui, which was waged with only limited help from Mexico City.[64] With its scant population, shifting internal frontier, and dynamic economy, the north was the land of the self-made man where, compared with central Mexico, achievement counted for more than ascription, where the rich (both Mexican and foreign) could expect bonanzas, and where even the poor enjoyed some mobility and opportunity.[65] In Monterrey, it was noted, the sons of the wealthy did not waste their substance, but studied business (often in the US) and went into the family firm.[66] Here, if anywhere, the Porfiriato saw the birth of a vigorous 'national bourgeoisie'. Hence, major commercial and industrial cities − like Monterrey, Chihuahua, Torreón − prospered, seeming to ape the ways of North America; the Church kept a low profile (Torreón was practically churchless); and the authority of the central government was grudgingly tolerated, sometimes sourly resented. Traditionally, the north had stood for federalism, liberalism and anti-clericalism, often in opposition to Mexico City. Under Díaz, these commitments were strengthened and with them the potential opposition of the north to the centre.[67]

Further south, as Mexico narrows towards the Isthmus, the two Sierra Madre ranges merge in a knot of convoluted peaks and valleys, crossed and further complicated by an east-west volcanic seam which had thrown up some of Mexico's greatest and (in the case of Paricutín) most recent mountains. Here, the Mesa Central had formed the heartland of the Aztec empire, of the colony of New Spain, and of independent Mexico. And, despite the growth of the north, the central plateau still contained the bulk of the population in the days of Díaz. In seven central states, together with the Federal District, one-third of the population inhabited one-fifteenth of the country's area.[68] Here, the pattern of settlement and society reflected the broken nature of the landscape. The Spaniards had built their ordered, gridiron cities, centred around church and plaza, in the temperate valleys, often following pre-Columbian precedent: Mexico City usurped the place of Tenochtitlán, Puebla inherited the religiosity of neighbouring Cholula, becoming a city noted for its churches, its Catholicism, and its conservatism. Most of the state capitals of the central states were, like these, old colonial cities, steeped in history: Guanajuato and Querétaro to the north of the capital, Toluca and Morelia to the west, Oaxaca to the south and Jalapa to the east. Some (which Lejeune labelled 'Catholic', compared with the 'American' cities of the north) failed to take up the economic challenges of the Porfiriato and remained administrative, ecclesiastical and cultural centres with sluggish economies, often declining artisan industries, and sometimes dwindling populations; others (the 'European' cities) embraced change and achieved new levels of prosperity.[69]

Outside the cities, three centuries of Spanish rule saw the hacienda emerge as the dominant, though by no means the sole form of rural tenure, as it amassed the better valley lands, dispossessing Indian villages, converting villagers into peons, and pushing the major areas of independent Indian settlement into the sierras. In the valleys, the hacienda raised crops to feed the cities, the mining camps, and later foreign markets: wheat and barley in the high Toluca valley, sugar in Morelos, maguey on the plains of Apam in Hidalgo, coffee on the temperate slopes around Jalapa. In addition, a vigorous class of middling landowners – *rancheros* – developed, particularly on the plains of the Bajío, watered by the River Lerma. Here, though the silver mines of Guanajuato were in decline, and with them the ancillary artisan industries of Celaya, León and San Miguel, *ranchero* agriculture nevertheless prospered, creating a distinctive pattern of agrarian tenure and social organisation.[70] In the Bajío, too, the economic influences of the Mexico City and Guadalajara markets met, their contrary tugging paralleled by a certain regional, cultural and political rivalry. The people of Guadalajara (some 120,000 to Mexico City's 471,000 in 1910) were almost ostentatiously well-off, notably devout, and seemed distinctly Spanish in appearance. Travellers noted few Indians (Indian settlements had always been rare in the Bajío) but a good many attractive blondes; altogether, the people seemed 'a great deal more refined than their compatriots in Mexico City', whose authority – like the *norteños* – they did not suffer gladly.[71]

South and east of the populous central plateau the land falls away to the broken country of the southern Sierra Madre which, less imposing but no less inhospitable than the northern ranges, cuts a broad swathe of rugged, under-populated land almost from coast to coast. To the east of the capital – and despite its relative proximity – the state of Guerrero enjoyed a long tradition of political autonomy, facilitated by geography, and later revived by the Revolution. It also contained within its borders (as did all such mountain states) 'outlying districts [which] are never visited by either the 134 jefes or the Governor . . . really independent communities which, if left alone, behave according to their own notions'.[72] Similarly, in Oaxaca, the arid, cactus-strewn sierras were the home of some of the largest Indian populations, while the valleys were the preserve of white and mestizo, merchant and *hacendado*. Government also emanated from the valleys, where the administrative centres lay – like the city of Oaxaca, ringed by mountains and hostile *serranos*, 'the ancient enemies of the town people'.[73]

Internally divided, Oaxaca was nevertheless jealous of its independence and suspicious of the claims of Mexico City – less so, perhaps, when a Oaxaqueño like Porfirio Díaz ruled in the National Palace, more so when northern interlopers appeared, as they did in 1914, and when the mountain barriers and the deficient communications facilitated a regional resistance in which different social and ethnic groups collaborated. The same was true of Chiapas, also a highland, Indian state, closely tied to Guatemala, and only recently and imperfectly linked to the Mexican heartland by the Panamerican Railway; and of Yucatán, too, cut off by the swamps and jungles of the Isthmus, oriented by trade towards the Caribbean and the US, and possessed of a vigorous regionalist, even separatist tradition which the Revolution served to revive.[74]

The mountains dominate the Mexican heartland. But from their highest points around Mexico City they fall away gradually towards the south, precipitately to east and west. Travellers riding the double-headed locomotives which, in the days of Díaz, zig-zagged down from Esperanza, on the Puebla/Veracruz border, to Orizaba, Atoyac and the port of Veracruz, descended from cool peaks to temperate slopes to torrid lowlands in a matter of hours; on the 260 mile trip from the capital to Veracruz the altitude drops by 8,000 feet, and the temperature rises by some 2500? Fahrenheit.[75] But the descent from the mountains to the coastal or isthmian lowlands, from the *tierra fría* to the *tierra caliente*, brought more than a change of climate; it meant also a change in ethnicity and population, in flora and fauna, in drink and disease.

The hot lowlands, especially the broad flood plain alongside the Gulf, had been sparsely populated during colonial times, attracting neither Indian nor Spaniard. But in the late nineteenth century growing demand for tropical products lured men into the lowlands, just as the mines had lured them to the inhospitable north centuries before. In southern Veracruz, Tabasco and Campeche plantations were set up to produce rubber, cotton, and tropical fruits; companies began to exploit the resources of the forest; and Yucatán, with its unique limestone formation, came to base its entire cash economy on the cultivation of henequen (sisal) to supply the farmers of the American Mid-West with binding twine.[76] With the development of these new crops, huge plantations were carved out of near-virgin tropical country, watered by broad, turgid, flood-prone rivers like the Grijalva, the Papaloapam, and the Usumacinta. Alone in Mexico, this region had more water than it needed, but the water had not yet been harnessed, and its very abundance only encouraged disease and the encroachment of the rain forest. Engineers working on Lord Cowdray's railway across the Isthmus of Tehuantepec doused the railway sleepers with petrol to stop them sprouting, and a quarter of those who built the railway terminus at Salina Cruz, on the Pacific coast, died within two years.[77] Here, foreigners came as managers and planters, but Porfirian hopes of white settlement were disappointed.[78]

Mexicans from the plateau, too, inured to the respiratory and gastric diseases prevalent there, rapidly succumbed to the malaria and yellow fever (the *vómito*) of the tropical lowlands. In Guerrero, it was noted, 'nearly all the inhabitants of the inland plateau have an exaggerated dread of the coastlands' – a dread that was not, perhaps, so exaggerated for under-nourished peons, who, unlike European travellers, were at the mercy of the lowlands quinine racket, and who too readily switched from the nutritious *pulque* of the highlands to the firewater of the tropics.[79] Yet in the same state – as the Revolution was to reveal once again – 'the people of the coast find it very difficult to campaign outside their own region', that is, when they ventured into the mountains.[80] Granted these territorial imperatives– and the absence, outside Yucatán, of a settled, Indian population in the lowlands – the new plantations had difficulty securing labour. Some Indians could be coaxed down out of the mountains, as the German coffee planters of Chiapas found; and for some poor communities the opportunity of seasonal work in the *tierra caliente*, however hard and unhealthy, offered an economic lifeline. Hence an annual flow of labour from highland to lowland became a feature of the Porfirian rural economy.[81] But since the free flow of labour proved inadequate, the plantations also relied on more coercive methods: forms of forced labour, penal servitude, and the ensnarement of nominally 'free' contract labour by the system of debt peonage, which reached its harshest in southern plantations like those of the celebrated Valle Nacional.[82]

Porfirian Mexico was thus ethnically and physically diverse; and the analysis of its diversity could be pushed further – to go beyond region and state, to encompass village, valley and *barrio*, each of which was capable of eliciting powerful loyalties. Tannenbaum gives the example of eleven neighbouring pueblos in Hidalgo, characterised by different economies, different reputations, and different politics.[83] Since, after 1910, the Revolution was fundamentally linked to local factors, a great variety of responses was possible; and the problems which this implies for the national historian of the Revolution, in his work of analysis, are analogous to those faced by Díaz – and by his revolutionary successors – in their work of government. During a generation of dictatorship, Díaz strove to create a strong, centralised government whose writ would run the length and breadth of the country. He succeeded, at a price. For, in turn, he created an opposition which, no longer confined to a town or a state, sought to emulate the national standing of the regime, and to create a national opposition transcending local particularism. The Porfirian regime – and its enemies – whose mortal struggle is now to be recounted were, in a paradoxical sense, mutual allies against the recalcitrant localism of Mexico and of the Mexican people.

THE REGIME

The Porfirian regime gave Mexico a generation of unprecedented peace and stability. The Pax Porfiriana was, of course, a flawed peace, based on recurrent repression as well as popular consensus; nevertheless, the continuity of government, local and national, and the absence of serious civil war, contrasted with the endemic political conflict of the fifty years after Independence. Díaz knew the old days: he had fought against the conservatives and their French allies in the 1860s, against his fellow-liberals, Juárez and Lerdo in the 1870s, finally battling his way to the presidency. A Liberal by affiliation, Díaz displayed more appetite for power than adherence to principle and, once president, he resolved to curb factionalism, to blur the liberal-conservative battle-lines, and to create a strong, centralised regime around his own person.[84] For Mexico, it was the end of ideology. Old Liberals died off or were harassed into silence or grew fat on the spoils of office; the Church was conciliated and allowed, tacitly, to recover some of its old importance, political, social and economic. The slogan of the Porfiriato summed it up: 'mucha administración y poca política' – 'plenty of administration and not too much politics'.

In the early days Díaz had a deft touch. He played off rival provincial factions, perpetuating divisions where it suited him, throwing the weight of the 'centre' behind a favoured party, thereby creating a loyal client.[85] The caciques and generals who had riveted their control on to particular states – Alvarez in Guerrero, Méndez in the Puebla sierra, the Cravioto clan in Hidalgo – were patiently prised from power or cajoled into alliances, or, when they were allowed to die in peace, succeeded by Porfirian appointees. Some, like the Craviotos, who never crossed the President, survived for decades. Others, one-time enemies of Díaz, saw the advantage of detente. In Chihuahua, Luis Terrazas (one of the north's self-made men, he was the son of a butcher) had opposed Díaz during the liberal infighting of the 1870s and the president accordingly maintained anti-Terracista administrations in the state through the 1880s and 1890s. Meanwhile, by judicious investment and marriage, Terrazas built up an empire of cattle ranches, flour and textile mills, banks and factories worth over 27m. pesos. Old rancours faded: Terrazas became state governor again in 1903 and was succeeded by his son-in-law Enrique Creel in 1907. Political hegemony now complemented economic power, as the

Creel–Terrazas oligarchy came to dominate state politics, local government and the courts.[86]

At the other end of Mexico, in Yucatán, Olegario Molina – 'a man who has made not only himself but all his family, down to the nephews and sons-in-law of cousins' – created a similar politico-economic empire, based on henequen. Though a member of the 'Divine Caste' of richest planters, Molina could not compare with Terrazas for sheer landholdings; but he and his son-in-law, Avelino Montes, served as Mexican agents for the International Harvester Co., the monopolistic buyer of Yucatán's henequen.[87] In addition to his economic muscle, Molina became state governor in 1902; one of his brothers was *jefe político* of Mérida, another President of the United Railways of Yucatán; lower in the clan, the son of a cousin served as Inspector of Mayan Ruins – in which capacity, he told two English travellers, 'he had never been to Chichén Itzá, but . . . he had satisfactory photographs'.[88] The Creel–Terrazas and Molina–Montas oligarchies were – sheer wealth apart – only exceptional in that they finally added national to local preferment: Creel served as Foreign Minister, Molina as Minister of Fomento (Development) in the penultimate Díaz cabinet.

Most local elites remained staunchly local. Over the years, however, as the political mobility of the civil wars gave way to the *immobilisme* of the late Porfiriato, so they grew older, tighter, and more exclusive. In San Luis Potosí, the Díez Gutiérrez brothers alternated in the statehouse for twenty years; Sonora was dominated by General Luis Torres, who served five terms as governor, with a Torresista front-man filling in between each term.[89] The Rabasas ran Chiapas: Ramón governed, one son was boss of San Cristóbal, another of Tapachula (where he had a monopoly of the slaughter-houses to add to his tram concession in Soconusco), a nephew served as a state deputy, as *jefe* of Tuxtla Gutiérrez, and as commander of the state *rurales*; a brother-in-law was mayor of Tuxtla and a sister ran the Escuela Normal.[90] Brother Emilio, the intellectual of the family, figured prominently in the Científico elite of Mexico City. In Puebla, an old companion-in-arms of Díaz, Mucio Martínez, held the governorship for eighteen years (this was no record: Cahuantzi, in Tlaxcala, served twenty-six and others over twenty), enriching himself by operating illegal saloons, brothels, and the state *pulque* monopoly. He and his official accomplices – notably his Chief of Police, Miguel Cabrera – were bywords for corrupt and arbitrary government, even by Porfirian standards; 'with governors like Mucio Martínez', declared an opposition spokesman, 'revolution is a duty'.[91]

But Díaz made it clear that the perpetuation of these great satrapies depended on his goodwill. In the early days he weeded out governors of doubtful loyalty; thereafter, re-elections and replacements only went ahead after Díaz had weighed local reports and petitions, exercising the ultimate veto of the 'centre'.[92] Where necessary, he created counterweights to incumbent caciques: the young, ambitious and loyal General Bernardo Reyes was sent as chief of operations in the north east in order to offset the influence of Generals Treviño and Naranjo, and to bind these distant states to the central government; Treviño and Naranjo turned from public life to private business and their many clients were prised from power. But there was a revealing postscript. Elected governor of Nuevo León, Reyes enjoyed two decades of uninterrupted power – a model ruler and a prop of the Porfirian establishment. But when men began to talk of Reyes as presidential timber, Díaz was swift to act, and among the decisive measures he took in 1909, in order to eradicate Reyes as a political threat, was the appointment of the aged General Gerónimo Treviño as military commander in the north east. The wheel had come full circle; in the end, as in the beginning, the divide-and-rule principle kept all the strings in Díaz's hands and these hands had only to twitch, at the apprehension of an over-mighty subject, for the threat to be removed.[93]

If, in the last analysis, the 'centre' prevailed over these local oligarchies, Díaz certainly took care not to antagonise too many provincial caudillos at one time; he buttressed their authority so long as they remained loyal, and he was not too bothered when state governors – who on their visits to the capital strove to convey an impression of culture and civilisation – drank, domineered, grafted, and abducted. Loyalty, rather than civic responsibility, was the chief desideratum. Hence, a large proportion of Porfirian governors – maybe 70% – were presidential favourites, imported into alien states, where their prime allegiance was to their president and maker, rather than to their provincial subjects: Antonio Mercenario of Guerrero, for example, knew the state merely as overseer of the Huitzuco mines, owned by Díaz's wife; his successor, Agustín Mora, was another outsider, from Puebla.[94] Local opinion might be outraged, but governors tended to be loyal, even servile.[95] As a result, when the Revolution came, it was not, like so many Latin American revolutions, the work of ambitious state governors (Urquiza riding out of Entre Ríos to topple Rosas, Vargas seizing power from Rio Grande do Sul in 1930), rather, it was an upswelling of popular feeling directed not only against Díaz but also – even more so – against the creatures he had installed in the state palaces of the Federation.

The army, the other great source of Latin American revolutions, offers a comparable case. At the outset, the Porfirian regime had a military complexion: three-quarters of the state governors of 1885 were generals, even if only two or three were career soldiers. By 1903, however, the complement of military governors had fallen from eighteen to eight and those who survived and prospered politically were those, like Reyes, who displayed administrative talents as well as military skills.[96] Meanwhile, the military establishment itself was cut back: the number of generals by a careful quarter, the total strength by a third, from thirty to twenty thousand. Even this was paper strength, for when, in 1910, the army was called upon to face its biggest test, only 14,000 or so men could be put into the field.[97] Auxiliary forces, too, like the state militias had been savagely pruned (in the interests of centralisation) and, as peace reigned and municipal government decayed, the once vigorous local defence forces had fallen into disuse.[98] This run-down of the bloated armed forces of the 1870s made political and budgetary sense, eliminating the gang of power- and peso-hungry generals which had battened on the treasury since Independence. And it worked militarily: thanks to the new railway network, Díaz could despatch troops into areas of disaffection and stifle revolts with unprecedented speed and efficiency. But this low-cost strategy involved risks which were dramatically revealed in 1910–11, when revolts proliferated, and the army, confined to the major towns and the vulnerable railway lines, proved inadequate to maintain the regime.

Díaz's was not a military regime. True, the army played an important part in maintaining the Pax Porfiriana: it had fought no foreign opponent since the French quit Mexico in 1867, and officers like Reyes and Victoriano Huerta won their laurels and secured presidential favour by 'pacifying actions' and punitive expeditions, in which rebellious Indians or political dissidents were the victims.[99] But the regime enjoyed other – civilian, *caciquista* – institutional bases and the army was in no sense an autonomous political actor: it took its orders from Díaz and carried them out loyally; rarely did officers, like Heriberto Frías, denounce in public the repressive actions they had to perform in practice.[100] Indeed, the army underwent gradual professionalism (in the 1900s, along Prussian lines) and it became less a bastion of conservative privilege, more a *carrière ouverte aux talents*, especially middle-class talents.[101] At the top, Díaz's generals grew old (by 1910 all the divisional generals were in their seventies, veterans, like Díaz himself, of the mid-century civil wars); they had acquired European spiked helmets and waxed moustaches to match their European munitions and European military manuals; under their leadership the army served as a loyal arm of the dictatorship, devoid of political pretensions. The Revolution changed all that.

What the Revolution failed to change – if we compare the 1900s and the 1920s – was the position of the rank-and-file, who were for the most part reluctant conscripts, rounded up by the authorities to meet required quotas, or even dragged from the gaols. Since most were Indian or mestizo, foreign military opinion disdained them as quasi-colonial levies (an estimation which was not altogether wide of the mark).[102] Not surprisingly, they were unreliable. When a picket of press-ganged troops was set to guard a prison work gang, an additional police detachment had to keep an eye on the troops; when soldiers were sent to Salina Cruz to protect a gang of West Indian labourers, whose presence the local workers resented, 'the first request of the officer in charge was to have strong blockhouses built, as the only means of preventing his soldiers from running away and marauding in the neighbourhood'.[103] For the common people, forced service in the army was among the most feared of punishments, and one that a good many rebel leaders (such as Zapata and Calixto Contreras) had suffered.[104] A few significant individuals thereby gained some familiarity, not with the arts of war, but with the internal working of the army, and the army acquired a mass of sullen conscripts, many on the look-out for the first opportunity to desert.

In the old days, when Díaz was young, the power of the military had been rivalled by that of the Catholic Church. But the liberal victory in the civil wars of the 1850s and 1860s had broken the economic power of the Church, stripping it of its huge landed wealth, and laws now curtailed the Church's ability either to educate outside church schools, or to pray, process and preach outside church buildings. The defeat of the conservatives left the Church in political limbo, shunned by the liberal rulers of Mexico and compelled, by its adherence to Pius IX and the Syllabus, to abjure them.[105] But as a moral force, capable of influencing the hearts and minds of men (and even more of women), the Church remained powerful and Díaz, keen to maintain a somnolent political climate, had no intention of going the way of doctrinaire, priest-baiting Liberals. On the contrary, his regime witnessed a gradual, though never total, detente between Church and state. The laws and the landed status quo remained (too many Liberals had a stake in that for any change to be contemplated) but the rules were gently bent, or overlooked, especially in states where devout Porfiristas ruled, and clerical garb reappeared on the streets, church bells were rung, religious lessons were tacked on at the end of the day in secular schools. Díaz sanctioned detente in Mexico, just as Pope Leo XIII did globally: the Archbishop of Mexico, exiled by the liberals, returned to officiate at Díaz's wedding; when the old prelate died in 1891, Díaz attended his funeral.[106] Some die-hard Liberals denounced this backsliding, just as some more radical Catholics began to question the social abuses of the Porfiriato; in the course of the 1900s, as the following chapter shows, both became more vociferous. Till then, the Church–State conflict remained muted, to the advantage of the regime, and Díaz, if he had not won a fervent ally in the Church, had at least disarmed a potential opponent.

The regime's neglect of constitutional requirements, evident in the case of the Church, was even clearer in the operations of Mexico's supposedly representative democracy. Díaz's Mexico was thus a leading member of that great tribe of 'artificial democracies', states in which political practice diverged radically from imposed, liberal theory.[107] Mexican politics were shot through with fraud, graft and nepotism; vices in the eyes of the regime's critics, but sources of strength to Porfirian rulers, complementing brute force, and so deeply entrenched that they easily survived the overthrow of the Porfirian system. It was expected that men in power, nationally and locally, would protect and advance their families and *compadres*, that political and judicial decisions would be influenced by considerations of personal gain, that concessions and contracts would be awarded according to criteria other than

the purely economic. The *mordida* – the 'bite', or bribe – was an integral part of
business and politics: Lord Cowdray, the British oil magnate, probably never
'bribed any of the Mexicans', commented an ingenuous (and mistaken)
diplomat, '[but] he sometimes gave valuable presents and he appointed
prominent Mexicans to positions which did not involve much work in his
businesses'.[108] But, in indulging in such methods – greasing palms, trading
favours and recruiting clients – foreigners merely followed the local rules. The
bonds of blood, *compadrazgo* and clientelism (the most ubiquitous of the
allegiances mentioned earlier) stretched across Mexican society: 'each
employee represents a whole hierarchy of protectors'.[109] Out in the sticks, for
example, muleteers needed the favourable recommendation of the local
political boss to secure trade; state governors, as we have seen, advanced their
friends and relatives wholesale; officers in the rural police – in defiance of
regulations – commanded over and promoted their own sons and nephews.[110]

Hence, when the bastard son of the *jefe político* of Tulancingo (Hgo) was
threatened with arrest by the *jefe* of neighbouring Tenango del Doria, the
response was typical: 'son,' his father said, 'I am the *jefe político* of Tulancingo
and the Governor of the state is Pedro Rodríguez; I am his intimate friend and
we shall succeed in ousting that jefe in Tenango . . . who has ordered your
arrest'.[111] The outcome is unknown; the story – told by a 'garrulous,
simple-minded individual' – may even be apocryphal; but it is in keeping with
the mores of Porfirian Mexico. Politics was less a high-minded, Gladstonian
striving in the public interest, than a source of power, security and patronage,
in a society where opportunities for advancement were often limited. A
growing number of Mexicans, however, deplored this state of affairs and
sought to close the chasm between constitutional precept and political
practice; for, as long as constitutions remain, however neglected and abused,
authoritarian regimes (be they artificial liberal democracies or pseudo-workers'
states) can hardly expect their subjects to maintain indefinitely a 'willing
suspension of disbelief' regarding matters political and constitutional.
Eventually, as Díaz found, the constitutional chickens come home to roost.

For a generation, however, it worked. Within the central government, the
executive, with Díaz at its head, was all-powerful. The Supreme Court,
commented a critic, was more 'courtesan' than court; in this it reflected the
position of the judiciary as a whole.[112] Opposition groups in Congress – still
vocal in the 1880s – were gradually silenced, as their members were harassed
and as rigged elections guaranteed an increasingly loyal legislature. Relatives
and cronies of the president packed the Chamber, and fellow-Oaxaqueños rose
high in government and administration. Local factions who sought to field a
candidate for state governor, and who therefore needed Díaz's support, could
do worse than pick a native of Oaxaca – 'that favoured spot . . . so productive of
statesmen' – even if the governorship was that of San Luis.[113] At both state and
national level, therefore, the legislature was effectively appointed by the

executive and its members were cyphers, 'I doubt', remarked an Englishman in Durango, 'if 1% of the inhabitants could tell their names'.[114] The irrelevance of Congress became a byword. When one Federal deputy had failed either to attend the Chamber or – more surprising – to collect his salary for two months 'they sent an urgent messenger and ascertained that he had died eight months before he was ever elected'; another apocryphal story, perhaps, but one that is no less revealing.[115]

Political power, during the Porfiriato, was concentrated in a small coterie surrounding the dictator – a national oligarchy paralleling the state oligarchies already mentioned. First elected to the presidency in 1876, after a revolt against Lerdo and the evils of re-election, Díaz secured his own re-election on seven occasions; following the presidential term of his old compadre Manuel González (1880–4) he ruled for twenty-seven consecutive years. Early presidential rivals, González, Dublán, Pacheco, Romero Rubio, were beaten off and by the 1890s Díaz's personal dictatorship was not only established but was clearly seen to be established. Now, as the president entered his sixties, a new political generation, familiar with and moulded by the years of peace, came to the fore, replacing the old generals and caciques. They paused to wonder what would happen (what, in particular, would happen to them) when the lynchpin of the system was removed; in 1897 their fears were stimulated by an unsuccessful attempt on Díaz's life and Finance Minister Limantour, on a trip abroad, learned that foreign bankers were also worred about the political succession.[116]

The 1890s thus saw the first attempts to place the regime on a surer institutional footing. In 1892 a group of Díaz supporters formed the Liberal Union, which advocated the president's third re-election in return for certain concessions which, they argued, would strengthen the regime, ensure continuity of government and avert the 'terrible crisis' of succession which they foresaw when Díaz was removed from the scene. Even some critics of the regime regarded their proposals as 'noble and pure'.[117] A third re-election, the Liberal Union conceded, meant a sacrifice of democratic hopes, but this was warranted by the situation; peace, now established, had to be preserved, and Mexico could not implement the full democracy of the 1857 Constitution without risking anarchy. Future reforms depended on continued peace and material progress. Hence, though the Liberal Union made moderate political proposals, advocating the immovability of the judiciary and the creation of a vice-presidency, its chief concern was for continued economic development: more railways, a rationalised fiscal system, the suppression of internal customs barriers, European immigration, and further cuts in the military budget. This insistence on the primacy of material progress and on the need to match political reforms to the level of economic development revealed the positivist influence at work among the Porfiristas of the Liberal Union. Hence, claiming a Comtian and 'scientific' view of society, they acquired their nickname: the Científicos.[118]

But this move towards a party organisation (which some hoped would be seconded by conservative, Catholic interests, creating an embryonic two-party system) was soon thwarted and the mild reforms were ignored or compromised away. Perhaps the last, best chance of gradual change, guided from above, was thereby lost and personal rule, lacking institutional supports, persisted. Even when Díaz conceded the vice-presidency in 1904, he made sure that its incumbent was (as he admitted himself) an unpopular *adicto*, who posed no threat to the president: Vice-President Corral began unpopular, remained unpopular, and Díaz took pains to keep him uninformed and uninfluential.[119] Fearful of rivals and jealous of his untrammelled power, Díaz thus perpetuated a variety of personal rule which, after the manner of the Virgin Queen, kept the succession an open and potentially explosive question.

But this was not the end of the Científicos. Though their proposals of 1892 foundered, they were clearly the coming men, a new generation (most of them were born in the 1850s) who now stepped into the shoes of the moribund liberal veterans of Díaz's own generation. They were also a new type: urbane, cosmopolitan, articulate and well read. Led (unofficially, for they constituted no formal political party) first by Díaz's father-in-law, Romero Rubio, and then by Finance Minister Limantour, they acquired a comprehensive range of political, administrative and business posts, amasssing huge wealth and, supposedly, huge influence. Over time, their positivist emphasis on economic development squeezed out their moderate political reformism and they emerged as the foremost advocates, apologists, and beneficiaries of Mexican capitalism. The Científicos have often been portrayed as corrupt *vendepatrias*, representatives of a *comprador* bourgeoisie which – unlike the national bourgeoisie of the Revolution – delivered the Mexican economy into foreign hands.[120] Certainly the Científicos favoured foreign investment, which grew some thirty-fold during the Porfiriato, with the US supplying the greatest share.[121] Of total direct foreign investment, about one-third went into railways, a quarter into mining, the remainder into banks, utility companies, property ventures, textile factories and oil. The Científicos involved themselves directly in these operations, handling concessions and contracts and serving on company boards: Pablo Macedo, for example, President of the Federal Congress, was director of two banks, of the Aguila Oil Co., the Panamerican Railway, the Buen Tono cigarette firm, the Mexican Light and Power Co., and the Light and Power Co. of Pachuca; Fernando Pimentel y Fagoaga, Mayor of Mexico City in 1910, served on the board of four banks, of the Chapala Hydro-Electric Co., the San Rafael Paper Co., the Industrial Co. of Atlixco, the Sierra Lumber Co., and the Monterrey Smelting Co.[122]

But the Científicos were not simply profiteers masquerading as positivists. They had a genuine vision of a dynamic, developing Mexico. They saw foreign investment as a crucial factor in this development, but they looked to Europe to offset American influence and they anticipated the day when – as Limantour and Pablo Macedo argued – domestic capital, already dominant in some sectors, would assume a greater, determining role within the economy.[123] By the 1900s, indeed, a new economic nationalism emerged in Porfirian–Científico circles: protective tariffs were raised, the bulk of the railways were merged and taken under government control, and the debates over the new Mining Code indicated that the Científicos' design to nationalise the process of economic development was real and not just rhetorical.[124] Furthermore, both Científico thinking and government policy recognised that development also depended on factors which were 'non-economic'. Crime, alcoholism, illiteracy, squalor and disease were subjects of lively debate and study: Justo Sierra championed educational reform (and the Porfiriato witnessed a modest but significant improvement in educational provision); preventive medicine and urban sanitation were overhauled.[125] Achievements in these fields were variable and limited, in particular, the Científico strategy of development encountered major, 'structural' barriers which it showed no desire or capacity to dismantle. Their demolition was not to come until after the Revolution.[126] But it cannot be denied that the Científicos had a programme of development which – however unjust or misconceived – went beyond personal peculation and collective *entreguismo*. It was a programme, furthermore, which later revolutionaries plagiarised at will and it was certainly not a formula for standpat conservatism. Politically inflexible and authoritarian, the Científicos were economically progressive, dedicated to the principle of 'progress' and capable, it seems, of imparting a similar dedication among their minions.[127] Indeed, it was as much their fervent commitment to social and economic change as their resistance to political reform which brought about their eventual downfall.

For by 1910 the position of the Científicos proved to be precarious. Over the long term their economic strategy appeared to be vindicated: during the Porfiriato, as population grew at 1.4% per annum, economic production increased at a rate of 2.7%, exports at 6.1%.[128] Mexico experienced a phase of export-led growth not unusual in Latin America during these years and this enabled Limantour, Finance Minister since 1893, to convert a situation of chronic governmental bankruptcy into one of unprecedented fiscal and budgetary stability. In the course of the 1890s Limantour balanced the budget, reformed the treasury, abolished internal tariffs and overhauled the country's banking institutions. In 1905 he placed Mexico on the gold standard, eliminating the fluctuations in value of the peso, hitherto based on silver. By 1910 the Mexican government had reserves in excess of 60m. pesos and could borrow at 5%; indeed, when the Revolution broke out, Limantour was in Europe, negotiating a reconversion of the national debt at 4%.[129] Limantour's success depended to a large extent on global trends which – as the recession of 1907 displayed – were beyond his control. But even then Díaz retained his faith in Científico theory and practice: sound credit and a healthy budget were essential ingredients of the Pax Porfiriana, which preceding regimes had lacked, to their cost. In the financial world, therefore, where Díaz's own abilities were limited, the president readily deferred to his team of loyal and efficient technocrats. [130]

Politically, however, the Científicos were weak and, by 1910, bitterly unpopular, the very term 'Científico' having become a general term of abuse, indicating a Porfirista, reactionary, or almost any political opponent associated with the old regime. Unpopular village officials were 'Científicos', often misspelt. [131] Apart from their greed and graft, the Científicos were supposed to have ensnared Díaz, making him their pliant puppet. Down in Oaxaca, where Díaz's friends, high and low, were still numerous, Limantour was 'universally considered a dangerous man, a sinister factor . . . dictating the policy of the President'; Limantour was forced to complain to Díaz himself of the 'daily attacks whose instigators (whom you and I know well) try . . . to portray you before the whole world as a puppet manipulated by the "científicos"'. [132] Some historians have taken these polemics at face value. Yet it is clear that the Científicos, for all their wealth and contacts, enjoyed limited political power, and their position was always conditional on the favour of Díaz himself. They were rooted in Mexico City, where they held their cabinet or congressional posts and managed their legal and business affairs; with the exception of Creel and Molina (and maybe Rabasa) they exercised no power in the provinces, though their unpopularity knew no such bounds. The loathed Científicos remained an intellectual, technocratic elite, confined to the metropolis, their influence 'deriving from the only authentic source of power, which was Porfirio Díaz'. [133] This dependence, indeed, was heightened in the closing years of the regime. While politics remained the prerogative of narrow camarillas, national and local, the Científicos prospered, but as the issue of the succession began to agitate the political nation and as new political movements got under way, they faltered. They lacked popularity, they lacked support among Porfiristas in the provinces, they lacked the charisma and common touch which, in the novel situation of political mobilisation, counted for more than seats on the board or a well-stocked law library. Open – even half open – politics did not suit them. Limantour, passed over for vice-president in 1904, when he had fallen victim to a hostile press campaign, was no more popular in 1910. [134] There was no question of the Científicos surviving the fall of their master: all that remained of them after 1910 was the opprobrious label and the developmentalist ideology, soon to be taken up by others.

The Científicos' crucial weakness was their neglect of the provincial grassroots. Díaz knew better: his regime depended, at root, on the tight control exercised over the municipalities of the country by political bosses, the *jefes políticos*, appointed by the executive. It was through these three hundred or so key officials, 'who, at the moment of action, were indispensable political agents', that the Porfirian regime exercised its social control and it was in reaction to these many petty 'Díazpotisms' that local opposition and revolutionary movements often developed.[135]

Mexico's municipalities had longstanding democratic traditions, tracing back to the self-governing Spanish towns and Indian villages of the colony, and later enshrined in the liberal constitutions of the nineteenth century. But, particularly since the days of Bourbon centralism, power-hungry administrations had cut back the authority of municipal government, of mayor and town council. By the 1900s, outright executive appointees had replaced elected officials in certain states, such as Chihuahua.[136] Elsewhere, elected officials only secured election through the good offices of the executive, that is, of the *jefe político*. As a result, local elections became a sham, conducted amidst apathy and indifference, and municipal authorities became the supine servants of the executive, irremovable, unresponsive to local opinion, and starved of funds.[137] The strings of local power were gathered in the hands of the *jefe político* and only in regions where centralisation had made less headway – in the sierras and the remote south – did municipalities retain some of their old freedom and autonomy.

The character of the *jefe* varied from place to place. Like many Porfirian officials, *jefes* often owed their position to family connections: Luis Demetrio Molina, of Mérida, had uncle Olegario to thank; Silvano Martínez of Uruapán (Mich.) had married the daughter of state governor Mercado.[138] Such family relationships penetrated deep into the fabric of local government. Some muncipalities – like Guachóchic, in the Chihuahua sierra – were nests of nepotism, in which a couple of related families monopolised political, fiscal and judicial offices: Urique, in the same region, represented 'el colmo de compadrazgo', where a single family ran the beef trade and held all federal, state and municipal posts.[139] Increasingly, as the power of national and state governments grew, these local hierarchies depended on – often were created by – forces external to the *municipio* itself. Standing at the apex of the local hierarchy, the *jefe político* sought to reconcile its interests (usually the interests of the well-to-do) with the growing demands of the 'centre'. Where such a reconciliation could not be effected, the regime faced the opposition of entire communities, from top to bottom.[140] More often, the *jefe* governed to the satisfaction of the well-to-do and to the disgust of the *pelados*.

Most *jefes* were imposed from outside, by the 'centre'. Some were military men, like Colonel Celso Vega, the middle-aged army regular who ran Baja California Norte, or the disastrous Brigadier-General Higinio Aguilar, an old veteran of the French Intervention, who lasted two and a half months as *jefe político* at Cuernavaca (Mor.), antagonising the population, until a fraud charge removed him from office.[141] There were also suave *jefes*, who impressed foreign travellers with their culture: the antiquarian Andrés Ruiz of Tlacolula (Oax.) whom, it was said, the local people 'trusted and liked', or the 'well-read Cicerone', Enrique Dabbadie of Cuautla (Mor.), who proved no literary slouch

when, facing political opposition in his district in 1909, he ordered the
mounted police to break up demonstrations and arrested a crowd of 'local
merchants, workers, clerks [and] peons . . . some without charges being filed,
most simply because of their reputations'.[142] Curbing the opposition in this
way was one of the main tasks of the *jefe político*, particularly in the last years of
the Porfiriato, when political passions were rising. Puebla, seat of the corrupt
and arbitrary Martinista administration, became a centre of political dissidence, which the Martinista *jefe*, Joaquín Pita, sought to contain. When the
governor's car was stoned in the streets of the city, Pita (dismissing the political
signficance of the affair) had thirty alleged culprits consigned to the army.[143]
At election time he personally closed down polling booths which might
deliver an anti-government vote and had their rash supervisors arrested.[144]
The *jefe* of the Chihuahuan mining town of Batopilas similarly disfranchised
the opposition, denying them booths and sending a list of miners thought to
be sympathetic to the opposition to the American manager, in the hope that he
would apply suitable pressure. Though there were precedents for such action,
the manager declined: foreign businessmen were chary of direct involvement
in the flux of Porfirian politics.[145]

Foreign businessmen did, however, take steps to cultivate the local *jefe*, and
they valued his co-operation in the maintenance of order: the *jefe*, it might be
said, stood in the front line of the Porfirian 'collaborating elite', performing a
function no less vital than that of the Científicos.[146] Some *jefes* – like an earlier
incumbent at Batopilas – defused strike agitation by diplomacy and exhort-
ation; Carlos Herrera at Orizaba, and even Joaquín Pita at Puebla, showed an
awareness of the problems of the textile workers and a clear desire to combine
repression with sympathy.[147] In this respect – and particularly where the
textile workers were concerned – they reflected a more general change taking
place in Porfirian official attitudes towards labour. But elsewhere, most
notably, it would seem, in the wild and remote mining camps of the north,
jefes preferred the stick to the carrot and 'mine managers openly boasted of
these methods to timid investors'.[148] The *jefe político* of Mapimí, for example,
broke a strike at the Peñoles mine by riding into town with the police,
dragging the strikers from their homes, and beating up the furnacemen who
refused to work at the old rate: a case of *trop de zèle*, it would seem, for the
company were prepared to concede a pay rise, after a suitable delay.[149]

In addition to political surveillance and peace-keeping, the *jefe* could fulfil
a number of informal functions: 'he was the local authority of the central
government, the boss of the town and often its moneylender, pawnbroker,
house agent, merchant and marriage broker at the same time, and all greatly to
his own profit'.[150] Some resisted the gross temptations of office and exercised a
benevolent despotism over their districts. Demetrio Santibáñez, despite an
earlier record of political repression in southern Veracruz, 'ruled the district [of
Tehuantepec] with firmness and tact', settling complex conjugal disputes with

threats and blandishments, rattling off official letters on his typewriter, while stocking his private menagerie with parrots, monkeys and geckos. Santibáñez governed with the support of a Tehuana *cacica*, thereby, it seems, guaranteeing his popularity: a few years later, when the Revolution gave the chance, his son was made *jefe político* by popular acclamation.[151] There were other *jefes* – like Juan Francisco Villar of Uruapán, who had 'practised Democracy in the full flood of Dictatorship' – who were the objects of popular esteem and recall.[152] Equally, there were cases where the *jefe* was exonerated of abuses committed by other officials: the corrupt judicial authorities of Parral, the police chief who was a 'real tyrant' at Jiménez (Chih.).[153]

As these examples suggest, there was considerable scope for individual variation, which in turn might be translated into a varied pattern of revolutionary response after 1910. Given the opportunity, many communities were discriminating in offloading some officials, retaining, even recalling others. Yet, even here, it seems, the system contained a quantum of oppression which it was hard to avoid: if the *jefe político* escaped censure, then the police chief, *juez de paz*, or tax-collector incurred opprobrium; the licence to oppress was not eliminated, simply shared around. It was particularly evident, too, in certain recognisable and recurrent cases, where the imperatives of social and political circumstances defied individual tact or reputation. In regions of acute agrarian tension, for example, the *jefe*, as appointee of the centre and upholder of law and order, was easily converted into an ally of expansionist landlords.[154] Similarly, where a small commercial elite held a community and its rural hinterland in an economic vice, the *jefe* partnered mercantile exploiters – at Acapulco for example.[155] But the *jefe* was most acutely and specifically resented in regions where he acted as the arm of an entrenched state oligarchy, enforcing a new and rigid centralism in defiance of municipal interests and independence: in Chihuahua, where Governor Creel replaced elected with appointed *jefes municipales*, creating a tribe of 'veritable sultans'; or in Sonora, where the Torres administration likewise dismantled elected local government in a state where political literacy and expectations were on the increase.[156]

In circumstances like these, the *jefe político* appeared as a tyrant subverting local liberties. Hence communities preferred that a local man should occupy this crucial office, for a local man might display some degree of social responsibility, and, after 1911, demands to this effect came thick and fast, coupled sometimes with declarations that 'this pueblo refuses to be abandoned into the hands of a stranger who comes from outside'.[157] During the Porfiriato, however, outsiders predominated, and the chief criterion for appointment was loyalty to the executive – to the state governor, and to Díaz himself, who took a close interest in the selection of *jefes políticos*.[158] The Porfirian regime, bent on centralisation, knew no other way of operating. As for its opponents, some sought the end of centralisation and the consequent abolition of the *jefaturas*, others would retain but democratise the system, making it answerable to its subjects. Meantime, the regime judged a *jefe* according to his success at managing elections, maintaining order, silencing political opposition and labour unrest. If he failed in these respects – as Dabbadie appreciated at Cuautla – his remunerative employment was at an end; similarly, municipal officials who went against their governor's wishes were soon out of a job.[159]

Loyalty to Díaz rather than responsibility to subjects was the hallmark of the system: for *jefes políticos* 'the sole desire is to keep the Centre happy, and the Centre is happy so long as there is no revolution and not too many bandits in the countryside. The rest is neither here nor there'.[160] If keeping the Centre happy allowed, even encouraged, more enlightened rule, as it apparently did with Herrera at Orizaba or Santibáñez at Tehuantepec, that, for the locals, was a fortunate bonus. More often, as in Durango, the *jefes* were 'men who, to say the least, could never be elected', while some, like Rafael Cervantes (San Juan Guadalupe, Dgo), Jesús González Garza (Velardeña, Dgo), Cipriano Espinosa (San Felipe, Gto), Ignacio Hernández (San Miguel Allende, Gto), were known tyrants, spurs to local rebellion.[161]

The position of the *jefe* lent itself to corruption. In Oaxaca, a prospective appointee, aware that the official salary of 150 pesos a month was inadequate, had to tout himself around the local planters and businessmen, seeking retainers in return for services to be rendered.[162] Others supplemented their income with fines, some of which were diverted into the *jefe*'s pocket. Complaints against petty, arbitrary fines were legion: in the prosperous towns of Sonora and the booming oil port of Tampico; in Guanajuato, where Indians were fined for coming into town wearing their baggy drawers; in Chihuahua where drunks were mulcted twenty-five pesos, and *arrieros* were fined for watering their burros at public springs.[163] Joaquín Pita, it was said, made so much money fining the people of Puebla that he paid his boss, Governor Martínez, for the privilege, rather than receiving a salary, while the *jefe* of Soconusco was reckoned to have accumulated a personal fortune of a quarter of a million pesos in three years, dispossessing people of their land and extorting excessive fines.[164] Early in 1911, his fortune made, he quit the region for Mexico City, fearing assassination.

Apart from such quasi-judicial peculation, the *jefe* enjoyed other means of making money. Dabbadie, in Cuautla, embezzled political funds (the Revolution brought to light many similar malpractices); increased, often arbitrary taxes were a constant complaint in Chihuahua and elsewhere; Aguilar lost his job at Cuernavaca for 'defrauding the feeble-minded heir to a Cuernavaca fortune'.[165] Even if some of these allegations were untrue, or exaggerated, they indicated something of the public image of the *jefe* and of his stewardship. Certainly *jefes* followed gubernatorial example and prevailing political mores in blurring their official and private functions. In Yucatán, the *jefe político* of

Acanceh managed a Molina plantation, while another ran a butcher's shop which local people were obliged to patronise, to the detriment of competitors and customers alike.[166] In Chihuahua, too, local officials, appointed by Governor Creel, were on the payroll of Creel's private companies.[167] Sonoran officials – *jefes*, judges, police chiefs – ran liquor stores and gambling houses.[168] The *jefe*'s control of prison work gangs also proved lucrative: one *jefe* used forced labour to pave a road through his brother's hacienda; another had prisoners build him a private house; *jefes* in Guerrero reaped profits supplying work gangs for the Chilpancingo–Acapulco highway.[169] Perhaps most lucrative, certainly most infamous, was the trade in *enganchados*, 'hooked' labourers who were consigned, by force or fraud, to the semi-slave plantations of the south. Ten per cent of the labourers in the notorious Valle Nacional were reckoned to have been sent there by Rodolfo Pardo, *jefe político* of nearby Tuxtepec, who 'by the illegal sale of lands and people has amassed a large fortune'.[170] The *jefe* of Pochutla, which lay 'ankle-deep in dust under the blazing sun' of the Pacific, ran a similar trade, while further afield at Pachuca – a large, run-down mining town on the central plateau, where the miners' acquaintance with liquor and unemployment helped business – the *jefe* annually sent 500 labourers south for plantation work.[171]

There was one final prerogative of the *jefe* which, if less profitable, was no less gratifying to the official or galling to the people in his charge: the *jefe*'s droit de seigneur. 'To possess by force or deceit', it has been said, is the essence of *machismo*, and the *jefe político*, along with other members of Porfirian officialdom, had ample opportunity to play the *macho*, again blurring public and private activities.[172] The caciques of Azteca (Mor.), for example, 'took advantage of poor girls. If they liked a girl, they got her – they always enjoyed fine women just because of the power they had. One of the caciques died at eighty in the arms of a fifteen-year-old girl'.[173] A *jefe* at Mariscal (Chis.) celebrated his birthday by 'inviting' a young woman to his house, while his men ran her *novio* out of town; his counterpart at the Yucateco port of Progreso, Colonel José María Ceballos, aroused a 'very keen hatred' among the local people, not least because of his 'questionable attitude towards the young girls of Progreso', and his propensity to arrest their fathers in order to further his suit.[174] Similar kinds of sexual exploitation had impelled rebels – like Pancho Villa – on their early outlaw careers. In the case of Ceballos it was his libidinous pursuits, rather than the forced conscription, exorbitant taxation, heavy fines and 'arbitrary and dictatorial behaviour in general', of all of which he was guilty, which finally brought his downfall. For in 1914 the daughter of a Progreso butcher, Lino Muñoz, spurned the *jefe*'s advances: the father rebelled rather than face reprisals and, recruiting fifty men, he captured the port, paraded Ceballos in the square, and had him shot. The Revolution thus came to Progreso after the manner of a Corsican vendetta.

In the main, Porfirian officialdom's sins of commission weighed most heavily on the *pelados*, the common people, who suffered arbitrary fines, arrests, impressment, deportation, even – in notorious cases like Tepames (Col.) – murder.[175] They conceived a bitter hatred of the regime, in its local manifestation, and the Revolution was therefore characterised both by sudden, violent, popular uprisings against such officials and also by a more general popular hostility to the Porfirian system, and to would-be restorers of that system, whose legitimacy had been irretrievably squandered. This popular reaction must be seen within the general context of Porfirian economic and agrarian policy (the subject of chapter three). The *gente decente* on the other hand, the respectable, literate, propertied people, resented Porfirian official-dom somewhat differently. Some, it is true, suffered arrest and imprisonment for their political views. Antonio Sedano, a 'respected merchant' of Cuerna-vaca, who dabbled in opposition politics, was arrested 'for not having washed down the street' in front of his store; Ponciano Medina, arrested by the *jefe político* of Tuxtepec (Rodolfo Pardo again) for participating in an opposition demonstration, chose to pay a fifty peso fine rather than to go to gaol, 'since his social and financial position would not allow his dignity as an honourable businessman to be outraged'.[176] He was gaoled just the same. In general, however, the *gente decente* escaped the more extreme abuses. Their chief complaint was likely to be the unfair, sometimes capricious incidence of taxation, which could weigh heavily on small businessmen and artisans.[177] It was perhaps for this reason that 'Commerce' was linked to 'the People in general' as the joint victims of the corrupt city government of Puebla, or that the *jefe* of San Miguel Allende was said to have 'all the middle and lower class subjugated'.[178]

The *gente decente* complained more of Porfirian sins of omission, of official derelictions of duty. The businessmen of Enseñada, for example, were sick of the extravagance and ineptitude of *jefe* Celso Vega, a military mediocrity, who was held responsible for a smallpox outbreak in the region.[179] In Chihuahua, the authorities at Ciudad Camargo tolerated drunkenness and abduction; the *jefe* of the Benito Juárez district of the state could never be found in his office; the muncipal boss at Carichic failed in his duty to support the local schools; at Cusihuaráchic, a fast-growing mining town, the *jefe* was a wastrel who kept only two policemen on the payroll, and they slouched about in sandals and sloppy shirts. Chihuahuan *jefes* in general, critics complained, failed to supervise their districts, preferring to sit immobile in the *cabecera* (the head town), save when they left 'to come to the capital for some banquet'.[180] What the respectable, literate people of Chihuahua wanted was not less government, but more, better, responsible government. What such people also wanted was a government which not only honoured its constitutional obligations (an obvious but central point), but also lived up to its progressive, 'developmenta-list' rhetoric. Científico advocacy of hard work, hygiene, sobriety and 'pro-gress' – values to which respectable critics were also strongly attached – was daily belied by the facts of life in small towns, like Potam (Sra), where the drunk police chief could be found with his cronies – the judge, postmaster and schoolteacher, the 'influential, governing class' of the community – drinking, playing billiards, fixing deals, while outside the streets remained unswept, the streetlights were inadequate, and the only centre of recreation was the saloon. In such towns, 'inefficiency and dishonesty were the order of the day', while, despite the regime's philosophy, 'all evolution was a sin, and every effort to break with custom a crime'.[181] Científicos like Sierra would have shared the sense of outrage. For critics of this kind, it was not that Científico social philosophy fundamentally erred (Científico political authoritarianism was, of course, a different matter), it was rather that the regime had failed to implement the philosophy, that it appeared to tolerate in practice the ingrained vices it condemned in principle.

It was additionally vexing for the *gente decente* that they had no say in the election of local officials, hence no control over their conduct. Sustained pressure, if it came from the right sources and was articulated in the right way, might dislodge an intolerable local boss. Díaz was prepared to cast the occasional *jefe*, like the occasional state governor, to the wolves, in order to assuage public opinion – and *pour encourager les autres*. Peculation and oppression had to be nicely judged, as Higinio Aguilar learned to his cost at Cuernavaca.[182] The people of Villa Aldama (Chih.) showed how to set about removing a hated political boss. They mounted an impressive, decorous demonstration, bringing over 250 protesters to the state capital and handing in a petition to the governor; on returning to Villa Aldama their train was met by 'a group of ladies and señoritas of our better society, with palms and flowers'. Clearly, this was no rabble and since, in the words of the governor, the people of Villa Aldama 'had always given proof of a model peacefulness and notable submissiveness and obedience to the constituted authorities', he agreed to accede to their petition and remove the offending official.[183]

But the government did not like doing this too often. Many more petitions and complaints were ignored; some egregiously offending officials (in particular, one suspects, those who chiefly offended against mute *pelados*) survived and prospered.[184] And from the point of view of the protesters – even successful protesters – this was a clumsy, expensive and uncertain method of effecting changes in local government. When the proposed re-election of unpopular city officials at Tampico produced vocal complaints in December 1910, the ticket was withdrawn and new candidates were substituted. These were elected 'in the usual form'. Not surprisingly, the townspeople remained dissatisfied, since 'they claim that they had no voice in the selection of the new men on this new ticket'.[185] What thinking, respectable citizens wanted was not this vague and uncertain right of veto (a right that could only be exercised occasionally and discreetly), but regular consultation through the polls, as the Constitution provided. Hence arose the original slogan of the 1910 revolution, *Sufragio Efectivo, No Re-elección*, and the reiterated cry for *Municipio Libre*, free local government.

In maintaining, in defiance of the Constitution, a closed, *caciquista* form of politics, the Porfirian regime had constant resort to repression, perpetrated by the army or the police, particularly the mounted police, the *rurales*. In some towns, such as Parral, the police chief called the tune and incurred popular hostility.[186] Elsewhere, at Potam, for example, or Puebla, he acted as ally and crony of the *jefe*. The death of Miguel Cabrera, Puebla's chief of police, provoked scurrilous verses in 1910:

> Cabrera arrived in hell, in his bowler hat and frockcoat,
> And a witch said to him: 'Why haven't you brought Pita?'[187]

Porfirian police methods were crude: suspects had been known to die in custody (Cabrera had been involved in one famous case) and there were allegations of torture, though in this respect Díaz, and his regime, were mild in comparison with Latin American dictatorships of then and now.[188]

If the regime was even less a police state than it was a militarist state, nevertheless it maintained a degree of covert political surveillance, particularly in the later years, as opposition grew and the president, perhaps, became more suspiciously dictatorial. Plain-clothes policemen watched opposition demonstrations, like those of the Anti-Re-electionist students in 1892; in the provinces, governors, *jefes políticos*, and military commanders monitored local subversion, reporting to Díaz members of opposition groups and subscribers to opposition newspapers.[189] Governor Martínez of Puebla was particularly zealous in the collection of political intelligence: he employed a retired policeman, turned newsagent, to furnish the names of those who read the wrong papers; he supplied Díaz with a complete run of the oppositionist *Regeneración*; he sent his hired thugs to pay nocturnal visits on suspect citizens. As new opposition parties developed in the 1900s, they were promptly infiltrated, as were some Masonic lodges. *Jefes* sent delegates to opposition party conventions (when they were permitted), while the military commander at Juárez hired a 'seductive lady' to worm her way into the Liberal Party and monitor their plans in the US. Political exiles such as these were closely watched (as were their families in Mexico) and there were even attempts at assassination on foreign soil.[190]

Within Mexico, the growth of political activity in the 1900s was matched by a parallel growth of secret police activity, of which people were well aware. In Yucatán, the rise of the 'universally detested secret police' added a new dimension to the old *caciquismo*: it was reckoned that Governor Molina had recruited 700 agents in a city of 50,000 (Mérida), where they 'were used for political and worse purposes by the Governor'.[191] Creel had his secret police in Chihuahua, too, said to be better known than the uniformed variety, and 'recognisable from miles away'.[192] Nevertheless, Porfirian rulers were tolerably successful at sniffing out disaffection and quashing revolts, like those of 1906 and 1908, organised by the Liberals. The first flicker of the 1910 revolution was easily doused as well. Porfirian political intelligence was thus adequate for pinpointing known oppositionists. It failed, however, to convey an accurate, general picture of political conditions and unrest and it failed because the kind of reports which governors, *jefes* and police chiefs liked both to file and to receive were ones in which the strength of the opposition was deprecated and derided, that of the regime taken for granted. A generation of peace had instilled a fatal political hubris and the regime, insulated from the reality of its own unpopularity, was encouraged to disregard mounting political and social unrest. Hence the 1910 revolution came as a surprise.

When it came, the regime proved equal to the challenge in the cities, where most known oppositionists were gathered and where they could easily be apprehended. But in the countryside, soon to be the locus of rebellion, the situation was different. Opposition here was more anonymous, inarticulate, and often unforeseen. Its supposed antidote was the rural police, the *rurales*, the showpiece of the Pax Porfiriana. The *rurales*, established in the 1860s as the Juárez government's answer to endemic banditry, had by the 1900s become a symbol of the Porfirian regime's *machismo* and efficiency. Foreigners, especially foreign ladies, were susceptible to the *rurales'* fine mounts and dashing *charro* outfits – tight trousers, brief leather jackets, wide sombreros, bandannas, cummerbunds and assorted weaponry. Parading through Mexico City, with sparks flying from their horses' hooves, they cut a fine figure and the romantic aura (cultivated by the official press) was only heightened by the prevalent belief that many *rurales* were themselves ex-bandits, now given 'the congenial occupation . . . of hunting down other robbers and malcontents'.[193]

The truth was more prosaic. The early *rurales* had included some ex-guerrilleros, though few bandits. By the 1890s the majority of recruits were *campesinos* and artisans (the latter disproportionately represented), many coming from the declining towns of the Bajío.[194] Their activities were less glamorous too: in 1908, for example, the First, Second, and Seventh Rural Corps were engaged escorting railway and factory paymasters, keeping order during Holy Week fiestas or on hacienda paydays, policing local elections, quelling revolts against unpopular authorities, conveying prisoners across country (chiefly to the penal colonies on the Tres Marías islands off the Tepic coast) and chasing rustlers and criminal fugitives. The occasional petty train-robber was the closest to the bandit quarry of the good old days.[195] Some *rurales*, it is true, lived up to the image. Corporal, later Major, Francisco Cárdenas peers impassively from the pages of Casasola, ruggedly handsome in embroidered *charro* jacket and waistcoat and a broad-brimmed sombrero. In 1910 he hunted down the elusive bandit–rebel Santañón and killed him on the banks of the Huasuntán River; three years later he collected an even more prestigious trophy.[196] Yet even Cárdenas' heroics were perhaps, like his jacket, embroidered and there can be no doubt that the *rurales* of the late Porfiriato were in general older, fatter, and less dashing than their image suggested. They were not averse to beating helpless peons (some used that favourite Latin American *bastinado*, the bull's penis), nor to liquidating prisoners by means of the *ley fuga*, the 'shot while trying to escape' formula which saved the authorities the embarrassment of a trial.[197] But Paul Vanderwood has ably documented their many failings, evident in the Gobernación archive, if not in the pages of Mrs Moats and Mrs Tweedie: their predominant illiteracy and one-in-three desertion rate, their combination of adolescence and senility, their drunkenness, delinquency, ill discipline and incompetence.[198]

The deportment of the First Rural Corps, on the eve of the Revolution, did not differ much from the average.[199] Its commander had enlisted in 1869; one of his corporals was a veteran of the War of the Reform (1857–60). But, an inspector concluded, the demands placed on the officers were not extreme: 'posts in the Rural Police ... as they are carried out at the moment are real sinecures, since the commanders of the detachments, once they establish themselves in the places allocated for residence, apart from procuring a small fortune in the shortest possible time, and at any cost, delegate all the duties of the service to subordinates'. The Corps' tasks – patrolling the railways, haciendas and textile factories of the Puebla–Mexico region – were poorly performed. Trains went unescorted (the *rurales* preferred to lounge in the stations) and managers believed their factories were menaced by labour agitation. The factory workers despised the *rurales*, while the peons of the Oaxaqueña plantation resented their well-paid employment as field managers and foremen. It was in this (strictly illegal) capacity that the only energetic detachment of the Corps exhausted their horses patrolling the plantation perimeter and bent their sabres belabouring the field hands. Discipline in the Corps was lax, or of a crude, pecking-order variety; nepotism was rife; and officers, generally illiterate, behaved like petty tyrants. Ignorant of the rule-book, they beat their men, reviewed them in shirt-sleeves, neglected their horses, drank, gambled, attended cockfights and ran up bills at the local bars – that is, if they did not, like Corporal Francisco Alvarez, at Atotonilco, run a *cantina* of their own. The men wore 'peasant garb' (no tight trousers and cummerbunds out in the sticks) and lived in squalid barracks, often with their families. Here, one corporal had been laid up with rheumatism for six months. While Corporal Alvarez ran his bar and Corporal Gutiérrez policed the plantation, Corporal Pacheco, who had been stationed at Necaxa for no less than eight years, had built up so many connections that the town was polarised into Pachequista and anti-Pachequista factions. Indeed, relations between the rural police and the civil authorities were not always cordial, and were frequently corrupt: Alvarez, receiving the inspector in bed, boasted of having the judiciary of Atotonilco in his pocket.[200]

Clearly, the *rurales* were unprepared for the supreme test of 1910. Their job was to police the countryside; they were, supposedly, the fleet, remorseless pursuers of bandits and rebels; they were the regime's first line of defence against subversion in the countryside, where political intelligence was poor and which the Federal army, with its troop trains and artillery, could not easily penetrate. That they failed in 1910 was partly because of their unpopularity at the grassroots (an admirer, with unconscious irony, likened them to 'the Irish Constabulary or . . . that splendid corps, the Guardias Civiles in Spain').[201] But failure can also be attributed to their acquisition, over the years, of new, peace-time habits; to their accumulation, in particular localities, of sinecures, contacts, retainers, kickbacks; to their growing preference for the quiet life in La Simpática Michoacana (Corporal Alvarez's *cantina*) over that of the hungry, saddle-sore bandit hunter.

The *rurales*, as Vanderwood remarks, were a typical Porfirian institution, a blend of self-interest and oppression tempered by inefficiency, sloth and complacency, displaying an overriding loyalty to the dictator. They may serve as a more general allegory of the regime. By 1910 Mexico's rulers had grown flabby, overweening, unpopular and often unaware of their unpopularity, for too long the monopolists of power and privilege. It was a government of old men: Cahuantzi, governing Tlaxcala, was eighty, Bandala in Tabasco was seventy-eight, Mercado, of Michoacán, was reckoned to be too senile to sign his name on state papers.[202] Old and sick men filled the cabinet, where four senior ministers had enjoyed an average of twenty years apiece in office.[203] As for Díaz himself, now seventy-nine, he had once enjoyed undeniable popularity – as the hero of the French Intervention and the creator of peace and progress; in Oaxaca, and probably elsewhere too, he still enjoyed support.[204] But by the 1900s this popularity – and with it the legitimacy of the regime – had waned, not least because of the social stresses consequent on rapid economic change. These stresses, to be considered in the next two chapters, could neither be mediated nor repressed. The Díaz regime was not a military dictatorship, nor a police state: it depended on some lingering legitimacy, as well as on coercion, and the coercion was selective and limited, not indiscriminate. Hence the financially successful rundown of the army, and the recognition, even by opponents of the government, that 'General Díaz has used absolute power with great moderation', that he 'is not a tyrant – a bit rigid, but not a tyrant'.[205] Indeed, a fully-fledged police or militarist state might have coped with the challenge of 1910 better than Díaz's ramshackle civilian/*caciquista* regime could.

But this was a failure of political mediation, as well as of military repression.[206] Barrington Moore has identified a species of 'strong conservative government', committed to state-building and economic development, but bent on 'trying to solve a problem that was inherently insoluble, to modernise without changing . . . social structures'.[207] The Porfirian regime, entertaining similar objectives, went even further in conserving both social structures and political mechanisms. If the Científicos represented one face of the regime – economically progressive, developmentalist, forward-looking – the corrupt *rurales* and arbitrary *jefes* displayed another, which was politically haggard, with rheumy eyes fixed on the past. Yet the social consequences of development had to be mediated through the political system; protests of increasing vigour had to be either accommodated or repressed. As it was, the Porfirian regime refused to accommodate aspiring, articulate groups (its sins of omission), while, in the last resort, it failed to repress aggrieved, declining groups, the chief victim of the regime's sins of commission. Like some saurian monster, the regime lacked a political brain commensurate with its swollen economic muscle; hence its extinction.

2

The opposition

OUTSIDERS AND DIE-HARDS

Articulate political opposition to the Díaz regime never altogether died during the long years of peace and stability. But most challenges to the status quo came at local not national level. Díaz himself was re-elected to the presidency on six successive occasions between 1884 and 1904, but no serious opposition developed or was allowed to develop at any time. In 1890, when the executive belatedly lifted the constitutional ban on the re-election of the president and state governors, the state legislatures rubber-stamped the proposals and opposition was slight.[1] The presidential re-election of 1892, coinciding with the novel Científico plans for party organisation and an institutionalised succession, witnessed greater political activity, as *gobiernista* efforts to impart a veneer of respectability to the inevitable re-election provoked counter-demonstrations in which the students and artisans of Mexico City were prominent. After this mild flurry, subsequent re-elections of Díaz in 1896, 1900 and 1904 proceeded smoothly and on each occasion the dictator amassed huge majorities by the usual methods.[2] The only serious politicking took place within the Porfirista camarilla, as would-be successors jockeyed for power; national politics remained the monopoly of a tiny minority.

With the politics of the centre thus constrained, the provinces alone offered examples of political opposition which occasionally achieved results. Just as odious local officials might be removed by a sustained display of carefully orchestrated protest, so opposition movements directed against incumbent state governors sometimes won victories. In 1893 popular antipathy to Governor Garza Galán and his *jefes políticos* in Coahuila bred opposition and finally a spate of revolts. Since some important local families were involved, Díaz sent Reyes to investigate and both agreed that Garza Galán should be replaced.[3] But, as Díaz told a *potosino* delegation which opposed the re-election of Governor Díez Gutiérrez in 1896, 'it was not a simple matter to procure changes in the state governments'.[4] Ensconced oligarchs clung tenaciously to power; only occasionally and judiciously would the centre throw its weight behind the opposition; more often, attempts to oppose gubernatorial re-election brought swift repression – as the opponents of Mercado in Michoacán learned in 1896, those of Dehesa in Veracruz in 1900, those of Mucio Martínez on several occasions in Puebla. Reyes, though he helped topple Garza Galán, was ruthless in crushing opposition to his own re-election in Nuevo León.[5] Old-style móvements of local opposition, such as those which contested political impositions in Guerrero, thus tended to fade away, the victims of Porfirian natural selection.[6]

The centre, so long as it remained the arbiter of provincial politics, sifting reports, protests and petitions, weighing the merits of incumbent against opposition, could tolerate a degree of political heterodoxy in the system. Indeed, granted the farcical nature of elections, this was the only process whereby public opinion could be crudely evaluated. An excess of unpopular governors was a liability; conversely, by occasionally sacrificing a governor, Díaz reinforced the power of the centre and demonstrated that he was the only political immortal in the system. Such local opposition movements therefore represented no serious challenge to the regime. They were generally personal-ist movements of limited objectives, concerned to evict a knave from the state palace. Ideological statements were ancillary to that end and rarely constituted a general indictment of Porfirian government.

If they could not challenge the regime, and if, in the main, they were ignored, harassed and where necessary crushed, these local movements did however maintain a tradition of protest to which certain groups and families – the political 'outs' of the system – remained committed for decades. Some 'outs' – like the Terrazas – made their peace with the dictator; others – like the Maytorena and Pesqueira families of Sonora – battled to wrest control of the state's fortunes from the Torres machine until finally they were driven into the arms of the Revolution, an embrace of expedience rather than of revolutionary passion.[7] In Durango, Lic. Ignacio Borrego, son of a prominent liberal general of the 1850s, capped a career of opposition journalism and oratory by supporting the Revolution; Eduardo Neri achieved power in Guerrero where his uncle Canuto had failed back in the 1890s.[8] Lower down, municipalities were split by similar clientelist tussles. At Pisaflores (Hgo), the Alvarados enjoyed growing economic and political dominance, to the chagrin of the Rubios; after thirty years of conflict the Revolution gave members of the 'out-faction' an opportunity to turn the tables.[9] It may be presumed that, in a closed political system like that of Díaz, in which – to use the appropriate jargon – elites circulated sluggishly if at all, 'out-factions' of this kind were ubiquitous. An old Mexico hand recalled the Sunday evening *paseo* in a provincial town, where the young people promenaded and flirted, their parents observed, and 'at one end of the square the solid citizens, such as the *jefe político* and his cronies and the priest and his cronies gather[ed], while at the other end the out-of-office malcontents and the eggheads congregate[d], with the bandstand in between the two factions'.[10] Such perennial opposition groups could supply important recruits to revolutionary movements. In particular, they could supply men of wealth, influence and political experience ('leadership cadres', if you like) – men like Maytorena and the brothers Pesqueira in Sonora. But such recruits, motivated by clientelist and personal concerns, were hardly disposed to be the originators of revolution. They were too few in number, too circumspect, and they had existed for too long – albeit uncomfortably – under the Porfirian dispensation. Furthermore, during their long quest for state or municipal power, the regime had shown itself well capable of coping with them. For Díaz they were old familiar irritants rather than the germs of a new terminal disease. They might board a bandwagon that was off and rolling, but they would not put their shoulders to the wheel to start it off.

If limited, local, clientelist opposition was common, ideological opposition – based on sure principles, a broad critique of the regime and a platform of reforms – was rare, until the very conclusion of the Porfiriato. Through the 1890s there could be heard only the muted voices of the die-hard liberals – voices crying in a positivist, Porfirian wilderness – and the perennial but passive Catholic opposition. While Díaz had successfully eliminated independent liberal opinion in Congress, printed criticism of the regime continued, sporadically and ineffectually, harping on the usual liberal themes: the inertia of the legislature, the revival of clerical influence, and – the central point – the suffocation of all independent political life, *poca política* in fact.[11] For years, Filómena Mata fulminated against Porfirian abuses in the pages of *El Diario del Hogar*; Juan Sanchez Azcona's *El Diario*, founded in 1906, became the first daily to campaign on social issues; the satirical press, all but killed off in the 1880s, staged a revival under the leadership of Daniel Cabrera's *El Hijo de Ahuizote*.[12] Theirs was a risky business. Mata suffered thirty incarcerations in Belem gaol: so frequent and predictable were his visits that, it is said, he installed his own bed in the prison.[13] But Mata, a one-time ally of Díaz, was more fortunate than Dr Ignacio Martínez, who published an anti-Díaz paper in Brownsville, Texas, where four attempts were made on his life before a Porfirista gang finally 'riddled [him] with bullets' in 1890.[14] But co-option was more usual and more effective than elimination and a good many critical journalists – Duclos Salinas, Zayas Enríquez, Wistano Luis Orozco – all made their peace with the regime and later came out in its defence.[15]

Catholic opposition, meanwhile, was polarised between the old nineteenth-century opposition to liberalism and 'atheism', the Catholicism of Pius IX and the Syllabus, and the new 'social' Catholicism inspired by Leo XIII and *Rerum Novarum*. The former were placated by Díaz's neglect of the Reform Laws and gratified by the regime's commitment to order and centralism. Still, some Catholic journalists, parish priests and seminarists continued to denounce the irreligious republic and the materialism of the Científicos. While this did not

crystallise into an organised political force, it encouraged reservations concerning the regime in the hearts of the devout and it afforded a basis for later
Catholic politicisation, which the Revolution would stimulate.[16] Social
Catholicism posed a greater threat to the regime and its policy of ideological
anaesthesia. In the course of the 1900s a series of Catholic congresses met to
discuss contemporary social problems: illiteracy, alcoholism, peonage,
working-class pay and conditions. Exponents of social Catholicism – or 'white
socialism' as its critics termed it – went further in investigating such problems
and attempting remedies by way of night schools, recreation centres and
mutualist societies.[17] The Catholic press meanwhile provided the most
consistent voice of moderate opposition to the regime: Victoriano Agüeros'
pioneer *El Tiempo*, and the Catholic daily *El País*, which in the 1900s enjoyed
the largest circulation in Mexico and the second largest in Latin America.[18]
While later generations of historians may feel gratitude for the 'dirt' they
published about the Díaz regime, the regime itself was unenthusiastic – as
were many conservative Catholics too. Clerical favour gave *El País* a degree of
protection, but its journalists still faced imprisonment if they went too far.

The rise of social Catholicism in the 1900s was a feature not only of global
trends within the Catholic Church, but also of specific developments within
the Mexican polity. Prior to 1900, ideological opposition to Díaz was
individual, sporadic and ineffectual. But the 1900s, and particularly the years
1908–10, witnessed a radical change. Three successive opposition movements
– the Partido Liberal Mexicano (PLM), the Reyistas (Partido Democrático),
and the Maderistas (Partido Anti-reeleccionista) – mobilised a degree of
popular support, based on coherent, national programmes, that was
unprecedented in the Porfiriato. For the first time in a generation the
opposition took the battle to the centre and opened up the whole question of
access to national power – hitherto a question guarded by political taboo. As a
result, the centre could no longer perform its traditional role, that of
maintaining equilibrium in a centralised, autocratic system, in which institutional, representative procedures had never been allowed to develop. Local
political conflicts, once capable of rapid, dictatorial settlement by the centre,
now multiplied and began to merge in a national struggle for supremacy. The
sombre prophecy of the Catholic opposition paper *El Heraldo*, made nearly
twenty years before, was vindicated: 'why do we attack re-election? Because it
is preparing the most dreadful civil war which the nation has ever suffered.'[19]

THE NEW OPPOSITION: I THE SOCIAL CONTEXT

The raw material for the politicisation of the 1900s lay in the burgeoning cities
of Porfirian Mexico and, to a lesser extent, in some regions of commercialised
ranchero agriculture. Throughout the Porfiriato the population of the country
grew by some 61%, that of the state capitals by 88%; between 1895 and 1910

the number of major towns (those in excess of 20,000 population) grew from twenty-two to twenty-nine, thus enabling the urban population (similarly defined) to increase by half a million, from 1.2 to 1.7 million.[20] Urban growth was far from uniform. While old metropolises like Mexico City and Guadalajara swelled and new boom towns like Torreón, Tampico and Cananea grew prodigiously, other communities, by-passed by the railway or unable for other reasons to participate in the Porfirian economic miracle, stagnated and shrank – notably in Jalisco, Zacatecas and San Luis.[21] Within states and regions, too, demographic fortunes varied: Guaymas throve while Ures stagnated; Torreón grew from a small *ranchería* in the 1880s to a city of 23,000 in 1900 and 43,000 in 1910 and, while Gómez Palacio prospered alongside, Ciudad Lerdo languished.[22] But it was the steady growth of established cities, rather than the febrile expansion of boom towns like Cananea, which was most significant. Between 1895 and 1910, when the national population increased at 1.2% per annum, Chihuahua City grew at between 5 and 6%, Veracruz at nearly 5%, Monterey and Mérida nearly 4%, Mexico City, Guadalajara and Aguascalientes at around 2.5%.[23] From a broader perspective, the absolute growth registered between the 1870s and 1900s is even more striking: Chihuahua City from some 12,000 to 30,000 (1871–1900), Durango from 12,000 to 31,000 (1869–1900), Monterrey from 14,000 to 79,000 (1869–1910), Mexico City from 200,000 to 471,000 (1874–1910).[24]

Urban growth accompanied and encouraged a range of phenomena: improved communications both between and within towns, as railways and trams replaced the pack-mule and mule-drawn carriages; a quickening and diversification of commercial life and industry; improvements in municipal service, at least in the major cities, as paved roads, piped water, drains and electric light appeared; a marked expansion of shops, schools and colleges, of banks and law firms. If politics languished, the pace of city life accelerated: smart hotels replaced the old *mesones*, cars appeared on the streets, the cinema offered a new diversion. Newspapers, magazines and cultural periodicals proliferated: 202 in 1884, 543 in 1900, 1,571 in 1907, an increase over twenty-three years from one per 54,000 inhabitants to one per 9,000.[25] Readership was limited, but growing: 14% of Mexicans were reckoned to be literate in 1895, 20% in 1910. Some states recorded much higher percentages, both absolutely and relatively: Coahuila 17 and 31%, Chihuahua 19 and 28%, Sonora 23 and 34%.[26] As these figures suggest, Porfirian educational policy (much maligned since the Revolution) had made some headway and Científico concern for education as a means to further national development was not wholly rhetorical.[27]

In particular, the capital and the cities of the north grew and prospered. Following the liberal abolition of corporate property, Mexico City expanded far beyond its old colonial core: the valley was drained, new markets were built, entrepreneurs created a swathe of new suburban *colonias*, radiating out from the Zócalo and, though the capital contained only some 3% of the Mexican population, it boasted one-fifth of the country's doctors and lawyers, a quarter of its periodicals, and almost half of its scientific and literary societies.[28] But there were equivalent developments, on a less grand scale, in other cities, especially those of the north. In 1850 Monterrey had a population of less than 20,000, one industrial establishment (with a capital of 7,000 pesos) and one major warehouse.[29] By the mid-1890s, as commercial expansion was succeeded by industrialisation, in which Mexican and foreign businesses participated to mutual advantage, the population had reached 48,000 and included 89 lawyers, 153 teachers and 2,000 merchants; by 1909 there were over 300 schools and 1,000 commercial houses serving a population of 70,000. A thriving economy, fostered by Governor Reyes, and a large industrial proletariat (to be distinguished from the artisans and sweated labour of many Mexican cities) gave Monterrey a distinctive appearance: 'here one does not encounter that unwashed, ill-clad mob which, unfortunately, one observes in some parts of the Republic . . . in Monterrey, in general, everyone has a decent appearance: the worker and the artisan display well-being and an appearance of dignity and personal decorum'.[30] A far cry, in other words, from the *pulque*-sodden rabble of cities of the central plateau.

Monterrey ('Mexico's Chicago') and Torreón (the latter with its busy industries, expensive hotels and dearth of churches conveying a distinctly 'American appearance') were the outstanding examples of trends exhibited by other northern cities. Chihuahua City, at the end of the 1890s, was a 'booming capital' of some 25,000, with a foundry, textile and brewing companies (several of them components of the Creel-Terrazas empire), public telephones and trams, three banks, forty-nine town houses valued in excess of 10,000 pesos, and nineteen weekly publications nursing the city's culture. It enjoyed the services of thirty-five lawyers, an average of one lawyer to 700 inhabitants (approximately the same as Mexico City; in Monterrey the ratio was 1:500, in Guanajuato 1:1,000).[31] Smaller towns, too, if favoured by trade and communications, underwent similar change: west coast ports like Guaymas and Mazatlán or the state capital of Sinaloa, Culiacán, which, having emerged from the ravages of the French Intervention, bandit attacks, and the liberal infighting of the 1870s, now had a population of 14,000, electric light and drinking water, spacious streets and plaza, a textile factory and two sugar refineries, a theatre, several schools and colleges, and a couple of newspapers.[32]

The quickening of economic life and the improvement in communications affected even smaller, more remote rural communities. Among the *rancheros* of northern Guerrero, some families managed to expand their holdings, establish small factories (flour mills, distilleries, ice-plants), build roads, irrigate, and acquire superior education for their children. A similar commercially successful group – a 'peasant bourgeoisie' – emerged in the Sierra Alta of Hidalgo.[33] In the case of San José de Gracia, the arrival of the railway at Ocotlán gave an impulse to economic development: new fortunes were made, old wealth augmented; San José now had its 'dozen rich men', farmers and merchants who imported foreign luxuries (felt hats and brass bedsteads, photographs and phonographs), who built houses with iron-railed balconies, who disdained their fathers' beards and went clean-shaven, save for curled-up Kaiser Wilhelm moustaches.[34] *El País* began to circulate and a few people ventured to travel to Zamora and Guadalajara. In 1905 a stranger arrived in the town, a *catrín*, who wore a wide-brimmed hat and who, when he called at some of the houses, was surprised to be kissed on the hand. The local people took him for a priest; he was in fact a salesman for Singer sewing machines.

Central to this process of social change was the growth of the Mexican middle class, particularly the urban middle class. To state this is to risk criticism, first from sceptical historians, weary of 'rising middle classes', and second from acute theorists, who point to the vagueness of the 'middle class' label. The first objection must be answered by deploying empirical evidence. As for the second, it is not clear that the 'middle class' label is any vaguer than other analytical categories, which of necessity take slices from a continuum of social reality. It may be less 'scientific', in that it departs from Marxist usage (where the middle class are likely to be disaggregated, both analytically and historically, into bourgeoisie and petty-bourgeoisie, as will be discussed later).[35] And it certainly implies a basic tripartite division of society (upper, middle, and lower class) in preferences to any basic duality (bourgeois, proletarian; landlord, peasant) and thus follows the preferred model of many contemporary writers, such as Julio Guerrero and Francisco Bulnes, as well as of subsequent commentators like Iturriaga and Córdova.[36]

The middle class were endowed with a measure of property, education and respectability: the men wore suits and ties, read the newspapers and claimed some knowledge of the world outside their own community; they were merchants, shopkeepers, *rancheros* (it would be wrong to consider them purely as a 'humanistic' middle class, scorning trade and profit), as well as government officials, lawyers, journalists and teachers. They belonged to families which kept up appearances and enjoyed some local standing, without claiming the opulence or lineage of the grand *hacendado*, with his estates, town houses and trips to Europe; families who fought proletarianisation tooth-and-nail and who, like their nineteenth-century predecessors, looked down on the lower classes – the sordid *pelados* of the cities, the peons and Indians of the countryside – with mingled fear, distaste and pity.[37] Though this was not a new class, the economic growth of the Porfiriato augmented both their numbers and their importance. Statistical evidence, though available, is of limited use, granted the looseness and subjectivity of class definitions and the unreliability of census material, particularly with regard to 'professionals'.[38] On the basis of the 1895 census returns, Iturriaga suggests that the middle class comprised some 8% of the population (three-quarters of these being

urban), as against 1% upper class and 91% lower class.[39] The middle class of
Porfirian Yucatán, according to one reliable authority, was particularly small,
no more than 5% of the state's population.[40]

If statistics can give rough orders of magnitude, they cannot, in this
instance, evidence change over time. But there is ample 'impressionistic'
evidence: contemporaries repeatedly commented on the 'rise of the middle
class', some using these very words, some describing the phenomenon
differently, but all clearly referring to the same, obvious process of social
change. The British vice-consul at Guadalajara observed in 1911, that ten
years earlier 'the palm hat and cotton trousers were predominant on every main
street while European costume was confined to the few ... within these ten
years we have seen the peon on the main street become a rarity, while the
European garb is everywhere ... In fact, a middle class, hitherto lacking, has
sprung into being.'[41] Some foreign observers went further, linking the new
middle class to the onset of revolution: 'the rise thereof is a phenomenon of
recent years, the years of peace. But for this middle class there would have been
no Revolution'; it was 'the middle classes ... [who] have made the old
Porfirian system impossible. It is they who inflame the low people against the
high.'[42] Díaz himself expressed the opinion – whether sincere or not – that
'today (1908) Mexico has a middle class, which she did not have before',
though he drew no revolutionary conclusions from the fact.[43] Recently,
historians have been at pains to stress the importance of middle-class mobilisation before and during the Revolution.[44] The character and significance of
this mobilisation, however, have often been misconstrued. Having sketched
the social context in which the new opposition of the 1900s developed, it is
therefore necessary to explain how and why the expanding middle class
contributed to the political ferment of the 1900s.

THE NEW OPPOSITION: 2 THE PARTIDO LIBERAL MEXICANO

The first bout of organised opposition in the 1900s arose out of a 'local and
relatively unpublicised' imbroglio in the state of San Luis.[45] Here, in the
summer of 1900, the local bishop publicly and impoliticly declared that the
Reform Laws were now a dead letter. The liberal, anti-clerical conscience,
dormant but far from dead, was pricked. Camilo Arriaga, scion of a well-off,
impeccably liberal family, who had served eight years in the Federal Congress
until a clash with Díaz over the same issue – Church/state relations –
occasioned his dismissal, took up the challenge and called for the organisation
of Liberal clubs throughout Mexico in order to stem the tide of resurgent
clericalism. Locally, Arriaga's manifesto was signed by over a hundred
respectable individuals: doctors, lawyers, engineers, teachers, junior army
officers, journalists and students; they included a fair smattering of Potosino
high society. Nationally, some fifty clubs, located in thirteen states,

responded to the call, though the bulk of them were in San Luis and neighbouring Hidalgo, where, it might be noted, Arriaga had managed the family mines at Pachuca. In February 1901 delegates to the First Liberal Congress packed into a San Luis theatre where they heard, in addition to the predictable anti-clerical tirades, some vocal attacks on the Díaz regime and the abuses of its officialdom. The most outspoken of these came from Ricardo Flores Magón, an Oaxaqueño student-politician and journalist who, with his brother, had just begun the publication of a mildly oppositionist newspaper, *Regeneración*.[46]

The Congress radicalised the Flores Magón brothers and they in turn sought to radicalise the Liberals – to turn 'plain "priest-baiters" into anti-Díaz militants', as they later claimed.[47] Two results followed. The Congress was at once split, the 'priest-baiters' declining the role of militants and, as the moderates drew back, the Liberal organisation made the first of many lurches to the left – a tendency which eventually took it to the extreme of the political spectrum, its old 'liberal' label a confusing relic of former times. The leftward shift of 1901, however, went no further than the broadly liberal objectives set out in the manifesto of the liberal 'Directorate', the Club Liberal Ponciano Arriaga. The club, named after Camilo Arriaga's illustrious liberal grand-father, urged citizens to unmask the corrupt and arbitrary conduct of government officials and advocated the candidacy of a 'talented and progress-ive' liberal in the 1904 presidential elections, a candidate who might return to the path cut by Juárez and the great liberals of the past and 'so long ago abandoned'.[48] A second manifesto was published, convening another Liberal Congress, to meet in February 1902. A tenuous national movement was in the making.

But now the second effect of radicalisation became clear. The Liberals' overt attack on the regime invited repression. Liberal clubs in six states were closed down by the police; individual Liberals were arrested, fined or jailed; the opposition press came in for a bout of closures, arrests, beatings and (it was said) murders. In San Luis, the Club Ponciano Arriaga was broken up by the *jefe político* and fifty police as it prepared for the second Congress. Arriaga and his Potosino collaborators spent much of 1902 in jail, while 'a dying opposition press carried out a flanking attack against the Díaz government, hitting, pulling back, and often being suppressed'.[49] Though the movement was not dead, it had lost the broad impetus of 1901. Divisions began to appear over the wisdom of opposing Díaz's re-election in 1904 and over the general strategy the liberals should adopt. Militants and moderates debated, and the repression continued.

In the course of 1903–4 the principal Liberals – Arriaga, the Flores Magón, Juan and Manuel Sarabia, Antonia Díaz Soto y Gama – migrated to the US. Here, publishing and mailing *Regeneración*, eluding Porfirista agents, Pinker-ton men and Federal spies, the group drifted further left, influenced by contact

with American and Spanish anarchists. Arriaga, disturbed at these developments, broke with the Flores Magón.[50] Hence, when the Partido Liberal
Mexicano (PLM) was formally constituted (September 1905) and its programme published at St Louis Mo. (July 1906), it was the work of a small,
exiled, radical group, committed to revolutionary action. Its provisions –
apparently toned down for public consumption – went far beyond the liberal
nostrums of 1901: it demanded not only free speech, the enforcement of the
Reform Laws and an end to re-election, but also the suppression of the
jefaturas, the abolition of conscription, progressive tax reforms, improved
education, 'protection for the Indian', agrarian reform, and a range of labour
legislation embodying an eight-hour day, minimum wages, accident compensation and a ban on child labour.[51]

In the light of later developments – notably the Constitution of 1917 – the
PLM, their programme and their activity have been retrospectively invested
with great historical significance. Not only were they responsible for the first
organised, national opposition, they also recruited in the mining camps and
textile factories, fomenting strikes, and they were involved in abortive local
revolts in 1906 and 1908. Above all, their advocacy of social reforms
prefigured later revolutionary plans and provisions. 'There can be no doubt,'
one historian writes, 'that these propaganda efforts and the PLM-inspired
strikes and revolts . . . contributed to the undermining of the Díaz regime.'[52]
Such a conclusion is natural. When an *ancien régime* falls amid social upheaval,
historians are soon busy amongst the rubble, digging up the 'roots of
revolution'. The tendency is to look for and find ideological statements (these
being easily recoverable) which match with later revolutionary thinking – as in
the cases of Rousseau and the *philosophes*, the Enlightenment thinkers of
Bourbon Latin America, the Russian slavophiles. But there is an obvious
fallacy here: ideological similarity does not imply a causal connection; *post hoc*
does not mean *propter hoc*. It may be that later revolutionary activists drew on
the existing pool of ideas to justify what they did for different (often
'non-ideological' reasons) or it may be that both ideologues and activists
stemmed, as separate and distinct branches, from a common trunk, without
the one enjoying causal priority over the other. Causal connections cannot be
inferred from a simple ideological congruence – comparing the 1906 Plan of St
Louis and the 1917 Constitution, for example. Rather, they must be shown to
thread through the actions and decisions of men in the intervening years. In
the case of the PLM, this thread is hard to locate. The initial Liberal Congress,
though significant in what it promised, failed to make a real impact on the
country.[53] Díaz, Governor Escontría of San Luis, and General Julio Cervantes,
the military commander, showed no anxiety as the Congress met.[54] Of course,
the spread of Liberal clubs in the provinces, and the repression they endured,
showed that the authorities, witnessing the coalescence of a broad liberal
opposition, were taking no chances. But the important point is that the

repression succeeded. The break-up of the San Luis Club had the desired effect: within a month, San Luis was tranquil, the affair was regarded with indifference, and Governor Escontría left the state for a visit to Mexico City.[55]

Nationally, too, political life went on unruffled. Díaz's re-election in 1904 proceeded smoothly and was notable less for any organised, grass-roots opposition – as the Liberals had urged – than for the battle within the Porfirian elite between the Científicos, who favoured Limantour for the new vice-presidency, and their enemies, who backed General Reyes. Díaz, nominating Corral, disappointed both. Equally, the municipal elections of 1907 were conducted in the usual manner and caused no fuss.[56] Furthermore, the repression of the PLM, by converting it from a potentially broad alliance of liberals into a radical rump, increasingly left-wing in thought and revolutionary in practice, deprived it of support and sympathy. Moderate liberals, like Francisco Madero, who had contributed to PLM funds, deplored its leftward drift, its sectarianism, its penchant for armed revolt.[57] Sympathisers, like the clerk, merchant and mechanic of Parral, who 'had subscriptions to *Regeneración* and wanted to help the San Luis Club', recoiled from the prospect of revolution, which they considered hopeless.[58] Meanwhile, the government could point to the unpatriotic intriguing of extremists on foreign soil, could hint at US connivance, and could denounce the PLM-inspired revolts as the work of tramps, illiterates and bandits – and each revolt an advertisement for the iron hand of the regime which swiftly put them down.[59] Essentially, the PLM was a liberal opposition *manqué*. At the outset, it exercised a broad appeal; thereafter, it still attracted sympathisers by virtue of its anomalous 'Liberal' label – even if, as he frankly admitted, Madero was unsure of the *emigrés'* policies.[60] Even dissident Catholics might adhere to the PLM.[61] The party's social radicalism and commitment to revolution, far from winning support, deterred would-be adherents, but, for most of the 1900s, it represented the only articulate, national opposition confronting the regime. People joined or read *Regeneración*, *faute de mieux*. This in itself was an achievement for the Liberals, but it would be wrong to infer that every reader of *Regeneración* was a paid-up PLM activist, living proof of the Liberals' pervasive political influence. On the contrary, events after 1908, the year of the Liberals' second abortive revolt, revealed how marginal they were to Porfirian politics and how indifferently they had represented the broad, middle-class demand for political reform.

THE NEW OPPOSITION: 3 THE REYISTAS

The response of liberals to Arriaga's appeal in 1901 had shown that there existed a reservoir of support for a moderate, national party, committed to some degree of political change – even if it was retrospective change, aimed at the restoration of forfeited constitutional rights. By 1908, conditions favoured such a party even more. The economy was in recession, Díaz was now seventy-seven; in two years time there would be presidential elections for a further six-year term, which, even the most committed Porfiristas had to admit, the president might not survive and, since 1904, the vice-president and heir-apparent had been the unpopular Ramón Corral. In the run-up to the elections of 1910, therefore, increasing attention was focussed on the question of who was to be Díaz's running mate and presumed successor.

Díaz himself encouraged a renewal of political activity with the famous interview he gave to the American journalist James Creelman early in 1908. The Mexican people, he declared, had demanded his long tenure of office, but it was now time for a change; Mexico now had a middle class, and the country was ready to enter upon an era of political freedom. He, Díaz, proposed to retire at the end of this term (1910) and 'if an opposition party were to arise in the Republic, I would regard it as a blessing and not an evil'.[62] In theory, this was good positivistic thinking: the regime had achieved stability and economic growth and it was now time for the Mexican people to enjoy their deferred democratic rights. But, in fact, Díaz's analysis was clearly made 'with tongue in cheek' and most of the promises were broken within months: the interview cannot be taken at face value.[63] A variety of ulterior motives has therefore been suggested: that the interview was simply for foreign consumption; that it was part of a devious plot to draw the opposition into the open; that Díaz wanted to be in a position to choose between rival political movements.[64] An interpretation with the merit of simplicity is that Díaz was too old and out of touch to know what he was doing. It is certainly possible that he anticipated a rush of supporters begging him to remain in office, after which the bland promises could be consigned to oblivion; at any rate, the government acted as if this was the case. The interview had hardly sunk into sceptical Mexican minds when the re-electionist machine swung into action: state governors, ignoring the president's self-denying ordinance, began to report local press demands that Díaz stand in 1910; the Governor of Jalisco appealed for re-election as a 'national necessity' and by the end of the year he was seconded by the governors of all the states of the Federation. It was agreed that they would all, simultaneously, launch the re-electionist campaign via newspapers, public speeches, and official clubs initiated by the *jefes políticos*. In October, Díaz made as if to bow to popular pressure, declared that the Creelman interview embodied no more than personal desires, and agreed to 'sacrifice' himself for the nation once again. In November, the National Porfirista Circle officially launched Don Porfirio's presidential candidacy.[65]

It was as if Creelman had never set pen to paper. And, through 1908, it looked as if the old man had turned the trick. For his speciously reluctant return to the political fray provoked no significant opposition and for a time it seemed that 1910 would pass off as had 1904, 1900, 1896 and all the earlier re-elections. But Díaz could not halt his advancing years, and the Creelman interview had given aid and comfort to those who shuddered at the prospect of Corral and who, for reasons of personality or principle, were ready to do battle over the vice-presidency. Whatever motives lay behind it, Díaz's statement wrought 'a fundamental transformation in the public mind . . . [and] by its effects on the intellectual classes was the psychological origin of the revolution of 1910'.[66] Old, remote, imperfectly aware of the changes at work in Mexican political society, Díaz had committed a 'cataclysmic error of judgement'.[67]

The chief beneficiary of the Creelman interview was General Bernardo Reyes. Now in his late fifties (and youthful by Porfirian standards), Reyes had been born into a prominent liberal family of Jalisco and had made himself an illustrious career in the army and in politics. He was Díaz's chosen instrument for the destruction of the Treviño/Naranjo *cacicazgo* in the north east, where he went on to serve as a progressive and energetic governor of Nuevo León, fostering local industry, improving public education and health, showing some concern – in paternalist, Bismarckian fashion – for working-class grievances.[68] But he was no lover of political heterodoxy. Preparing his own re-election as governor in 1903, he ordered the mayors of the state to proceed with 'the greatest severity' against opponents and an anti-Reyes demonstration in Monterrey provoked a riot, police repression, arrests, and a subsequent congressional inquiry, which absolved Reyes unanimously.[69] For two years Reyes served in the cabinet as Minister of War, endearing himself to the army and creating the Second Reserve, a kind of territorial army which reached a peak complement of 30,000 before it was disbanded, at Díaz's insistence.[70] It was at this time that Reyes emerged as the chief counterweight to the Científicos and as Limantour's rival for the vice-presidency. Reyes clashed with Limantour over the army budget and with the Minister of Justice over the trial of journalists who had attacked the Second Reserve, which in Científico eyes seemed like a private Reyista army. Partisan newspapers supported the two sides, impugning Reyes' militarism and ambition and Limantour's foreign ancestry.[71] Díaz therefore acted: Limantour was indispensable at the treasury, but he was denied the vice-presidency; Reyes was sent back to govern Nuevo León, though with an increased salary to show that there were no hard feelings; the Second Reserve was abolished by presidential decree.

But Reyes' popularity, and his reputation as a potential successor to Díaz, survived his removal from the cabinet. As 1908 drew to a close and Díaz's decision to run for president had still not been seconded by an official nomination of a running mate, political speculation and activity gathered pace, with the name of Reyes continually cropping up.[72] Reyes himself, well-schooled in Porfirian politics, enthusiastically endorsed Díaz's presidential candidacy and confined himself to somewhat cryptic and demure statements on the subject of the vice-presidency.[73] If he coveted national power (and later events suggested that he did) Reyes knew the way to get it was through the favour and support of the centre, not by rabble-rousing in the provinces. Reyismo therefore developed in the shadow of an ostensibly reluctant leader.

Reyismo's first formal embodiment was the Partido Democrático, set up in Mexico City in January 1909 by a mixed bunch of *gobiernista*, Reyista and opposition politicians. The party manifesto contained familiar liberal proposals with a leaven of social reform: the suppression of the *jefaturas*, municipal freedom, improved primary education, the enforcement of the Reform Laws, accident compensation for workers and the creation of a Ministry of Agriculture.[74] The manifesto named no candidates, but it was clear that the party supported Reyes as Díaz's vice-presidential partner. And, to start with, it created no great stir. The personnel behind the party represented an interesting combination of personalism and principle: there were men with close government and Científico links, like Manuel Calero and Querido Moheno, who, while maintaining complete deference towards Díaz, questioned the prolonged domination of the elderly Científicos and called for new political reforms and organisations which would ensure future stability. They echoed, twenty years on, the advice the Científicos themselves had given at the time of the Liberal Union; they favoured a gradual, conservative accommodation with changing conditions; they were, in a sense, Porfirian Peelites. But there were also bolder reformers, like Sánchez Azcona, editor of *El Diario* and (since late 1908) *México Nuevo*, and Francisco Sentíes, whose polemics had shown a relatively advanced concern for agrarian reform. For them, the Democractic Party represented a force for democratic reform. Finally, there were adherents like Heriberto Barrón, opportunists with an eye to the main chance.[75]

Such a combination had its advantages. The presence within the party of known *gobiernistas* like Calero led wits to translate the COPD (Centro Organizador del Partido Democrático) as 'Con Orden de Porfirio Díaz', but this presence gave the party an air of respectability and some guarantee against repression. Independent oppositionists were sceptical, and disdained the party as one of scheming opportunists.[76] But the real test of the party's character came when it went to the country. Here, it proved unexpectedly successful at recruiting broad support, often in spite of its timid leadership. Whatever the complexion and aims of its founders, the Democratic Party appealed to the same middle-class constituency which the PLM had aroused, only to disappoint. It was therefore well placed to pick up the pieces of the Liberal debacle of the 1900s.

Early in 1909 the Díaz machine began preparing the ground for the president's re-election, sponsoring provincial clubs which would send delegates to the national convention scheduled for April.[77] Reyes himself still maintained a guarded silence. Together, these factors impelled the Reyistas to action: they needed to create an impression on Díaz and Reyes alike, forcing the two into the desired political embrace. *México Nuevo* sought to counter the re-electionist propaganda of the official press and to make an impact on 'mass consciousness' — though it also had to publish the occasional kind word about Corral to guarantee survival.[78] At the same time the first official Reyista club was set up in the capital, soon to be succeeded by many others. The most important, the Popular Sovereignty Club, had as president Francisco Vázquez Gómez, a top Mexico City doctor who had treated Díaz, who was also a landlord and a railway concessionaire, and as vice-president José López Portillo y Rojas, an ambitious young Porfirista, ex-president of Congress.[79] By mid-summer 1909 there were half-a-dozen Reyista clubs in the capital, despatching speakers to the provinces and organising their own propaganda in Mexico City. This reached its climax on 18 July, in a ceremony supposed to commemorate the death of Benito Juárez. The Masonic lodges of the capital — heavily Reyista — declined to attend the official ceremony and mounted their own, which turned into a full-blown Reyista demonstration.[80]

But it was in the provinces that the Reyista impact was most notable. The Reyistas of Guadalajara began to organise early in 1909 and were soon reinforced by speakers from Mexico City. Governor Ahumada took steps to obstruct them and made sure that the press proclaimed their mission a failure. Reyista support, he intimated, did not include men of substance, but simply 'people who carry no weight, like students, lawyers without clients, and others of that ilk' — the raw material, from a *gobiernista* perspective, of most Porfirian opposition movements.[81] But the Reyistas were undeterred, claiming that their support in Jalisco (Reyes' home state) was great and growing among workers, artisans, men of letters, professionals, businessmen, farmers, industrialists, soldiers, police and federal employees. The red carnation, the Reyista badge, was all-pervasive.[82] And vigorous proof of this came when Re-electionist speakers arrived at Guadalajara to preach political orthodoxy. A crowd of 3,000, including all the students of the city's *Liceo*, met them at the station, shouting abuse; the *jefe político* attempted in vain to clear the mob, arresting forty demonstrators. For four successive nights Reyistas roamed the streets of Guadalajara with cries of 'viva Reyes!' and 'muera Corral! muera Díaz!'. The Governor, forced to admit that 'the Reyista movement is on the increase', expelled students who refused to relinquish their political activity, and wished that he had the services of a good *gobiernista* journalist to counter Reyista propaganda. By August 1909 Guadalajara was seen by outsiders as the focal point of the Reyista movement and the government, its own propaganda proving futile, even counter-productive, resorted to the usual tactics — forcibly closing Reyista clubs and jailing the local Reyista leaders.[83]

In the state of Veracruz (traditionally liberal and hostile to Mexico City and governed by the anti-Científico Teodoro Dehesa), Reyista speakers were welcomed in the major cities. At Torreón, too, where the military commander reported the 'majority of the inhabitants' were Reyistas, a crowd of 8,000 turned out to demonstrate for Reyes and, in the heat of the moment, the customary formula (Díaz/Reyes) gave way to overt attacks on the president himself, as well as on Corral.[84] By the end of the summer, Reyista clubs had been established in a dozen cities and towns, particularly in the north east, where Reyes' personal influence was strong and where the pre-conditions for a reformist opposition party were favourable in fast-growing commercial centres like Monterrey, Parras, Múzquiz, Cd Juárez and Torreón. As this political geography suggests, the urban middle class were strong for Reyes. In Puebla, for example, it was the 'middle class, great and small' who showed most enthusiasm, led by Dr Espinosa de los Monteros and a local journalist who had fallen foul of police chief Cabrera. At Tepic, on the west coast, a merchant set about forming the local Reyista centre; soon, even the judiciary of the territory were reckoned to be 'Reyista to the marrow of its bones'. At Mazatlan, further north, the merchants of the port were solidly for Reyes.[85]

To be more precise, particular sectors of the middle class responded to Reyes' appeal. Ex-members of the Second Reserve (itself a largely middle-class institution) remembered their old chief fondly and supported his campaign.[86] More seriously, the Federal Army was riddled with Reyismo. Ten officers, who had written to the president of the Central Reyista Club putting themselves 'unconditionally' at his orders, were despatched to distant postings in the malarial tropics of Quintana Roo or in the front line of the campaigns against the Yaquis – an action which provoked fierce exchanges between the official and independent press. In Guerrero, the Federal commander, a Reyista, refused to attend a Re-electionist club installation; another Federal officer resigned his commission rather than quit his post as a vice-president of a Reyista club.[87] Even officialdom did not wholly escape the contagion; the judges of Tepic, as already noted, were Reyista; the mayor of Cananea led a Reyista movement in the mining town which was reckoned to be 'very powerful'.[88] And, while Reyismo exercised a strong attraction to the middle class – lawyers, merchants, freemasons, doctors, Second Reservists, army officers – it also appealed to their sons, and to educated youth in general, and depended on student support for its city parades and demonstrations.[89] In addition, upper-class 'outs' saw the advantages of a movement promising limited change within the system. In Sonora, José Maria Maytorena started a Reyista centre of Guaymas (his allies were Carlos Randall, a merchant, and Eugenio Gayou, a mining engineer). Re-electionist speakers, safe enough in Hermosillo, got a hot reception when they ventured to the southern port.[90] At Durango, Ignacio Borrego welcomed Reyista propagandists and presided over the local club; down in Yucatán the old Cantón clan, a longstanding opposition faction of conservative origins, boarded the Reyista bandwaggon in opposition to Governor Arístegui, Molina, and the Científicos.[91]

The government was rattled. Here was a broadly based movement, proclaiming the candidacy of one of the foremost members of the Porfirian establishment, mobilising a degree of national support that was unprecedented and creating, as one observer put it, a form of political 'animation of which one had lost all recollection for many long years'.[92] The Reyistas were not rabble-rousing subversives, plotting insurrection in Texas or California; they were solid, respectable, middle-class citizens, who, in the main, still affirmed their loyalty to Díaz. Yet Reyismo clearly represented an attempt to wrest from the centre its traditional stranglehold on major political decisions and appointments. By 1909 it was no longer possible for state governors and *jefes políticos* to control local politics, insulating their districts from outside influence, eliminating opponents, hatching out Re-electionist political clubs every election time (clubs which lasted just long enough to endorse the official ticket and then, like the mayfly, their political procreation over, die a swift death). Rather, the Reyista clubs were vital and independent, bucking official control, and the novel *gira electoral*, aided by a resurgent opposition press, broke down the political isolation of states and districts, importing outside speakers, linking established local oppositions to a national network. The disaffected lifted their heads and took heart. Local complaints and grievances began to find expression in the Mexico City press – even those emanating from distant Chiapas.[93] For the first time in over twenty years politics were a national and not a circumscribed local affair.

For the government, this was a new and worrying development, a 'sudden step from complete electoral inertia to an aimless and unrestrained agitation', as Limantour put it, rather extravagantly.[94] It countered with several measures. First, there was an attempt to beat the Reyistas at their own game, as *gobiernista* speakers were sent to Guanajuato, Tehuacán, Puebla and into the lions' den of Guadalajara. Such speakers could always count on some sort of audience – a claque of students on government grants, postal or other public employees, plus hired supernumeraries – but still the results were poor.[95] The debacle at Guadalajara has been mentioned; at Puebla (July 1909) a pro-Corral demonstration attracted 'a very reduced group of *empleados* who, faced with the prospect of dismissal which would bring starvation in its wake, submitted, not without grumbling, to the inexorable order of their boss [Governor Martínez]'. The dangers of this policy became apparent at Guaymas, where the hired claque finished up crying 'viva Reyes!'. Indeed, Corral's unpopularity even influenced Re-electionist groups like the state committee of Oaxaca, which declined to endorse Corral's vice-presidential candidacy, despite official pressure.[96]

Meanwhile, the official press joined battle with the opposition and new organs like the aggressive *El Debate*, run by Luis del Toro, helped initiate a trend towards a new, savage political journalism. Reyes was denounced as a potential military tyrant, the Reyistas as subversives bent on the destruction of public order.[97] And, now that mass political support was a factor to be reckoned with, government overtures towards the urban working class – particularly on the part of Guillermo Landa y Escandón, Governor of the Federal District – assumed additional importance. Conciliation of working-class grievances was now necessary not just to avert industrial conflict, but also to counteract Reyes' undoubted appeal to the workers.[98] The government's conversion to mass politicking, however, was tardy, out of character, and unsuccessful. It therefore had to fall back on the old and tried methods. Reyistas – including highly respected men like Benito Juárez Maza, son of the great liberal president – began to complain to Díaz of *atropellos* ('outrages' – one of the commonest words in the political vocabulary of the time); Díaz brazenly advised that such matters be dealt with in the courts. José López Portillo y Rojas, a leading figure of the Jalisco and Reyista establishments, was arraigned on a trumped-up charge. The example of Jalisco, where Reyista agitation could only be met with repression, encouraged the Governor of Zacatecas to ban all political demonstrations in his state.[99]

The weak link in the Reyista machine, and the key to the government's campaign against it, was Reyes himself. The general had never vocally encouraged the movement which carried his name; equally, he had not actively discouraged it. By mid-summer 1909, his silence was growing embarrassing: Reyista clubs and sympathetic journalists began to ask for a clear statement of intent, while the official press, led by *El Debate*, made fun of Reyes' 'total dumbness'.[100] Reyes, however, was a quintessential product of Porfirian machine politics. He was prepared to let his supporters create a 'Reyes boom' in the hope that it would influence Díaz, but he did not dream of influencing Díaz at the head of a popular opposition movement. He had spent too much of his career successively quashing such movements. So he protested his loyalty to the president, insisted that Díaz must pick his own vice-presidential candidate from among his close collaborators and deplored rabble-rousing as unpatriotic and subversive.[101] Reyes would only accept the guerdon of succession at the hands of Díaz himself – crowned, like the heirs of the Capetian kings of France, in the life-time of their father. But Díaz, to the last, jealous of power and suspicious of over-mighty subjects, remained committed to Corral; indeed, the progress of Reyismo – an insolent, factious demagogy – seems to have steeled Díaz against compromise at a time when compromise was eminently feasible and in the long term interests of the regime. The sacrifice of Corral for Reyes would have cost Díaz few friends, would have temporarily deflated the opposition, and would have settled the succession issue. Reyes, it may be presumed, would have been a faithful vice-president, as he had been a faithful governor and minister, and a subsequent Reyista regime would not have differed radically from its Porfirian predecessor. Indeed, Reyes' authoritarian/ progressive record in Nuevo León suggests that he was the ideal candidate to continue the 'revolution from above' strategy of modernisation. But instead, Díaz let himself be ruled by *amour propre*: he decided to behead the Reyista movement and put an end to its troublesome activity.

At the end of July 1909 Reyes was on his country estate near Galeana, south of Monterrey, plotting a coup, some imaginative gossips whispered, but more probably deliberately avoiding a big Reyista demonstration in Monterrey which, had he been present, might have forced him to declare his hand.[102] Now, Díaz sent General Gerónimo Treviño to command the third military zone in the north east (a nice piece of spite, this, in view of Reyes' removal of Treviño back in the 1880s). Reyista heads began to roll (Governor Miguel Cárdenas of Coahuila; the military commander at Guadalajara) and a noted critic of Reyes replaced the incumbent district judge at Monterrey – a prelude to concocted legal proceedings against the General himself.[103] There were Reyistas who urged their leader to resist political elimination by force of arms and they included his politically shrewd son, Rodolfo. But Reyes accepted the bitter cup meekly. Charitable biographers have put this down to patriotism and personal loyalty to Díaz; others have imputed cowardice and vacillation, casting Reyes as Mexico's General Boulanger. Both contain elements of truth. Reyes was both a product and an instrument of the Porfirian system, in whose service he had shown a certain energy and statesmanship. But outside, or against the system, he was like Antaeus held aloft – weak and uncertain, recoiling from the limbo of opposition politics, fearful of committing himself to the embrace of popular movement. Popular movements always rattled him, good Porfirista that he was: the first outbreak of real opposition to his regime in Nuevo León had left him (notwithstanding his statements to the contrary) nervous and visibly agitated, prone to violent over-reaction and, in Díaz's own words, 'having lost his head and gone mad'.[104] It was too much to expect that, six years later, Reyes would have either the nerve or the inclination to cross over the barricades.

THE NEW OPPOSITION: 4 MADERISMO

If Reyes was ill-cast as the leader of a popular opposition movement, his successor, the inheritor of the Reyista mantle, was better suited. Francisco Madero was another man of the north east, in his case born and bred there, the product of one of Mexico's dozen richest families, the owners of cotton and guayule plantations, mines and rolling mills, distilleries, flour mills and textile factories.[105] The Maderos were the cream of the enterprising, northern Mexican landed elite: 'their name is found linked to all the major enterprises of the north of the Republic' – such was the impression of an Italian traveller. Of impeccably liberal lineage, the family had supplied the state governor of Coahuila in the 1880s – Francisco's grandfather, Evaristo, now the old patriarch of the clan – and, though they subsequently concentrated on commercial rather than political affairs, they were linked by ties of blood and interest with some of the leading members of the Porfirian establishment, including Limantour and General Treviño.[106] In no sense were they 'outs'.

Francisco, born at Parras in 1873, was the eldest of fifteen children. He went through the conventional, cosmopolitan education of sons of such

wealthy, progressive but religious families: a Catholic education at Saltillo and
Baltimore, five years in Europe, chiefly Paris, a stint at Berkeley studying
agriculture. On his return to Mexico at the age of twenty he began to play a
prominent and successful role in the Madero economic empire, developing
properties in the San Pedro area, introducing American machinery to handle
the cotton crop, organising local planters in their litigation over the waters of
the Nazas, and writing studies of cotton cultivation and irrigation, which
combined learning and practical insight.[107] By the time he was twenty-eight,
and about to be married, he had built up a personal fortune of over half a
million pesos. Clearly, he was no idle visionary.

But if Francisco had turned out a dutiful, successful and conformist member
of the family on the surface, he was, as an individual, a complex character, and
one whose eccentricities invited ridicule. He was short (about five foot three)
and had a piping voice; despite his mastery of business practice, he also
engaged in esoteric interests which made him seem, in some eyes, a crank –
spiritualism, theosophy, homoeopathic medicine.[108] In 1901, when he was
twenty-eight, his mother's narrow escape from typhoid brought on a personal
crisis which led him to renounce drink and tobacco (of both of which he had
been over-fond, by his own account) and to take the drastic step of selling off
his wine cellar. More important, two years later Reyes' brutal treatment of
demonstrators at Monterrey induced a comparable political conversion.
Already known for his enlightened and humanitarian treatment of employees,
Madero was now shocked out of what he called his 'criminal indifference' to
public affairs and propelled into a political career.[109]

For six years this took the shape of local politicking, a dedicated, disappointing struggle against the abuses of *caciquismo* and artificial democracy in
his home state of Coahuila. First, Madero formed a political club in San Pedro
('the little city of the big capitalists', it was called), named it after Benito
Juárez, and instituted weekly meetings at which he expounded his views: that
the centre had abandoned the municipalities, denying them their constitutional rights of self-government, that only the free election of mayors and
town councils could guarantee the people a healthy political future.[110] The
appeal was that of classic liberalism (Madero's own writing was shot through
with references to Juárez and the Constitution of 1857) coupled with the
parish-pump grievances of men of property and public spirit: the need for more
schools, for water wells and a piped water supply, for fire-fighting equipment,
for the imposition of fines on saloon-keepers whose cantinas habitually
disgorged drunks onto the city streets.[111] Admittedly, this programme was
drawn up with a view to impending municipal elections; Madero's own
horizons were far wider. But, as noted in the previous chapter, the urban
middle class were particularly aggrieved at Porfirian sins of omission: the
inadequacy of public services, the dearth of municipal spirit, the offences
against good taste which abounded in an ill-governed, corrupt township. San

Pedro's administration had not kept pace with its economic development, but when Madero and his men of goodwill attempted to elect a reputable mayor they were thwarted by all the traditional devices: arbitrary shifting of election booths, police intervention, attempts (once the independents achieved a majority) to reach a back-room deal, and finally, the imposition of the official candidate in spite of all.[112]

Undeterred, Madero and his allies in the Club Benito Juárez went on to participate in the Coahuilan gubernatorial election in opposition to Governor Miguel Cárdenas (1905). The scope of their activities widened: a weekly paper, *El Demócrata*, began to appear; a convention of anti-Cárdenas elements was held; Madero – learning the ways of Porfirian politics – explored the possibilities of a deal with the government which would bring some genuine independents into the state legislature on the coat-tails of a Corralista governor.[113] Again, disappointment. The deal misfired and Cárdenas won a tightly controlled election. Afterwards came the arrests: the editor of *El Demócrata* preferred exile to jail and Madero, with a warrant out for his arrest, was only saved by the influence of friends in high places.

Even as he progressed from municipal to state politics. Madero became involved in the tenuous, still-forming network of national opposition. As early as the summer of 1905 he was seeing the independent political clubs of Coahuila, which had participated in the gubernatorial election, as the nucleus of a national party which would contest the 1910 presidential campaign. Building from the grassroots was a sound strategy, but experience showed that, so long as the centre retained liberty of action, it could quash or manipulate isolated, local independent movements at will. So the fight had to be taken to the centre.[114] For a time, Madero contributed to the PLM exiles in the US, though he admitted to being unsure of their precise aims and strongly opposed any idea of armed revolution.[115] He established contact with opposition journalists like Sentíes, Sánchez Azcona and Paulino Martínez, and angled for the support of prestigious names like Fernando Iglesias Calderón, son of the short-lived president of 1876.[116] Finally, with the stimulus of the Creelman interview, Madero penned this contribution to the spate of contemporary books and political pamphlets: *The Presidential Succession in 1910*, published in January 1909 and swiftly distributed around sympathisers, potential sympathisers, and some probable opponents, like Díaz himself.[117]

The book reviewed Mexican history – with the customary obeisance to Juárez and other liberal heroes – denounced militarism and absolutism as endemic political vices and, coming on to contemporary issues, made a plea for an independent Anti-Re-electionist Party which could work for a democratically chosen vice-president (and presumed successor) to Díaz. Towards Díaz himself, Madero was charitable, recognising the peace and economic progress he had helped provide and the relative moderation with which he had exercised power. The usual developmentalist concerns of the educated middle class –

concerns which liberals shared with their Porfirian opponents – were rehearsed: the evils of drink, the need for more and better education, the backwardness of Mexican agriculture.[118] In addition, Madero cited well-known examples of Porfirian repression: Tomóchic, Cananea, Río Blanco. To this extent, it cannot be said that 'social' issues were entirely neglected. On the other hand, the main theme, and certainly the proffered solutions, were essentially political – at times almost spiritual. Despite undoubted economic progress, which Madero fully recognised, the Mexican people were still living in benighted political ignorance, showing a purblind neglect of the common weal. Civic virtue had been sapped; corruption was rife. Echoing Cato the Elder, Madero summoned his fellow-citizens to rediscover their public spirit and redeem their prostituted political inheritance. The inheritance was that of nineteenth-century liberalism – still adequate, in Madero's opinion, for the problems of the twentieth century; the aim was 'the realisation of the great democratic ideal'; and the means were free and fair elections, municipal freedom, and a respect for states' rights.[119]

To some, this has seemed, and seems, a limp ideology and programme, out of date even when it was propounded. But to Madero, and to many like-minded liberals, it was a bold crusade, requiring faith and daring.[120] And in many senses they were right. First, the programme struck a vibrant chord, which chimed in with the still powerful tradition of Mexican liberalism – hence its undoubted appeal. Second, by promising No Re-election throughout the political hierarchy – from local caciques to the great national cacique in the presidential palace – the programme threatened major change, as Madero recognised. Adherence to the law and the Constitution would not make for a quiet life, but would imply inevitable political turbulence, the price and the proof of political freedom.[121] Madero was prepared to consider a *transacción* with the old regime (as he had done during the Coahuilan state election) and he did not advocate armed revolution, but his programme represented a real and profound threat to the workings of the Díaz dictatorship.[122]

Towards Reyes, whom many fellow-liberals applauded and followed in 1909, Madero was suspicious and hostile. Reyes' treatment of political opponents in 1903 had prompted Madero's political conversion and he never ceased to regard and attack Reyes as an undemocratic militarist whose regime, were it ever to materialise, would prove more absolutist and military even than Díaz's.[123] Thus, as the 'Reyes boom' got under way, Madero limped behind, critical of Reyes, regretful of the support the general received from genuine independents, and concerned to build up his own Anti-Re-electionist Party in the shadow of Don Bernardo's more populous and impressive party. The Democratic Party had been founded in January 1909; Madero's Anti-Re-electionist Centre ('party' was thought to be premature) appeared in Mexico City in May. Reyista and Maderista provincial tours both began in the summer, but the Reyistas attracted more publicity and were more immediately successful at founding provincial clubs. To the government, Reyes appeared the principal enemy – a general, an ex-minister, with an extensive clientele and an established power base in Nuevo León – while Madero was hardly taken seriously. Indeed, his decision to risk an enviable social position by a career in opposition politics, combined with his known personal eccentricities, led some hard-headed Porfiristas to conclude that Madero was *un loco*. [124] Reyes, who had brushed with Madero during the 1905 Coahuilan election, considered him 'stunted, ugly and rancorous', the runt of the Madero litter; grandfather Evaristo who, like most of the family, did not share Francisco's political views, compared his grandson's defiance of the government to 'a microbe's challenge to an elephant'. [125]

Partially protected by such disdain, Madero set about publicising the Anti-Re-electionist cause, drawing on his own ample funds. In June 1909 *El AntiRe-eleccionista*, a weekly edited by José Vasconcelos, began to appear and, in the same month, Madero undertook his first national speaking tour, sailing from Veracruz to Yucatán (on board ship he handed out homoeopathic medicines to sea-sick passengers), thence to Campeche, back to Tamaulipas and Nuevo León. A spell of organising and propagandising in Coahuila at the height of the summer left Madero sick and exhausted, compelled to convalesce for a month at Tehuacán, 'le Vichy méxicain', but at the end of the year he was off again on an extended trip through the western and north-western states, visiting Guadalajara, then through Sinaloa and Sonora to Chihuahua. Finally, in the spring of 1910, Madero campaigned through the north-central states of San Luis, Durango, Zacatecas and Guanajuato. By then Madero had passed through twenty-two of the twenty-seven states of the Federation, and spent at least a few days campaigning in eighteen of them: an unprecedented phenomenon. [126] Locally, too, Maderistas followed their leader's vigorous example: Anti-Re-electionist speakers trekked out of Puebla, north into the sierra, south into the valleys of Tehuacán, Atlixco, and Tepeaca; in the mountains their campaign prospered and thirty-seven clubs were reported to have been set up, but down in the hot valleys they faced the hostility of watchful authorities, and had to preach and convert covertly, like the early Christians. [127]

In the course of these hectic months, the Anti-Re-electionist Party became established as the major opposition to the Díaz/Corral ticket in the 1910 elections. Their political campaign in 1909–10 prefaced the revolutionary military campaign of 1910–11: it was now that the politicised middle class made their decisive contribution to the gestation of the Revolution. To appreciate how this came about it is necessary to turn away from narrative and to present an analysis of the personnel of Maderismo, as they swelled and jostled in the anteroom of power.

The first point to make about the Maderistas is that – *pace* Córdova – many of them were ex-Reyistas, disillusioned by the *gran rifiuto* of their putative leader. [128] In his propaganda Madero consciously wooed the Reyista rank-and-file, while excoriating Reyes himself. At Torreón, he wrote to his brother in July 1909, 'since there were some of the principal Reyistas there, I made a distinction between Reyes and the Reyistas, speaking well of the latter, while putting Reyes in his place'; as a result, Madero went on, some of the Reyistas at once tore off their red carnations and 'trampled them underfoot'.[129] In August 1909, as Reyes' star went into decline, Madero publicly called on all Reyistas 'of good faith' to unite with the Anti-Re-electionists.[130] Not suprisingly, it was the principled rather than the personalist supporters of the general who most readily responded. For those who sought a genuine, democratic political movement, wrote Sánchez Azcona, the switch from Reyes to Madero was easily made – 'it would be no more than changing the colours of the flag, the name of the leader' – and his own *México Nuevo* itself became an organ of Maderismo towards the end of 1909.[131] Many individuals followed the same route: Francisco Vázquez Gómez in Mexico City, Francisco Múgica, young Reyista journalist of Michoacán, the students of Puebla – typified by Juan Andreu Almazán – whom Dr Espinosa of the Central Reyista Club found drifting away on the tide of Maderismo.[132] At Guadalajara, the old Reyista heartland, the Governor complained of the demagogic activities of men like Celestino Padilla, 'of the extinguished Reyista party, who today are Anti-Re-electionists'.[133] As this overlapping membership suggests, Reyismo and Maderismo were closely related phenomena, both products of a distinctive social milieu.

Geographically, Maderismo was a northern, especially a north-eastern movement. Madero's propaganda tours considerably broadened its appeal, but it always retained disproportionate strength in Coahuila, the Laguna, Nuevo León and Chihuahua (roughly in that order). As early as July 1909 Madero regarded the party's foothold in these areas as 'very solid'; Anti-Re-electionist clubs were being established in many north-eastern towns (Múzquiz, Lampazos, Sabinas, Lerdo, Torreón, Viesca, Matamoros, Villa Aldama, Monterrey, Bustamante); 'within three weeks,' Madero predicted early in August, 'there won't be a pueblo in Coahuila without an Anti-Re-electionist club'.[134] Here, in addition to the region's general socio-political character and the specific stimulus of a gubernatorial contest in Coahuila occasioned by the fall of Miguel Cárdenas, the Madero name and family influence counted for a good deal. Thus, despite his father's and grandfather's antipathy to his politics, Madero's party spread according to the pattern of Madero economic interests, radiating from the Parras–San Pedro region east towards Monterrey and west into the Laguna, where Francisco had farmed his cotton estates and helped organise his fellow-planters back in the 1890s. Brother Gustavo proved an energetic (ultimately a too energetic) fund-raiser for the movement, even extracting contributions from Madero's apolitical sisters; a cousin, Jesús González, served as president of the Monterrey Anti-Re-electionist Club; while the appointment of General Treviño – 'my relative and friend', as Madero called him – to command in the north east raised Maderista hopes further.[135] Government propagandists seized on this aspect of the movement, commenting on the Madero family's history of commercial greed and expansion, its desire to 'monopolise money and power to conserve their village seigneurie'; the millionaire Maderos, they alleged, could always drum up support, since those who 'got on the wrong side of these gentlemen soon find themselves out of a job'.[136] This was an exaggeration, an application of hoary Porfirian methods to a new form of voluntarist political association. But there was a kernel of truth. Madero was not afraid to use his money (and his family's, when he could get it) to further his political ends, and his extensive contacts in the north east helped the movement and gave it an aura of respectability. The Anti-Re-electionists were no PLM *sans-culottes* and Madero, contrary to some accounts, was no dreamy visionary, incapable of operating in the messy world of practical politics.

Madero's whistle-stop tours also got their best reception in the north and north east: at Monterrey and Torreón (a scene of 'delirious enthusiasm', wrote Madero), at Chihuahua City (2,000 people packed into a theatre) and Parral, where the town's merchants declared a public holiday to accommodate local celebrations.[137] The north-western expedition experienced mixed fortunes: the Madero name carried less weight beyond the Sierra Madre Occidental and the authorities were disposed to be tougher. Sinaloa, in the summer of 1909, was in the throes of a gubernatorial election and Maderismo did not make any real headway here until 1910. In Sonora, Madero was well received in oppositionist Guaymas but faced a frosty reception in Hermosillo, where the authorities did their best to sabotage Maderista plans and a mere 400 gathered in an 'obscure little square' of the city, where they had to put up with the shouted abuse of a hired government claque.[138] Sonora, later to play a decisive role in the Revolution, was not therefore notable for its overwhelming commitment to Maderismo.

If the north stood in the van of Maderismo, the Anti-Re-electionists were also making headway in the cities of the central plateau (even before Madero's final campaign through the mining states of the centre–north). South of the Isthmus, however, save at those points on the Gulf coast touched by the first *gira electoral*, Maderismo was non-existent. This geographical balance is reflected in Madero's own extensive correspondence. A list of Maderista correspondents, sent to Filómena Mata in August 1909, includes five (out of a total twenty-two) from the north east, two from Chihuahua, eight across the central plateau, four from the Veracruz–Oaxaca region, a mere two on the west coast, and one in Yucatán.[139] A year later, following his release from jail, Madero received an avalanche of letters of congratulation, the great majority from Maderista clubs or declared supporters. Of 150 such letters, 24 came from Mexico City, 22 from Coahuila – the latter, with less than 2½% of the country's population, contributing 15% of the correspondence.[140]

The preponderance of the north reflected not only Madero's personal roots, but also the more developed, urban and literate character of northern society: it was a function, above all, of Maderismo's middle-class composition. The national leadership of the Anti-Re-electionist Party was generally well-off and well educated. It included 'upper-class' adherents like Madero and Vázquez Gómez; Alfredo Robles Domínguez, a wealthy landowner with properties in Mexico City and Guanajuato, president of the San Miguel del Monte Mining Co.; and Manuel Urquidi, an engineer from a 'distinguished family' of the capital, who in 1910 was directing an irrigation project in Michoacán.[141] Other members of the party directorate have been classified as 'petty-bourgeois intellectuals from low status groups': Felix Palavicini, José Vasconcelos, Filómena Mata, Paulino Martínez and Luis Cabrera.[142] Provincial Maderistas were in the main solidly middle class (in some cases upper class); by virtue of their solid respectability and prosperity they bear comparison with the Radical cadres of early twentieth-century France. In Pachuca, for example, the club president was a lawyer, and the vice-president a 'capitalist' and Masonic Grand Master.[143] In Oaxaca, where the state committee was presided over by another lawyer, its members included four *licenciados* (one edited the local opposition newspaper), one professor, one engineer, one graduate of the Military Academy, five students and two artisans – a tailor and a printer.[144] Doctors and professors also figure among Maderista correspondents in the states.[145] But there were entrepreneurs too. At the Yucatecan port of Progreso, for example, the boss of the Navigation Co., Ismael García, was a Maderista who 'has at his disposal a large number of labourers who depend for their livelihood on the unloading and other jobs supplied by this company, labourers whom Sr García influences in favour of the National Anti-Re-electionist Party in Progreso'.[146] Furthermore, Madero's correspondence (and that of Maderistas like Robles Domínguez) teems with *licenciados* and *ingenieros*, merchants and small businessmen: J. G. Hermosillo, veteran Maderista of Múzquiz, manager of the Eagle Pass Lumber Co.; Angel Arch, Maderista organiser in Jalisco, a dealer in rice, maize and chiles in Guadalajara; Gonzalo González, of the Jalapa Liberal Club, a 'merchant and commission agent' supplying the haciendas of the region. Ponciano Medina, the 'honourable businessman' of Tuxtepec, arrested for an excess of Maderista zeal, has already been introduced; a prosperous shopkeeper of Otumba (Mex.), a dealer in hardwear, lost his position in the judiciary for putting out flags and crying 'Viva Madero!' in 1911.[147] In addition to these individuals, who could point to club membership or even gaol sentences as proof of their Maderismo, there were many more fellow-travellers, sympathisers and hangers-on who moved on the fringes of the party and corresponded with its leaders: company directors and managers, doctors and chemists, storekeepers, and occasional *hacendados*.

As the example of Progreso suggests, Maderismo could also attract working-class support or, more strictly, it attracted artisan and working-class support. Rodney Anderson has shown how Anti-Re-electionist support spread among industrial workers in 1909–10, particularly among the textile workers but also among railwaymen, miners, printers and electricians. In some factories, between a quarter and a half of the labour force were reckoned to be actively involved. Workers figured prominently in Maderista demonstrations, particularly in Puebla and Orizaba, and in 1910 they paid the price, suffering arrests and consignment to the army.[148] But perhaps more important were the artisans, to whom the Maderista programme of free elections, individual rights, and education was particularly appealing. The literate, skilled artisan – typified by Silvestre Dorador or Gabriel Gavira, and well depicted in Posada's woodcuts – was an object of Madero's particular favour. He singled out that 'chosen element of the working class which aspires to improvement' as an important source of support and it is clear that the aspiring artisan felt more kinship than antipathy for the public-spirited urban middle class which dominated Maderismo.[149] In Puebla, the shoemaker Aquiles Serdán was president of the Club Luz y Progreso; his treasurer was a carpenter and the three committee members included a factory (almost certainly a textile) operative, a student, and another shoemaker.[150] At Orizaba, where the Club Ignacio de la Llave had grown out of a workers' mutualist society, the carpenter (or cabinet-maker) Gabriel Gavira was president, the saddler Rafael Tapia treasurer, and the committee included Camerino Mendoza (a shopkeeper) and Francisco Lagos Cházaro (described by his colleagues as a 'picturesque Bohemian').[151]

Working-class Maderismo had an obvious economic dimension. Its very success indicated that the workers perceived a connection between political reforms and economic betterment and recruitment was most noticeable in factories with a history of labour problems. This will be explored more fully in the next chapter.[152] As regards the middle-class adherents – who provided the great majority, the backbone of the movement – the economic dimension is much less clear. Yet, despite the marked absence of economic grievances from Maderista manifestos and of economic policies from Maderista programmes, both in and out of government, some historians have persisted in analysing Maderismo in economic terms, as a protest movement of the downwardly mobile, of the impoverished middle class, of the *lumpenbourgeoisie*.[153] The evidence presented here, however, points the other way. Maderismo was more the expression of a rising middle class, comfortably off, and demanding its place in the political sun. Of course, such a demand carried economic implications for, particularly in a society like Porfirian Mexico, political power could advance economic interest. Whether the middle-class demand for open, responsible politics was an end in itself or a means to advance middle-class economic interest, is a difficult question to answer, requiring, as it does, that the historian open windows into men's souls, and divine their inner motives (of which even they themselves might be ignorant). My own impression, for which evidence will shortly be advanced, is that a great many Maderistas (Madero being the most obvious example) sought reform as an end in itself, because it was right and the status quo was wrong; conversely, had they sought power for its own sake or as a source of economic pay-offs, an orthodox Porfirian political career would have been the logical choice. Madero, in fact, repudiated such a choice, denounced Porfirian materialism, and squandered his wealth pursuing what – to his financially hard-nosed family – seemed Quixotic political dreams.[154] And what goes for Madero goes for a good many of his well-to-do collaborators: rational economic self-interest could not justify support for Maderismo in 1909–10.

Of course, the Maderistas were not blind to social and economic questions. They recognised their existence even if, in speech, manifesto and article, they propounded *political* remedies for their solution. In the main, these questions concerned lower-class groups, not the *gente decente* of Maderismo: proletarian wages and conditions, agrarian dispossession (for example, of the Yaqui Indians), the government's sins of commission (repression, conscription, deportation, forced labour) which weighed upon the *pelados*. Such concerns reflected middle-class social conscience, not middle-class immiseration. Taxation, it is true, figured as a middle-class and Maderista grievance – in San Luis, Yucatán, Chihuahua – and, later, the equalisation of taxes became a feature of some Maderista state governments in 1911–13.[155] But this was only one plank, and far from being the broadest, in the Maderista platform. Alone, it cannot take the weight of an 'economic' interpretation of Maderismo.

There are, however, at least three alternative 'economic' hypotheses which have won considerable support, even though all have the demerit of stressing latent functions – that is, they require that Maderismo respond to aims that are largely covert, maybe even unconscious, and for which there is scant empirical evidence.[156] The first, and without doubt the most appealing, concerns the 1907–8 recession, which brought unemployment, bankruptcy, and a general reappraisal of Porfirian economic policy and of its reliance on export-led growth. The recession certainly hit the working class and some sectors of the peasantry, but its effect – both economic and political – on the middle class is harder to fathom. It is too glib to assume that recession automatically breeds protest; it might engender quiescence and political docility. There had been recessions before (the drop in GNP was more severe in 1898–9 and 1901–2 than in 1907–8) and these had not coincided with waves of political mobilisation.[157] Maderista polemics, furthermore, did not concentrate on the slump and it would have been irrational if they had. There was no way the Díaz government (or indeed, any government, in these pre-Keynesian days) could dominate the business cycle and to suggest that the Maderistas claimed power on the grounds of superior ability at economic management is to substitute anachronistic speculation for inductive argument. No such claim was made; indeed, the evidence suggests that Maderistas had not only benefited from

Porfirian economic policy, but also regarded it as the one area of the regime's policies which they could endorse.[158] No doubt the slump, by affecting a section of the middle class and well-to-do, facilitated Maderista recruitment, but examples are notoriously hard to find. Cockcroft cites Pedro Barrenechea, yet he was a staunch Porfirista. Ruíz cites Bulnes' dubious figures of graduate unemployment and intellectual indigence yet, even if the data are accepted, they do no more than permit an inference; they do not establish proof.[159] Many Maderistas were committed to opposition long before the 1907–8 recession. The timetable of middle-class protest was determined not, in some mechanistic fashion, by the curves of the business cycle, but by the political chronology of the 1900s – the Creelman interview, the impending 1910 elections.

The other two economic hypotheses may be taken together. They concern the supposed 'status demotion' suffered by middle-class opponents of the regime, particularly in situations where upward mobility was frustrated by 'rich, monopolising foreigners'.[160] But 'status demotion', as used by Cockcroft, is a notoriously vague concept; at times it assumes the Protean characteristics of 'relative deprivation', that other passe-partout of revolutionary etiology.[161] 'Status demotion' (when it is not used simply as a long-winded alternative for 'poverty') implies some incongruence between social expectations and rewards, entailing 'social frustration and a decline in status'.[162] It can apply to individuals who, apart from being badly off, are also forced to accept 'clerical posts', jobs as 'nameless adjuncts' in foreign companies, or similarly demeaning employment; it is, of course, a common explanation of middle-class malaise in developing countries, popularised in particular by Edward Shils.[163] But it can also apply to individuals 'making some degree of economic progress (who) were denied the higher status they felt they deserved'.[164] To the extent that this sought-after status is political – that is, to the extent that the Maderistas were a rising class, seeking access to political power through the ballot box – the analysis is broadly correct, but there seems little point in confusing the issue with talk of 'status demotion'. Marx, after all, did not clutter up his analysis of the ascendant European bourgeoisie with such superfluous and theoretically anomalous concepts. Otherwise, we are left with the proposition that people on the way up and people on the way down are 'status demoted' and therefore prone to opposition politics. Yet in any society not rigidly defined by caste barriers, and particularly in a society like Porfirian Mexico which was undergoing rapid commercialisation, a large slice of the population will fall into one or other category. It is therefore not difficult to take a narrow sample of oppositionists and note that they are either rising or falling and therefore disaffected. A similar, selective exercise could be undertaken with Porfiristas, to prove the opposite. As another authority worthy of deference has put it, social life being so complex, 'it is always possible to select any number of examples or separate data to prove any proposition one desires'.[165]

Examples can be selected; contradictory generalisations can be swapped to and fro. 'Mexico does not suffer from the "crisis of intellectualism"', a French observer concluded, 'Every educated Mexican is able to find himself a position and to earn a handsome living.'[166] In the absence of any hard, quantitative data on middle-class unemployment, decline or frustration, the only recourse is to consider the individual cases – a primitive, but unavoidable methodology. Cockcroft's case really rests on two: Luis Cabrera and Félix Palavicini. Cabrera is said to have 'experienced this sense of status demotion personally', finding his career blocked by the 'cliquish Científicos'.[167] Yet Cabrera, on the eve of the Revolution, was serving as attorney to the Anglo-American Tlahualilo Company in its protracted dispute with the Ministry of Fomento over the River Nazas waters. This was no 'clerical post', nor did it make Cabrera a 'nameless adjunct' to a foreign company. In 1910, it should be noted, following the presidential election and the apparent defeat of the Maderistas, Cabrera turned his back on opposition politics, publicly stating that 'I would be failing in my obligation as a member of society if I did not retire to private life, dedicating myself to my private business interests, for I have never thought to turn myself into a professional politician.'[168] There is an additional twist, which makes this quest for a simple correlation between private circumstances and public posture appear all the more doubtful. In representing the Tlahualilo Company, Cabrera came up against the Fomento lawyers, Jorge Vera Estañol and Manuel Calero – both active politicians of decidedly conservative persuasion, here representing the nation against foreign, corporate landowners. Furthermore, the battle against the Tlahualilo Company had previously engaged the energies of Francisco Madero, as leader of the 'lower river' planters of the Laguna.[169]

As for Palavicini, his autobiography, published twenty-five years after the Revolution, seems to carry much of the weight of the status demotion argument.[170] It is true that Palavicini's conversion to Maderismo followed the decision of the Ministry of Education to cut off a grant, earlier awarded for research into industrial education. But, even assuming that these events were causally linked, not merely coincidental, it is surely dubious to infer a general theory of revolutionary motivation on the grounds of one bad break. Palavicini, after all, was no intellectual proletarian. He came from a respectable Tabasqueño family; he qualified as an engineer and spent two years on a government-sponsored trip to Europe, where he represented Mexico at the International Geographical Congress at Geneva in 1908.[171] In April 1911, when the Revolution was in full cry, Palavicini took advantage of the appointment of a new Minister of Education to solicit a post in the ministry. These may be the actions of an ambitious young professional, but they do not constitute firm proof of a condition of social frustration and status demotion. Actually, both Cabrera and Palavicini had done reasonably well under Díaz – hence their eagerness to return to their respective careers when it seemed that the challenge of Maderismo had failed. Yet this lively concern for career was in no way incompatible with certain political ideals and sympathies. Cabrera (a point often overlooked in the search for economic motives) was the nephew of the veteran opposition satirist Daniel Cabrera; Palavicini had been a political animal from an early age, starting an opposition newspaper in Tabasco when he was only twenty.[172]

The error of conflating private career and public politics is especially clear when it comes to the role of foreign interests in Mexico, which allegedly frustrated the upwardly mobile (like Cabrera), reducing them to 'nameless adjuncts', while also eliminating competing Mexican entrepreneurs. Frustration bred opposition to Díaz, the darling of the foreign imperialists.[173] With regard to the first argument (frustrated mobility), this hypothesis, like the status demotion hypothesis of which it forms part, tries to have the best of both worlds: Mexicans are deprived of jobs by foreign companies, *ergo* resentful; Mexicans (like Cabrera or Vasconcelos or Díaz Soto y Gama) are employed by foreign companies, *ergo* resentful at having to truckle to foreigners. Yet there is no evidence (bar some *ex post facto* rationalisation) that such employment was resented; in many areas, in fact, it was coveted.[174] Furthermore, it did not require personal experience of foreign employment to generate economic nationalism. Maderismo displayed only mild signs of economic nationalism, chiefly with regard to the oil industry and the Mexicanisation of the railways. In both cases, furthermore, Maderistas merely shared in a general, modest shift in economic thinking, which affected the Porfirian establishment no less than themselves. Economic nationalism, such as it was in these years, offered a poor criterion of differentiation between Maderista and Porfirista.[175]

The whole notion of a Mexican backlash against foreign penetration (whether on the part of exploited workers or a frustrated national bourgeoisie) is greatly exaggerated and errs in regarding Mexican and foreign interests as locked into a 'zero-sum game', in which the gains of one equalled the losses of the other. In fact, as Cockcroft himself shows, Mexican and foreign enterprises were more often complementary and reinforcing and the Mexican response to foreign investment – which brought jobs, money, orders – was more often collaborationist than hostile.[176] The Maderistas were no exception. Many came from the northern states where US investment was extensive and many had prospered in liaison with American interests. The Madero family co-operated with foreign capital both as private individuals and, after 1911, as national politicians. Like many northern progressives, they sought to emulate American enterprise, not to liquidate it.[177] This is not to say that foreign interests were immune to Maderista criticism. Rather, they faced criticism for specific abuses – for maltreating their workers, for conniving at political repression – in much the same way that Mexican employers were criticised.[178] Thus, although the empirical evidence advanced in this chapter could support the hypothesis of Maderismo as a political movement of the emergent national bourgeoisie (the progressive entrepreneurs of the north), a crucial factor is missing: the element of economic nationalism which, to the extent that the Maderistas displayed it, they shared with other, Porfirian groups. Despite many assertions – but little proof – to the contrary, the mainstream political opposition of the 1900s had no intention of breaking with Porfirian policy with regard to economic development and the role of foreign interests within it.

The quest for deep socio-economic explanations is sometimes a flight from reality and historians can sometimes be too clever for their own good, searching for profound causes and latent functions when it is the overt and the obvious which require attention. Madero and his supporters harped upon *political* themes; in office they concentrated almost entirely on *political* reforms. Among the indentifiable Maderista leadership – which is a large group – most were economically secure, even affluent, the beneficiaries, not the victims of Porfirian economic progress. Not surprisingly, they wanted such progress to continue. On the other hand, many had records of political opposition stretching back into the lean years of the early 1900s, if not before: Madero in Coahuilan local politics, Palavicini in Tabasco, young Francisco Múgica in Michoacán, where he continued a liberal family tradition, lampooning Governor Mercado in student flysheets.[179] Political opposition antedated the slump of 1907–8 and political opposition, far from opening avenues of advancement, closed them off.[180]

Maderista motivation – though it related to a recognisable social class, that of the rising middle class, urban and rural – was itself profoundly ideological and cannot be reduced to the objective economic interests of that class, still less of individual members of that class. Indeed, it is arguable that this ideological motivation ran against such objectives. Throughout Mexico, though particularly in the north, there were serious-minded, politically literate families, nurtured in the strong tradition of Mexican liberalism. They looked back at the liberal heroes of the past and felt ashamed of the political death-in-life which their country now experienced. It was appalling, one liberal declared, that political and social abuses were still rampant in Mexico 'well into the twentieth century . . . in an epoch when it is said the apogee of civilisation has been attained, and in a country which boasts of its culture . . . and of the progress it has achieved'; 'if Hidalgo and Juárez were to rise from their graves and witness the abominable slavery which their sons suffer, they would return to their tombs bursting with indignation'.[181] As this quotation neatly illustrates, the liberal oppositionists of the 1900s had one eye on the Mexican past – the past of Hidalgo and Juárez – and one on the global present, the epoch of western, liberal capitalism. Córdova rightly stresses the backward-looking character of Maderismo: 'the Revolution in Mexico is born along with a burning defence of the past' – though a past which, as usual, had been suitably sanitised and mythologised.[182] Hence the constant invocation of the great liberal names of the past (Arriaga naming his club after grandfather Ponciano, Madero his after Juárez, Gavira's in Orizaba taking the name of the Veracruzano liberal Ignacio de la Llave); hence the repeated references to the Constitution of 1857, not only by educated and well-to-do *políticos* like Madero and Urueta, but also by working-class Maderistas.[183] Opposition intellectuals penned biographies of Juárez or converted ceremonies in homage of Juárez into anti-Díaz demonstrations. Later, rank-and-file revolutionaries would quote Juarista slogans and revolutionary manifestos would remind Díaz of his own liberal promises of thirty-five years before.[184] Such ideological statements could mask class or clientelist interests. To the industrial workers, Maderista liberalism might appear (rather as the liberal reforms of the nineteenth-century Chartists appeared to British workers) as a 'knife and fork question'; to political 'outs' it offered a possible entrée to power. But to the majority of the Maderista middle class, the primary appeal was ideological, and ideology acted as an autonomous and important variable. Through the long and bitter civil wars of the nineteenth century, liberalism had put down deep roots, which were all the stronger for liberalism's close association with the patriot cause. It had acquired a numerous and dedicated constituency, concentrated in traditional liberal families, communities, and regions; a staff of propagandists in the press and public schools; and a set of texts, slogans, and ritual festivities, all of which underpinned the movement.[185] Mexican liberalism represented much more than a tepid conformity; it could still be a vigorous faith, complete with prophets and martyrs, historical revelation, and a Manichaean image of the eternal clerical, conservative enemy.[186]

It was additionally invigorated by foreign example. To the literate middle class, the Díaz dictatorship seemed increasingly incongruous in a world where liberal democracy was the norm – at least in 'civilised' states. In particular, the France of the Third Republic and the US of the Progressive Era served as models. France had long been established (in Mexican as well as French eyes) as the fount of culture and civilisation. Mexican *políticos* loved drawing French parallels and citing French texts; a dose of French education was highly valued.[187] But the closer, almost overwhelming example of the US was more potent still. A somewhat fearful admiration of American economic might was common among educated Mexicans, both Porfiristas and their opponents. In particular (I would argue), northerners, who were most directly familiar with the American model, sought to emulate it south of the border. Though this might involve a degree of nationalist resistance to American economic penetration, it involved yet more collaboration and the attempted inculcation of 'American' values – hard work, thrift, hygiene, entrepreneurialism, initiative. Sometimes this emulation even implied the classic liaison between Protestantism and the progressive, capitalist ethos.[188]

Such 'developmentalist' concerns could unite Porfiristas and Maderistas.

But the Maderistas also revered American constitutional government and saw it as inseparable from American economic dynamism: 'we must imitate American practices,' Madero wrote, 'above all that adherence to the law which her rulers display, if we are to become as great as they'.[189] Oppositionists contrasted Mexican electoral fraud with North American honesty. *El Correo* compared Mexico with 'civilised France, correct Argentina, and our neighbours to the north, where the government is for the people and where effective suffrage is respectfully complied with'. As a result, the paper concluded, 'industry in these countries progresses, agriculture achieves notable advances, and the nation in general marches forward in solid prosperity'.[190] It was an up-dated, peripheral version of the old Victorian vision, whereby constitutionalism would unlock the latent energies of autocratic states, encouraging them upon a path of vigorous capitalist growth.[191]

But, apart from any economic pay-offs, the North American political example inspired – and rankled. Salvador Alvarado angrily described the meeting between Díaz and President Taft on the border in October 1909: Taft soberly dressed, with two grey-uniformed adjutants, Díaz loaded with medals, surrounded by a lavish military escort: 'on the one hand, all the simplicity of a true democracy, on the other, the pomp and vainglory of an oriental sultanate'.[192] For many Maderistas, furthermore, these revealing comparisons were based on personal experience. Madero had rounded off his European education with eight months at Berkeley. Chihuahua's leading Anti-Re-electionist, Abraham González, was an American college graduate, as were fellow-Maderistas in the state.[193] Among the Maderistas of Sonora, Maytorena, Gayou and Juan Cabral had all been educated in the US; the Aguirre Benavides family, relatives, business associates and political allies of Madero, sent their sons to study commerce in San Antonio; many other oppositionists had attended American mission schools in northern Mexico – Moisés Sáenz and Braulio Hernández were perhaps the most celebrated.[194] Such men were patriots, even nationalists, but they were not anti-American. Like all educated Mexicans (Porfiristas included) they entertained doubts and dislikes concerning the 'Colossus of the North', but they did not dismiss the *gringos* as Protestant ogres and materialist barbarians, as their conservative Catholic cousins were wont to do.[195] On the contrary, they appreciated (and in the case of the Maderos and Aguirre Benavides, emulated) American economic initiative and they entertained a high opinion of American democracy, recently rejuvenated by the Progressive movement. Noting the 'fairly deep' impression of Progressivism in the writings of Madero and others, Womack justly translates 'Sufragio Efectivo, No Re-elección', the Maderista slogan, as 'a real vote and no boss rule'.[196] To put it another way, the revived liberal opposition of the 1900s, drawing on Mexican precedent and foreign example, sought to subvert the Porfirian motto 'mucha administración y poca política' and replace it with their own variant: 'mucha política y buena administración'.[197] As such, Maderismo was above all else a profoundly political and ideological movement.

CHALLENGE AND RESPONSE

In the past, the occasional state election had caused a political rumpus, as dissatisfied groups mobilised to oust an unpopular governor. In 1909, four such electoral contests were scheduled, and they were to be conducted in conditions of unparalleled political ferment. Though the national Maderista leadership did not play a prominent part in these elections, the Maderista example encouraged local groups – the perennial 'outs', the aspiring middle class – to additional efforts and the government was placed on its mettle. The 1909 battles over the state executives of Coahuila, Sinaloa, Yucatán and Morelos were dress-rehearsals for the 1910 battle over the national executive.

Venustiano Carranza, the opposition candidate in Coahuila, had held lower political office under Díaz; he had recently been strong for Reyes; he only approximated to Maderismo when he failed to get the support of the centre in his bid for the governorship. Madero, for his part, was also lukewarm and, though the Anti-Re-electionist clubs of Coahuila backed the Carranza candidacy, they did so with less than total enthusiasm and seemed to be husbanding their resources for the impending presidential election. Still, they put up a good show and, according to one account, ran up a majority for Carranza; but the *jefes políticos*, reinforced by the army, had their instructions to support the official, Corralista candidate, Jesús del Valle, and he was declared elected. It was an imposition which the people of Coahuila did not forget in a hurry and it brought more recruits to Madero's already powerful following in the state.[198]

In Sinaloa a particularly bitter struggle was fought between *gobiernista* elements, backing the local *hacendado* and industrialist Diego Redo, and the journalist José Ferrel, supported by the usual opposition coalition of ex-Reyistas, professionals and students, who went down to the usual illicit defeat. Though Ferrelismo had all the hallmarks of a local Maderismo, Madero himself had made little headway in the state so far. Early in 1910, however, in the bitter post-election aftermath, Madero visited Sinaloa, where many responded warmly to his speeches and converted their recent local into a national opposition allegiance. 1910 saw the spread of Anti-Re-electionist clubs in the state and growing government repression; in June the Maderista activist Gabriel Leyva was caught by *rurales* in northern Sinaloa and shot 'while trying to escape'. Maderismo had its first martyr.[199]

Violence also flared in Yucatán. Here, the familiar political objections to the incumbent governor, Muñoz Arístegui, were compounded by economic grievances, brought on by the fall in the price of henequen which was attributed to the Molina–Montes liaison with the International Harvester Co.[200] Middle-class opponents fused with a powerful 'out' faction, the conservative Cantón family, in the Independent Electoral Centre – 'a group of people belonging to the best families in Yucatán' – which ran a Cantonista candidate against the incumbent.[201] Madero, never averse to a pragmatic deal, advised the Yucatecan Anti-Re-electionist leader, the poet and journalist Pino Suárez, to back the Cantón candidacy in return for a promise of support in 1910. The Cantonistas made the running, and Governor Muñoz responded in the customary way: opposition leaders were shadowed night and day; government lawyers ransacked the criminal archives to find compromising evidence against them; Indians were herded into town to parade in gobiernista demonstrations. Eventually, when members of the opposition were driven into rebellion, their conspiracy misfired and the leaders were rounded up. But this was not the end of political violence in Yucatán.[202]

The fourth gubernatorial conflict, in Morelos, was potentially the most serious. Here, in the warm valleys across the Sierra de Ajusco from Mexico City, the progress of the sugar industry had created profound social tensions. But, as with the Mexican Revolution as a whole, it required a crisis over the political succession to bring these tensions to the fore. This came with the death of Governor Alarcón, whose 'stern but benevolent rule' ended in December 1908, the 'Mexican country diet [having] corroded his insides and killed him of gastro-enteritis at fifty-seven'.[203] When Díaz backed the candidates of the sugar planters – the effete, inept Pablo Escandón – the opposition gathered around the leading political 'outs', the Leyva family. General Francisco Leyva, hero of the French Intervention and one-time governor of the state, had fallen from power after a quarrel with Díaz in the 1870s; now too old (he said) to re-enter politics, he allowed his son Patricio, an agronomist and civil servant, to enter a contest of unprecedented ferocity.[204] Old allies of the Leyvas re-emerged: like the Sedanos of Cuernavaca, father and sons, a family of 'moderate prosperity' holding minor posts in the state administration; while in Cuautla and the surrounding towns schoolmasters, village lawyers and one-time municipal officials joined the movement. The respectable city professionals made the running but, as Leyvista clubs spread through the state, country people began to second their initiative. The motives at work – well described by Womack – were the same as those which impelled Reyistas, Maderistas, Ferrelistas. Each district, like each state, contained a lump of indigestible opposition – indigestible, that is, in the dyspeptic politics of the Porfiriato. For some, the grievance was poverty; for some, a long exclusion from politics; for others, resentment against local officials. Taken together, however, 'these disaffected families formed a vague community of opposition . . . the articulate and the prominent among them were town folk . . . with white collars, shoes, underwear and important if shaky connections with the establishment . . . [the] rural families . . . usually kept quiet and let the clerks and shopowners and editors and lawyers do the talking'.[205]

Meanwhile, the growth of these local coalitions was greatly facilitated by the climate of national politics. Democratic Party members and newspapers endorsed Leyva, and even Escandón was driven to publish a sweet-sounding programme (the work of a Reyista) designed to appeal to the prevailing mood: free speech, free municipal government, better primary education, civic improvements, tax reform. But the *gobiernistas* of Morelos, like their national counterparts, could not compete with the opposition on these terms; their eleventh hour conversion to reform politics lacked credibility. So, in Morelos, Escandón had to achieve victory by the old and tried methods: the disruption of opposition demonstrations, the arrest of opposition leaders and their deportation to Quintana Roo, the final, inevitable electoral chicanery. In this sense, the government could still defeat local oppositions, but it could no longer snuff them out in provincial obscurity. Routine matters, like state elections, were routine no longer. And with Reyes tamely accepting defeat (he resigned his governorship in November 1908, leaving Mexico for a military mission to Europe) Madero emerged as the pre-eminent opposition leader, who could no longer be ignored, derided or tolerated.

Thus, while Madero's first trip along the Gulf coast had been relatively trouble-free, his visit to the west at the turn of the year encountered greater obstacles. At Colima, a rally had to be held outside the town, and mounted police patrolled ominously; at Guaymas the authorities vetoed the use of any public place (including the beach) and Madero spoke from an open coach.[206] In the autumn of 1909 Madero's newspaper, *El Anti-Reeleccionista*, was closed by the government, in 1910 the Governor of Zacatecas banned all Maderista activities in the state. Hitherto, the authorities and their opponents had played a cat-and-mouse game, but a game with its lighter moments. When Governor Martínez ordered all the electric lights at Puebla railway station to be doused at Madero's arrival, the Maderistas welcomed him with blazing torches.[207] But now the gloves were coming off. In April 1910, as Anti-Re-electionist delegates from all over the country converged on Mexico City for the party convention, Corral initiated criminal proceedings against Madero over a longstanding land suit (it was a transparent ploy, which the government was soon forced to give up) and local Maderista activists were picked up by the police, some of them en route to the convention.[208]

The convention took place in mid-April, when over a hundred delegates gathered to debate the party programme and decide on its electoral ticket. Already, the rapid spread of Maderismo, and its absorption of different local oppositions, were creating divisions and dissensions in the party. In particular, there was a split over the question of opposing Díaz's presidential candidacy. Madero's initial plan had been to concede the presidency and contest the vice-presidency, and some of his more moderate supporters (including Emilio Vázquez Gómez, brother of Francisco) clung to this strategy until the elections. Others, especially some young Maderistas, favoured a thorough-going opposition, with the Anti-Re-electionists fielding serious candidates for both offices. Madero himself was ambivalent – perhaps deliberately and astutely ambivalent. The choice of strategy would depend in part on Díaz's response. [209] He reassured supporters that there would be no *transacción*, no compromise, and when the convention had met, it voted Madero as the Party's presidential candidate by a wide margin – a nomination which he accepted in a 'vibrant, impassioned and stirring speech'. [210] Yet, even then, Madero was prepared to meet Díaz in a private interview, fixed up by Governor Dehesa, at which he offered to withdraw his candidacy and revert to the original formula (Díaz/Madero) if the president would guarantee fair and free elections. But Madero came away disappointed, the dictator, decrepit and ill-informed, showing no disposition to compromise. A final opportunity to arrange a peaceful political succession was thereby lost, and Madero emerged from the meeting believing that it would require a revolution to oust the obstinate old dictator. [211]

In fact, Madero had for some time recognised that armed resistance might prove the only means of toppling Díaz. This is not to say that he welcomed this conclusion (on the contrary, he believed a revolution would constitute a 'national calamity'), nor that he acted in deliberately devious fashion, as has been suggested. [212] Díaz must be made to realise that total intransigence would incur the risk of revolution; perhaps this realisation, coupled with the political pressure of the Anti-Re-electionist campaign, would force him to compromise. If not, the responsibility rested with Díaz. Meantime, the Maderistas would press on with their peaceful campaigning, even if the outcome looked increasingly bleak, their electioneering increasingly formalistic.

After nominating Madero, the convention selected Francisco Vázquez Gómez as running mate and proceeded to approve a programme. This contained the usual liberal nostrums: respect for the Constitution, better education, free suffrage, measures to aid agriculture with credit and irrigation, to improve the lot of the workers by curbing gambling and alcoholism, the reinvigoration of municipal life through the suppression of the *jefaturas*. [213] It was an entirely political plan, save in its enlightened concern for social abuses; it offered neither agrarian reform nor economic nationalism. In May, with the convention wound up, Madero embarked on a final campaign tour through the cities of central and northern Mexico, the last push before the elections scheduled for late June.

It was now a political battle *à outrance*. A crowd of 10,000 welcomed Madero to Guadalajara, 25,000 to Puebla. [214] Surviving newsreels show scenes of real popular enthusiasm. Madero's speeches became more forthright and provocative, and the government responded with more heavy-handed measures. All Anti-Re-electionist demonstrations were banned in Coahuila, similar repression occurred in San Luis, Aguascalientes and Nuevo León;

persecution was particularly severe in Puebla, scene of the recent Maderista triumph, where entire club committees were consigned to gaol, and some individuals to the army.[215] As tension and repression mounted, there were sporadic resorts to violence, deplored and discouraged by the Maderista leadership. An Anti-Re-electionist revolt was put down in Tlaxcala; Gabriel Leyva, goaded into rebellion, was shot in Sinaloa, a purely local uprising at Valladolid (Yuc.) was blamed on the Maderistas.[216] At the beginning of June, after a final, tumultuous reception in Mexico City, Madero headed north; 16 June found the candidate and his entourage at Monterrey, closely shepherded by the police. That evening Madero was arrested (it came as no surprise) and charged with insulting the president and fomenting rebellion; according to one account, not entirely trustworthy, Corral was all for a summary application of the *ley fuga*.[217] Madero's was only the most prominent of many arrests, which have been estimated at between 5,000 and 60,000; when the elections were held late in June nearly half the Anti-Re-electionist Central Committee was in gaol or hiding, and most of the opposition press had been closed down.[218]

The election results surprised no-one. In the primaries, Díaz had secured 18,829 votes to Madero's 221. Towns in the Maderista heartland were said to have voted thus: Saltillo, 110 for Díaz, 0 for Madero; Monclova, 84 for Díaz, 0 for Madero; Parras (Madero's home town), 65 for Díaz, 0 for Madero.[219] Maderista complaints abounded: at Huamantla (Tlax.) enrolment was completely defective, independent votes were nullified, and the electoral officials refused to accept protests; at Mapimí (Dgo) the Anti-Re-electionist chief was gaoled and only one-third of the electorate received voting slips, and these with strict instruction as to how to vote; at Parral (Chih.) a platoon of *rurales* and a regiment of cavalry arrived on the eve of the elections, and an official told the citizens how to vote with the friendly admonition, 'if you don't sign, I shall make a note of you'.[220] All told, the Maderistas were able to collect nearly two hundred documents from nineteen states alleging electoral malpractices, which were submitted to the Federal Congress with a futile petition that the election be declared null.[221] Meanwhile, with the danger past, Madero was released on bail in the city of San Luis.

It was a bleak scene which confronted the defeated candidate. His party was in disarray, his protests to the government were ignored. The brothers Vázquez Gómez (who had never been keen on opposing Díaz himself) were flirting with a Díaz–Dehesa formula – a last-ditch effort, which counted on some support in high places, to oust Corral. Madero would have none of it. But what options were open? In the wake of the abortive election, political apathy seemed to prevail.[222] Cabrera declared that it was the patriotic duty of all citizens 'to return once again to their occupations as soon as the campaign is over'; he certainly did not waste any time himself.[223] Other Maderista luminaries, like Palavicini, had already recanted.[224] In Mexico City, the Centennial orgy was getting underway.

It seemed as if the great hopes, first aroused by the Creelman interview, nurtured by dozens of local clubs and newspapers, disappointed by Reyes, revived by Madero, were now irrevocably dashed. The logic of the situation, which Madero had earlier perceived, and by April 1910 accepted, demanded some kind of armed resistance. If the force of enlightened public opinion had failed to budge Díaz, if the speeches, rallies and reasoned arguments – all the weapons of the liberal arsenal – had proved ineffective, then the only alternative was force. For the solid, sober, frock-coated Maderistas, this was a bitter truth. A revolution, observed Dr Vázquez Gómez, 'we ought to avoid at all costs'; his brother dissuaded militant Maderistas from contemplating such a course.[225] A revolution was unpalatable not only because it would jeopardise property and order, both of which the Maderistas leaders held dear, and not only because it risked playing into the hands of the degenerate, illiterate masses; it was also unpalatable because it could not possibly succeed.[226] This was the accepted wisdom on all sides.[227] All previous insurrections against the central government had been successfully, often bloodily repressed: what chance did the Maderista doctors, journalists, engineers and shopkeepers stand, where mighty caudillos and belligerent Indians had met their match? As an observer in San Luis put it: 'the discontented are the middle class who have quite a definite idea of their own desires. They wish a new and free election, a free press, and the abolition of the feudal system of property and taxation. But . . . they would not of their own initiative resort to force to secure these ends.'[228]

The Maderistas faced at national level the same dilemma which had confronted the local Cantonista opposition in Yucatán shortly before. Having marshalled their opposition coalition, having proceeded with impeccable legality, they found their efforts being thwarted and their persons threatened. In Yucatán they had discussed what to do:

somebody proposed . . . that the only way of making front [sic] to armed force, when all guarantees had been apparently suspended, was with armed force. Nobody accepted the idea of what would be looked on as a revolution. It was dangerous – nobody was partisan of shedding blood, and, even if everybody had been so, there was no money, time, nor . . . people expert in a movement of that sort. So it was decided to keep on working as we had done.[229]

So thought most Maderistas in 1910. But Madero thought otherwise. Where Reyes had drawn back from revolution in 1909, 'stunted, ugly' Francisco Madero (Reyes' words) accepted the logic of the situation. While still in gaol, he began discussing plans for a rebellion, though he and his close supporters agreed that they lacked the wherewithal for immediate action.[230] For two months Madero remained under bail in San Luis, forbidden to leave the city limits. Late in September, Congress completed its scrutiny of the election results and declared Díaz and Corral elected. A week later, disguised as a labourer, Madero jumped bail and travelled third class by train to the border. On 7 October he crossed the international bridge in Laredo, where he was met by a small group of Maderista *émigrés*.[231]

October was spent drafting a manifesto to the Mexican people – the Plan of San Luis Potosí – a terse document which rehearsed the efforts of the Anti-Re-electionists, denounced the Díaz dictatorship, and declared Madero to be provisional president, the recent elections being null and void. Pending new elections under the aegis of the provisional government, all existing laws and contracts made by the Díaz regime would stand – this 'to avoid as far as possible the disorders inevitable in any revolutionary movement'.[232] One clause promised the restitution of illegally acquired landholdings but, in other respects, 'social' questions went unmentioned; the Plan was essentially a political statement, a response to the thwarted democratic hopes of 1909–10, a call to arms for the revindication of constitutional rights. Distributed clandestinely early in November, the Plan set a precise time for the revolt against Díaz: 6 p.m. on 20 November 1910.

Time was short. From his base in San Antonio, Madero negotiated the purchase of arms in New York; he sent agents into Mexico to link up with potential rebel leaders; he appointed provisional governors for certain states. Preparations were made for his own triumphal return to Mexico, which would follow an attack on the border town of Cd Porfirio Díaz. The fall of Porfirio Díaz City would preface the fall of Porfirio Díaz Mexico.[233] Early in November, Madero received a letter from his brother Manuel, in Parras: the family were undertaking a 'recreational trip' to Europe, would Francisco care to join? Francisco politely declined, since he had a revolution to lead.[234]

3

𝕊𝕊

Popular protest

The revolt which sprang from Madero's call to arms initiated a fully fledged 'social' revolution, comparable to the Russian Revolution and unprecedented in Latin America at that time. Its 'social revolutionary' character derived from mass participation and from its expression of genuine popular grievances, both of which were evident from the start.[1] There was no clear, chronological distinction (as has often been posited) between initial 'political' revolt and subsequent 'social' revolution; on the contrary, the two were coeval.[2] Indeed, without mass popular participation the Maderistas could not have overthrown Díaz and their respectable reformism would have remained on a par with similar movements of urban middle-class protest – the Argentine Radical Party, for instance, or Rui Barbosa's Liberal Republicans in Brazil, who launched their challenge in the same year as Madero – moderate movements, directed against incumbent oligarchies, liable to be co-opted or crushed. To understand how the Maderistas avoided this fate, only to confront another – that of sponsoring social revolution – which was in many ways even more unpalatable, it is necessary to investigate the character of popular protest on the eve of the Revolution, a task which, granted the relative lack of sources and the nature of the problem itself, is difficult and daunting.

THE COUNTRYSIDE: HACIENDA AND VILLAGE

The key to the social revolution lies in the countryside. Where Maderismo was predominantly urban, the revolution was predominantly rural. 'It was the earthy peon,' commented an observer, 'spendthrift of his own life and inured to an incredible degree of hardship who fought the war of the revolt'.[3] Some historians have concurred: 'the Mexican Revolution found its energies in the villages and the millions who fought were primarily moved by the idea of land reform'.[4] This is not quite the platitude it might seem – or would have seemed twenty years ago. Recently, historians have been at pains to de-emphasise, sometimes to eliminate altogether, the role of autonomous, agrarian revolt in the Revolution of 1910–20. The agrarian factor has sometimes been buried in

78

compendious lists of 'social' causes, lists lacking any hierarchy of importance.[5] Alternative factors of dubious validity (such as 'anti-imperialism') have been promoted above it.[6] Frequently, agrarian revolt is limited to the single, allegedly untypical case of Zapatismo.[7] And a prestigious authority (an expert on 'peasants', if not on Mexico) has ventured the incredible assertion that 'the bulk of the peasantry ... was not much involved in the revolution of 1910–20'.[8]

Such arguments may stem from ignorance and even qualified 'Mexicanists' run the old risk of listening to the articulate, literate voices of the past, while neglecting the inarticulate and rustic. Zapatismo demands a hearing, but many lesser Zapatismos are ignored. But these arguments also stem from the fructiferous ground of revisionism-for-its-own-sake, the seed-bed of so many theses and learned articles. In particular, it would seem, the success of a good historian in debunking the revolutionary orthodoxy of the 1920s had encouraged lesser historians to attempt (on the basis of far less evidence) a parallel debunking of the Revolution of 1910–20.[9] The cynical, manipulative state and the passive, manipulated peasantry are thus projected backwards into a decade when they did not exist. On the contrary, the evidence of contemporary observers was unequivocal from the very outset. 'It is very remarkable', one noted in 1911, 'that during the whole of the revolutionary movement it is the agricultural classes who have furnished the militant element.'[10] An earlier generation of historians – notably Frank Tannenbaum – argued along these lines and this generation would be better advised (in this case) to build on their solid analyses, rather than to attempt a slick demolition.[11]

Mexico was a predominantly rural society in 1910. Government resided, news was made and archives accumulated in the towns, but these contained only a fifth of the country's population.[12] Mexico's labour force was primarily agricultural, secondarily artisan and only thirdly industrial; for every hundred rural workers, there were perhaps a dozen small farmers and a dozen artisans, four factory operatives (at least one a woman), three miners, one *ranchero*, and a quarter of one per cent of an *hacendado*.[13] What is more, the agricultural share of the labour force was actually rising in the last decade of the Porfiriato, for reasons which will become apparent. As regards this rural mass, conditions and relations of production varied according to location, population density, and crop. Available sources are patchy and the information they convey is sometimes contradictory,[14] but two general tendencies stand out in the agrarian history of the Porfiriato. First, landownership became more unequal as land gravitated from villager and smallholder to *hacendado*, cacique and (sometimes) *ranchero*; second, the real wages of rural labourers, as well as the terms enjoyed by tenants or sharecroppers, tended to deteriorate.[15]

The first of these salient trends spanned the entire period, while the second only became clearly apparent after the 1890s. Both, however, must be linked to major changes taking place in the Mexican economy during the Díaz regime. With the onset of political stability and the rapid creation of a railway network, the commercialisation of agriculture accelerated. The first trunk line, connecting Mexico City and Veracruz, was completed in 1873. By the early 1880s, the boom years of construction, nearly 2,000 km. of track were laid per annum. Total length of track reached 13,000 km. in 1898 and 19,000 km. in 1910.[16] The social effects of this development were profound. Though the railways were criticised for many failings – high tariffs, price-fixing deals, and general inefficiency – they wrought a transformation in Mexican society and one which, as contemporaries noted, was inextricably linked to the origins of the Revolution.[17] The locomotive replaced the mule train, beggaring many *arrieros*, freight bills were cut, often dramatically, hitherto local economies were stitched together to form regional, national, even international markets.[18] Sonoran wheat was shipped to the capital, Puebla *mantas* (transported by steamship as well as locomotive) reached Yucatán, cargo could be seen leaving Guadalajara for Orizaba, 800 km. away across country; and *pulque* from the plains of Apam flooded into Mexico City, to gratify the capital's thirst for half a million litres a day.[19] There were small but neat illustrations of the growing economic integration of the country: in Chiapas, an altar to the Virgin of Guadalupe was decorated with two green glass insulators; the pine-board huts of Indians in the Sierra de Ajusco, separating Mexico City from Morelos, were roofed with 'the cut-up tins of the ubiquitous Standard Oil Company'.[20]

The growth of the railways, coupled with political stability and rising demand, both national and international, made possible the Porfirian economic miracle. Under Díaz, population grew at 1.4% per annum, production at 2.7%; foreign investment rose from less than 100m. to 3,400m. pesos; the volume of money in circulation rose eightfold, while prices doubled.[21] Though there was a significant degree of import-substitution industrialisation, particularly in the fields of cotton textiles, liquor, and tobacco products, it was the export sector which grew fastest, registering an annual increase of 6.1%, about double the figure for world trade.[22] The old export staples of gold and silver fell from two-thirds to one half of total exports, as non-precious metals and primary products increased in import-ance. The new mines of the north pioneered the production of lead, copper and zinc, while in agriculture, rubber, chicle, chickpeas, and livestock grew fastest, supplementing the established exports of henequen, coffee, vanilla and hides.[23] And, by the 1900s, oil was coming on tap in significant quantities.[24]

Agriculture, responding vigorously to domestic and foreign demand, began to display a dual character. Aggregate figures of growth were unimpressive, a mere 21% over thirty years, 1877–1907.[25] But while the production of staple foodstuffs – maize, beans, chile – remained static, despite population increase, exports rose by nearly 200%. Between the 1870s and the Revolution, for example, henequen exports rose from 11,000 to 123,000 tons; tropical fruits from 1,000 to 10,000; caucho and guayule, the two principal forms of rubber, from nothing to 8,000 and 5,000 tons respectively. Tobacco and cotton production also rose in response to domestic industrial demand.[26]

Mexico, of course, was not alone in experiencing this growing integration into world markets and a consequent commercialisation of agriculture,[27] but the social consequences were in some respects distinctive. Landlords found themselves facing new market opportunities – and not simply in the export sector. Dante Cusi, a go-ahead Italian immigrant, farming the Hacienda de Uspero in Michoacán, had hitherto made his money selling rice in Pátzcuaro, the crop transported in big Studebaker waggons, each hauled by a dozen mules, whose noisy progress through the local villages was a great spectacle for the inhabitants. But the arrival of the railway at Uruapán opened new horizons: 'this meant that produce could be sent all over the country, wherever demand existed and prices were better, rather than being limited to local consumption alone, as had been the case, consumption that was paltry and bitterly competed for by small farmers. Without the railway, it would have been useless to go on increasing the harvests.'[28] In Morelos, the railway brought revived trade, higher wages and a boost for the charcoal business at Tepoztlán; in the rest of the state, where sugar was king, it enabled the planters to ship in modern refining machinery and ship out more sugar to Mexican and the world markets.[29] The sluggish performance of the San Luis mining industry was offset by the boom in agriculture, as *hacendados* built railway feeder lines, sank wells, established sugar refineries and, in addition to supplying maize to the expanding urban markets of central Mexico, began to produce fibre (lechuguilla), cotton, wool, kid-leather, and tropical fruit.[30] The latter came from the Huasteca, where, in the space of ten years (1893/6–1903/6), coffee production almost doubled and tobacco production more than quadrupled. But, as the case of Tepoztlán indicates, it was not just the big *hacendado* who prospered. The *rancheros* of northern Guerrero entered the market, increasing and diversifying production; those of the Sierra Alta of Hidalgo, raising corn, cattle, coffee and sugar-cane, stimulated a 'rapid expansion of local commerce', even in this remote area.[31] Quiet, bucolic communities like San José de Gracia were sucked into a regional, then a national, market economy, exporting pigs and cheese from the new railway station at Ocotlán to destinations as far afield as Mexico City.[32] Here, and elsewhere in rural Mexico, 'getting rich became fashionable'.[33]

Getting rich had always been fashionable; the difference was that now more people – albeit still a small minority – could get richer, and do so quicker, than in the past, and without relying on fortuitous mining bonanzas.[34] This raises a number of important points of theory and interpretation which must be touched on. The increased demand for agricultural products, stimulated by population growth and industrialisation (both inside and outside Mexico), and facilitated by improved transport and communications, acted upon an agrarian society already possessing clearly defined social, economic and juridical features. The effects of such demand – ubiquitous in the 'world system' of the later nineteenth century – were far from uniform and were determined by these local features, which varied between countries and also within countries. Mexico responded differently from Argentina or West Africa, Yucatán responded differently from Sonora. As a protagonist in a recent debate has stressed, it is mistaken to analyse the process of peripheral incorporation into world markets according to some simple economic determinism (incorporation brings development/underdevelopment) without giving due attention to the 'particular, historically developed class structures through which these processes actually worked themselves out and through which their fundamental character was actually determined'.[35]

In the case of Porfirian Mexico, the countryside had for three centuries been dominated by two key institutions, the hacienda and the village.[36] During the colonial period the hacienda had acquired much of the best valley lands. In some more populous states, like Puebla, its dominance prevented any expansion of village holdings or peasant agriculture.[37] In the north, where the sedentary Indian population was limited and scattered, the hacienda embraced vast, untilled acres.[38] But, despite frequent encroachments, clashes and prolonged litigation, the village survived as an independent entity, often retaining land. In particular, it survived in the more remote, mountainous regions, but it also proved capable of resisting the hacienda in certain lowland areas, like the valleys of Oaxaca.[39] Indeed, the survival of the village was in some senses necessary for the prosperity of the hacienda for – considerations of social stability aside – the village provided seasonal and temporary labour and, some would argue, assumed the burdens of the reproduction of labour power.[40] A relationship was thus established which – be it a 'symbiosis' or an 'articulation of modes of production' – proved durable over long periods of time, while economic and demographic pressures were broadly favourable.

The colonial – or 'traditional' – hacienda operated within limits determined by its economic environment. Demand was weak, communications were poor, hence production was kept low.[41] Within these limits, *hacendados* (or their managers) sought to maximise profits. They switched from share-cropping to rentals to demesne farming according to circumstances; they played the market to get the best return and were not indifferent to other forms of investment.[42] Hence, there was an active land market and a frequent turnover of ownership.[43] But profit could only be sought within the limits of the system. Hacienda expansion served a purpose in assuring a supply of labour (from dispossessed Indians) and in weakening peasant competition in the grain market; no doubt sprawling acres also appealed to seigneurial sentiments.[44] But the basic characteristics of the traditional hacienda – its inefficiency and untapped potential – were the result of inexorable economic circumstances, not of some prior, determinant 'feudal mentality'. Such a mentality, to the extent that it existed, was the child of circumstances, not vice versa.

Hacienda and village had thus co-existed, in the presence of weak market forces, for three centuries before the time of Díaz. Then, in the last quarter of the nineteenth century, both the level of demand and the rural entrepreneur's capacity to meet his demand were dramatically augmented. In stressing this development – which was intimately bound up with the origins of the Revolution – it is worth inserting a brief theoretical note. It has long been debated whether the traditional hacienda was 'feudal' or 'capitalist' ('feudal' in the Marxist, rather than the stricter historical and juridical sense).[45] For A. G. Frank, the presence of strong market relations is sufficient to denote capitalism, hence Mexico and Latin America had been capitalist since the Conquest; Wallerstein would broadly agree.[46] Both the theoretical and the empirical implications of this argument are important for an understanding of Mexico's development and of the origins and character of the Revolution.[47] Critics of Frank have pointed out that his analysis rests at the level of circulation and that it neglects the relations of production; they rightly stress the importance of non-capitalist relations (serfdom, peonage, service tenantries) which underpinned hacienda production, even production for the market.[48] Some commentators, ignoring Frank's tireless warnings, continue to regard hacienda production as late as the early twentieth century as 'feudal'.[49] But they necessarily recognise the hacienda's external links with capitalism and contrive to square the circle with the notion of the 'articulation of modes of production' – an approach which has the merits of almost limitless flexibility and a certain superficial sophistication.[50] Better 'AMP' (as its users, great aficionados of the capital letter acronym, are wont to term it) than a surrender to feeble compromise: 'quasi-feudal', 'semi-feudal', 'subcapitalist' or 'seigneurial'.[51] 'AMP' can at least promise a degree of fidelity to Marxist theory and a recognition of the complexity of historical reality, on both of which counts it may represent an advance on Frank. It is, however, notoriously difficult to 'operationalise' in that, while the different modes of production may be identified (often in rather banal descriptive fashion), their 'articulation' remains something of a mystery.[52] As so often is the case, theoretical sophistication has been acquired at the expense of clarity and forthrightness.

The workaday historian must confront these problems, if only because of the currency and strong connotations of terms like 'feudal' and 'capitalist'. For the historian working on 'peripheral' societies, be they in Africa, Asia or Latin America, there is a strong case for taking Chirot's advice to dispense with the 'hopelessly petrified Marxist model'. Unfortunately, Chirot escapes the Marxist frying pan only to be consumed in the flames of Wallerstein's 'world system' – arguably a worse fate still.[53] But self-immolation is not essential; the historian is not obliged to subscribe to a general, a priori theory. The historian should, of course, frame hypotheses and make them clear, but this activity is quite consistent with a certain theoretical and terminological agnosticism. The historian's concern is with lower-level generalisations, hypotheses and models, and these can often be analysed, with equal 'fruitfulness', from different theoretical perspectives. And, ultimately, it is 'fruitfulness' – the pay-off in terms of historical understanding – which counts. A theoretical perspective derived from (say) Hegel or St Augustine is likely to prove barren, even lethal, when it comes to historical understanding. Marx or Weber or Gramsci offer much more and their respective contributions may depend on the nature of the particular historical problem. Granted that the historian's task is not to validate or disprove any grand theory (no single piece of empirical history could do that anyway), but rather to understand *wie es eigentlich gewesen* in some historical period, then a degree of controlled (not promiscuous) theoretical eclecticism is fully justified – even recommended.[54]

The traditional hacienda, therefore, reacted to market forces (at the 'level of circulation'), while relying on non- (or, if the teleology is permitted, 'pre-') capitalist relations (at the 'level of production'). Both theoretical approaches contain a partial truth. But, equally, both miss out on certain vital developments: the rapid commercialisation of agriculture which occurred in the later nineteenth century, subverting the status quo ante, and bringing about a change which was both quantitative and qualitative. For Frank, integration into the market is a datum from the sixteenth century, subsequently there can only be oscillations in the degree of integration.[55] For his opponents, the most significant social change is associated with transformation of the relations of production, which, in the Mexican and, perhaps, the Latin American case, did not take place until the second or third quarters of the twentieth century.[56] Both, because of their respective theoretical positions, fail to recognise the importance of agrarian commercialisation in the later nineteenth century, which most historians would stress.[57] Indeed, if a theoretical *point d'appui* is sought, from which this historical development may be assessed, the historian – following the precept of controlled eclecticism – could do worse than consider Weber's 'spirit of capitalism'; for an ethic of this kind, devoted to 'the earning of more and more money', to the destruction of 'traditionalism', and to the subversion of 'the old leisurely and comfortable attitude towards life', clearly affected Mexico's landlords, both great and small, during this period.[58] The ethic was even evident in forms of 'developmentalist' ideology which, by their insistence on thrift, hard work, hygiene and 'progress', could be seen to act as a surrogate Protestantism.[59] This is not to say that the ethic was determinant. Its relation to economic action may have been one of 'elective affinity' or, if the causal primacy of the economic 'base' is accepted, one of rationalisation and reinforcement. No matter: the point is that the new ethic *indicated*, even if it did not *create*, the new economic circumstances in which the rational pursuit of profit enjoyed vastly great potential and demanded a 'hard frugality' and commitment to bitter competition.[60]

As demand grew and communications improved, landlords were well placed to take advantage of both – as they had done of the disentailment of ecclesiastical lands in the preceding generation.[61] Agrarian commercialisation thus reinforced many aspects of the pre-existing system of land tenure and exploitation. In some regions, *ranchero* farmers benefited and their role will be considered shortly. But, unless such *rancheros* are to be classified (as they have been, at the risk of some misunderstanding) as a 'peasant bourgeoisie', it cannot be said that peasant agriculture in Mexico responded to commercial opportunities in the vigorous fashion of peasant farmers in other parts of the world – West Africa, for example.[62] Rather – for perfectly rational reasons – the Mexican peasantry resisted commercialisation. The chief actors and beneficiaries, in fact, were the *hacendados*, whose pre-existing political and economic dominance conferred overwhelming advantages under the new commercial dispensation. Furthermore, these advantages could be realised without any immediate or significant break with familiar practices. The existing labour supply could be increased to boost output; patterns of labour recruitment, tenancy and sharecropping could be juggled and modified, as they had been in the past, without being revolutionised; and landholdings could be extended, or the cultivation of existing land stepped up. With regard to both land and labour, therefore, increased production implied linear development, more of the same, not a revolution in technology or labour use. Such a strategy could be adopted, with every prospect of profit, because of the existing character of the agrarian political economy and its untapped potential.

Hacienda labour was of three main kinds: resident workers (*peones acasillados*), temporary workers, and renters or sharecroppers.[63] Resident workers, farming the hacienda demesne land, formed the core of the labour force, but their condition varied as between central and northern Mexico on the one hand and Mexico south of the Isthmus on the other. In the first case, the peons lived on the estate, billeted in quarters around the big house, attending the hacienda chapel, forbidden – in one hacienda – to set foot outside its boundaries, required – in another – to sing a hymn to the owner's patron saint before starting work in the morning.[64] Here, if anywhere, the old paternalism of the colonial hacienda survived. The peons (Eric Wolf argues) saw the *hacendado* as a surrogate father and identified with his power and wealth; they regarded the ravishing of their daughters by the *hacendado* as a mark of favour; they tended the grave of a dead master.[65] But, by the later nineteenth century, such personal, paternalist bonds were loosening.[66] Commercialisation and absenteeism took their toll; in the north, the ending of the Indian wars weakened the ties between landlord and peon; and, by 1910, *hacendados* began to complain of the unreliability of their labourers (some blamed the decline of religion).[67]

By then, economic dependence rather than any deferential sentiment bound the peon to the estate. Furthermore, this economic dependence was only partially – and probably decreasingly – the result of outright debt peonage. In the early nineteenth century, it is true, *hacendados* had expanded the colonial institution of debt peonage (whereby a worker received an advance against wages and could not leave the estate until the debt was paid off).[68] Thereby, landlords guaranteed themselves a labour force in regions of low population (like Coahuila) or of Indian population, reluctant to submit to hacienda work (Oaxaca, Yucatán). In the latter cases, debt peonage acted alongside territorial expansion to prise the Indian out of the village and into the hacienda. But, as much recent research has shown, debt peonage was an ambiguous relationship, capable of different interpretations. It could act as a mechanism for perpetuating a harsh form of servile labour or it could indicate the bargaining power of workers, who themselves ran up credit and who were accommodated by landlords keen to retain a stable labour force.[69]

Despite legislative attempts to limit the scale of debts, they remained significant, even in central and parts of northern Mexico, until the Revolution.[70] Complaints against the landlords' juggling of the figures – in order to increase and perpetuate debts – were common; it was said that hacienda schoolteachers were warned against teaching too much arithmetic.[71] No doubt such abuses existed. But by the 1900s debt peonage had lost much of its earlier utility, at least in the more populous parts of the country. As population increased, and real wages fell, landlords could rely on market forces to secure labour. In many cases they found it more profitable to switch from demesne farming to renting and sharecropping. Some haciendas clung to peonage out of inertia, while others abolished the institution without damaging their profitability. In Tlaxcala, indeed, peonage appeared to correlate with feckless, inefficient labour, while free market recruitment secured more sober and industrious workers – those, perhaps, who had converted more fully to the time and work discipline required of commercial agriculture.[72]

As real wages fell, so the position of the resident peon improved, at least relatively. He was guaranteed a degree of security – a roof, food, work, sometimes a plot of land to cultivate. Some resident workers, such as the *acomodados* of the Hacienda de Bocas (SLP), the *realeños* of Morelos, the shepherds and cowboys of the north, were particularly privileged as regards wages and conditions and they identified with and, in some cases, took up arms on behalf of the hacienda.[73] For the peons lower in the hacienda's strict hierarchy, considerations of security militated against disobedience or defiance: though there was certainly physical abuse on the sugar estates of Morelos, it was fear of eviction which represented the biggest sanction.[74] Furthermore, the internal discipline of the hacienda helped maintain docility. Peons worked in gangs (*cuadrillas*), often under close supervision. On some haciendas, ethnic and tribal divisions among the workers could be exploited and there were field managers, like Fausto Gutiérrez of Tlahualilo, 'adept at playing off the petty jealousies and underlying hatreds of the peons'.[75] For these reasons, resident peons – even when they were not privileged 'trusties' – rarely challenged the authority of *hacendado* and *mayordomo* and rarely figured in movements of rural protest during the Porfiriato. They seemed, in the words of one employer, 'not high in the scale of civilisation, but . . . quiet, strong and industrious'.[76] Their chief failings, a survey revealed, were idleness and an excessive taste for drink, both of which 'progressive' elements, Porfirian and Maderista, were keen to extirpate.[77]

But peon docility, resting on economic dependence and close supervision as much as any declining deference, was not immutable or absolute. Real grievances were voiced, when the opportunity arose, against the *cargadilla* (the inflated debt), against the company store and its manipulation of prices and credit, against harsh overseers, who despised and maltreated their workers.[78] Such grievances often focussed on Spanish employees, who held key positions as storekeepers, clerks, managers and foremen. The old Mexican antipathy to the *gachupín* was greatly exacerbated by this social confrontation in the Porfirian countryside, and Spaniards – far more than Americans – bore the brunt of popular xenophobia in the years after 1910.[79] Furthermore, although resident peons lacked the organisational advantages of free villagers, and although their most immediate and vocal demands concerned wages and conditions, they were not indifferent to the appeal of land reform. Some, after all, were fairly recently dispossessed villagers, sharecroppers or tenants. Others, cleaving to an old tradition, 'aspired more to a plot of land than to an increase in wages'.[80] Though time might erase such a tradition, it was also the case that worsening conditions and fears of unemployment – vivid enough in the 1900s – might enliven it; land reform, as Martínez Alier has demonstrated, might hold out the prospect of security for economically precarious workers.[81] It would be wrong to infer that only 'peasants' favoured land distribution, while 'peons' or 'proletarians' scorned distribution in favour of unionisation and wage increases. Reality was more complex and the potential of popular support for a *reparto* extended far beyond the traditional villages.

Peonage reached its most extreme and oppressive form in the south, as a direct result of the increased demand for tropical agricultural products. Here, in southern Veracruz, Tabasco, Campeche, Yucatán and Chiapas, was the closest parallel to the second serfdom of Eastern Europe, as the demands of the market, mediated through an appropriate social and political structure, strengthened and extended servile forms of labour.[82] Here, plantations could count on a flow of labour from outside: criminals, vagrants, Indian prisoners-of-war, political dissidents, even sexual deviants, despatched from the centre and north by profiteering officials and labour contractors.[83] In addition, planters used cash advances to coax the local Indians out of the sierras of Chiapas and the interior of Yucatán, and developed a form of debt bondage which (as even Bauer admits) had little of the ambiguity of its equivalent elsewhere in Mexico.[84] Only by means of advances – accompanied, often

enough, by drink, cajolery and intimidation – could the Indians' attachment
to subsistence farming and antipathy to the labour discipline of the plantation
be overcome. Such advances, explained the German planters of Chiapas,
countered the 'natural indolence' of the sierra Indians.[85] The Germans of
Chiapas, of course, were facing a local version of a secular, global problem: that
of converting subsistence farmers, accustomed to a 'natural' economy, into
plantation workers, inured to the discipline of commercial production.[86]
Slavery was impossible, attempts to import foreign contract labour failed,
domestic forced labour had to be supplemented by local recruits, formally free,
in effect servile.[87]

The peonage which lay at the end of this road, even if it was only temporary,
had few of the redeeming features of peonage in the centre or north of the
country. It is clear that, even allowing for a certain muckraking enthusiasm,
the denunciations of southern peonage penned by Turner and others rang true
– as Madero averred.[88] Again, discipline was harsh, maintained by overseers
fond of the lash and the riding crop. Drink provided the main solace and life
expectancy was short. Of the labourers destined for the tobacco fields of the
Valle Nacional, so the local Indians recalled, 'many went in but few returned'
and, though the region was particularly notorious (the stevedores of Veracruz
struck, alleging that 'they are being turned into a Valle Nacional'), it was not
unique.[89] Debts piled up; in Jonuta (Tab.) many peons owed over 400 pesos,
the equivalent of more than three years' wages. Clearly, these could never be
redeemed and some peons suffered corporal punishment, it was alleged, for
requesting redemption.[90] Again, debts were augmented by crooked book-
keeping (one manager was said to add the date at the top of the page to each
peon's debt) and, in defiance of the law, debts became heritable, thus
legitimising a *de facto* slavery.[91] The system worked and was still working on
the eve of the Revolution, because of the planters' domination of society,
which was not seriously challenged either by urban interests or by a strong
independent peasantry. Planters bought each others' peons by transferring
their debts from one *libro de hacienda* to another. There was an 'unwritten law'
among the henequen planters of Yucatán that they would not give shelter and
employment to runaways; and in the same state, as in the slave society of old
Brazil, the planters employed professional fugitive hunters who readily
invaded private houses in pursuit of their prey.[92]

If sheer immiseration produced rebellion, regions like the Valle Nacional
would have been in ferment. But, as several commentators have pointed out
(perhaps a little too sweepingly), the debt-peon country of the south did not
make a prominent contribution to the popular revolution; liberation, when it
came, came from outside, not from below. Neither deference nor economic
dependence can explain this quiescence. Rather, the plantocracy had grown a
carapace of social control and repression which, in defiance of concerted
challenges from within, could only be dismantled by alien interlopers. The

harsh discipline (Spaniards, Cubans and *canarios* were again prominent), the combination of public and private violence, the planters' domination of local politics, maintained the plantocracy; while the peons, shipped into a strange malarial environment, lacked common origins, common traditions, even a common tongue, and the weakness and remoteness of free villages in the south made escape and resistance almost impossible. Indeed, it is unlikely that the peons of the south developed a countervailing culture, based on combined accommodation and resistance, as did the slaves of North America; unlikely that, after the manner of those slaves, they achieved 'success at forging a world of their own within a wider world shaped primarily by their oppressors'.[93] The plight of the peon, certainly in the new, exploitative plantations of Veracruz, Tabasco and parts of Yucatán and Chiapas, thus corresponded more closely to that of Elkins' quiescent slave – uprooted, oppressed, overwhelmed within a 'total institution' – than did the real condition of the slaves of the American south.[94]

Rigid, stratified and ostensibly stable, the plantocracy was not immutable or unchallenged. There were pockets of 'peasant' resistance in western Tabasco, in the sierras of Chiapas, in the Yucateco interior and on the Isthmus. At the time of the Revolution there were sudden, bloody outbreaks on the plantations themselves, reminiscent of the slave rebellions of Cuba and St Domingue.[95] Underlying, unspectacular changes also occurred. High levels of indebtedness represented a burden and a risk for the plantations and servile labour of this kind, deficient in the necessary 'work ethic', was not the most productive.[96] Towards the end of the Porfiriato, it seems, some planters came to see the advantages of free wage labour, and a few even switched to such a system, relying on higher wages to attract recruits and piece rates to boost production.[97] Foreign plantations, in particular, which lacked some of the political, 'extra-economic' advantages of their Mexican equivalents, took the lead.[98] That they could do so, without intolerable risks, depended on certain new factors: higher profits, lower wages and, linked to the last, a growing supply of labourers prepared to undertake plantation work. This last factor was not simply demographic, it also reflected the gradual inculcation of the work ethic throughout the preceding years, as the planters, by force and cajolery, dragged the Indians out of their 'natural indolence' and broke them to the new discipline. Such a development was incipient in 1910 and servile forms were still the norm, however. Continued profitability, as well as downright inertia, underwrote the system. The transition from servile to free wage labour would have been slow and gradual, had not the system's internal dynamics received some powerful shocks from outside.

It is reasonable to assume that the inculcation of the new work ethic depended, above all, on the growth of seasonal, migrant labour. Haciendas had always relied on additional inputs of labour to supplement the *peones acasillados* during periods of planting and harvesting and this was additionally attractive as population grew and real wages fell. Often, indeed, the resident peons formed only a small minority of the hacienda's peak labour force.[99] But, whereas haciendas in more populous regions could draw on village labour (they could even use the inducement of renting out plots of land, once the patrimony of the village), those less favoured by the local land/labour ratio had to recruit further afield.[100] In the south, as we have noted, such recruitment was overlaid with abuses and coercion. But even here, and *a fortiori* elsewhere, genuine inducements were necessary, particularly if seasonal migrations were to become regular. In the Zongólica district of Veracruz, landlords in the *tierra templada* could draw their temporary labourers from the surrounding villages, while down in the hot country they had to rely on migrants drawn – not, it seems, by cash advances and debts – from the populous highland regions of Puebla and Tlaxcala.[101] Similarly, the impoverished villagers of Naranja trekked down to the Pacific coast for seasonal work which, however hard or unpleasant, afforded a valuable source of income.[102] Work of this kind inculcated new disciplines but, as Favre has shown for the Peruvian sierra, the income thereby granted served to reinforce, not dissolve, the solidarity of the migrants' village community.[103]

If, from this angle, migrant wage labour possessed an ambiguous character, from the point of view of the *hacendado* dependent on such labour it compelled new, 'modern' approaches, in which monetary incentives triumphed over coercion or forms of *de facto* service tenantry. The go-ahead *gachupín*, Don Juan de la Fuente Parres, who farmed two haciendas in the northern part of Mexico state, drew his labour 'from as far away as Toluca and Zinacantepec by a reputation for high wages and fair treatment'. Laguna cotton planters like Madero, dependent on regular migration from the Bajío, paid better wages and provided schools, medical services and other good works.[104] Though these have been termed 'paternalist', their style should be distinguished from the older, traditional paternalism which governed the life of the *peon acasillado*.[105] The latter sacrificed mobility for security; in times of recession his insulation from the money economy afforded a real protection and the hacienda guaranteed his food supply.[106] Migrant wage labourers could seek out better, more remunerative employment, but they were at the mercy of the market and when this slumped, as it did after 1907, they faced unemployment and beggary. There was ample evidence of this in the Laguna region in 1908–9.[107] Enlightened employers like Madero might strive to alleviate hardship (again, foreign enterprises often took the lead) but they were in business to make money, not to dispense charity, and they could not defy the combined effects of recession and drought. In such circumstances the 'new paternalist methods' (which were, at bottom, good business practice in times of labour shortage) began to look pretty thin. Workers were shed, from haciendas as well as mines, and the north paid the penalty for its high level of mobile, free wage labour. The problem was compounded by the repatriation to Mexico of thousands of the country's most intrepid migrants: the *braceros* who, since the late 1890s, had carried labour mobility to its logical conclusion and flocked to the US, most of them illegally, and hence in numbers which cannot be precisely fixed.[108]

The hacienda demesne, cultivated by resident peons and hired labourers, often formed only a small proportion of the estate, even in highly commercial enterprises. The García Pimentel properties of Santa Clara and Tenango, which produced a million pesos worth of sugar in 1909, devoted only 10% of their area to cane cultivation, two-thirds of which lay fallow at any one time. Of the remainder, some 20% was mountain and forest, 30% pasture, and a little over 40% non-irrigated land given over to sharecroppers cultivating corn.[109] Such a breakdown was not untypical for Morelos. Indeed, in Mexico as a whole *hacendados* strove to diversify production, not in search of some 'feudal' self-sufficiency, but in order to spread risks and maximise market opportunities. Hence the creation of sprawling estates which produced a variety of crops by a variety of methods – estates whose sheer size and multifarious activities impressed foreign visitors.[110] Within such a system, sharecropping and rented tendencies performed a vital role, for they offered a means of utilising non-irrigated land surplus to the requirements of demesne production of transferring risks from owner to tenant. Sharecropping appears to have been the more common resort, though tenancies were preferred, for example, in northern Guerrero.[111] The terms of sharecropping agreements varied from place to place and according to the nature of the crop and the relative inputs (with regard to seed, animals and tools) of landlord and tenants, but it is clear that sharecropping had grown in scale during the Porfiriato and, by 1910, was ubiquitous.[112]

Sharecropping was particularly prevalent in the Bajío, traditionally the granary of Mexico, where population surplus gave landlords a strong bargaining position. Around León, it seems, virtually all the corn produced on the eve of the Revolution was the work of sharecroppers, while the irrigated demesne lands were given over to wheat.[113] It would be wrong, however, to infer from this the internal dissolution of the hacienda – a capitulation, perhaps, to the Chayanov principle.[114] Some haciendas were fragmented, by sale or inheritance, but 'fragmentation' into sharecropping tenancies was a different matter, so long as the landlord retained control, as often he did. Sharecropping offered a means to 'delegate responsibility' and risk, 'without prejudicing ... control'.[115] The element of risk became clear, for the tenant as for the migrant worker, in the lean years of the 1900s. Already, population growth had shifted the terms of sharecropping agreements to the advantage of landlords. Now, poor harvests (to which tenants of *temporal*, non-irrigated land were particularly vulnerable) compounded the problem. In Guanajuato it was reckoned that most sharecroppers were in debt; some were forced to sacrifice their precarious independence and become peons or wage labourers.[116] In such circumstances, the division of the crop could be fraught with tension, as the landlord claimed his due and the tenant wriggled to avoid or minimise payment. 'It was particularly as regards the claim made by me, as representative of the owners of the Hacienda,' a manager recalled, 'that I felt the resentment of the toiler at yielding any part of his produce to another merely because that other held some document of title to the land and could enforce it by the invocation, if necessary, of the power of the law.'[117] In Durango, in 1901, sharecroppers 'rebelled', rejecting terms and seeking better landlords.[118] Throughout the previous century, it appears, protests emanating from within haciendas more often concerned tenants than peons, an indication not only of the tenants' grievances but also of their great capacity for resistance and their valued, if precarious, independence.[119] Later, sharecropping regions like the Laguna and the Bajío were afflicted by a high level of violent, though often ill-directed, revolutionary activity. One estate-manager was in no doubt that 'the system was obviously one that lent itself throughout to some of the abuses that bred the Revolution'.[120] In northern Guerrero, too, the classic, village-based agrarian movement was largely absent, but grievances over rents provided a numerous rural contingent to revolutionary armies.[121]

Hacienda control of labour – peons, migrants, villagers, sharecroppers – depended on a range of political, 'extra-economic' powers.[122] *Hacendado* involvement in politics was starkly evident. Landlords dominated the politics of San Luis and clearly used their influence in specific agrarian conflicts; the planters of Morelos, even where they did not hold office, called the political tune in the state; lower in the rural hierarchy, caciques combined landed fortunes with local political power and well-to-do *rancheros* controlled regional politics.[123] At a more general level, too, the power of the state served the landed interest with regard to the tariff, agricultural credit, taxation and, above all, agrarian legislation.

Even haciendas specialising in a particular cash crop – sugar in Morelos, zacatón in Mexico state, lechuguilla in San Luis – raised staple crops too. Hence they, and the cereal-producing estates of the Bajío, benefited from rising prices for corn, wheat, beans and chile and, as in the days of the colony, made their biggest profits in times of dearth.[124] But now, with world cereal prices falling, inefficient Mexican producers required protection against cheap foreign imports. This they received, as did politically powerful landlords in other countries whose broad pattern of agrarian development resembled Mexico's.[125] The duty on corn and wheat, it was reckoned, represented an annual premium of some eight pesos per hectare cultivated. In addition, differential railway freight rates favoured export goods over those destined for internal consumption.[126] On both counts, the price of staple foodstuffs was forced up, while foreign competition was discouraged. The cereal farmers of the Bajío, therefore, received a higher profit per acre (46%) than their equivalents in the American corn belt (26%), even though the latter were more than twice as productive. [127] While it made sense to boost exports in response to mounting demand, it made equal sense to limit the production of staple crops, making a large profit on low production. Hence, it has been argued, corn production fell from 2.7m. tons in 1877 to 2.1m. tons in 1907, during which period the population grew by 5.2m. [128] Consequently, in the last twenty years of the Porfiriato the price of staples more than doubled and, with the poor harvests of 1908–9, which occasioned the steepest price rises, imports of foreign corn reached unprecedented heights. [129]

Fiscal inequality was pronounced in the countryside. Taxation figured prominently among the grievances of rebellious Indians in the nineteenth century (though, by the later years, other complaints became more vocal). Middle-class reformers protested against such inequality and some concluded that Henry George's 'single tax' would provide a solution. [130] Certainly, existing taxes on land were unbalanced and often insignificant. It was said that the vegetable sellers in the city market of Guanajuato paid more to the treasury than all the *hacendados* of the state, that the smallholders of Tenango paid more *pulque* tax for their new maguey plants than did the huge maguey plantations of Otumba. [131] Tax assessments, perhaps never very realistic, failed to keep pace with rising land values. The 'great latifundium' of La Gavia in the valley of Toluca, reckoned to be worth 6m. pesos, paid tax on an assessed value of 400,000 pesos; the Porfirian authorities in the territory of Tepic admitted that cadastral ratings were hopelessly out of date and that the current assessments (1910) needed to be increased at least tenfold. [132] Landowners naturally sought to preserve such a state of affairs. Visiting tax inspectors were offered roast kid and the best tequila so that they would approach the matter of tax assessment in a benign mood. [133] Cadastral revision became an important part of reformist policy after 1910.

Big landowners were also favoured in the allocation of credit. There were economic reasons, of course. They could put up the biggest security and the banks maintained it was not worth while lending to small farmers. [134] But there were personal and political reasons too. Bankers, businessmen and landowners cohered in a tight oligarchy and, commented an acerbic Frenchman, 'tout pour nos amis et rien que pour nos amis' might provide an appropriate device for Mexico's bankers. [135] Thus, while smallholders failed for want of credit, funds were channelled from the banks and the state agricultural development agency, the Caja de Préstamos, into the swollen estates. [136] The *hacendados* themselves were greedy for funds. Some, conforming to the old stereotype, wasted their substance in conspicuous consumption: balls, fiestas and trips to Europe; imported champagne and fox-terriers, Parisian fashions and oriental rugs; new, palatial hacienda buildings, landscaped gardens, country retreats on the shores of Lake Chapala and town houses in the new, chic Colonia Juárez of Mexico City. [137] But many also embarked on extensive capital investment. They built railway feeder lines, irrigated, and established processing plants for henequen, sugar, zacatón, coffee, *pulque* and spirits.[138] The sugar planters of Morelos in particular indulged in a 'fever of mechanization' and some boasted of having invested half a million dollars in a single project.[139]

Where the income of the estate proved inadequate to cover such large outlays, *hacendados* readily mortgaged property to raise cash. Since, throughout the Porfiriato, land values rose rapidly, the collateral available for such loans continued to grow and some landlords increased their debts and renewed them time and time again. By 1910 many of the great estates were heavily mortgaged – like those of the newly elected Governor Redo of Sinaloa, who hoped to use his position 'to save the great patrimony that he [has] loaded with debt to the last peso'.[140] Following the 1907 recession, too, hacienda income fell and the banks, prodded by Limantour, cut back credit and called in loans, to the irritation of some major borrowers.[141] It is not likely that this had a profound effect on the origins of the Revolution. Few *hacendados* came out in clear opposition to Díaz and most of those who did had a record of opposition antedating the financial troubles of 1907–10.[142] The crisis did, however, reveal the shaky state of agricultural finances and underline the way in which *hacendados*, eager for credit, had been encouraged to expand their holdings for reasons over and above those of production.

The third and most important area of government favour was that of legislation. Though the Constitution banned peonage, several states legislated in a manner that sanctioned and only modestly controlled it. Sonora allowed cash advances up to the value of six months' wages, Tamaulipas to the value of a year's.[143] Several states passed measures against vagrancy, which empowered the authorities to arrest the unemployed and consign them to the army, to public work, or to private employment on haciendas or in the mines.[144] But such compulsion – common enough in agrarian societies split between commercial and subsistence agriculture – was of secondary importance in Mexico, granted the growth of population and, above all, of the landless population.[145] And here government policy was most effective in promoting hacienda (and *ranchero*) expansion at the expense of the villages, thereby swelling the pool of landless, unemployed labourers.

Already, in the 1850s, the reformist liberals had set out to dismember the concentrations of land held by the Church and the corporate villages. The Church lands were disentailed, but the conversion of village holdings to individual, freehold tenure proved to be a long, often violent process. Resistance and rebellion hindered the disentailment in the 1850s and 1860s; political instability and economic uncertainty dulled landlords' appetites.[146] But with the coming of the Pax Porfiriana, the railways and enticing market opportunities, the attack on communal property was renewed *à outrance*. Porfirian legislators pandered to the new territorial gluttony. A law passed at the height of the railway boom (1883) and ostensibly designed to promote colonisation of remote regions, empowered the executive to grant contracts to surveying companies which, in return for locating and surveying public land (*terrenos baldíos*) for which no private title existed, would receive one-third of the land in question, the remaining two-thirds to be auctioned by the government on the open market. In theory, the land was to be divided among colonists in lots of not more than 2,500 hectares. In fact, this rarely happened and a subsequent law (1894) recognised this, removing the 2,500 hectare ceiling, and defining as 'public' all land which, even though it might be occupied, was not strictly delineated by legal titles.[147] Meanwhile, executive circulars urged that the process of disentailment, the conversion from corporate to individual tenure, be carried to a conclusion and state governors, like those of Guerrero, worked consistently to this end.[148] Under these laws companies and individuals could 'denounce' and thereby acquire a stake in land for which no title existed and such land included not only the virgin expanses of northern desert and southern jungle, but also the village lands held by custom, or the fields which squatters had occupied and made their own. Now only impeccable titles, produced before a court of law, could prove ownership and, even then, the vagaries of Porfirian justice had to be taken into account. *Hacendados* who coveted a contiguous field and who knew the law – or, better still, the judge – could denounce it as public land and stake a claim. And if the occupier – villager, squatter, shepherd or woodcutter – could not prove his case, the field went the way of Naboth's vineyard. This was all the more likely to happen where political and landed wealth were concentrated in the same hands. Local caciques were well placed to take advantage of the new agrarian laws; so too, were governors like Molina in Yucatán, Terrazas in Chihuahua, Flores in Guerrero, and Espinosa y Cuevas in San Luis.[149]

The 1880s and 1890s thus witnessed a land-grab of unprecedented proportions, as 'the gates were thrown open for land speculation on a huge scale'.[150] Throughout the Díaz regime, nearly 39m. hectares of untitled land were converted into private property, an area equal to that of California, and comprising one-fifth of the surface area of the country.[151] Most of the remaining corporate village landholdings were 'fractioned' into freehold plots. Across the face of Mexico, land became a commodity, to be bought, traded and accumulated; land values, buoyed up by rising agricultural demand and prices, rose steeply; and landholdings became increasingly concentrated into few hands, ensuring landlessness for the great majority.[152] The consequent agrarian problem lay at the heart of the popular revolution. Científicos like Limantour and Rabasa, anticipating the views of some recent historians, denied that such a problem existed or they conceived it in purely technical terms, concerning productivity and output, and recognised no causal link to the upheaval of 1910–20.[153] González Roa thought differently: 'the fundamental cause of Mexico's bad organisation, and of the character of its internal revolutions, must be sought in the agrarian question'.[154] González Roa was right. But the search is not easy. It will be attempted in the final part of this section under four headings: first, an overview of land tenure on the eve of the Revolution, noting the dominance of the hacienda; second, a consideration of the local implications of varying forms of land tenure (hacienda, *rancho*, village), particularly with reference to the subsequent geography of revolution; third, the national implications of hacienda production; finally, and perhaps most important of all, the social conflict attendant upon this process of rapid agrarian change.

By 1910, landownership had reached a state of unprecedented concentration. Four-fifths of Mexican rural communities and nearly half the rural population were located within hacienda boundaries. They were not simply landless, but were also subject to the political and social control of the estate; they were, in effect, hacienda labour compounds.[155] Some haciendas were well endowed with such hacienda pueblos: San José el Zoquital (Hgo) contained twenty-two, San Antonio y Anexas, in the same state, seventeen.[156] Though some were, as it were, reared in captivity, the offspring of the hacienda itself, others were once independent pueblos, absorbed by the voracious estate to become new *cascos*, hacienda nuclei, complete with church, tienda, workshops and houses. Such was the fate of several old pueblos in Durango: San Diego de Alcalá, which became the El Maguey hacienda, Presidio del Pasaje, now one of the component haciendas of the great Santa Catalina latifundio, and San Bartolo, once head of a *municipio*, now a politically anonymous hacienda *casco*.[157] Hacienda domination was most marked in northern and north/central states, where the sedentary Indian population had been small, and where the Spaniards had carved their great estates out of the Gran Chichimec: Zacatecas, for example, where 76% of the rural population lived on haciendas, or San Luis (82%).[158]

On the central plateau and parts of the south, however, the Indian village, and its mestizo counterpart, still survived in numbers; clipped, circumscribed, surrounded by the hacienda, it could not be wiped from the map as a discrete entity, and it never lost its pretensions to self-government and economic independence. But survival took many forms. Some villages retained ample lands, some possessed no more than the *fundo legal*, the ground on which the village buildings stood. Landless independence, though distinct from incorporation within the bounds of the hacienda, was precarious. The village might have its own 'elected' officials, its secular and sacred hierarchy, but lack of resources placed it in pawn to the estate. Such *pueblos enclavados* were increasingly common by 1910. Jonacatepec, once a flourishing centre of the mule trade, stood and stagnated in the middle of the Garcia Pimentels' huge domain (Santa Clara hacienda began eight yards from the last village street).[159] The *municipio* of Rincón de Ramos (Ags.) lay 'completely surrounded' by the hacienda El Saucillo, which embraced 35,000 hectares: the people worked as *arrieros*, carried wood and charcoal from the mountains, or became hacienda sharecroppers.[160] In Durango, Sauces de Salinas was squeezed between hugh latifundia; at San José Gracia, Canatlán (Dgo), a hacienda boundary stone stood at the foot of the church tower; the inhabitants of Villa de Reyes (SLP) complained that the owner of the Gogorrón hacienda, with which they had a longstanding conflict, had literally tried to fence them in.[161]

There are no authoritative figures indicating the proportion of free (non-hacienda) villages which retained land or which, like Jonacatepec and Rincón de Ramos, eked out a precarious landless existence, dependent on some measure of hacienda employment. In the shadow of the sun and moon pyramids, one study has shown, 7 haciendas and 22 villages shared some 10,000 hectares in the fertile valley of Teotihuacán. But the 7,500 villagers held only 10% of the land, enough for a little over 400 of them to cultivate plots of 2 to 2½ hectares each, leaving the rest landless and dependent on hacienda or non-agricultural work. Some have estimated that this rate of landlessness (about 90%) was typical for the central plateau as a whole.[162] McBride hazarded some informed guesses which suggested that about a third of the rural population held land in Mexico, Michoacán, and Veracruz, rather more than a third in Oaxaca, but less elsewhere.[163]

The picture lacks detail but the general outlines are clear. Free villages survived in considerable numbers, especially in central Mexico. But they were increasingly squeezed by expansionist haciendas, so that only a minority, possibly a small minority, and certainly a declining minority, retained landed resources. A community's success at retaining its land depended on a variety of factors: its accessibility, the quality of the soil and its suitability for commercial exploitation, legal skill, political contacts, and collective tenacity. Many regions were afflicted by bitter agrarian conflicts, in which haciendas were pitted against villages; such regions were often of key importance in the revolution and will be considered shortly. Conflict was most pronounced where expansionist haciendas encountered strongly entrenched villages. Conversely, it was weaker where the hacienda dominated, or where the village survived intact, with ample land, or where one or both of these institutions were absent. On the basis of this schema it is possible to sketch a crude map of revolutionary ecology.

Where the hacienda ruled, it left its mark on local society. In the south, we have noted, the plantocracy faced no serious threat to its hegemony – in Yucatán, Campeche, much of Chiapas and southern Veracruz. Some northern regions were comparable. Wistano Luis Orozco contrasted the fortunes of Jerez and Villanueva, both in the state of Zacatecas, where the hacienda was powerful. Jerez had escaped hacienda domination. It was picturesque and prosperous, with fine churches and houses, an active commerce, a college, theatre, jail, hospital and public gardens; its surrounding fields (in October) were stocked with maize, beans and squash; its men were fat and its women

beautiful. Villanueva, further north, occupied a better location, but presented
a sad contrast. It was ringed by six large haciendas, comprising nearly a quarter
of a million hectares; all had company stores which monopolised commerce
within their confines, all save one kept a jealous hold on its resources, refusing
to let out pasture land. The biggest possessed not only their own chapels but
also their own cemeteries 'so that they do not even contribute their corpses to
Villanueva'. So Villanueva stagnated, its traditional industries decaying, its
people miserable, deprived and socially divided. Such contrasts, Orozco
maintained, were not uncommon: west of Guadalajara, for example, Ameca
prospered within a diversified rural economy, while Cocula languished in the
lap of a bloated estate.[164]

The local impact of the great estate was not, therefore, confined to
dispossessed villages. Hacienda self-sufficiency prejudiced local trade, the
tienda de raya took potential customers away from local shopkeepers.[165] Not
surprisingly, middle-class interests were said to favour the emancipation of
commerce and an end to the 'feudal system of property and taxation', and there
were cases of landlords feuding with local shopkeepers.[166] What is more, the
dominant hacienda prejudiced free, liberal politics. *Hacendados* might
disdain political office themselves, but they could buy their way into power
and turn out their *cuadrillas* of peons at election time if required. Three or four
big landowners, Orozco observed, could run a district as they pleased and,
under such conditions, the middle-class hopes of decent municipal government were dashed. At Jonacatepec, for example, the political authorities were
in the pocket of the Garcia Pimentel. Officials, like the *jefe político* of Cuquío
(Jalisco), who tried to take an independent line were likely to find themselves
out of a job, the offended landlords having communicated their displeasure,
along with a suitable sweetener, to the state governor. 'Democracy', Orozco
concluded, fifty years in advance of Barrington Moore, 'is impossible in a
population fixed in a feudal mould.'[167]

But, if the dominant hacienda inhibited local political and economic
development, at least outside its own boundaries, this did not necessarily
generate serious popular protest and resistance. The southern plantations were
not alone in possessing effective methods of social control and many great
estates, like those of the Aguirre of Tepic, remained intact until outside forces
were brought to bear.[168] Till then, challenges from internal dissidents or
external reformers were silenced or ignored. Or, it might be suggested,
popular discontent, lacking the organisational base of the free village, assumed
more anarchic forms, such as banditry.[169]

At the other end of the spectrum were regions where property was relatively
divided, and the estates, if not altogether absent, co-existed with small-
holdings or village communal farming, without threatening their independence. Here, too, the absence of severe agrarian tensions was reflected in
regional participation (or non-participation) in the popular revolution. Or, to

be more accurate, participation, when it occurred, assumed different forms and modalities. But regions of greater agrarian equality were far from uniform. In particular, it is possible to differentiate between those in which traditional (usually Indian) villages survived, retaining sufficient land, and those in which equality had developed with the growth of a prosperous *ranchero* class – a 'peasant bourgeoisie' or 'village elite', as they have been termed.[170]

The first category is of great importance and will receive fuller analysis in the next section of this chapter. These were regions in which, chiefly by virtue of their remoteness, traditional communities had retained land and the threat of the hacienda was limited. In Oaxaca, for example, 85% of the rural population lived in free villages outside hacienda boundaries, and many such villages, even some in the valleys, had managed to hold on to land. Agrarian conflicts, when they occurred, pitted village against village, not village against hacienda.[171] Such land division, complemented by strong, semi-autonomous *cacicazgos*, seemed to have beneficial social effects. In Oaxaca, an observer noted, 'the property is divided, each inhabitant had his "milpa" filed ... [and] the Zapotec villages do not suffer from the wretchedness which desolates the other tribes of Mexico'.[172] This by no means ruled out revolutionary participation, but it determined that such participation would not follow the agrarian pattern, but would be *sui generis*, a distinct form of *serrano* rebellion, which will be analysed subsequently. The same generalisation holds, *mutatis mutandis*, for rebellions which emanated from other regions of highland parochialism – in Puebla, Chiapas and, above all, the Sierra Madre Occidental of Chihuahua and Durango. Most, but not all, contained a strong Indian element. But, more important, they shared a common social and political character, in which village autonomy, based on a significant measure of agrarian equality, was central. To put it another way: *serrano* movements could only develop in the absence of the hacienda.

But the absence – or weakness – of the hacienda could have other social and political consequences. In Nuevo León, it was noted, 'property is very divided and thus poverty does not exist'.[173] Both premise and conclusion might be qualified, but they contained an important truth. Nuevo León possessed a tradition of land subdivision antedating the Porfiriato; the growth of industry and proximity to the US weakened the incentives for land concentration.[174] It was no coincidence that the state, prominent in civilian reformist politics, played little part in the popular revolution. The same was true of Aguascalientes; the subdivision of rural property, coupled with urbanisation and industrial development, inclined the *hidrocálidos* to electoral rather than armed conflict.[175]

In these two cases the beneficiaries of agrarian equality were white/mestizo farmers, not Indian communities. Elsewhere in Mexico, too, a prosperous *ranchero* class developed in the course of the nineteenth century; *ranchos* – which might range up to 1,000 hectares in size, but which carried connotations of family ownership and exploitation – numbered 6,000 in 1810, 14,000 in mid-century, and 50,000 in 1910.[176] During the Porfiriato *rancheros* responded positively to commercial opportunities, expanding the production of cash crops, extending their holdings, and sometimes taking on wage labour: in Guerrero, Hidalgo, Michoacán, Mexico state and elsewhere.[177] As already noted, they shared some of the characteristics of their urban middle-class equivalents, despite their rustic manners: a concern for 'progress', an interest in education, and a receptivity to political appeals and information.[178] But the social consequences of the emergence of this class varied in certain crucial respects, depending on location.

The *ranchero* (who has become something of the darling of agrarian historians, Englishmen in particular) was a Jekyll and Hyde character. In his better known incarnation he represented rural middle-class virtues: hard work, diligence, solid respectability, independence. Enjoying conditions 'far better' than those of the common peons, the *ranchero* was distinct from and often hostile to the opulent *hacendado*. *Rancheros* like those of La Puerta de Medina (Mex.) had successfully banded together to resist hacienda encroachments. Policies of fiscal equalisation and honest municipal government naturally appealed to them.[179] Beyond this, their politics might diverge. *Rancheros* of Guanajuato, Michoacán and Jalisco (who together, comprised one-third of the Mexican *ranchero* population) tended to be strongly Catholic, hence (according to the old political shorthand) 'conservative'; those of northern Guerrero, the Sierra Alta of Hidalgo and parts of the north were traditionally liberal.[180] So long as Church-State relations were kept off the political agenda, however, the *rancheros'* shared interest in honest, stable, constitutional government, which would respect rights, property and votes, bulked larger than any ideological division. When asked of his community's attitude towards the Revolution, a *ranchero* from Mexico state 'replied that his fellows took no interest at all in the affair; that they were all right as they were and did not like such "revueltas"; all they wanted was to be left alone'.[181] This ostensibly passive sentiment did not imply quiescence. *Rancheros*, liberal and Catholic, became involved in civilian politics and regions of *ranchero* agriculture were notable for their commitment to peaceful, electoral politics in 1911–13. They were also notable for the relative absence of revolutionary violence, unless and until that was imported from outside; then the *ranchero* often proved to be a doughty combatant, especially on home ground. As the Orozquistas found in Sonora in 1912 and the Carrancistas (sometimes, too, the Zapatistas) found in central Mexico after 1914, the invasion and subjugation of *ranchero* country was no easy matter, even if the *ranchero* victims had shown no belligerent tendencies previously.

If the Dr Jekyll *ranchero* resembled Kipling's Saxon – stolid, quiet, slow to anger but fearsome when roused – his transformation into Hyde was brought about by a simple change in the cast. *Ranchero* agriculture had benefited from the break-up of corporate landholdings. Individuals had thereby acquired land from 'extinguished' communities – sometimes their own, sometimes adjacent villages, especially Indian villages. In the former case, the *rancheros* (often mestizos) might emerge as the local caciques, lording it over the (often Indian) population. In the imminent discussion of agrarian expropriation and conflict, it will be noted, several examples of *ranchero* expansion will appear, in Guerrero, Oaxaca, Morelos, Sonora, the Huasteca. In such circumstances, *ranchero* politics were not governed simply or principally by old ideological allegiances, by reformist inclinations, or by antipathy to the *hacendado*; rather, it was the enmity of recently dispossessed villagers which dictated *ranchero* responses and which, whatever formal political labels were attached, gave them something of a 'counter-revolutionary' complexion. In the absence of a popular agrarian challenge, *rancheros* could cultivate their gardens, defend their homes and mother Church, or feud amongst themselves (the examples of Michoacán and Hidalgo); in its presence – in Sonora, Guerrero, Oaxaca, the Huasteca – *ranchero* defence of property, though quite consistent in itself, demanded some heavy-handed repressive measures. So, Ambrosio Figueroa fought against Zapatista agrarianism; his brother Rómulo advised the *agraristas* of Guerrero that if they wanted land they should buy it and, brother Francisco inquired, 'if suffrage has been made effective, if taxes have been modified, and order has been restored, what more do these men want?'[182]

The character and intensity of the Revolution thus varied according to the prevailing form of land tenure. But before examining, in more detail, some illustrative examples of local agrarian conflict and rebellion, it is worth pausing to take in the national scene. The expansion of the hacienda and the growing concentration of landed wealth had important consequences for Mexico's political economy. Orozco's critique of the local effects of hacienda rule – its eclipse of commerce and representative government – carried weight at national level too. In the realm of politics, it was not simply that the landlord could fix elections and control municipal government; his social and ideological control of the peons, his capacity to interdict outside political information and influence, also abstracted them from the nation state, denying them a role as subjects, let alone citizens, and checking the development of national allegiances.[183] To this extent, the hacienda, like the self-contained mining town, was an 'anti-national' institution.

In addition, the hacienda exercised a decisive influence on Mexico's pattern of economic development and represented the most outstanding failure in the Porfirian strategy of modernisation. True, commercial agriculture boosted exports, though not as much as some Porfiristas had hoped.[184] But the circumstances and parameters in which it operated guaranteed inefficiency; 'low pay, poor agriculture, dear product', as Genaro Raigosa summed it up.[185] The *hacendados'* (and, to an extent, the *rancheros'*) increasing control of land, coupled with population growth, ensured a supply of cheap, landless labour, whose real wages fell after the 1890s. Abundant labour ruled out technological improvement, save in the field of processing. In Jalisco, for example, it cost 8% more to farm with machinery than to rely on hand harvesting, in Yucatán, planters stuck to the old steam-driven rasping machines in preference to the new petrol engines, since the supply of timber fuel was met by dependent labourers on their estates.[186] Meanwhile, as landlords switched to export crops, the production of staple foodstuffs fell and their price rose, further squeezing real wages. In times of dearth, such as 1908–9, some *hacendados* made healthy profits.[187] The government, obliged to enter the market to boost grain supplies, displayed anxiety and the 1900s saw widespread comment on the agrarian problem. But, in official (and some non-official) circles, the problem was seen as one of output and efficiency, not fundamental structures. The government urged greater productivity and more exports; *hacendados* formed chambers of agriculture, discussed new technical methods and, in some quarters, advocated the abolition of debt peonage.[188] But, even had such a reform been nationally legislated (which it was not), it would not have undermined the hacienda as the dominant form of land tenure. Only in the Bajío were there reports of the impending demise of the hacienda as a territorial unit and these, I suspect, were much exaggerated.[189] On the eve of the Revolution, therefore, there was no indication that the Porfirian strategy of development would not continue, certainly in the countryside, as it had done for decades and that the regime would not persist with its 'revolution from above', seeking modernisation without parallel changes in the agrarian social structure.[190]

The implications of this strategy, furthermore, extended beyond the countryside. Low wages, dear food, and the very structure of hacienda production inhibited the growth of a domestic market and thus of Mexican industrialisation. By the late Porfiriato, peons were devoting between a half and three-quarters of their income to the purchase of food, leaving only an exiguous surplus for the purchase of goods.[191] The operations of the *tienda de raya* further constrained purchasing power and confined it to the hacienda. Frustrated entrepreneurs complained of the 'damned wantlessness' of the Mexican people.[192] Hence, in the one industry (apart from pulque) which catered to mass demand – that of cotton textiles – growth slowed in the early 1900s and became negative after 1907.[193] The over-production, wage cuts and unemployment experienced in the textile industry were thus in part the result of chronic agrarian inequalities. And textiles were simply the biggest and best example; in San Luis, it was noted, 'several factories have . . . met with disaster for lack of a market for products'.[194] Again, there is no evidence to suggest that the Porfirian regime either conceived of or resolved to carry out decisive policies to deal with this problem. To that extent, the regime was a prisoner of its own development strategy, even now that diminishing returns had set in. But that is not to say that the problems, or 'contradictions', of this strategy doomed it to a prompt demise or that the agrarian and associated social grievances of the 1900s made a radical break inevitable. 'Contradictions' only become insuperable in retrospect and regimes (especially regimes of this traditional, authoritarian type) can display remarkable stamina in the face of economic failings and popular displeasure. The crucial additional factor, which enabled these factors to assert themselves, was the political crisis of 1908–10 and the failure of the political nation to agree on who should succeed Díaz.[195]

The crisis broke while agrarian change and consequent tension were still acute, just as the First World War engulfed Tsarist Russia while Stolypin's 'wager on the strong' hung in the balance. In time, Lenin argued, Russian agriculture would become polarised between 'Junker-bourgeois' landlords and well-off peasant farmers (*Grossbauern*) on the one hand and rural proletarians on the other – by which time the revolutionary potential of the countryside would have been spent.[196] The same was broadly true of Mexico: the continued expropriation of the peasantry, the expansion of hacienda and *rancho*, the growth of free wage labour, would eventually have led to a similar tripartite division in the Mexican countryside – in some regions, indeed, it clearly took shape.[197] But, meantime, this process of change excited strong grievances. There were not wanting precise and sombre precedents. When the Caste War broke out in Yucatán in the 1840s (again, the stimulus came from national political crisis and dissension among the *ladino* rulers) it was the frontier Maya, the Huits, who fought to preserve a precarious economic and political independence in the face of hacienda expansion. They took the lead, while the plantation labourers of western Yucatán, long expropriated, 'civilised', whipped and wheedled into an acceptance of *ladino* rule, not only spurned rebellion but even took up arms in defence of the status quo.[198] As Nelson Reed's classic study makes clear, 'what was dangerous was not long oppression, but sudden acculturation, the forced march from one world to another'.[199] The revolutionary north west affords an interesting example of shifting antipathies and responses. Here a section of the Yaqui tribe rebelled in the hope of recovering lost lands, declaring war on the *yori* (whites/mestizos) in general, both Mexican and American. The Mayo Indians of Sinaloa, more fully 'acculturated', behaved differently. Following the loss of their lands to Mexican *hacendados* back in the 1890s the Mayo rebelled, acquiesced, and lapsed into a form of messianic quietism; yet the loss still rankled in 1910 and the local *hacendados* remained the target of Mayo hostility. Meantime, however, the American United Sugar Co. had appeared as a third party, competing with the *hacendados*, forcing up wages, poaching labour, finally bankrupting many of their rivals.[200] The Mayo were gratified to receive better wages and to witness the decline of their old enemies. Hence, between the Mayo leader Bachomo and the American manager Johnson 'there arose a strange rapport', based on common hostility to the native landlords and 'the Indians intimated' – after the accidental killing of one of Johnson's compatriots – 'that they regretted [it] . . . as they considered all Americans "buen amigos" [sic]'.[201] It was not the case that all landless labourers were deferential and docile, nor that they were concerned solely with the improvement of wages and conditions by means of the 'quasi-urban methods of trade unionism'.[202] Peons – especially if they were recently expropriated peasants or if they suffered chronic unemployment – could respond to the appeal of the *reparto* along with villagers. But it seems clear that the most acute agrarian tension and rural rebellion were concentrated in regions where land expropriation had proceeded vigorously and recently, and where it represented a live issue, and not in regions where it was merely incipient, nor where it appeared as an accepted, irrevocable feature of the rural scene. Hence the particular significance of the generation following the 1880s, which witnessed widespread expropriations and growing inequality in the countryside, and which in turn determined much of the incidence of rebellion after 1910. The Díaz regime – in the jargon of strategic studies – faced a 'window of vulnerability' and serious political crisis thus carried the risk of social revolution so long as the window remained open. It was still open in 1910 when Madero summoned the Mexican people to arms.

Conflicts between hacienda and village were nothing new: one, in Querétaro, was settled in 1879 after 318 years of contention.[203] But the legislative and economic changes of the later nineteenth century generalised and exacerbated this phenomenon. Furthermore, although the 1850s and 1860s witnessed the first big spate of disentailment of village lands, and the consequent agrarian protest and rebellion, the process continued throughout the Porfiriato.[204] In Puebla, where such litigation was common, the villages of the valleys had largely been deprived of land; in the sugar country of the Matamoros valley 'impoverished farmers and now-landless peasants turned envious calculating thoughts towards the *hacendados'* land'.[205] Similarly, in Hidalgo, *ranchero* farmers prospered in the northern sierras, while haciendas and despoiled villages – such as Amealco – clashed in the lowlands.[206] In the central regions of Tlaxcala, Buve observes, 'landgrabbing and the application of the Liberal Desamortization Laws kept [the] peasant tradition of protest alive' and, during and after the 1890s, it was further stimulated by overpopulation, unemployment, and a rising tax burden.[207] Many communities in Mexico state also lost their land: Chalco was additionally prejudiced by the draining of the nearby lake, which deprived the Indian fishermen of an ancient livelihood.[208]

'Such instances', Hans Gadow observed, after his extensive travels in the 1900s, 'are not uncommon', and Paul Friedrich has provided an invaluable study of one in particular.[209] The village of Naranja lay on the western edge of the central plateau, in the Tarascan country of Michoacán. In the early Porfiriato its inhabitants (numbering some 750) continued to raise staple crops on the village land, to fish Lake Zacapú, to weave mats and baskets from the marsh reeds. It was a tight, self-contained community, deeply suspicious of mestizo outsiders and, while it was no egalitarian Utopia (land and power were unequally shared), it enjoyed a measure of economic and political independence under traditional authorities, which, if oligarchic, were also indigenous and in some senses responsible to community opinion. In the 1880s, however, the Noriega brothers (Spaniards again) acquired some of the village land titles, apparently with the collusion of the mestizo storekeepers of the village. Under the aegis of the *baldío* laws they drained the marsh and acquired, or sold, the alluvial land; hence 12,000 hectares finished up in the hands of *hacendados*, while only 400 remained to the Tarascan villages; Naranja itself was left with a narrow ribbon of land, hemmed in on all sides by five estates, and 'essentially deprived of the ecological niche where it had nestled for hundreds of years'.[210] Furthermore, while the Noriegas were prepared to sublet peripheral land to a few Indian sharecroppers (the privileged and trustworthy families), they preferred to import mestizo peons for demesne work (men who 'scorned everyone who spoke Tarascan'), thus denying the villagers employment. Deprived, too, of the resources of the lake and marshes, the Naranjenos had to search for work among the neighbouring haciendas, or make the two-day walk down to the hot country at Los Bancos. The 1900s were the hardest years: the poorest had only squash and quelite weed to eat, women braided straw incessantly in the hope of raising some cash in local markets, the villagers, old-timers later recalled, began to look like 'Apaches'. And within the pueblo itself economic divisions were emphasised, as the remaining plots of land tended to gravitate into the hands of the half dozen 'haves', who sold food to the 'have-nots'. Naranja thus experienced the twin scourges of Porfirian agrarian change: the loss of village lands to the estate, and the growth of a new, pronounced inequality within the community itself.

Both were also evident in Morelos, but here the agrarian conflict and revolutionary response were particularly endemic and sustained, embracing an entire state, rather than a single village or valley. For this reason (among others) commentators have been misled into seeing Morelos and Zapatismo as unique cases.[211] But they were not. In briefly sketching the origins of Zapatismo, my object is not to amend or augment the classic studies of Womack and Warman but rather to display how the movement shared common origins and common forms with lesser agrarian movements, which cropped up across the entire face of the country.[212]

Sugar haciendas had co-existed with subsistence villages in Morelos since the sixteenth century. But, by the 1880s and 1890s, heightened demand, better communications, and favourable political conditions created pressures for plantation expansion that proved inexorable. By 1908, Morelos produced over a third of Mexico's sugar and was, after Hawaii and Puerto Rico, the most productive cane sugar region in the world; the seventeen owners of the thirty-six major haciendas owned a quarter of the state's area, and virtually all the best land. Morelos' once variegated rural society – 'sugar plantations, traditional villagers, farm settlements, single independent farms, day labourers' hamlets, country towns' – gave way to an imminent 'planters' Utopia'; and, for the villagers converted to peonage or sharecropping, 'the social difference between the old and the new oppression was as profound as the difference between a manor and a factory'.[213] Hamlets and villages blocking hacienda expansion were absorbed or annihilated: thirty communities disappeared in the ten years following 1876, and the process of agrarian *Gleichschaltung* did stop there. Cornfields, pastures, and orchards were poached by the planters in their quest for land, water and labour; the judiciary and the Ministry of Fomento smoothed their path; and villagers, having run the whole gamut of legal resistance, culminating in appeals to Díaz himself, found themselves arrested, and their leaders deported to Quintana Roo. Thus, towns like Cuautla and Jonacatepec became tightly ringed by haciendas. Yautepec had its water supply fenced off by the Hacienda of Atlihuayán (an Escandón property). Communities boasting three centuries and more of history and tradition were wiped off the map: Tequisquitengo, flooded by a hostile *hacendado*, leaving only a church spire poking above the waters; Acatlipa, Sayula and Ahuehuepán, whose ruins 'hidden darkly in the fields of high, green cane ... rotted into the earth ... their demise ... a fearful lesson, leaving the villagers no hope of rest'.[214] Then, in 1908–9, the death of Governor Alarcón and his replacement by Escandón afforded the opportunity for political mobilisation and, ultimately, agrarian revolt; a microcosm of the national sequence.

Morelos has attracted deserved attention because of the strength, stamina and, in a sense, the success of Zapatismo. Lesser agrarian movements have been neglected since, in many cases, they were repressed, defeated, or driven underground. Their relative failure, however, should not detract from their importance in any analysis of the causes, as against the effects, of the Revolution. It is not easy, however, to proceed in any more 'scientific' a manner than that of enumerating examples; there is no way of quantifying or achieving a statistical measurement of agrarian protest and rebellion. John Coatsworth has come closest, demonstrating that there were at least fifty-five 'serious conflicts' between villages and haciendas during the seven years of railway boom, 1877–84; some 60% of these occurred within 20km. of the closest (sometimes projected) railway line, thus illustrating the close connection between railway building and the increased demand for land which spurred expropriation.[215] Most took place in central Mexico (Hidalgo and Mexico state figured prominently), and several districts appear which would later acquire revolutionary notoriety: Jonacatepec (Mor.), Tamazunchale (SLP), Acayucán (Ver.), Cd del Maíz (SLP). Coatsworth's analysis halts, and railway-building began to slow down, in the mid-1880s. But there is no reason to assume that this period was *sui generis*, or that the trends of the time were purely associated with railway construction, rather than with the general social and economic effects of such construction, which continued long after.

Furthermore, it is clear that expropriation and protest were not confined to the central plateau, and that they involved mestizos and smallholders as well as Indian and traditional villagers. Naranja has been mentioned, but other pueblos in Michoacán nursed agrarian grievances, often associated with the invasion of their woodland (an invasion stimulated in a very direct fashion by railway construction which required ample timber for sleepers).[216] Governor Mercado had thrown open woodland for private exploitation, thus depriving Indian pueblos 'of the one resource they possessed in order to subsist', and occasioning violent incidents.[217] Elsewhere in the state, for example at the Hacienda La Orilla, arable lands were in dispute between the local people and the estate management; the Indians of Acuitzeramo complained of the loss of their *ejidal* land to *hacendados* of the district; the landlords and caciques of Los Reyes Ecuandereo, an Indian spokesman reported, 'not content with despoiling us of our lands, attempted the extermination of our unfortunate race'.[218]

In neighbouring Guerrero, where, it is true, rents were the chief source of rural conflict, there were instances of hacienda–village confrontation, particularly, and significantly, in the sugar-producing region around Taxco.[219] Here, it may be presumed, *hacendados* had a greater incentive to make profits by demesne production of a cash crop, rather than to rely on income from rents. In Oaxaca, too, agrarian conflict affected the sugar estates of the Cuicatlán region, as well as valley haciendas elsewhere in the state: around Etla, Ejutla, in the Atoyac valley near Zaachila, and in the isthmus country of Guichicovi.[220] There is also evidence of agrarian dispossession and protest in parts of Tabasco (in the western districts of Cárdenas and Huimanguillo), in southern Veracruz (around Acayucán, and in the Sierra de Soteapán), and further north in the same state.[221] Here, a particular trouble spot was Papantla, Mexico's chief producer of vanilla, and the scene of repeated agrarian disturbances throughout the nineteenth century. In the 1890s the activities of a surveying company provoked rebellion; a thousand Indians were reckoned to be up in arms in 1896, demanding the 'division of lands', and the movement, imperfectly quelled in the 1890s, revived in the 1900s.[222]

Papantla may be seen as representative of a more generalised, regional, and basically Indian *agrarismo* which stretched northwards along the line of the Sierra Madre Oriental, through the Tres Huastecas, to the Veracruz–San Luis–Tamaulipas borderlands. Here, amid the rough hot country where the plateau tumbles down to the Gulf lowlands, the Huastecs had maintained a degree of political and economic independence throughout the colonial period. The nineteenth century, however, witnessed new outside pressures which galvanised major rebellions, notably in the 1840s.[223] Again, in 1856, Tantoyuca was the scene of an 'anarchist' Huastec revolt, while in 1879–81 the Indians of Tamazunchale mounted an agrarian revolt against local *hacendados*,

to the cry of 'muera a todo el de pantalón'.[224] Repression, tempered by
conciliation, brought peace, but, as the state governor pointed out, the local
Indians still coveted their lost lands and resented the presence of mestizo
landlords, 'none of whose rights to possess and work the land they recognise,
even though they have acquired them through just and legal procedure'.[225] In
the following decade economic pressures increased with the completion of the
Tampico–San Luis railway link; the valleys of the Huasteca became a 'great
cattle-raising region', where cattle from the north were fattened for slaughter.
Barbed wire and new strains of grass were introduced by progressive *hacendados*, and beef from the Huasteca went to feed the miners of Pachuca.[226] In
addition, American colonists settled at Valles, on the north-west border of the
Huasteca; Italians cultivated coffee at Xilitla and Axtla; and, in the 1900s,
British and American oil companies began to stake out claims in the
petroliferous territory inland from Tuxpán and Tampico.[227]

The outcome of these complex inter-relationships in the Huasteca is far
from clear, despite the efforts of skilled researchers.[228] Certainly there were
Indian groups – like the Santa María Indians of the Tantima/Tantoco/Citlal-
tepec region – who maintained a belligerent independence, reminiscent of the
Yaquis, both before and during the Revolution; and, just three months before
Madero's call to arms, there were clashes between troops and Indians at
Tamazunchale (again), there being a 'general understanding that the trouble is
caused by officials taking away the lands belonging to the native Indians. It is
stated that there is always revolution in Tamazunchale.'[229] But, in addition to
this Indian population (and Indians, as an observer noted, 'refractory to
organisation'), the Huasteca possessed a growing class of *rancheros*, middling
landowners who, like their counterparts elsewhere in Mexico, might look
favourably upon political reform, without contemplating social revolution.
Huasteca families like the Santos and Lárraga, prominent after 1910, fell into
this category and, it seems, they pursued their careers at least in part by
mobilising Indian clienteles, with the promise of agrarian restitution.[230]
Eventually, this form of clientelist recruitment reached its apogee in the
Pelaecista movement of 1914–20.[231]

Agrarian resentments and resistance could thus be channeled into ostensibly
inappropriate rebel movements, in which different castes and classes merged.
So far, the bulk of the examples given have contained a significant, even
preponderant Indian element. But the agrarian tendencies of the Porfiriato
were no respecters of ethnic personality; they affected mestizo smallholders as
well as Indian villagers. In the central and western parts of the state of San
Luis, for example, the Moctezuma family, smallholders farming on the slopes
of the Sierra Gorda near Cd del Maíz, were driven into a running battle with
local *hacendados*, members of the Potosino political elite who in 1898
denounced their land as *baldío*.[232] After a celebrated court battle the Moctezumas won their case, but in 1908 President Díaz's nephew, Felix Díaz, again

claimed that the land was public, initiating a second bout of litigation which was still in progress (despite the arrest of the leading Moctezumas by the local authorities) when the Revolution broke out. Close by (though for somewhat different reasons) friction developed between the smallholders of Palomas, led by the Cedillo family, and several of the same *hacendados*, owners of the Montebello and Angostura estates; the ensuing conflict was to have momentous political results for the state of San Luis.[233] Meanwhile, in the eastern part of the state, the mestizo community of Villa de Reyes clashed with the go-ahead Spanish *hacendado* Felipe Muriedas, whose Gogorrón estate had swallowed up the community's lands, denied its inhabitants water, and seemed bent on the economic extinction of the place.[234] There were frequent violent incidents, successive state governors and local authorities backed Muriedas, and members of the community, including 'merchants and indus- trialists' as well as farmers, were obliged to take refuge elsewhere, on account of the 'persecutions and attacks which are daily committed against our pueblo'.[235]

Eastern San Luis, an arid plateau noted for mining rather than agriculture, was ecologically part of the north rather than the Mesa Central. Yet, as this example suggests, agrarian conflicts linked to hacienda expansion were not unknown in this region too, despite occasional statements to the contrary. In the main, it was not so much the creation of massive latifundia – such as the four which dominated Baja California – which generated conflict, as lesser, specific expropriations of land already occupied and tilled by Indian villagers or mestizo smallholders.[236] Furthermore, it might not require extensive expropriations and consequent rebellions to generate a broader agrarian movement, a single instance might prove a sufficient *casus belli*, and one effectively belligerent community (like Cuencamé) could act as a pole around which other potential rebels – peons, sharecroppers, bandits, migrant workers – might coalesce to form a broad and formidable rebel host. In the sierra of western Chihuahua, it will shortly be argued, agrarian grievances formed an important part of a more general repudiation of Porfirian government. The ensuing rebellion, of great importance in the genesis of the Revolution, was not quite essentially agrarian (in the way that, say, Zapata's was) and for that reason it requires separate treatment. But the *serrano* rebels of Chihuahua shared many of the grievances exhibited by agrarian revolutionaries: the commercialisation of agriculture (again, the exploitation of forest resources was important), the penetration of the railway, the acquisition of village lands by big landlords or (more commonly) local caciques, who combined growing economic with growing political power.[237]

But there were also classic agrarian conflicts and rebellions in the north too, and, though they were less numerous than in the centre, they often had a revolutionary impact out of proportion to their numerical weight. In other words, it was often those pockets of the north which most resembled the centre

– the more populated, often Indian, agricultural regions, rather than the seats of mining, smelting, industry and commerce – which came to the fore after 1910. The Laguna region, for example, had long before established itself as Mexico's chief cotton-producing zone; subsequent conflicts centred around the allocation of the waters of the River Nazas between landlords, or the terms of sharecropping agreements between landlord and tenant. By the 1890s, however, a new factor appeared in the shape of guayule, the hardy, northern rubber plant, which flourished in the dry conditions of the Coahuila/Durango borderlands. Commerical exploitation began in the mid-1890s, as *hacendados* (led by the Maderos) gave over their poorer, upland fields to guayule. Processing plants were established at Torreón, Gómez, Viesca and Parras, where 'poisonous miasmas' polluted the air and offended the townspeople.[238] But there was money in guayule, exports rose, prices rose (six-fold in a few years prior to 1910), and travellers commented on the ubiquity of the spiky guayule shrub 'which has created so many fortunes in the last few years'.[239] Some rural communities, however, suffered more than offended nostrils. The pueblos of Santiago and Cuencamé lost their lands to the Sombreretillo Hacienda in 1905, chiefly as a consequence of the guayule boom; village leaders who protested were consigned to the army, among the Calixto Contreras, a dark Ocuila Indian 'of sinister aspect and sidling looks' who, along with Cuencamé's local lawyer-intellectual, Severino Ceniceros, became prominent in the turbulent revolutionary history of the Laguna after 1910.[240] A little to the east, at San Juan Guadalupe, a similar story unfolded. The local caciques leased the pueblo's guayule-producing lands to commercial interests, thereby creating 'daily difficulties [with the latter] . . . and absolute misery for everyone'; perhaps for this reason the inhabitants took to drink and acquired a reputation as drunken brawlers – *los borrachos*.[241] The guayule boom helped lay the groundwork for revolution in one further respect. Throughout the region, the plant grew in open, non-irrigated country, encouraging poaching which in turn led to gunfights and machete battles, useful training for activities after 1910. One freelance guayulero, Gertrudis Sánchez, became a pioneer revolutionary on the Coahuila/Zacatecas borders in 1911.[242]

Across the Sierra Madre to the west, the territory of Tepic – only recently brought under the heel of the central government – experienced numerous agrarian conflicts. At Camotlán the Espinosa y López Portillo family had kept up 'a tenacious persecution of the Indians . . . in order to drive them from the village, trying to lay hands not only on their fields but also on the municipal buildings and the church'. In 1910 the family called on the authorities to vindicate their property rights by force, in 1911 the Indians rose in rebellion against them, their employees and tenants.[243] The pueblos of Sentispac and Mexcaltitán had been swindled out of their title deeds by the sub-prefect of Tuxpan, leaving them in abject poverty, their villages squeezed between the latifundia of the Aguirre and Fernández del Valle. These families, combining huge landed and mercantile interests, dominated the territory until 1913/14, when they were ousted by the Revolution.[244] Similar episodes were enacted in Sinaloa to the north where, a local historian asserts, agrarian conflicts were central to the Revolution.[245] At Escuinapa, to take one example, the villagers complained that their land titles, dating back to 1712, had been seized, that the *fundo legal* had fallen into the hands of local caciques, and that their fishing rights had been suppressed.[246] They now possessed 'not an iota' of land, they had to rent plots of land for their huts, and they had to buy firewood at steep prices. Their problems, it could be said, typified those of the new landless of the late Porfiriato. For these were fairly recent developments (fishing rights had been suppressed in 1888), and the villagers had no doubt that the blame lay with Díaz:

in the colonial period, the Independence, the American and French interventions and the Reform, the Indians suffered not the slightest incident, until the Dictatorship of the Government of General Díaz, in which it was all reprisals, outrages, and abuses without limit.

But the greatest indignation and resistance in the north-western region came from the Yaqui Indians of Sonora. Yaqui rebellion had been common enough during the nineteenth century (as in Yucatán and elsewhere it often coincided with national crises, and depended upon a degree of white/mestizo incitement).[247] But in the latter part of the century Yaqui revolt grew more serious, particularly under the leadership of the cunning opportunist José María Leyva (alias Cajeme), who served in national campaigns in the 1850s, 1860s and 1870s before leading the Yaquis onto the warpath in the 1880s. By then, the penetration of the Yaqui valley by Mexicans and foreigners was creating a situation of endemic agrarian conflict, which persisted throughout the Porfiriato; bloody battles were interspersed with ephemeral truces, and, after Cajeme was killed according to the *ley fuga*, Juan Maldonado (alias Tetabiate) and Luis Buli continued the struggle into the 1900s.[248]

The agrarian origins of the Yaqui wars were plain enough, even to General Reyes, sent to deal with the troubles in 1881.[249] With the defeat of the Apaches, the onset of the railway, and the favourable political and legislative climate of the Porfiriato, the way was open for the expropriation of the Yaquis' traditional lands in the river valley. Denounced as *baldíos*, these came into the possession of *hacendados*, politicians and American interests: 400,000 hectares went to the Torres family, the Sonoran oligarchs, 547,000 to the Richardson Construction Company of Los Angeles.[250] It was hoped and expected that, like the Mayo Indians of Sinaloa, the expropriated Yaquis would become peaceful peons. Attempts were further made to appease the Yaquis by settling them in approved pueblos in the valley, but the Yaqui pueblos were soon invaded by whites and mestizos who outnumbered the Indians. The Yaquis, compelled to find employment in the mines, the cities, or on the plantations, objected to being penned within a parcelled fragment of their old patrimony: 'God gave the Yaquis the [whole] river', they declared, 'not an allotment each', and they claimed the lands stretching from the river up to the Sierra Bacatete, amongst whose canyons the Indian guerrillas took refuge during the interminable wars.[251]

Increasingly, therefore, the valley lands were incorporated into the thriving commercial economy of Sonora. Yaqui pueblos (and sacred places) like Bacum and Cocorit were carved up among mestizo settlers; the Richardson Company brought in American colonists who grew vegetables, fruit and chickpeas (another boom crop of the late Porfiriato) for the Californian market, but, since they farmed 'in the heart of the ancient tribal lands of the Yaqui Indians' they did so under the watchful eyes of a Federal garrison.[252] As has been mentioned, the Yaquis polarised: the *mansos* (tame Yaquis) worked in the valley; the *broncos* (wild Yaquis) remained under arms, raiding, hiding in the mountains, sporadically working on haciendas during truces, but vowing to 'die before handing over our lands, even if it means killing all the *yori* (whites)'.[253] By the 1900s, the campaigns had reached a new level of brutality. The Federal authorities (to the chagrin of some *hacendados*, who balanced need for Yaqui labour against fear of Yaqui attack) resorted to familiar anti-guerrilla methods: concentrating the civilian population, deporting prisoners-of-war as far afield as possible, in this case to Yucatán.[254] Atrocities multiplied. The Federals, newly equipped with Mausers, massacred women and children; Governor Izábal boasted of the tortures used to extract information from prisoners. Such measures were justifiable: did not the Yaquis flay their victims and hang them with ropes made of their own skin? Had they not (according to the Catholic *El País*) forfeited any claim to membership of the human race? Aguilar is surely right to see in the Porfirian regime's prosecution of the Yaqui campaigns a crusading, ideological (and, one might add, racialist) commitment over and above any simple political expedience.[255] This commitment notwithstanding, no conclusion was reached prior to the Revolution. The year 1908 brought an uneasy peace and a brief calm, brought on by repression, temporary exhaustion and, quite probably, the downswing in the economy, which curtailed demand for Yaqui labour in both Sonora and Yucatán.[256] But, like most Yaqui peaces, it was no more than a lull. In 1910, as in the past, national crisis and mestizo civil war gave the Yaquis a renewed opportunity to press their old agrarian claims, whether as recruits to mestizo forces (*manso* revolutionaries, as it were), or as independent guerrillas, *bronco* revolutionaries of the sierra, dedicated to the defeat and expulsion of the *yori*.

So far, in this brief survey of agrarian dispossession and conflict, the hacienda has been cast as the chief villain. But it was not alone. The same forces which impelled hacienda expansion also encouraged the rise of prosperous, entrepreneurial *ranchos*; and the *ranchero* especially when he assumed the guise of local cacique, could prove just as effective a solvent of village autonomy as the great landlord. In some cases *ranchero*/cacique aggrandisement proceeded by way of internal differentiation, as communities polarised (like Naranja) into a handful of *ricos* and a mass of poor. Alternatively, *ranchero* communities (usually mestizo) filched the land of neighbouring (usually Indian) villages. The first process was greatly facilitated by the disentailment of village lands for, in many cases, the inhabitants sought to comply with the law, while safeguarding the community's lands, by vesting the titles in the name of trustworthy *vecinos*, who proved they could not be trusted. Many of Guerrero's 'village elite' made their fortunes in this way. Clemente Unzueta of Tlaxmalac exploited his position as representative of the community to acquire the best lands, augmented them by a shrewd combination of purchase, marriage and *baldío* denunciations, and thus established himself as the cacique 'in whose hand power was always held, directly or indirectly'.[257] Of sixteen similar representatives chosen by the communities of Chaucingo and Quetzalapa, only one proved trustworthy, while the others used their position to confine the rest of the inhabitants to inferior land.[258] The state governor's prediction that the disentailment would stimulate 'that powerful agent, individual interest' was proved correct.[259]

Where disentailment did not create caciques *de novo*, it greatly strengthened the power of existing caciques, who were favourably placed to exploit the law to their own advantage. Crescencio Rosas bought up the lands of Cachuamilpa (Gro) when they came on the market in 1894 (many of these disentailments were still proceeding in the 1890s, some even in the 1900s); Tepoztlán, in Morelos, resisted hacienda encroachments but lost its lands to Tepozteco caciques who, 'with the support of the state and federal authorities, prohibited the villagers from using the communal lands in order to secure a cheap labour supply for themselves'.[260] In certain cases already mentioned, such as that of San Juan Guadulupe, Sentispac and Mexcaltitán, caciques appropriated, or appropriated and then alienated, the community lands. More examples will be noted in the following analysis of *serrano* rebellion. What is more, the *ranchero* cacique, once established in power, could follow the same stratagems as the hacienda in his quest for land, labour and power; advancing seed and oxen to needy villagers (as the *jefe político* of Ejutla did), then using his political power to foreclose on their land when the harvest failed.[261] The disputes over rent which were the salient form of rural conflict in Guerrero may well have reflected a similar situation, characterised by *ranchero* manipulation of a favourable market position established since the disentailment. Conflict over land ownership and rent were not, perhaps, so distinct as has sometimes been suggested; rather, they could represent successive phases within a continuing process of expropriation and land concentration.[262]

This process was also pushed along by the transfer of land from community to community; indeed, many of the ostensibly neutral, even meaningless, inter-village disputes which littered the Mexican countryside may have arisen from such circumstances. Jamiltepec, on the coast of Oaxaca, for example, feuded with Poza Verde and other neighbouring pueblos. The conflict was described in partisan terms (according to the Jamiltepec version, the Pozaverdeños were mere bandits), or it was redefined according to current national labels – Zapatista, Carrancista, Constitutionalist and so on. Yet, it will be argued, the dispute centred on land ownership; the cattlemen and *ranchero* farmers had expanded their holdings at the expense of their rivals, thus incurring their hostility and armed opposition.[263] An even clearer case was that of Ometepec, on the Guerrero coast, where a mestizo pueblo had acquired (in the course of the 1880s and 1890s) the community land of Igualapa and Huehuetán, thus provoking a violent, rebellious response.[264] It is plausible (though it would require further research to prove) that in regions like the Huasteca or Acayucán, where similar mestizo metropolis/Indian satellite relations prevailed, amid evident agrarian conflict, a comparable phenomenon was taking place.[265]

A final point should be made concerning the *ranchero* and his relations with the rural mass. The *ranchero* has been depicted as a Jekyll and Hyde character, stolid, prosperous and hard-working in regions of agrarian tranquillity, avaricious, expansionist and unpopular in regions of agrarian tension, where he might play the role of a surrogate *hacendado*. Such a portrait, if starkly drawn for effect, is broadly valid. But it misses one important feature. *Rancheros*, even *ranchero* caciques, maintained close personal ties with local people, they had an intimate knowledge of factions, grievances and feuds, which was denied the rich, absentee *hacendado*, with his rare or, at best, recreational visits to the estate.[266] In some cases, this proximity merely aggravated resentment and made revolutionary reprisals all the swifter after 1910. But, elsewhere, there were *rancheros* – even enterprising, entrepreneurial *rancheros* – who enjoyed the sympathy of local people: like Marcial López of San Juan Guelavía in the Tlacolula valley (Oax.), for example, who cleverly manipulated the cargo system in order to acquire control of the village *ejidal* land but who, 'though he had robbed the villagers of their properties (nevertheless) gave them work and treated them in a way that was never despotic'; thereby building up an 'indisputable, respected' authority in the region.[267] Indeed, when revolutionary forces appeared in 1915, burning López's land titles and releasing the villagers from their financial obligations to him, 'not one left the debt unpaid'. In certain highland regions, furthermore, the authority of *ranchero* caciques remained even firmer, safe from the solvent of commercialisation.

In the right circumstances, therefore, the *ranchero* could emerge as the natural leader of popular forces, forming a hybrid yet effective revolutionary coalition. In the Huasteca, for example, *ranchero* families like the Lárraga and Santos raised popular armies, which blended the contradictory elements of middle-class (*ranchero*) reformism and popular, Indian agrarianism. In the

Laguna, the creole rancher Luis Moya allied with Contreras and his Ocuila Indians; Obregón's later alliance with the Sonoran Yaquis represented a similar coalition.[268] *Ranchero* leaders could achieve this union because they possessed political resources which the vast majority of *hacendados* lacked. In particular, they possessed the common touch; to an extent 'they shared the dress, deportment and speech of their economic subordinates'; and, to the extent that they did not, they could often achieve a fictive, rhetorical identification (Obregón, again, is a good example).[269] Opulent *hacendados*, in contrast, were too remote, citified and – by their own lights – refined; witness Pablo Escandón's ineptitude in governing Morelos in succession to the canny Manuel Alarcón.[270] *Ranchero* leaders, understanding country matters and capable of eliciting popular respect, were thus uniquely placed to represent local people, to channel their grievances and to captain their rebellions. Of course, the fundamental aims of leaders and led often diverged. *Rancheros* who operated in a context of popular agrarianism ran obvious risks – as the Sonoran allies of the Yaquis found out. *Ranchero* reformism and Indian agrarianism easily parted company. But if – by means of promises, concessions and propaganda – the *ranchero* could stay in the saddle, the political rewards were considerable. For in the new revolutionary politics ushered in by the fall of Díaz, the capacity to lead (and some would say to co-opt) a popular following was crucial for success. The common touch now counted as never before. If, as Tannenbaum and Friedrich have argued, the Revolution found its fundamental energies in the villages, it acquired its political style from the *ranchero* community. In a sense (and the point is not original) the revolutionary populism of the 1920s was born down on the farm.[271]

THE SIERRA

Rebellions stemming from agrarian grievances were central to the popular revolution of 1910–20. But there were also forms of rebellion (which I have elsewhere termed *serrano*) in which agrarian grievances were non-existent, or at best formed part of a more general complex of motivations.[272] Many such rebellions emerged from the mountains and foothills, hence their name, but they were not exclusively confined to highland regions. They may be discerned in the jungle hinterland of Yucatán, or the remote coastal regions of Chiapas, wherever the authority of state and landlord was tenuous, enabling peasant communities to maintain a jealous independence. They also displayed many of the characteristics of frontier society (or, at least, frontier society of a particular variety): relative freedom of mobility, a familiarity with violence, resistance to urban political control and culture.[273] *Serrano* society was still fundamentally peasant society, in that it was based upon low-status rural cultivators, producing for subsistence as well as for the market, and controlling (not necessarily owning) their own means of production.[274] But, granted the human and natural resources of such regions, pastoral farming was likely to play a greater role than in the lowland, hacienda zones. It can be seen from this description that Mexico's *serrano* society – like Mexico's sedentary village society – was by no means unique, that it bore comparison with other places and ages (even with Pyrenean communities of the fourteenth century).[275] It may also be said to correspond roughly to Eric Wolf's 'peasantry located in a peripheral area outside the domains of landlord control' or, even more roughly, to some of Joel Migdal's 'inward-oriented villages'.[276] And, though many *serrano* communities were Indian, some – notably those of the Sierra Madre Occidental – were mestizo; as with the case of agrarian rebels, it was political and economic forces which generated protest, crossing and often ignoring ethnic divides. Ethnicity affected the character of the protest, but it did not determine who the protesters would be.

While lowland communities, close to towns, had of necessity formed relationships with landlords and state officials, *serranos* were better able to keep these influences at bay. While demand was limited and communications were poor, landlords had no incentive to penetrate the mountains and jungle, and until the time of Díaz, the state lacked the co-ordination and the capacity to launch a sustained assault on these redoubts of parochialism. So they survived: under the aegis of Indian and mestizo caciques in the sierras of Oaxaca and Puebla and the inhospitable lowlands of the Isthmus and the Yucatán interior; in semi-autonomous, pioneer communities in the mountains of the north, like the military colonists who populated the Sierra Madre Occidental in defiance of the Apache.[277] The local urge to independence, conflicting with the state's unremitting, if sometimes ineffectual, quest for obedience, produced numerous *serrano* rebellions, from the colonial through the independence periods and down to the Porfiriato. Following the Caste Wars, the 'defensive society' of the Cruzob resisted *ladino* penetration of Yucatán for decades; Indians (like those of the Minatitlán district of southern Veracruz in 1853) rebelled in protest at the imposition of *alcaldes de razón* – *ladino* officials – in their villages in 1853.[278] Many nineteenth-century Indian revolts represented a similar protest against the community's incorporation into mestizo civil society and against the consequences which swiftly followed: taxes, forced recruitment into the army, vagrancy laws, and, often enough, agrarian dispossession.[279] But there were also mestizo protests of a similar kind, such as the Tomóchic revolt of 1892. Here, although both religious fanaticism and land expropriations have been seen as the causal factors, it seems clear that the villagers' basic grievances were against the high-handed local authorities, and their corrupt, clientelist network. Taxes were augmented, and vagrancy laws applied in arbitrary fashion, clients of the caciques enjoyed favours (they could pasture their burros in the village cornfields with impunity), and five Tomochitecos were summarily executed for a bandit attack which they did not commit.[280] Once the revolt had begun, it took over 1,000 Federal soldiers almost a year to subdue a village of less than 300.

Revolts against political domination, and in favour of 'communal autonomy', were common enough in Mexican history.[281] They reflected the forward march of the state (be it colonial or independent), a march that, despite its frequent halts, detours and retrogressions, gradually pushed forward political frontiers, embracing new populations and achieving a more complete, centralised authority, based in Mexico City and the many provincial metropolises. Under Díaz, the pace quickened. Governmental stability and improved communications gave Díaz greater power than any previous ruler of the country. *Serrano* communities – like their agrarian cousins in the lowlands – faced new pressures, in the face of which they could adopt various strategies: outright resistance, passive resistance, the invocation of powerful local *patrones* which might intercede on their behalf, or simple surrender. The third strategy, it would seem, was most successful at preserving a significant measure of autonomy. Well-to-do caciques – Indian or, more often mestizo, but sharing, if only for self-interested reasons, a commitment to the *serrano* cause – acted as a bulwark against the advance of the central government: Juan Francisco Lucas in the Puebla sierra, the Meixueiro and Hernández families in the Sierra Juárez of Oaxaca, the *finqueros* of Chiapas, who afforded some protection to Indian autonomy and supported the cause of San Cristóbal against the pushy, upstart capital of Tuxtla Gutiérrez.[282] Such *cacicazgos* – old-style but effective – even survived in the more 'modern', integrated north, in the Sierra Madre Occidental, and they kept alive parochial sentiments in some lowland regions, like the Juchiteco district of the Isthmus of Tehuantepec.[283] In Mexico, as elsewhere in Latin America, the old-style cacique (to be distinguished from the new, 'modern' caciques thrown up by the institutional revolution of the 1920s) was thus anti-national, a barrier to integration and a *bête noire* of ardent nationalists.[284]

The pace and intensity of integration varied from region to region. The pressures exerted on the *serrano* communities of the north were greater than those of the south and, as a result, the timing and character of the respective *serrano* rebellions differed. The northern *serranos* took the lead against Díaz in 1910–11; the southerners stumbled into revolution in subsequent years, reacting sometimes against conservative, neo-Porfirian pressures (in the Puebla sierra 1913), sometimes against new, revolutionary threats (Oaxaca, 1914), and sometimes taking advantage of contingent revolutionary upheaval to validate old claims and recover old liberties (Chiapas, 1912). Despite their many undeniable differences, however, these revolts revealed certain common threads. Initially, it is the northern *serranos*, the pioneers against Díaz, who demand attention, but it is necessary to establish the common threads, which will be picked up again in subsequent chapters, as the *serranos* ride to battle again.

The western Sierra Madre, running up through Zacatecas and Durango to Chihuahua and the border, was a remote, hostile environment, characterised by a bloody history.[285] In the early Porfiriato the Apaches had poured out of the mountains, devastating Carrizal, Galeana and down to the Laguna, and it was from sierra towns like Galeana, where tough frontiersmen populated a region of 'rocky piedmonts and silty bolsons' that the Indian fighters were recruited for the battles at Tres Castillos and Casas Grandes, which finally broke Apache resistance.[286] Across the mountains in Sonora, endemic conflict with Indians and bandits bred a comparable frontier population.[287] This heritage of recent violence – apart from imparting skills and attitudes suitable for revolution – tended to fortify the solidarity of communities and regions; caciques and landlords depended on the strong right arms of their retainers, and they in turn respected the leadership displayed by those in authority.[288] Sierra society thus exhibited 'semi-feudal' traits – 'semi-feudal' not in strictly Marxist terms, but in the classic sense of a society partially organised for warfare, on the basis of localised, personal military hierarchies.[289] Nowhere was this clearer than in the settlements of military colonists established in the sierras of Chihuahua.[290] While such a situation persisted, furthermore, the authority of landlords and caciques remained firm and legitimate, buttressed by the popular belief that their organisational role justified their superior status.[291]

But with peace came change. In place of the Apaches, new pressures impinged on sierra society; they emanated not from the mountains to the north, but the plains to the west, from Chihuahua City (itself, in some senses, a fulcrum for the growing power of Mexico City), and they were represented not by painted savages but by frock-coated politicians, generals in gold braid, rail-laying gangs and uncouth gringo prospectors. In the 1880s and 1890s the railways appeared, their tracks crushing the sacred plants of the Tarahumara Indians, their belching smoke obscuring the noonday sun. Bad luck was sure to follow.[292] With the advent of the railway, old colonial mining dumps could be profitably reworked and brand new mining towns appeared – like Batopilas, the 'tight little community' autocratically ruled by its boss, Alexander Shepherd.[293] Vast areas of 'public' land were now expropriated, and these formed the basis of the new northern latifundia: Terrazas' block of six haciendas in the Galeana region, Phoebe Hearst's estate in the Babicora basin, Limantour's 170,000 hectares in the Guerrero and Bocoyna districts. The lure was less arable land than pasture and timber. The Limantour property, for example, included pine, fir, and oak, and, having begun the deforestation of the mountain slopes, its owner sold out to the Cargill Lumber Co.; William Greene acquired timber concessions in the Galeana and Guerrero districts and brought in the North Western Railway, which curved from Chihuahua City through the foothills and sierras up to the border at Juárez, touching the timber towns of Temosáchic, Pearson (now Mata Ortiz) and Madera. Though remote, this was not unpopulated territory, the North Western touched seventy centres of settlement and, while some were new company towns, many were old, proud, established communities.[294] Beyond the sierras, too, communities accustomed to a rough, independent, frontier style of life now had to accommodate rapid change, as woods and prairies were demarcated and fenced off, as entrepreneurs, Mexican and foreign, undertook a more intense exploitation of local resources, as, above all, political authority became mightier and more meddlesome.

Here, as elsewhere in lowland Mexico, agrarian expropriation was common, though it did not dominate popular grievances as it did in Morelos, or other particular regions of the central plateau. Agrarian expropriation was but one part of a more general assault on local independence (a degree of independence which central Mexican communities had long ago forfeited). Where it occurred, expropriation followed the familiar dual pattern, loss of land to neighbouring haciendas, or to indigenous caciques. The people of Aldama fought a long battle with the Hacienda de Tabaloapa over springs and woodland which the hacienda had denounced; at San Carlos, near Ojinaga, Governor Creel (as he then was) had expropriated the *ejidal* land which 'the inhabitants of that place assert to be their property, according to titles which they present and the immemorial possession they enjoy', such that Creel needed to keep a *rurales* detachment stationed there to enforce his claim.[295] There were frequent clashes, too, as big landowners, engaged in cattle rearing, fenced off grassland and water sources, denying them to the common use of peasants. The people of Santa María de las Barbizas, having lost their land titles to a typical, corrupt *tinterillo* now had their community, its roads and remaining plots fenced off with barbed wire, and even faced eviction from their huts; Manuel Terrazas, of the famous family, fenced off his ranch, barring both a well frequented road and waterhole, and ordered the arrest of *arrieros* who continued to pass that way – an order which the local authorities readily enforced.[296] In a similar incident, which forms part of a long and dramatic story, the English landlord William Benton fenced off his Hacienda Los Remedios, denying passage to the villagers of Santa María de Cuevas (who claimed that part of the hacienda land was theirs anyway); there were threats made against Benton's person, some villagers set about pulling down fences, and Benton summoned the *rurales* to defend his property. Benton, known to be a choleric individual, openly denounced his enemies as 'protagonists of old atavisms [who] want to make theirs what is not theirs and who, like Proudhonne [sic] hold property to be theft'.[297] Here, too, the local authorities backed Benton, fining the villagers for pasturing or watering their animals on hacienda land.

The new regime of barbed wire, which infringed old customs of grazing, watering and woodcutting, also affected sierra communities.[298] Here, however, it was the rise of new caciques, who monopolised scarce village resources, which caused most resentment. Tomóchic had rebelled against the tyrannies of the Chávez *cacicazgo*.[299] Bachíniva languished under the control of Luis J. Comadurán and his compadre Pablo Baray: these, the inhabitants complained, were 'years of noose and knife [with the caciques] abusing all laws, municipal, civil, universal, human and divine, converting municipal property into [their] own and the citizens into pure slaves'.[300] Bachíniva was to be a staunchly revolutionary pueblo in 1910–11. The same was true of Temosáchic, where one individual, Encarnación Quesada, had taken illegal possession of most of the community's lands, to the detriment of the villagers who now lacked pasture for their flocks.[301] Three individuals, backed by the corrupt authorities, had achieved a similar monopoly at Janos.[302] Furthermore, where mestizo communities of this kind lost out, it is hardly surprising that Indian groups, like the Tarahumara, faced dispossession and exploitation at the hands of caciques at Bocoyna, Guachóchic, and elsewhere.[303] And, while it is true that northern *serrano* rebellions were principally mestizo affairs, they could draw on useful and sometimes numerous Indian recruits.[304]

These expropriations, it should be stressed, were often recent events: at Janos, the *ejidal* lands had been denounced in 1906, following a state law of 1905; William Benton was wrangling with the people of Santa María and Creel with those of San Carlos in 1909–10. And these developments were particularly linked to the local political hegemony achieved by the Creel–Terrazas interests in the 1900s. One authority has stated that 'Díaz-potism' (*caciquismo*, Porfirian-style) was no worse in Chihuahua than elsewhere.[305] But this seems unlikely. Levels of protest and rebellion clearly varied according to the severity of local *caciquismo*. And *caciquismo* was more severe in Chihuahua, and thus more capable of generating a revolutionary response, for four reasons: first, political and economic hegemony were combined to an unusual degree; second, this hegemony had been fairly recently achieved; third, the Creel–Terrazas oligarchs, far from being standpat conservatives, were in fact eager progressives, in the sense of seeking change and 'progress', according to their own notions; and fourth, because the people of Chihuahua, especially the *serranos*, were particularly sensitive to the new burdens placed upon them, and unusually capable of mounting effective resistance in response.[306] These endogenous factors – rather than the alleged effects of foreign economic penetration – determined that Chihuahua, and most notably the regions of the Sierra Madre which spilled over into Sonora and Durango, would play a prominent role in the Revolution.[307]

The drive towards political centralisation got under way in the 1880s, following the defeat of the Apaches, and with the government's substitution of appointed *jefes políticos* for elected local officials. Partly in consequence the 1890s were a decade of considerable unrest particularly in the Guerrero district of Chihuahua, west of the state capital, in the foothills and mountains of the Sierra.[308] When Enrique Creel, Terrazas' son-in-law, became Governor in

1904 he resolved to modernise, strengthen and centralise the state government yet further. Executive control of even minor municipal appointments was extended, a new tax farming system was introduced, the aggregate level of taxation rose. In matters of administration and economic development, Creel and his family were self-consciously progressive. They fostered industry, boosted the state's education budget and encouraged urban improvements.[309] Of course, they did not allow democratic niceties to obstruct the path of progress overmuch – hence the mounting resentment of middle-class liberals. Furthermore, like later Mexican administrations eager for progress and material development, their sincere and, in some respects, successful advocacy of change was compromised by unavoidable corruption and self-seeking. The material, out of which they would create a modern, dynamic Mexico (or Chihuahua) was flawed – by nepotism, clientelism and graft, not least within the bosom of the family itself – and as a result Terracista progressivism often appeared hollow and hypocritical.[310]

For the common, country people, the benefits were few, the burdens many, and the abstract appeal to 'Progress' carried little weight. 'To take a step in the direction of progress', complained petitioners from Bocoyna, where 'the general custom and right' of free grazing of animals had been banned, 'is it necessary to commit an arbitrary act?'[311] At the political level, Creel's 'fever of reforms and projects' excited widespread opposition.[312] To the abuses of the old *caciquismo* were added the new grievances of unprecedented political centralisation and erosion of municipal independence: 'in trying to nullify small *cacicazgos*', commented a critic, Governor Creel 'gave strength to a *cacicazgo* that was greater, oppressive, insatiable, devouring'.[313] The growing strength and scope of government required additional taxation, and at the same time facilitated tax collection. Grievances over taxes had fuelled revolts in the early 1890s, and the then governor, Miguel Ahumada, had made cuts; now, Creel not only increased the tax take, but also ensured that it would operate regressively (not least because many of Chihuahua's major companies had been encouraged to establish themselves with tax concessions and exemptions). In 1911, it was reckoned, the state's tax burden was eight times the level of 1892, and its incidence was more inegalitarian.[314] Complaints about taxes were common and, at San Andrés in March 1909, a serious revolt broke out, with taxes as a principal grievance and the tax-collector (who also managed some Creel timber interests in the district) a chief victim.[315]

The San Andrés rebels were reckoned to be popular throughout the mountain region and, once defeated, they found a welcome in neighbouring pueblos; an indication, it was thought, of the general disgust against the local authorities which prevailed there, and of which the San Andrés revolt was merely an advanced symptom.[316] Certainly popular complaints against arbitrary, corrupt and oppressive caciques were legion, and can easily be traced to communities which, two years later, were to be in the forefront of the

Chihuahua *serrano* rebellion: Cd Guerrero, Namiquipa, Temosáchic, Bachíniva, Cuchillo Parado.[317] Though the *serrano* rebels of 1910 assumed national
labels, they fell squarely within an old tradition, whose text might be taken
from the words of Cruz Chávez, the Tomóchic leader of 1892, who told
travellers that his people simply wanted that 'no-one should interfere with
them, nor bother them for anything, nor meddle in their affairs'.[318] It was a
tradition which Creel, in seeking to curtail local particularism, had only
enlivened.

Once under way, *serrano* rebellion displayed two distinctive characteristics.
First, as a rebellion directed against an external political agency (of which the
cacique and his camarilla might figure as local representatives) such rebellions
were often capable of mobilising very nearly the entire community – including
better off, respectable families who resented alien impositions no less than the
pelados. Communities were not polarised (the imposed officials/caciques hardly
constituted a significant numerical faction) and *serrano* movements easily
spanned classes.[319] To put it differently, vertical divisions (between governing
and governed regions) prevailed over horizontal (class) divisions. *Serrano*
protest was therefore often led by men of property and status: Meixueiro in the
Sierra Juárez, De la Rocha on the mountain borderlands of Sinaloa and
Durango, the Mascareñas family of northern Sonora.[320] The traditional image
of the landlord leading his retainers to battle still had a certain reality in the
sierras, while in the lowlands the progress of absentee, commercial farming
and market relations had consigned it to the dustheap of history.

At the same time and by the same token, *serrano* movements often contained
a significant bandit element. This reflected not only the violent character of
serrano society (of which more in a moment) but also the potential for broad
alliances, embracing landlord, peasant, *arriero* and brigand. Banditry was not
confined to the mountains (during the Revolution it flourished in lowland
areas, too, like Tabasco and the Bajío, possibly acting as a surrogate form of
popular protest) but it enjoyed historic links with *serrano* regions. The Sierra
Azul and Ajo mountains, spurs of the Sierra Madre in northern Sonora had
'been the haunts of bandits from time immemorial'; the mountains of western
Durango, where Heraclio Bernal, the celebrated brigand of the 1880s, had
roamed, remained a region 'where the government has never been more than
superficially imposed on the old bandit stock'; in the sierras of Tepic, where
old men could remember the extensive rebellion of Manuel Lozada in the
1870s, *rurales* were still striving (with limited success) to extirpate banditry in
the 1900s.[321] Indeed, there were recognisable generations of banditry evident
within a given geographical area. When Doroteo Arango, a sharecropper on
the Hacienda de Gogojito (Dgo) clashed with his landlord he rode off into the
mountains and took up as an apprentice with the established brigand of the
Canatlán region, Ignacio Parra, whose lineage stretched back further:[322]

Mucha guerra Parra dió / Era valiente y cabal
Perteneció a la cuadrilla / Del gran Heraclio Bernal.

Doroteo Arango, alias Pancho Villa, became the most famous bandit–rebel of the Revolution. But he was far from alone, and banditry flourished, adding its contingent to the Revolution, wherever local conditions inhibited the authorities and made a life of rural crime viable. A recent study has stressed, with some justification, the mercenary, careerist element in Porfirian banditry.[323] But it surely goes too far, especially when it interprets the phenomenon as an expression of individual enterprise and initiative: 'banditry . . . expanded the economic horizons of people and . . . enticed them to leave a dreary life for one of adventure and opportunity. It put them in touch with others, people with big ideas, and it awakened them to new possibilities. In sum, banditry released individuals from their traditionalism.'[324] But a degree of mercenary self-interest (which it may be worth noting as a corrective to rosy, romantic portraits of Robin Hood style bandits) is by no means incompatible with 'traditionalism' (whatever that may mean), nor is it sufficient grounds to depict the Porfirian bandit as if he were a graduate of business school.[325] Indeed, it is arguable that the bandit and bandit–revolutionary were no less – and sometimes were more – narrow, blinkered and 'traditional' in outlook than ordinary peasant rebels. And, in the light of available biographical evidence, it is mistaken to regard most bandit careers as the result of deliberate, individual choice, a release from boredom into excitement, rather than as an existence compelled by circumstances, and one that was invariably rough, occasionally dramatic, and usually brief. Most bandits, in other words, had banditry thrust upon them.[326]

'Social' bandits – those 'considered by their people as champions, avengers, fighters for justice, perhaps even leaders of liberation' – recently became academically fashionable and are now, it seems, somewhat *passé*.[327] The vagaries of historiographical taste, however, are a poor guide to any given historical reality. Social bandits were common in Porfirian and revolutionary Mexico, and the kinship between social banditry and popular rebellion was close – so close that the two can scarcely be differentiated.[328] In the days of Díaz, it was not confined to the northern mountains either. The country roads of Puebla (a state noted for its brigands in the earlier nineteenth century) were still plagued by 'gangs of robbers' in 1910, and there were villages like San Miguel Canoa which lived upon cattle rustling and where bandits could be sure of welcome and protection; thus, all too often, 'the bandits, being well familiar with the country in which they operate, and often protected by unarmed people who, moved by fear, lend them assistance, succeed in evading the forces sent to pursue them'.[329] Likewise, there were parts of Guerrero where bandits throve and *rurales* preferred not to go.[330] It is furthermore clear that – whatever the truth of the Puebla report – bandits did not necessarily rely on intimidation to gain support. Indeed, if they did, it is not likely that they would have survived long. The coastal lagoons of Chiapas, for example, were the haunt of outlaws, smugglers and 'bad Indians' who kept up a constant and successful resistance against the *rurales* sent to combat them.[331] As the report of a frustrated *rural* officer indicated, there could be no doubt as to the 'social' character of this banditry:[332]

in addition to the fact that I know nothing of the terrain I am traversing, I also face the opposition of all the people of the villages and ranches which I pass . . . since the people protect the criminals whom they employ to avenge their grievances against the authorities and outsiders (*forasteros*) for matters concerning the common land of this village.

Irrespective of specific services rendered, bandits often enjoyed a certain mystique and popularity. In a *macho* society, they were the essence of *machismo*; amid the violence of the sierras, they were adepts; above all, under a regime of overweening oligarchs and officials, they snapped their fingers at the authorities. When a northern mine manager got his men to vote in a mock presidential election he found (it was said) that 150 voted for the long dead Juárez, 100 for a popular bullfighter, and 50 'for one of the most notorious bandits in the section where the mine was located'.[333] The story is probably apocryphal. But the image it conveys of popular heroes – mythical liberal patriots, *toreros* and bandits – rings true.

When popular rebellion was on the agenda, the bandit – with his special skills, local knowledge, and popular reputation – was often prominent. The flotsam of the sierra drifted onto the scene at Tomóchic in 1892, impelled by narrow self-interest, or plebeian sympathy with the rebels, or a combination of both; hence the Tomochitecos found 'their numbers augmenting daily with the discontented of the sierra pueblos, those persecuted by the police, even bandits like Pedro Chaparro (who) joined them with men and money, simply at the prospect of booty'.[334] When the Revolution came, Pancho Villa and several of his gang debouched onto the plains of Chihuahua; Tomás Urbina, a crony of Villa and 'a highly successful bandit and highwayman' mopped up the towns on the Chihuahua–Durango borders; and Rosario García, 'a thief and a murderer . . . and an outlaw for the last five years' descended from the Sierra Madre into the Sahauaripa district of Sonora.[335] For men like Villa – well-armed and tough who, only weeks before, had been raiding around Parral – the Revolution meant a change of title, not of occupation.[336]

Such a change of title did not mean a change of heart. Bandits did not become social revolutionaries overnight – in the sense of pledging themselves to a radical social programme. Rather, the presence, often the prominence, of bandits in *serrano* movements further reinforced their classlessness and, ultimately, their political aimlessness. As Hobsbawm himself has noted, the fact that (some) bandits represent a form of social protest does not make them carriers of social revolution.[337] Rather, the careers of many bandits indicate a necessary degree of liaison with the establishment, or at least, a section of it. Outlaws may be outside the law, but they do not necessarily operate outside the local political and social hierarchy. Arango/Villa, for example, cultivated and counted on the sympathy of woodcutters and ranchers, *hacendados* and hacienda foremen.[338] In Tepic – traditional bandit country – it was 'public knowledge that the bandit Catarino [González], throughout his criminal life, enjoyed the sympathy [cariño] of the common people and of some good society', such as José María Ramírez, who owned far-flung rural properties in the territory and who, out of fear for these properties and for his own life, not only declined to join in the pursuit of González but also forewarned him of the danger.[339] Some bandits even aspired to seigneurial status themselves. Teodoro Palma, the 'gentlemanly highwayman' of Guachóchic, 'never dared go down to the lowlands because he "owed so many dead", as the saying goes'; yet up in the sierra he was the 'lord of the manor', dwelling in a fortified house complete with private chapel, affecting blue waistcoats and scarlet rosettes in his sombrero. Travellers passing through the region could, if they were favoured, count on his assistance against other brigands.[340] Later events suggested that Pancho Villa, as well as Urbina, entertained similar aspirations.

In this respect, it is valid to talk of bandit 'upward mobility'; though there was nothing particularly modern (and a good deal that was 'traditional') about such mobility; furthermore, it was not incompatible with a form of 'social' banditry, so long as the aspiring bandit did not, in his ascent, forfeit popular support. And this was not inevitable. The aspiring bandit became the new cacique even – in times of civil war – the new *caudillo*. Sierra society readily tolerated such a transition. *Serrano* rebels sought no major restructuring of society (of the kind that, say, agrarian radicals espoused when they divided up the haciendas), still less did they advocate a classless Utopia. Their objective – bearing in mind the text of the Tomóchic revolt – was to free themselves from the impositions of the central government. They shared with northern frontier society in general not only an aptitude for violence but also a 'regionalist mentality hostile to any outside influence, hyper-sensitive to interference from the central authorities'.[341] Since regionalism (or, better, parochialism) was paramount, since 'vertical' divisions took precedent over 'horizontal', entire communities acted as one against the common, alien enemy; Temosáchic, for example, 'form(ed) a single body' in opposition to Encarnación Quesada.[342] A successful *serrano* rebellion could therefore be the work of a morning, as the handful of caciques or officials were expelled and acceptable local replacements were installed. Certainly this could imply a shift in economic power too (from the caciques or officials to the inhabitants), but it did not subvert the social order inside the community. Nor did it threaten the social order outside, unless, by a cumulative process of *serrano* revolt, more and more districts extracted themselves from the control of the government. As a result, *serrano* rebellions lacked ideological ballast. They had no agrarian programme, no national blueprint. Political institutionalisation was beyond them. Successful *serrano* movements, like successful bandits, were therefore often accommodated into the status quo, sometimes co-opted by conservative forces, and rarely capable of achieving lasting gains.

But what the *serranos* possessed, above all, was a capacity for resistance greater than that of any other popular group – lowland peasants, peons, city workers. Foreigners commented on the spirit of independence evident among the Chihuahuans (comparing it with the apparent apathy of the Indians further south), and they attributed Chihuahua's rebellious disposition to the fact that 'the inhabitants of these wild regions are not so longsuffering as many of their brothers'.[343] Though not lacking in a kind of corporate solidarity, *serrano* people were freer, more mobile (after the bandit, the *arriero*, the muleteer, was the symbol of mountain mobility) and, above all, more accustomed to fighting. This last attribute – perhaps too easily overlooked in academic retrospect – was crucial. For the *serrano*, the transition from peaceful protest to guerrilla warfare was less traumatic, and usually more successful, than for other groups; hence, *serrano* regions were to be the leading sectors of the popular revolution of 1910–11. In particular, the *serranos* of Chihuahua had the advantage of belonging to a 'frontier' region, in both senses of the word. They came from 'that dangerous zone, where two Mexican states border two American territories, a country of wild Indians, outlaws, rustlers, where the most inoffensive passers-by are, at the very least, smugglers'.[344] The quotation dates from 1886, but it was still partially valid for 1910. The international frontier offered possibilities of escape and supply, the internal frontier generated a tradition of 'self-defence in an isolated environment exposed to violence and social disruption'.[345] On the eve of the Revolution, the *hacendado* William Benton complained, rustling was endemic; a visitor to San Andrés complained that the local people – rough, lewd and lawless – were a breed apart, such that even 'those in the interior of the Republic who have an evil reputation cannot compare with these [of San Andrés]. They [of the interior] at least know how to respect authority and the police.'[346]

Serrano toughness was complemented by *serrano* military tradition. The Tomochitecos had fought for Juárez as far afield as the state of Hidalgo, the sons of Guerrero (district) had first brought Terrazas to power in Chihuahua, Oaxaqueño *serranos* had been the architects of Díaz's victory in 1876.[347] Throughout the Porfiriato and the Revolution, the Juchitecos of the Isthmus supplied a stream of tough recruits for mestizo generals.[348] Sierra society nurtured fine horsemen (notably the *vaqueros* of the north) and expert shots; many inhabitants possessed their own hunting rifles and some even had access to old arms caches, hidden away in the mountains after some previous political skirmish.[349] The Tomochitecos were only peasant farmers, but they threw a scare into the Federal troops sent against them:

they are a terrible lot ... they know their Winchesters inside out; since they were children they have kept up a constant struggle against Apaches and bandits; they can run like a deer through the sierras without putting a foot wrong; but they are excessively ignorant and proud.

Twenty years later, the Oaxaqueño *serranos* received similar grudging accolades from their victims in the valley.[350] *Serrano* sharpshooters might have been incapable of organising and carrying through a popular revolution; but they were the ideal recruits to start one off.

WORKSHOP, FACTORY, MINE

For many country people subsistence farming or relatively secure hacienda employment afforded a measure of security against inflation and economic recession. But equally there were many – probably, though not definitely, a growing number – who depended on wage labour and who were exposed to the vicissitudes of the market.[351] The same was obviously true of urban, industrial workers – with the caveat that Mexican industry (broadly defined for the moment) spanned a wide range of activities, in which vestiges of unfree labour and 'paternalist' control were still present, compromising the free exchange of goods and labour in perfect market conditions.[352] In general, however, it is valid to analyse Porfirian urban, industrial labour in terms of wages, prices, conditions, and levels of employment – categories which, though they are of importance in discussing the role of peon and peasant, do not enjoy the same predominance in the analysis of the Porfirian countryside.

It is also generally valid to stress the urban location of the working-class groups examined in this section. Thus, at the risk of some confusion, two discrete variables are being conflated: first, we are dealing chiefly with proletarians, selling their labour in the market (some artisans would constitute exceptions to this generalisation), second, we are dealing chiefly with residents of large 'urban' communities (again, there would be significant exceptions, some mining communities were no more than villages). As this admission makes clear, 'urbanism' – without it necessarily constituting a 'way of life'[353] – is seen as an independent variable which, at least for the purposes of immediate historical understanding, should stand alone and should not be disaggregated into supposedly anterior categories.[354] In other words, there were distinctive features to Porfirian urban life, which stamped city-dwellers and which – over and above class, political or religious allegiance – imparted a degree of shared 'urbanity', distinguishing them from their rural counterparts. The fact that 'urbanity' can (and later will) be seen in terms of a collection of attributes (literacy, mobility, rationality and so on) does not invalidate it as a presently useful concept: first, because such attributes, while not confined to the towns, were strongly concentrated there and, second, because contemporaries on both sides of the divide saw urban/rural distinctions and conflicts as crucial for any explanation of Mexican society during the Revolution.[355] In many situations, therefore, an urban worker felt more identification with an urban petty-bourgeois, or even bourgeois, than with a rural peon.

The cities were the showpieces of the Porfirian regime: it was here that the cohorts of foreign observers, typified by the indomitable Mrs Tweedie, witnessed and admired Mexico's new sophistication and material prosperity, the business houses and retail stores, the electric lights and tramways, the paved roads, theatres and public buildings (especially those recently and pompously unveiled during the Centennial celebrations). In the city, even the *rurales* looked smart and efficient, and it was in the city, too, that government was carried on, and that the protest politics of the late Porfiriato flourished, mobilising the growing, urban middle class. The latter, in the main, benefited from the economic growth and ostensible prosperity of the epoch. But for the mass of the urban population – the industrial workers, artisans, domestic servants, casual labourers and unemployed – the prosperity was often more apparent than real, and historians have seen, in the strike, riots and labour violence of the late Porfiriato, the birth-pangs of the Revolution.[356] After 1910, it is further argued, the urban workers made a major contribution to the Revolution, even if they did not play the hegemonic role assigned them in certain scenarios. In fact, it will be argued here, the revolutionary commitment of the urban workers has been both exaggerated and misconceived.

Not that the urban workers lacked reason to protest. The last decade of the Porfiriato, it is clear, was a period of markedly rising prices and declining real wages. Some writers have seen this as merely the final phase in a secular trend, dating from the early nineteenth century.[357] Not only is this probably incorrect, it also lacks any explanatory power (of the kind the writers attribute) with regard to the revolution of 1910. After a century of progressive immiseration (and assuming immiseration and rebellion to be directly related), one must ask not why the revolution occurred in 1910, but rather why it did not occur earlier. More convincing and relevant are the figures for the decades immediately preceding the upheaval, decades during which the revolutionary actors grew up and formed their opinions. These figures show that while wages, buoyed by the railway boom of the 1880s and the rapid industrialisation of the 1890s, tended to rise in the late nineteenth century, a reverse trend had set in by the 1900s. Now, railway-building was much reduced, industry contracted, villagers evicted from their lands swelled the pool of labour, and the expanding sectors of the economy (the export-oriented mines and plantations) could not absorb the surplus. Indeed, the shift within industry from artisanal to factory production (a shift most evident in textiles) actually resulted in a net fall in the industrial labour force at a time when production continued to rise. Between 1895 and 1910 the total number of textile workers (of all kinds) fell by 50%, while the ratio between artisans and factory operatives changed from 2:1 to 1:4.[358] In the last decade of the Porfiriato, the industrial labour force as a whole remained static, in absolute terms, and fell relative to the agricultural. Meanwhile, population continued to rise (though less rapidly in the 1900s); landless migrants made their way to the cities, helping to swell the urban masses; and the growth of this propertyless, under-employed proletariat depressed the level of wages throughout the economy.[359]

Within this general picture, however, there were important variations, both sectoral and geographical, the 'proletariat' was no more homogeneous than the 'peasantry'. Wages varied according to locality (being higher in the north, where labour was more scarce) and according to occupation. Whereas real wages, agricultural and industrial, may have fallen by as much as one-third during the 1900s, there were groups like the miners who fared rather better:[360]

Real Minimum Daily Wage in (a) agriculture (b) industry (c) mining

1899	35c.	49c.	48c.
1910	26c.	33c.	63c.

These figures, like all Porfirian statistics, can be no more than suggestive, but they were borne out by the monetary commission which studied the effects of Mexico's conversion to the Gold Standard in 1905 and which found that, while agricultural wages (outside parts of the export sector) had remained static, those of miners and certain skilled workers had risen.[361] There were similar divergences within the textile industry, though for the mass of the factory operatives money wages had generally remained constant, while real wages had fallen significantly.[362]

The fall in real wages derived principally from the rise in food prices (food constituted 60-70% of many workers' expenditure).[363] Again, there has been a tendency to interpret this as a secular trend, dating back at least to the 1870s, and brought about by inefficient and inadequate hacienda production of staples. But, as John Coatsworth has shown, such an interpretation, based on an exaggerated estimate of food production in 1877, cannot be sustained.[364] Food production roughly kept pace with population increase, at least until the turn of the century. By the 1900s, however, and quite possibly because of changes in hacienda crops, per capita production began to fall. Production of corn peaked in 1897, with 2.4m. tons (184 kg. per capita), ten years later 2.1m. tons were produced (144 kg. per capita). Production of beans registered a similar decline after 1901.[365]

The consequent fall in living standards was compounded, after 1907, by economic recession and a series of poor harvests. Whatever the effect of the recession on middle and upper-class groups, there can be no doubt that working-class incomes and levels of employment suffered considerably, and that the results were particularly keenly felt in hitherto dynamic regions, like the north. Mining was curtailed, in some places halted altogether, and there were widespread lay-offs. A thousand miners were out of work in Pachuca, Cananea shut down, there were closures and bankruptcies in Oaxaca. In Puebla, one-third of the textile operatives were laid off.[366] Cities like Torreón, once notable for their economic dynamism, now swarmed with beggars.[367] In addition, the 1908 and 1909 corn harvests proved deficient, particularly in the north, forcing up prices and necessitating a high volume of foreign imports.[368]

Most of the working class therefore faced a real drop in living standards during the 1900s, and particularly after 1907. But it would be wrong to infer, in glib fashion, that the Mexican proletariat was on the verge of armed revolt in 1910. Such an inference requires that objectively deteriorating conditions produce political revolt according to some neat economic equation; it assumes that revolt – rather than other forms of defence and protest – is the outcome; and it overlooks the degree of economic recovery achieved by 1910.

On this latter point, aggregate figures suggest a fairly complete economic recovery by 1910.[369] Specific, local evidence varies: the towns, especially the mining towns, of western Chihuahua were still depressed and plagued by beggars in 1910; concern for employment was to figure prominently among revolutionary priorities in that region.[370] Elsewhere, the signs of recovery were clearer. By late 1909 confidence had revived in the Laguna, buoyed by a good cotton harvest; at Monterrey (March 1910) employers complained of a shortage of skilled labour, and observers noted a return flow of *braceros* from the US; in the territory of Tepic (July 1910) the economic crisis 'which has affected all the Republic . . . has now completely disappeared, and businesses have resumed their usual course'.[371]

But, irrespective of the degree of recovery between 1908 and 1910, it remains methodologically dubious to infer rebellion from falling living standards, especially when the evidence is presented in the form of aggregate statistics. It seems that historians – having necessarily disabused themselves of the notion that objectively bad conditions must breed revolution – have gone on to espouse a 'relative deprivation' theory which is only a marginal improvement.[372] Once, a catalogue of bad conditions (which certainly abounded in Porfirian industry) explained the Revolution. Now, it is a *deterioration* in conditions and pay which carries the burden of explanation. Yet, just as bad conditions were a secular, global phenomenon so, too, periods of falling living standards were common enough in Mexico as in the rest of the world; yet they rarely produced serious revolt, let alone revolution. In the specific context of late Porfirian Mexico, furthermore, falling living standards elicited different responses among different sectors of the population, for they were mediated through a range of different and complex factors – occupational, geographical, ideological, political and so on. In San Luis, for example, it does not appear that the undoubted privations of 1908–10 led to a generalised, revolutionary ferment; rebellions were localised, and responded to specific factors, often of long standing, and not directly associated with the economic recession.[373] The industrial proletariat, it will be argued here, sought to protect themselves by means other than armed insurrection, yet it cannot even be argued that declining living standards bred a new, sydicalist militancy – for, as is often the case, recession brought a drop in the incidence of strike action.[374] In some instances, indeed, recession bred a clientelist dependency on the company, rather than militant confrontation.[375] Thus, while declining living standards were clearly of importance, and in specific cases can be causally related to revolutionary commitment, it is necessary to go beyond aggregate figures and their presumed consequences, and examine working-class politics *in situ*. Only that way can the effect of broad economic trends, filtering through different and discrete circumstances, be properly analysed. For the sake of brevity, I shall focus on three particular industrial groups: the artisans, an important but often neglected group, and the textile operatives and miners, both of which have received considerable attention, not least by historians who would stress their contribution to the gestation of the Revolution.

In 1910, artisanal workers still greatly outnumbered factory operatives: according to the census of that year, there were less than 60,000 factory employees and 32,000 textile workers compared with (for example) 67,000 carpenters, 44,000 shoemakers, 23,000 mat-weavers (and the same number of potters), and 18,000 hatters.[376] These groups included some of the worst casualties of Porfirian progress: they were the human equivalents of the stagnant or declining towns bypassed by the new railways and outstripped by their more favoured commercial rivals. The traditional artisan, protected by distance, local poverty and, possibly, ingrained custom, could survive in the face of industrialisation.[377] But the urban artisan, catering to a mass market, had no defence. Their lot was apparent in the towns of the Bajío where artisan crafts – weaving, hat-making, leatherwork – had long flourished in conjunction with the mining industry. Now, the mines were past their peak and, with abundant local labour available, agricultural wages were low. In León, the pre-eminent manufacturing town of the region, the population of 70,000 was heavily dependent on artisan industry, making hats, serapes and shoes – nearly 10,000 persons were engaged in shoemaking alone. Much of the work was done on a domestic, putting-out basis and travellers, observing 'the workers of León work[ing] at home, in their miserable tenements', commented on their disunity, their primitive technology, and their pitifully low returns.[378]

The development of large textile factories at Querétaro and Puebla/Veracruz subjected the Bajío weavers to intolerable competition (just as they had crushed their own, local artisanal industry); in the country as a whole there was a 26% fall in the number of weavers between 1895 and 1910.[379] New shoe factories in Mexico City and San Luis undercut the leather workers, while soap-, wax-, and candle-makers faced industrial competition, or outright obsolescence.[380] The result was increasing poverty, unemployment, and out-migration. Guanajuato offered a large contingent to the army of *braceros* who sought employment in the US; the Bajío became the chief recruiting ground of the *rurales*, and the towns and cities of the region presented a dismal aspect:[381]

what right-thinking man has not been moved by the patent misery of the pariah of León, of Irapuato, of Celaya, of Querétaro, by the plaintive tone of those unfortunates who, in the stations of the Central Railway, offer one the most exquisite pieces of work for the lowest prices imaginable?

By no means all the artisans of Porfirian Mexico were in such straits. Village artisans, as already mentioned, might prosper in the absence of industrial competition, and they could assume prominent roles as allies, even leaders and ideologues, of peasant rebellion – men like Felipe Neri in Morelos, Orestes Pereyra in the Laguna.[382] Equally, there were urban artisans who benefited from the economic boom of the Porfiriato (carpenters and construction workers for example) and who might aspire to the ranks of the middle class.[383] Men like Gabriel Gavira, proud of their literacy and political awareness, and displaying concerns similar to those of the artisans of Europe, especially Latin Europe, were prominent in the formation of political groups and mutualist societies during the late Porfiriato.[384] The village artisan thus merged with peasant rebellion, the aspiring, urban artisans with middle-class political protest. But for the great mass of declining, artisanal workers, neither allegiance exercised much appeal. At the same time organised, collective self-defence was hard to achieve. Units of production were small, and conducive to an individualist ethic, mutualist associations were notoriously weak and ill-financed; compared with 'proletarian' groups like the miners, railwaymen and textile operatives, the artisanate proved incapable of collective, economic action against the merchants, middle-men or employers who held them in pawn.[385] The putting-out workers in particular were driven by the logic of their position to compete with each other in a descending spiral of immiseration, in which collective action was weak or non-existent.[386]

But, in the absence of unions or political affiliations, the artisans displayed a predisposition towards revolutionary violence (that is, collective violence exercised within a revolutionary context) considerably greater than that of the more 'advanced' proletarian groups. To that extent they made a contribution to the history of the Revolution which was distinct and important, even if it has been largely neglected in historical accounts. Though it was the peasant, the villager, the peon who did the bulk of the fighting after 1910, the urban masses made their presence felt principally through riots and the threat of riots; and within the urban masses the artisanate was particularly prominent, just as the declining manufacturing cities of the Bajío were particularly prominent in the spate of riots which hit Mexican cities in the spring of 1911, setting a trend that would continue so long as the social revolution was on the march.[387] Mesmerised by the proletariat and their nascent unions – the germs of future society – historians have overlooked this phenomenon, the archetypal protest of the pre-industrial urban 'mob', with numerous parallels in the history, not only of Mexico, but also of Europe.[388] They have overlooked it, in part, because the artisanate constituted a declining class, scarcely capable of the more 'modern' associational forms of action which characterised both proletarian unions and middle-class political parties.[389] Yet this status they shared with the peasantry, the shock-troops of the Revolution. In this respect, the impulse to physical violence which lay at the heart of the Revolution (which made it a revolution) derived, in city and countryside alike, from the action of declining, 'conservative', groups, who resented the deleterious effects of progress and who fought, often wildly and seemingly 'anarchically', to defend their ancient, threatened position.[390]

This point becomes clearer as the analysis shifts from the artisan to the fully-fledged industrial proletarian. The rapid industrialisation of the 1890s created the first, mass industrial proletariat in Mexico, particularly (though not exclusively) in the textile industry, where, in the Puebla/Veracruz region, some ninety factories employed 30,000 workers.[391] Three giant enterprises stood out, representing the new shape of textile production which was now highly capitalised and electric-powered: Río Blanco (1892) and Santa Rosa (1898), at Orizaba, both based on French capital and containing 1,000 and 1,400 looms respectively and Metepec (1902), at Atlixco, a Spanish company with over 1,500 looms.[392] The scale of these industrial operations was unprecedented: the French interests at Orizaba were reckoned to employ 10,000 people in a town of 40,000, and Río Blanco alone gave employment – when times were good – to 6,000.[393] Notwithstanding their size and technical modernity, these factories drew upon an older, 'paternalist' industrial tradition, which recognised few inhibitions on management control of factory life. Like hacienda paternalism, this could cut both ways, it might afford a measure of security for workers, or it could guarantee industrial tyranny; much depended on the character of individual management.[394]

Management was still capable of significant variation after the modernisation and expansion of the 1890s, but the inexorable trend was towards 'stricter industrial regimes for the workers and harsher personal practices'.[395] Like the hacienda, the Porfirian factory developed as new, more intense methods of production were grafted upon existing, 'traditional' practices, and the result displayed numerous contradictions. Management clung to its old prerogatives: factories were run 'in the old traditions of capitalism', whereby managers hired and fired at will, exacted fines for negligence, discounted wages for holidays, and kept records of possible trouble-makers. As on the hacienda, the *tienda de raya* served to recycle cash within the enterprise, and the very character of the company town (in which management exercised real political as well as economic power) facilitated close supervision and control; at Culiacán, as in many of the larger textile districts, the workers lived in company shacks and the bosses 'take an interest in the private lives of their men'.[396]

In some instances, the parallel with the hacienda may be pushed further. At Metepec the factory was located on the site of an old hacienda and its labour was drawn from the surrounding villages, converting peasants into proletarians. It was, in a sense, an industrial *rus in urbe*. In cases like this (apparent also in Tlaxcala) the gap between worker and peasant was less marked, the urban–rural divide was blurred, and the potential for common revolutionary action was correspondingly greater.[397] Here was Mexico's closest equivalent to the 'hyphenated' worker–peasant who played so important a part in the industrial unrest and revolution which overtook Tsarist Russia.[398] At Metepec, and elsewhere, Spanish managers shared some of the attributes of Spanish *mayordomos* and *administradores*, and Spanish shopkeepers and usurers were, as in the countryside, the objects of popular hatred.[399] But the Spaniards, it would seem, merely reflected particularly starkly the prevailing attitudes of industrial management, which regarded its work force as lazy, benighted, feckless and (in the literal sense) vicious. Hence, industrial relations were primitive, confrontationist, and overladen with crude stereotypes.[400] Like the peon, the worker had to be strictly disciplined, the vices of drink, absenteeism and negligence had to be extirpated; unionisation was tantamount to sedition. In the main, management proved even more intractable than the government in its attitudes towards labour, and in its determination to cling to the old, 'paternalist' prerogatives, even as industry entered upon a new phase of mass production.

For, by the 1900s, the textile industry began to pay the price for its recent, rapid expansion. Mexico had now achieved virtual self-sufficiency in the production of non-luxury textiles: the share of the market accruing to foreign imports fell from 31% in the late 1880s to 11% at the turn of the century and less than 3% in 1910.[401] But, as already mentioned, the domestic market was limited and, by the 1900s, was actually contracting as purchasing power declined. Facing the threat of over-production, the textile companies reached price-fixing agreements in order to maintain profits despite weak demand, and they cut labour costs by means of lay-offs, shorter hours and lower pay. In one Orizaba factory, for example, average wages fell from 1.71 pesos a day in 1902 to 1.59 pesos in 1907, despite the intervening inflation, and between 1907/8 and 1909/10 the total number of workers employed in Mexican textile mills fell by 11%.[402] Like their landlord counterparts (and there were obvious overlaps between the two groups) Mexico's industrialists counted on making continued profits from a limited, protected market, to the detriment of employees and consumers alike.[403]

The ruthless cutting of labour costs was more feasible in central Mexico, granted its surplus population, than in the sparsely inhabited north and, in the course of the 1900s, it provoked major clashes between the companies and the textile workers, who now displayed an unprecedented degree of organisation. These clashes – and particularly the troubles at Río Blanco in 1906–7 – have been seen as antecedents of the Revolution, the assumption, tacit or otherwise, being that labour disputes radicalised the industrial workers, drove them into the arms of radical groups like the PLM, and finally impelled them to armed revolt after 1910.[404] But these assumptions are not altogether warranted. Industrial confrontation did not necessarily imply political radicalism; the influence of the PLM, never particularly great, tended to fade over time; and the factory operatives, as the following chapter indicates, made little contribution to the armed revolt.

The textile workers had organised and struck on many occasions prior to 1906, their activities following a switchback cycle rather than a gradual, unilinear progression.[405] After a period of ostensible quiescence, 1906 saw the creation of the Gran Círculo de Obreros Libres (GCOL) at Orizaba: a broad association which went beyond the self-help activities of the mutualist societies, and which had close contacts with the PLM.[406] But it was the industrial situation rather than PLM dreams of radical revolution which pushed the textile workers into strike action in the closing months of the year. The GCOL aired the usual grievances: low pay, long hours, fines, harsh regulations, company stores; strikes were called at Orizaba, in the Federal District, and at Puebla.[407] When the Puebla strike broke out in December, and soon spilled over into neighbouring Tlaxcala, the textile companies, marshalled by the powerful French interests at Orizaba, resorted to a lock-out, with the clear intention of breaking the GCOL once and for all. 'Now', an industrialist commented, 'is the opportune time to throttle these movements – at their beginning'; if the lock-out succeeded, he went on, 'the strike is dead in Mexico'.[408] Virtually the entire textile industry was thus paralysed, and 30,000 men were thrown out of work, to the consternation even of many hard-nosed conservatives.[409]

The immediate antecedent of the violence at Río Blanco, therefore, was not a strike but a lock-out; it reflected the intransigence of the employers rather than the militancy of the workers. Furthermore, the initial influence of the PLM within the GCOL had waned. Díaz's government was not congenitally hostile to all labour organisation, but it would have no truck with revolutionary subversion. In the summer of 1906, therefore, several of the radical GCOL leaders were arrested, and the union fell under the leadership of moderates who strove, with some success, to achieve official recognition from both state and national authorities.[410] When the PLM launched revolts in Coahuila and Veracruz, the textile workers did not stir. Rather, the GCOL petitioned Díaz to arbitrate in the current industrial dispute and, when Díaz agreed, it was the resistance of the employers to arbitration which had to be overcome.[411] The president's ruling was not quite the sell-out (to the industrialists) it has often been said; in providing for uniform wage rates within the industry, limiting child labour, and curbing deductions from the pay-packet, it partially met the workers' complaints, if, in other respects, it deferred to the industrialists' desire to monitor their work force. Above all, however, it marked the definitive entry of the state into the field of labour relations, and indicated 'the regime's willingness to break with its past *laissez-faire* labour policies in order to impose a settlement sufficiently attractive to the workers, but one which did not wreak any harm on the basic economic interests of the industrialists'.[412]

The GCOL delegation and the majority of the workers were prepared to accept the president's ruling. The factories opened and work restarted. A minority, however, opposed the settlement and (though accounts differ and contradict one another) possibly sought to prevent fellow-workers from returning to the factory. Violence broke out, a mob headed for the company store, and, when the employees opened fire, the store was looted and gutted. Alternatively, the store employees invited retribution by their insulting treatment of workers who were hungry, hard-up, and a week away from pay-day.[413] With the arrival of police and Federal troops on the scene, calm was soon restored, but later in the day other company stores were attacked, and there was a certain amount of inter-factional fighting among the workers themselves. The military, usurping the position of the *jefe político*, who was thought to be too tolerant of the workers' excesses, gave themselves up to the kind of repression more usually reserved for rebellious Indians and *campesinos*: between fifty and seventy workers were killed, either in skirmishes or subsequent, summary executions.[414]

The Río Blanco affray did not obey revolutionary motives. Not only was the influence of the PLM now in abeyance; it does not appear that any political objectives were at stake.[415] It represented, rather, a bloody industrial dispute, brought about by the employers' intransigence, the workers' internal divisions, and the military's preference for heavy-handed repression. As a 'precursor' of the Revolution, it is chiefly noteworthy first for the bad publicity it won the regime (Río Blanco could join the roster of Porfirian atrocities), and second for the way in which the workers' assault on the company stores (and not, it should be noted, on the factories themselves) prefigured so much of the urban, industrial violence of the revolutionary period.[416] Río Blanco thus made a small contribution to the erosion of the regime's legitimacy, while at the same time anticipating events that would become almost commonplace within a decade. But Río Blanco itself did not march on to a violent rendez-vous with revolutionary destiny. On the contrary, within a couple of days 80% of the workers had gone back and, though strikes continued, premised on the usual grievances, there was no repeat of the sudden, extraordinary violence of January 1907. The workers, chastened, kept their heads down, and the regime, while maintaining a sizeable garrison on the spot, avoided further heavy-handed action; industrial disputes and political subversion were different, in the eyes of both the government and the workers.[417]

The point deserves emphasis, for it supplies the key to the industrial proletariat's revolutionary – or, more often, non-revolutionary – stance. The main thrust of working-class organisation was in the direction of unionisation and 'economist' aims, not political radicalism. In the Mexican, as in many other contexts, Lenin's theory of 'trade union consciousness' is no less valid for being somewhat shopworn.[418] Sporadic confrontation and violence – not necessarily indicative of political radicalism – arose in the course of industrial disputes, in which the intransigence of employers (sometimes deplored by the government itself) was often the key factor. The workers' own attitude was captured by the song of Guillermo Torres, a Río Blanco textile operative:[419]

> y no somos anarquistas, ni queremos rebelión,
> [sino] menos horas de trabajo y buena distribución

> we are not anarchists, we do not want rebellion,
> [but] a shorter working day and a better deal.

Consequently, there is scant evidence of PLM influence among the textile workers after 1906; the workers made no move in support of PLM insurrectionary movements in 1908; and, in that year, PLM mouthpieces were scathing about the passivity of the industrial proletariat.[420]

This marked preference for industrial, syndical activity over revolutionary, political commitment, well established in the 1900s – and no doubt reinforced by the bitter experience of 1907 – was carried into the years of civil war after 1910: the industrial workers preferred to organise and strike, rather than to engage in revolutionary violence. Not that 'economism' was in any sense a soft option. Management clung tenaciously to its old prerogatives, resisting unionisation; the state of the labour market – especially in central Mexico and after 1907 – militated against organisation; and, as the fate of many unions and mutualist societies showed, the financial and logistical problems involved in building up such associations were immense.

If the workers' chief concern was to improve wages and conditions, and – as Anderson stresses – to assert their basic human dignity in the face of abuse and contempt,[421] this did not mean that the industrial proletariat was apolitical. Rather, politics took second place to these basic concerns, and politics tended to be liberal and gradualist (sometimes even Porfirian) rather than radical and revolutionary. Although anarchist and anarcho-syndicalist influences were at work – more so among the big city artisans than the new factory proletariat – these were more vocal than effectual, and the dominant ideology of the Mexican working class was still liberalism. Workers' demands for industrial justice, in 1906 and after, were couched in liberal terms, with many references to the spirit of 1857 and the 'Constitution of Benito Juárez'.[422] Gabriel Gavira, co-founder of an Orizaba Liberal Club with a strong artisan and proletarian membership, recalled how, early in 1910, a bookseller marketed a million copies of the Constitution, at 10c. apiece; soon 'there wasn't a single worker who had not availed himself of a copy, and the Club had to explain and comment on the articles which referred to the rights of man, of the Mexican, and of the citizen'.[423] The people, Gavira explained, 'revered the Constitution of '57, because they believed that therein their rights could be found inscribed'.

Again, therefore, we receive a reminder of the continuing appeal of liberalism on the eve of the Revolution, even outside its traditional, middle-class constituency. And it would be wrong to jump to the facile conclusion that the workers were being lured up the cul-de-sac of 'false consciousness'. Liberalism offered the workers not only the promise of free elections, and thus a voice in politics corresponding to their growing numbers; it also offered them the right to strike, to organise, to escape some of the more arrant abuses of old-style, autocratic capitalism which still prevailed in many factories. Articles IV and V of the Constitution could be taken as a guarantee of the right to strike, but this right had been abrogated under article 925 of the Porfirian penal code.[424] In addition, the patriotic aura of liberalism appealed to workers who so often confronted foreign superiors: French and Spanish retailers at Orizaba, Spanish managers at Metepec.[425] Thus, 'from the industrial workers' perspective what they needed was not a new ideology, but a revitalisation of their version of nineteenth-century Mexican liberalism'.[426]

Progressive politicians were well aware of the political receptivity of the working class. Reyes, as governor of Nuevo León, had legislated for a minimum wage and accident compensation; while this responded more to Bismarckian than strictly liberal objectives, and reflected Reyes' commitment to stable industrial development, it did not go unnoticed or unappreciated by the workers themselves. Though the Reyista movement of 1908-9 was primarily one of the urban middle class, it also attracted working-class adherents, especially in Mexico City.[427] *A fortiori*, the Anti-Re-electionist Party, with its strong commitment to liberal reforms, excited such support in 1909–10. Madero and the Anti-Re-electionists were not blind or indifferent to social issues; their labour policy, adopted at the 1910 party convention, promised accident insurance, factory schools, and the continued Mexicanisation of the railways.[428] But their chief appeal was one of open politics, and respect for constitutional rights. For the workers, as Madero recognised in his famous May 1910 speech at Orizaba, this implied freedom to organise, to create 'strong unions so that, united, you will be able to defend your own rights'.[429]

Moved by this appeal, workers turned out at Maderista rallies and joined Maderista clubs in large numbers. By the summer of 1910 there were at least thirty working-class Maderista associations (some of them, like Gavira's, transformed mutualist societies), and there were four in Orizaba alone, where the French employers were clearly worried at the 'bad effect of the prolonged [Maderista] propaganda' in the factories.[430] Conversely, the Maderista rebels placed high hopes in the workers of Puebla and Veracruz. But the respective hopes and fears proved largely groundless. Despite 'worker-peasant' rebellions in Tlaxcala, the majority of the textile operatives remained inert and showed no greater disposition or capability to take up arms for Madero in 1910 than they had for the PLM in 1906 and 1908.[431]

Of course, there was more to the Revolution than fighting, even if, without the fighting, there would have been no Revolution at all, and it is the men who took up arms and fought who should command most attention. In this respect, the textile workers, the classic proletarians of Porfirian Mexico, do not stand in the forefront of the drama.[432] They achieved a limited impact on the revolutionary process, however, by organising, striking, and developing some political muscle, as the Revolution conferred unprecedented opportunities for unionisation and mobilisation. But it is important to realise that this represented a direct continuation of efforts begun during the Porfiriato – and, to an extent, facilitated by the regime. Opposition politicians – Reyista, Maderista – in no sense monopolised working-class support, and it would have been remarkable if they had, granted the power and patronage at the disposal of the regime, and the obvious advantages to the workers of an amicable, if clientelist relationship with the authorities.

And the authorities were not blind to the attractions of working-class support, particularly as the urgency of the labour question became apparent in the course of the 1900s. As well as mediating in the textile dispute, Díaz commissioned two inquiries on labour conditions in the industry.[433] One was undertaken by Teodoro Dehesa, Governor of Veracruz, who, like Reyes, displayed a lively interest in working-class politics.[434] *Jefes políticos*, too, saw the utility of handling labour unrest with a certain tact and sympathy.[435] In particular, the authorities were keen to channel working-class grievances into peaceful, apolitical channels, and the encouragement of semi-official mutualist societies (mild Porfirian equivalents of the Zubatov 'police unions' of Tsarist Russia) was a favourite ploy.[436] Dehesa managed to get a client elected as president of Gavira's Liberal Club (he provoked a split by insisting on apolitical mutualism); Guillermo Landa y Escandón, Governor of the Federal District, arbitrated in disputes, visited factories, sponsored and subsidised mutualist associations.[437] Oligarchs noted for their wealth, conservatism and corruption, were similarly enlightened on the labour question: Cahuantzi,

Molina, Creel, Corral.[438] Of course, their enlightenment was informed by self-interest. The authorities did not hesitate to infiltrate police spies into mutualist societies, to ensure that proletarian self-help did not spill over into political radicalism.[439] But the fact was that the urban working class were considered worthy and capable of redemption, in a way that the peasantry were not. Peasant protest was more likely to be repressed, and harshly repressed, and there were no comparable attempts to sponsor peaceful political association among the peasantry. Any such sponsorship would have been thought to be both unnecessary and impractical. On both counts, as it happens, the Porfirian leaders were wrong, but their error was shared by most Latin American *políticos*, who awoke to the social threat as well as the political utility of working-class mobilisation long before they came to perceive the rural masses in a similar light.[440] An earlier point is thus borne out: city-dwellers, whether proletarian or bourgeois, shared a degree of common culture which facilitated quite durable cross-class alliances.

The workers, for their part, did not disdain official overtures. On the contrary, and quite naturally in view of their weak position, they welcomed and solicited them. The GCOL had shown more enthusiasm for government arbitration in the textile strike of 1906 than had the management; in 1909 and 1910 textile workers sought the intercession of local *jefes* at Atlixco and Orizaba.[441] Landa y Escandón's efforts in Mexico City met with a mixed, but in some respects warm response: 5,000 workers from 78 factories were reckoned to be enrolled in his Grand Mutualist Society in the summer of 1910.[442] Workers also turned out for official, patriotic rallies in 1909, endorsed a Díaz/Reyes ticket for the 1910 elections, and gave modest, maybe grudging, support to the Re-electionist cause during election year.[443] Maderismo, it is clear, exercised a much stronger appeal. But the incipiently organised working class did not and could not ignore the power of the regime to reward its friends and punish its enemies. Before the Revolution, therefore, there were already signs of a tactical detente between government and labour – an urban phenomenon, for which there was no rural equivalent. And the Revolution itself served to accelerate the process, not to initiate it *de novo*.

The Mexican mining industry employed between 80 and 90,000 men during the 1900s – almost three times as many as the textile industry.[444] But mining was more dispersed throughout the Republic and lacked any single concentration comparable to Orizaba. Sonora, it is true, contained a few, big copper mines, Coahuila produced the bulk of Mexico's coal, Chihuahua, Durango, and Hidalgo were notable for silver. But within such states, production could be scattered, and could embrace a range of enterprises of different sizes and characters. Chihuahua alone, for example, contained 4,000 mines.[445] Generalisations are therefore risky. Furthermore, lists of strikes – easy enough to compile – are not of themselves informative.[446] Strikes and occasional violent incidents were bound to occur with so large and variegated an industry, and they did not necessarily indicate a militant, organised, still less a politically radical workforce. They must also be set against situations in which attempts at unionisation were successfully resisted (at Batopilas for example), or where companies maintained a form of clientelist, paternalistic control over their employees.[447] The Revolution often served to reinforce rather than dismantle such control, at least in the short term.

The mining sector embraced a range of different activities: from the Guggenheim interests which 'blanketed northern Mexico', with silver, lead, and copper mines and smelters in half a dozen states, to the gold-panners of the Balsas Valley (where intruding whites, thought to have designs on the local women, sometimes ran foul of Indian rough justice) and the American family firms and individual prospectors of the north and north west, characters straight from the pages of B. Traven.[448] The conditions and wages of the miners varied accordingly. But two common characteristics were shared by most operations, and helped shape the miners' response to industrial and political conditions.

First, the miners were far from constituting a perfect proletariat, dependent solely on the sale of their labour power, and schooled to the time and work discipline of modern capitalism. Mexican mining (like Mexican textile production) was not fully modern and capitalist. The labour force was often temporary and transient; for some rural communities, the mines offered a source of seasonal income in the same way that the plantations did. In Oaxaca, for example, villagers worked in the mines during the slack winter months; in the Chihuahuan sierra, the able-bodied young men of Tomóchic migrated to the mines of the Rayón district, attracted by the higher wages.[449] Individuals like Pancho Villa and Pascual Orozco had both worked stints in foreign-owned mining companies; for Villa, it was only one job in a long succession of legal and illegal occupations.[450] The problems faced by the companies in maintaining a fixed, regular and conscientious labour force reflected yet again the process of transition from an agrarian and often subsistence economy to one based on the cash nexus and industrial discipline. Some mines even relied on contract labour, hired and paid in advance, after the manner of classical debt peonage.[451] And even in the most modern, corporate enterprises, management had difficulty in securing regular attendance, curtailing absenteeism, and eliminating the bad old habits of San Lunes.[452]

A Mexican mining camp of the 1900s, therefore, might contain a high proportion of drifters, transients, migrant villagers, part-timers, even Indians. The diversity and fluidity of the labour force, combined, often enough, with the remoteness and isolation of the work site, made labour organisation difficult. Parallels with plantation agriculture again spring to mind. But the important point to stress here is that the category 'miner' was and is vague, hence lacking in explanatory precision. There would be little point in trying to explain Pancho Villa's revolutionary career in terms of his brief acquaintance with mining. More contentiously it would be argued that excessive attention has been paid to the occupational antecedents of, say, Manuel Diéguez, who figured in the Cananea mine affray of 1906, and that Diéguez's revolutionary commitment (especially his supposed economic nationalism) has in consequence been misunderstood.[453] A miner, in other words, might also be a liberal, a villager, a bandit, an individual with a grudge against the political authorities. The key to revolutionary commitment – assuming it can be found at all – may reside in any one or any complex combination of these attributes. To exalt industrial occupation is, perhaps, an ethnocentric prejudice, inapplicable in a society where specific occupations were less permanent, vocational, and determinate of life-style.[454]

This point is reinforced by a consideration of the effects of the 1907 recession. The mining industry was, at least for a time, hard hit; mining centres like Pachuca and Parral languished, and many small communities in the Sierra Madre Occidental had still not recovered by 1910.[455] Coincidentally, the north in particular suffered bad harvests and high food prices. It is not clear how far these conditions created a positive impulse to political revolt: the basic grievances in the northeren sierra were not related to immediate, 'knife-and-fork' questions (as might be expected if the recent recession and unemployment dominated revolutionary thinking), but rather to the form of corrupt political domination which had been imposed on communities over a longer period. Certainly the rebels were aware of the problem of unemployment, and sought to counteract it, but the gravamen of their charges against the Porfirian regime was that it had imposed an intolerable *caciquista* oppression, not that it had failed to regulate the economy to produce full employment, nor even that it had neglected to cushion the effects of recession.[456] Indeed, articulate opponents of the regime, like the editorial team of *El Correo*, did not believe that the government should involve itself in economic trafficking in pursuit of some notional common good: the latter was best served by the hidden hand of the market.[457]

Thus, the argument that the recession proved the 'watershed of rebellion', radicalising unemployed miners and the like, remains somewhat conjectural and overly dependent on contemporary assumptions about unemployment and governments' responsibilities in the matter which may not be appropriate to Porfirian Mexico. The argument is particularly dangerous because, at first sight, there appears to be a clear correlation between unemployment and revolutionary recruitment. In 1910–11, and throughout the subsequent years of revolution, the closure of mines (and other enterprises) usually boosted revolutionary recruitment, just as the provision of continued employment acted as a deterrent to armed rebellion. It was not that the miners were hostile to the Revolution, on the contrary, like the textile workers, they took advantage of the situation to unionise and press for economic gains, and they showed a lively interest in the new, open politics ushered in by the revolutionary triumph. But they almost never rebelled *en masse* (as, for example, some rural communities did); they never converted the mines into armed revolutionary camps (as the Bolivian miners were to do in the 1950s); and, so long as work was available, they showed a distinct preference for work and pay over armed rebellion – even when proselytising revolutionaries visited the mine.[458] This cautious, 'economist' response to revolution was not, it seems, unique to Mexican mines, or Mexican workers in general.[459]

Unemployment, on the other hand, stimulated revolutionary recruitment if only for the simple reason that it released men from existing ties and placed an added premium on the meagre pay received by rebel troops. Workers (like those of Mexico City in 1915) who had spurned the Revolution for years, were compelled to shoulder arms under the dire pressure of circumstances. Clearly, such recruitment cannot be satisfactorily explained in terms of occupational membership and grievances. Unemployment *released* men into the Revolution, creating (literally, in this case) a reserve army of the unemployed which, in a state of full employment, would not have existed. In the case of the miners, therefore, it is risky to attribute too much to the specific nature of pre-revolutionary employment: the bad conditions and health hazards (both, by objective criteria, appalling), the nature of the company town, or, above all, the supposed antipathy to foreign ownership and management.[460] Neither Villa nor Orozco, despite their pre-revolutionary antecedents, based their later careers on their mining experiences; even Diéguez, who had participated in the events at Cananea, proved to be solicitous of foreign mining companies and strict towards labour militants. Indeed, in those relatively unusual cases where, early in the Revolution (1910–11), mining communities supplied recruits to the rebel forces from among the unemployed, it may be more appropriate to subsume such 'ex-miners' (who, of course, might also be ex-farmers, ex-shepherds, ex-rustlers, ex-bandits) into the more general category of the loose, shifting, *serrano* society – the 'flotsam of the sierra', typified by Pancho Villa. For, it may be presumed, when lay-offs had to be made, it was the more recent recruits, the migrants and drifters, who would go first – not the core of fully proletarianised labour. Thus, just as the most revolutionary sector of the textile workers was precisely that which retained most contact with rural society – the 'hyphenated' peasant-workers – so, too, the miners and mining communities which displayed an untypical enthusiasm for armed revolt were often those closest to the *serrano* model and furthest removed from that of modern industrial capitalism. We shall return to this point in a moment.

The second common characteristic of mining enterprises was their self-contained, often isolated existence. 'Urbanism' – and its associated literacy and political awareness – was less marked among the miners than, say, the artisans of the big cities, or the self-consciously literate railwaymen, who constituted the aristocracy of labour.[461] With this went, often enough, a form of autocratic management. Alexander Shepherd ran Batopilas in cahoots with the local *jefe*; Cananea, under William Greene, 'was a principality and Bill was its feudal lord'; the Buick boys of El Tovar, loathsome American adolescents in their father's employ, behaved like a self-confessed 'couple of little tyrants . . . and sacked on the spot anybody who wasn't behaving as we thought he should be'.[462] In many cases, the company owned not only the mine but also the miners' shacks, the water and electricity plants, the hospital and school, even the municipal offices.[463] Even more than the hacienda, therefore, the mining town was an 'anti-national' entity, abstracting loyalties from the state and conferring them, often enough, upon foreign interests. Middle-class criticism of foreign companies was frequently premised not on their detrimental *economic* effects (which were not always so apparent) but rather on this patriotic and political consideration: foreign interests were enclaves obstructing national political integration.[464]

The miners saw things differently. Life in the company town, like life on the hacienda, could offer a certain basic security, but much depended on the character of the individual boss. Some managers, like Shepherd at Batopilas, were tactful and apparently successful at conducting industrial relations (according to the crude principles of the time). Even the Buick brothers failed to get their deserved come-uppance. The employment alternatives – on the hacienda or in the teeming cities – made the Mexican miner tolerant of abuses which in other circumstances might appear insupportable.[465] Nevertheless, some bosses went too far. John Hepburn, the wayward scion of English nobility, 'vacillated between authoritarianism and complete disinterest [sic]' in his management of the Pinos Altos mines, in Chihuahua. He antagonised the local officials, arbitrarily decided that payday would come fortnightly rather than weekly, and ruled that half the miners' wages should be spent in the company store.[466] There were protests, a riot; Hepburn was killed; and the *rurales* visited swift retribution upon the miners' ringleaders. Years later, when Pinos Altos had passed into the hands of the Creel/Terrazas interests, the manager was still being urged to go carefully, especially in the introduction of new methods and the correction of old abuses.[467]

Though the Pinos Altos incident occurred nearly twenty years before the Revolution, it indicated a pattern which would be followed after 1910. In those instances where the miners went beyond peaceful economist measures and resorted to violence they did so in order to correct specific abuses and settle specific scores – sometimes against managers, sometimes against local officials, sometimes against both. With regard to management, their grievances were usually the old, familiar ones concerning wages, conditions, the operations of the *tienda de raya*, the tyranny of overseers; with regard to the officials, miners shared the same grievances as the mass of the common people, upon whom the burdens of *caciqusimo* rested. Never did a mining community attempt to take over and operate the mine for its own benefit, and virtually never was foreign ownership (as against foreign management) an issue among the miners' grievances. In other words, the miners might dislike certain American managers, Spanish shopkeepers, and Chinese labourers, but they showed no desire to eliminate foreign enterprise *per se*. Anti-imperialism was not a noticeable feature of the ideological baggage of the Mexican miners, or, indeed, of most other working class groups.[468]

When violence erupted in mining communities it was, therefore, 'spontaneous' (in the sense of lacking formal organisation: it might have been brewing for years previously) and 'primitive'. It was also most marked in those mining centres which were experiencing stagnation or decline, and where management was individual, capricious and benighted. Conversely, the larger, more modern and corporate mining interests of the north tended to enjoy labour relations and less overt violence. In 1910–11, for example, the revolution prompted violent outbursts at Mazapil, Concepción del Oro, Angangueo (Mich.), Hostotipaquillo (Jal.) and – nearly – Pachuca. Concepción had a record of bad labour relations, Pachuca and Angangueo were experiencing renovation after a long period of decline, Hostotipaquillo was a backward enterprise in the far west.[469] The mining town which, proportionately, made the biggest contribution to the 1910 revolution was not one of the corporate giants, but the small, stagnant community of Aviño in the state of Durango.[470] These incidents, furthermore, bear comparison with the riotous events which occurred in the Bajío towns at the same time, in which the artisans, similarly experiencing hard times, unemployment and, often enough, official oppression, took to the streets in brief, 'spontaneous' outbursts. While the miners of the large camps – the copper mines of Sonora, the coal mines of Coahuila – turned to unionisation and peaceful protest, their numerous colleagues in smaller mining communities followed a much older tradition of urban violence; and, certainly at the outset of the Revolution, they made a greater contribution to the popular movement by means of their 'primitive' 'pre-political' behaviour than the more 'modern', economist trade unions.[471]

Paradoxically, the famous case of Cananea, so often invoked (in painful solitude) as evidence of the miners' or the proletariat's commitment to radical politics and armed revolution, fits this general picture. The strike and repression of 1906, which have been seen as key precursor elements in the genesis of the Revolution, arose for local, industrial reasons; as at Río Blanco there were political influences at work but their significance, probably exaggerated, was certainly short-lived; and the causal connection between the whole episode and the revolutionary upheaval which began in 1910 is somewhat tenuous.[472] First, it must be recognised that Cananea was a distinctive untypical enterprise. Copper mining did not get under way at Cananea until the late 1890s, when the local population was less than a thousand; by 1906, on the eve of the troubles, the company employed 5,360

Mexicans and 2,300 foreigners, mostly North Americans and a few Chinese.[473] Labour relations acquired a special character: not only were the Chinese bitterly unpopular, as they were throughout northern Mexico, but in addition, the unusually high proportion of American employees, concentrated in the skilled jobs and receiving better wages, provided a stimulus to unionisation and protest. It was the Americans, to start with, who pioneered strike action against the company in 1903. Furthermore, the American presence and the proximity of the American border enabled syndicalist ideas to penetrate Cananea; and, if it is difficult to estimate the influence of the Western Federation of Miners south of the border, it is likely that the American example gave the Cananea miners a sophistication – in terms of organisation and ideology – which their comrades in the rest of Mexico lacked. Thus, not only did the Cananea workers look better off and receive better pay than other miners; they were also better organised and more conscious of the advantages of unionisation.[474] Finally, the Americans' monopoly of skilled jobs and enjoyment of higher wage rates spurred Mexican unionisation and protest. As on the railways, where a similar situation prevailed, and where the employees were also unusually articulate and well organised, there were growing demands for equality of pay and opportunity – for 'Mexicanisation', not of the company itself, but of the work force.[475]

These factors predisposed the Cananea miners to militancy. And, although the enterprise was a large one, its management (in 1906) was not distinguished for its prudence or its professionalism. William Greene, the proprietor, was an ex-miner, ex-gambler and ex-Indian fighter; with a combination of luck, native wit and an eye for the main chance he had bought his way into Sonoran copper and cattle and successfully 'founded an empire on prospectuses and bluff'.[476] Jobs went to his old frontier cronies, with no concern for their book-keeping abilities. Despite the resulting inefficiency, the company prospered in the early 1900s, buoyed by the rising demand for copper. But, meantime, the good veins were rapidly depleted and, as the town swelled in size, social tensions increased. In 1906 these came to a head. Once again, the hand of the PLM has been discerned at work. Certainly, Cananea had its Liberal Club, organised by Lázaro Gutiérrez de Lara, and, early in 1906, Manuel Diéguez and Esteban Baca Calderón, known opponents of the regime who were in touch with the St Louis junta, established the Unión Liberal Humanidad, which sought to articulate and capitalise on the miners' grievances.[477] But the ULH was no mass, industrial union: most of its (small) membership were skilled artisans and white collar workers, like Diéguez himself, typical PLM constituents.[478]

In May 1906 the miners' longstanding grievances were exacerbated by a management decision to change work contracts in such a way that jobs were threatened and work loads increased. A strike was called (Diéguez deemed it unwise), the mines were paralysed and, as Greene considered the workers' demands for better pay, promotion, and Mexicanisation, the strikers paraded in the streets of Cananea. As they approached the carpentry shop (where the men had not struck) the American manager barred the entrance and turned hoses on the demonstrators. They in turn rushed the building and the Americans inside opened fire, killing two. The demonstrators then set fire to the building and in the ensuing blaze four Americans died. Shortly after, a few blocks away, another clash occurred, in which the company manager and a small group of employees exchanged fire with the protesters, who had now acquired guns. There were thirteen more deaths. Meanwhile Greene, anticipating trouble, had summoned a detachment of Arizona rangers from Bisbee, just across the border, and the Governor of Sonora, unable to send Federal troops to Cananea at once, allowed the Americans to enter Mexico after a token swearing-in as Federal/Sonoran recruits. Not surprisingly, the arrival of these foreign forces, along with Mexican police and *rurales*, failed to quieten the situation, and further fighting continued until regular troops under General Luis Torres, the old Sonoran oligarch, arrived to garrison the town. Next day the men went back to work, their demands unmet, save for the removal of three unpopular foremen. The supposed leaders of the strike narrowly avoided the death sentence and instead were committed to the dank cells of San Juan de Ulúa for periods of up to fifteen years: the Revolution cut short their sentences in May 1911.[479]

Cananea invited conspiratorial explanations. The Porfirian government, true to form, blamed political subversives (it gave grounds for extradition proceedings against the Liberals in the US); the American mining press denounced 'anarchistic agitators, possibly incited, with the assistance of mescal, by the Western Federation of Miners'; Greene even pointed a finger at his American business rivals.[480] It seems clear, however, that the Cananea affray, like its Río Blanco counterpart, was not planned or directed: it simply happened. Liberal agitation may have laid some of the groundwork (that is impossible to evaluate), but there were not wanting cogent, local factors making for confrontation. The PLM leaders in the US do not appear to have played a part; Diéguez opposed the strike and Baca Calderón asserted that the Cananea Liberals sought to control a strike movement which they had in no sense initiated. As Anderson concludes, 'the evidence seems to indicate that the strike was spontaneous and not a conspiracy of the PLM to begin the revolution against the regime'.[481] As at Río Blanco, a political and conspiratorial colouring was given, *ex post facto*, to what was essentially a bloody industrial dispute.

If the causes were primarily local and industrial, what were the consequences? Cananea, like Río Blanco, has generally been seen as a fatal blow to the Porfirian system. Even Anderson (whose own evidence often points another way) succumbs to the familiar view that 'Cananea may well have been the watershed of the Old Regime', and most other commentators dispense with the subjunctive.[482] Certainly there was a general outcry: Madero included Cananea along with Río Blanco in his litany of Porfirian abuses and, more interestingly, there were vigorous protests in the press, conservative and Catholic as well as liberal and oppositionist.[483] The main thrust of this criticism, however, was directed against Governor Izábal and his decision to allow American forces to enter Mexico and fire on the strikers of Cananea: the miners excited more patriotic sympathy as victims of American intervention than they did radical solidarity premised on their proletarian demands. Locally, Governor Izábal and his clique lost what little legitimacy they enjoyed, and to that extent Cananea contributed to rising political discontent in Sonora.[484] But Sonora, as it turned out, did not play a pivotal role in the 1910 revolution. Nationally, the impact of Cananea is hard to measure. It provided grist to the opposition mill, and it gave added piquancy to the 'social question' now exercising enlightened minds – Porfirian as well as liberal and Catholic. The government, while condoning the repression at Cananea, began to seek subtler ways of controlling labour agitation; even the Mexico City theatre began to explore 'social' themes.[485] But this mood (the depth of which should not be exaggerated) was not necessarily the mood from which revolutionaries sprang. In Chile, scene of similar ugly incidents in the 1890s and 1900s, the 'social question' was also topical; but Chile underwent no consequential popular revolution.[486] Indeed, a roughly contemporaneous discovery of the working class and its discontents occurred within many Latin American polities in the period, and in all cases (bar Mexico) existing political structures proved capable of repressing and/or accommodating the fresh demands to which this gave rise. The novelty of Mexico's pattern of development lay elsewhere.

This novelty will be discussed in a moment. As for Cananea (and Río Blanco) the really important question is what happened in the aftermath of the troubles – during the four year interval preceding the Revolution, which proponents of the 'precursor' theory tend to skip over. The Revolution – it has been suggested, and it will be shown – was a highly localised affair, usually deriving its impetus from local grievances. Leaving aside the supposed effect of Cananea on the public mind and national politics (a matter inviting conjecture but defying assessment) it is necessary to trace the causal and chronological links which join the 1906 incident with the 1910 Revolution. Did Cananea – or Río Blanco – lay the groundwork for revolutionary movements in the mines of Sonora or the textile mills of the centre?

In both cases, the government removed the strike leaders, and what PLM influence there had been rapidly faded. At Cananea, furthermore, the economic situation depressed labour militancy and prevented further outbreaks. In the wake of the strike management was reshuffled and Louis D. Ricketts (who, for all his scruffy appearance had a Princeton doctorate and solid experience of mining in the American south-west) was promoted to permanent manager; he took pains to improve labour relations, raising wage levels and cutting the North American share of the labour force from 34% (1905) to 13% (1912).[487] At the same time (one indisputable consequence of the strike), William Greene's personal empire collapsed and his share in Cananea was bought out by the Cole-Ryan group, which set about an extensive programme of rationalisation and improvement: when the 1907 recession forced a cessation of production in October, the company set about installing new furnaces which substantially increased both capacity and efficiency.[488] This marked an important caesura in the life of Cananea. For its part, the new management, responsible to corporate ownership rather than personal whim, proved more adept than the old; by a policy of 'circumspect neutrality' the company lasted through the difficult years of the Revolution surprisingly well, and, though there were inevitable dislocations and stoppages, there was no repeat of the 1906 affray.[489] From the miners' point of view, the 1907–8 stoppage and the company reorganisation implied a big turnover: from a total population of some 20,000 in 1906, Cananea fell to around 13,000 in 1907, pulling back to 15,000 in 1913. Copper production followed a similar trend.[490] On the eve of the Revolution, therefore, the labour force at Cananea was smaller, more Mexican, more efficient, and probably a good deal different from the labour force which had witnessed or participated in the 1906 strike. The period between strike and Revolution was, therefore, one of change, reorganisation, and relaxation – not simmering discontent presaging a revolutionary outbreak. It is probable, too, that the memory of 1906 and, even more, the experience of contraction and unemployment in 1907–8, encouraged quiescence rather than militancy.

Furthermore, where a continuity of personnel can be established, the picture is by no means as neat as many accounts suggest. Manuel Diéguez, the leader of 1906, freed from gaol in 1911, returned to become mayor of Cananea and a prominent revolutionary general. By 1916 he had risen to become military commander in Sonora. But he did not, it is clear, regard himself as an armed tribune of the proletariat; he was no Mexican precursor of Bolivia's Juan Lechín. Indeed, his relations with the mining companies of Sonora were cordial and, when confronted by wage demands on the part of the Cananea miners, he was quoted as saying: 'they are agitators and do not wish to conform to our governmental wishes; I am afraid they have to be disciplined presently'.[491] Strikes and armed revolts; labour leaders and revolutionary commanders; these were different phenomena and different breeds, obeying different motives and objectives.

There is a final, important point of similarity between Cananea and Río Blanco. In both cases the workers' will to armed revolt was weak, and their famous, though untypical, resorts to violence were the result of particular, provocative circumstances, in which their chief concerns were limited, economist ones. But in both cases, too, the workers readily responded to the new political movements of the late 1900s. Whatever the influence of the PLM at Cananea, it is clear that Reyismo and later Maderismo made considerable headway there. By the summer of 1909 Cananea's Reyista movement was reckoned to be 'very powerful'; its leader, an officer in the local garrison, was a fellow-*tapatío* and a friend of Bernardo Reyes. Madero, however, was confident that the Anti-Re-electionists would corner the market in opposition politics at Cananea: a local branch was established and it soon received the imprimatur of a police raid.[492] Under the leadership of Juan Cabral and Salvador Alvarado, both educated, white-collar workers, the Maderista cause prospered, and peacefully entered upon power at Cananea in 1911.[493]

Thus, in general, the Cananea miners eschewed armed revolt, and, when they went beyond the day-to-day economist struggle (a struggle not to be undertaken lightly or without risk), they looked to a brand of reformist politics, usually of middle-class or 'bourgeois' provenance. This was a perfectly rational strategy, and it got results. Revolutionary leaders, building on Porfirian precedent, appreciated the support of organised labour, and, as the careers of Manuel Diéguez and others revealed, labour organisation afforded a springboard into local and national politics. The route from the *sindicato* office to the gubernatorial palace – or even further up the road of political preferment – was already being mapped out. This was possible because the urban workers, especially those in the larger, corporate enterprises, displayed an early awareness of the new politics which the Revolution brought into being; and because alert politicians, particularly those of Sonora, soon appraised and began to cultivate this fresh political force, which contributed little to the overthrow of the old regime, but which was to be instrumental in the construction of the new.

THOUGHTS ON THE CAUSES OF THE PEASANT DISCONTENTS

For obvious reasons, the workers of the new industrial complexes – Cananea, Río Blanco, the railways – had no inherited ideals of the good industrial life to which they made appeal: they had to develop and absorb ideologies (liberal, anarcho-syndicalist, socialist) as they went along, and they had to experiment with new organisation forms and political stratagems – mutualism, syndicalism, clientelist dependence on the state. Their vision had to be forward and their discourse innovative. In the terminology of the Tillys, they were 'pro-active', that is, they advanced 'claims for rights, privileges or resources not previously enjoyed'; to this end they formed 'special purpose associations' (such as unions) which achieved a complex 'articulation of objectives, programs and demands'; and this strategy, as it turned out, implied 'attempts to control rather than [to] resist different segments of the national structure'.[494] To put it differently, more crudely, and with caution, they were more 'modern'.[495]

Such ideas and strategies contrasted with the 'reactive' stance of the peasantry, whose norms were nostalgic, whose models derived from past experience (suitably mythologised, no doubt), and whose objectives were in some senses conservative, even reactionary.[496] It should be noted that many artisans, some agricultural proletarians, and even some miners stood closer to this pole than to the Cananea–Río Blanco norm. As regards organisation, the peasantry resorted to forms of 'reactive' resistance and violence which were communal (i.e., based on community rather than special associations, and thus displaying a spatial rather than an occupational loyalty). And it was, essentially, this 'reactive' collective violence which underwrote the Revolution. The empirical evidence for this assertion is scattered throughout the book. Here, I intend simply to present some very general, comparative comments about its role and character.

Mexico alone of Latin American countries experienced a popular, agrarian revolution prior to the Second World War and it did so because in Mexico a range of factors – none of them individually unique – combined in a distinctive revolutionary constellation. These factors were principally endogenous. This is not to ignore the impact of foreign economic penetration or of Mexico's integration into world markets, both of which, as I have already suggested, were crucial in stimulating economic and social change during the Porfiriato. But Mexico was not alone in experiencing this impact; it was, rather, the mediation of these exogenous forces within domestic social, economic and political structures which was distinctive. At the more narrowly political (I would be prepared to call it epiphenomenal) level, exogenous factors – though emphasised by some recent writers – are of secondary if not tertiary significance.[497] There is simply insufficient evidence to prove that US policy, domestic US political alignments, or even the *Grosspolitik* of the European powers causally determined the Revolution. As for the argument that the Mexico Revolution (among other revolutions) was somehow causally bound up with the First World War ('it is not accidental', Goldfrank observes, with sublime imprecision, 'that more than the Mexican Revolution occurred in the period around World War One'), this argument omits, *inter alia*, the four years by which the outbreak of the Revolution preceded the outbreak of the war.[498] My negative contention – to the effect that exogenous factors were of very limited relevance in the gestation and birth of the Revolution – will receive additional support later. For the moment, it is the positive contention and the endogenous factors which demand attention.

Most Latin American societies experienced closer integration into world markets in the latter part of the nineteenth century and, with this, a growing commercialisation of agriculture and a rising demand for land and labour. Different responses resulted. Where land was relatively abundant[499] and local labour scarce, landlords had to attract manpower from afar: either under coercive conditions (Brazilian and Cuban slavery; the indentured labour of

Peru) or by creating money incentives (Argentina and Uruguay). The planters of São Paulo contrived to switch from the one to the other inside a decade, as slaves gave way to European *colonos*.[500] Alternatively, landlords could draw upon local (or 'peri-local')[501] labour. In Peru the coastal plantations, initially reliant on slave and indentured Chinese workers, came to depend on labour drawn from the relatively populous sierra, thereby creating a system in which coercion and incentive combined in proportions which are hotly disputed.[502] Chilean landlords, meanwhile, facing less imperative marker signals than, say, their Argentine counterparts, could rely upon existing local labour, whose relative abundance made *inquilinaje* contracts positively attractive to rural workers.[503]

Mexico contained analogues of all these types. Northern Mexico, with its highly monetised, free labour economy corresponded roughly to the southern cones, while the coercive systems of the south, of 'Barbarous Mexico', resembled slavery. Equally, there were some southern planters, like the German *cafetaleros* of Soconusco (Chis.) who relied on incentives rather than outright force or fraud to coax Indian workers from the sierra: Soconusco paralleled Peru, and Soconusco, we may note, remained relatively tranquil during the Revolution.[504] The landlords of central Mexico, like their Chilean counterparts, could depend on an abundant (and increasing) supply of local labour, and a near monopoly of land; hence the market favoured the landlord (leaving forms of coercion at a discount) and, as with the Chilean *inquilinos*, the position of the 'internal peasantry' – the *acomodados* of Bocas or the *realeños* of Morelos – was in some respects enviable.[505]

But while these discrete elements were familiar elsewhere, the Mexican mix was distinctive. The matrix of popular, agrarian revolt lay – as both Wolf and Tannenbaum have argued – in the villages: the villages of the central plateau and, I would stress, those of other regions which were in important respects comparable (in Sonora, Sinaloa, the Laguna, the Huasteca). But, as has already been argued, the village was a necessary but far from sufficient condition for sustained agrarian revolt. Village-based regions could prove quiescent as well as rebellious, or they could adopt different modes of rebellion, in which agrarian grievances were relatively unimportant, and in which resistance to political centralisation was paramount (the *serrano* revolt).[506] As these variations suggest, there is little point in focussing exclusively on the social location or affiliation of rural rebels or in creating typologies along this single axis (tenant farmer, smallholder, sharecropper, peon, proletarian) in the belief that revolutionary or non-revolutionary conduct will neatly correlate with these categories. As global studies by Wolf, Stinchcombe, Steward, Paige (and, no doubt, others) have shown, the correlations vary greatly from place to place.[507] One man's revolutionary 'middle' peasant is another man's conservative kulak; for some, the rural proletariat is the carrier of revolution, for others, it goes the way of political reformism and trade unionism.[508]

Rather, the revolutionary participation of discrete groups can only be properly analysed within the more general framework of agrarian social and political relations; the analysis, in Corrigan's terms, must be 'relational' rather than 'positional'.[509] Paige is therefore correct to focus on landlord-peasant relations, rather than on peasant types; but it is necessary to take one further step and to substitute diachronic for synchronic analysis. Paige's typology of landlord-peasant relations, though illuminating, is somewhat static; it conceives of specific patterns of such relations, and gives less attention to the dynamics of change from one pattern to another.[510] Yet it was this kind of change, undergone by an agrarian society in flux, which precipitated the Mexican Revolution.

In Mexico's case, agrarian revolt was intimately linked to agrarian commercialisation, itself stimulated by national and international demand, foreign investment, and the development of the country's infrastructure. Here, exogenous economic factors are crucial, but they stand – both causally and chronologically – at some distance from the revolutionary upheaval itself. This process of change was a characteristic feature not of early nineteenth-century, still less colonial Mexico, but rather of Porfirian Mexico, of the era of political centralisation, land concentration, and the consequent dispossession of villages in favour of *hacendados*, *rancheros* and caciques. As a result, peasant revolt (a familiar enough event in Mexican history) displayed a change of emphasis. True, agrarian revolt, provoked by land disputes, was an ancient phenomenon, with a continuous history throughout the nineteenth century: Ecatzingo (Hgo) in 1834; in Mexico, Puebla and Oaxaca ten years later; Yucatán, the Huasteca and Juchitán in the late 1840s; Zacapoaxtla (Pue.) in 1855–6, the Lake Pátzcuaro region in 1857, Pachuca and elsewhere in 1869.[511] The Yaqui agrarian revolt had endured for over a century before its final settlement in the 1920s. As this last example suggests, continuity was sometimes evident as between some of these old, early nineteenth-century revolts and those of the revolutionary decade. But discontinuity was also – perhaps more – evident. Old regions of popular agrarian revolt (such as Yucatán) had been pacified by the 1900s. And new centres of opposition, whose grievances were specifically associated with the changes taking place since the 1870s, came to the fore: the rash of revolts provoked by railway-building, analysed by Coatsworth; Morelos; the rebellious outbreaks of 1910–15 which, more often than not, traced to recent dispossession – Cuencamé, Naranja, Ometepec, and many others which will appear subsequently. The Indians of Escuinapa (Sin.), who claimed that they had 'suffered not the slightest incident, until the dictatorship of the Government of General Díaz, in which it was all reprisals, outrages and abuses without limit', perhaps protested too much, but the chronological implication of their complaint was clear and not untypical.[512]

To a lesser extent the same may be said of *serrano* revolt. The *serrano* revolt was an ancient, global phenomenon, the secular product of state-building and centralisation. Tilly comments on rebellions undertaken by 'communal groups jostled and outraged by the commotion of state-building'; Mousnier examines revolts in France, Russia and China which (he argues) resisted the advance of the state and mobilised entire communities, from top to bottom.[513] In Mexico, too, the advance of the state, both colonial and independent, met with constant resistance. Popular revolts in the early nineteenth century were frequently premised on resistance to political incorporation and to its most obvious manifestation, taxation. The Tzotzil rebellion of 1869, which promised its followers that 'no-one shall have authority over them or demand taxes of them', was thus typical of a whole genre.[514] Revolts of this kind, usually mounted by 'Indians', and in opposition to the state and its fiscal demands rather than to rapacious landlords, were common throughout the 1840s and 1850s: in Mexico state, 1844; around Chilapa (Gro), 1849; in Hidalgo at the time of the Revolution of Ayutla (1854).[515] Thereafter, however, and certainly during the Porfiriato, such revolts became less common. There were two principal reasons for this. First, *serrano* resistance tended to follow a rough generational sequence. Resistance gradually gave way to incorporation and, once political autonomy had been lost, it was hard to recover, for the state did not easily or often relinquish its conquests. During the second third of the nineteenth century, as the Mexican state faced a series of crises (the Mexican-American War, the War of the Reform, the French Intervention), so its power fragmented and, as Buve has suggested, the peasantry enjoyed opportunities to assert their rights and independence.[516] But thereafter Díaz resumed the work of state-building and centralisation: a process which, granted its unprecedented rigour and success, stimulated further *serrano* resentment, even while it stifled *serrano* protest. Old regions of (usually Indian) particularism were now subjected to the control of the state, and the tradition of protest died. There was no independent Tzotzil rebellion during the Revolution, and the Maya of the Yucatán interior, the victims of a long war of attrition, made a minimal contribution. Different movements – often mestizo, and located in the pioneer north, rather than the Indian south – now stood in the forefront of local resistance to state encroachment. We shall also note how, during the Revolution and over a shorter time scale, *serrano* revolts again followed a regional and chronological sequence, as the initial 'revolutionary' movements of 1910–11 gave way to successor movements which, though located elsewhere, and often of different ethnic make-up and supposedly 'reactionary' character, nevertheless obeyed the classic *serrano* rationale: collective, parochial resistance to the state, be it Porfirian or revolutionary.

It is secondly significant that, within the general context of Porfirian and revolutionary rebellion, agrarian factors became more important, while other grievances (notably taxation) tended to recede. It is worth stressing the point that, unlike many earlier peasant revolts, not only in Mexico but also in Latin America, Asia or medieval and early modern Europe, those of Porfirian and revolutionary Mexico centred upon and derived their character from the struggle for land. Access to land was at issue in a way that it was not, say, in 1381, or in twentieth-century Vietnam.[517] Conversely, taxation – a good indicator of state-building, and cause of frequent rebellions in Mexico's past – was less important. For, with the political and financial consolidation of the Porfirian regime, the end of civil war, and the rapid growth of the economy, the fiscal basis of the Mexican state both shifted and became more secure. Tax collection became more efficient, less arbitrary and desperate. Traditional taxes, such as the *alcabala* and the *capitación* (head tax), vestiges of the colonial era, gave way to import duties, stamp taxes and property taxes, all of which were boosted by economic growth.[518] The decline in importance of the head tax, which was highly regressive and had weighed heavily on the rural poor (especially the Indian population), was of particular significance: in Chiapas, for example, where it had figured among the grievances of the Tzotzil rebels of 1869, the *capitación* became less remunerative as other forms of revenue swelled the state treasury.[519] A central feature of popular, especially Indian revolt, evident throughout the colonial period, the Independence movement and the early nineteenth century, thus faded.

Anti-tax protest did still play a part in *serrano* rebellion, as the case of Chihuahua illustrates. But now the focus had shifted away from the Indian south to the more remote, pioneer regions of the white–mestizo north. And here the problem was not one of an ancient tribute being exacted by precarious regimes fighting for survival; rather, fiscal extortion was the work of a strong, centralising, progressive regime (Porfirian–Terracista), and it was but one element in a general assault on local autonomy.[520] In general, however, taxation was a less contentious issue than in the past: the Porfirian state was fiscally stronger than its predecessors, and, for its rural subjects, fiscal oppression was less provocative than agrarian dispossession. It is to this central point that we must now turn.

Agrarian dispossession was nothing new in Mexican history. But, as Eric Wolf has argued, it now occurred on an unprecedented scale, stimulated by agrarian commercialisation (whose effects were further compounded by population growth).[521] Agrarian protest and revolt therefore took place in regions of commercialisation where profit-seeking landlords (*rancheros* as well as *hacendados*) afforded new market opportunities, clashed with established peasant communities. Clashes of this kind (as Paige and Huntington have, in their different ways, pointed out) assumed the characteristics of a zero-sum game: first, because land was a finite resource, coveted by both sides, second, because dispossession of the peasantry was a vital element in landlord strategy, in that it created surplus labour, while also eliminating peasant competition in the market.[522] Landlord and peasant – unlike industrial capitalist and proletarian – had no common interest (however ostensible or short-term) in collaboration and increased production.

Meanwhile, secondary to the outright dispossession of the peasantry, went the general deterioration of rural wages and (perhaps more important) of sharecropping and tenancy terms, hence a general decline in rural living standards. Any Marxist formulation of this process of change must therefore embody (at least) two concepts: first, the antagonistic relationship of two modes of production (created not by the articulation of these modes, but rather by the breakdown of an earlier articulation, under the impact of the market); and, second, the conflicts generated within the hacienda system, as landlords extracted a greater surplus from direct producers – tenants, sharecroppers and, to an extent, *peones acasillados*. This latter conflict, as Paige illustrates, was potentially violent, since the extra-economic coercion deployed by the land-lord involved the backing of the state, and its logical outcome was, in Paige's terminology, the 'agrarian revolt'.[523] But, leaving aside the contentious concept of 'extra-economic coercion', it should be stressed that such conflicts, fought *within* the hacienda system, between the landlord and the 'internal peasantry', were of secondary importance; the dominant conflict and motor of the agrarian revolution was the expansion of the hacienda (and rancho) system *as a whole*, at the expense of the independent, 'external peasantry', and hence the transformation of 'external' into 'internal' peasants, or even rural proleta-rians. Here again, of course, the state played a crucial role, legitimising and abetting agrarian expropriation. But such a conflict, generated by the advance of one 'mode' at the expense of another, cannot be analysed according to the dynamics (or 'laws of motion'?) of a homogenous single mode.[524] Equally, that now fashionable school of articulation theory which, in a manner strangely reminiscent of its arch-enemy, structural functionalism, conceives of modes meshing together like well-oiled cogs in a complex capitalist ('in the last analysis') gearbox, is no more appropriate.[525] Better Luxemburg's formu-lation: less articulation, more conflict, corrosion and assimilation.[526]

As Luxemburg's own cases illustrate, agrarian confrontation of this kind was a global, secular phenomenon. Russia, in particular, offers many parallels which cannot be pursued here.[527] Within Latin America, however, Mexico was the outstanding example: why? In Uruguay and Argentina (outside the north west) there was no large, established peasantry. In Chile, both established peasant communities and also the pressures of market and population were weaker: though the hacienda ruled, its rule (especially if Bauer is preferred to Loveman, as I believe he should be in this instance) was relatively lax and tolerable, with regard to both the internal and external peasantries.[528] Peasant protest was largely unknown in Chile at least until well into the 1960s, by which time demographic, market and political circumstances had changed dramatically. In Peru, where peasant communities analogous to those of Mexico existed, the spatial separation of peasantry and commercial agriculture mitigated the social consequences of their collision. While it is true that expropriations occurred on the coast, provoking sporadic, violent resistance (one analysis goes so far as to draw parallels with Zapatismo), the coastal planters' chief need was for peasant labour rather than peasant land; and to this end they looked to the populous sierra, whence migrant Indians were lured down to the lowland valleys.[529] Such migration, however, far from dissolving highland communities, could actually serve to reinforce them (a pattern which had parallels in Mexico – among the Huicholes, for example – but on a smaller scale).[530] Peasant communities could thus survive, even prosper, by 'raiding the cash economy', as Scott calls it.[531] Meanwhile, attempts at expropriation undertaken by the pastoral haciendas of the sierra appear to have been resisted with considerable success. Here, conditions did not whet landlords' appetites as elsewhere: large-scale commercial farming was risky and often unprofitable, and the peasantry – for all the divisions extant both within and between communities – was capable of dour resistance, legal, economic, and political. National governments, such as Leguía's, recognised and in turn reinforced this defence of the peasant community.[532] In these respects, as I have already suggested, Peru paralleled Chiapas, where highland communities, though linked to a dynamic, commercialised, capitalist sector (the coffee region of Soconusco), were perpetuated rather than pulverised by this relationship.[533] Here (if such terms are to be used) the respective modes of production did not collide, but articulated with at least the appearance of reciprocal benefit; the landlord/peasant dyad was not a simple, antagonistic zero-sum game; and Chiapas, like Peru, did not experience sustained agrarian revolt.

It was, rather, the close, antagonistic juxtaposition of commercial haciendas/*ranchos* and a populous, established peasantry, typified by Morelos, much of the central plateau, and certain key regions of the remainder of Mexico, which was distinctive and productive of agrarian revolt. Perhaps the closest analogue in South America is to be found in the Cochabamba valley of Bolivia, where strong market forces acted upon a profit-seeking landlord class, and a numerous, established peasantry.[534] Cochabamba, of course, was to be one of the chief centres of agrarianism in the Bolivian Revolution. Protest thus stemmed from the irrevocable breakdown of the old hacienda/community 'symbiosis' (or 'articulation'), from the landlords' consequent loss of legitimacy, and from the uncompromising conflict which ensued – a conflict all the more clearcut since, in these circumstances, the expansionist landlords frequently controlled the political apparatus. Granted the close contiguity of hacienda and community, and the landlords' local political monopoly, there was little opportunity for the peasantry to seek sympathetic *patrones*, who might defend their interests. Such clientelism was feasible in less commercialised, highland regions, it often formed an integral part of *serrano* rebellions, but it could not bridge the class divide in zones of agrarian polarisation.[535]

Hence, the intransigence of peasant rebels: Zapata's obdurate resistance to

compromise; the undiluted claims to landownership made by peasant spokesmen, to the dismay, surprise or indignation of observers. In Veracruz, peasants
considered the acquisition of their lands by 'outsiders' to be an 'ineffable
injustice', while in Sonora the Yaquis claimed the entire river valley, which
had been given them by God.[536] Again, this was no Mexican peculiarity.
'Traditional peasant politics', it has been observed, 'cannot be insinuated into
"modern" politics; wrongs cannot be only partly righted. Justice must be
untarnished by compromise'.[537] In practice, of course, compromise might
ensue; peasants, more than most, have to be realists, and this may require that
they come to terms with 'modern politics'. But it is essential to stress the moral
(hence intransigent) nature of peasant protest in its inception. This was not
simply a manifestation of peasant conservatism, nostalgia or religiosity (points
which will be considered in a moment). Rather, as James Scott has shown in his
cogent study of peasant rebellion in south-east Asia, the moral bases of peasant
protest derive from the logic of subsistence farming, its attendant insecurity,
and the perennial – often seemingly illegitimate and capricious – threats posed
by the state and the landlord class.[538] For these actors, obeying imperatives
whose validity the peasant did not recognise (the capitalist market; *raison
d'état*), threatened destitution or drastic changes in status and income, thereby
violating the 'moral economy' on which peasant society depended.[539] I shall
return to this, the 'moral' dimension of protest, in a moment.

The peasant community, be it Indian or mestizo, was important in
providing the cell of revolution, in both classic agrarian and *serrano*
movements. It was not just that forms of communal tenure (whose importance
varied greatly from place to place) or corporate civil/religious hierarchies came
under sustained attack from engrossing landlords and the expanding state; it
was also the case that the very existence of the community actively facilitated
resistance, and that, without such organisational facilities, resistance was at a
discount. The community, it could be said, afforded both the *casus belli* and the
modus operandi of the revolutionary war.

Before developing this argument, it is worth noting an ostensible paradox.
'Peasant studies' often stress the corporate solidarity of the community (which
might be conducive to resistance). But they also – and recently more
vigorously – emphasise quite contrary tendencies: Bamfield's 'amoral familism', the 'all-pervading individualism' of Fanshen, the proto-capitalism of
MacFarlane's English 'peasants'.[540] Mexico, whence came the notions of the
'limited good' and the 'culture of poverty', is no exception.[541] Paige thus
follows an established but still lively tradition (one tracing back to the
Eighteenth Brumaire, if not before) in stressing the divisions, conflicts and
rivalries evident in peasant societies, especially those afflicted by a 'predatory
upper class'.[542] For Paige, as for Marx, the proletariat is likely to display
greater class solidarity and revolutionary commitment than the classic
peasantry. But again, such analyses err by imputing attitudes and modes of

behaviour to discrete social groups, rather than to social groups located in specific historical circumstances. Inwardly divided communities may display a degree of solidarity *vis-à-vis* the outside world; *pace* Paige, the presence of a 'predatory upper class' may actually encourage such solidarity, rather than provoke atomisation and conflict. Tilly, in contrast, notes the 'visible presence of an antagonist' as a factor in this direction.[543]

This was certainly the case in Morelos, where the pressure of the plantation relegated old, intra-peasant feuds to second place (they were never entirely eliminated, as the history of Zapatismo reveals) and where, later on, the return of land to the villages, and the curtailment of plantation expansion, stimulated renewed internal conflict, not bucolic harmony.[544] Communities thus combined 'individualist' and 'solidarist' tendencies and, depending on circumstances, one or other tendency might prevail. The feuding 'amoral familists' of yesterday could become the peasant guerrillas of today, but equally, there was no guarantee that guerrilla solidarity might not give way to 'amoral familism' again tomorrow. After all, post-revolutionary peasantries, beneficiaries of land distribution, have been noted more for their social and political quiescence (even 'petty bourgeois' conservatism) than for their corporate revolutionary commitment: witness nineteenth-century France and twentieth-century Bolivia.[545] To talk of peasant solidarity, therefore, is not to imply a *gemeinschaftlich* idyll, nor to impute timeless, inherent characteristics.

It is nevertheless the case that, in Mexico as elsewhere, corporate village structures, seen by some as divisive and inhibiting factors, were often of vital importance in providing modes of organisation and protest. Here, I do not refer simply to *formally* corporate or communal structures (communal land tenure, civil/religious hierarchies, the *cofradías* and *barrio* organisations beloved of anthropologists, the importance of all of which varied from place to place), but also to the *informal* solidarity generated within peasant society, despite internal divisions, by the logic of subsistence agriculture and the presence of external threats, which in turn led to forms of collective action undertaken by the community, rather than by (say) occupational associations.[546] And such action was not confined to the classically corporate, Indian village of the centre/south, it was evident, too, in white–mestizo communities elsewhere, such as Tomóchic, Bachíniva, or Palomas. For there is no doubt that the peasant community, for all its internal divisions, possessed resources which could be mobilised for resistance. Traditional village leaders served as the mentors of popular rebellion, village 'intellectuals' as ideological spokesmen.[547] In the sierra, caciques like De la Rocha (Sin.), Lucas (Pue.) or the Mapache leader Castañón captained vigorous popular movements (as 'Che' Gómez did in the lowlands of Tehuantepec). The elders of the villages of Morelos exercised a controlling influence over the Zapatista revolt; the Cedillos, *rancheros* of Palomas, led a powerful, sustained agrarian rebellion in San Luis.

This leadership was local and home-grown. As such, it may be analysed in terms of Weber's notion of 'traditional' authority,[548] and, as such, it both exemplified and helped shape the character of the popular movement, which thereby differed in important respects from a movement led by some exo-genous 'vanguard', such as a Communist party. The prominent role of local, traditional leadership indicated both the weakness, in Mexico, of any such potential vanguard (not only was there no CP; there was also no liberal/nationalist/bourgeois vanguard capable of mobilising the peasantry behind a coherent party), and also the continued vigour and legitimacy of such leadership throughout the country. The *serrano* caciques and village elders had not, in other words, gone the way of China's contemporaneous scholar-gentry and squandered their moral and political capital.[549]

At the same time, traditional leadership went with and reinforced a 'traditional' ideology. Peasant revolt was certainly not 'non-ideological', it did not (indeed, could not) lack political ideas and a broad, normative vision which informed its action, nor, by the same token, can it be said to have been 'pre-political', if that somewhat patronising yet popular term denotes an inability to grasp political realities and conceive of ideological alternatives to reality.[550] The Mexican peasantry did not, it is true, cleave to socialism, or form mass parties led by well-organised political cadres (or captained by Popkin's 'political entrepreneurs'). If such actions are the hallmark of 'poli-tics', then the Mexican peasantry, along with the numberless multitude which also fall into this promiscuous category, was indeed 'pre-political'.[551] But in no sense was this (or probably any other peasantry) apolitical. Aristotle, of course, was nearer the truth in seeing man as generically political, while Gramsci's emphasis upon the universality of ideological attributes among all classes (and, I would go further, of the role of 'organic intellectuals' within classes, the peasantry included) is apposite in the case of Mexico popular protest.[552]

But the peasantry's reliance on traditional authority (rather than modern party cadres) and on its own 'organic intellectuals' (rather than the party ideologies and organisers whom Gramsci had in mind) had important consequences for the popular movement. Traditional authority could stifle as well as canalise sentiments of popular rebellion (needless to say, modern party cadres are not blameless in this regard either: some Communist parties have proved adept at stifling popular protest). Thus, caciques could represent and mobilise but they could also control and repress. Parish priests, following an ancient tradition, could sometimes act as allies and spokesmen of popular revolt, sometimes (as revolutionary orthodoxy would have it) as the loyal partners of landlords and political bosses.[553] Traditional authority – cacical, clerical, corporate – was therefore inherently ambivalent; like those forms of nineteenth-century religious dissent analysed by E. P. Thompson, it could both foment and suffocate popular protest.[554] But, in the decade 1910–20 (and especially 1910–15), when 'objective' conditions made for revolt rather

than quiescence, such authority frequently provided the necessary organisation and inspiration for rebellion. And, in the absence (at least until late in
the Revolution) of an exogenous alternative, of any 'modern' political mobilisation, this was a crucial role. Conversely, where such authority was weak or
absent – among the debt-peons of the south or the artisans of the Bajío –
protest was more sporadic, anarchic and aimless. It will also be noted that
popular movements which outgrew and sloughed off this traditional, organisational carapace, risked going the same way: Villismo was a major example.

Peasant revolt, under such traditional leadership, displayed characteristics
familiar in other, comparable historical contexts. It was parochial, lacking a
national vision, and it was here that the 'outside agitators', so keenly seized
upon by contemporary landlords as well as by latter-day sociologists, could
play a valuable role, as Magaña did for Zapatismo – not in generating political
awareness, which already existed, but rather in 'provid[ing] the power,
assistance and supralocal organisation that helps peasants *act*'.[555] In addition,
the ideological accoutrements of traditional authority, or of the 'organic
intellectuals' of the insurgent peasantry, were antique and motley. This made
them nonetheless revolutionary, for garbled and archaic ideas, if sufficiently
powerful and appropriate, can still serve in the overthrow of regimes. As
Lawrence Stone has observed concerning the ideas and myths of the English
Revolution:[556]

the fact that these notions were cast in an antiquarian mold does nothing to alter one
way or another the degree of radicalism or conservatism which they represent. This
must be judged against the contemporary situation and it makes no difference
whatever whether the idealised Golden Age is in the past or in the future. All that
matters is the degree to which the vision differs from the reality of the present.

Clearly, Stone goes too far: the distinction between 'pro-active' and 'reactive'
protest, between forms of protest which are innovative and forward-looking on
the one hand, and traditional and retrospective on the other, has already been
emphasised; but his central point – that either or both forms can be genuinely
revolutionary – is surely valid. And for that reason it would be wrong to deny
'reactive' peasant movements revolutionary status, as some commentators have
chosen to do.[557]

The point is worth making as there can be little doubt that, in Mexico as
elsewhere, peasant protest was generally backward-looking, nostalgic, and
'traditional' (though not 'apolitical', still less 'spontaneous', as often
alleged).[558] The ideology of protest, furthermore, was often vague, ostensibly
inconsistent and inarticulate. Some Mexican peasant movements, it is true,
displayed a veneer of more formal, sophisticated political thought: the 1869
Chalco revolt, led by the self-styled 'communist–socialist' Chávez López; the
rebellion led by Alberto Santa Fe ten years later at San Martín Texmelucán,
which has been seen as the 'apex in the development of nineteenth-century

agrarian revolutionary ideology'.[559] Both movements were influenced by Anarchist thought, both enjoyed links with urban radical groups and both occurred in regions east of Mexico City where, both then and later during the Revolution, urban, working-class and rural peasant protest interacted to a greater extent than elsewhere. But it would be wrong to contrast these unusually articulate revolts too starkly with those 'which articulated little and merely resulted in land seizure'.[560] First, formal manifestos, cataloguing the abuses of governments and landlords, prescribing remedies, and embracing certain general political ideas, were not uncommon: they emerged from Olarte's revolt (Papantla, 1836), that of Eleuterio Quiroz (Sierra Gorda, 1847–9) and Lozada's prolonged insurrection (Tepic, 1857–81).[561] They came thick and fast again after 1910, following established patterns and formulae, written up by the *tinterillos* who served the leaders of the Revolution. Secondly, the relative absence (or occasional presence) of clear-cut, committed ideological statements should not be regarded as so important anyway. To an extent, these may have depended on the vagaries of individual leadership (or the even greater vagaries of archival preservation). Ostensibly mute, inglorious rebellions may have been badly served by their *tinterillos*, or simply suffered the loss of their documentation; in practice, they may not have differed much from their more articulate and sophisticated cousins.[562] Certainly, one must be cautious about dismissing them as mindless jacqueries.

Furthermore, the absence of formal, rigorous ideology did not render peasant revolt non-ideological, or intellectually inert (if it did, consider how many middle or working-class political movements would fall into the same category). In Mexico as elsewhere, peasant grievances tended to be specific, local, concrete, and judged against some retrospective norm.[563] But this clearly did not make peasant demands 'apolitical' (the relation of political power to, say, agrarian grievances was all too clear). Equally, peasant protest was rarely 'spontaneous' (as I understand the term): more often it derived from longstanding disputes, which may have undergone years of litigation before breaking out into violence. Communities with histories of protest through the 1880s, 1890s and 1900s soon came to the fore after 1910, and local people were often thereby able to predict the incidence of revolt and quiescence in the neighbourhood. And plans and petitions (the latter perhaps the best source of peasant grievances) made up in moral outrage and invective what they lacked in formal ideological exegesis: denunciations of Díaz (or lesser tyrants and traitors), assertions of communal rights, invocations of both abstract principles of justice and concrete historical precedents. It was the task of the 'village intellectual' precisely to articulate these rights, proclaim these principles, and recall these precedents, and all, to a significant extent, were built upon the bedrock of the moral economy, after the manner of popular demands elsewhere.[564]

Formal ideologies – liberal, socialist, anarchist – were rarely invoked, though they filtered through, glossed, bowdlerised and conflated. Zapatismo, though later tinged by anarcho-syndicalism, drew principally upon traditional liberal and patriotic ideas, and had no difficulty in reconciling these with rural Catholicism. Many popular rebellions displayed a similar liberal, patriotic lineage: they harked back to Morelos, Hidalgo and Juárez, quoted liberal aphorisms, and recalled the heroic struggles against the nineteenth-century conservatives and their French allies. Again, there were abundant precedents: Julio López, Hart's 'communist-socialist', stridently proclaimed himself 'a true liberal (and) a true patriot' and 'a faithful defender of the Constitution'; 'Independence, Liberty and Nation' was the slogan of his rebellion.[565] Perhaps he sought ideological respectability but, more likely, it was his enemies who, denouncing him as a 'rabid socialist', traduced the record.[566] Not for the first time, perhaps, radical historians have been taken in by the scare-mongering of an earlier generation of conservatives.[567]

The practice of popular rebellion was also redolent of liberalism – of the 'secular ritual' which paralleled the rites of the Church.[568] Victorious rebels would parade in the plaza, paying homage at the foot of the statue of Hidalgo or Juárez; street names would be changed, the pictures on the walls of the *ayuntamiento* replaced, and liberal and patriotic anniversaries would be fervently commemorated, with the resident intellectual or orator declaiming from the bandstand. We are reminded again, therefore, of the pervasive appeal of liberal and patriotic ideas and symbols in Porfirian and revolutionary Mexico, an appeal which embraced peasants, workers, middle class and elite. Liberalism in particular was sufficiently elastic to accommodate different, often antagonistic classes. As recent Marxist scholarship has tended to emphasise, class and ideology do not necessarily effect neat, one-to-one fits (liberal bourgeoisie, socialist proletariat and so on).[569] But the belated realisation that ideology is more than a mere superstructural passenger upon the relations of production does not warrant a retreat into the vapid idealism of discourse theory. Ideology is relatively, not wholly autonomous; it is (as I have stressed) important, but not paramount; above all, it can no more be successfully analysed *in vacuo* than can the relations of production, whose pre-eminent role it has tended to usurp. Idealism is no improvement upon crude economic determinism. Obviously (to the historian, at any rate) ideology and class relations must be studied in unison.[570]

Such is the case with Mexican liberalism which, while it afforded a large section of the peasantry the closest it possessed to a formal ideology, also informed Científico, working-class and later 'revolutionary' thinking and practice.[571] Liberalism, which sanctioned attacks on peasant rights in the name of progress and the market, also legitimised consequent peasant protest with the invocation of liberal heroes, liberal traditions, and liberal principles of constitutional rule.[572] Perhaps this indicated the lamentable 'false consciousness' of the peasantry: but, not only do I doubt whether peasant consciousness was either false or lamentable; more important, I doubt whether historians should presume to rewrite historical scripts, prompting the actors and imposing new, preferred roles upon them.[573] History, as we have been reminded, is what 'happened to happen', not what we would have liked to have happened.[574] Patriotism and nationalism displayed a similar elasticity. Again, a congeries of ideas and symbols pervaded different social groups, affording ideological sanction for a variety of (often conflicting) policies and modes of behaviour. While traditional patriotism, for example, co-existed happily enough with Catholicism (both found expression in the ubiquitous Virgin of Guadalupe)[575] the revolutionary nationalism of the late 1910s and 1920s went to war against the Church, which it conceived as a threat to the claims of the nation state. Patriotism or nationalism figured within the 'discourse' of Porfirismo, Maderismo, Huertismo, Zapatismo and Carrancismo – all socially and politically distinct movements. Historical actors did not follow consistent ideological principle: any analysis which imagines that they did, which focusses excessively on the level of ideas and 'discourses', or which engages in the facile task of compiling ideological genealogies, is bound to err.[576] But that is not to deny the importance of ideology, whether in the realm of Científico developmentalism, Maderista politicking, or Zapatista revolt.

On the contrary: in the context of the present discussion, ideology – along with organisation – was of great significance in the gestation of peasant revolt. Peasant participation in the revolution depended heavily on the capacity for organisation and on the articulation of common interests and aims (to an extent it might not matter whether these were couched in liberal, Catholic, anarchist, or whatever hybrid terms). As Tilly has noted, rebels required a 'common lore, grievances, and political experience', successful revolts were underwritten by an evident 'solidarity and articulated interest'.[577] Barrington Moore likewise has stressed the importance of organisation and the moral support which this engenders.[578] In Mexico, the village – for all its internal divisions – faced sustained, sometimes lethal threats; the shared plight of the villagers bred solidarity and varied forms of resistance, non-violent and violent. Ultimately, bereft of clientelist patronage or political alternatives, the village looked to its own, internal resources for ideological expression and military organisation. Thus, when rebellion seemed feasible (when the 'calculus of force' looked more favourable),[579] it was the village which formed the cell of revolution, and the moral economy of the peasant which gave it its normative basis.

The corollary of this argument is that the importance of 'objective', especially quantifiable, economic factors can easily be exaggerated. Yet many standard analyses of the Mexican Revolution focus on precisely these factors. In doing so, I believe, they fall into the common error of believing that 'popular radicalism can be encompassed in cost-of-living series'.[580] Such raw economic data (where they are available) are certainly important, the broad economic trends which they encapsulate were intimately bound up with popular protest, but such protest can only be analysed through the mediation of social and political factors, which are often neglected. Different analysts have come up with different explanatory keys of this kind: at one extreme, a supposed secular decline in living standards since 1810; at the other, the 1907 recession and the bad harvests of 1908–9.[581] But, as already suggested, these are not convincing arguments. The crucial period for analysis is neither a century, nor a couple of years, but rather the generational span of the Porfiriato. And this span is crucial not only because of the economic changes which then affected the countryside, but also because these changes were widely regarded as illegitimate. Protest and revolt did not correlate neatly with deteriorating objective conditions or increasing, quantifiable rates of exploitation (as measured, for example, in real wage rates). Subjective considerations of justice and legitimacy were also involved (so too, it goes without saying, were considerations of feasibility, the end result of the 'calculus of force'); these subjective considerations determined the targets as well as the timing of popular protest and, without them, protest could not get off the ground.[582] Schematically, it could be said that revolt possessed an economic, an organisational and a moral dimension: it occurred not just when times were bad, and when resistance seemed worth a try, but also when the badness of the times engendered a kind of moral outrage leading to resistance. In such a scenario, revolt could even occur when the calculable chances of success were very limited and when, if participants behaved predictably as 'rational peasants', passivity might have been expected.[583] Equally, there were many cases of passivity when revolt was feasible.

This is to broach the question of legitimacy. In Mexico as in most of the world, conditions had never been easy for the mass of the people. But, in Mexico as elsewhere, conditions of poverty and powerlessness had been tolerated, sometimes in situations where resistance *was* possible.[584] Skocpol also points to the antithesis: 'even after great loss of legitimacy has occurred a state can remain quite stable – and certainly invulnerable to internal, mass-based revolts – especially if its coercive organisations remain coherent and effective'.[585] In fact, these antithetical cases are probably rare (South Africa is a valid, but exceptional example)[586] and Porfirian Mexico is patently a contradictory case, even if one notes how decrepit the Porfirian régime's 'coercive organisations' had become by 1910. More than Skocpol cares to admit, I believe, states (and structures of authority more generally) depend for their survival on more than coercion; and, while it may not be easy empirically to unravel where and why men are coerced into obedience and where and why they are not, I would agree with Scott, Moore and others who see 'issues of compliance and legitimacy [as] analytically distinct'.[587] In other words, there is a factor making for the stability of states and systems of authority over and

above coercion and the compliance which it compels: some may choose to follow
Weber and talk of legitimacy; some may prefer to talk in terms of 'consensus',
'false consciousness', 'mechanical and organic solidarity', or 'ideological
hegemony'. These are all perspectives on the same problem, and explanations
of an ancient phenomenon, what Hume called 'the easiness with which the
many are governed by the few; and the implicit submission with which men
resign their own sentiments and passions to those of their rulers'.[588] Conversely, each school has its chosen antithesis: ideological or hegemonic crisis,
crisis of legitimation, breakdown of consensus, dissolution of the social
contract. The year 1910 was one of these. To understand its significance, the
historian must ask, not simply 'why men rebel', but also 'why men obey'.

Under Díaz, poverty and powerlessness increased. The mass of the people
grew poorer (certainly after the mid-1890s) and their capacity to influence
events, never great, became even more exiguous. But for this process to
culminate in rebellion, it had not only to be accompanied by tactical
opportunities for protest and revolt, but had also to engender deep feelings of
injustice and outrage. Such feelings were subjective, were conditioned by
particular circumstances, and cannot be reduced to 'relative deprivation' (or
the more specific and supposedly appropriate variant, 'decremental deprivation') according to some neat formulation.[589] Poverty and oppression might
be old, familiar afflictions, but in some circumstances they were perceived as
particularly gratuitous and offensive: not necessarily where they were most
acute, but rather where rulers were demonstrably indifferent to their subjects,
where abuses lacked any apparent justification, where, in Barrington Moore's
words, subjects faced 'violent and capricious interference in their daily lives'
and concluded that they were getting a 'raw deal'.[590] It was not exploitation
per se, but ostensibly new, arbitrary, unjustified exploitation which provoked
resistance. Parallels abound, from Vietnam to East Africa.[591] Closer home,
Nelson Reed's comment on the origins of the Caste War bears repetition:
'what was dangerous was not long oppression but sudden acculturation, the
forced march from one world to another'.[592]

Yucatán, in this respect, afforded a massive and ominous premonition of the
1910 Revolution. And, as Reed's metaphor suggests, it was traumatic changes
in status, rather than progressive, economic immiseration, which stimulated
revolt.[593] It was not simply that wages fell or rents rose in Porfirian Mexico: it
was rather that once-independent villagers and smallholders now found
themselves in pawn to the hacienda or under the heel of the cacique; thereby
they lost both the autonomy they had formerly enjoyed, and the basic security
afforded by possession of the means of production. They were forced across the
threshold from independent peasant to dependent peon status.[594] And, even
where this resulted (as occasionally it did) in better material rewards, these did
not necessarily compensate for the psychological penalties.[595]

Thus, by 1910, protests against the twin processes of agrarian commercialisation and political centralisation were sufficiently profound and widespread to convert a summons to political revolt into the tocsin of social revolution. Porfirian policy had served to generalise such protests, while disregarding (in the main) forms of paternalist appeasement. Hence the legitimacy of the old order was spent. The people of Bocoyna queried the benefits of 'progress', recently thrust upon them; the people of Chihuahua as a whole denounced – not ancient tyrannies – but rather the 'fever of reforms' let loose by the Creel–Terrazas regime.[596] By 1910, similar denunciations of lesser caciques were common, in Chihuahua and elsewhere. In Morelos, the paternalistic rule of Alarcón had given way to the unthinking administration of Pablo ('let-them-farm-in-a-flowerpot') Escandón.[597] Plantation agriculture continued apace, but where Alarcón had wisely placated, Escandón wantonly provoked. Often, as we have noted, the lofty contempt of the likes of Escandón carried strong racialist overtones, reminiscent of colonial attitudes. Now, racialism justified not paternalistic supervision but rational economic exploitation, and considerations of social stability took second place to profit-maximisation. Hence landlord aphorisms: peons are machines that run on *pulque*; Indians only hear through their backsides; hence, too, the proposed genocide of the Yaqui nation. And such attitudes, reinforced by positivist education, were by no means confined to the agrarian elite.[598] The result, for a large section of the peasantry, was harsher, dehumanising treatment, and the ultimate justifying goal (for exploitation, like war, is usually validated by some grand design, loftily moral rather than basely monetary) was 'progress', the leitmotiv of Porfirian landlords and *políticos* alike.

These, the dominant ideas of Mexico's 'modernising elite', can be recovered and examined, since that elite was literate and articulate and the material consequences of its policies in the countryside can also be described, even quantified (hectares expropriated, real wages depressed). As for the *campesinos*, their reaction can be assessed – at least partially and with difficulty – in the sporadic revolts which punctuated the Porfiriato, and in the great coalescence of popular protest which came after 1910. This (in part because of the difficulty) historians have increasingly neglected. But what is even harder to penetrate is the *campesino* mentality: the psychological reaction to changes in status; the manner in which (as I have suggested) mounting injustice generated moral outrage. Conventional history and memoir largely neglect these crucial but intangible issues. It may be inferred that the well-documented attitudes of the elite (contemptuous, racialist, dogmatic, authoritarian) at the very least exacerbated growing material deprivation; but some social psychologists would go further and suggest that 'expressive' concerns for status and self-respect and esteem are even more fundamental, and thus capable of provoking resentment when they are infringed.[599] Oral accounts are certainly suggestive of such resentment: against harsh overseers (Spaniards especially), racial contempt, sexual abuse, the power of the hacienda to hire and fire at will, the loss of personal independence associated with the loss of land.[600] Warman's interlocutors from Morelos:[601]

remember the [hacienda] administrators and Uncle Tom employees [*empleados serviles*] with disgust. They have never forgotten the injustice in which they lived and they talk articulately about the despoliation and exploitation to which they were subjected. For most of them the revolution was an inevitable process.

By way of analogy, it may be worth recalling the non-material grievances which, as Anderson has shown, carried weight with the urban workers: treatment which denied them their humanity, ignored their complaints, and hedged them about with arbitrary restrictions.[602] And it was precisely the more 'traditional', 'paternalist' industrialists (rather than, say, the new foreign corporations) who, by cleaving to their old interventionist and coercive attitudes while at the same time reacting to the strict discipline of the market, were most responsible for creating such grievances. Thus, as in nineteenth-century German industry, worker militancy sprang more from the market-induced breakdown and distortion of an older, 'paternalistic' order, than from the creation *de novo* of classic, capitalist enterprises.[603] And the Porfirian countryside – even more than the towns – was the scene of a massive breakdown and distortion of this kind, as the market impinged upon a powerful, entrenched landlord class, and a peasantry endowed (to varying degrees) with corporate solidarity, capacity for resistance, and a vigorous alternative moral vision.

Over the years, therefore, the rulers of Porfirian Mexico had undermined the legitimacy upon which (in default of a large, efficient repressive apparatus) they depended. This was revealed, suddenly and surprisingly, in 1910. Landlord–*políticos* like Terrazas found themselves helpless, fearful of arming the *campesinos* whose fathers had been faithful retainers. Others were shocked by the transformation of deferential peons into (as they saw it) bloodthirsty savages: and, though the transformation was often mythologised and embellished, it contained some real truth, as the people of Ometepec or the Cicerol family of Catmis found to their cost.[604] Elsewhere – in much of the south, for example – caciques and landlords still ruled, and clearly did not rule by fear alone. The same was true even in some regions affected by Zapatismo: the hacienda of San Felipe del Progreso, for example, run by conscientious landlords who combined profit-maximisation with the maintenance of 'traditional obligations' towards their peons, survived the Revolution without internal upheaval.[605]

It is impossible – and somewhat pointless – to establish which was the norm: Ometepec or San Felipe, revolt or quiescence. The indisputable fact is that the loss of legitimacy of the old regime, and of its chief actors and beneficiaries, was sufficiently serious and extensive to bring about its overthrow and to open the way to a genuine popular revolution. And, just as 'psychological' or 'moral' factors played their part in the gestation of revolution, so, as we shall see, the revolution embodied important 'moral' or 'psychological' or 'expressive' dimensions – elements, one could say, of 'the world turned upside down.'[606] Adherents of the old order were not just ousted, they were also humiliated. Old, deferential habits gave way to a new, plebeian insolence. And the rise to power of popular leaders gratified their peasant followers even as it appalled the well-to-do.[607] It is as necessary, though often as difficult, to grasp this 'psychological' aspect of the process of Revolution, as it is to appreciate the analogous 'psychological' factors which went into its creation.

The 1910 revolution was not presaged (as some simplistic theories of revolution would have it) by mounting premonitory symptoms: there was no cumulative fever leading to a revolutionary outbreak.[608] If anything, the incidence of popular rebellion was less in the 1900s than it had been early in the Porfiriato, the PLM revolts of 1906 and 1908 had been easily quashed, and neither Cananea nor Río Blanco were genuine symptoms of mounting popular insurgence. Hence the constant assertions – by opponents as well as supporters of the Díaz regime – that revolution was impossible.[609] But, despite its ostensible solidarity, the regime was something of a hollow shell. What legitimacy it had once enjoyed had been squandered, and it had not acquired a military capacity sufficient to offset this loss. When the opportunity for rebellion was afforded by Madero's political campaign and call to arms (a purely endogenous factor, we should note: the Revolution was not initiated by war or international crisis, regrettable though this may be for some analysts)[610] then the accumulated resentments of a generation flooded out, unchecked by barriers of deference. Hence the political crisis of 1909–10 led logically to the social crisis of 1910–15. Thereafter, pending the creation of new forms of legitimacy (or ideological hegemony, or consensus, or a renewed social contract) *force majeure* would prevail. That was what the Revolution was all about.

Yet the final outcome of the Revolution (which may be briefly anticipated here) revealed a fundamental paradox. Over time, the Revolution displayed a fickle propensity for rewarding late-comers and lukewarm adherents (and even some downright opponents), while spurning many of its pioneer supporters. The popular elements which contributed most to the overthrow not just of Díaz but of the entire Porfirian order came from threatened and declining groups, the casualties of Porfirian economic and political development: first, the *agrarista* peasantry, the villagers, sharecroppers and smallholders who had suffered from the rapacity of *hacendado*, *ranchero* and *cacique*; second, the *serranos* who, besides facing economic hardship, unemployment and, in some cases, agrarian dispossession, rebelled in defence of their freedom and independence and in opposition to Porfirian *caciquismo* and centralisation; third (much less important, but worthy of mention) the urban artisans, whose progressive immiseration drove them not towards unionisation and 'economism' but rather towards sporadic collective violence, and occasional, individual revolutionary commitment. These groups, and in particular the first two, provided the rank-and-file of the Revolution and ensured that it would be a rural revolution, and in many instances an agrarian revolution, in which the struggle over land and water was central.

Conversely, there were groups unable or unwilling to chance a revolutionary commitment: in the countryside, the resident peons on the great estates, and the debt-peons of the southern plantations (who, to varying degrees, were held in check by bonds of coercion or clientelism); in the towns, cities and larger mining camps, the industrial proletariat, who showed little inclination to play the role of a revolutionary vanguard. Yet, so far as the common people were concerned, it was this last group who would become the chief beneficiaries of the Revolution, while those who took up arms and shed their blood usually received few — or at best belated — rewards for their efforts. For, if the Revolution depended essentially on the mass support of declining, threatened, 'traditional' groups, it was itself a powerful engine of continued modernisation and development: it accelerated the very processes which its pioneer, popular supporters sought to resist. Cronos devoured his children; the Revolution swallowed up its progenitors.

4

𒁹𒁹𒁹

The Madero revolution

The focus now shifts away from structures, processes, and grand comparisons; narrative supplants analysis; *l'histoire événementielle* takes over. But, in order to explain events, it will be necessary to refer back to previous generalisations, while the latter depend for their valdity on the empirical evidence presented here.

On 3 November 1910 a young Mexican, accused of murdering a woman, was dragged from gaol in Rock Springs, Texas, and killed at the hands of a lynch-mob; this incident provoked demonstrations and anti-American attacks in the cities of Mexico, which immediately preceded (and which, some say, were causally linked to) the revolution which began later in the month. Anderson is no doubt correct to see these events as indicative of the *inquietud* then prevailing in Mexico; there had been comparable ugly incidents in the past which had failed to provoke such a strong reaction.[1] But now, in the wake of the Anti-Re-electionist campaign, the fraudulent elections, and Madero's call to arms, the Rodríguez killing assumed national political significance and was seized upon by the disgruntled opposition. The demonstrators, the American Ambassador believed, were anti-Díaz rather than anti-American; domestic political motives were similarly detected at Tampico; and the targets of the mobs included governmental institutions such as *El Imparcial*.[2] Thus, while issuing reassurances to the US, the regime could not let itself be outflanked by the patriots in the streets. In some towns the authorities tolerated or even connived at anti-American demonstrations (at Guadalajara the police were reported to have been 'pointing out to the mob the residences of Americans and helping to gather stones to throw'), and the official press vied with the opposition, which included the Catholic *El País*, in denouncing the US.[3]

Certainly these events reflected the *inquietud* of the times (it is significant that in a stable, conservative city like Oaxaca the authorities wasted no time and showed no compunction about halting the protest at its inception), but their connection with the imminent armed revolution is tenuous.[4] They were certainly not symptoms of a mounting fever that was to culminate in a catharsis of popular, xenophobic rebellion. The preferred victims in 1910 (as in subsequent anti-American outbreaks) were the official representatives of the US Government or, occasionally, symbols of *Yanqui* culture and religion, but not American economic interests.[5] Thus, consulate flags were pulled down, the premises of the *Mexican Herald* were stoned, and in Guadalajara the mob attacked the Methodist College.[6] Yet Sonora, host to heavy US investment, was free from anti-American outbursts, while at Monterrey, the Consul-General reported, 'nothing but the most cordial relations, perfect quiet and good order prevail'.[7] The most serious troubles occurred in the capital and in Guadalajara, a seat not of American investment but of strong Catholic opinion and of a vocal middle class which had already distinguished itself in the anti-Díaz politicking of the previous year. Only among Mexico's railwaymen was there a genuinely 'economic' anti-Americanism which contributed to the November protests.[8] Otherwise, the overwhelming feature of the protesters was their urban middle-class (often student) origin. Students organised a major demonstration in Guadalajara, they joined with the railwaymen in San Luis, and 'university students, small shopmen and the better class of artisans' were prominent in the Mexico City riots.[9] Not only did such literate, urban groups comprise the classic 'nationalist' constituency, nurtured in the secular schools of the Porfiriato; they were also the main source of the civilian opposition of 1908–9 which, repulsed in its electoral confrontation with the regime, now sought to attack by more circuitous routes.

But such groups were not the stuff of armed revolution. Their protests were easily contained (especially where the authorities sought to contain rather than to connive), the current issue soon faded and, above all, there was no resort to organised rebellion. The students went back to college, the artisans to their workshops. The November demonstrations were less the start of the Revolution than the last somewhat desperate fling of the old civilian opposition, already defeated. More significant, if less well-publicised, were the concurrent agrarian troubles in the Huasteca; the campaigns of the bandit/rebel Santañón in southern Veracruz, or the rebellion of Juan Cuamatzi in Tlaxcala (May 1910) which united peasants and 'peasant-workers' in armed opposition to the regime.[10] The Cuamatzi rebellion was crushed, and Santañón was soon to be hunted down, but their challenges to the regime anticipated both the style and the character of the Revolution more surely than the evanescent urban protests of early November.

FAILURE

This was not perceived at the time. Madero's political strength had been in the towns, and it was in the towns that he and his close collaborators placed their hopes, and that the summons to armed revolt had most immediate effect. Early on 18 November, two days before the scheduled uprising, the first shots of the Madero revolution were fired in the old colonial and industrial city of Puebla, east of the capital. A police detachment came to search the house of Aquiles Serdán (by trade a shoemaker, by family tradition a convinced liberal) and the occupants resisted; Miguel Cabrera, Governor Martínez's notorious police chief, died in the initial exchanges and, in the ensuing siege, the defenders were gradually picked off and finally compelled to surrender. No help came to the beleaguered household: the factory workers of the city, though tainted with Maderismo, made no move, and plans which the local Maderistas had made to attack the barracks and seize the strategic church towers of the city (throughout the Revolution churches were usually the key buildings in urban warfare) came to nothing. Serdán himself was captured and shot. [11]

On the banks of the Rio Grande Madero received the news tearfully, while in Puebla a broadsheet congratulated the dead Serdán on consigning to 'the bosom of all the devils the craven assassin . . . Miguel Cabrera'. [12] That Puebla was rid of its unpopular police chief, however, was small consolation for Maderista sympathisers, to whom it seemed that the swift repression of the Serdán conspiracy had nipped the revolution in the bud, leaving the Pax Porfiriana intact. [13] For Serdán's failure was replicated, less gloriously and bloodily, in other Mexican towns. The pre-emptive moves by the authorities which had forced Serdán into resistance scotched other Maderista plots. Would-be revolutionary leaders were arrested in Mexico City, Pachuca and Orizaba, and they included Alfredo Robles Domínguez, detailed by Madero to organise the rebellion in central Mexico. Documents found on prisoners supplied evidence – said the Mexico City press – of 'vast projects for overthrowing the present government'. [14]

But for the conspirators the truth was more prosaic. Abel Serratos, a travelling salesman, had been sent to rouse Orizaba in rebellion; arrested, roughed up, and sent to Mexico City, he was confronted by the chief of police (Díaz's nephew, Félix) and by his chief fellow-collaborator who broke down, 'fell to his knees and with tears in his eyes blamed [Serratos] for all the arms which had been bought'. [15] At Orizaba, meanwhile, there were further arrests and the strong Federal garrison easily beat off an attack on the barracks (indeed, the attack may have existed largely in the imagination of the commanding officer). [16] It was plausibly supposed that the local workers remembered the bloody events of four years before and had no taste for a second dose of Porfirian peace-keeping; thus, Maderista organisers who counted on armed working-class support were as disappointed at Orizaba as they had been at Puebla. [17]

The experience of Colmenares Ríos, Maderista and would-be revolutionary, was probably not untypical of these early days. Part of the same conspiratorial network as Serratos, Colmenares left Veracruz six days before the scheduled uprising, laden with copies of the Plan of San Luis, heading for a promised arms cache in the interior.[18] He learned of the arrest of his colleagues and, after a tortuous journey through the Puebla sierra, came to Orizaba, where he found the workers in disarray rather than open rebellion. So he continued south, heading for the hot lowlands of the Isthmus, where he had worked on the Tehuantepec Railway and thus knew the ground well. There he linked up with seventy disorganised, poorly-armed guerrillas operating among the plantations of Tabasco. But, for reasons already suggested, the plantation country of the south was unreceptive to revolution. Harried by superior Federal forces and decimated by desertions, the band dwindled to a score of disheartened men, and, after a final disastrous defeat, Colmenares decided to dissolve the group and return to Veracruz, a failed revolutionary. His mortification ('I am deeply pained and mortified' by failure, he declared) might have been less if he had been aware of how many fellow-Maderistas had faced the same predicament. Juan Martínez, for example, a village lawyer from Huejanapam and a confederate of Serdán, arrived at Puebla on 19 November, only to be told by the train conductor of yesterday's gun battle; he found himself a wanted man, his house was ransacked by the police, and he went into hiding, relinquishing revolutionary ambitions.[19] Others were less fortunate. Gerardo Rodríguez, a factory worker of Paso del Macho (Ver.), met with fellow-plotters on the evening of the 20th at the spot on the Mexican Railway where they proposed to hold up a night munitions train. But, as elsewhere, the authorities were tipped off, the tyro train-robbers were scattered, and Rodríguez, escaping to La Tejería, was there recognised and arrested.[20]

The roster of failed revolutionaries could be extended, but the point – that the repressive capabilities of the old Porfirian machine were by no means spent – is clear enough. Many plots were uncovered, their participants arrested; many rebellions were extinguished before the rebels could acquire sufficient men, arms, or territorial security – the guerrilla *focos* of modern theory. The high incidence of failure among these early, largely city-based uprisings meant that many of Madero's political collaborators were now *hors de combat*. Some, like Crescencio Jiménez of the Yucatán Anti-Re-electionist junta, had been behind bars since the Porfirian crackdown in the summer of 1910; they were now joined by key men like Robles Domínguez and José Inocencio Lugo, Maderista 'general co-ordinator' in the state of Guerrero.[21] Others, like Colmenares Ríos, found the path of revolution a *via dolorosa*, and yet others feared to tread it at all. The punctilious Maderistas of Morelia, led by an engineer, planned a coup for the spring of 1911, but, as the countryside around began to pullulate with rebellion, Morelia itself remained politically inert, a 'quiet, deaf-mute city', unresponsive to Maderista agitation. And the Maderistas declined to sally out into the barbarous countryside, preferring to await official endorsement from Madero in the north for, without it, they feared, they would constitute simply 'an armed faction which might be taken for banditry'.[22] There were similarly inactive Maderistas in Guanajuato and

Mexico City too, while in Puebla, after the death of Serdán, Lic. Felipe Contreras performed the sort of services to the cause which all too many Maderistas found congenial:[23]

during the development [of the revolution] Sr Contreras did not cease making propaganda among the middle and upper classes. He wrote energetic, reasoned articles against the dictatorship in the independent press and on the day when the armistice was reached . . . or a little before he wrote a notable article in which he called for the resignation of General Díaz. This is a sketch of his work for the revolution.

The successful rebels of 1910–11, of course, did not spend their time penning elegant articles, they did not await official endorsement from the north, and they did not worry about acquiring criminal reputations – many had them already. In contrast, the doctors, lawyers, engineers and chemists who had staffed the Anti-Re-electionist Party made poor revolutionaries, particularly once the failure of the original urban strategy made it clear that the revolution would be rural or it would be nothing. These – the 'Platonic revolutionaries', as the Governor of Chihuahua called them – were inhibited by ties of business and family (not only were they respectable, they were often middle-aged too); they were quite right to doubt their own ability as *guerrilleros*.[24] As a result, their revolution-by-the-rulebook was soon super-seded by more aggressive, popular outbreaks in the countryside, where alternative forms of collective protest, based on old grievances and traditions of resistance, were more feasible. It was time for the common people of the countryside – like Gulliver pinioned by the ligatures of the Lilliputians – to stir, break their bonds, and discover the extent of their new power.

THE FIRST *FOCO*

This is apparent if we turn to the areas of successful insurrection in the closing months of 1910, to the pioneer regions of the Mexican Revolution. These were concentrated in the mountain districts of western Chihuahua and Durango, and the Laguna country on the Durango/Coahuila borders – regions where Maderista organisers had not anticipated great success.[25] Here, too, the urban strategy had been tried and had failed. Two hundred men attacked and briefly held the Laguna town of Gómez Palacio before being driven into the hills; Parral was subjected to a bloody, abortive attack. At once, Federal comman-ders adopted a policy of shooting prisoners, and at Lerdo there was some critical comment when rebel corpses were left to rot in the city park, by way of example.[26]

Thereafter the success of the rebels stemmed from their adoption of a rural strategy. Not that this was a calculated option, rather, it responded to the immediate force of circumstances (comparisons might be made with Mao's odyssey to Yenan, or Castro's taking to the Sierra Maestra) and to the social and geographical origins of the northern rebel leaders and their followers. In Chihuahua, the mountains and foothills of the Sierra Madre provided the cradle of the Maderista revolution, and the revolutionaries were products of tough, troublesome *serrano* communities. The outstanding leader in 1910–11 was Pascual Orozco, a tall, powerful, taciturn young man (he was barely thirty) who came from the rebellious district of Guerrero, west of the state capital. Orozco had 'sprung from sturdy, middle-class, farmer folk' and he and his family enjoyed some status in the locality. But he differed from the middle-class Maderistas of the cities: he was barely literate, his father – though a minor office-holder and would-be *político* – had run a village store, and Pascual's own reputation was that of an honest and capable *arriero*, in which capacity he would have known the mountain trails intimately.[27] When the Maderista organiser in the state – the well-to-do philosopher–farmer Abraham González – set about recruiting in 1910, he approached Orozco, who was known to harbour anti-government sentiments. But Orozco's resentments were directed less against Díaz, in distant Mexico City, than against Joaquín Chávez, the longstanding cacique of the Guerrero district, client of Terrazas, and Orozco's rival in the local freight business, hence, when introduced to González, Orozco pledged his support in order 'to liberate the district of Guerrero from the cacique . . . Don Joaquín Chávez'.[28] Private grudges merged with political discontent, and one of Orozco's first actions, as his forces began to mop up the small mountain villages along the North-Western Railway, was to ransack Chávez's house at San Isidro.

Near the American border, meanwhile, Toribio Ortega led the villagers of Cuchillo Parado (a traditionally liberal *pueblo*) in revolt and González, the nominal Maderista commander in the state, joined up with the young Protestant academic Braulio Hernández. These two were a cut above the average rebel leader, they were 'much respected citizens', according to an American report, but the forces they assembled in the Ojinaga district, numbering a thousand by Christmas, were typical 'mountaineers', men 'who know every trail over the mountains in which they are located'.[29] Deep in the Sierra Madre itself, José de la Luz Blanco 'pronounced' near the old trouble spot of Temosáchic, where he counted on a good deal of local (including some Indian) support, while Cástulo Herrera was deputed to lead the revolution on the 'red altiplano' of San Andrés.[30] Herrera's lieutenants, however, included Pancho Villa, who readily effected the conversion from sierra drifter and bandit to revolutionary *guerrillero* (days before, he had been raiding the environs of Parral), and who soon led upwards of 300 men, recruited without much difficulty from the villages around San Andrés. Herrera's authority over this burgeoning force, never strong, faded as Villa established himself as the ranking rebel leader of the district, scouring the local ranches for arms, and linking with Orozco to resist the Federal advance into the sierra in mid-December.[31] Meantime, Tomás Urbina, an illiterate peon-turned-bandit and crony of Villa, separated from Herrera's command and headed south into western Durango, capturing the small villages and mining towns – Inde, Guanaceví, El Oro – his efforts seconded by recruits from the Tarahumara and Tepehuanes Indians.[32]

The Durango–Sinaloa mountains produced their own crop of revolutionaries – Domingo and Mariano Arrieta, Conrado Antuna, Pedro Chaides, Ramón Iturbe. The Arrietas, who were to play a major role in the years to come, were *rancheros* of some local repute but little wealth or education: Mariano, an illiterate, farmed at Vascogil, while Domingo, like Orozco, was an ex-*arriero*; both happily admitted that they were neither 'learned thinkers nor . . . profound moralists'.[33] Iturbe was of different stamp: a young man up from the Pacific coast (he had worked as a clerk in the Culiacán city gaol) he served his revolutionary apprenticeship in the sierra before descending to the lowlands of Sinaloa in the spring of 1911, by which time he had 2,000 men under his command and, for all his youth and previous obscurity, was thought to have 'accomplished more than Madero himself . . . [and might] be another Porfirio Díaz in embryo'.[34] And there were lesser *cabecillas*, too, whose names or origins remain uncertain. Also uncertain is the precise nature of their following. It is clear that recruits were readily made in sierra towns and villages like Temosáchic and Cd Guerrero, where there resided *gente muy revolucionaria*.[35] The contribution of Indian groups (discounted by many historians) was not insignificant. But the bulk of the forces of Villa, Orozco, and the Arrietas came from the white/mestizo population of the sierra communities: they were ranchers, peasant farmers, shepherds, muleteers and bandits. Many, it was pointed out, 'have not been men of fixed occupation in the past', hence classification by employment is difficult and probably inappropriate.[36] But, equally, large collective contingents were supplied by peasant communities like Cuchillo Parado and Bachíniva, and the longstanding agrarian grievances of certain of these communities lent the revolutionary movement as a whole – even in its northern, *serrano* form – a distinct, if not dominant, *agrarista* colouring. As the Governor of Chihuahua lamented in December, 'all the lower stratum of the people' were agitated by revolutionary appeals, which promised them 'public offices and the distribution of lands, cattle and wealth, on socialist lines'.[37]

Industrial workers (broadly defined) did not join the revolution in large numbers, save in exceptional circumstances. Not that they were hostile: in Chihuahua, a French engineer noted, 'the mine-workers, without joining (the revolutionaries) are nevertheless sympathetic to them'; cries of 'Viva Madero' and 'Muera Díaz' could be heard daily in the lumber camps of the high sierra.[38] But here, as elsewhere in the country, the miners did not rebel *en masse*, after the fashion of some peasant communities. The only major exception to this was the small, declining mining community of Aviño, which supplied a hundred men to the revolution in February 1911. But Aviño was run by an inept

Englishman 'of somewhat warm and excitable disposition', as even his compatriots admitted; he had antagonised the local people in various ways, not least by substituting payment in tokens for cash wages. Furthermore, as the recent history of the company showed, employment at Aviño was precarious and could not act as a disincentive to rebellion.[39] In the larger mining camps, where management tended to be more enlightened and employment both more secure and better paid, revolt was uncommon. Similarly, the people of the timber towns like Pearson and Madera were reckoned to be *gente tranquila*, 'fully dedicated to their work in a very peaceful manner'.[40]

Even without the armed support of the miners, the Maderista guerrillas soon converted the whole mountain chain stretching from the border down towards Tepic and Zacatecas into a zone of rebel dominance, where Federal power rapidly wilted and withdrew. By December, the Chihuahuan rebels were 'masters of the sierra, where they find a refuge from San Andrés to Ciudad Guerrero'; Luis Terrazas registered alarm as his interests in the Guerrero region slipped out of government control.[41] While Federal troops could, thanks to their superior fire power, win pitched battles (as they did in the cemetery of Cerro Prieto on 11 December) they lacked the will and the mobility to disperse the rebels once and for all. As a British lumber company manager observed, it was like the Boer War all over again: well-armed but sluggish regular troops confronting elusive sharpshooters, familiar with the terrain.[42] This last factor was crucial, enabling Orozco, for example, to trap a Federal troop-train in the Cañón Mal Paso, or José de la Cruz Sánchez to lure a large Federal force into the Cañón Galindos Vinata where, hemmed in, nearly two hundred men were massacred.[43]

Under such pressure, the Federal reconquest of the sierra was abandoned. As the rebels began to threaten the main railway link between Chihuahua City and Juárez, the Federal commander, Navarro, pulled his troops out of the mountains, effectively renouncing government control in the regions west of the state capital. The latter began to fill up with *hacendados* and their families who had evacuated the danger zone; Terrazas despatched his land titles to Mexico City in seventeen strongboxes.[44] But now, early in 1911, a stalemate was achieved, the Federals held the plains, where they were still formidable, but the Maderistas had established control — had secured their guerrilla *foco* — in the mountains. It was something no rebellious group — save the Yaqui Indians — had achieved for thirty years. And the Maderistas, unlike the Yaquis, proclaimed a political message of national significance, which could not now be ignored. As the correspondence of the Chihuahua state government clearly reveals, the 1910 (Maderista) revolt inspired official anxiety, even panic, where the 1906 and 1908 (Magonista) insurrections were occasions for official self-congratulation. The success of the northern *serranos*, of 'instinctive *guerrilleros*' like Villa and Orozco, had put the revolution on the map, alarmed the regime, and rescued the name of Madero from possible oblivion.[45]

In Durango, too, the early rebel victories came in the mountainous west, and Díaz's statement to Congress, attributing these victories to the nature of the terrain, contained a partial truth.[46] But Díaz could not plead the same excuse when, with the civil war in Chihuahua temporarily stalemated, the 'chief centre of unrest' shifted south, to the Laguna plains.[47] Here, there were centres of classic agrarian revolt – such as the 'plague spot' of Cuencamé, as one planter put it – where villages clashed with expanding commercial enterprises; there were ranches involved in conflicts over the Nazas waters; and there was a large pool of migrant and proletarian labour, for which – perhaps in the manner which Martínez Alier has analysed in the Cuban case – a *reparto de tierras* exercised a distinct appeal, not least by way of offering security against unemployment.[48] Cuencamé itself fell to a force of 500 rebels led by Luis Moya, 'a small rancher' from the locality, in mid-February; soon, the Cruces hacienda received a visit from 120 Maderistas, 'all from Cuencamé', reported the manager, 'and a rough and ignorant lot of bandidos'. It was now that Calixto Contreras, 'of sinister aspects and sidling looks', the leader of the 4,000 or so Ocuila Indians resident in Cuencamé district, embarked on his long revolutionary career: 'the immediate cause of the outbreak', it was observed, 'was a bad landgrab from the Ocuila Indians by some wealthy neighbouring landowners'.[49] Cuencamé's contribution to the Laguna revolution was outstanding, but not alone. Other pueblos soon went over to the revolution, ousting their incumbent officials, and local people could usually predict which they would be. It was no surprise, for example, when Peñón Blanco, in Cuencamé district, pronounced for the revolution since 'the people of this place had grievances of long standing against the Government' – though the precise character of these grievances is unknown.[50] By mid-March 1911, as such incidents multiplied, the Federals found themselves bottled up in the garrison towns of the region, while beyond the towns and their tenuous railway connections the rebels held sway, their numbers conservatively estimated at 1,000 in the mountains to the west, 2,000 in the Laguna itself, and growing all the time; in military encounters so far 'the revolutionists have had things all their own way'.[51]

The rebellion was rural, popular, and significantly agrarian. Its leaders came from the common people, their authority was local and 'traditional', and their Anti-Re-electionist credentials were dubious: Contreras, the Ocuila leader; Ceniceros, a village lawyer turned revolutionary 'intellectual'; Orestes Pereyra, a tinsmith, whose features were scarred by fire; Enrique Adame Macías, a self-proclaimed *campesino*; Sixto Ugalde, 'an unlettered man of great valour and ability'.[52] Their followers, too, were common people from the countryside: 'although it is a well-known fact', it was observed, 'that the revolutionists have many sympathisers in the large cities, none have joined their cause, it is made up wholly of country people'.[53] Agrarian resentments were seen to be at the heart of the upheaval too, since the rebels espoused the old, emotive ides of the *reparto de tierras* and, without some satisfaction of these resentments, it was thought, the Laguna revolution could not be curbed.[54]

Hence, as authority collapsed and the zone of rebel operations spread, the long-incubating grievances of the country people came to life: Moya's men killed the manager of the López Negrete hacienda; the Guichapa cotton estate, near Rodeo, was sacked and its *administrador* wounded; seventy rebels under Pereyra called at Zaragoza (one of the constituent haciendas of the Tlahualilo estate), summoned the peons from the fields, lined them up, and declared that they were looking for Cecilio González, the *administrador*: 'they were angered against him because he has been talking too freely against them and also because the people said that he was hard on them'.[55] Once begun in the early months of 1911, this process of agrarian *reparto* and reprisal continued spasmodically for years to come, and the Laguna rebels retained a certain anarchic, popular character while others (such as those of Chihuahua to the north) underwent professionalisation. To John Reed, who encountered them two years later, they seemed 'simply peons who had risen in arms'; to an ex-railwayman and revolutionary gangster like Rodolfo Fierro they were 'those simple fools of Contreras'.[56] And they retained a rough, even fearsome, aspect (no doubt enhanced by the trophy – a beribboned, severed head – which Contreras hung from his railway car).[57] Meanwhile, in Durango as elsewhere, the contagion of rebellion did not enter the mines. At Guanaceví, in the rebel sierra, mining operations continued; at the Guadalupe Mines the company made ad hoc, forced payments to the rebels, as companies were wont to do throughout the Revolution, but the employees 'were treated very well' and 'were able to continue operations, which was decidedly popular' with the local people.[58]

This typical contrast between (putting it crudely) agrarian upheaval and industrial peace was thus established early on. So were other essential features of the popular revolution. As their control spread, the rebels wrought a revolution in local government. And it seems likely that the scope and profundity of the Chihuahuan revolution reflected the scope and profundity of the Terrazas *cacicazgo* (so even some Porfirians admitted).[59] In other states – such as San Luis or Tabasco – resentment against the state (as compared with the national) administration ran less high.[60] Hence, from the earliest days of the Chihuahuan revolution, as the rebels occupied the lumber towns of the sierra, they were busy 'changing all of the Government officials, putting their men in office, in charge of all Government business'; the fate of incumbent officials might follow that of Urbano Zea, killed at Cd Guerrero, or they might be run out of town, leaving in their place 'common people (*gente ordinaria*) who are made Provisional Authorities at whim'.[61] The same pattern was followed in the Durango mining towns of Topia, Tamazula and Santiago Papasquiaro, while Tomás Urbina, though not the most dedicated democrat, having taken Inde and Guanaceví *a fuerza y sangre*, 'summoned the people to elect their representatives, thus leaving provisional authorities (installed), with various detachments to provide the necessary guarantees'.[62] At Peñón Blanco, in the Laguna, as we have seen, the people effected their own changes; Trinidad Cervantes allowed the inhabitants of San Juan Guadalupe to recall a popular old *jefe* in place of the hated incumbent, and Luis Moya ranged as far south as Zacatecas, changing the officials in all the pueblos through which he passed.[63]

With the change in local officials often went the opening of the local gaol (releasing political and non-political prisoners alike), and sometimes the destruction of legal and municipal archives, the symbols not only of Porfirian officialdom but also of the voracious hacienda; all these practices had ancient precedents.[64] The gaol was flung open and the archives were burned at Topia in March, the same happened at Parral, where the town's sixteenth-century charter went up in flames.[65] Otherwise, the popular revolution tended to be orderly and restrained, targets were deliberately selected, the rebels policed their new conquests, presenting cash or, at worst, signed receipts for sequestered goods, sometimes dealing harshly with outright bandits. Anti-foreign sentiment was not apparent, and, in the small towns and villages taken by the Maderistas, the mob had not yet made its mark (though occasionally the local people seconded the military efforts of the rebels when they attacked).[66] Thus, the incipient northern revolution (which antedated even Madero's appearance on Mexican soil) revealed many of the classic features of the popular revolution as a whole: the dominance of local (state or municipal) concerns; the preponderance of rural elements; the distinct agrarian content; the implementation of grassroots political change, albeit haphazardly, sometimes at bayonet-point; the absence of xenophobia.

The government's response to this, the most serious military threat for over thirty years, was initially complacent. Díaz readily denounced the rebels as 'desperadoes' and 'bandits' and, noted the British Chargé, 'quite ignored the very possibility of an imperfection in his administration'.[67] Luis Terrazas anticipated later Pavlovian reactions, categorising the rebels as 'communists'.[68] And the first official instinct was to repress. Federal reinforcements were funnelled into Chihuahua and General Navarro was sent on his abortive mission to drive Orozco into the mountains and oblivion, burning the houses of rebel sympathisers as he went. In Chihuahua City the gaol was crammed with political prisoners suspected of 'sedition', and fears of mob disorders first began to stir. In Juárez and Durango the military started taking over civilian posts (a process that was to be carried to the limit two years later) and in Durango the calm of a Sunday afternoon concert in the plaza was broken by a cry of 'kill the *jefe político* and the chief of police'.[69] But, despite these premonitory symptoms, the authorities remained in control in the cities.

By the end of January 1911 it became clear that this revolt would not be snuffed out as so many had been previously. The Federals had relinquished the sierra, and the main railway line between Chihuahua City and Juárez was now threatened by Orozco, who had moved his forces north-east; the state capital, though secure, felt increasingly isolated, with business panicky, the mines lacking dynamite (the army banned shipments which might fall into rebel hands) and food prices rising.[70] For the second time in two years business slumped and the threat of unemployment and street disorders increased. With the Federal presence in the state increased from 1,000 to 7,000 in the space of four months, civil—military relations were at a low ebb; clashes between the troops and townspeople were narrowly averted and, if this were not enough, thirteen people were killed in a mass break-out from the city gaol at the end of February.[71]

More serious, from the government's point of view, were signs of disaffection in the army. Forty-five men of the 18th Regiment had gone over to the rebels in the countryside, and there were similar stories from Durango and Sonora where, as the revolution spread over the peaks and high valleys of the Sierra Madre, government troops holding one of the key passes at Sahuaripa broke and fled in the face of the first rebel attack.[72] This, too, was to become a familiar phenomenon as the manpower demands of the Federal Army encouraged 'drafting among the criminal and improvident classes' in Mexico City, who naturally made reluctant heroes.[73] And the first of many attempts to raise local volunteer forces to combat the rebels in Chihuahua and Durango came to nothing. Landlords, lamented the Governor of Chihuahua, indulged in the rhetoric of self-defence, but took no action, fearing revolutionary reprisals on their properties.[74] Luis Terrazas went further, equipping trusted hacienda peons as vigilantes, but was disgusted to find that 'even the servants themselves are contaminated and only a very reduced number can be counted on as loyal. To arm the disloyal ... would be entirely counter-productive, since they would go over to the enemy, armed and equipped.'[75] Even an offer of two pesos a day (well above the average daily wage) plus arms and horse failed to get recruits.

It was suddenly made abundantly clear that the legitimacy of the old order was spent. The newly-appointed American consul at Chihuahua, sounding out opinion in the state, detected 'almost universal discontent with political conditions', 'the people with whom I talked', he went on, 'declare that the only supporters which the government has are the office-holders', and even some of these were beginning to waver, like the chief of police at Juárez, who had recently resigned and crossed to the US.[76] At Parral 95% of the people were reckoned to be for the rebels and against the regime; and there were similar reports from Durango and the Laguna.[77] Repression having failed, the government now tried conciliation – which had settled some troublesome local protests in the past. In January 1911 the popular ex-Governor of Chihuahua, Miguel Ahumada, returned in place of the Terracista incumbent; he appealed publicly to the rebels – in particular to the 'virile sons of Guerrero who have taken up arms animated by a good cause' – to desist from fratricidal conflict on the understanding that they would in future be able to choose their own *jefes políticos* and municipal presidents – a clear recognition of *serrano* grievances.[78] In Mexico City there was talk of impending cabinet changes and the dismissal of 'a number of the more obnoxious governors'; overtures went out to the nominal leader of the revolution, Francisco Madero, via his more conservative family, who had no stomach for such upheaval.[79] But it was too little and too late. The northern rebels and the people of Mexico more generally were not impressed by this piece of Porfirian prestidigitation; they demanded not a cosmetic change of personnel but a more fundamental reform of the method of selection, which would admit of popular representation. Concessions of this kind in fact served to undermine the regime further, and to encourage revolutionary morale; in the beleaguered garrison towns of the north, they added to the growing uncertainty.

On the military front, meanwhile, stalemate prevailed. The rebels had free run of the northern countryside, where they 'seem[ed] to have . . . a welcome among the common people', while the Federals clung, limpet-like, to the major towns and railways, much of their activity devoted to keeping the Chihuahua–Juárez section of the Central Railway open. Even here, as they escorted repair gangs along the exposed track, the Federals found that, once out of the city, they were 'in hostile territory'.[80] So far, pitched battles had been rare. Perhaps 2,000 men had fought at Cerro Prieto, on the North-Western Railway, on 11 December, when, after several hours of fierce combat concentrated around the village cemetery, the combined forces of Orozco, Villa, and José de la Luz Blanco were repulsed by the Federals and forced to seek shelter in the sierra. The Federals' superiority in artillery and the rebels' (especially the Indian rebels') military inexperience were seen as crucial to the outcome.[81] Again, in February, Orozco failed to stop General Rábago from reaching Juárez with reinforcements.[82] Now, if the revolutionaries were to maintain momentum and credibility, it was vital for them to quit the security of the mountains and their guerrilla operations and to challenge the Federal Army in open battle, at the gates of the cities of the plain. It was also necessary for Madero, still in the US, to return to Mexico and assume personal leadership of the movement he had initiated but not, so far, participated in. A new phase in the progress of the revolution was about to begin, and one that would bring its swift extension throughout the rest of the Republic.

MADERO RETURNS

After his flight from Mexico in October 1910, Madero had achieved no more than most of his fellow civilian *políticos*. On 18 November he had left San Antonio to rendez-vous (so it was planned) with several hundred Coahuilan rebels, who would assault Cd Porfirio Díaz. Close to the border, however, the party lost their way and spent a chilly night wandering aimlessly; when, next day, they finally met with the Coahuilan contingent (a mere ten men, led by Madero's uncle, Catarino Benavides), they learned of the death of Serdán in Puebla, and decided that it would be suicidal to stick to the original revolutionary plan. So, like many of his supporters, Madero had to take stock of the situation, relinquish the initiative, and wait upon events. He returned to San Antonio.[83] For a couple of months, Madero and his entourage lived a peripatetic existence in the American south and south west, shifting from San Antonio to New Orleans, Dallas to El Paso. So far, the US authorities had taken no action against the Maderistas on American soil: for which reason the Díaz government despatched complaints and protests, and later historians wove elaborate theories of *gringo* connivance in the Madero revolt.[84] In particular, it has been suggested, American disenchantment with Díaz — based on the dictator's supposed discrimination against American and preference for European interests — prompted support for the Revolution on the part not only of the Taft administration but also of specific companies like Standard Oil. And, in the era of dollar diplomacy, this congruence of opinion was not purely coincidental.

A balanced history of the Revolution, however, need consider these points only fairly briefly. In general, the US government was reluctant to get involved in Mexican revolutionary politics (there were exceptions, but 1910–11 was not one of them); and the ability of the US to influence these politics was both limited and uncertain. Of course, American recognition of regimes, or of the belligerent status of revolutionary factions, carried weight, particularly with regard to the supply of arms across the border. But these decisions depended chiefly upon Mexican events and initiatives: at no point can it be said that US policy (whether in 1910–11 or 1913–14) was primarily responsible for making or breaking a regime south of the border. Still less could Standard Oil, or any other American corporation, make a similar claim. As has already been suggested, the Revolution was a fundamentally endogenous process: a fight (as a Mexican participant put it) 'fought with the hunger and abnegation of the Mexicans, with no more'; a fight (according to an American observer) that was 'entirely a Mexican fight . . . Mexicans fighting Mexicans [in] . . . their own family quarrel'.[85] At certain junctures (but only at certain junctures) American influence counted, but it was clearly secondary in causal importance to the domestic factors which determined the course of the Revolution.

The evidence for American disenchantment with Díaz and active support for Madero is poor and equivocal, often it derives from the speculative reports of hostile foreign diplomats.[86] It is true that, particularly in the last years of the Porfiriato, Científico economic strategy involved moves to limit American penetration of the Mexican economy and to encourage the entry of European capital as a counterweight.[87] American investment, however, continued to rise, and economic nationalist measures like Limantour's Mexicanisation of the railways posed no real threat to American economic hegemony. American policy-makers (who could be thoroughly vague about the aggregate level of American investment in Mexico) still preserved an image of Díaz as the patron and protector of US interests, which was not so far wrong.[88] It is therefore hard to conceive of any American administration – let alone the cautious, legalistic Taft administration of 1910 – flirting with revolution out of resentment at Porfirian economic policy. A more emotive issue was the treatment of American nationals in specific instances. With the spread of American trade and investment overseas, American presidents began to mouth (without the same grandiloquence) the sentiments of Palmerston's 'Civis Romanus sum' speech: if US diplomacy was to 'respond to modern ideas of commercial intercourse', Taft told Congress, it must be based upon 'the axiomatic principle that the Government of the United States shall extend all proper support to every legitimate and beneficial American enterprise abroad'.[89] This might involve protests at supposedly prejudicial legislative or judicial decisions (some, like the Tlahualilo case, dragged on for years). But it was rather cases of physical attacks on American persons and property which quickened the diplomatic pulse, excited public opinion, and raised the spectre of direct US intervention in Mexico.

With the Revolution, the question of protecting American persons and property – not just inside Mexico but also along the border – became of paramount importance in Mexican–American relations.[90] But prior to November 1910 there was no cause for the US government to desire the overthrow of Díaz on these grounds. The Pax Porfiriana was proverbial, and the border was tranquil. Some writers, it is true, have detected a rising tide of xenophobia during the late Porfiriato, when 'popular hostility [to Americans] became widespread and open', but, as already suggested, such xenophobia is notoriously hard to substantiate.[91] Even in those rare cases where labour disputes took on a violent, anti-American cast, Díaz coult not be faulted for the swift repression he visited upon trouble-makers (e.g., Cananea). Rumours of a general anti-American uprising, which were current in 1906, proved groundless.[92] And, even during the genuine anti-American protests of November 1910, the State Department absolved Díaz, blaming 'Mexican reactionaries [sic]', and Taft's faith in the fellow-president with whom he had personally conferred the previous year never faltered: 'I cannot conceive a situation', he told his Secretary of State, 'in which President Díaz would not act with a strong hand in defence of just American interests.'[93] Thus, not only was there no very good reason for an American 'destabilisation' of Díaz; more important there is no very good evidence either.[94]

The appearance of American support for Madero derived from the freedom with which Maderistas in the US were able to move, propagandise, purchase arms, and ultimately, cross into Mexico to foment revolution. This was the nub of Porfirian protests in Washington and Mexico City.[95] But Taft, a strict constructionist, was bound by American law, which severely limited the capacity of the administration to interfere with the Maderistas. They could not, for example, be arrested for slandering Díaz or for buying arms; the neutrality statutes required that they be apprehended mounting an armed expedition, and this was not easy to prove, save where individuals were caught *in flagrante delicto*.[96] Within the terms of the law the Taft administration sought to maintain a genuine neutrality, and American officials on the border did their best to seal the frontier against filibusters. But the border was long, surveillance on the Mexican side was poor or non-existent, and the population north of the Río Grande (especially the Mexican population) was sympathetic to the Revolution.[97] For Díaz, as for subsequent Mexican regimes, accusations of American connivance with the revels served as a useful alibi; but it cannot be maintained either that the US government worked for the fall of Díaz, or even that the *de facto* implementation of American law tipped the balance in favour of the rebels. The rebels fought and won their own battles, and, as the best analysis of the problem reveals, 'the Díaz regime fell because of its own corruption and its inability to defend itself or enforce its laws, not as a result of American support for the regime's opponents'.[98]

There remains the question of Standard Oil, who supposedly helped (or offered to help) Madero because of Díaz's generosity to British oil interests. This generosity is easily exaggerated.[99] More important, the evidence for Standard Oil's complicity is of the worst kind. In April 1911 an individual told a Department of Justice secret agent that he was acting as a broker between Standard Oil and the Madero family, offering up to 1m. dollars in return for commercial concessions.[100] It was a detailed, cloak-and-dagger story, complete with clandestine meetings in Texan parks and Turkish baths; it suggested that Francisco Madero had approved the negotiations, and it attributed to Alfonso Madero the incredible statement that 'the *insurrecto* government had requested of the Federal government to secede [sic] fifteen of the states of the Republic of Mexico commencing on the US border', by way of achieving a peace settlement.[101] Either Alfonso Madero was a fool as well as a traitor, and Francisco (who usually gave concession-mongers short shrift) was a consummate hypocrite, or, alternatively, the report was inaccurate, if not entirely spurious.[102] (Certainly spurious stories flourished in the American border towns during the Revolution.) As for the cash itself, Peter Calvert has shown that no loan was in fact made (Standard Oil, of course, categorically denied it, and the State Department was inclined to accept the denial), and it seems likely that the Maderista war-chest derived from the Madero family fortune, some of which was ill-gotten, but not ill-gotten by the promise of post-revolutionary economic privileges.[103]

Legal niceties notwithstanding, American tolerance of Maderista activities had its limits. Originally it had been planned for Madero to re-enter Mexico in February 1911, when Orozco looked likely to take Juárez. But Juárez did not fall and Madero was denied a triumphal entry. By now, Madero's infractions of the neutrality laws made him a wanted man in Texas and, irrespective of the military situation in Chihuahua, he had to go south to avoid arrest.[104] Once again, plans were torn up and action was dictated by events. On 14 February the self-styled president slipped into Mexico just east of El Paso, leading about a hundred men, linking up with José de la Luz Blanco. Riding stolen Terrazas horses the small force made its way in bitter cold across the huge, semi-desert cattle ranches towards San Buenaventura, their numbers gradually augmented by fresh recruits.[105] Early in March, Madero decided to make his mark by attacking Casas Grandes, the most important town on the North-Western Railway, where his 600 or so men would face a Federal garrison only slightly inferior in numbers.[106] But, unfortunately for Madero, a Federal cavalry force of several hundred was coincidentally making for Casas Grandes too.

Thus, after the rebels had attacked at dawn on 6 March, and a fierce, fluctuating battle at last began to turn in their favour, the Federal reinforcements arrived, raking the Maderistas with machine gun fire, pinning them down in the irrigation ditches around the town. Equipped in the main with Winchesters and old Springfields, the Maderistas could not match the Federals' firepower; rebels occupying an adobe building were shelled into surrender by Federal artillery. At the end of the day, when the Maderistas broke and fled, they had lost up to a hundred men dead and captured, and a large part of their valuable supplies. Madero, slightly wounded in the arm, was lucky to escape.

Casas Grandes, the first pitched battle of the Revolution, revealed that the rebels were ill-equipped, in terms of arms and organisation, for such engagements; and that the Federals' monopoly of machine guns and artillery gave them a decisive advantage in open country which it would require great efforts, losses, and skill to overcome. Precisely the same lessons were meted out to the rebels in Sonora (many of them were Chihuahuans) in subsequent weeks: to José de la Luz Blanco at Agua Prieta (12 March), to Ramón Gómez at Navojoa (12 March), to Anacleto Girón at La Colorada (22 March), to Cabral, Rojas, the brothers García and others at Ures (23–26 March).[107] On the other hand, the Federals' failure to follow up their victory at Casas Grandes was typical of their over-cautious, static strategy – a strategy encouraged by the Federal commanders' nagging uncertainties about the terrain, the temper of their troops, even the political future of Mexico. And in defeat the revolutionaries did not lose heart, though they gained wisdom. An American who visited Madero's camp in the secure territory west of Chihuahua City three weeks after Casas Grandes found their numbers increased, their spirits high, their discipline exemplary.[108]

Meanwhile, as the Revolution spread in Durango and the Laguna, Federal troops were diverted to maintain communications from Chihuahua south, and Madero moved north towards the key border port of Juánez. Again, the depleted Federal garrison surrendered the countryside and dug in; by mid-April the Maderistas had ringed the city. But by now the Chihuahuan theatre was only one of several – if still the most important, by virtue of the rebels' numbers and the presence there of the titular revolutionary leader. Díaz could no longer concentrate on Chihuahua, confident of the failure of revolts elsewhere. The success of Orozco and his fellow rebels in Durango had maintained revolutionary morale and momentum, inspiring the would-be, the failed, and the potential rebels of the centre and south, while at the same time depriving these areas of Federal troops: the barracks at Juchitán (Oax.), which normally housed 2,000 to 3,000 troops, contained only a battalion, and garrisons in Guerrero and Veracruz were similarly depleted.[109] It had been shown that rural insurrection could succeed where urban coups had failed and, as others followed this example, all Mexico north of the Isthmus began to experience political turbulence. By failing to crush a number of localised revolts in the north (revolts of the kind he had readily quashed in previous years) Díaz had incurred a national revolution. The Pax Porfiriana was irretrievably ruptured, the legitimacy of the old order was shown to be spent. President Taft, moved by his alarmist ambassador, ordered troops to the border and ships to Mexican waters, to guarantee American lives and property; however this might be interpreted, it dealt another blow to Díaz's sagging prestige.[110]

PATTERNS OF REVOLT

But if Díaz faced a national revolution, it was not that of a centrally directed movement or party. It consisted rather of a multiplicity of local uprisings, responding to local circumstances and grievances, and assuming national significance by virtue of their sheer extension throughout the country, and their nominal adherence to Madero's name and plan. Another leader and another plan (it was plausibly supposed) could well have elicited a similar revolutionary response.[111] This adherence was all the more nominal since, with the bona fide Maderistas, the civilian *políticos* of 1909–10, largely unable or unwilling to take the lead, new men, with tenuous or non-existent Maderista credentials, now came to the fore; men whose prominence depended on local status and popularity and who, in the eyes of sour conservatives, were down-at-heel reprobates: 'rogues or killers escaped from justice, ignorant ranchers, coarse muleteers, bankrupt crackpots, failed students and professionals'; such were the men who 'captained the guerrilla bands and formed the inner councils of the revolution'.[112] Though a caricature, this contained a lot of truth, as the individuals themselves were sometimes prepared to admit. If they were short on education (as the Arrietas conceded), they were long on temerity, for sobriety and caution were no attributes of these pioneer revolutionaries of 1910–11. It was, as Gabriel Gavira put it, with typical bravado, 'we, the madmen, who went with Madero', who were 'the initiators of the movement'.[113] Hence, many were young: family men were more likely to stay at home (unless, as with one individual, it was the mother-in-law who drove a man to revolution); sons rose in rebellion, sometimes against their parents' wishes.[114] Thus, if civilian Maderismo carried the stamp of respectable middle age, while Porfirismo had connotations of senility, the revolution was the work of young men, in their twenties and thirties (those few civilian Maderistas who continued to prosper in the climate of revolution were young men, like Almazán and Pedro de los Santos); hence political conflicts began to assume generational as well as class, regional, and ideological dimensions.[115] And for many of these new leaders the name of Madero meant little more than a vague source of legitimacy and an opportunity to confer a national label on local squabbles, often of many years' standing. The chickens of Porfirian economic development and political centralisation were coming home to roost, summoned by Madero's call to arms.

The revolution, therefore, was variegated, localised, and amorphous. But it did not lack regular, recurrent patterns, and those already established in the north were soon followed elsewhere. The northern revolution was not – as is sometimes maintained – *sui generis*.[116] Of prime importance in the generation of popular rebellion was the agrarian question. This was true of parts of the north too, not only the Laguna (where it was freely admitted) but also in certain of the sierra pueblos of Chihuahua and Durango.[117] But whereas here resentment at the monopolisation of land, water and pasture formed part of a greater antipathy to *caciquismo* and centralisation, the essential fuel of *serrano* rebellion, it was elsewhere the case that agrarian dispossession, and hence the classic agrarian revolt, provided the central, dominating features of popular insurrection.

In Morelos, for example, Maderismo had made slight impact (albeit Leyvismo can be seen as a local surrogate), Madero's appeal to arms had no immediate effect and 20 November passed off peacefully. But, by the end of the year, news of the northerners' success encouraged dissident elements in Morelos to test the strength of a faltering government (to engage, as Scott puts it, in the 'calculus of force'):[118]

of the hundred pueblos in the state in 1910, there was probably not one that was not involved in a freshly embittered legal dispute with a neighbouring hacienda. And in the current confusion many desperate villagers calculated whether they might serve the cause better by taking direct action. That they would calculate in favour of revolt was most likely around traditional centres of independence and agrarian discontent.

Several rural strikes occurred, but were defeated. In the mountains north of Cuernavaca – in the spit of barbarism separating the Mexico City *haut monde* from their weekend villas in the Cuernavaca valley – Genovevo de la O recruited twenty-five men, though he alone had a fire-arm, a 0.70 calibre musket; while north of Tlaltizapán Gabriel Tepepa, a hacienda foreman, a veteran of the 1860s wars, with a great local reputation, rose in revolt, occupied Tepotzlán, ransacked the houses of the village caciques, burned the municipal archive, and then made for the hills, safe from government reprisals.[119]

Meanwhile, in the municipality of Ayala (which had a reputation for belligerence and independence) the more 'politically-minded' farmers began to discuss what they should do in the light of recent events in the north and in Morelos itself. Among them was Emiliano Zapata, municipal president of the village of Anenecuilco. Zapata was just over thirty; slight, quiet, fond of the dandified *charro* outfits of the Mexican countryside. He came from a well-known local family, one that was comfortably placed by Morelos' low standards, and one that had played a distinguished part in the Wars of Independence and the Reform as well as the French Intervention; at his baptism, Emiliano's god-parents had been the manager of the big Hospital hacienda and his wife.[120] But relations with the big house had cooled and, just recently, Zapata had led eight of his fellow-villagers in an armed seizure of land held by the hacienda but claimed by the village. And, thanks to the current political uncertainty in Morelos and Mexico as a whole, the authorities had temporarily acquiesced in this *de facto* reform. Zapata's reputation grew, other villages contributed to the Anenecuilco defence fund and benefited from Zapata's armed assistance.[121] By the turn of 1910–11, as news of the northern revolution filtered through, an armed truce existed in the countryside around Cuautla, the villagers and the hacienda field-guards confronting each other in circumstances of potential rural civil war.

So far, Zapata strenuously denied any connection with the Madero insurrection. But events were moving fast. Other rebel groups (notably the Figueroa brothers) were making headway in neighbouring Guerrero and, with the cane harvest approaching its climax, the government reinforced its garrisons in Morelos. Having established a formal liaison with Madero (more a tepid alliance of mutual interest than a warm embrace), Zapata and his collaborators met at the annual Cuautla fair in mid-March and made plans for an immediate uprising. Next day, Zapata led a revolt at Villa de Ayala: the local police were disarmed, the people convened in the plaza, where the intellectuals of the rebellion, the schoolteachers Torres Burgos and Montaño, harangued them, combining an appeal to the Plan of San Luis Potosí with a cry from the heart: 'down with the haciendas! long live the pueblos!'. Not that the Morelos rebels entertained radical ideas of doing away with the hacienda, which was an integral part of their rural society, rather, they sought to restore the balance between hacienda and village, upset by the rapid expansion of the plantation during the Porfiriato.[122]

The rebel column moved south from Ayala, collecting recruits along the way, entering Puebla to pick off the villages along the Interoceanic Railway, harvesting men, material, discipline and experience until they could assault the strategic heart of Morelos, the city of Cuautla: the necessary guerrilla preparation for the hazards of pitched battle and siege. In general the revolt was orderly and disciplined, even if gaols were opened, archives occasionally burned, and some commercial establishments (especially those of the Spaniards) ransacked.[123] But to the local planters it seemed, as one put it, that 'the peons, thinking the Administration is powerless [are] . . . taking advantage of the opportunity to revert to what was the normal condition in Mexico and above all in the state of Morelos in the old days, brigandage'.[124] Respectable opinion in Mexico City concurred that the Morelos movement constituted neither a revolt nor a revolution (which would imply political objectives). A British diplomat contrasted the 'brigand bands of Morelos and Puebla' with decent, orthodox rebels like Madero; Limantour blamed 'local rancours' (in a sense he was right); *El País* maintained that the Morelos 'Indians' 'revolted not to sustain the principles of the revolution but to generate a war to the death against property, especially agricultural property, and to divide it up'.[125] The distinction between Maderismo and Zapatismo was valid, if crudely put, and terms like 'brigandage' or 'anarchy' (which *El País* went on to use in describing the condition of Morelos) may be taken as elite shorthand for decentralised, autonomous, popular rebellion.[126] For, clearly, this was what was occurring in Morelos in 1911. The rebel leaders may not have been peons, nor even village farmers: Felipe Neri had worked a hacienda kiln, José Trinidad Ruiz had preached the (Protestant) gospel, Fortino Ayaquica was a young textile worker, Francisco Mendoza a 'rancher-rustler', Jesús Morales 'a paunchy, blustery, saloon-keeper from Ayutla'.[127] But their forces were drawn from the country villages (initially from the free villagers, for the recruitment of hacienda peons came later), the leaders had deep local roots, and their aims were strongly agrarian: early in the summer of 1911, for example, Mendoza began to carve up the hacienda land at Palo Blanco among the villagers of Axochiapam.[128] What is more, as these leaders organised the incipient popular revolt, the respectable, civilian oppositionists of Morelos, those who had staffed the Leyvista movement, played no conspicuous part.[129]

If Morelos produced the most virulent popular revolt (and certainly the one best researched), it was not a unique case. In nearby Tlaxcala, too, the progress of the railway and consequent agricultural commercialisation affected villagers and smallholders, notably in the southern part of the state, where the hacienda had previously not been strong.[130] In addition, 'peasant–artisans' were threatened by factory textile production. The 1900s had seen a spate of revolts in the state and, with the onset of the Madero revolution, the same leaders and districts were prominent. After initial reverses (Juan Cuamaxti, whose 1910 revolt has been mentioned, was killed in February 1911), the Tlaxcalan rebels established control of the countryside: Benigno Centeño and Francisco García in the Atoyac valley; Isidro Ortiz and others in southern Tlaxcala; Gabriel

Hernández and Francisco Méndez in the north. Again, it was the regions of free villages, rather than the hacienda-dominated valleys which produced the most revolutionary activity; for the villagers enjoyed a relative freedom of manoeuvre and had experienced recent, cumulative threats to their position, both of which the hacienda peons lacked. [131]

Nor was the agrarian revolt confined to the central plateau. The Huasteca had witnessed recurrent struggles over land and Tamazunchale, a centre of revolt in the 1880s, knew rebellion and repression again in August 1910. [132] The Madero revolution now offered a new opportunity and a new official banner. Fighting broke out at Tancanhuitz and Tantoyuca within days of the uprising and, if other groups in the region held back (as Zapata, of course did, until mid-March 1911) it was often out of circumspection rather than satisfaction with the status quo. [133] By the new year, with the authorities making many, possibly counter-productive, arrests, it was common knowledge that 'the Huasteca district is very disaffected', that 'the whole valley of the Pánuco, known as the Huasteca are [sic] in favor of the insurgents and prepared, when necessary, to join them'. [134] A hundred *rurales* were rushed to Valles, where they made 'a great many arrests', and troubles were reported from Tantoyuca, Tamazunchale, Tantima, Chicontepec – all familiar names from the rebellious past. [135] By the spring, 200 rebels were at large around San Dieguito; Pedro Antonio de los Santos, a young law student (and a rare convert from civilian to revolutionary Maderismo) led 500 near Valles; Alberto Carrera Torres, a 24-year-old schoolteacher, headed a movement in southern Tamaulipas. [136] And, a little to the west, the Cedillo brothers (soon to ally with Carrera Torres) were beginning to mobilise sharecroppers around Cd del Maíz. [137] The precise character of these movements – especially those of the Huasteca proper – is hard to establish. However, it is clear that, while San Luis had a high proportion of hacienda peons, it was the Indian villagers and *rancheros* of the Huasteca, and the *campesinos* of Ciudad del Maíz, who proved most rebellious; furthermore, observers discerned few links or similarities between these rebellions and Madero's respectable political revolution in the north and they began to fear for the future. 'It seems', wrote one, [138] 'that the repression of many years has resulted in a reaction, hastened by the disturbed conditions elsewhere, that no ordinary terms of peace can stop, and that there is a danger of a prolonged period of reprisal and accounting.'

In seeking to explain the pattern of revolt, it is also worth noting that as these eastern regions of San Luis developed popular movements which, fulfilling the fears quoted above, were to survive the fall of Díaz, the arid, upland, mining country to the west, where lay the state capital, remained relatively quiet. Though the PLM had been born there, and though Madero's revolutionary plan carried its name, the city of San Luis and its hinterland were untroubled by rebellion, even when the state was 'denuded' of troops by demands from elsewhere. [139] True, public opinion was generally hostile to

Díaz (attempts to raise pro-government volunteers failed here as well), and repression was severe — by mid-April the San Luis city gaol contained over 1,000 prisoners, including 100 or more migrant workers, arrested as they made their way north, not to join the revolution, but to labour in the Texas cotton-fields.[140] But the anti-Díaz elements in the cities (and the mining camps) did not see themselves as *guerrilleros*, and took no initiative; though there was 'revolutionary feeling everywhere among all classes . . . the people here will not originate any disturbance, but will join the revolution if it should spread to this state'.[141] San Luis thus provides additional, negative evidence against the *révolution minière* thesis.[142] And, when revolutionary forces began to make their presence felt in northern and western San Luis, they were intruders from outside, like the guayulero, Gertrudis Sánchez, and the liberation of the state capital was performed by the Guanajuatense school-master, Cándido Navarro. So much for the 'cradle of the revolution'.[143]

The states of Sonora and Sinaloa, lying cheek-by-jowl on the west coast, offer a similar, illuminating parallel. Here, Sinaloa (and, in Sonora, the Yaqui Valley) compared with the Huasteca: a region of agrarian tension, of popular and *ranchero* revolt. Sonora (with the important exception of the sierra country shared with Chihuahua) had a mining and commercial economy, a prosperous, literate mestizo population, and did not, as a result, witness great upheaval. Though Sonoran public opinion ran strongly against Díaz, and the revolution-aries' liberal demands exercised a powerful appeal, taking up arms was another matter, and armed revolution was hardly good for business. Thus, while Sonora (like San Luis) has claimed a pre-eminent revolutionary role, this claim must rest almost entirely on the events of 1913, not of 1911, for Sonora's contribution during the first flush of popular revolt was unimpressive. The political opposition of 1909–10 went the way of most such oppositions. Some, like Benjamín Hill of Navojoa, were already in gaol when the revolution began. Others, like the Guaymas triumvirate Maytorena, Randall and Venegas (an *hacendado*, small businessman and editor respectively) fled to Arizona to avoid arrest; so, too, did Salvador Alvarado and Juan Cabral of Cananea, though they showed somewhat greater enthusiasm to return to the fray.[144] Other Sonoran oppositionists, such as the two subsequent presidents Adolfo de la Huerta and Plutarco Elías Calles, took no part in the Madero revolution, though de la Huerta signed a protest when over-zealous police invaded a masked ball attended by *porteño* high society.[145]

Hence the Sonoran revolution of 1910–11 (in contrast to that of 1913) tended to be alien and acephalous. The first rebel successes (and these did not come until the turn of the year) were the work of Chihuahuans, or *serrano* Sonorans. Rosario and Juan Antonio García, for example, came from an extensive, well-known family of Sahuaripa: Juan Antonio was reputedly a 'very popular chap' in the vicinity, so, probably, was Rosario, for he had killed the chief of police of Nacozari Viejo a few years before. In American eyes, however,

he was 'a thief and a murderer ... and an outlaw for the last five years'.
Though Sonorans, the Garcías were in touch with Pascual Orozco (Sahuaripa
was as close to San Isidro, Orozco's home town, as it was to Hermosillo or
Guaymas) and they entered Sahuaripa in January 1911 declaring that they had
come to carry on 'the great liberating task which had begun in the state of
Chihuahua'.[146] Further north, the Chihuahuan José de la Luz Blanco crossed
the mountains, took El Tigre, and advanced on Agua Prieta; Perfecto Lomelín
moved to Nacozari; and a third Chihuahuan, José Cardoso, led the revolution
in the Altar district.[147] From the Chihuahuan mining town of Dolores,
Alejandro Gandarilla (another associate of Orozco) and Antonio Rojas both
chose to head west rather than east.[148] Though they operated in Sonora, they
derived from the same sierra society which had shaped Orozco and his kind.
They may be seen as the first of several waves of Chihuahuan rebels who came
westwards over the mountains during the Revolution (the Orozquistas did so
in 1912, the Villistas in 1915–16), taking the logical, if laborious path when
the plains of Chihuahua were blocked, and alarming the more peaceful,
civilised people of Sonora. Sonora produced its own modest quota, too, in
1910–11: Miguel Matrecitos was a classic *serrano* rebel who launched a
family-based revolt in the Moctezuma district (it was soon put down), and,
with more caution, Cabral and Alvarado kitted out an expedition in Arizona,
crossed to Mexico in January 1911, and began to operate in the Sierra de Ajos.
In this they could claim to represent the pioneer Sonoran revolutionaries of
1911, and their pioneer status, coupled with their north Sonoran origins, set
them aside from the *porteño* Maytorena, who maintained a prudent *attentisme* in
Arizona, and this created a potential rift in the rebel ranks.[149]

But, despite its later revolutionary pre-eminence, Sonora's contribution to
the Madero revolution could not at all compare with Chihuahua's and its
notable export surplus of *serrano* rebels. General Torres, Governor of Sonora,
was of the same mind: 'everything', he told the American consul in March
1911, 'depended on conditions in Chihuahua', if the Federals could crush the
insurrection there, Sonora could revert to peace and order.[150] Torres was not
simply passing the buck. Facing the Federals in open battle, the Sonoran rebels
had suffered a series of defeats in March, which forced them to revert to
guerrilla operations. There was no immediate hope that they could wrest
control of the state from the Torres clique. What is more, Torres promised free
and fair elections for April – a promise backed by the authority of Vice-
President Corral.[151] This was a smart move. Public opinion in Sonora favoured
reform and was sympathetic to the Maderista movement: at Nogales (February
1911) 'the great majority of the inhabitants are in favour of the [rebel]
movement'; at Alamos (March) 'nearly all the citizens not in Federal employ
... may be considered as sympathisers with the revolutionary movement'.[152]
Rurales operating along the border found the local people's support for the
rebels an insuperable problem. But most Sonorans – progressive and busi-

nesslike – would have preferred change to come in peaceful, evolutionary channels. Notwithstanding their familiarity with frontier violence, they did not rush to join the Revolution and they were alarmed when, as at Sahuaripa, 'robbery and rapine' seemed to be on the revolutionary agenda.[153] In Sonora – as in the comparably progressive, commercial state of Nuevo León – the respectable progressives allowed the revolutionary movement to pass, by default, into the hands of coarse plebeians: rural workers, 'miners and ranchmen from the more isolated mountain districts', men distinct from the civilian opposition of 1909–10, and from the official revolutionary junta in Arizona.[154] But, as the battles of March 1911 showed, these plebeian forces could not defeat the Federals in the open, even if the Federals, for their part, could not mount an effective anti-guerrilla campaign. The Sonoran revolution hung fire, with the majority of the state's inhabitants looking on, until outside events took control. The final collapse of the old regime thus took place without any major rebel victory being scored over the Federals in Sonora; the state's entry into the Revolution (so different from its glorious role two years later) was halting and indecisive.

The fundamental reason for this, as already suggested, was that Sonora's grievances were primarily political; the people were sick of 'local rings and chronic feeders at the trough'; and Governor Torres (one of the 'chronic feeders') touched to the heart of the problem with his offer of free elections.[155] Only among the Yaqui did there exist the kind of profound resentments, the consequent 'moral outrage', and the capacity for collective resistance which sustained prolonged popular rebellion elsewhere, such as in Morelos. In fact, the perennial conflict between Yaqui and Mexican had entered one of its periodic lulls following the 'peace' of 1908. But with the outbreak of the Madero revolution there were Yaqui leaders and war-parties in the mountains ready to take advantage of the situation, even if Luis Buli, the pre-eminent chief, had been corralled by the state government and obliged to serve, with his men, as Federal auxiliaries.[156] Before long it became clear that the revolution followed the long tradition of Mexican civil wars which offered the Yaquis both the temptation and the opportunity to press their claims for land, water and autonomy. In March, revolutionary agents were arrested for fomenting revolt among the Yaquis and there came the first reports of Yaqui contingents going over to the revolution; soon, war-parties were descending from the mountains to raid the haciendas of the Guaymas valley.[157] The Yaqui rebellion thus gathered strength in tandem with the national revolution, its chiefs claiming that Madero had promised them the restitution of their lands in return for support; but Maderista control over their allies was scarcely evident as, in May, their forces began to seize the small towns and stations along the Southern Pacific Railway. By June there were reckoned to be over 1,000 Yaquis at large in the valley, demanding both the restitution of their lands and the return of Yaqui deportees from Yucatán.[158] White/mestizo communities, witnessing this recrudescence of the old Yaqui peril, demanded reinforcements, and it became a prime concern of the new, post-revolutionary state government to settle the Yaqui question, whether by force or diplomacy. But the Maderista rulers, like their Porfirian predecessors, soon found how much harder it was to assuage than to incite Yaqui belligerence. [159]

In Sinaloa, too, the Mayo Indians took advantage of the situation to settle old scores with the landowners and caciques of the Mochis region, establishing themselves as an independent force under Felipe Bachomo. [160] But while in Sonora the Yaqui rebellion represented an isolated, anomalous centre of popular, agrarian revolt, the Mayo movement in Sinaloa merged into a more general picture of social upheaval; Sinaloa, it has been suggested, was 'the state where Zapatismo — that is, the agrarian ideas of the south — prospered most'. [161] This is not easy to prove. But there can be no doubt that revolutionary bands, of popular and plebeian character, proliferated in the state. In addition to Ramón Iturbe, whom we have already encountered, Manuel Sánchez and Justo Tirado revolted south of Mazatlán, and Crescencio Gaxiola at Guamuchil, near Culiacán; Juan Banderas began a notable career among the haciendas of Badiraguato; while the usual descent from the mountains to the plains carried with it *serrano* outsiders, in this case so-called *chileros* from Durango like Herculano and Nabor de la Rocha. [162] Such leaders were not peons, but still less were they men of education or political prominence: Salazar and Cabanillas (also Sinaloan rebels) had been a cobbler and carpenter respectively; Juan Banderas, 'a great, burly, burr-head', and later a *compañero* of Zapata, and Juan Carrasco, who succeeded Banderas as the ranking rebel in Sinaloa, were both cowboys; though the American consul in Mazatlán, with the usual consular concern for police records, rated Carrasco a criminal, and most of the Sinaloan leaders as outlaws, for almost all had 'more or less open accounts with the government for crimes unpunished'. [163]

But, as in the Huasteca, matters were more complex than this. If the prevailing tone of the Sinaloan revolution was plebeian, its leaders also included men of property and status: Justo Tirado, a landowner of liberal antecedents (though a rough-and-ready character); José María Ochoa, scion of an established but declining family of El Fuerte; and the de la Rocha clan, who enjoyed a long-standing *cacicazgo* in the Durango mountains. [164] Later, we shall encounter landlord-rebels who were patently counter-revolutionary (the 'last-minute' revolutionaries of summer 1911). [165] But these Sinaloan pioneers were of different stock. They did not join the revolution to save their skins, or to contain peasant revolt; on the contrary, they took decided risks, and were able to mobilise their tenants, retainers and followers in a fashion that Luis Terrazas would have envied. And they could do so because, unlike Terrazas or the planters of Morelos, they had not sundered the bonds of paternalism and gone in search of progress and profit. The Ochoa family was a casualty of Porfirian development, while Tirado's son was 'a virtual illiterate'. [166] Herculano de la Rocha was a classic *serrano* cacique: a grizzled, grey-haired old man, with a scrubby beard, *huaraches* on his feet, a red bandana covering one empty eye-socket, who rode down from the mountains to begin a long revolutionary career accompanied by a brother, a son, a daughter, a nephew, and a retinue of 'dwarves, cranks, wild and beautiful women and brave mountaineers'.[167] The precise motives for their revolutionary commitment cannot be plumbed. Some, like Tirado, boasted an ancient, liberal affiliation; and some, in all probability, nurtured particular grudges against the authorities. The fact that they were landlords was important, but not all-important. Like the *rancheros* of the Hidalgo sierra – and unlike the second-generation sophisticates of Morelos – these retained sufficient characteristics in common with their popular followers (note the description of de la Rocha), and, what is more, they could share with them a common antipathy to Porfirian centralisation, modernisation, and pacification, all of which tolled the knell for traditional, *serrano caciquismo*.[168] But equally they stood apart from the political opposition of 1909–10, from the city professionals and businessmen, the writers and talkers, who represented a very different type of well-to-do. The latter were Mexico's Whigs; the pioneer landlord rebels were Mexico's Jacobites, rural backwoodsmen, sometimes boorish and rough-hewn, who spurned progress but who could, in times of armed rebellion, whistle up a following from among their ramified family and retainers. Thus, landlords though they might be, they could logically ally with popular, even *agrarista* forces, and contribute to the overthrow of the old regime. By the spring of 1911, as these assorted rebels battened their control onto the Sinaloan countryside, laid siege to the towns, and extended their operations down into the rough Tepic territory, observers – while noting the customary, prevalent feeling against Díaz – also lamented the growth of 'a condition which allows the disorderly to plunder the law-abiding elements', and predicted a descent into the endemic anarchy which Mexico had experienced between 1810 and 1876.[169] If, for some, this was an appalling prospect, there were others who welcomed (and thus assisted) this rending of the Pax Porfiriana and partial reversion to the bad old days. Despoiled *campesinos* and old-style caciques were not wholly unnatural allies in this violent attempt to put back the clock.

The emergence of these new men in almost all the states of Mexico north of the Isthmus was one of the remarkable features of the Madero revolution; in the space of a few months, as the winter snows melted and the summer rains began, a new political generation was born. The revolution which they staffed was far from monolithic, and cannot be encapsulated in a few neat generalisations. But, granted its growing extension and variety, the historian of the (national) revolution cannot afford to describe its many component parts in even the modest detail with which the pioneer rebellions of 1910–11 have been so far treated. At this point, therefore, we shall try to maintain the national–provincial dialectic which is so vital for an understanding of the revolution (without sinking into a morass of descriptive detail) by shifting the analysis away from the question of cause and origin (clearly important in studying the pioneer rebellions) and towards that of means and tactics. For, as the revolution spread, these show a certain uniformity throughout the country; they tend to unite the many disparate movements which multiplied in the early months of 1911 and, at the same time, they shed an oblique light on the character and composition of the constituent rebellions of the Revolution, which, in default of more direct illumination, often remain obscure.

The build-up and operations of rebel bands such as those which infested Chihuahua, or Morelos, or Sinaloa, followed patterns which recurred throughout Mexico. First, they were clearly rural in origin, even if a few of their leaders (still a distinct minority) had migrated from town to countryside to escape Porfirian vigilance. Initially, they were poorly armed, incapable of resisting Federal or *rural* forces, dependent on speed, mobility, local co-operation and intelligence. Their first task was to secure weapons, hence the frequent raids on outlying haciendas and the quest for hidden caches of arms, some of them old relics of previous rebellions, some of them, as it turned out, purely mythical.[170] Rebel forces in Chihuahua, close to the border, could count on illicit supplies from the US but, even so, Madero's men faced Federal mausers and machine guns with inferior weaponry (as at Casas Grandes) and, as they ringed Juárez, they were said to be 'quite destitute of any munitions of war'.[171] Indians from the Chihuahua sierra – according to one, perhaps fanciful, account – went armed with 'arquebuses of the time of the Conquest'. In the Laguna, too, the rebels had to face the Federals equipped with 'any old thing' they could lay hands on; when Gertrudis Sánchez began his peregrinations through the Coahuila/Zacatecas borderlands, 'all [his] men rode bareback, and their arms were cudgels of dry maguey'.[172] Whatever the source and size of the Maderista war-chest, it did not guarantee a well-equipped army. And lack of guns and ammunition constricted activities even more in the south. This was the case in Veracruz, as it had been during the Valladolid uprising in Yucatán, when church railings were ripped up to serve as pikes.[173] Small groups of marauders in the marshy borderlands of Tabasco and Veracruz went armed with the ubiquitous machete and cheap shotguns, which they loaded with nails, pebbles and any ammunition they could steal. But, in general, the south was tightly controlled by government and planter; the rebels' attempts 'to gather arms from the villages and hamlets was impossible, since the authorities and the government forces had already done it'.[174] Many would-be rebel movements did not get beyond this initial stage of searching out and sequestering guns and cartridges, horses and *burros*, the sinews of guerrilla war in Mexico.

The shortage of arms dictated rebel strategy. After the first optimistic assaults on Parral, Gómez Palacio and elsewhere, towns were given a wide berth. The rebels concentrated on remote haciendas and villages, they would attack, while their ammunition lasted, and then run for the hills. In the Laguna, an observer noted, 'they are poorly armed [and] have but little ammunition . . . the policy of the rebels seems to be to rob and run'; hence the ready equation of rebellion with brigandage.[175] Sánchez kept his tatter-demalion forces out of sight when he called at lonely haciendas, claiming strength far in excess of reality.[176] In the Nombre de Dios district of Durango a lone horseman rode up to a hacienda employing a hundred peons; he claimed to lead 150 rebels, 'who had remained out of sight to avoid frightening the ladies of the house'; he demanded – and got – arms, ammunition, and a few recruits. After he had ridden off, it transpired that he was alone. But, thus equipped, he made for Muleros, took the town, and destroyed the municipal archives. Such deeds of bravado were possible, it was thought, because of 'the sympathy of the people in general [towards the rebels] and the frightened condition of those who have property to lose'.[177] It was, in other words, the general hostility of the population towards the regime – not simply the failings of the repressive apparatus, still less some mysterious international conjuncture – which brought the collapse of the old order.[178] And, as the revolution progressed and the panic of the authorities augmented, there was scope for bigger bluffs: Juan Cabral stood at the gates of Cananea with 200 men, claiming to have 1,500; Enrique Aguirre (by his own account, it is true) rode into Tepezintla, in the Huasteca, brandishing a pistol, informing the authorities that he was 'a Maderista captain and that if the town was not handed over at once 400 armed and mounted men would enter, in response to which the Mayor replied that the town was in my power'.[179] Thus far had the hollow shell of Porfirismo crumbled.

Speed also compensated for the rebels' inferior hardware. Many of the northern revolutionaries (and some southerners, too, like Zapata) were natural horsemen; when José de la Luz Blanco crossed the sierra from Chihuahua he brought with him 'the best [horses] that have ever been seen in the state of Sonora'.[180] Many of Urbina's men (leaving aside his 'Indian infantry') were *vaqueros*, capable of riding sixty-five miles across rough country with empty bellies, and this was true of rebels throughout the north (*vaqueros* like Banderas and Carrasco of Sinaloa spring to mind), 'men whose daily vocation makes them good horsemen and marksmen'.[181] And their Tarahumara Indian scouts, it might be added, were capable of prodigious feats of endurance on foot.[182] But this mobility – contrasting with the static strategy of the Federals – was not confined to the north. In Guanajuato, Cándido Navarro led a vigorous revolutionary movement in the region north of Silao. Guanajuato and the Bajío more generally were characterised by a widespread artisanry and mining industry (Navarro, though a schoolmaster, had also worked as a watchman at the mines of La Luz), and by diverse land tenures; 'traditional' villages were scarce and though the region produced abundant rebellion, banditry and urban rioting, the basis for a sustained, organised, agrarian movement, such as

Zapata's, was lacking. Save in rare individual cases, the membership and motivation of revolts like Navarro's are therefore hard to penetrate. [183] At San Felipe, for instance, his followers were thought to be 'men . . . of the middle class', at Silao they were 'peons'. [184] Such reports may have been more accurate and less inconsistent than it would appear at first sight. Membership, it seems, changed according to locality: a nucleus of mobile guerrillas (about half of Navarro's men were mounted, with rifles) would be supplemented by local sympathisers, who participated in skirmishes, helped drive out unpopular authorities, and then returned to their homes. This practice, which obfuscated the counting or categorisation of rebel bands, was common elsewhere. [185] And, when coupled with the (full-time) rebels' speed of movement, it presented the Federals with formidable problems. Navarro led 300 men across thirty miles of rough country between the Hacienda Ramona and Silao in fourteen hours at night; after a battle, they marched on to La Luz (another ten miles) next day, and moved on again the same night, 'a very remarkable achievement', local people thought. Indeed, the moves were so rapid that many concluded there were two separate bands operating in the vicinity and it was clear that neither the *rurales* (whose job it was to patrol the countryside), still less the Federals, could track them down. So, too, on the Puebla–Hidalgo borders, the forces of Gabriel Hernández easily outran Federal pursuers by cutting across country. [186]

Mobility could compensate for lack of munitions in the early months. But the moment came – at different times in different regions – when the rebels had to venture out of the bush and meet the Federals in the open. Otherwise, they could not hope to capture towns, or to destroy Díaz's army, and thus the regime – though bruised and battered – could hope to survive. Even if a negotiated settlement were to be considered (as soon it was) captured towns would represent important bargaining counters; indeed, when talks began, government spokesmen could address those across the table as 'rebels who are not yet in possession of a single important city'. [187] Local leaders, too, had to make their mark, in case a negotiated peace supervened: 'to guarantee the Ayalan position in Morelos, Zapata now had to take towns, not just to raid them'. [188] Finally, towns (especially the border ports) represented sources of funds and *matériel*.

But pitched battles with the Federals had gone badly, and the reduction of towns presented particular difficulties. Rebel artillery was almost non-existent; not until April did the revolutionaries of Chihuahua, the most advanced in the field, attempt to equip themselves with artillery, using the machine-shops of the lumber company at Madera, one of their first conquests, to build two makeshift cannon out of car axles; while the intrepid Antonio Villareal made off with a cannon from an El Paso public park. [189] But this sort of ordnance it was almost safer to face than to fire. [190] It was easy, therefore, for the Federals to dig into towns like Juárez and rely on their superior fire-power.

Improvised dynamite bombs were one answer, particularly in the mining districts where explosives were readily available. Ramón Iturbe blasted his way into the sierra town of Topia, block by block, reaching the centre without exposing his men to direct Federal fire; it was the same technique which the people of Alamos (Sonora) feared as Benjamín Hill's forces approached, fresh from using 'their nitro-glycerine method of attack' at Navojoa.[191] Once a town was taken, dynamite bombs could also provide a lethal defence: they took a heavy toll of Federals equipped with Mausers and dum-dum bullets who sought to recapture Madero's home town of Parras early in May.[192] Meanwhile in Mexico City – which was spared these horrors – the government press denounced the rebels' use of 'infernal machines' as being somehow 'underhand' and 'unchivalrous'.[193]

In addition, the rebels might hope to sneak into a town covertly (as they did at Acapulco, only to be driven out again), or they could surround it in the hope of starving out the garrison and wearing down the government's morale.[194] This, as it turned out, was the way to end the military stalemate. By mid-April 1911 government confidence had been sorely eroded, public opinion was running strongly against Díaz, and, if the rebels could not in the foreseeable future crush the Federal Army, no more could the Federals expect to crush the rebels. But, for reasons soon to be considered, a long war of attrition was unacceptable to the leadership of both sides; instead, a few more rebel successes, a further wilting of Porfirian morale, would ensure a swift, too-easy revolutionary triumph; the long war of attrition would be postponed for three years. This became clear at Juárez, on the northern border, whose siege and final fall precipitated the ouster of Díaz and opened the floodgates of revolution throughout the country.

VICTORY

By mid-April 1911 the Maderista forces in the north held Cd Juárez in check; General Navarro, the Federal commander, had received and rejected a surrender demand. But now diplomacy began to assert itself. In the past, when local rebellions flared, Díaz had sometimes tempered repression with conciliation; now, faced with a national rebellion he could not defeat, he had to attempt conciliation on a national scale. For, not only were the holders of power and property showing grave concern, Díaz himself was now showing signs of physical decline. There were indications 'of both health and intellect failing' at the end of 1910 and, as the wearing weeks went by, the old dictator seemed weak, inactive and absent-minded. When the supreme crisis broke in May, Díaz was confined to bed, suffering agonies from an ulcerated jaw.[195] Under pressure from his advisers, he began to make concessions.

In January, Miguel Ahumada had replaced Alberto Terrazas as Governor of Chihuahua, where he pointedly dissocated himself from the old Creel–Terrazas machine and appealed for peace. Some moderate, non-belligerent, reformist opinion believed that this was change enough, and that the rebels could now lay down their arms with peace and honour.[196] In March, more governors were sacked, including Mucio Martínez of Puebla. Next, the cabinet was purged and prominent Científicos removed. A bemused Congress heard the president promise democratic and agrarian reforms. As a final sop, Vice-President Corral left for Europe on grounds of failing health.[197] But, as when concessions were made locally, these did not have the desired placatory effect and, if anything, they encouraged the revolutionaries further. At Veracruz and Acapulco, it was reported, the cabinet changes made scant impact on public opinion; at Tampico they were construed as signs of official anxiety; while in war-torn Sinaloa this last-minute liberalisation only served to stimulate 'some dozen . . . pronunciamientos [since] it was considered as proof of weakness on the part of the government'.[198] Maderista spokesmen were careful to encourage this impression and Madero dismissed the changes as too little, too late.[199]

Finally, Díaz bid for a negotiated settlement. Peace talks had been in the air since early in the new year: in February, members of the Madero family (exiled to the US, but unsympathetic to Francisco's revolution) recommended peace to the rebels, without success; in March, Limantour offered terms to the Maderos (his old friends) and to Dr Vázquez Gómez, but, while they were interested, Francisco Madero was not. Now, in April, with the rebels threatening an attack on Juárez which could embroil the US (fighting at Agua Prieta had already caused American casualties and protests), Vázquez Gómez repeated his plea for an armistice and peace talks; Oscar Braniff and Toribio Esquivel Obregón, representing the government, came to El Paso to repeat Limantour's offer and, after some debate, the revolutionary leadership agreed to an armistice covering the Chihuahuan theatre, while peace negotiations were held.[200] For nearly two weeks (24 April–7 May) a shaky armistice prevailed in Chihuahua while, in the rest of the country, the revolutionary build-up continued, amid growing panic and political uncertainty.[201] At Juárez the talks increasingly focussed upon and finally stuck at the question of Díaz's resignation: required by the rebels, rejected by the government. Corral and any number of ministers and governors might be thrown to the wolves, but not the president. On 7 May, with the extended armistice running out, Díaz categorically refused to resign and Madero, announcing the breakdown of the talks, ordered his army to march south, away from Juárez and the border, presumably towards Chihuahua City.[202]

But at this point Madero failed to carry his men with him. The Maderista army, which was neither accustomed nor amenable to static discipline, had now been encamped around Juárez for three weeks. Food and funds had been running low and Madero had found it necessary to decree a five year prison sentence for desertion – the first indication that rebel morale was sinking.[203] Among the various *cabecillas* who commanded the army, loyalty to Madero was conditional and sometimes outweighed by local or personal commitments. Madero's appointment of José de la Luz Soto as general commander in Chihuahua had had to be withdrawn to avoid offending Orozco, and the men of Bachíniva quit Juárez for their homes in the sierra when their *jefe*, the quarter-master general of the Maderista army, was demoted for alleged peculation.[204] As the talks dragged on and the armistice was twice renewed, the Maderista troops began to fear a government plot to buy time while reinforcements were brought up from the south. Díaz and the Federals could not be trusted; there were stories of a *soldadera* treacherously shot while taking food to her man in the Maderista front line.[205] News of the rapid spread of the revolution elsewhere must have galled these pioneer revolutionaries, now bogged down for weeks outside a northern border port. Orozco's men, certainly, resented the inactivity and were spoiling for a fight; they saw Juárez as ripe for conquest (the Federals were outnumbered two to one) and they dismissed the American threat.[206] So, as Madero began to move south on the morning of 8 May, some of his forces instead turned about and engaged the Federal defenders, and this soon led to a full-scale assault on the town. It is not clear whether the military chiefs had precipitated the conflict, or taken advantage of a spontaneous clash, but, whatever the cause, Madero was powerless to halt the attack. By dusk the rebels held the outskirts and had begun blasting and boring their way through the adobe houses towards the centre. The next morning found the Federals pinned down in a few key buildings, including the church; on 10 May, now besieged without supplies in the barracks, they agreed to surrender.[207]

The capture of Juárez was a great fillip for the revolution. Establishing the town as provisional capital of the Republic (as Juárez had done back in the days when it was Paso del Norte) and naming a cabinet, Madero could credibly pose as the head of an alternative government. As the most important link between Mexico and the US, and the spot most favoured by American journalists seeking local colour in relative comfort, Juárez conferred prestige and publicity; the second of which (since the rebels policed the town well) was generally favourable.[208] More significantly it offered a port for the introduction of arms, and a proof that Federal-held towns were not impregnable. The Díaz government rushed to renew negotiations, and Madero (for reasons which will become apparent) was ready to respond. A new armistice was concluded, covering the whole country. The pressures on Díaz became intolerable; urged by his colleagues and facing the hostility of the Mexico City mob, he conceded his resignation. It was agreed that Francisco León de la Barra, a non-Científico, Catholic lawyer and diplomat, should take over as provisional president and convene elections, and that the new government should study and seek to satisfy public opinion in the different states. On this basis – notoriously vague, save for the change in the national administration – hostilities would cease and the demobilisation of the rebel army commence. At 10 p.m. on 21 May, the principals, accompanied by newspapermen, met at the Juárez customs house, only to find the building closed and in darkness; car headlights were switched on and by their light the famous Treaty of Cd Juárez was signed, bringing to an end thirty-five years of Porfirian rule.[209]

Meanwhile, as Madero's army invested Juárez, dozens of local revolutionary movements gathered momentum elsewhere, unaffected by the Chihuahua armistice, though encouraged by the government's evident anxiety. As the news from the north – especially the fall of Juárez – spurred them on, so their collective impact softened the regime in its attitude to the Maderista demands, yet, paradoxically perhaps, the runaway success of the revolution also pushed Madero and his advisers in the direction of compromise rather than intransigence. The welter of events talking place in April–May 1911 cannot be recounted in any detail. It is only possible to suggest the flurry of revolutionary activity and to extract certain significant themes: first, organised rebellion; then riot and jacquerie. But this should be sufficient to prove a vital, if contentious point: that the *transacción* which ended the Díaz regime represented not the logical culmination of a narrow, controlled, political revolution, but rather the alarmed reaction – on the part of elites on both sides – to a mounting social upheaval.

This upheaval now affected virtually every state in the federation. The Huimanguillo and Cárdenas districts of Tabasco, for example, now produced a vigorous rebel movement and, if the Federals contrived an important victory there in late April, the Maderistas recovered to take Pichucalco in May; while Chiapas boasted a rebel army of 300 which captured Ocosingo, their grievances, according to a consular cable, 'local displeasure alleged abuses prefects, dissatisfaction state officials'.[210] Rebellion was compounded by additional problems. Tabasco suffered an outbreak of smallpox and, though it is not known if this was causally linked to the revolution (as so many later outbreaks were to be), it was certainly the case that the virtually besieged inhabitants of Acapulco and Mazatlán (where food was short and the summer rains were beginning) feared imminent epidemics.[211] In such towns, prices were high and morale was low: like the Mazatecos further up the coast, the people of Acapulco witnessed the entire rural hinterland fall under rebel sway. Here, rebellions (often of agrarian origin) flickered, flared and spread: at Ayutla, Ometepec, and San Marcos; court records (usually the first target of such revolts) were rushed to Acapulco; and by May the port was isolated and the revolutionaries were encroaching on its outskirts. Nevertheless – or perhaps as a result – the citizens refused to join a volunteer force for the defence of their home town.[212] Meanwhile, in the regions north of the Balsas River (which looked towards Morelos and the central plateau rather than to the hot country and the coast) two strong, better organised rebellions developed. Jesús Salgado rose in arms with 55 men at Arcotepel on 2 April; he took, *inter alia*, Apaxtla, Tetela del Río and Arcelia (the latter on 17 April, by which time Salgado led

325 men); then Totolopam, Ajuchitlán, and Tlalchapa (22 April; 1,758 men).[213] Such was the speed of revolutionary recruitment and conquest in the spring of 1911. Close by – too close, as it soon transpired – the Figueroa brothers of Huitzuco were mopping up the region east of Iguala. As *rancheros* with some local influence and reputation in their own hilly corner of Guerrero, they had a long record of opposition to Díaz appointees; they graduated to Maderismo, and thus combined a commitment to middle-class reformism (more typical of the cities) with a capacity for rural resistance (which they shared with the caciques and *rancheros* of the countryside); an unusual, but powerful union. While Francisco Figueroa, a teacher, had written a biography of Juárez, his brother Ambrosio ('a man of scant education') had been forced by his opposition activities to quit Guerrero for Morelos, where he worked on a Ruiz de Velasco plantation and served in the local army reserve, thus acquiring some useful contacts, as well as a familiarity with soldiering.[214] After beating off a *rurales* attack on Huitzuco in February, the Figueroas extended their control over north-eastern Guerrero, and began to spill over into Morelos.

Here, of course, they encountered Zapata, and, although a working agreement was reached, it was clear – not least to the alert planters – that the Guerrero and Morelos rebels were only lukewarm allies. Still, Zapata left Jojutla to the Figueroas while he concentrated on Cuautla, picking off the outlying towns, raiding into Puebla, finally massing some 4,000 troops – 'largely untrained, undisciplined, impatient gangs' – for an assault on the strategic heart of Morelos. For almost a week, while Madero negotiated at Juárez, Zapata's men hurled themselves against the Cuautla defences and finally occupied the ravaged city on 19 May.[215] Apart from contributing significantly to the demise of Díaz, the revolutionaries of Guerrero and Morelos had established themselves as forces to be reckoned with in the politicking that would follow the peace.

Puebla, to the east, was the scene of repeated Zapatista incursions, which supplemented the indigenous revolutionary efforts of Francisco Bertrani (Teziutlán), Benigno Centeño (Texmelucán), Esteban Márquez (Libres) and others. By the middle of May, seven of the twenty district seats (*cabeceras*) were held by the rebels and four more were under threat; the American consul in Puebla reckoned, a little extravagantly perhaps, that there were up to 20,000 rebels at large in the state.[216] But state boundaries meant little to the rebels: several of Zapata's closest allies were *poblanos*, and the revolutionaries of Puebla, Tlaxcala, Hidalgo and highland Veracruz shuttled in and out of each others' states, fighting, collaborating and occasionally quarrelling. In Veracruz some of the failed revolutionaries of November 1910 now began to make their names (though there were others, like Heriberto Jara, who held back until as late as April). By then, Gabriel Gavira had arrived back in Veracruz on a fruit boat from New Orleans, where he had sought refuge; Camerino Mendoza made his way overland from the Texas border; Rafael Tapia and

Cándido Aguilar, after weeks of swimming against the tide and comparing their local failure with the northerners' success, quite suddenly found recruits outnumbering deserters, villages and small towns falling into their hands, and cities like Orizaba now within their sights.[217] Oaxaca, too, witnessed several significant uprisings and Sebastián Ortiz, in hiding since November, was able to emerge from the mountains and join up with the rebels of Tuxtepec.[218]

Further north, regions of relative quiet now began to experience revolt. Western San Luis, so far more tranquil than the Huasteca, was caught in a pincer move, as Gertrudis Sanchez came south (his 7 followers of mid-March augmented to some 40 in late April, nearly 200 in early May) and Cándido Navarro headed north from Guanajuato; in addition, San Luis began to produce rebel contingents of its own.[219] Similarly, the prolific Laguna revolution started to fan out into southern Coahuila: Enrique Adame Macías led 850 men in a successful assault on Parras, held it against a Federal counter-attack, and then began to move troops towards Saltillo. Smaller groups, meanwhile, were operating around Galeana, Arteaga, and Monclova.[220] Much of Coahuila, and most of Nuevo León and Tamaulipas, however, remained quiet, as did much of Jalisco; regions which had distinguished themselves during the phase of political opposition, 1908–10, thus receded from view during the armed revolution.[221]

But the extension of the revolution was most dramatic, significant and thus worthy of analysis in Durango and the Laguna. By mid-April, Durango swarmed with rebel bands; the state capital was threatened and prominent citizens made the first of many attempts to raise a volunteer force to supplement the small Federal garrison.[222] But – like a similar scheme floated at Mapimí – it came to nothing.[223] Within a week, in fact, the governor and city officials had resigned and, among the 'prominent citizens', the once stiff upper lip was all a-quiver. Demands were made that the Federals evacuate rather than convert the city into a battlefield. Just as alarming as the prospect of a pitched battle was the fear of mob rule. A speedy, peaceful revolutionary takeover was now seen as infinitely preferable to either: after all, the Arrietas, who had just taken Santiago Papasquiaro after heavy fighting (in which the Federals, 'without the sympathy of a single person in the place', put up a brave resistance), had maintained good order, punished looters, and treated prisoners and government officials humanely. Such examples gave grounds for cautious optimism, and the proximity of the rebels made for a wonderful new objectivity in the assessment of their character. And this was particularly the case in Durango in April–May 1911, when food prices were soaring, when there were as many beggars on the streets as in the depression days of 1908, when the city gaol was crammed with 800 prisoners, and when three policemen had been murdered in five days. The fears of the well-to-do were thus focussed less on the rebels outside than the 'rough element' within, who were thought to be 'very hard to control'; indeed, the rebels offered a means of control which, in the circumstances, might prove more effective than the shaky garrison and the dwindling police force.[224]

But the Federal commander, displaying more initiative than many, stayed put, sealing the city with barbed wire and blockhouses, contriving to make his garrison seem bigger than it was.[225] While lesser towns in the state fell, and while Madero still parleyed at Juárez, the fighting reached the outskirts of Durango and the feelings of panic within increased. The acting governor (of two weeks standing) tried to resign but the legislature refused to accept his resignation; the 'solid men of the community' floated the 'absurd' idea that the foreign consuls take over the government of the city; all the time, the lower classes displayed keen anticipation of the impending rebel attack.[226] But they were to be disappointed. The siege went on until the Juárez Treaty was concluded and publicised at the end of May, bringing immense relief to the propertied classes of Durango, who proceeded to sound the church bells, call out the city band, and drink to the restoration of peace. On the penultimate day of May the rebel troops began to file in, bearing an assortment of weaponry – shotguns, machetes, some with just a knife stuck in the belt, and, though they rode ostentatiously on the pavements and frequented the cantinas, they were generally peaceful and orderly.[227]

But close by in the Laguna a similar story produced a different denouement, which showed that the fears of the propertied classes were not groundless. By the end of April, Torreón was a Federal island in a sea of rebellion, defended by 200 Federal troops and 50 police, *rurales* and volunteers.[228] Its triplet towns of Gómez and Lerdo had just fallen: Gómez to Jesus Agustín Castro (who thereby returned victorious to the streets he had hastily evacuated after an abortive attack in November), Lerdo to Pablo Lavín who, though 'most courteous' to American residents, went through the familiar routine of opening the gaol and burning the municipal archives; other *lagueros* were extending these customs to Parras and points east. A Federal counter-attack on Gómez was parried with great aplomb, and the rebels began to mass for the assault on Torreón.[229] As contingents from all over Durango and the Laguna began to converge, the Federal commander, General Lojero, grew jumpy; in the dead of night on 14/15 May, during a heavy rainstorm, he ordered a sudden evacuation – so sudden that some Federals were left in the front line unawares.[230] At dawn the citizens of Torreón awoke to find the army gone, and the amazed Maderistas began to troop in. The chief of police, three city officials, and a Federal captain left behind in the rush sought asylum in the American consulate. Outside, huge crowds formed and began to ransack Chinese properties and attack Chinese immigrants on the streets, the city *canaille* abetting the Maderista soldiers. The rebels claimed that the Chinese had sniped at their forces (which was unlikely); a rebel *jefe*, Jesús Flores, was said to have made a speech 'in which the Chinese were depicted as dangerous competitors for the common people of Mexico', concluding 'that it would be best to exterminate them'.[231]

Even if such a speech was never made, its sentiments still accorded with a strong popular antipathy to the Chinese, which became evident in dozens of attacks and killings during the years of revolution. It was against the Chinese (and the Spaniards), not the Americans (still less the British) that xenophobia ran strong, and was translated into violent action. No American, it is worth noting, was killed or harmed in Torreón, and damage to American interests (in what was a very Americanised town) totalled only $US22,000. Yet dozens of stores had been looted, a casino and bank ransacked, the courthouse and *jefatura* put to the torch. When Emilio Madero (Francisco's brother) arrived, restored order, and began to count the fatalities, a 'feeling of awe befell all Mexicans with the death list of Chinese swelling from minute to minute'.[232] Over 250 Chinese had died in the pogrom (more than all the American civilians to be killed in ten years revolutionary violence) along with a good many Maderistas (they included Jesús Flores), some Federal stragglers and bystanders.[233] For months afterwards, goods stolen during the sack of Torreón appeared in the more questionable shops of San Pedro and (one assumes) other Laguna towns.[234]

Though the Chinese, forming tight, introverted but prosperous colonies within the towns of northern Mexico, suffered repeated persecutions, the Torreón massacre was the biggest of the Revolution; indeed, it was probably the biggest civilian massacre since that of the Alhóndiga in October 1810 (when, again, the foreign – *gachupín* – inhabitants of a prosperous city were butchered by Indian and mestizo hordes from the rural hinterland). Yet the events of Torreón only represented in extreme, xenophobic form what was taking place throughout urban Mexico in the late spring of 1911. In almost every state the collapse of authority brought riots or the threat of riots; the repeatedly voiced fears of the 'prominent citizens' proved all too legitimate; and the targets of the mob were uniformly consistent – the gaols and government buildings, officers and officials, moneylenders, pawnbrokers and the small shopkeepers who supplied the urban poor with basic essentials. Many of these were Spaniards, some (in the north and north west) were Chinese: hence the popular xenophobia which bypassed the real agents of economic imperialism, the American or British company managers. Urban riot was so ubiquitous, however, that it deserves brief, separate analysis, which follows.

RIOT

The importance of urban violence during the Revolution has not been recognised. Some would regard the action of the mob as marginal, and confined to Mexico City (the best-known case); histories of the Revolution may mention examples in passing, but without drawing inferences.[235] It could be objected, of course, that riots and rioters – however fashionable in academic circles – were peripheral to the revolutionary process; that, however numerous, they were apolitical, ineffectual, and pointless. There are two replies to this. First, many riots or near-riots (especially those of 1911) were specifically political, and they frequently achieved their objectives, that is, the downfall of unpopular officials. Examples will be given. But there were also ostensibly 'apolitical' riots, often more bloody and violent, which, though they might include 'political' victims, also ranged more widely, taking in an array of 'economic' targets: the shopkeepers, pawnbrokers and ethnic groups just mentioned, as well as factory owners and members of the propertied class generally.[236] To observers, these often seemed expressions of wanton violence and aggression; usually they fizzled out, or were repressed, without registering real gains, without even formulating any real objectives; racial or other crude psychological stereotypes derivative of Le Bon might be employed by way of explanation. The historian, who does not risk being robbed, and who can consider the matter more dispassionately, should not be so dismissive; in particular, the historian should not reify 'the Revolution' (that is, the articulate, organised, speech-making, regime-building Revolution) and neglect all the diverse movements – rural as well as urban – which do not fit within this rubric. For, in fact, these movements were both important in their own right, and instrumental in the formation of the 'official', reified Revolution. Urban riots were among the most significant expressions of urban, working-class resentment during the Revolution; arguably, they involved more people and had more direct impact than either unionisation, or organised participation in revolutionary armies (the means by which it is usually supposed that the working class made its presence felt). In particular, they contributed powerfully to the *grande peur* of the well-to-do, and to the general erosion of hierarchy and deference which were central to the Revolution. Finally, it is worth noting that the riots of the Mexican Revolution – like those of pre-industrial Europe – displayed recurrent features and a certain internal logic; even the most violent, 'apolitical' upheavals obeyed motives which are susceptible to rational analysis.[237]

With the spread of rebellion and dissolution of authority of 1911, the response of the urban worker was often to take to the streets, just as that of the peasant was to retreat into the village. But the peasantry possessed corporate traditions which might channel and sustain protest; the apparently aimless protest of the proletarian reflected the anomie of city life, particularly in key regions.[238] For riots followed a clear ecological pattern. Most of the towns affected were those suffering economic decline: decayed industrial centres like Celaya, San Miguel Allende or León, or failing mining towns like Pachuca. Torreón was far from declining, but the depression of 1908, with its attendant unemployment and misery, was a recent memory, and the whole Laguna region, despite its high wages, contained a large, seasonally employed, migrant population.[239] By sundering city and countryside, and generally dislocating economic activity, the Revolution revived unemployment (or heightened existing levels) and sharpened popular hostility to familiar enemies: officials, employers, usurers, retailers. The reappearance of beggars on the streets of Torreón (and, perhaps, the spate of attacks on policemen) were harbingers of mob protest. Furthermore, the revolution encouraged a new uppishness among the common people. Petty tyrants of years' standing were being ousted and humiliated; egalitarian ideas were circulating. It was said (according to one account from Durango) that 'if the revolutionists win out [the peon class] are made for life', we shall note similar sentiments associated with rural protest in 1911.[240] And, as the rebels rode their horses along the pavements of Torreón, or travelled in the trams without paying, so the common people of the city also seemed to swagger in the streets, 'displaying an improper equality ... [and] obliging ladies and respectable people to walk in the middle of the streets' (which, now the rains had come, resembled a quagmire); all this because they believed that 'the hour had come in which we are all equal'.[241] Economic and political upheaval, transmitted from the countryside to the city, and coupled with this new spirit of insubordination, set the scene for the urban riots, and these involved not simply material acquisition, but also revenge and humiliation, displays of 'moral outrage', and demonstrations that the world – if not yet turned upside down – was certainly in the process of rotating.

The towns of the Bajío were worst hit. On the eve of the rebel entry into Cd Manuel Doblado (Gto) the people took to the streets, burned the courthouse and tax office, and opened the prison gates.[242] 'Revolutionaries' under Bonifacio Soto restored order.[243] Almost at once, a deputation of citizens from San Francisco del Rincón arrived and begged Soto to put their house in order too, 'in view of the fact that a movement of numerous workers was making itself felt, workers who because of the lack of a market for their goods, meant to commit vandalistic acts'. Soto obliged, 'firmly repressing the workers' movement ... preventing them from opening the prison and saving business from damage'.[244] In the same state, the *jefe político* of Celaya feared that the entry of the rebels under Fernando Franco would be the signal for mob outrages: the police force was non-existent, and the gaol was crammed with 'over 200 notorious criminals who, united with the masses would cause great damage, taking advantage of the confusion of the rebel entry'.[245] These fears were not groundless. There had been an attempted prison break-out a few weeks before at Celaya. And, a revolutionary sympathiser reported, the Spanish industrialist Eusebio González rightly feared[246]

that the workers at [his] important factory, La Soria, might commit outrages ... since the assistant *jefe* at La Soria was practically appointed by Sr González ... and is thoroughly hated by the local people on account of the abuses he has perpetrated, and it is natural that Sr González, who is scarcely loved by his workers, should fear for his interests.

It seems clear from these accounts that it was the destitute artisans – the weavers and leather-workers – who made the Bajío a hotbed of urban unrest, much as it had been a century before. Though times had changed – and mining, for example, had declined in importance – it was still the case that the Bajío population, being more subject to the vicissitudes of the market than to the constraints of the corporate village, were prone to vent their protests violently in the streets, and, as already suggested, syndicalist self-defence was hardly a viable course for the artisanate.[247] It is also clear that the revolution had worsened their plight: as at Celaya, so at León, the biggest manufacturing city of the region, the handicraft workers were 'on the point of starvation for several months because . . . their market in the north had collapsed'. Riots were only narrowly averted at León, but at Pénjamo, on the Michoacán border, seventy Maderistas joined with a 'rabble of about a hundred on foot' to sack the municipal buildings and two pawnshops, until 'the better people of the town' formed vigilante patrols to restore order.[248]

One final trouble-spot in Guanajuato deserves attention, since there happen to be good accounts, from different perspectives, which suggest how and why such riots occurred.[249] San Miguel Allende was a town of some 20,000, dominated (a Maderista reported) by a tyrannical *jefe político* (a crony of the longserving Porfirian governor) and a police chief fond of dealing out beatings, forced labour sentences, and terms of service in the army. Under their stern authority San Miguel remained peaceful until mid-May 1911 (Cándido Navarro's force was operating to the north west and did not impinge on San Miguel). Then, on 17 May, news came – prematurely, as it happened – that peace had been concluded at Juárez. The *jefe* reluctantly conceded permission for a public celebration and 600 people gathered outside the municipal palace carrying a white flag inscribed with a message of peace; there were some *vivas* for Madero, but all was orderly. Then, Miguel Zamora (a Maderista, and, according to a hostile account, a drunk Maderista) began dispensing mescal to the crowd and 'invited them to adopt an inconvenient and dangerous attitude'. A lawyer, Miguel Herrera, who reputedly had personal reasons for wishing the legal archives destroyed, joined Zamora on the rostrum and

invited the mob to let everyone out of prison and commit all kinds of outrages because 'the people were free; they were the masters of everything; they could dispose of other people's lives and property according to their whim, and there was no law other than their will'.

The people grew excited at hearing these egalitarian 'infamies'; when the *jefe* came forward to hear their grievances he was pelted with stones. Now thoroughly drunk, the mob tried to rush the gaol, the guards fired on them, and one rioter was killed. Repulsed at the gaol, the rioters broke into the Municipal Treasury, the law courts and the *Jefatura*, they rifled strongboxes and put the Treasury to the torch, they went back to the gaol, smashed down the doors and liberated the occupants (all 'really dangerous men', the hostile account explains). At this point the parish priest came forward and urged the mob to disperse to their homes. He was on the point of succeeding ('because the lower class always show respect for ministers of the Catholic faith') when the lawyer Herrera mounted a public bench and began to declaim against the clergy and assert that the public funds belonged to the people by right. There ensued, for some tense moments, a classic encounter of the Red and the Black, of jacobin and cleric, in the riot-torn streets of San Miguel. At the end, honours were even. The crowd began to disperse, looting shops as they went. The women's gaol was now opened and the governess's house ransacked; a Spanish moneylender was cleaned out. Zamora robbed the railway station, then thought better of it and returned the money. Herrera, realising the gravity of the situation, caught the next train to Mexico City and anonymity. Soon after, troops of Bonifacio Soto arrived to guarantee order.

The Maderista reply agreed as to the main events. Zamora admitted emptying the prison and destroying the archives (both were common revolutionary practices) but he placed the blame for the troubles squarely upon the town's officials. Once the protest had got under way, it had proved impossible to halt the looting. Herrera, claiming to be a casual traveller, prevailed upon to speak in praise of the Liberating Army, blamed liberal indulgence in mescal for the riots; but he confessed to surprise at these events, since San Miguel was 'a fairly respectable town, mostly factory workers who could read and write'. In fact, particularly when viewed in the national context, the events at San Miguel were not at all surprising: a comparable combination of long-term political *caciquismo* and economic hardship on the one hand, and of immediate political crisis and a certain democratic euphoria on the other, generated similar violent protests throughout urban Mexico.

Gertrudis Sánchez, for example, quelled disorders at Matehuala and Concepción del Oro, and used the threat of mob rule to secure the peaceful surrender of Mazapil.[250] Events at Concepción are perhaps dignified by the term 'disorders'. Here, a mob uprising was fully expected: Luis Gutiérrez, a local revolutionary (later a prominent general) advocated an attack on the town on the grounds that the rebels 'would win the action and then the people would riot, wanting to settle scores [*tener venganzas*] with the Authorities and certain individuals', which they did. The mob bayed for the blood of the municipal president and his officials, the commanding Federal officer, wounded in the rebel attack, was caught by the mob, grotesquely mutilated, and dragged by his feet through the town, after which his unrecognisable corpse had to be wrested from the mob 'with some fury and energy' by the revolutionary commander. Meanwhile, at La Paz, in the same region, commercial houses were sacked (the Spaniards again suffered) and the court records went up in smoke; at Salinas, on the western border of San Luis, Maderistas joined with local people in gutting the municipal palace, the courthouse and the post office. Again, the parish priest tried and failed to stop the disorders. Despite an 'exodus of all the decent people in the place' the British salt company managed to continue work, but it was hampered by the rapid disappearance of its Spanish clerks, who could not be induced to stay 'as at any moment the mob may go for them'.[251] Spanish textile factories on the outskirts of Acapulco and at Metepec and Atencingo (Pue.) were sacked and, in the latter case, several Spaniards were killed.[252]

Of the several mining towns badly affected by riots, it tended to be the smaller and/or declining ones which predominated. At Pachuca the prison was opened and (it was reported) drunken miners went on the rampage. Enrique Aguirre, who fetched Maderista forces under Gabriel Hernández to restore order, was invested with a tricolour sash by the city's well-to-do in recognition of his services, and young General Hernández, who ordered thirty of the principal rioters to be shot, was similarly feted, and given a parade of honour led by 'elegant señoritas mounted on sumptuously caparisoned horses'. The Spanish colony of Pachuca, who had suffered most from the riots, collaborated closely with Hernández, even to the extent of supplying advice and secretarial help in the restoration of the city's government.[253] Mining centres in west-central Mexico – generally smaller and poorer than the big camps of the north – were also affected by the collapse of the regime. At Los Reyes (Jal.) a female employee was reported raped, dynamite bombs were placed in the manager's house, and only the presence of private company gendarmes prevented worse trouble.[254] Among several towns in Michoacán hit by riots was Angangueo, where 'the local mob wrecked the place'.[255] Again, a minor incident (the arrest of a drunk) sparked off a riot in which the usual victims were sought out; the *jefe político* maintained that the riot was apolitical and dissociated from the revolution; Madero and the leaders of the official revolution would no doubt have agreed. According to the *jefe*,[256]

the object of the rioters [was] not . . . the support of the revolutionary movement, which pursued a political end, but rather . . . they dedicated themselves to pillage and destruction, in that, having destroyed all the furniture and most of the archives in the public buildings . . . they busied themselves sacking Felipe Llaguno's pawnshop and the poolroom and cantina La Cosmopolita of the Spaniard Benito Abascal . . . Men, women and children were engaged in quietly carrying away [from the pawnshop] the goods that remained after the sack, as if it were a quite honourable thing to do.

At Angangueo and other Michoacán towns, like Uruapán, Maderista troops co-operated with officials in restoring order, punishing the culprits, and attempting – without much success – to recover looted goods.[257]

It is worth noting that the big mining and manufacturing centres of the north experienced much less trouble. In part this may have been because the northern revolts were more organised and extensive; hence the transition from Porfirian to Maderista authority could be more rapid and efficacious. But, as

Torreón showed, this was not always the case. More important, the miners and industrial workers of the north were less disposed to take violent, direct action. Not only was that not their style, they were also less hard hit – even though the north was the chief locus of revolution – by economic dislocation and hardship. Major companies could weather the storm better than the impoverished artisans of the Bajío. Thus, when the Cananea Copper Co. was forced to stop operations in February, it took steps – encouraged by the state government – to spread some work around and avoid mass unemployment.[258] Though the collapse of the old regime did not go uncelebrated in the mines of Sonora (there was a drunken spree at Nacozari), the incidence of violence was less marked than in the centre-south. Cananea itself was peacefully occupied by Cabral's forces and there was 'no disorder or evidence of animosity towards Americans'.[259] When, soon after, Cananea began to experience unrest, the protagonists were unpaid Maderista soldiers, not malcontent miners, and when the miners became active, it was as trade unionists, not as rioters. Elsewhere in the industrial and commercial cities of the north business managed to keep going, with favourable results: at Monterrey, it was noted, 'there has not been the least manifestation of disorder'; at Matamoros, where trade with the US was brisk, 'everything is moving as if there had been no trouble in this locality'.[260]

Broadly speaking, then, it was the older industrial and administrative towns of central Mexico which were most affected by such riots, and it was declining, impoverished groups which supplied the manpower (somewhat as in the countryside). Working-class groups associated with newer, large-scale, progressive industry (and thus often with foreign investment: railways, mines, oil) chose to behave differently.[261] Thus, while there was a certain crude congruence in terms of social participation in urban and rural violence (putting it over-simply, 'declining' groups were responsible in both city and country-side), there was an obvious geographical divergence. Agrarian revolt was most pronounced in regions of dynamic commercial agriculture (such as Morelos) and most insignificant in remote, subsistence-farming sierras (e.g., those of Oaxaca); in the cities, capitalism and popular violence were less intimately associated, at least in spatial terms. While the peasant could perceive an immediate enemy (the expansionist *hacendado* or *ranchero*), the artisan's real foe (the factory owner) might be located hundreds of miles away. The impoverished Bajío weaver attacked, not the distant textile factories of Veracruz, but the local shopkeeper, pawnbroker, official, or entrepreneur (the last of whom, paying artisans on a putting-out basis, was more merchant than industrialist); and grievances, as in Europe, often focussed on issues of consumption rather than production.[262] The victims and beneficiaries of Porfirian progress, juxtaposed in the countryside, were more effectively segregated in the cities; hence there were few examples of Luddism or machine-breaking, as might have been expected.[263]

When urban violence occurred, it was often the Maderista forces who appeared as the saviours of order and property. There were exceptions, when the rebels joined with the mob, as at Torreón and Salinas, but in the latter instance, it should be noted, the delinquent Maderista commander was subsequently executed by his fellow-Maderistas. The behaviour of Hernández at Pachuca or Sánchez at Concepción was more typical. Similarly, the Maderista leader Miguel Zamora aborted a miners' riot at the Aurora Mine, in the Puebla sierra; Rafael Tapia entered Orizaba 'in order to prevent popular disorders'; and at Parras, where the houses of hated officials were sacked, 'the damage [was] . . . done principally by the people of the town and not by the revolutionary bands . . . the disorders was soon stopped and the town well policed [by the rebels]'.[264] Sometimes, this meant straightforward repression, all the more redolent of Porfirian practices when the acting policemen were men of dubious revolutionary credentials, like Bonifacio Soto. But often the moral authority of a *bona fide* revolutionary commander sufficed to calm the situation. Cándido Navarro restored order at Matehuala with only thirty men, where a larger, unpopular Federal garrison had been helpless.[265] And, as examples of Maderista responsibility accumulated, public opinion (that is, the opinion of the respectable, literate classes) reacted favourably. At Durango, as we have seen, the city elite decided that they preferred the rebels they did not know to the mob they did. In Mexico City, during the final peace negotiations,[266] 'no-one seems to have any great fear of the revolutionaries, but the general apprehension, showed by all parties, is lest there should be a mob uprising, but all parties are so unanimous in this fear that . . . they will not hesitate to unite for the purpose of crushing it should it take place'.

In fact, Mexico City and the major provincial cities did not escape mob outbursts. But they differed from – and were much less serious than – the wild affrays which occurred in the Bajío towns and in certain mining centres, as already described. In part this was because the larger cities had larger garrisons, and attracted larger (and hence more disciplined) Maderista forces; in part, these forces, or at least their leaders, may have sought to present a favourable impression on entering local metropolises. But, more important, the raw material for urban violence was less evident and, where troubles did occur, they tended to be more narrowly political, directed against specific office-holders and representatives of the old regime (whose swift removal could often guarantee peace), not against the social, economic and political establishment *in toto*. The major cities thus revealed, once again, their attachment to political renovation and reform, and their horror of social convulsion.[267]

In the northern state capitals of San Luis and Saltillo trouble threatened but was averted by the Maderistas' stern control of the situation. The arrival of Cándido Navarro at San Luis 'caused popular disturbances which degenerated into disorders'; a 'multitude of the lower class of people' gathered outside the banks and warehouses (ominously, so it seemed) but no serious trouble occurred.[268] So, too, at Saltillo, after the signing of the peace treaty, huge crowds gathered in the streets, somewhat the worse for drink, and police had to keep them out of the post office building; more demonstrations greeted the entry of the Liberating Army. But, observers were pleased to note, 'the populace seems to have a wholesome fear of the revolutionaries, as they seem to be men of more vigor and self-respect than the members of the former police force or the Federals military force'. Calm was further guaranteed by the prompt resignation of Governor del Valle and his replacement, first by a Saltillo banker (who happened to be an obscure relative of Madero), then by the Maderista Venustiano Carranza.[269] Thus, where responsible Maderista troops made a peaceful entry, and the more odious representatives of the old regime a graceful withdrawal, the political transition was effected without violence; the same was true in small as well as large communities; and a gratified spectator in Mexico City commented that 'the transfer of the powers of government is proceeding with far less disorder than might well have been expected', though, he added with a certain sombre prescience, 'the future is . . . still full of gloomy possibilities'.[270]

On the other hand, in cases where the armistice kept the Maderistas outside the city gates, and entrenched Porfirian officials tried to brazen it out, trouble was likely, pending the installation of new, acceptable authorities. For, while the Plan of San Luis had repudiated all branches of Porfirian government, empowering the revolutionaries to name new state governors, the Juárez Treaty embodied no such written commitment; only the resignations of Díaz and Corral were guaranteed in print; the renovation of the rest of the political establishment (for many people a more vital objective) depended on vague, verbal assurances.[271] Even assuming such assurances were well-known, they were little consolation. Public opinion was running strongly against entrenched officialdom, and the latter's defiance frequently invited direct action and specifically 'political' riots.

Three days after the signing of the Treaty, for example, crowds gathered on the streets of Guadalajara, ostensibly to celebrate the peace. Before long a mob confronted the governor's palace, crying 'Viva Madero!' and 'Muera Cuesta!'. In the belief that the mob might rush the building, a picket of *rurales* opened fire, killing five. Popular hopes that the occupants of the city gaol could be sprung were disappointed, but Governor Cuesta Gallardo felt compelled to tender his resignation at once.[272] A similar incident threw Tampico into a panic, and hinted at future developments in the port. When the peace treaty supervened, Tampico was still in Federal hands, and there was anxious speculation whether the 'bandits' who had sacked Tula would reach the city in advance of the more respectable Maderistas from Tantoyuca – to whom the Chamber of Commerce had extended an urgent invitation.[273] Then, on the afternoon of 28 May, the authorities conceded permission for a Maderista demonstration (a fairly sure recipe for trouble, but still probably safer than a blank refusal). Two thousand people turned out on the streets and the gathering culminated in an attack on the city gaol,[274] which the police resisted, killing half a dozen attackers. The crowd scattered, regrouped and were dispersed again. It was now gone midnight and the city went to bed with shops boarded up and rumours current that 'the labouring men from Doña Cecilia, which has been the hotbed of the Maderistas, would return at 10 a.m. to avenge the death of their comrades'. Next day the fearful mayor led a delegation to Doña Cecilia (now Cd Madero) where he talked to the men (mostly port and oil workers), urging peace and quiet, which for a time Tampico got. Nevertheless, some criticised the mayor's diplomacy, since it gave the impression (accurate though it was) 'that the officials of the city are afraid of the lower elements'.

Tampico continued to live in fear of the rabble across the tracks. Troops guarded the gaol, banks and business houses, and the German colony begged the captain of a visiting merchant ship to prolong his stay at the port. In fact the Germans – and the other foreign residents – were in no danger, the only xenophobia associated with the troubles was directed against the Bahamian immigrant labourers who competed with the local workers for jobs on the docks; as with the Chinese of Torreón, it was coloured scab labour, rather than foreign, capitalist employers, who excited most resentment. Not until 150 Federal troops arrived from Monterrey and seven of the Doña Cecilia leaders were arrested, could Tampico rest easy. Henceforth, the energy and resentment of the Tampico workers were channelled into more peaceful political and industrial action: the men of Doña Cecilia continued to pose a threat which the owners of property and employers of labour had to meet, but their *modus operandi* changed and, arguably, became more effective. In both Guadalajara and Tampico, the examples given here, the 'political' riots of 1911 ushered in, not a period of violent social upheaval, but rather one of generally peaceful politicisation and mobilisation, characterised by more 'modern', associational interest groups.[275]

Lesser 'political' riots occurred elsewhere, often in small communities.[276] But, logically, the biggest and most significant took place in the capital. During the months of revolution, Mexico City remained at peace; but, as already noted, there were growing fears of popular violence, and the campaign against the Zapatistas – now at the very gates of the city – took second place to the policing of the streets.[277] Here, too, the peace treaty forestalled a rebel entry. According to its terms, Díaz agreed to resign by the end of May, handing over to de la Barra. But the mob was not disposed to wait. On the night of 24 May crowds gathered, crying for the immediate resignation of the president; police strove to maintain the Pax Porfiriana to the bitter end, and demonstrators in the Zócalo were mown down by machine-guns and mounted charges.[278] At midnight, pouring rain dispersed the crowds more effectively. Next day, however, the streets began to fill up again. Ill, bed-ridden, surrounded by moping friends and relatives, Díaz decided it would be prudent to resign at once. At 4 p.m. on 25 May he submitted his resignation and the Porfiriato ended. The anger of the mob turned to jubilation. Within an hour, the ex-president had boarded an armed train bound for Veracruz and, ultimately, France; the nation against which he had won his laurels at Puebla nearly fifty years before.

JACQUERIE

It is a cliché of Mexican historiography (though an apt one nonetheless) that as Díaz boarded ship at Veracruz he remarked: 'Madero has unleased a tiger; let us see if he can control him'.[279] Indeed, even when said in May 1911, this was close to a cliché; back in March, for example, the American consul at Mazatlán watched rural Sinaloa revert 'back to first principles' and asked himself much the same question.[280] How far it crossed Madero's habitually optimistic mind we do not know, but certainly the scene confronting him as he began his triumphal progress south from the border was a daunting one. Towns and cities were racked by riots (Parras, Madero's birthplace, was one of them). Major revolutionary movements had developed in states which had not figured prominently in Maderista plans, and where the rebels' subordination to Madero was tenuous and soon to be proved temporary; in the Laguna the assorted rebel contingents would not agree among themselves, still less to defer to their distant, nominal leader in Juárez.[281] Revolutionary movements like Zapata's were pursuing their own local objectives without much regard for Madero's national political preoccupations.

The divergence of interest and loosening of control were particularly evident in the agrarian field. The Plan of San Luis contained no more than a passing reference to the restitution of illegally acquired land; on the strength of this – and, rather more, one suspects, on the strength of Madero's appeal to arms and the opportunity which it afforded – agrarian movements stirred into life, or advanced from fitful to strenuous and sustained activity. In areas where they were strong, 1911 now witnessed the beginning of *de facto* agrarian reform, of a local, anarchic, often customary kind: April and May 1911 were months 'when the great country estate saw itself threatened on all sides'.[282] In Morelos, the best documented but far from the sole case, Zapata authorised and supported the villages' recovery of lost lands: 'in the days that followed, armed parties of sharecroppers and poor farmers began invading fields in the central and eastern districts of the state. The defenceless plantation managers and peons resident on the land the squatters claimed had no alternative but to meet the revolutionary demands.'[283] In the Laguna, where agrarian grievances had helped swell the many Maderista contingents, similar seizures took place. By July, 'quite a number of haciendas have been taken possession of by the working class who claim that, as the Maderistas have won, they have the right to take and are, in fact, owners of the land'.[284]

But, apart from the better known and organised agrarian movements, there were also varieties of jacquerie: local vendettas, land seizures, attacks on landlords and their employees, perpetrated by the rural poor with scant Maderista credentials. Their resentments were similar to those which fuelled revolt in Morelos, the Laguna, the Yaqui valley, but for various reasons they failed to achieve the same degree of scope and organisation. Sometimes, repression was too effective, sometimes the area of agrarian disaffection was too small – maybe just a village or a valley – and its inhabitants could do no more than mount a unilateral attack against a solitary cacique or landlord. Such intensely local movements, lacking even the pale 'political' colouring of Zapatismo, and vengefully directed against specific individuals, were readily categorised as banditry. But it was in form rather than in origin that they differed from the classic agrarian movements, and they deserve a mention no less (indeed, rather more) than the riotous artisans of the Bajío. But they are not easy to get at. In some cases a village revolt against its caciques helped propel the community into a more coherent revolutionary movement; it presaged a more formal revolutionary commitment.[285] But in many other cases such revolts were as circumscribed in time as they were in space. During a brief, coruscating flight they illuminated the locality, alarmed the well-to-do, and by their glare attracted historians interested in such pyrotechnics. But they soon fell to earth, guttering out, permitting the place to revert to Stygian dark and obscurity.

Many incidents occurred on the fringes of bigger rebel movements, right across the face of the central plateau. On the Puebla–Morelos border rebels sacked the 'big house' of a Tenango hacienda in reprisal against the manager, and at Atencingo seven hacienda employees were murdered.[286] In the Apam region of Hidalgo, a region dominated by big maguey plantations, rural banditry (so-called) was extensive; a conscientious Maderista commander lamented that his forces were inadequate[287] 'to maintain their policing duties in the face of the banditry which has taken control of this important district, which includes over fifty haciendas, which are constantly requesting protection for their persons and property'. The manager of the Hacienda Espejel, in this district, was fortunate to be out in the fields when Maderistas called at the 'big house': there they broke open the office safe, smashed desks and drawers, ransacked the house, leaving the dining room in ruins, the dainty porcelain figurines in fragments. They had come (it was reported) looking for the *hacendado*, muttering against him, declaring that they desired to leave him strung up in the entrance to his hall, and to despatch the *administrador* 'a puros machetazos'.[288] The Contreras family of Epazoyucán (Hgo), also landowners and managers, were victims of another, less brutal vendetta.[289] In the Malinche district of Tlaxcala *hacendados* were being arrested and held to

ransom, while in the Puebla sierra near Huejotzingo the villagers of Xalmili-
lilco clashed with the neighbouring Hacienda de Santa Aña.[290] Here, when
Maderista troops entered the district, the villagers went to the hacienda to
fetch provender; the manager (del Rivero, another Spaniard) refused and, as
tempers rose, he opened fire on the villagers, wounding some. A siege ensued:
del Rivero bolted the door and, with a colleague, took up a firing position on
the roof. Someone sounded the church bell and all the villagers rushed to the
fray. Hopelessly outnumbered, del Rivero and his partner tried to escape out
the back, but they were caught and killed.

West-central Mexico had not produced major rebellions in response to
Madero's summons. Though many no doubt shared the common antipathy to
Díaz, the ranchers of Jalisco were lukewarm about revolution. Salvador
Gómez, a would-be *tapatío* rebel, had to go to Chihuahua to make his
contribution, since in his own state 'the people have not revolted . . . there are
no supplies of arms and ammunition: property is divided up, the owners of
ranches and haciendas take it upon themselves to pursue rebels, and the people
are by nature very patient'.[291] Michoacán was more active, but organised rebel
forces did not appear until late in the day, and were sometimes captained by
dubious 'revolutionaries'. But there existed a strong undercurrent of popular –
often Indian – agrarianism, which ran independently of and counter to the
official, political revolution in these states. By the summer of 1911 there were
bands of 'armed Indians organised for the purpose of dispossessing landowners
around Lake Chapala . . . [claiming] lands once belonging to their ancestors,
because "Madero promised we should have them"'.[292] In Michoacán the
problem was more acute, and the acquisition by private interests of timber-
land was a common grievance. In April, Rafael and Antonio Ibarrola, lumber
dealers from Sevina, were attacked by revolutionary villagers who, they
recounted, dragged them from their ranch, striking them with pistols,
machetes and daggers, took them to the plaza, and there 'tried to hang us from
the trees', until 'at the plea of certain women' they were allowed to flee, badly
hurt, to Pátzcuaro.[293] Somewhat later, squatters invaded the lands of the
Hacienda de la Orilla, taking over fields without paying rent, pasturing their
animals, cutting wood on the slopes of the hills. They claimed that they 'were
acting within their rights, since the Revolution had offered the division of
lands to the working class'.[294] At first the management did nothing, then,
when an *administrador* thrashed one of the squatters for poaching a deer, the
squatter returned with a rifle and killed him. Other Michoacán estates
experienced less serious troubles: crop-stealing at Charahuen, fears of an
outbreak at La Cantabria, which for the moment did not materialise.[295]

Most Michoacán haciendas got through 1911 unscathed. That they did so
was often thanks more to counter-measures, combining repression and
diplomacy, than to the absence of agrarian grievances (as is sometimes
assumed). The state governor supplied a detachment of troops for Cantabria,

and trouble was postponed for a year. At La Orilla, the local prefect prevailed upon the manager to change all the *administradores* on the property and he himself toured the district exhorting (and warning) the people 'to be good citizens, so that they would earn the consideration of their bosses, and to show respect for other people's property, so that they would not merit punishment from the masters'.[296] A similar campaign of pacification was mounted at state level by the Maderista commander, Marcos Méndez, a civilian *político* lately turned 'revolutionary', who made up for his inactivity prior to May by frenetic peace-keeping thereafter. He quelled riots at Uruapán and Zamora and, he claimed, had averted widespread rural rebellion:[297]

since the Indians of Michoacán were somewhat aroused against the Mercado admin-istration, because it despoiled them of their woods, the only inheritance they had to live on . . . I calmed their agitation, telling them I would do all in my power to have these woods returned to them, thus preventing thousands of Indians, who asked to join me in the struggle, from proceeding to exact vengeance.

No doubt, this was an exaggeration, but it caught something of the climate of the times. Faced with simmering popular revolt, those in authority had to wheedle and promise, as well as repress. When the crisis passed, the wheedling stopped, the promises were forgotten.

Thus, throughout the country, the revolution afforded an opportunity for local disputes to revive, for squabbles over land to take a violent turn. Fears of Indian jacquerie, if sometimes exaggerated, were not groundless. Round the turn of the year 1910–11, the old conflict between the Espinosa y López Portillo family and the Indians of Camotlán (Tepic) intensified, involving the family, their tenants and employees, the villagers and the local authorities; it matched, in microcosm, the trajectory of the national revolution. Finally, in April, a group of Indians attacked the property, killing two tenants.[298] Perhaps this would have happened, revolution or no. But the timing suggests otherwise; and there is one well-documented, comparable case which precisely illustrates the capacity both of the Maderista revolution to stimulate and of the Maderista leadership to repress such local agrarian revolts.

On the Guerrero coast, close by the borders of Oaxaca, Enrique Añorve of Ometepec declared for the revolution and took command of local Maderista forces.[299] At the same time, Liborio Reyna, said to be a lawyer, enlisted the villagers of nearby Huehuetán and Igualapa, who had suffered the loss of their communal lands to the people of Ometepec, and elsewhere. The Reyna family were in fact among the losers, the Añorves among the beneficiaries.[300] Personal and political interest alike therefore compelled Añorve to warn Reyna against subversive agitation, 'making him see that the promises of the revolution would be satisfied when the new government was cemented on the basis of respect for other people's rights' (Juárez's dictum here serving the interests of the propertied status quo). But when the revolution took Añorve north to Ayutla and Acapulco, Reyna won over the junior officer left in command, got himself named *jefe político*, and then encouraged the Indians of Huehuetán and Igualapa to recover the lands they claimed had been robbed from them. The process of recuperation soon led to violence. The chief of police at Huehuetán (an ally of Reyna) delivered an ultimatum to the mayor of Ozuyú: the title deeds of the disputed lands would be returned to the Huehuetecos or they would 'smash those who resisted handing them over'; the mayor of Igualapa similarly demanded the return of titles to land comprising a third of Igualapa's patrimony and warned that if the present owners refused, they would be dealt with by force.[301] When the appropriate titles were not handed over, the Indians went on the rampage, seizing the documents, occupying the land, and wreaking vengeance on the landowners. A Spaniard, 'a man who had committed no crime other than that of collaborating with his efforts and labour in the growth of this rich part of the country', was killed by the Huehuetecos, who appropriated his land; Gregorio Medina, a native of Huehuetán, who had refused to help his fellow-villagers in a lawsuit against the Spaniard, was tracked down in Ometepec and 'riddled with bullets', the Indians dividing his property amongst themselves and 'invoking the name of the revolutionary cause'. Even a Catholic priest, a *ranchero* who had bought 'a small fraction of the land which had formed part of the extinct community ... of Igualapa' (for which reason the villagers 'hated him fit to kill'), was murdered and his body left mutilated (they were less respectful of the cloth down on the Costa Chica than in the cities of the Bajío).[302]

At Pinotepa Nacional, just across the border in Oaxaca, a company store was ransacked and the Indians (some from Igualapa, some from Pinotepa itself) killed a town councillor; their hatred, said a Maderista officer, was directed especially against 'the landowners and local authorities, notwithstanding the fact that they were all now Maderistas'.[303] But this presumed community of political interest meant little in a situation of social conflict, with strong racial overtones. A Pinotepa shopkeeper locked himself and his neighbours indoors, fearing that the Indians would fulfil their threat 'to kill the municipal president and other authorities and get rid of the *gente de razón*, especially the landowners', but the Indians forced their way in, seized the shopkeeper's land titles, along with a pistol, ammunition and a supply of Russian cigarettes, and they forced the shopkeeper to mark down his prices.[304] Though there was no killing, the mestizos of Pinotepa felt particularly indignant that their own Indians had made common cause with the invaders from Igualapa.

In fact, the violence was not entirely gratuitous. If the coveted title deeds were promptly handed over there was usually no bloodshed. This was not pointless, atavistic savagery. Dozens of title deeds were recovered by the Indians (though not for long: there lay the pointlessness) and almost all dated from the late 1880s through to the 1900s: the heyday of land concentration, following the laws of 1883 and 1894, the advent of peace and the railway, the rapid commercialisation of agriculture. The landlord victims admitted that the lands in question had belonged to the 'extinct community' of Igualapa but maintained (probably quite correctly) that they had been legally acquired (and as such, the Plan of San Luis was irrelevant). And they were not opulent grandees like the planters of Morelos: they were ranchers, shopkeepers, small merchants, even a priest. Many claimed to be Maderistas, and no doubt were. Apart from the Añorve family itself, the victims included Prisciliano García, later a Maderista colonel, who had been driven from his house and *milpa* while the Indians had made off with 128 pesos-worth of cotton and chile, as well as the titles to his land 'which used to belong to the commons of Huehuetán.[305] Briefly recovering their patrimony, the Indians divided up the lands, herded their cows onto the pasture, tore down barbed wire fences, and destroyed banana groves and canefields.

But their triumph was short-lived. After the peace treaty was concluded, Enrique Añorve returned from up the coast, now a victorious officer, soon to be 'Commander-in-Chief of the Army of the Costa Chica'. Like many of the victims of the revolt, he was a good Maderista, but for him and his kind Maderismo stood for political liberalism and its achievement was that it had overthrown 'a monarchical, centralist government' (as Juárez had done fifty years before). It was to be regretted that, in the process, 'the Nation fell into the most fearful chaos and state of genuine anarchy' and the revolution had been taken advantage of by 'bewigged criminals (*ladrones togados*), highwaymen, parricides, arsonists and assassins'.[306] Añorve proposed – and proceeded – to clear all this up, at least around Ometepec. Reyna fled and the fugitive landlords drifted back. Their title deeds were returned to them, new authorities and garrisons were installed to guarantee the peace. What retribution was visited upon the rebellious Indians is not known. But it was not quite the end of the story: a second bout of local agrarian conflict, similarly camouflaged under national political labels, disturbed the region four years later.[307]

The chaos deplored by Añorve was most pronounced in central and northern Mexico, where the revolution had made most impact. Beyond the Isthmus the situation was somewhat different. Even here, rebellion was now on the agenda. But the plantation and peonage were strong, and the free village correspondingly weak, and, since the free villages generally provided the cells of revolution, and the peons (as in Morelos or Tepic) tended to remain quiescent, the south did not experience sustained popular movements.[308] Instead, rural protest remained patchy, sporadic and inconclusive, but it certainly occurred, and both plantocracy and government had to reckon with it.

Perhaps the most vigorous movements were to be found in western Tabasco, notably the districts of Cárdenas and Huimanguillo: marshy, wooded country, dotted with tobacco, fruit and rubber plantations, as well as *ranchos* and smaller settlements. Somewhat like the Brazilian *sertão*, and in contrast to the classic plantation regions such as coastal Yucatán, this was a zone of relative mobility, endemic violence and (it has been suggested) a certain anomic individualism; if organised peasant movements were absent, banditry and petty *caudillismo* could flourish in the climate of revolution.[309] Certainly, after initial defeats and disappointments, rebel activity got up steam in the spring of 1911. Three leaders were prominent: Manuel Magallanes, son of a liberal *guerrillero* of the 1860s, who now revived the family traditions; Ignacio Gutiérrez, reputedly 'an Indian who has been harshly treated in the past by petty officials'; and Domingo Magaña, who had something of the character and charisma of the social bandit, and who proved to be militarily the most successful of the three.[310]

Late in 1910, pioneer rebel bands were prowling the rubber plantations of western Tabasco (Gutiérrez, and possibly Magallanes and Magaña, were among them); they extorted the usual quota of guns, ammunition, saddles and mounts, and also recruited from among the able-bodied workers, 'all of whom', complained one manager, 'are owing to us'.[311] In the spring, as rebel activity picked up after serious reverses, Magaña now stole the local headlines: he robbed Spanish merchants at Reforma, raided plantations, and freed the peons, thus paralysing agricultural work. Fellow-Maderistas, who preferred a more orderly revolution, were highly critical: in freeing peons, Magaña usurped the powers of Congress to legislate 'concerning the fairest way to solve the problem of rural workers'; in kitting out his men with red ribbons in their hats and jackets, he proclaimed they were Magaña's *gente* and defied the Plan of San Luis; in freeing the prisoners from Pichucalco gaol and openly consorting with 'unsaintly women' in Reforma, he flouted decent opinion and revealed a certain plebeian coarseness.[312] But, for all his peccadilloes, Magaña displayed some social conscience. Demobilised in the summer of 1911, he took up the cause of the dispossessed Indians of Tabasco, pressing for reforms, especially from the Federal government, since 'all the authorities of the Canton have gone hand-in-glove to exploit this indigent race'.[313]

These western districts of Tabasco were to resume their rebellious activity at a later date. But for the moment, political concessions – of the kind attempted, without success, in the revolutionary north – encouraged quiescence. Here, as in San Luis, it mattered that the state governor was a popular individual, not a crook or a tyrant. Abraham Bandala, the long-serving Porfirian governor, was not much loved; but in January 1911 he was replaced by Policarpo Valenzuela, a robust eighty-year-old, a 'self-made man of broad and progressive ideas', who had worked his way up from woodcutter to millionaire, and now owned several plantations.[314] Reputedly of Indian extraction, Valenzuela was 'exceedingly popular with all elements of the state and especially with the medium and lower classes' (even Madero agreed he was a distinct improvement on Bandala).[315] His appointment – in a state whose Maderista revolts may best be seen as pale reflections of northern *serrano* rebellion – helped assuage revolutionary protest for the time being. Despite its limitations, the Tabascan revolution of 1910–11 was both organised and extensive by southern standards. Elsewhere, rural protest remained inchoate, and was easily contained. In March 1911 there was reported to be 'considerable unrest' in the Valle Nacional, the *enganchados'* graveyard, but nothing came of it.[316] Eastern Tabasco, Campeche, and Chiapas were generally quiet: planters and caciques alike retained power and parried what feeble thrusts were made against them.[317] When peons of the Carpizo family plantation at Champotón (Camp.) tried to press for better wages in the spring of 1911, the owner neatly turned the prevailing conditions of unrest (which may or may not have prompted the peons' demands) to his own advantage:[318]

he misinformed the state authorities, telling them that we [the peons] had intended taking up arms against our bosses, then in the afternoon we returned from work, ten of us were locked up in the plantation gaol . . . and the authorities ruled that we should be exiled from that coast, five of us being sent to Veracruz . . . and five to Frontera.

In Yucatán, too, rural protest was contained (though not without occasional, violent incident) and, as in Tabasco, a deft political manoeuvre gave the status quo ante a new lease of life. The state had already experienced considerable political unrest associated with the gubernatorial campaign of 1909–10 and culminating in the Valladolid revolt of June 1910.[319] Though Díaz cited the Valladolid revolt among the charges brought against Madero at the time of his arrest, it was in fact a purely provincial affair, quite distinct from the national strategy of the Maderista leadership.[320] But the grievances of the Yucateco rebels matched those of the Maderista rebels already examined: grievances against arbitrary local officials, against high taxes, against the continued politico-economic rule of the Molina clan and their puppet governor Muñoz Arístegui. In addition, almost all classes in the state suffered from the fall in the price of henequen.[321] Nevertheless, the Valladolid uprising was bloodily suppressed, the survivors fleeing to sanctuary with the Huits, the independent Maya of the interior.

In 1911, local revolts broke out once again, though now the rebels assumed a Maderista label and signed receipts for sequestered goods 'Don Pancho Madero will pay it all'.[322] Though, of all the Mexican states, Yucatán was particularly remote and provincially jealous, the manner of its revolutionary participation was in this respect not radically different from that of other regions, where the chief effect of the (national) Madero revolution was to afford aid, comfort, and legitimacy to existing (local) rebellions, actual or potential. Such rebellions displayed the usual continuity of location and style; it was the remote, inland settlements (what might be termed, socio-politically, the Yucateco sierra), far from the civilised, commercial coast, that were most affected; and, again, a crude, retributive justice was apparent. At Peto in March 1911 the people chopped down the *jefe político*'s door with their machetes, forcing the *jefe* to flee, then murdering his secretary 'in circum-stances which cannot be related'. At Temax the *jefe* was tied to a chair in the plaza and riddled with bullets.[323] Though these initial confrontations took place in the small towns of the interior, the rebels – fearful of Federal reprisals and mindful of the lesson of Valladolid – soon took to the countryside, recruiting both peons and deserters from government forces (labourers press-ganged and armed by the state administration, who changed sides in such numbers that the practice was soon dropped). Only in Mérida, the seat of government, could the regime raise volunteers, as had been done at the time of the Caste War. Rebel forces now roamed the interior with apparent impunity, living off the plantations, with the Federals confined to the main towns.[324]

The rebel contingent from Peto made the biggest impact. About a week after their local *coup de main* they attacked the Catmis hacienda, a large sugar and henequen enterprise owned by the Cicerol family, landowners who 'have the reputation of having treated their laborers very cruelly'; for which reason 'the uprising was a combination of revenge, rebellion and robbery'.[325] Catmis also included a large contingent of Yaqui deportees, who at once responded with the characteristic belligerence of their tribe, seizing the plantation's stock of Winchesters and joining the attackers. Catmis soon fell, and reports filtered out that the rebels had given themselves over to a drunken orgy. The Cicerol brothers therefore led 150 troops – supplied by the state governor and mostly forced conscripts – to recover their property. But, in Yucatán as elsewhere, the Porfirian planter could not play the role of feudal seigneur. At Catmis they were greeted by shots and cries (directed at the conscripts) of 'come and join us, brothers . . . long live liberty'; as a result of which many of the government troops switched sides. After several hours fighting, the Cicerols' force was 'badly defeated'; Enrique and Arturo Cicerol, seeking refuge in a friend's house, were betrayed to the rebels and dispatched, Yucatecan style, *a machetazos*; it was said, in fact, that 'they were killed by the weapons of their own servants'.

This violent, personalised attack had something of the quality of the slave revolts which (at rare intervals) affected Cuba or the American south in the nineteenth century: responding to cruel treatment (rather than, say, to agrarian dispossession), and mounted by servile plantation labourers rather than by free villagers, they tended to be sudden and explosive, lacking declared objectives and generally incapable of building on initial success.[326] At best, the insurgents might escape into the interior, where the Huit communities were the closest Yucatán possessed to the *quilombos* of Brazil.[327] Furthermore, as in slave societies, such revolts invited immediate attention from a well-developed repressive apparatus, linking government and plan-tation (in that force had always counted for more than legitimacy in such societies, the loss of legitimacy experienced by the Porfirian regime was less problematic in Yucatán than, say, Morelos or Chihuahua). And such revolts also encouraged politicians, planters, and property-owners in general to sink their more superficial differences in order to maintain social stability. Such was the case in Yucatán. The Catmis rebellion worried the planters (it cannot be over emphasised that, even where the landlord class survived 1911 materially intact, its collective psychology was jolted) and it dealt a severe blow to the government's prestige. The planters petitioned for energetic measures to combat rural anarchy, and they stepped up their campaign for the removal of Governor Muñoz Arístegui; Díaz, never entirely deaf to the demands of influential groups, least of all in 1911, bowed to the pressure and sent General Curiel (who had contacts with the Yucatecan opposition) to replace the unpopular incumbent. Curiel was welcomed enthusiastically; his arrival heralded a political reshuffle, as Muñoz's underlings were sacked and oppositionists promoted in their place; a political amnesty was decreed, taxes were cut, the secret police disbanded. The planter class was satisfied and the political reforms gratified urban, middle-class opinion. Many of the rebels reached terms with the new administration.[328] Yucatán, its political rancours laid to rest, its plantation/peonage system intact, enjoyed almost complete peace for three more years.

This was true, *mutatis mutandis*, for much of southern Mexico. There were political conflicts, regional squabbles, isolated outbreaks of violence (the most important will be considered later), but in general they could not compare with the organised revolutionary movements begun elsewhere in Mexico during 1910–11 and often sustained thereafter, and the plantation of the south faced nothing like the same challenge which confronted the hacienda of the centre and north. The 'so-called peonage conditions' prevalent in the south might receive criticism in the liberal press, but they appeared to be 'borne without a murmur by the laborers'.[329] This could reflect a genuine legitimacy and acceptance (the quotation derives from Chiapas, where some more benign, voluntarist forms of contract labour flourished); but, often more important in maintaining the system and averting popular rebellion, was geographical isolation and (most crucial of all) 'the absolute physical control of the situation by the large proprietors'.[330] Here was a regime most obviously reminiscent of Skocpol's typical state: dependent on force, largely invulnerable to internal popular rebellion, and capable of overthrow only through the providential intervention of outside forces.[331] Certainly there was little danger of the southern plantation system dying, as it were, by its own hand; not until the revolutionary contagion was imported from outside did the system's vitality begin to fail.

THE STATE OF THE NATION (1911)

Thus Madero, negotiating at Juárez, then heading south to the capital, saw his revolution for liberal democracy degenerating into riot, banditry, and jacquerie. This he had never intended; he had always given Díaz credit for rescuing

Mexico from the chaos and *caudillismo* of the nineteenth century; he had in all sincerity reassured his grandfather that 'our cause is the cause of order and our party is the one which will be the best guarantee of peace and the best support of the law'.[332] Democracy was to be the saviour, not the solvent, of the social order; it was to rescue Mexico from the perils of prolonged personal rule: thus it could exert a strong appeal to enlightened men of property who (like the Científicos of the 1890s) favoured an institutionalisation of politics. But now, in 1911, it seemed to be delivering different goods. Madero's grandfather was soon reminding the new government of its duty 'to repress any new movement which seeks to introduce disorder . . . punishing its authors with the greatest severity'.[333] And Madero himself, in concluding the peace treaty rather than pushing ahead with a total military solution, showed that his concern for order and legality (and for property and social stability), as well as his aversion to ochlocracy, the rule of the rabble, were as strong as ever.[334] He also showed a humanitarian outlook and a realistic awareness that, if the war went on and the Federals dug in and defended the major cities (as they were to do in 1913–14) a military solution would be protracted and bloody. There was finally the consideration that the agricultural cycle had now entered its period of greatest activity and this, throughout the revolution (though particularly in the early years, when 'amateur' armies were the norm), acted as a constraint on campaigning. It was not just the *hacendados* – like those of Morelos or Veracuz – who wanted a speedy demobilisation so that planting could start; some of the Maderista rank-and-file were also keen to get back to their *milpas* now the rains had started.[335]

Various factors therefore encouraged Madero to accept a negotiated peace which historians of different persuasions have justly criticised, pointing out that it represented a deal with the old regime which robbed the revolution of the fruits of victory and established a compromise government in which conservative elements could block reform.[336] Since historians, by definition, work with the benefit of hindsight, it is legitimate for them to argue that, objectively, the treaty had this effect. It is less legitimate for them to enter the realms of subjective, counter-factual hypothesis and argue what Madero *should* have done: held out for draconian terms, perhaps, eradicating the old regime in its entirety, even if this meant prolonging the civil war by months or years. Lacking hindsight, Madero could not have foreseen the consequences of the treaty, furthermore, it is difficult to imagine he and the Maderista leadership opting for the alternative, counter-factual, draconian course (in historical terms, therefore, it is a null hypothesis). While some of this leadership (Venustiano Carranza, for example) later claimed that they opposed the treaty, for just the reasons mentioned here, this was not at all evident at the time.[337] There does not appear to have been an immediate, contemporary outcry against the Juárez settlement: lower down, among provincial Maderistas or the people at large, there were plenty who, like the Revolutionary Junta of

Jacala (Hgo), saw it as a matter of 'rejoicing', 'this event being in all respects a happy outcome for the nation'.[338] Like Munich, the Juárez agreement seemed a good idea at the time, only later did it become a dirty word. And, given the circumstances (in particular, the threat of a runaway revolution) some sort of *transacción* was likely in 1911; historians are right to analyse its effects, but wrong to castigate Madero – as a whipping boy for the Maderista leadership as a whole – for doing what he was bound to do. The character of Maderismo was such that its leader could not do otherwise.

With the treaty signed, the Maderista leaders recognised their own responsibility as nominal directors of the revolution to bring some order out of the chaos. Madero himself, though lacking any official status under the interim regime, was fully prepared to use his considerable influence in aiding President de la Barra in the interests of peace and stability. The overwhelming problem was that the Liberating Army constituted a military hydra, with dozens of individual *cabecillas* exercising local, personal authority, and defying co-ordination. Already, in Chihuahua, with the campaign in full swing, Orozco had objected to Madero's promotion of José de la Luz Soto and Giuseppe Garibaldi (grandson of the great Italian patriot) and had quarrelled with Villa; the attack on Juárez had happened in defiance of Madero's orders; and, once inside, Madero and Orozco had clashed over the question of the captured Federal General, whom Orozco wished to execute. At one point, it was reported, Orozco pulled a gun on Madero and the revolutionary forces seemed likely to split into warring factions.[339]

In addition, Madero faced the problem of independent groups of Magonistas who were operating in Chihuahua, Sonora and Baja California under the auspices of the PLM. This division had existed from the outset of the revolution; while some Magonistas joined Madero's rebellion, the Magonista leadership in the US denounced Madero as a bourgeois opportunist.[340] The strength of Magonismo is hard to assess and perhaps easy to exaggerate. Some historians emphasise the role of the PLM during both the politicking of 1900–10 and the fighting of 1910–11; Professor Cockcroft, for example, argues that Magonista *guerrilleros* kept the revolution going prior to February 1911 when 'the Madero wing of the revolution' (Orozco excepted) 'did not succeed'.[341] In that the civilian Maderistas largely failed in their attempts at insurrection, and Madero remained in the US until February, Cockcroft is right, but he is wrong to appropriate the early, pioneer successes for the Magonistas. He argues his case two ways. First, there were indisputably Magonista rebellions, led and staffed by Magonistas, quite distinct from the Maderista organisation. But their only clear achievement was the capture of Mexicali (Baja Calif., N.) by a filibustering raid in late January; to call this 'the biggest single victory against Díaz on the battlefield' is stretching matters; it promotes an odd, peripheral, 'conventional' action above the sustained, successful guerrilla war of Chihuahua.[342] Secondly, Cockcroft appropriates a number of ostensibly Maderista leaders for the PLM. Certainly there were a few committed Magonistas who shunned Maderismo: Prisciliano Silva refused to take orders from Madero and, faced with arrest, preferred to quit Chihuahua for the US; it is argued that Luis García and the men of Bachíniva split from the revolution and went home to their mountain pueblo at least in part because of their Magonista affiliation.[343] But such cases are exceptional; as regards the more prominent revolutionaries cited by Cockcroft, the evidence for their Magonismo is tenuous, resting primarily on an article of Enrique Flores Magón written twenty years after the event. A comparison of the revolutionary roster of 1910–11 with Flores Magón correspondents of the 1900s does not reveal much overlap and where an overlap does appear (a letter sent, a copy of *Regeneración* received) its significance should not be exaggerated.[344] For many rebels, grievances against the regime were longstanding and, in the mid-1900s, the PLM represented the only articulate national opposition. But browsing through *Regeneración* did not make a man a PLM militant, and a veneer of Magonismo, acquired (in a handful of cases) in the 1900s, should not be allowed to colour later events too strongly. After all, it was the 1910 Maderista revolt which turned into a revolution, not the PLM insurrections of 1906 or 1908.

Magonismo did not play a major role in the military overthrow of Díaz. But it did create another distinctive thread in the tangled skein of the Madero revolt, especially in Chihuahua.[345] Outside Chihuahua, Madero's influence was even more tenuous, even more incapable of sorting the threads into a coherent pattern. His name might be used by way of justification (e.g., in the signing of receipts in Yucatán), but the loyalty of most of the rebel rank-and-file was to the locality from which they had sprung and to the leader who had recruited them, who led them in battle, and who was familiar with the immediate grievances which had compelled them to take up arms. Even within the larger, conglomerate 'armies', rebel contingents carried the names of individuals: 'de Lara's company', 'Casavantes' company', 'the *gente* of Don Sixto (Ugalde)'; or they might adopt regional names, like Martín Triana's 'Cuerpo Armado Laguna y Cuencamé Unidos'.[346] As John Reed noted three years later: 'the soldiers all look up to some one General under whom they are recruited, as to their feudal lord. They call themselves his *gente* – his people; and an officer of anybody else's *gente* hasn't much authority over them'.[347] Loyalty to the *jefe* influenced the behaviour of the men of Bachíniva; it compelled the men of José de la Cruz Sánchez to refuse to serve under another officer; it helped give the Morelos revolution its stamina.[348] And *jefes* (like Domingo Magaña of Tabasco, whose troops wore special red insignia) were not above pandering to this personal and territorial imperative.[349] Hence the high incidence of intra-revolutionary squabbles, between leaders and men competing for power in close proximity; squabbles which, though they sometimes involved real social and political differences, often centred on personal supremacy and prestige, and the demarcation of respective spheres of influence.[350]

At any rate, Madero, at Juárez, had claimed to negotiate on behalf of these motley forces whom, with the conclusion of the treaty, he had to cajole into acceptance, subordination and demobilisation. From the border, and again from Mexico City, he appealed to the Mexican people for peace, urging his men to exchange the gun for the vote ('a new weapon which you have won'), and to 'consider as an enemy of the institutions and of the highest interests of the people anyone who seeks to disturb [public] order'.[351] Leading Maderistas now collaborated with the government in the attempted restoration of peace: orders went out to suspend hostilities, provide receipts for sequestered goods, to repair railways, to guarantee property rights. A circular sent to rebel *jefes* in seventeen states forbade the popular practice of opening gaols (the Plan of San Luis had provided only for the liberation of *political* prisoners) and Trinidad Rojas, commander at Amecameca (Mex.) was set the impossible task of recapturing 185 inmates released from Chalco prison. Irresponsible acts of this kind, it was stressed, 'would prejudice our noble cause'.[352]

For such policies to succeed, it was first necessary to impose some order on the Liberating Army itself, which, like the rain-forest of Tabasco, had sprung up wild, unchecked and prolific, and now had to be cut back. In the north, longer campaigns (and occasional sieges) had created larger, better organised military units: Emilio Madero's Second Division of the North had a complete officer corps; Orozco's army, boasting eight qualified doctors, also showed signs of professionalisation.[353] But most rebel groups were smaller and looser in structure; when two (or more) *jefes* met on the confines of their territories, or at the gates of a coveted city, there was no sure method of ensuring disciplined co-operation. Accordingly, Robles Domínguez, on Madero's behalf, sought to create some order and hierarchy. The rebels of Puebla were told to keep out of Tlaxcala; Puebla itself was partitioned between Agustín del Pozo in the north and Camerino Mendoza in the south east; Manuel López (Ver.) was subordinated to Gabriel Gavira, Francisco Llanas (Mex.) to Gabriel Hernández, and so on.[354] Civilian Maderistas were appointed as special peace commissioners to sort out the conflict in particular states: Múgica in Michoacán, Bonilla in Sinaloa.[355] Múgica's tasks were typical of the time: he wrought changes in local government at Tancítaro, Jiquilpan, Maravatío, Zinapécuaro and Zamora, in which latter town he also halted a riot and settled a strike by the tram drivers; he persuaded dissident rebel *jefes* to accept Salvador Escalante as Maderista commander in the state and acted as broker between Escalante and the Federal commander; he averted a clash between Maderista troops and police at Yurécuaro, arranged the pursuit of bandits around La Piedad, and finally arrested and placed on trial the fractious Maderista leader Marcos Méndez. At the end of it all Múgica could legitimately boast that he had 'complied with his duty as a good revolutionary, first as agitator, then as pacifier', though it must be said that his pacification was more extensive and successful than his agitation.[356]

Elsewhere, pacification was less successful. And even where it succeeded, it succeeded at a price. The process of creating chains of command, of halting what the government saw as abuses, alienated many rebels in the field. Juan Andreu Almazán, a rare middle-class *guerrillero*, who had quit medical school in Puebla to fight for the revolution in the south, felt he had been slighted in the allocation of authority; he had done more for the cause than any other rebel in Guerrero (he claimed, unconvincingly); and 'it hurts me that I am superseded and that others are found to be placed as my superiors'.[357] Disgusted, Almazán was soon up in arms again. The very moves to restore peace thus produced additional conflict: the country witnessed the first bout of a recurrent disease, whereby the attempted rationalisation of a sprawling, spontaneously created popular army and the resolution of all its local rivalries and anomalies, served to create more dissidents and the raw material for a second conflict. Furthermore, an integral part of this 'return to normalcy' policy was the strict curtailment of land seizures and attacks on rural property. Though he was not blind to the agrarian problem, Madero believed that this, like other problems, should be settled legally and peacefully; meanwhile, property should be protected. The new governor of Morelos was told (not that he took much telling) to evict fifty *campesinos* who had invaded the canefields of the Hacienda Maltrata; rebels in Puebla were ordered to cease their depredations on the Hacienda de Tejahuaca, near Atlixco; at Amecameca they were instructed 'to cease all acts of expropriation on the lands of the Hacienda Guadalupe'. Similar orders went out to Zapata.[358] Landowners were even empowered to claim against the government for damages done by revolutionary forces; some, it was said, took advantage of this facility to restore the compromised finances of their estates.[359] From the very outset, therefore, the new regime guaranteed the hacienda and set its face against *de facto* agrarian reform which failed to obey the (as yet unspecified) rules.[360]

The process of pacification and organisation went both ways. As they dispatched orders around the country, the Maderista leadership had also to deal with a flood of requests for cash, supplies, and authorisations (especially to enter towns). There were maybe 60,000 rebels under arms in May 1911: where the peace settlement had left them in the countryside, which it often had, they faced major problems of shelter and supply (since they could no longer live off the land), but billeting them in the nearest town, which probably contained a Federal garrison, created further problems. Hilario Márquez wanted to enter Jalapa 'since there are more supplies there for the support of my troops'; Domingo Magaña had 1,500 men at Huimanguillo short of supplies, stricken with malaria and needing billets; a little to the north, outside Acayucán, Pedro Carbajal's forces were being molested by malaria and Federal forces at the same time.[361]

But state governors (often newly installed) were reluctant to admit to their cities bands of rebels fresh from living off the country; where Federal or *rural* detachments remained, there was a real danger of armed clashes, peace treaty or no; and in cities like Veracruz, where the gaols were crammed full and stocks of ammunition ran high, frightful results were envisaged.[362] Conflicts and confrontation were therefore common: the rebel Manuel Paredes wanted to occupy Jaltipán (Ver.) but would only do so if the *rurales* evacuated first; at Potam (Sra) the arrest of a Maderista *jefe* by Federals nearly provoked a renewal of hostilities.[363] Government fiat could not bring such recent enemies together: mutual enmity was still strong, as rebel commanders like Juan Banderas asserted, and as incidents like the Puebla massacre proved.[364] President de la Barra, collaborating with Robles Domínguez, was scarcely sympathetic to rebel demands and imprecations: Cándido Navarro was told he might not enter León, as he wished, other *jefes* were banned from entering Tlaxcala and Jalapa.[365] But orders from the 'centre' no longer carried the weight they once did. Sometimes they were downright impractical: the forces of Dolores Huerta could not be concentrated, as ordered, as they were scattered throughout the Puebla sierra. In other cases, rebel leaders spurned central direction. Isidro Ortiz and his 500 men intended taking Tlaxcala and Zacatelco irrespective of orders to the contrary: they were, a Maderista agent reported, 'very dour folk', with whom any kind of deal would be hard to arrange – typical country people, in fact, not unlike the Zapatistas.[366]

These tortuous problems of organisation and pacification, which were to be so productive of conflict, had barely been taken in hand when Madero began his triumphal progress to the capital, arriving on 7 June. For Madero (strictly a private citizen, but momentarily revered as the embodiment of the revolution) and for interim President de la Barra, it was time to thrash out a political settlement, one that would fill the huge lacuna left by the Juárez Treaty. The fighting (it was hoped) was over, the Liberating Army awaited demobilisation, where it had not already demobilised itself and started to drift home. 'The issue of change', as Womack observed, '(had been returned) to the voluntary dimension of politics.'[367] The struggle between Maderistas and Porfiristas, radicals and conservatives, liberals and Catholics, would now be fought out on the hustings rather than the battlefield, with speeches, votes, bribes and deals, rather than with Mausers and machetes. True, the threat – often the reality – of force was never far away. But the peace settlement had still fundamentally altered the rules of the game, so that political rather than military resources were now what counted.

It is for this reason essential to conclude the chapter with a review of the political situation as the new regime took power; and it is particularly necessary to consider the situation at local level (the national settlement will be analysed in the following chapter). Two points stand out: the prevalence of 'last-minute rebels' – *revolucionarios de la última hora* – who had battened their control onto certain regions usually in May 1911, thereby constituting themselves as powers to be reckoned with under the new regime; and, at the same time, the widespread changes in local government which amounted to a grassroots political revolution of great significance, promoting men and ideas that would also figure prominently in the months and years ahead. Together, these phenomena were antithetical: the last-minute rebels were generally conservatives, wedded to the status quo ante; the new holders of municipal power often represented popular interests and stood for change. As antitheses, they did not cancel each other out, rather, in their manifold local variations, they created a situation of great heterogeneity and political tension. Both sprang from similar circumstances: the runaway success of the revolution and the collapse of local Porfirian regimes in April–May 1911. The pioneer rebels, as we have seen, experienced many failures and reverses. But by the spring and late summer (the tempo varied by region) the revolution began to look like a winner. By April in the north, and by May further south, the revolutionary band-waggon began to roll: revolutionary commitment now became easy and opportune. 'Since the signing of the armistice', Madero wrote to Orozco 'it is incredible the number of forces which have rebelled in many parts of the republic ... and those soldiers have not been put to the test.'[368] Now, the revolution could even assume some light-hearted, musical comedy touches, but, beneath the hilarity, the struggle for local power went on as doggedly as ever.

Something of the political climate of May 1911 is illustrated by the brief odyssey of Marcos López Jiménez through the state of Mexico.[369] Delaying his revolutionary commitment until mid-May, López Jiménez left Mexico City with eight companions, heading east; raiding haciendas for arms and supplies, they came to Atlacomulco, entered the town without resistance, and went through the usual procedures – confiscating the treasury, reading out the Plan of San Luis, offering the people the opportunity to replace their officials (which they declined to do). But if the revolution in Atlacomulco was to be no revolution at all, at least it could be done with style: a band was assembled, a national flag procured from the municipal palace, and the Maderistas marched through the streets to the sound of patriotic music, 'thus provoking unlimited enthusiasm', López Jiménez wrote to Madero, 'with deafening hurrahs going up for you and for liberty'. Local officials signed a repudiation of the Díaz government, a portrait of Díaz was removed from the *ayuntamiento*, and festivities culminated in speeches at the foot of the statue of Hidalgo. No secular, patriotic ritual was overlooked. After lunch (for this was a morning's work) the Maderistas headed for Temascalcingo, 'where we continued with exactly the same procedures as we had used at Atlacomulco': more bells, bands and delirious enthusiasm. Next day (21 May) the triumphal progress was cut short by news of the peace settlement. For most of June the company – now numbering sixty-seven – was billeted on the Hacienda Solís, while their *jefe* attended the fiesta of welcome for Madero at San Juan del Río and went to Mexico City for instructions. On the last day of June his men (now down to thirty-five) were discharged, each receiving five pesos and a peso for each day's service; their horses were (supposedly) returned to their owners, their guns to the government. A few veterans therefore went home with sixteen or seventeen pesos, some with only nine or ten; none, it seems, had heard a shot fired in anger.

Now that the path of revolution seemed strewn with roses, it attracted some dubious travellers. There were Maderista late-comers, like López Jiménez, who perhaps deserve the benefit of the doubt; there were out-and-out bandits – not just vengeful *campesinos*, traduced by the label, but criminals like the 'declared bandit' Camilo Barloza of Ahualco (SLP);[370] and, most important of all, there were political opportunists, the last-minute revolutionaries, who, discerning the drift of events, swam with the tide, thereby (at worst) staying afloat or (at best) attaining the upper reaches of power and influence. Not every landowner, official, or cacique who joined the revolution was necessarily a cynical time-server; there were idealistic liberals (like Madero), members of well-to-do 'out' families (like Maytorena or the Pesqueiras of Sonora), who combined self-interest with a solid revolutionary conviction, and old-style caciques (like de la Rocha) whose grievances against the regime made them natural and effective leaders of popular rebellion.[371] But there were also calculating opportunists who sought, *in extremis*, to colonise the revolution and who can be identified on the basis of the timing, location and character of their revolt.

When, for example, Lieutenant Colonel Severiano Talamantes went over to the rebels with his 400 troops at Alamos, Sonora, in January 1911, this was not the act of a time-server: it was too early in proceedings, Sonora was hardly ablaze with rebellion, and Talamantes himself had a long record of political involvement and rebellion.[372] The defection of the *jefe político* of Canatlán (Dgo) two months later, however, is more suspect: a member of a prominent family (the Patoni), he had held office for years; Topia and Tepehuanes, not far away, had fallen to the rebels, who were regularly visiting Yerbanis and Peñón Blanco (where the *jefe* had run away); the *jefe* of Torreón had just been sacked by the government for failing to dominate the situation. There was not a lot a *jefe político* could do in Durango in March 1911: defecting to the revolution was simply one of the more imaginative moves.[373] Next month, a little higher in the mountains, there was a classic, pre-emptive coup at San Dimas. There, in a stretch of country which the Arrietas had practically made their own, 'local forces of the government' took over the town 'calling themselves Maderistas'; 'these revolutionaries', adding the American consul, 'consisting of the best men in the district'.[374] In regions such as these, however, where the revolution was more bitter and prolonged and where political divisions were more sharply etched, there was less scope for such tactical turnabouts; bona fide rebels had fought their way to power, and there was a more complete renovation of local government.

Elsewhere the scope for dissimulation and compromise was greater. In May, in the quiet north east, 'prominent citizens' were reported organising their own private forces (though it was not at all clear whom they proposed to fight); Pablo Santos Jr, who was 'quite influential in the locality' formed a 'revolutionary' band at Sabinas, north of Monterrey, which was reckoned, significantly, to be more Reyista than Maderista.[375] Thus it was possible for the old regime to survive, as it did at Linares (NL) 'under cover of a belated and shameful adhesion to Maderismo'.[376] And among those tardy recruits were a good many Federals and *rurales* – like the infantry lieutenant who pronounced for the revolution at Monclova, thus incurring a fight with his loyalist sergeant, or the entire body of the state *rurales* of Hidalgo.[377] Late in the day, even retired army officers began to join the Liberating Army, pressing for promotion and apprehensive 'that, once the revolution is over, their services will not be taken into account'.[378] In many parts of central Mexico, where the revolution had some of the characteristics of a nine-days wonder, such 'revolucionarios de la última hora' cropped up in almost every state. Late in April, following overtures from the Maderista junta at Zautla, the Federal colonel Miguel Arriaga pronounced at Zacapoaxtla, receiving a glowing tribute from the town orator. Though the *jefe político* fled, it does not seem that local officials were changed, and Arriaga's troops (he claimed 1,400 but had nearer 300) spent their time hunting down bandits and guarding the Zaragoza–Pochintoc railway. Known Maderistas denounced Arriaga as a 'last-minute revolutionary', a partisan of old Governor Martínez, who was now plundering the sierra Indians in worse fashion than the Porfirista caciques.[379] New officials, appointed after the fall of Díaz at Cuetzalá, were arrested and removed by Arriaga; their persecutor, they complained, was 'a pensionary of the Díaz government' who, 'when he saw that the opportunity for getting on was slipping away from him, and that the only legacy which remained to him was the hatred which the people felt towards him', decided to join the revolution, appropriated the public funds, and began a predatory campaign in the district.[380] It was logical that Arriaga should ally with the brothers Márquez, similar 'last-minute revolutionaries' or 'reactionaries', also from Puebla: they agreed zones of influence and even exchanged troops.[381] Thereafter, the brothers headed down from the sierra into Veracruz, where Hilario sought to defend the train carrying President Díaz to the coast, and Esteban, having entered Jalapa, 'happily put himself at the orders of [the Federal] General García Peña', held a banquet in his honour and, when Federal–Maderista friction led to a shoot-out in the city, sided with the Federals against the rebels.[382] In Tlaxcala, meanwhile, Colonel Miguel Arrioja (not to be confused with Arriaga) offered his services to 'pursue banditry' in the state, old Governor Cahuantzi enthusiastically endorsed him (while denouncing rebel

subversives like Isidro Ortiz and Carmen Vélez), and even prevailed upon the
Maderista leadership in Mexico City to appoint Arrioja chief of (Maderista)
forces in Tlaxcala; such was the importance which 'pacification' now assumed
in official thinking.[383]

West-central Mexico also deserves mention in this catalogue of opportunism. Indeed, it produced the most prestigious last-minute revolutionary of
the lot: Manuel Rincón Gallardo, hacendado, son of a general, and well-
known in Mexico City society (where the news of his rebellion, at Encarnación
de Díaz, in May, produced a 'sensation').[384] His fellow-rebels included Luis
G. Llianes, a renowned 'sportsman' (sic) and José Castro, nephew of another
general and son-in-law of Díez Gutiérrez, ex-Governor of San Luis. In
Michoacán, too, where – even the state historian admits – the revolution was a
short-lived affair, it attracted landowners, retired Federals, even the Porfirista
prefect of Santa Clara who, having rebelled on 10 May, rose to become chief of
the Maderista forces in the state. Particularly in the region north of Lake
Pátzcuaro, reported an American:[385] 'there has been considerable revolutionary activity . . . and there are a number of bands. In general, the leaders are
"Hacendados" or men of good position in the community and we have heard of
no outrage being committed by these bands.' Though the importance of this
phenomenon must be recognised, it should not distort analyses of the entire
revolution.[386] Opportunist landlord-rebels were a distinct minority in
1910–11 (and, as already suggested, they must be distinguished from other
landlord-rebels of different stripe); it would be quite wrong to deny the
Maderista revolution its popular and radical character on their account.
Equally, it would be wrong to infer from this phenomenon a general
dissatisfaction on the part of the landlord class towards Díaz, or a general
proclivity towards rebellion. The great majority of landlords supported the old
regime as long as it was feasible to do so. Indeed, the very phenomenon of the
last-minute, landlord revolutionary is indicative less of the dissatisfaction and
rebelliousness of this class, or of the inherent moderation, even conservatism of
the Madero revolution, than of the threat to their interests which the landlords
now perceived, and which they sought to counter by a tactical adhesion to the
revolution itself; if they could not beat it, they would have to join it.

The best example, with which this survey can be concluded, came from
Guanajuato, where, some weeks after Cándido Navarro began to dominate the
northern part of the state, two 'revolutionary' leaders, Bonifacio Soto and
Alfredo García, came to prominence in the centre. Both were men of property
and influence in the Silao district, García was another ex-Federal officer, and
their efforts were directed towards maintaining and increasing this influence,
while preserving law, order, and property. They organised a 'vast, ramified
movement', recruiting men from their haciendas, or those of their supporters,
who 'are people of good social position, related by ties of friendship and
kinship with the most important families of the state of Guanajuato'.[387] By

their own admission, Soto and García were more concerned to shore up the status quo than to change it. They encouraged the removal of some Porfirian officials ('revolutionary' credentials had to be acquired somehow) but otherwise their role was conservative: Soto boasted of his police actions at Cd Manuel Doblado (where he put down a riot) and San Francisco del Rincón (where he averted one), he toured the *cabeceras* not to foment rebellion but 'in order to pacify the inhabitants and avoid popular uprisings'.[388] Not surprisingly, the big estates around Silao enjoyed tranquillity and 'the "*Hacendados*" in this district', so the American consul thought, 'are rather in favour of the revolutionists'.[389] After the peace treaty was concluded, the conservative administration of Governor Castelazo 'requested their co-operation, which they willingly gave, despite the fact that this government did not enjoy the sympathy of the people, being a continuation of the (Porfirista) administration of Governor Obregón González'; García continued to drill the troops, while Soto served as *jefe político* at San Miguel Allende; they remained champions of the conservative interest in the continuing battle against popular movements in the state.[390] That they did so was in many respects a tribute to the strength of popular upheaval and rebellion in Guanajuato.

One of the principal objectives of popular rebellion — against which conservatives like Soto and García struggled — was the renovation of local government. This was not a 'narrow', 'political' issue, indicative of a 'narrow', 'political' revolution. With particular control of a community often went control over land and water, law and order and many important aspects of community life. Grievances against local officials, especially *jefes políticos*, were probably the most common determinants of revolutionary commitment, and the ouster of these officials constituted the most common item in revolutionary practice. What the north, as we have seen, pioneered in 1910–11, the rest of the country followed in the spring of 1911. In Veracruz, it was reported: 'these officials seem to have great power and the resentment of the discontents [sic] is directed more against them than against any other class. There does not seem to be so much resentment against Díaz personally as against the system of government which he represents;'[391] hence 'constant changes of *jefes políticos* of different districts' were taking place. This was March, by May minor political revolutions had become endemic in the state. Manuel López, for example, declared for the revolution at Teocelo (canton of Coatepec); having taken the town, with only a dozen soldiers, he authorised the local schoolteacher (who happened to be a friend of Francisco Vázquez Gómez) to name new local authorities; forty Maderistas signed the document approving their appointment.[392] From Teocelo they marched on, touring the local villages, deposing existing authorities, naming Maderista municipal presidents, tax-collectors, judges and other officials. In this way they passed through Quimixtla (10 May), Chichiquila (11 May), Yuhuacán (13 May), Ayahualulco (14 May), Calcahulco (15 May), Tlacotepec and San José Coscamatepec (both 16 May). In most cases the old officials voluntarily surrendered power or ran away, allowing the Maderistas to assume control bloodlessly and decorously; the only assaults on property occurred in a couple of pueblos where the municipal archives were put to the torch. López covered a limited patch of ground south of Jalapa. But there were plenty of analogous movements operating in the rest of Veracruz.[393] Gabriel Gavira, heading south from Altotonga, performed similar functions at Huatusco, Atoyac, Córdoba and ultimately Orizaba; in the south, Guadalupe Ochoa changed local authorities in the canton of Minatitlán; Manuel Paredes brought democracy to Sayula, and Pedro Carbajal to Oluta.[394] To the French consul in Veracruz, the sight of revolutionary chiefs perambulating from village to village installing new officials 'by means of instantaneous elections' seemed to denote a state of anarchy.[395]

But it was happening everywhere. The problem for the historian is to assess the real scope and significance of these changes and to consider how far they – taken with other manifestations of popular insurgence – qualify the picture of the Madero revolution as one of minimal change, as they necessarily must.[396] On paper, these changes were impressive. Quantitative assessments are extremely difficult: Salvador Escalante, Maderista military commander in Michoacán, claimed that by the end of May 1911 eleven of the state's sixteen districts were controlled by the rebels and that new authorities had been installed in all of them.[397] It is unlikely that Michoacán would have experienced greater political change than most states north of the Isthmus, and, on the basis of evidence already advanced (nonetheless impressive for being 'impressionistic'), states like Chihuahua, Durango, Morelos, Puebla, and possibly Veracruz had all undergone sweeping changes in local government.[398] At a conservative estimate at least half the local regimes of Porfirian Mexico (north of the Isthmus) must have been overturned.

The character of these changes is another matter. Often, popular ex-officials were recalled: Francisco Cantú came back to replace the hated *jefe político* at San Juan Guadalupe (Dgo); petitioners at Jiquilpam called for the return of Francisco Villar, who had governed decently in the 1900s; at Tehuantepec a riotous gathering forced the resignation of the incumbent *jefe* and the appointment of the son of one of his predecessors.[399] Such cases illustrate not only the variability of Porfirian officialdom, but also the moderation of popular demands; 'structural' reform went no further than the abolition (in some cases) of the office of the *jefatura*.[400] People had little time for Utopian tomfoolery, they sought reasonably decent, honest government according to the provisions of the Constitution. Where previous officials were not recalled (as often they were not), posts usually went to representatives of the political opposition of 1909–10, generally men of some standing and education who had proved their opposition to the regime without usually contributing to its military overthrow. At Teocelo, the schoolmaster friend of Vázquez Gómez determined the political succession; at Zoconusco (Ver.) the

Baruch family (known oppositionists and friends of the Magonista, Hilario Salas) shot to power; at Jalacingo (Hgo) the new town council members were all Anti-Re-electionists, including a *licenciado* and professor.[401] At Mazapil, liberated (political) prisoners were at once invested with authority.[402] Hence civilian Maderistas (including some of the failed revolutionaries of 1910, like Abel Serratos)[403] now came into their political inheritance, and if, at the outset, this caused no aggravation (often, it was the rebels in the field, the military Maderistas, who made these appointments), the prevalence of this trend at all political levels – municipal, state and national – eventually provoked a major rift within the loose Maderista coalition.

It is also pertinent to consider how representative these changes were; how far they reflected popular wishes, how far they substituted one local elite for another. As already suggested, the new appointees had not risen from the ranks of the rabble, and frequently it was the 'most honourable citizens' or the 'principal men' whom the revolutionaries consulted – as Trinidad Rojas did at Chalco, or Gertrudis Sánchez at Concepción.[404] The new appointments sometimes had a distinctly inbred look. At Zoconusco, where Eduardo Baruch served as secretary to the Maderista commander, two of the five new officials were also Baruchs; at Chapulhuacán, in the Hidalgo sierra, it fell to Gumersindo Angeles to convene a meeting in the portals of the municipal palace, where some two dozen people chose him to be mayor; of the twenty-six signatories of the authorising document, six were also members of the Angeles family.[405] And, even in revolutionary states like Puebla, there were no doubt plenty of communities (like San Juan Xiutetelco) which the rebels bypassed, having received a message that the authorities there were acceptable and sympathetic to the revolution, and where the status quo thus survived, whether out of popular approval or official dexterity.[406] But these qualifications should not be pressed too far. The selectivity with which communities responded to the rebels' offer of reselection bespeaks a real degree of choice. Within the same district (such as Chalco) some dismissed their auxiliary judges, some retained them; and, within towns, some officials went while others stayed.[407] New policies – albeit on the modest scale permitted to municipal authorities – also suggest a new departure. At Chalco the Maderista appointees rented a new building for the school and ordered a clean-up of the meat market; at Atlacomulco the authorities (old incumbents, confirmed in power) took advantage of the revolutionary situation to break their fiscal dependency on El Oro, a move which was locally popular; and there were many other instances of genuine municipal innovation.[408] Even where elite replaced elite, it does not follow that the change was irrelevant, or that the mass of the people were indifferent: the election of the Baruch state at Zoconusco was effected by a 'huge crowd' and the accompanying official documents received an impressive list of signatures; in communities like San Juan Guadalupe, which languished under the control of an alien Porfirian despot and his cabal, it is not unreasonable to suppose a perceived identity of interest even between the 'principal citizens' and the common people.[409] Finally, the climate of the time made political fixing difficult. Towns like Atlacomulco received two visits from revolutionary forces in quick succession. And – certainly until the conclusion of the peace treaty – the Maderista national leadership encouraged the wholesale replacement of Porfirian officials.[410] Thereafter, revolutionary *jefes* were instructed to support the newly installed authorities, and some state governments continued to urge renovation throughout the summer. The governor of Yucatán boasted that new *jefes* had been appointed 'by popular acclamation'; in San Luis the Maderista Governor Cepeda sent commissions out to the villages 'to inform me if the people are or are not satisfied with their authorities, so that an immediate remedy might be found'.[411] Múgica, sent as peace delegate to Michoacán, had just such a brief from the Federal government.

But such policies responded as much to a desire for peace and quiet as to a thirst for local reform and renovation. Initial changes and concessions had to be made but, particularly with the peace treaty concluded, the whole thrust of Maderista official thinking was towards stabilisation first, then peaceful, electoral change – effected through the ballot box, not by acclamation in the plaza. On the last day of May, Cándido Navarro was rebuked for changing the *jefe político* at León and peremptorily instructed: 'confine yourself to maintaining the authorities in places occupied up to now by our forces, respecting the authorities of the previous government in towns which have not been occupied'.[412] Thus the effect of the treaty, at municipal as at state level, was to freeze the political situation, postponing further changes until elections could be held. But 'unliberated' communities, cheated of revolutionary change, and of the parades, celebration, music and drink that went with it, were not always disposed to accept postponement and promises. Through June, many communities appealed to rebel leaders to effect their liberation: Acámbaro (Gto), Jilotepec (Mex.), San Juan Evangelista (Tab.).[413] Many took the initiative themselves: at Atzcapotzalco, close by the capital, plots were hatched to overthrow the unpopular *jefe* from within; at Orizaba, with its large, politically conscious proletariat, demonstrations forced the *jefe* to resign; further south, a Maderista commander was ordered into Acayucán 'to avert riots' since 'public opinion is growing increasingly excited in anticipation of the desired (political) change'.[414] Again, we note the efficacy of 'political' riots – which did not necessarily require the intervention of revolutionary troops. At Chilmahuacán (Mex.), while the old town council was closeted in the *ayuntamiento*, debating whether or not to resign, impatient crowds gathered outside and mounted a hostile demonstration; twenty *rurales* were summoned to hold back the press but, fearful of the outcome, the old regime caved in and tendered its collective resignation.[415] And when such change finally came, and long-serving caciques –

like Antonio Núñez of Tuxpan (Ver.) – packed their bags, there were scenes of joyful celebration.[416]

After June 1911, as the government's 'return to normalcy' policies began to bite, such incidents became less common. But this did not denote satisfaction. The chorus of complaints against those caciques who had survived went on. At Zumpango (Mex.) the old *jefe* clung to power, and even gaoled the small Maderista detachment left to garrison the town; at Jilotepec, the promise that 'a son of the People' (or of the *pueblo*) would be made *jefe* remained unfulfilled two months later.[417] Where the revolution had been more brief and the political turnover less complete, the old regime lived on: at Tampico, where it galled the common people, at Monterrey, at Cd Porfirio Díaz, where there were protests at the continued employment of Porfiristas in the customs, the *rurales* and the judiciary.[418] What is more, there were cases of Porfiristas not simply surviving but even making a political comeback. In parts of Veracruz, such as Perote, for example, the old caciques hung on; partisans of ex-Governor Dehesa still held office at state level; and, thanks in part to their influence, conservatives were able to 'win' local elections at the end of 1911.[419] We shall note more examples of Porfirian *revanche* during the liberal politics of the Madero presidency. And occasionally (even more provocatively) conservatives ousted by force shot their way back to power, as they did at Tehuantepec.[420]

Such local squabbles, which had been at the heart of the civil war in 1910–11, went on even after the treaty formally ended hostilities; in the months ahead, it could be said, politics were the continuation of the war by other means. Madero paid the price for his alacrity in settling with the old regime by inheriting a country racked by political conflict, devoid of the consensus which his proposed liberal experiment required. A partial revolution had taken place, one which had brought to power – notably in rural and revolutionary districts – new authorities more amenable to public opinion, and one which had produced a new generation of populist leaders,[421] parvenus who had led the Maderista guerrilla movement, and thereby acquired a certain power and prestige. But it was only a partial revolution; old Porfirista caciques survived, or plotted a comeback. The centralised system of Don Porfirio, based on the pre-eminence of the Federal executive, its provincial appointees and favourites, was shattered; though many of its creatures remained, they now had a fight on their hands, and one in which they could no longer rely on the *ultima ratio* of the 'centre', but had rather to look to their own resources. And, moving up from the municipalities to state and national politics, the picture was again one of flux and confusion; much would depend on how de la Barra and his presumed successor Madero chose to govern, and on who attained power in the states of the Federation, in the wake of the defeated and departing oligarchs.

One thing, in the prevailing uncertainty, was certain. The climate of politics – of society in general – had changed.[422] It was not that the national government of de la Barra or even Madero broke so radically with the Porfiriato. But enough people had been impressed by the progress of the revolution (in its many guises) prior to May 1911, and this profoundly affected their outlook and conduct. The Madero revolution was not, as so often asserted, a narrowly political, ineffectual episode, for, whatever Madero's own intentions, it is clear that many of the participants looked beyond political reforms, or interpreted them in a potentially radical fashion. From the start, a powerful agrarian content was evident, *serrano* rebels sought to roll back the powers of the state, and the destructive forces unleashed in riot-torn towns and cities reflected the grievances of the urban poor. Even where the revolution seemed to display predominantly 'political' features – for example, in the pervasive changes in local government – these cannot be dismissed as 'narrowly political', the concern of a coterie of intellectuals and *bien-pensant políticos*, and no more.[423] For these, too, attracted the keen attention and participation of much wider groups – of 'the masses', to use a vague but convenient term. The Díaz system – its peace, its skewed prosperity, its economic growth and agrarian policy – depended on the maintenance of an authoritarian, unrepresentative polity, in which key decisions were taken by a small, self-renewing oligarchy. Municipal democracy and free elections had no place, and their implementation, even partially, was political dynamite, which could blow the entire edifice to bits. Genuine popular representation as apparently practised in many communites in the spring of 1911, would bring to the fore troublesome populists at local, state, even national level. And with populists in the town halls, the state palaces, maybe even the Palacio Nacional, the dynamics of economic development could go into reverse, as villagers reclaimed land, as cash crops gave way to beans and maize, as labourers pushed up wages in line with prices, as the hacienda lost its cheap, sometimes coerced labour, its guaranteed high prices and tariff protection. Of course, at various points along the way, these trends could be halted or modified; if they followed logically, they did not follow inevitably from the initial democratic experiment; but if the experiment were carried through, if its opponents and likely victims did not bestir themselves . . .?

The fears of the beneficiaries of the old regime mirrored the hopes of the common people. To the villagers of Morelos and the urban *canaille* of the Bajío towns (as much as to the hacendado and the Federal officer) democratic reforms meant more than harmless liberal tinkering, devoid of 'social' significance, and a good many better-off, respectable Maderistas were beginning to agree with them. The political and social orders went together: the defence of municipal self-government in, say, San Juan Guadalupe was a necessary prerequisite for the recovery of the community's *ejidal* land, sold by the old town council; or for the liberation of sharecroppers gaoled by the local magistrate when they refused to pay debts incurred working his – the magistrate's – fields.[424] In these terms it would be possible to interpret the 1910–11 revolution as one of a species of social crisis, brought on by the rapid politicisation of the masses (especially the rural masses) within a hitherto authoritarian or semi-authoritarian state: Italy 1918–22, Spain 1931–6, Brazil 1963–4, Chile 1970–3.[425] The Madero revolution, then, was as much a revolution for what it promised as for what it achieved. The hopes of the common people were reflected – and the fears of the upper class heightened – by the new egalitarianism which seemed to infect society. In the Laguna the *gente decente* were obliged to walk in the middle of the muddy streets of Torreón; the lawyer Herrera expounded subversive notions of popular sovereignty to the San Miguel mob. Popular *corridos* suggested that, with the fall of Díaz, a new era had opened up, and conservatives deplored the weakening not only of political authority but also of social mores: peon soldiers now swaggered in the street, armed to the teeth, not only frequenting (as might be expected) the bars and the brothels, but also invading the preserves of the bourgeoisie – the theatres, cinemas and quiet city parks.[426]

There were many contemporary witnesses to the new uppishness of the common people. At Ometepec, 'the Indians fell into the grave error of believing that the Maderista power would support and protect them so that they could be free, so that they could cease paying all taxes, so that they could be absolute masters of the fields'.[427] Communities in Jalisco – not a very revolutionary state – were also affected. At the Los Reyes mines, reported the manager, 'the common people don't know and don't want to know about the peace treaty', they had picked up ideas from radical sheets like *El Cascabel* of Guadalajara, and begun to mouth slogans about the 'slavery of the workers'.[428] In August, at Lagos de Moreno, a mob tried to get free drinks from a cantina (so the story went); in the ensuing brawl, a customer was wounded by a bar employee who was consequently gaoled, whereupon a crowd of 200 approached the prison and appealed to the major in charge that 'since we are all Maderistas he should help them kill all the rich (since it seems someone has been filling their heads with socialist ideas) because, they allege, the rich were setting about killing the poor' – a reference, presumably, to the recent brawl.[429] Troops were called out to disperse the mob and 'light injuries' were sustained when the people tried to disarm the troops. Uppishness of a more orderly kind – though perhaps no less disturbing for that – was exhibited at Teziutlán, chief town of the Puebla sierra, where the local people (factory workers, artisans and small traders) set up a Committee of Public Safety which passed judgement on the local well-to-do, notably the Spanish landlords of the region.[430] Even down in peaceful Chiapas, drink and demagogy disrupted the quiet of a summer night when, a *cantinero* of Tonalá reported, twenty or thirty drunks rang the cathedral bells and shouted *vivas* for Madero, giving rise to fears that an attack on the gaol and a full-scale riot were imminent. The *cantinero* (presumably familiar with local gossip) explained to Madero that:

'there is no shortage of perverse people who are trying to exploit the gullibility
of the illiterate population, telling them that the glorious triumph obtained
by yourself marks the day when taxes no longer must be paid, and when
everyone is free to do whatever he pleases'.[431]

As has already been suggested, such descriptions, purveyed by the literate
and better-off, may be exaggerated; popular ideas and objectives were
generally moderate, and rarely bloodcurdlingly radical. But the very fact that
they were perceived to be so extreme and dangerous (either for what they
were, or for what they threatened in the future) was itself significant. Reports
of the restlessness of the common people said as much about their well-to-do
writers as they did about the common people themselves. And anxiety bred
action. Some alarmed citizens wrote letters to Madero; some began to look to
strong-arm conservatives (would-be national saviours, or local men-on-
horseback like Soto and García of Guanajuato); some tried to neutralise
corrosive ideas of equality and class war with their own counter-propaganda.
Following the riots at San Miguel Allende, the local notables convened a
public meeting in the theatre, at which Domingo Hernández (an admirer of
Madero) made a weighty speech, a classic exposition of moderate, mollifying
liberalism, clearly aimed at the destitute handicraft workers who had rampaged through the town a month before. Don Domingo at once recognised the
need to improve the lot of the 'proletarian classes' and to revive the 'small
industries' which had once flourished in San Miguel. Taking Switzerland as
his model, he extolled thrift, technology, investment, hard work and education; he called for free night schools, for the benefit of the workers, public
conferences, where useful ideas might be exchanged, and decent politicians
who were neither too lax – in tolerating drunkenness, for example – nor too
ruthless – in cramming the town gaol – but who would show initiative in
developing the town, and who could 'tighten the relations between capitalists
and workers.'[432] Don Domingo had a dream; he looked to: 'the day when
every son of the community possesses his own capital, his modest workshop,
his parcel of land to cultivate, acquired by saving and constant hard work –
then we shall all be peaceful men and no-one will want to stage revolutions'.
But he also had words of warning, which he delivered to his audience along
with an appeal to trust the new rulers of Mexico: 'if your situation has suffered
a radical change from the political point of view, do not expect that your
economic and social situation will change so rapidly: for that cannot be
obtained by means of laws and decrees, but by the constant and laborious
efforts of all elements of society.' It could have been Madero himself speaking
– or any one of the myriad Maderista civilians, the earnest, respectable men of
substance who had espoused the opposition cause in 1909 or 1910, who had
sympathised with but failed to join the armed rebellion, who had recoiled in
horror from the violence and social upheaval it engendered, and who now
sought to enter on their political inheritance and to begin to build a stable,

liberal, hard-working, sober and prosperous Mexico: Mexico in Switzerland's image.

But could they communicate this ideal? At the end of the speech a worker put several questions: what is law, what is society, what is democracy, what are our rights and duties? Facundo González drew great applause for this honest questing after truth, and, at the chairman's insistence, his name was published alongside that of Sr Hernández in the official brochure. But it is not recorded that he got any answers. Try as they might, the Maderista liberals could not sell their elevated, abstract ideas to down-trodden artisans, to the city lumpenproletariat, to dispossessed peasants and exploited sharecroppers, to the bandits and *vaqueros* of the sierras, to the degraded debt-peons and deportees of the tropics; men whose grievances and objectives were more concrete, immediate and urgent, and whose view of the world often ran counter to liberal principles of thrift, property, hard work and sobriety. Nor, of course, could the Maderistas convince the *hacendados*, the army officers, the politicians, bosses and bureaucrats of the old regime, for whom all this earnest reformism was so much sentimental yet subversive cant.[433] Preaching to sceptical congregations, the liberals could not but fail, and the story of the Madero regime, which follows, is the story of their failure.

5

𒁹𒁹𒁹𒁹𒁹𒁹𒁹𒁹𒁹𒁹𒁹𒁹𒁹𒁹𒁹𒁹𒁹𒁹𒁹𒁹𒁹𒁹𒁹𒁹𒁹𒁹𒁹𒁹𒁹𒁹𒁹𒁹𒁹𒁹𒁹𒁹𒁹

The Madero regime: (1) the Revolution goes on

THE NATIONAL SETTLEMENT

On the last day of May 1911 Díaz took ship from Veracruz, protesting to the last that his was the only way to govern Mexico. Prominent Porfiristas like Limantour and Landa y Escandón soon followed the path to exile, leaving Madero happy in the knowledge that 'the Científico party . . . no longer exists'. True, Díaz's coterie of able but unpopular technocrats, dependent in the last resort on their old political patron, had no place under the new regime, but their sacrifice had perhaps redeemed the political lives of others, less conspicuous and notorious. And, as will be shown, plenty of Porfirian oligarchs survived: Madero might have taken warning from the fact that, even as Limantour left, Luis Terrazas returned from Long Beach to his Chihuahua estates, reassured by de la Barra's assumption of the presidency.[1] The day after Díaz sailed, Madero began his triumphal progress south, pausing *en route* to receive news, despatch messages, meet with local revolutionary leaders, and attend fiestas held in his honour (a few hundred pesos spent by a pueblo might represent a sound political investment; though at Tulancingo the *jefe político* embezzled the funds raised for such a fiesta).[2] The progress culminated in a triumphal entry into the capital, which coincided with an earthquake; this 'very mysterious portent' worried the superstitious and gratified Madero's enemies (his supporters managed to interpret it as 'a sign of God's favour'), but it did not deter a huge crowd (one estimate put it at 200,000) from turning out to see Madero pass by 'in a luxurious coach complete with liveried, bewigged and powdered footmen', while the bells of ninety churches pealed out a welcome.[3] It was the kind of welcome, a sour opposition newspaper commented, usually reserved 'for the celebrated bullfighter Rodolfo Gaona', but it was an impressive and 'extraordinary affair' which made at least one Mexico City ten-year-old aware for the first time of the stirring events taking place in the political life of his country.[4]

Though de la Barra was formally president, Madero was the man of the hour. The crowds in the streets were genuine enough, their enthusiasm was

not the ersatz kind which distinguished Porfirian (and some later revolutionary) demonstrations; they rejoiced in the fall of Díaz and wanted to see his
conqueror, even if they were disappointed at what they saw – not a victorious
caudillo but a diminutive man in a bowler hat.[5] This did not deter – more like
it encouraged – political supplicants. 'At this moment', a French observer
noted, 'Madero reigns: his house is constantly besieged by more or less
importunate citizens'; in the crush, some of Madero's recent revolutionary
lieutenants could not get access to his person.[6] The courting and importuning
went on at lower levels too: Abraham González, the new Governor of
Chihuahua, confronted a 'multitude' competing for his attention; at Chalco
(Mex.) Trinidad Rojas was surrounded by 'innumerable people . . . thirsting
for justice'; a plantation manager from Veracruz congratulated Robles Domínguez, hoping that 'from this time on the whole path of your life is strewn
with roses and that you will not forget your old and good friends'.[7] Pent-up
grievances and ambitions, dammed during the Porfiriato, were now released in
precipitate flood.

Meanwhile, at all levels – but most conspicuously at the top – Mexico
enjoyed an uncomfortable dual power, the legacy of the peace treaty. This in
turn was reflected in political appointments and policy decisions. Though de la
Barra exercised formal (and not inconsiderable power), Madero, as the
revolutionary victor and presumed president-in-waiting, enjoyed immense
unofficial influence.[8] The cabinet was a hybrid, including two ministers (apart
from de la Barra) who were identified with the old regime, two relatives of
Madero ('Maderistas' by name rather than by proven conviction) and three
Anti-Re-electionists, including Emilio Vázquez Gómez at Gobernación. If
some of the faces were new, conservatism still prevailed. Furthermore, the
three 'revolutionary' incumbents were 'revolutionary' only by virtue of their
records of political opposition (and by no means unwavering opposition: note
the Vázquez Gómez' prevarications in 1910, their readiness to negotiate in
1911); none had served in the field.[9] Madero was satisfied with the composition of de la Barra's cabinet but many of his supporters – moderates included
– were disconcerted. To oust Díaz and retain the Porfirian oligarchy, warned
Robles Domínguez (no radical firebrand) would mean a 'half-measures revolution' and would invite a second upheaval.[10] The Maderistas of Guadalajara
were reported disillusioned by the 'Científico' presence in the administration;
so, too, was the veteran oppositionist newspaper *El Diario del Hogar*.[11] Yet
more significant were the protests emanating from the revolutionary forces in
the provinces. A rebel 'colonel' denounced the survival of Porfirista officials in
the Federal District; Enrique Adame Macías – a prominent Durangueño leader
and, as he told Madero, a simple *campesino* – regretted the political survival of
Porfirista luminaries like Vera Estañol; while a junta of Maderista chiefs,
including Almazán, Cándido Navarro and Gabriel Hernández, declared they
would use 'all the means at their command' to enforce the fulfilment of the

Plan of San Luis and to expel Científico elements from the administration.[12] Madero criticised his generals for interfering in politics and, at a personal meeting with them at Tehuacán, his peremptory manner encouraged mutinous thoughts.

Linked to the contentious question of cabinet appointments was the no less contentious issue of the vice-presidency: an apple of political discord ever since its creation in 1904. In 1910 Francisco Vázquez Gómez had run as Madero's vice-presidential partner. But now, relations between Madero and the Vázquez Gómez brothers – never that cordial – had deteriorated. Historians of the revolution – possibly too concerned to find ideological (as against 'Namierite') explanations of behaviour – have depicted the brothers as the guardians of the revolutionary conscience; even where their opportunism and dalliance with the Díaz regime are recognised, they are cast as the 'opponents of compromise', embodying 'the essence of radicalism'.[13] Certainly they took up cudgels for the disaffected Maderista military but – since Emilio, as Minister of Gobernación, had but recently been hurrying along their demobilisation – there appears to be a certain inconsistency, bred of opportunism, in their policy; it seems probable that, as the Vázquez Gómez and de la Barra fell out, and the brothers' indisputable ambition took fire, they began to resist demobilisation and speak up for the military with an eye to winning the latter's support – which they did. When de la Barra moved to dismiss his dissident interior minister – with Madero's support – the Almazán/Hernández/Navarro junta protested, though in vain; Navarro led 200 troops to the president's residence at Chapultepec, where de la Barra informed them that the deed was done; shortly afterwards, four Maderista generals (including Navarro) were arrested for allegedly threatening a violent riposte.[14]

The split between Madero and the Vázquez Gómez widened further with the former's decision to wind up the old Anti-Re-electionist Party in favour of a new Progressive Constitutional Party: a change of name rather than substance, but one which was received suspiciously by the brothers, who clung to the old Anti-Re-electionist Centre, and sought to convert it into a vehicle for Francisco Vázquez Gómez's vice-presidential ambitions.[15] Accordingly, when the 1,500 delegates of the PCP gathered in Mexico City at the end of August, there to formulate a programme and endorse Madero's presidential candidature, Madero selected as his recommended running mate a forty-year-old journalist and political activist from Yucatán, José María Pino Suárez. The PCP convention represented a first important step along the liberal democratic path Madero had envisaged since his early days in Coahuilan politics; the party would operate on the basis of active local branches, primary elections, and a representative national convention. But, as Maderista sympathisers set about creating the party structure in the summer of 1911, and granted the imprimatur of revolutionary success which the PCP carried, it tended to assume the character of a semi-official, bandwaggon party, whose ultimate success was guaranteed; it attracted the time-servers as well as the idealists. Nevertheless, it was an important step beyond the fly-by-night, elitist political groups which had backed Díaz's repeated re-elections. Maderistas in Michoacán and the sierras of Durango set about organising and propagandising; in the mountains of Oaxaca they worked by night, as by day the *campesinos* were busy in the fields.[16] On paper, the organisation was impressive, even if the Maderistas' enthusiasm led them to take liberties with figures: an individual in the Sierra de Ixtlán claimed to have established PCP clubs in twenty mountain pueblos; Tlaxcala was said to have seventy-two branches of the party; a more detailed survey of Puebla reveals twelve well-established clubs with a membership of some 1,500 and here, as in Guadalajara and Orizaba, a significant working-class element was apparent among the Maderistas.[17] The urban working class, which had not distinguished itself in the armed uprising, was alive to the possibilities of political mobilisation, as it had been in 1908–10.

Conversely, it did not follow that towns or regions prominent in the fighting would assume a comparable political prominence in 1911. Professor Pedro Ruiz had to inaugurate a Maderista club at the Durango mining town of Aviño, even though it had contributed a hundred men to the revolution in February.[18] This disjunction between military and civilian (or revolutionary and reformist) protest can be seen at a higher level too. Following the pattern of 1909–10, the north-eastern states of Coahuila and Nuevo León bulked large (relative to population) in the PCP, despite their antipathy to revolution; and the spread of Madero's party south of the Isthmus – to Chiapas and Yucatán, the home of Pino Suárez – took it into areas where the impact of the organised Maderista rebellion had been tangential.[19] And few *cabecillas* figured among the PCP delegates as they convened in Mexico City: the makers of revolution and the makers of democratic parties were distinct species. When the convention met, it unanimously endorsed Madero's presidential candidacy and agreed a liberal programme closely following that of 1910: free suffrage, free speech, educational reform, support for foreign capital (without the 'establishment of monopolies'), encouragement for small farmers and 'the division of the big estates, always with respect for the sacred right of property'.[20] This was amicable enough; the real storm arose when a Vazquista minority sought to block Pino Suárez's vice-presidential candidacy; which attempt, though it failed, rent the fragile fabric of the Maderista coalition. Not only did the Vázquez Gómez name carry weight (Emilio's opposition to Díaz, if spasmodic, dated back to 1892; the family had important contacts in Mexico City and San Luis, and their recent 'radical' stance had won them support in the Maderista army); it was also the case that Pino Suárez was a relative unknown (in Chiapas, a Maderista cabled, there was 'murmuring . . . [and] confusion . . . everyone is asking, who is Pino Suárez?') and the manner of his selection seemed to smack of Porfirian practice.[21] Recalling Díaz's choice of the unpopular Corral,

Vázquez Gómez grumbled at this new 'imposition'; an adviser warned Pino
Suárez that – mistaken though they were – 'the masses have already been
penetrated by the poisonous idea that the methods used by Sr Madero are
identical to those used by General Díaz'.[22] Though Madero tried to assuage
criticism, the damage was done: opponents seized on the 'imposition' of Pino
Suárez as evidence of Madero's autocratic, neo-Porfirian conduct, and, among
the spate of armed revolts which Madero soon faced, many contained, among
their alleged grievances, the downfall of the Vázquez Gómez.[23]

The ambitions of others, too, were quickened by the approach of the
presidential election. Bernardo Reyes, absent from the political scene for
nearly two years, returned to Mexico (with Madero's permission). For a short
time these two protagonists of the anti-Díaz opposition appeared to work in
concert: Reyes agreed to support Madero for the presidency, in return for
which Madero would appoint him minister of war; it was another *transacción*
which disturbed the more intransigent Maderistas.[24] But consistency was not
Reyes' strong suit; with mounting evidence of support for his candidacy, the
general went back on his self-denying ordinance and declared he would run for
president after all, and Madero, as the champion of liberal democracy, could
hardly say no.[25] There is no doubt that in the summer of 1911, as Madero's
popularity began to wane, Reyes was the chief beneficiary. The first process
was inevitable: the high hopes, even euphoria, of May/June 1911 were bound
to deflate as peace-making, demobilisation and political fixing got under way;
Madero's own mistakes and personal idiosyncrasies had only a secondary,
contributory effect. But how and why should Reyes benefit? It should be
stressed that the Reyista movement of 1911 was different from that of 1909.
The latter had mobilised the urban middle class in a progressive, anti-Díaz,
protest party; in 1911 Reyes appealed to ex-Díaz office-holders and well-to-do
conservatives. Middle-class support was also forthcoming; but from a worried
middle class which, far from demanding political rights from an entrenched
dictatorship, now sought to recreate that dictatorship, or, at least, a comparable tough regime which would re-establish order and end violence, demagogy
and uncertainty. Reyista clubs thus carried Vichyite names: 'Patria', 'Orden y
Trabajo'; and Reyes made a frank appeal to the nation on these lines, noting
that current 'realities and the demagogic threats which lie behind them, have
brought fervent demands for the restoration of peace and for the strengthening
of individual guarantees'; hence he now proffered his presidential candidacy.[26]

Talk of a Reyes come-back, and the casting of Reyes as the necessary strong
man, antedated even the fall of Díaz; in turbulent Sinaloa (March 1911) it was
reckoned that 'his return would restore order in a short time . . . many of the
guerrilla bands would scatter to their homes and others would be smashed
easily'; clearly, Reyes' record of Porfirian punitive actions was not forgotten.[27]
Sentiment was soon supplemented by action. In May – even before the signing
of the treaty – Reyista clubs were being set up in Guadalajara, one of the key

cities of 1909.[28] In June, with Reyes en route from Havana to Mexico, Tampico (scene of the recent troubles) witnessed 'a daily increase in the sentiment for General Reyes for President', especially among the middle class.[29] A national political survey conducted by American consuls in August 1911 gave further evidence of this second 'Reyes boom', in most states and cities the Reyistas ran a strong second to the Maderistas: in Veracruz, Aguascalientes, Mazatlán (60:25 was the consul's estimate), Oaxaca (65:25), San Luis (75:25), Topia (75:25). While Reyismo was weak or non-existent in Hermosillo, Juárez and Chihuahua, it was now more popular than Maderismo in conservative cities like Guadalajara or Durango, or those, like Torreón and Tampico, which had suffered serious upheavals, and where 'strong government' was now at a premium. At least a quarter, and sometimes over half, the 'political nation' (for these estimates clearly do not embrace the mass of the population) thus supported Reyes. And they did so because Reyes – unlike Madero – was seen as a guarantor of order and property. He 'is looked upon by many as the only man who will be strong enough to restore order' (Tampico), while 'people lack confidence in Madero's ability to control the situation'; at Acapulco, the 'better class' considered Madero a 'weakling' and looked to Reyes to 'pacify the country'; the 'stable elements' of Mazatlán hoped that Reyes would 'create a benevolent dictatorship along the lines of that of Díaz'.[30] Foreign interests, like Lord Cowdray's, agreed that with a Reyes administration 'a greater sense of security will prevail than if Madero is president'.[31]

Thus, within weeks of the fall of Díaz, a durable myth was manufactured: that Mexico could only be governed by a new Díaz, running a neo-Porfirian system. This became a basic tenet of conservative groups (landowners, propertied middle class, the army, church hierarchy and foreign businessmen) and it found practical application in the Huerta regime of 1913–14, which finally revealed it for the myth it was. Its rapid manufacture further illustrates that the Madero revolution had been a traumatic experience for many of these groups, and, it should be noted, they now included a good many middle class oppositionists of 1908–10 (Reyista and Maderista) who, shocked by the experience, put material interest before liberal principle and opted for stable authoritarianism rather than experimental democracy. The fact that Reyes, figurehead of the 1909 civilian opposition, now appeared as the man on horseback, merely eased the transition. Hence the general could count on much of his old constituency. And, apart from the anxious middle class, the back-pedalling Maderistas, there were Freemasons, army officers (including generals like Huerta and Velasco), and disgruntled political 'outs' who felt they had not received their just deserts from the revolution.[32] But the conservative character of Reyismo was reinforced by the recruitment of Porfiristas who, rather than face political exclusion, and debarred from the Madero bandwaggon, saw Reyes as a vehicle for their return to power. At San Luis 'most of the Díaz adherents are now Reyes followers'; in Campeche 'Reyes is a tolerably important factor with office-holders under the Díaz regime'; Porfirian oligarchs like ex-Governor Torres of Sonora now flirted with Reyismo.[33] They possessed money and political contacts. A vigorous Reyista campaign was mounted in Tabasco, where 'a number of the most prominent partisans of the late Díaz administration' took the lead, 'flooding (the state) with pamphlets and posters'.[34] Campaigning took a violent turn at Tapachula (Chis.) where Reyistas hired a marimba band and toured the streets crying 'Vivas' to General Reyes and swilling drink until dawn; next day, still drunk, they attacked the Casa Municipal during the inauguration of the new (Maderista) mayor; when their fire was returned five people were killed, and the surviving attackers fled to Guatemala.[35] Reyistas and Maderistas also clashed on the streets of Mexico City (when Reyes himself tried to calm tempers he was stoned by the Maderistas) and forty participants were wounded; in Guanajuato the Reyistas were howled down by their opponents and many arrests followed.[36]

Such affrays were hardly surprising so soon after the cessation of hostilities and the spate of urban violence already described. But they did the Maderista cause no good, they compounded fears of social upheaval and governmental irresponsibility, and, if Francisco Madero sincerely deplored the use of force by his supporters, it was said that his brother Gustavo, fonder of strong-arm methods, had organised political bully-boys to mount these (and subsequent) attacks. The myth, maybe the reality, of the *Porra*, was born.[37] As for Reyes (whose law and order platform was hardly advertised by these events) he let his supporters down again. With elections scheduled for October it was clear he could not overhaul Madero, though he might put up a good show. Along with other anti-Madero factions, therefore, he called for a postponement of the elections until peace was fully restored. If the logic was spurious (postponement would have prejudiced, not enhanced political tranquillity) the aim was clear: to await the further erosion of Madero's popularity. But when Congress rejected these demands, Reyes opted out of the campaign and left Mexico; the American Ambassador was moved to his second apposite comment: 'General Reyes, who came into the country as the nominal saviour of the old Díaz regime, seems to be, like Lord Salisbury, a lath painted to look like iron'.[38] But this was not the end of Reyes, nor of the myth of Reyes the saviour of Mexico. Settling in Texas, surrounded by his cronies, he plotted revolt, encouraged by reports of Madero's growing unpopularity and by promises of support from landowners, army officers and the well-to-do. San Antonio, recently the hub of the Maderista conspiracy, now became the 'Mecca of Reyismo'. But, as evidence of Reyes' rebellious intentions piled up, the US authorities – showing, perhaps, a little more alacrity than in 1910 – arrested his partisans and confiscated their weapons; Reyes himself, already arrested once and released on bail, seemed destined for gaol unless he quit the country.[39] So, like Madero the year before, he was forced to evade imprisonment by crossing the border and taking up arms. The result was a fiasco: with only two companions the general roamed the rugged desert south of Camargo; it was mid-December, with bitter cold nights, and the anticipated recruits never appeared. On Christmas morning, Reyes gave himself up to an officer of the *rurales*. His surrender, he said, marked the end of his public life. But Don Bernardo was wrong again; like some Santa Anna of the Revolution he bounced back, for one final fiasco.[40]

Reyes' departure did not entirely clear the field for Madero and Pino Suárez. Apart from the Vazquistas there were fringe parties – the Liberals, Liberal Radicals, Popular Evolutionists – parties that were barely liberal and certainly neither radical nor popular, and that exerted little influence.[41] But, in the short space permitted by the electoral timetable, the Catholics were able to mount an impressive campaign, backing interim President de la Barra for the vice-presidency (while declining to oppose Madero's presidential candidacy). At a time when 'political societies of all kinds are in formation', a British observer commented, 'perhaps the most noteworthy is the Catholic Party who are showing great activity and whose influence in the election will be important'.[42] This was a significant development. In a sense it was a throwback to the primordial division in Mexican political society, which had dominated throughout most of the nineteenth century: that between clerical conservatives and anti-clerical liberals, which Díaz had papered over, which the PLM, with its shortlived campaign of 1901, had threatened to reopen. Now, in conditions of relative political freedom, and with the Maderistas committed – at least in theory – to the full implementation of the 1857 Constitution, a clash was on the cards; even though Madero himself was a devout Catholic, had never pressed the anti-clerical issue, and had even received the help of the Bishop of San Luis at the time of his imprisonment. Indeed, as regards the nascent Catholic Party (formed in May 1911, it held its inaugural national convention in August),[43] Madero adopted an attitude of benign tolerance: he believed it would provide a healthy, democratic element in the new politics he envisaged for Mexico; he readily received Catholic leaders, sent them telegrams of congratulation when they won elections, and praised their efforts at political organisation and working-class proselytisation. In this respect he recognised and approved the currents of social Catholicism then stirring the Mexican church, which were apparent in the make-up of the Catholic Party.[44] So far as Madero was concerned, the Catholics were playing the game *comme il faut* and, Madero's father assured the Archbishop of Mexico, the church would be accorded complete liberty.[45] But for many Mexicans, including many Maderistas, the clerical issue was still a live one. Perhaps this represented a political atavism, an obsession with old quarrels, perhaps it even functioned as a diversion from more pressing social and economic questions.[46] But as the history of the Revolution showed, the political – and still more the social – influence of the Catholic Church was still formidable; recent revisionism notwithstanding, both the Church and the Catholic constituency contained their gimlet-eyed reactionaries as well as their benign progressives (the same was true of their opponents), hence the battle between clericals and anti-clericals was no mere charade, even if both sides erred in believing that its formal result would make much difference to either the secularisation or the Catholicisation of Mexican society. At any rate, the formation of the National Catholic Party revived old rancours, despite the progressive nature of its initial programme. Díaz's defusion of the clerical issue was shown to have been – like so much of the Pax Porfiriana – a holding operation rather than a final solution.

In a short time, the Catholic Party made a marked impact throughout the country. It was reckoned to have a bright future at Mazatlán and to hold the balance between Maderistas and Reyistas at Tampico; if weak in the traditionally secular north, it enjoyed great support in the devout, conservative cities of central Mexico: in Guadalajara, for example, where 'the Catholic Party is much in evidence', or in Puebla where, a supporter wrote regretfully to Madero,[47]

the reason why we have not achieved the desired success is that Puebla is a very religious city, and the clergy is your enemy, and under the guise of the Catholic Party . . . actively opposed Pino Suárez. In the churches, in sermons, they propagandised for de la Barra.

Such clerical intromission in politics became a bitter refrain (and a source of further, more virulent anti-clericalism). Maderistas in Oaxaca complained of the 'parish priests working against us', in Guadalajara they lamented the success of the Catholic Party 'which is . . . nothing more than the old Conservative party revived', in Chihuahua they hoped that the 'healthy elements of the Nation' could counter the Catholic challenge.[48] The anti-clerical conscience was by no means confined to Maderistas, there were Porfirian (neo-conservative) anti-clericals too, hostile to Madero but equally critical of Catholic electoral practice: the political sermons, the subtle suborning of devout ladies, the dragooning of ignorant Indians by the *cura*, the provision of voting booths inscribed 'here you vote for God'.[49] If sometimes exaggerated, the Church's powers of persuasion were considerable, and the hierarchy were not afraid to use them.[50] Thus they contributed to the mounting support for de la Barra (the candidate himself reckoned he was attracting 20% of the vote, a too modest estimate, as it turned out) and, after their initial good showing in the vice-presidential contest, they went on to greater successes in state and local elections, thereby confirming anti-clerical fears, while establishing one of the fundamental political (I stress political) divisions of the Madero period.[51] But there was more to the de la Barra candidacy than Catholic piety and clerical guile. He appealed – by his own account – to 'the quiet element in the population . . . made up of the best people ... who thought and observed but did not make propaganda or vociferate'; the Mexican silent majority, in other words.[52] And certainly, with the failure of Reyes, de la Barra emerged as the 'strong man' of the election, politically experienced and hostile to further disorder. The well-to-do of Irapuato, for example, backed de la Barra since he was 'a thoroughly competent man and [all the more] since he had been a collaborator of Díaz'.[53] De la Barra's hard-line policy as interim president enhanced this image, and won him support not only among the devout, but also among respectable, propertied groups at large.

The presidential election, held as scheduled in October, was peaceful and 'unquestionably ... among the cleanest, most enthusiastic and most democratic', in Mexican history; even the opposition press reported it to be 'free and spontaneous'.[54] When (the ballot being indirect) the electors convened to cast their votes, Madero won the presidency by an overwhelming margin, as everyone expected (98%), while the vice-presidential poll, reflecting divisions between Maderistas and Catholics and within the Maderistas themselves, gave a truer indication of the political climate: Pino Suárez 53%, de la Barra 29%, Vázquez Gómez 17%.[55] While the election was cleaner than anything that had gone before, this was not so great a claim, and the degree of genuine popular participation is hard to establish. A critical observer of the primaries in Mexico City concluded that 'little comprehension of voting methods existed'; the 'elections were marked by the absence of participation ... of the peon or labouring classes' – who, it was said, feared that signing their names on voting slips 'would involve identification for the purposes of taxation'.[56] This was perhaps too cynical; but the quietness – even torpor – with which the elections passed off throughout the country must give rise to some suspicions, especially in view of preceding events. In some areas, where old Porfirian bosses retained control, the Maderistas were harassed and the elections held according to the old methods.[57] But the sheer unanimity of results (in favour of Madero), and the frequency with which Vázquez Gómez won the towns and Pino Suárez the countryside, argue a degree of official (Maderista) fixing, or at least popular indifference.[58] Even in towns like Tampico, noted for their political effervescence, the election was a quiet affair: peaceful, partially but subtly fixed, with a low turn-out, a massive plurality for Madero, and a victory for Pino Suárez over Vázquez Gómez.[59]

The 1911 presidential election, therefore, while an improvement on its predecessors, was far from being an exercise in mass, democratic participation. Democratic processes could not be implanted overnight, and the apathy of the electorate reflected a certain scepticism about the whole business – a reaction which, as we shall see, reformers like Madero found hard to eradicate.[60] But scepticism and apathy were particularly pronounced in the national, presidential election (where the main result was a foregone conclusion anyway), and they cannot be taken to indicate a general, popular indifference to politics, especially local politics. That provincial concerns should predominate in states like Oaxaca or Yucatán, where 'people generally take little interest ... in national affairs', was only to be expected; but the same was also true of the less remote, politically literate north.[61] At Saltillo, for example, the summer of 1911 was one of intense political activity: clubs were busy hiring rooms and holding evening political meetings; a state convention was scheduled for August, when delegates from all over Coahuila would meet to propose a Maderista gubernatorial candidate. All this was novel in a city where 'formerly the interest of the common people in political affairs was not welcomed'; it indicated the politicisation achieved by the Madero movement and revolution, but activities were principally geared to local (state, not national) affairs, and the presidential election, here as elsewhere, was an anodyne event.[62] Granted the existence of 'many Mexicos', it was the constitution of the new regime at local level, not in Mexico City, which counted for most. As a shrewd American, trying to run a construction company in Durango as local instability mounted and the *políticos* of Mexico City shuffled the pack, was moved to comment: 'no matter what compromises are arranged in Mexico City among the politicians and financial and landed interests, the lower classes will not obey ... [here] each group has its local interests and local sedition, not national, is the motive'.[63] The 1910 revolution had responded to local grievances, the 1911 political settlement had to take them into account, or risk the consequences; it is to the panorama of local politics that we must now turn.

LOCAL POLITICS: (1) THE CONSERVATIVE REVIVAL

The state governors represented the arm of the executive in the provinces; often, under Díaz, they represented entrenched, oligarchic cliques, and were the chief targets (along with their local minions, the *jefes políticos*) of revolutionary hostility. Madero's plan had provided for their immediate replacement by provisional, revolutionary appointees, but this clear-cut procedure was obfuscated by subsequent events. Díaz, prior to his departure, threw some governors to the wolves, some resigned in anticipation of a rebel victory, some (despite the peace treaty's freeze on political appointments) were forced out by popular protest. In these cases, state legislatures faced the difficult decision of naming a successor (balancing their own conservatism against the demands of the people); subsequently, the decision devolved on to the national interim regime. Finally, all these decisions were provisional, pending the election of all state governors according to the new constitutional principles. The initial consequence of this sequence of events was confusion and a good deal of sporadic violence, as governors shuttled in and out of the state-houses like commuter trains: Oaxaca had five governors in three months before Benito Juárez Maza was constitutionally elected; Veracruz had half a dozen in as many months following the resignation of Dehesa (who had ruled for eighteen years).[64] Sonora experienced a two-day, followed by a one-day, governorship, before Maytorena finally came into his constitutional inheritance.[65]

But there were some patterns in this apparent chaos. The north, the seat of the revolution, experienced the most rapid and thorough change, initiated by Díaz's sacking of Alberto Terrazas of Chihuahua in January. Thereafter, as gubernatorial heads rolled, it proved increasingly difficult for Porfirista legislatures to install their own creatures or fend off Maderista claimants. Esteban Fernández of Durango resigned after sixteen years in office; his successor lasted a matter of weeks before a Maderista was installed. The old (older even than Porfirio Díaz), rich, and unpopular governor chosen by the San Luis legislature survived only days; in Coahuila the legislature's choice of a prominent banker was overruled by Madero in favour of Venustiano Carranza; and in Chihuahua no conservative dared oppose Abraham González.[66] Thus at state, as at municipal level, local revolutionary success ensured a real degree of political change. For, while the Maderista governors thus installed were no radicals, and their administration soon antagonised popular revolutionary elements, nevertheless they were not Porfiristas either; Maderista governors like Gayou and Maytorena in Sonora could underwrite a major shift of political power, affecting families, regions and factions (in this case, Guaymas superseded Hermosillo, and Maytorena's clients those of Torres), and achieving a real expansion in political participation.[67] As regards both personnel and practice, therefore, Porfirian *immobilisme* came to an end.

Further south, where the revolution had been more sudden and swift, Porfirian governors (and their minions) clung to power more doggedly. In Tlaxcala, there was 'general disgust' among the Maderistas at Cahuantzi's continuance in office throughout May; Policarpo Valenzuela, recently appointed governor of Tabasco by Díaz, lasted into mid-June, obstructing Maderista forces in the state; the tardy dismissal of Dehesa and his clients in Veracruz provoked petitions to Madero.[68] Though the oligarchs of the Porfiriato ultimately went, such delays were politically significant, for – in circumstances of governmental instability, local conflict, and rebel demobilisation – they could materially affect the disposition of political forces within the different states, as the *interinato* gave way to Madero's constitutional regime. By way of example, we shall briefly examine three states of central Mexico (Mexico, Guanajuato, and Morelos) where the outcome was a significant conservative revival, revolutionary defeat, and ultimately further social conflict.

In Mexico state, the political spoils were shared, though unequally. A Maderista, Munguía Santoyo became lieutenant-governor, but the governorship went (courtesy of the legislature) to Rafael Hidalgo, for many years *oficial mayor* of the outgoing Porfirian governor, now the ally of a cabal of state deputies (the so-called 'Científicos' of Toluca), who termed themselves Reyistas.[69] The governor and his clique sought a rapid demobilisation of the Maderista troops, they resisted Munguía's attempts to oust Porfirista officials and they blocked his attempts to investigate the disbursement of state funds under the old regime (particularly a large payment made to a Federal senator, and an intimate of Díaz, for school furniture which never arrived). The survival of these Porfiristas, now sometimes self-styled Reyistas, had its impact locally. At Zumpango the *jefe* ignored the new authorities appointed by the rebels and gaoled eleven Maderista soldiers; at Chalco the *jefe* menaced the new administration at Atlautla; while the caciques of the region were blackening the reputation of the ranking Maderista commander in the region, Trinidad Rojas, and striving to gain the ear of the interim president. Precisely the same tactics, we will note, were pursued by the Morelos planters in their conflict with Zapata.[70] At Jilotepec, finally, the old authorities remained in power, to the disgust of the population.[71] Late in June, therefore, the young Maderista general Enrique Adame Macías accompanied a deputation to Mexico City, where they put their case to the Interior Minister, Vázquez Gómez, imploring that 'the chief authority in this district should be a native of the community'. The Minister was sympathetic, gave appropriate instructions to the state governor, and the people went home happy.[72] Weeks passed, however, and nothing happened; a second deputation went to the capital and received more bland reassurances; still nothing happened. Then the petitioners learned that two townspeople 'in league with the officials of the late administration', had urged the governor to veto their request, since it was the work of 'four or so trouble-makers of low status', which he had done. Again, questions of old regime graft and corruption were involved – misappropriation of municipal funds, charitable donations to the hospital which had gone astray. As far as we know, these peculations were never uncovered, and the Jilotepec petitioners never achieved satisfaction. Local grievances, so often the spur to rebellion, were now aired more vehemently as a result of the revolution; but their settlement was still thwarted by Porfirian officials.

In Guanajuato the revolution had produced two radically distinct movements. Cándido Navarro had built up a formidable, fast-moving rebel force in the northern district of Comanguillo, whence they had headed north to take San Luis; by the end of May, when the peace treaty supervened, Navarro's men were reckoned to be 'spoiling for a fight and to have [had] just about enough of the taste of fighting to do something big'.[73] Navarro, an ex-schoolmaster and watchman at the La Luz mines, was a dedicated revolutionary with a strong popular following. To an independent observer he seemed 'a man of good character', 'an honourable man, though somewhat visionary'; he shared with many such populist leaders a certain taciturn diffidence, he was 'exceedingly suspicious', a man who 'seems to consider very carefully every statement he makes'.[74] But then he had much to be suspicious about. A peremptory

order from President de la Barra denied him entry into León; the composition of
the interim administration, as we have seen, offended him along with other
Maderista *cabecillas*; meanwhile, events in south-central Guanajuato were
hardly reassuring. Here, Soto and García led their last-minute, defensive rebellion, co-operating closely with interim governors Aranda and Castelazo; the
latter, in fact, had been placed in charge of García's properties for the duration
of the campaign, and, as governor, he took pains to promote his 'friends' within
the state. García continued to drill the troops, while Soto became *jefe político* of
San Miguel.[75] 'As for Soto', the governor openly declared, 'he is at my orders
and I pay his forces and . . . there is nothing I need fear from this good friend of
mine.'[76] But rabble-rousers like Miguel Zamora (who, after his part in the San
Miguel riots had been gaoled, only to be released by Navarro) and revolutionary
populists like Navarro himself were a different matter; the latter, in particular,
commanded a strong following in the state and was outspoken in his attacks on
Porfirista elements in the state administration.[77] The governor's predicament
was typical of many in the aftermath of the 1910 revolution:

I cannot be completely at peace, nor . . . can this state, while revolutionaries of the kind
of Navarro . . . remain in it . . . I say this because Navarro . . . is an ignorant man with
pretensions to education, ordinary in appearance and lacking in high ideals but, on the
other hand, he has shown a special knack for attracting the boorish elements of the
population and now enjoys such great prestige that, without exaggeration, I believe
the question of whether or not civil war flares up in this state depends on his decision.[78]

Thus, the old regime confronted the new generation of populists thrown up
by the revolution. And Madero, smarting from the criticism of young militants like Navarro, and committed to orderly government, was sympathetic to
the governor and his kind. He considered Navarro 'stupid' and 'a very dangerous man'.[79] The old and the new regimes conspired to conjure the populist
threat, to eliminate the 'ignorant [and] ordinary' from their anomalous, offensive positions of power. Late in July Navarro was arrested for alleged sedition;
documents were unearthed attributing his disaffection to the regime's failure
to implement Maderista promises, particularly with regard to political rights
and agrarian reform.[80] His imprisonment was in fact brief and it was not
enough to quell the mounting resentment and rebellion which now affected the
state. By the spring of 1912, 3,000 Federal troops were deployed combating
ex-Maderista rebels; the most disaffected region was around Silao, 'the old
camping [sic] ground of Cándido Navarro', and 'the men who are making all
the trouble are his followers', now led by Navarro's lieutenant, Jesús Armendariz.[81] Gradually, however, this renewed surge of rebellion was dammed. A
Federal spy infiltrated Armendariz' forces and shot the rebel leader in the back
of the head; his body was displayed on a cot in the main street of Silao: a classic
'bandit' demise.[82] As repression increased, and rebel leaders were killed or
arrested, the political gains of 1911 were dissipated. The officials appointed in

that hectic spring were too suspect, and the continued unrest gave conservative elements the chance to reassert their control. By April 1912 only one 'local authority of popular origin' remained in the state of Guanajuato.[83]

The revolutionary veterans of 1910–11 thus saw their military efforts and political gains subverted.[84] Before long, many of the regions and individuals which had been prominent in the revolution against Díaz opted for revolt against Madero too. Such revolts have often (and often rightly) been seen as agrarian struggles, directed against a regime which failed to carry through its alleged agrarian promises. But while the agrarian factor was important (we have noted its role in 1910–11, and even Navarro, in a state hardly noted for its *agrarismo*, alluded to its importance), it cannot be surgically separated from local political questions and appointments. Agrarian reform, like the agrarian expropriation which preceded it, hinged upon the political: upon the general rules of local politics (would elections be free or fixed? would municipalities enjoy autonomy or suffer *caciquista* domination?) and upon specific decisions (who would govern: entrenched Porfiristas? rural populists? or the ambivalent civilian Maderistas, whose concern for social stability tugged against their desire for political reform?). This becomes abundantly clear if we consider the best-known case of agrarian rebellion, Zapatismo. When the peace settlement was concluded, Zapata and his allies had just succeeded in their prodigious, costly assault on Cuautla.[85] For the moment, Zapatista forces dominated Morelos, and their dominance enabled villagers to right agrarian wrongs despite the opposition of planters and politicians. But with the establishment of peace and of the interim regime, the planters set about repairing their position, and central to their strategy was an understanding with Ambrosio Figueroa, the ranking Maderista leader in neighbouring Guerrero – a strategy dictated by the strength of the local, popular rebellion, which ruled out straightforward conservative resistance and required, instead, a certain co-optation of 'revolutionary' forces.[86] Zapata, committed to the villagers' cause, declined to co-operate, but Figueroa, a modest landowner in his own right, unsympathetic to agrarian demands, and enjoying previous contacts with the Morelos planters, proved more amenable. And the planters believed that 'it would be easy to play on his emotions and butter him up [*adularlo*] so that he would serve as their instrument'.[87]

The strategy displayed the defects of its virtues: suitably pliable, Figueroa carried little weight in Morelos, and, after the manner of many interlopers who were to plague the state in subsequent years, his cavalier treatment of local interests only generated further resentment and rebellion. But, for the moment, he provided the military muscle: troops were sent to garrison Cuernavaca and Jojutla in advance of the Zapatistas; Figueroa's lieutenants, Asunsulo and Morales, playing a role comparable to that of Soto and García in Guanajuato, 'kept order', shot one of Zapata's allies (a personal enemy of Morales, who had been levying the well-to-do of Jojutla), and bent their influence to secure the appointment of a conservative governor.[88] In this they succeeded. The new governor – chosen without Zapata's consultation and to his evident disgruntlement – was Juan Carreón, manager of the Bank of Morelos, and an unconditional friend of the planter interest.[89] Once installed, Carreón relayed to the central government alarming reports of Zapatista indiscipline and depredation (reports which Zapata justifiably queried), he sedulously cultivated Madero, and he co-operated with the planters in their call for a rapid demobilisation of the Liberating Army. As Womack observes, 'the speed and the extent of the planters' recovery of influence was astounding'.[90] Appreciating that, in the post-treaty circumstances, political contacts and influence were at a premium, Zapata travelled to Mexico City and joined the throng soliciting Madero. But in response to Zapata's demands for immediate land reform and the implementation of the Plan of San Luis, Madero counselled patience; the land question would have to be settled by gradual, constitutional methods and, meantime, Zapata's forces would have to be mustered out; at best, 400 of his 2,500 men could serve under their leader as Federal police, mopping up trouble in their own back-yard. Both the demands and the response were typical.

As Zapata reluctantly concurred and went home, the planters moved in on Madero, wining and dining him (he was one of their own, a landowner and businessman, albeit a somewhat gauche and eccentric northerner), and the Mexico City press began to titillate its readership with stories of Zapata, 'the modern Attila'.[91] In Morelos, the situation was tense and ambiguous. Despite the official mechanics of demobilisation (3,500 weapons handed in, 47,500 pesos disbursed in compensation), a Zapatista army remained covertly in being in the villages of Morelos, defending their agrarian gains, defying the planters, who complained to Madero of the villagers' 'socialist pretensions'. Some, in terminology scarcely more accurate, feared an imminent 'caste war'. As usual, Madero's inclination was to conciliate. But the dual authority which prevailed throughout the summer of 1911 denied Madero independence of action; instead it ensured a tug-of-war between Madero (who exercised some loose legitimacy over the Zapatistas) and the hawkish de la Barra. The latter – even before the Juárez treaty – had advised Díaz to compromise with the northern rebels (since Madero was a respectable fellow), thus releasing Federal troops for operations in the south where 'if handled with energy [they] will soon put an end to the brigand bands of Morelos and Puebla'.[92] Madero and Zapata were seen – rightly – as representing different revolutions; one could be talked round, the other had to be bludgeoned into submission. As president, de la Barra had not changed his mind and he was backed up by Vázquez Gómez's successor, the new Minister of Gobernación, García Granados. Ambrosio Figueroa was therefore appointed governor and military commander in Morelos, and Federal troops were dispatched under the command of General Victoriano Huerta, a career soldier with a sanguinary record, who saw the move not as a limited manoeuvre, to compel Zapatista demobilisation, but rather as 'a campaign of occupation'.[93] It was to be a test case for the repressive, root-and-branch policy which many conservatives believed would restore peace and order to Mexico.

Throughout August, the Federal troops advanced; the villagers – and some of the Mexico City press – protested; Madero strove to conciliate; de la Barra prevaricated. Suitably encouraged, Huerta forced the pace of events and advised the president it was essential 'to reduce Zapata to the last extremity, even hang him or throw him out of the country'. This, for Huerta, was an almost Pavlovian reaction to vexing political problems (though it was also suggested that his heavy-handed approach was designed to aid the political fortunes of Bernardo Reyes, of whom Huerta was an old partisan).[94] By the end of the month, Federal provocations had the Zapatistas spoiling for a fight and Madero, despairing of his arbiter's role, went off to electioneer in Yucatán. Spurred by the news of revolutionary sack and rapine at Jojutla, de la Barra and his cabinet now resolved on the 'complete extirpation of banditry' in Morelos, and Huerta was given his head; soon, the entire state was under military control and Zapata was driven into hiding in the mountains to the south.[95] Here, while the Mexico City press applauded the success of the campaign, Zapata cast about for revolutionary support, and proclaimed his grievances against the government, which precisely reflected the interdependence of political and agrarian factors. He demanded popular authorities and military commanders, the abolition of the *jefaturas políticas*, and 'what in justice the pueblos deserve as to lands, timber and water' – a claim which, he said, lay at 'the origin of the present Counterrevolution'.[96] In addition to the appeal exercised by this programme, Zapata's cause was served by the Federals' dogged advance through Morelos and into Puebla; not for the last time, repression stimulated Zapatista resistance and a Federal general proved to be Zapata's best recruiting sergeant.[97] When Zapata swooped back into Morelos in October, outflanking the Federals, he found ready recruits and was able to lead his resurgent army to the gates of Mexico City. Huerta was sacked and Madero – about to be inaugurated as president – made fresh overtures to the rebel leader. But the Federal Army (its officers liking repression better than diplomacy) continued freelance operations, and Madero, too conscious of the gulf separating the President of the Republic from a common rural *cabecilla*, would accept nothing less than unconditional surrender.[98] The prerogative of the central government and the *amour propre* of the political elite (both components of Maderista as they had been of Porfirista official thinking) ruled out a settlement.[99] Madero and Zapata, briefly united in their opposition to Díaz, went their separate, antithetical ways, and a war began in Morelos that was to continue for nine long years.

The story of Zapata has been better told elsewhere, and has become familiar. But too often the story is considered unique, when in fact it was typical. This is as true of the events of 1911 as of the agrarian origins of the rebellion. Zapata's plight mirrored that of other popular (often agrarian) rebels in other states. In Morelos, as in Mexico and Guanajuato, a conservative governor facilitated a conservative revival; Maderista demobilisation was hustled along, justified by garbled tales of indiscipline and disorder; rebel leaders of weaker populist conviction were co-opted to the conservative cause, where they complemented the Federal Army. As a result, erstwhile Maderista leaders like Zapata or Navarro were driven to rebel a second time, espousing just the same objectives as in 1910–11, but now, ultimately, in opposition to Madero.

LOCAL POLITICS: (2) THE LIBERAL INHERITANCE

The triumph of out-and-out conservatism was less marked in other states. If, at local level, the pattern of reform and reaction was chequered, state power usually passed (if not immediately) into the hands of bona fide Maderistas, or at least of men with proven opposition records: González in Chihuahua, Maytorena in Sonora, Juárez in Oaxaca, Cepeda in San Luis, Carranza in Coahuila, Guadalupe González in Zacatecas.[100] But credentials of civilian opposition were not enough. The most striking feature of the political settlement of 1911 was the promotion of civilian *políticos* over military *cabecillas*, of 'platonic' over practising revolutionaries, of age over youth, education over ignorance, respectability over *arrivisme*.[101] The middle-aged, middle-class Maderistas of 1909–10 floated to the top, the young, plebeian and popular leaders of 1910–11 – who had overthrown Díaz – were passed over. Not only did this policy disappoint both the personal ambitions of these leaders and the collective hopes of the followers, it could also jeopardise their safety, for in a good many regions the rebels had goaded local conservatives, planting a few *banderillas* without delivering the *estocada*, and they feared that once demobilised and stripped of power, they would fall victim to conservative reprisals (as indeed they did). Domingo Magaña of Tabasco begged that his officers – 'who *por cariño* stay by my side' – be given commissions in the state militia, since both 'leader and officers have powerful enemies [among the] defeated party . . . and [we are] at the mercy of the first assassin we meet'.[102] Such fears and resentments were aggravated as it became clear that the civilian Maderistas who took office were all to ready to conciliate vested interests, to disown their own ragged rank-and-file, and to insist on a swift demobilisation. As such, and despite their opposition records, they often seemed little better than standpat conservatives.

The allocation of national jobs produced first de la Barra's then Madero's hybrid administrations. Madero's cabinet retained a conservative core, it included no revolutionary veterans (i.e., belligerents) save Abraham González and Madero himself. Now, men like Miguel Díaz Lombardo, who had sat out the revolution in Morelia, became ministers; Jesús Urueta, who had sat with him, emerged as a leading Maderista spokesman, deputy and anti-Vázquista; Félix Palavicini, 'who left the cause when Madero led it to revolution was welcomed back with open arms'.[103] The central commitee of the PCP, numbering twenty-two, contained only one Maderista who had actively fought in the revolution: Eduardo Hay, who had been wounded and captured at Casas Grandes.[104] And, as already noted, the experience of the revolution (even – or especially – when viewed from afar) gave these erstwhile opposition-ists pause for thought. High-principled campaigns against the dictatorship were one thing, conniving at anarchy was another. Alberto García Granados, for example, seemed (in conservative eyes) 'a traditional anti-Porfirista and sincere democrat'; Madero welcomed his appointment at Gobernación, since 'his merit . . . from the point of view of the aspirations of the revolution cannot be disputed'; yet, as a minister and *hacendado*, he 'despised the rebels who had done the fighting' and sought to demobilise them as quickly as possible, if necessary at the prod of Federal bayonets.[105]

The wholesale preferment of respectable civilians, of few or no revolutionary credentials, was no surprise. It was assumed that poorly educated, sometimes illiterate, provincial *guerrilleros* were disqualified from high (and often low) political office. Enrique Adame Macías, who played an important role in the Laguna revolt and later contested the conservative post-revolutionary settlement, made a bad impression on the urbane Maderistas whom he met at an official banquet in June 1911, on the banks of Lake Xochimilco:[106]

being a simple man of the lower class, like almost all the revolutionaries, he appeared dressed in a double-breasted frockcoat and top hat, and so abused the available liquor that, on getting into a canoe, he fell into the water and got sopping wet, which produced loud guffaws on the part of the assembled company.

Clearly (it was felt), such bumpkins could not govern states, run ministries or mix with foreign diplomats. Yet in later years the experience of the Revolution was to show that parvenus who had battled their way to power could make competent *políticos*, certainly at provincial, often at national level: witness the careers of Cándido Aguilar, Joaquín Amaro, the Cedillos and the Arrietas. And, irrespective of expertise, it was politically essential for such men to share in the division of power if the revolutionary rank-and-file were to be satisfied and stability recreated. Here lay one of the major errors of the Madero regime: its failure to reward its friends (the populist leaders) and punish its enemies (the Porfiristas). This was not an error of the kind for which Madero has often been blamed: his failure to initiate sweeping social reform, to start the 'building of socialism' in Mexico. These alternatives lay so far outside the pale of Maderista thinking as to be irrelevant; it would be as appropriate to blame – say – Gladstone for the same sins of omission; and to suggest otherwise is to engage in polemic rather than historiography. But, as regards political preferment, the decision to exclude popular leaders had no such inevitability (was not 'over-determined'), it was contested bitterly, especially at local level, even some ranking Maderistas (the 'hawks')[107] doubted its wisdom, and, within a few years, it was significantly reversed, without producing civil chaos. On the contrary, it proved a necessary cement for the new revolutionary order.

But, for two principal reasons, Madero and his advisers declined to promote popular, plebeian leaders, and instead allowed the middle-class worthies to monopolise office. First, they held assumptions about who should and should not govern a model liberal regime; these assumptions, later eroded by events, excluded the young, the 'ignorant', the boorish from power. But secondly, they had to face the civilians' pressing demands for rewards and positions. Under Díaz, power had been jealously retained by small, closed, gerontocracies. Now, with the fall of Don Porfirio, the frozen glacier of Mexican politics began to melt and shift; middle-class opponents of the old regime awaited an avalanche of jobs and favours. As in the aftermath of every coup, revolution or election – but all the more when it was the first significant one for a generation – there was an orgy of political patronage. Crowds of supplicants, as we have seen, battened on Madero and his provincial lieutenants, Madero's wife and private secretary were lobbied, ministerial antechambers were 'jam-packed with hundreds of Maderistas who had never heard a shot fired', but who now claimed their reward.[108] The process began but did not stop in 1911. Tireless supplicants like Maximino Avila Camacho badgered Madero throughout 1912, travelled up to Mexico City from Teziutlán to press his case, boasted of his clerical skills, his excellent references (some from 'American companies with whom I have worked'), and his readiness to take on any job, 'even a dangerous one'.[109] In this case, preferment had to wait. But others were more immediately successful: a *jefatura* for Abel Serratos, failed revolutionary of 1910; a secretaryship (in the Federal District administration) for E. Bordes Mangel, who had helped draft the Plan of San Luis; a choice of second-class consulates for Benjamín Viljoen, Boer turned Maderista.[110] Lower in the scale of patronage, the printing office of the Chamber of Deputies went to Wenceslao Negrete, a 'good friend of the government'; Maderistas in Veracruz who stood firm for the regime during the abortive coup of October 1912 were recommended for posts in the customs service, always one of the chief reservoirs of official patronage.[111] In addition, the government could confer or withhold endorsement of aspiring politicians – would-be deputies, senators and state governors.[112]

The distribution of favours went beyond the specifically political and administrative, it could also include judicial and economic benefits, and it reflected the clientelism which pervaded Mexican society, and which the revolution had done little to alter. And here again, it could be said, the 'mobilisation of bias' worked to the advantage, not of the popular *cabecillas*, still less their *campesino* followers, but rather of the educated, worldly-wise, city-dwelling Maderistas: those who knew how the system worked (even if under Díaz their knowledge was of limited use) and who had access to the new sources of patronage.[113] The veteran journalist Silvestre Terrazas, long-time critic and martyr of the Creel–Terrazas regime in Chihuahua, now enjoyed Madero's support in his search for credit among the northern banks; a Mexico City editor, Alfonso Peniche, who cited two years spent in Belem as proof of his anti-Díaz convictions, claimed 500 pesos from the government for services rendered to the revolution.[114] The good offices of the regime could also speed litigation. The procurator of the Federal District was instructed to expedite a case involving a debt owed to the Maderista, Agustín Sánchez, who blamed 'the intrigues and chicaneries of the opposition party' for delays hitherto; while the Minister of Fomento was urged (by Madero's influential secretary) to do what he could to further a denunciation of public (*baldío*) land made by 'an excellent friend of the government who has furnished us very important services'.[115] This last case was particularly suggestive. Land concessions had comprised one of the chief weapons in the Porfirian assault on the villages, in response to which *campesinos* had protested and recently rebelled; now it was Maderista rather than Porfirista clients who could count on the blessing of the courts and administration in making such claims. A Maderista newspaper editor from Madero's home town of San Pedro requested governmental help concerning property he, as an absentee landlord, owned in the Yaqui valley: the local inhabitants, he feared, were going to 'play him a dirty trick' behind his back; the region was, after all, one of the main centres of agrarian disaffection in the country.[116] A worthy, propertied, newspaperman (from the 'little city of the big capitalists'), and the insurgent Indians of the Yaqui Valley: they represented polar extremes within a fragile coalition, rapidly assembled and only briefly held together by their common opposition to Díaz.

As the coalition fell apart, the civilian Maderistas got the lion's share of the spoils and this was particularly offensive at state (as against national) level, since the ambition of popular leaders and the grievances of their followers usually assumed a local focus; furthermore, the newly installed civilians usually enjoyed even less of a revolutionary record, hence even less prestige, than Madero himself (who had at least risked his life in combat). Throughout Mexico, therefore, the civilians found their authority cramped, their coveted political inheritance compromised, by surviving Porfiristas on the one hand (*políticos* and army officers or landlords and local notables, wedded to the old regime and critical of the new), and by parvenu, populist leaders on the other, who now expected a return for themselves and their *gente* after their successful revolutionary efforts. Faced with this dilemma, Maderista governors often chose to rely on conservative support in order to quell popular unrest – to call in the old regime to redress the balance of the new. The case of Morelos is, again, typical rather than exceptional, in that the respectable, civilian opposition of 1909–10, the Leyvistas and Maderistas, supported the policies of rapid demobilisation and pacification which drove Zapata and his allies to rebel. [117]

Other cases abound. In Hidalgo, both the interim governor, Jesús Silva, and his successor, Ramón Rosales, had impeccable opposition credentials and were men of property and standing (president and vice-president of the Pachuca Anti-Re-electionist Club, a lawyer and a masonic grand master respectively); both had been arrested when Díaz's police swooped in November 1910 (when Silva, it was said, recanted with indecent haste), and certainly neither had taken part in the armed revolt. [118] Attention shifted to the 23-year-old 'Indian' general, Gabriel Hernández who, after recruiting three supporters in his native village of Chignahuapán (Pue.), became the dominant leader in Hidalgo, amassed an army of several thousand, and entered Pachuca in triumph in May. [119] Hernández was the man of the hour, his arrival at Pachuca quelled riots, a sumptuous parade was held in his honour; as the victorious Maderistas posed for photographs (which was *de rigueur* in 1911) Hernández was captured for posterity, seated at a desk wearing an incongruous pith helmet, surrounded by older, paler, moustachioed mestizos. [120] As Gruening comments: 'Hernández, four weeks before an unknown village lad, now headed 3,000 men, many well-equipped, and controlled the entire state of Hidalgo', in Mexico he was termed (not necessarily in friendly fashion) 'el famoso de Pachuca'. [121] But Jesús Silva was governor, and soon under attack for his political appointments (of an old Porfirista, for example, as Lieutenant-Governor), for his retention of Porfirian tax officials and magistrates, and for his continuance of the *jefe político* system, which made nonsense of the promise of free municipal government. [122] At Junapam, to take one local example, the Maderistas had let the people elect a popular *jefe*, only to have their choice subverted by the governor, to the detriment (the people complained) of revolutionary principles. [123] Hernández, meanwhile, after a brief spell in the *rurales* (the only official role to which a young *cabecilla* might aspire) returned to his native patch, where he became involved in a violent feud with Miguel Arriaga, a paladin of the old regime, whose successful 'last-minute' revolt has already been mentioned. [124] Hernández was responsible for attacking the garrison at Cuetzalá, in the heart of Arriaga's fief, and he was implicated in his brothers' sacking of Arriaga's house in Zacapoaxtla. The precise nature of this dispute cannot be fathomed. Arriaga was now termed a 'Vazquista', Hernández a 'Maderista' (though he was thought to be on the brink of revolt against Madero in January 1913). But, as this usage suggests, these national labels were loosely and opportunistically applied. What is clear is that the rupture of the Porfirian order had revived old feuds and generated new ones, and, if some were purely 'Namierite' squabbles over local power and patronage, pitting like against like, others involved battles between old-style, Porfirian caciques (like Arriaga) and the new, young, revolutionary populists (like Hernández). [125] Such battles had a palpable social significance (it made a real difference who won) and there was little evidence in 1911–12 to suggest either that they were running down, or that the central government was imposing its will and terminating them. Rather, they continued with vigour, buffeting the central government, and compromising political stability. As an observer of these local feuds on the Puebla-Hidalgo border was moved to comment, both aptly and, in a sense, prophetically:[126] 'in my opinion, peace can never be established in this country until the government makes a general house-cleaning of all or the majority of those belonging to the "old regime", from the humble pen-pusher [and] telegraph operators to the most important personages'.

Similar troubles affected the Puebla heartland, further south. Here, in the summer of 1911, the new governor found that his authority was confined to three or four districts; the rest went their own way, a local Maderista observed, 'since the villages, guided by revolutionary elements, do not accept the magistrates, or the tax-collectors ... or the *jefes políticos*'.[127] Governor Canete's political appointments angered rebel leaders like Camerino Mendoza (on the Puebla–Veracruz border) and Francisco Gracia, of Atlixco; Gracia, though demobilised, strove to oust the local *jefe*, even though (the governor said) 'the best of Atlixco society is happy with his administrative record'.[128] In the state capital, the first major city to hear gunfire in 1910, friction between Maderista and Federal troops produced a bloodbath. Accounts agree that the arrest and attempted liberation of a rebel leader started the trouble, but they differ in stressing either the drunken behaviour of the Maderistas or the deliberate provocation of anti-Maderista elements, including the two sons of ex-Governor Mucio Martínez.[129] At any rate, the better equipped Federals – they included the crack 29th Battalion, which will reappear in equally grim circumstances later – 'mowed down' the Maderistas with machine-guns, killing over a hundred and driving the rest in flight from the city. Thus provoked, the fleeing rebels took it out on the factories and haciendas of the surrounding countryside and, once again, Spaniards were among the principal victims.[130] Madero, as it happened, arrived at the city next day on a pre-arranged visit. Already, *poblano* Maderistas (of the urban, respectable kind) had urged him to take vigorous action against disturbers of order – 'even against the revolutionaries' – for otherwise the 'interests of the Revolution' could not be guaranteed.[131] Now, as Madero contemplated a middle course, involving changes of command on both the Maderista and Federal sides, many of his supporters disagreed: tough measures, including the speedy demobilisation of the Liberating Army, were the only remedy for disorder and instability. As the paterfamilias of the Madero clan advised:[132]

the horrible events at Puebla give an idea of the state of mind prevailing in a great part of the country ... it is absolutely necessary for the central government to act with great energy to repress any new movement which tends to encourage disorder of any kind, punishing its authors . . . with the greatest severity. Only by such methods will it be possible to avert . . . unrestrained anarchy.

Evaristo Madero was not just huffing and puffing. Despite the formal return to legality, conflicts between Pofiristas, liberal, and popular Maderistas were endemic; as between the last two, the 'interests of the Revolution' looked different from the perspective of a middle-class, urban progressive and that of a rural populist, and a renewal of hostilities, on the basis of these fundamental disagreements, was always on the cards. In Mexico state, the governor complained of the insubordination of Maderista troops who, besides defying his authority, were said to be manufacturing dynamite bombs with a view to imminent rebellion.[133] Similar complaints emanated from Michoacán, where Governor Miguel Silva – a middle-aged doctor, complete with goatee beard and gold-rimmed spectacles – had brought to power on his coat-tails (the Partido Liberal Silvista) a crowd of 'doctors, lawyers, and other professionals, some farsighted landlords . . . and many men of the middle class', who staffed the executive, the state legislative and the judiciary. None of the state's military leaders received comparable rewards and, if some middle-class aspirations were satisfied, there were continued complaints that local Porfirista office-holders had been restored in defiance of popular wishes.[134] Reform and renovation in the towns and cities did not necessarily extend into the countryside. In Oaxaca, too, Benito Juárez Maza successfully campaigned for the governorship, backed by others of similar pedigree (like the ex-Reyista Jesús Urueta) and the familiar flock of professors and other middle-class worthies.[135] The new governor's conservatism (and his allegedly close relations with Díaz's nephew, Félix) caused adverse comment; his political appointments incited a furore down on the Isthmus and, as elsewhere, the revolutionary veterans of 1910–11 were driven to rebel again.[136] Angel Barrios and his fellow-*cabecillas* resisted demobilisation through the summer of 1912, turned down the offer of *rurales* commissions and finally raised the standard of revolt in November in the mountains around Cuicatlán, in the same region and with the same supporters as in the days of the Maderista revolution. They claimed to represent the purity of the Plan of San Luis, and denounced Madero for reneging on the promises of the revolution.[137]

The Maderista coalition also fissured along generational, as well as class or cultural lines – hardly surprising, since youth had fought the battles of the revolution. Populist leaders were usually in their twenties or thirties, the civilian *políticos* in their forties or fifties. But here an interesting and important sub-group demands attention. The main exception to the general argument presented here (that distinct groups undertook the politicking of 1909–10 and the government of 1911–13 on the one hand, and the popular mobilisation and guerrilla warfare of 1910–11 on the other) was constituted by a handful of young, civilian Maderistas, scions of respectable families, who combined the civilians' ambition, idealism, and political *nous*, with a capacity for guerrilla fighting, and thereby for genuine popular mobilisation. Thus, unusually, they straddled both camps. Juan Andreu Almazán, a medical student when the revolution broke out, took to the countryside, acting in loose alliance with Zapata; he built up his Brigada Serdán, styled himself, somewhat grandiloquently, as Madero's plenipotentiary in the south, and carved out a zone of influence on the Puebla-Morelos marches. Ambitious and guileful, Almazán was aggrieved when he received no preferment from Madero.[138] During the uneasy process of demobilisation, Almazán's forces clashed with Federals in Cuernavaca (a minor version of the Puebla fracas), and their leader addressed an audience of invited pressmen, denouncing the government's 'violent method of demobilisation', blaming Madero for being corraled by conservatives, and complaining that he (Madero) was 'casting all his partisans into an abyss'.[139] Zapata – or Magaña, or Hernández – no doubt felt the same, but none had convened press conferences to say so. And, as a friend, and a member of the middle-class political fraternity, Almazán could expect Madero's indulgence: after a brief period of detention, therefore, he was released, having 'reflected on and understood' his youthful error.[140] But within weeks, Almazán was back with Zapata, stirring up rebellion in the Puebla–Guerrero mountains; within months he had led several hundred men in a successful assault on Ayutla (Gro).[141]

Another aspiring student (of law) and friend of Madero posed similar problems for the authorities in San Luis. Pedro Antonio de los Santos came from a well-to-do family, steeped in politics, which had provided the leadership for a popular rebellion in the 1880s.[142] Now, in 1911, Santos established himself as a prominent Maderista leader, became state secretary, and, despite his tender years, declared himself a candidate for the governorship. With this in mind, it was alleged, he deliberately stalled the demobilisation of his troops, there were boisterous political demonstrations in his favour, and alarmed Potosinos implored Madero to summon Santos to Mexico City 'on any pretext' to keep him out of the way.[143] As it was, Santos' gubernatorial challenge faded and Dr Rafael Cepeda, the 'official' Maderista candidate, triumphed against negligible opposition. Though a genuine reformer, Cepeda incurred resentment by the manner of his election and the tough line he took with fellow-Maderista dissidents; by the late summer, it was noted,[144] 'there is some comment [in San Luis] on the fact that nearly all the Madero [sic] leaders who were active in this district have been arrested, the Maderista forces partly disbanded and partly moved to small towns, while the Federal force has been augmented'. Carrera Torres, Pérez Castro and Daniel Becerra, who led a 'Vazquista' revolt on Río Verde, were among the prominent rebels captured and gaoled during 1911–12; and in the same period the Cedillos were driven from vague opposition to outright rebellion.[145]

But while the Cedillo rebellion was classically agrarian, popular and plebeian, Santos – like Almazán – belonged to that diminutive group, 'many of them very young men' who, though they came from 'the middle or better class ... have supported seditious movements'.[146] As such, they were regarded – rather indulgently – as political delinquents rather than social subversives and 'when captured, they have not usually been punished, in fact at least four of them have been appointed or returned to office' in San Luis.[147] Now, as in the days of Díaz, or the endless *cuartelazos* of the nineteenth century, the political nation could tolerate a degree of dissension within its own ranks, without resorting to the brutal repression reserved for rebellious Indians and *campesinos*. In consequence, Santos could combine popular mobilisation with more orthodox political careerism; he angled for the post of police chief in the Huasteca (his brother represented the region in the Federal Congress); the family sought to advance their interests there, clashing with Governor Cepeda and his appointees, appealing to Madero, and thus embroiling president with governor.[148] Since several of the communities whose political destinies were being haggled over had records of agrarian disaffection, it may be that these fierce, ostensibly 'Namierite' squabbles rode upon the back of deeper socio-economic conflicts. Further local research might (or might not) reveal a connection, might, for example, show if Santos (like other Huasteca landowners) built a revolutionary career by capitalising upon and giving expression to popular grievances, as his family had done in the past.[149] In fact, the career was cut short by a hero's death in 1913. But Almazán survived, prospered, and after a chequered revolutionary history emerged as a key figure in the post-revolutionary state. Thereby he confirmed what a powerful amalgam was formed when political literacy was married to popular charisma, when, in consequence, popular forces could be mobilised *within* rather than *against* the prevailing state structure.[150] But this took time, and a hard education in the school of revolution. In 1911–12 these young, smart, rabble-rousing Maderistas – distinct, alike, from both their supine, middle-aged superiors and their rough, plebeian allies – represented a force for the future, but they were too few, and too junior, to affect the course of events; for the time being they were condemned to remain as isolated rebels and dissidents.

The character of the 1911 settlement and of the Madero regime may be finally and particularly well illustrated by the example of Veracruz, a key political state. Here, the sudden guillotine on revolutionary activity brought down by the peace treaty created a 'sentiment of disappointment or deception'; opinion was offended by the survival in office of Dehesa's creatures, and, as in Puebla and Cuernavaca, Federals and Maderistas fought in the streets of the state capital long after 'peace' had been concluded.[151] Thereafter, energies were channelled into fierce political conflicts, particularly concerning the state governorship. In the gubernatorial election, Francisco Lagos Cházaro (a 'picturesque Bohemian' and, like most Bohemians, solidly middle class) confronted Gabriel Gavira, a literate, aspiring artisan (a carpenter), who had progressed from mutualism and Anti-Re-electionist politics in Orizaba to become 'a self-styled general of the usual stripe', that is, a popular leader of some 500 men, at the head of whom he took Córdoba in May 1911.[152] If Santos and Almazán were unusual middle-class *guerrilleros*, Gavira was unusual by virtue of his working-class (more strictly, his artisanal) and his urban background. In running (like Santos) for the governorship, he displayed both daring and sophistication. Many popular, rebel leaders of 1911 were more diffident and deferential, especially in the centre/south: Gavira's friend Rafael Tapia, a saddler from Orizaba and another self-made *cabecilla*, meekly supported Lagos Cházaro because, he believed, state governors should be men of education. Tapia, in return, received a commission in the *rurales*; he knew his place and was rewarded according to his status.[153] Madero, too, supported Lagos Cházaro, since (Gavira observed) 'he preferred a priori the *licenciado* to the carpenter'.[154]

But Gavira pressed ahead and mounted a strenuous political campaign, travelling through the state in an unprecedented 'gira electoral', counting on his 'strong following in the interior among the lower classes'.[155] According to his partisans he was 'very highly thought of in the whole state, chiefly among the oppressed people (*la gente sufrida*), the working people' – which was hardly surprising in view of his background; while Lagos Cházaro depended upon 'the old caciques, in a word, the Científicos'.[156] After the election, both sides claimed victory but Lagos Cházaro was named the winner, and Gavira, following common practice, repudiated the result, 'pronounced', and took to the hills – appealing, with considerable success, for popular support, especially in the wild, upland country where the 1910–11 revolution had made most progress. This, Gavira stressed, was a local rebellion; he declined to adopt a 'Vazquista' label and he wrote to Madero deploring the President's excessive compromising with conservative interests, which had led to disillusionment and revolt.[157] But Gavira was soon hunted down by *rurales*, caught near Altotonga and committed to the notorious San Juan de Ulúa prison in Veracruz harbour. Madero wrote to the state governor congratulating him on Gavira's capture. But even during his nine months imprisonment (two of them spent in the dank airless cell where Juan Sarabia, gaoled for three years by Díaz, had contracted tuberculosis), Gavira figured in Veracruzano politics: he was visited and importuned by gubernatorial candidates in the summer of 1912; by his own account, his endorsement of Antonio Pérez Rivera (no radical, but 'honest and independent') ensured the latter's election.[158] This was entirely plausible. When Gavira was released during a general amnesty at the end of 1912 he received a 'great popular demonstration' in Veracruz; Governor Pérez Rivera trembled, fearing another Gavirista outbreak, and appealed to Madero to coax Gavira up to Mexico City, where the Veracruz state government would happily pay him a pension to keep out of the way. It was not so much Gavira as Gavirismo which was to be feared,[159] since Gavirismo . . . marks a division among classes in society, hence it is my desire that public demonstrations should not be held, which might awake and enliven passions which, with great tact, I am trying to get the people to forget, in order to make one family out of all social elements, a family which breathes the same ideals and shares the same aspirations.

Like Domingo Hernández of San Miguel the previous year, Pérez Rivera longed for the social stability and consensus of Switzerland, in place of the political and social ferment of Mexico. And Madero could not but approve these pacific sentiments, and their implied rejection of divisive class politics: he agreed that 'with nothing to do, Gavira would undoubtedly occupy himself with politics and would keep the state in a condition of constant ferment'.[160] But Madero did not think it necessary to seduce Gavira away to Mexico City, rather, from the distant security of the capital, he believed he could talk Gavira into returning to his carpenter's shop in Orizaba. That – rather than in the statehouse – was where Gavira and his kind belonged.

LOCAL POLITICS: (3) THE POPULAR CHALLENGE – THE NORTH

By and large, the civilian Maderistas – and the out-and-out conservatives whom they increasingly resembled – carried the day in central Mexico, successfully suffocating popular protest and rebellion. The relative conservatism of the Madero regime, therefore, was less the logical outcome of a puny, irrelevant revolution (which 1910 had not been) than the result of a hard-fought defensive action (even 'counter-revolution'), in which conservatives and civilian Maderistas, 'last-minute' revolutionaries and local caciques, collaborated in the interests of peace and order. But in the north, where the 1910 revolution had been stronger, where the pillars of the old regime had been partially demolished, and where Maderistas – military as well as civilian – had come to enjoy greater power, such 'counter-revolution' was both more difficult and more productive of resistance. Again, it will be necessary to focus on the principal cases: first Sinaloa, Durango and the Laguna; then (meriting individual treatment) Chihuahua, the cradle of the 1910 revolution.

Even before the signing of the peace treaty, Madero had sent Manuel Bonilla as his political emissary to Sinaloa, where he was to bring some order out of the revolutionary chaos.[161] Bonilla, an archetypal civilian Maderista (once director of the Culiacán Anti-Re-electionist Club, a minister under first de la Barra then Madero), returned to his home state and installed a 'political brother' as interim governor. As the summer progressed, attempts to demobilise the Maderista troops incurred 'the unanimous discontent of all the revolutionary elements'; Juan Banderas, the hulking, crop-headed, ex-*vaquero* who had risen to revolutionary prominence in 1911, urged Madero to halt Federal troop movements in the state 'since the forces I command here . . . still consider the Federals as their enemies'; finally, late in the summer, Banderas mounted a coup, ousting the governor, dissolving the state legislative (still a nest of Científicos), and installing himself in the statehouse, in defiance of the central government.[162] An American observer welcomed the coup: Banderas, he believed, 'is the strong man who will rescue the state from its chaotic condition'; he could do so because he 'is sprung from the rabble that now dominates, is its creature, and is the only one of the petty leaders who has ever opposed the rabble in its fury'.[163] A 'man on horseback' was required – but one of plebeian, not Porfirian origins. But the central government balked at this example of nascent populism: annoyed at the ouster of his protégé governor, Bonilla bent his ministerial influence against Banderas; commercial and propertied interests in Sinaloa (like the Reyista merchants of Mazatlán) added their opposition, denouncing a regime in which 'Banderas is all-powerful ... [and] does just as he pleases'.[164] Presidents de la Barra and Madero were both urged to remove Banderas to Mexico City – where his populist appeal would count for nothing – and Madero, displaying no inclination to support his lieutenant, rebuked him for his illiberal, strong-arm methods.[165]

Finally, a constitutional governor of the approved type was elected: José María Rentería, who was old (older than most Porfirian oligarchs), deaf, possibly senile, certainly inept, and no match for Bonilla's alleged intrigues; but at least he was liberal, well-to-do and respectable.[166] Banderas was first sidetracked into a mission in northern Sinaloa, then summoned to Mexico City and arrested for the murder of a Federal colonel; he was still in gaol over a year later, Madero having ignored both his pleas ('it is now over three years that I have left my family abandoned') and his recriminations ('I have never been your enemy, I have always been loyal to you ... [yet] I see that you are more generous to your own enemies').[167] It was another of the now familiar laments, combining injured pride, indignation and rueful disillusionment, as the veterans of 1910–11 contemplated the outcome of their revolutionary efforts. Banderas was not alone in his feelings. Justo Tirado, a rough-and-ready old landlord from Palma Sola, had armed his peons for the revolution in February 1911 and, with victory, installed his son ('an almost illiterate being') as *jefe político* of Mazatlán; now, Governor Rentería had him removed and retired to the countryside, indeed, by early 1912, it was reckoned, the governor had generally 'cleaned out the revolutionary jefes who had remained in offices that pay well'.[168]

But this political housecleaning was less feasible in the north than in the centre. Banderas' arrest triggered a wave of revolts: Manuel Vega, pronouncing at Navalato, claimed allegiance to Zapata's recently published Plan of Ayala, and linked up with other supporters of Banderas and veterans of 1910 like Antonio Franco and 'Chico' Quintero; their forces were said to include many 'Indians who had been despoiled of their lands', and they took Mocorito to cries of 'Viva Zapata!'. Further south, Tirado rebelled – in opposition, he asserted, to Governor Rentería, not President Madero – and allied with Juan

Carrasco ('a sort of foreman peon ... an uneducated man ... and a hard drinker'). Together, they threatened Mazatlán in the spring of 1912.[169] By then, the entire south of Sinaloa was overrun, as Juan Cañedo and his Tepic allies captured the smaller towns: Tominil (one of the first to fall in 1910), Concordia, Siqueiros and others.[170] Once again, the authorities proved incapable of defending the countryside: Nestor Pino Suárez, brother of the new vice-president, and a colonel in the *rurales*, set an example, giving his life in the campaign against Quintero; but other guardians of the peace, less committed to the central government, were reluctant even to engage the rebels (in some cases, they were their old revolutionary confreres of the previous year). Fifty *rurales*, sent to defend Concordia against Cañedo, stopped *en route* and got drunk instead; another detachment, stationed at the threatened town, broke and scattered when the attack came; at Mazatlán, the *rurales* chose not to resist Tirado but 'remained in their barracks and took no part ... saying it is nothing, only a personal affair to get rid of the governor'.[171] In this, Tirado succeeded: the central government gladly accepted Rentería's reluctant resignation, and 700 Federals were sent to restore order at Mazatlán. As Tirado and his allies – partly satisfied – withdrew, rebel detachments now headed north, reducing the 'entire Culiacán valley [to a] state of anarchy', capturing and looting the state capital before finally dispersing.[172] To an observer in neighbouring Durango (itself no haven of peace and order) it seemed that 'the whole state of Sinaloa, with the exception of the city of Mazatlán, is seething with revolution'; while from Mazatlán south, down into the fastness of Tepic, 'the entire country ... is filled with roaming bands of bandits'.[173] Here, communities lived in constant fear of attack. At Acaponeta – on the Mazatlán–Tepic railway – the church was so loaded with sandbag breastworks that 'fear is felt (that) the roof ... will fall in'.[174]

Though it is clear that rebellion was endemic in Sinaloa – and though key names and incidents can be related – it is not easy to probe the underlying causes (if there were any). Certainly the same leaders as 1910–11, and the same places (the Sinaloa–Durango–Tepic sierras; Palma Sola, Tirado's patch; Mocorito; and Navolato, the home of Manuel Vega) were once again prominent and, as elsewhere, it was the regime's (especially the local regime's) attempts to demobilise the Maderista forces and oust Maderista officials which provoked renewed rebellion. There was some evidence of *agrarismo* too. Vega subscribed to the Plan of Ayala, both he and Banderas later linked up with Zapata. Cries of 'Viva Zapata!', heard in the attack on Mocorito, were repeated when Cañedo assaulted San Ignacio in March 1912. Government officials habitually referred to the Sinaloan rebels as 'Zapatistas'.[175] When Cisneros (an ally of Tirado and Cañedo) lodged his headquarters at the Hacienda de Quimiches, on the Tepic–Sinaloa border, he 'ran the hacienda with a high hand ... declared all property "free" and prohibited all hauling of corn to Puerto del Río' – no doubt to benefit local consumers. The previous year, Dario Medina and his squad of 'men who call themselves Maderista soldiers' had similarly occupied the Tierra Blanca estate on the banks of the Culiacán River, appropriating the crops, getting drunk and spreading alarm.[176] Whether these were the unprincipled hoodlums portrayed by landlords and consuls, or agrarian rebels, whose seizure of land responded to more than mere predatory instinct, it is often impossible to say.

But the fundamentally rural and popular character of the rebellion is suggested by its fluctuations which, in 1911–13, follow the agricultural cycle; it bears out the old adage that 'no Mexican revolution can survive the harvest season'.[177] Popular revolts – in Sinaloa and elsewhere – typically occurred in the winter months, following the autumn harvest, when men were relatively free from agricultural duties; they peaked in the spring (when the exhaustion of winter food supplies may have encouraged a roving, requisitioning campaign); and they subsided with the summer rains and the planting season. It is interesting to note that both Madero's Plan of San Luis and Zapata's Plan of Ayala were November documents; Orozco's revolutionary *pronunciamiento*, soon to be considered, came in March; while political events determined this timing, the fate of the rebellions was clearly affected by their relationship with the harvest cycle.[178] In Sinaloa (and at local level the synchronisation was of course more marked) Cañedo and a clutch of fellow-rebels quit fighting in July 1912 and quite suddenly the situation seemed to be 'greatly improved'; but, it was pointed out, 'it is considered probable that there will be another uprising after the rainy season in November or December'.[179] Sure enough, the end of the year saw a recrudescence of rebel activity: several 'outbreaks' were noted in December, with small groups of *guerrilleros* raiding haciendas (as Fortunato Heredia raided Mochis); thus, when the new year (1913) brought national political upheaval, stimulating further revolt, the local auspices in Sinaloa were favourable.[180]

The decline in rebel activity in the summer of 1912 also reflected Federal repression. Banderas had been shipped to Mexico City (though this alone cannot explain the decline, as Olea seems to suggest); Dario Medina was caught, consigned to the army and removed from Sinaloa, over a hundred prisoners accompanied him, via Mazatlán and Manzanillo, to points south.[181] Other leaders were tracked down and killed, others were amnestied. But the amnesty – which the government appeared to use with some success in Sinaloa, as compared with Morelos – was a dangerous and deceptive device. In Sinaloa (and other states) rebels took advantage of amnesties to recuperate, work, and stock up on arms ready for the next bout of fighting; leaders like Cañedo were amnestied, rebelled, and were amnestied again; and, an indignant American complained, there were pardoned brigands like Osuna and Soto riding through the streets of Mazatlán on fine – probably stolen – horses.[182] The promise of peace – especially when it coincided with the summer rains – was often shortlived and illusory. But there was also war without quarter which, as it claimed revolutionary victims, also boosted the power and prestige of the Federal Army. For, while a few ex-Maderista *rurales* collaborated in the peace-keeping operations (as Ramón Iturbe did), the majority – where they had not themselves rebelled – were rightly considered too unreliable, and their units were wholly or partly demobilised in the course of 1912.[183] Thus the Federal Army shouldered the burden, and arrogated to itself growing administrative and political duties. On his arrival in June 1912, General José Delgado took *de facto* control of the state, appointing a new *jefe* in Mazatlán and even assuming the governorship himself for a few weeks; which prompted the observation that military rule had virtually been established in Sinaloa.[184] As it was, Delgado soon stepped down and fresh elections returned another typical civilian Maderista – Felipe Riveros, a 'well-to-do hacendado' – as governor.[185] But the observation was less inaccurate than premature: for the incipient militarisation of 1912, brought about by sustained rebellion and consequent repression, was carried to its logical conclusion in 1913–14.

Popular revolt was no respecter of political boundaries. Many of the rebels who fought in Sinaloa, in 1910–11 and again in 1911–13, were Durangueños (or *chileros* as the locals called them), who had descended from the ridged back of the Sierra Madre to make their name – as *serranos* did in other states too – fighting in the lowlands: men like de la Rocha, Antonio Franco, or Conrado Antuna. The latter, for example, had joined the attacks on Topia and Tamazula back in 1910; rewarded with a commission in the *rurales*, he rebelled again, at Topia, in April 1912, and then headed towards the plains; he made off with a large slice of the proceeds of the sack of Culiacán (comprising 'many mule-loads of loot'), only to be relieved of it by a fellow-Durangueño, Orestes Pereyra.[186] But meanwhile, the main action was taking place in Durango itself, and here the pattern was familiar. Three successive governors, of liberal, civilian provenance, strove to contain rural rebellion: Dr Alonso y Patiño, one-time director of the Durango city hospital; Emiliano Sarabia, an intimate of Madero who, the president regretted, was rarely sober after lunch; and Carlos Patoni, an American-educated engineer, son of a prominent liberal general, now approaching sixty.[187] Beneath them, a young civil engineer, Pastor Rouaix, served as *jefe político* in Durango; his counterpart in Torreón, in the heart of the Laguna, was Manuel Oviedo, another friend of Madero and secretary of the city Anti-Re-electionist Party (like many of his kind, he had spent the duration of the 1910 revolution in gaol); the mayor of Torreón was soon to be Adrián Aguirre Benavides, a well-to-do lawyer from a family intimately linked to Madero's by both business and marriage.[188]

As liberals, and often lawyers, these new office-holders sometimes impaired their already precarious positions by displaying a pedantic concern for legal and constitutional nicety. In the case of San Juan Guadalupe, for example, where Maderista troops had in April 1911 removed the unpopular authorities and installed popular substitutes, Governor Alonso y Patiño insisted on reinstating *jefe*, judge and tax-collector, all with back pay. As a result, 'not a single post in the public administration' of San Juan remained in the hands of a Maderista; 'from the humblest porter up to the chief authorities they are all the same as they were before', and – since the town had a rowdy reputation – the situation was tense and potentially violent. [189] But the new governor, supported by Emilio Madero, who had commanded in the Laguna, was adamant: the appointment of *jefes políticos* was 'not a question of popular election but of the exclusive prerogative of the government'; the people of San Juan were urged to calm down and 'help with pacification and the smooth progress of administration'. [190] Such were the priorities of the new regime. Municipal democracy, so recently revindicated, went by the board, and the Maderista executive soon slipped into the official jargon of the Porfiriato: 'pacification', 'prerogative of the government', 'smooth progress of administration'. At Parras, too, on the borders of the Laguna, the rebel chief Inés Sosa had established himself as military commander, even though (said a hostile witness) he was 'absolutely illiterate' and habitually drunk; he used his influence to threaten and arrest ex-Porfirian office-holders, and he incurred the opposition of the ex-mayor of the town. The latter appealed to Emilio Madero – the chief political broker of the region – who undertook to depose Sosa in favour of the mayor's son. But Sosa resisted 'and the rabble bawled "death to the authorities", protesting against his [Sosa's] dismissal'. [191] Only a large Federal presence could settle this stormy conflict. And, even after communities went through the required constitutional procedures and elected new authorities, the results were disappointing. An elected town councillor in Durango soon concluded that the *ayuntamiento* 'was in fact no more than a group of decorative figures . . . [and that] the [state] government did and undid whatever it liked, as if the council did not exist'. [192]

This reversion to Porfirian practice – after an actual and, even more important, anticipated shift to more democratic procedures – offended some of the urban middle class which had provided the backbone of civilian Maderismo; hence by early 1912 there was open criticism of the regime (local and national), 'even among the liberal party' in Durango, and some even talked of plots and rebellions. [193] But these did not materialise, and the middle-class liberal conscience was increasingly overshadowed by fears of further disorder. Twelve people were killed in street gun battles one night in June 1911; there was an abiding 'fear of mob violence from within the city'; and, as 1912 progressed, both Durango and Torreón were threatened by the build-up of powerful revolutionary forces in the surrounding countryside. [194] Hence, to the propertied urban middle class, Porfirian rough justice and tough government exerted an increasing appeal (the vogue for Reyes has already been mentioned) and the Madero regime's reversion to these methods incurred less opposition from recent democrats than might have been expected.

But in the rural areas, such a reversion seemed a bitter lesson, which provoked further rebellion. For, while the respectable Maderistas of the cities condescended to the rough, rural *cabecillas*, the latter despised and often ignored the new Maderista authorities: young men fresh out of gaol or (more often) old men stale from years of law and medicine. They resented, in particular, the authorities' deference to Porfirian interests: the decision, in Durango, to subordinate the revolutionary troops (pending demobilisation) to the Federal commander; the policy, in the Laguna, of appointing 'authorities as bad as or worse than those of Porfirian times', so that 'the people of the old regime continue in power and . . . the government goes on selecting people of this kind for public office'.[195] Hence, by July 1911, there were 'frequent clashes' between the civil and military powers in Durango; Calixto Contreras and his Ocuila followers ignored the governor and made arbitrary arrests of their enemies; peons were in possession of several haciendas 'claim[ing] that as the Maderistas won they have the right to take and are in effect owners of the land'.[196] This uneasy, dual authority, noted an American consul, was the logical outcome of a revolution which had brought to sudden prominence 'a large number of men who are absolutely unqualified, either by education or character' to hold political office; and this had come about because,[197]

the Mexicans of birth, wealth, education and character . . . Mexicans who were opposed to Díaz, instead of taking up arms, remained indifferent, allowing the poor and ignorant to do the fighting. The result is that those who did the fighting are those who are running affairs.

The clash between civil and military, urban and rural, middle class and plebeian, was all the more acute because here, as in Morelos, major social and economic issues lay behind the battles for place and power. Loot, wage increases and the 'apportionment of lands' had – according to one account – stimulated the Laguna revolution; now, with the revolution apparently victorious, respectable Maderista leaders were finding it hard to instill patience into their ragged followers. In consequence, it was reported, 'the rank-and-file are feeling that the only real vestige of these promises is the resentment that non-fulfilment has left in their minds'.[198] But fulfilment would have threatened the Laguna estates (in which the Maderos and close allies like the Aguirre Benavides had a stake); it would have implied the preferment of boorish popular leaders; and the Maderista leadership would countenance neither. At best, the revolutionary rank-and-file were promised eventual, gradual, peaceful reform. So, the demobilised troops wandered back to village and hacienda (some riding newly acquired horses marked with the 2D – Segunda División – brand), a few silver pesos gratuity in their pockets, feelings of disenchantment in their hearts. Some (like demobilised troops elsewhere, after other wars and rebellions) went home 'not from a desire to work . . . [but from] a determination to spread discontent and . . . to secure, for all, increased pay and short hours, conditions which were promised when they agreed to support the cause'.[199] Radical spokesmen, like the Magonistas, now found they had an audience in the Laguna which they had hitherto lacked, and Maderista officials were obliged to act like Porfirians once again, gaoling agitators rather than risk (as they termed it) a 'socialist revolution'.[200] By early 1912, the 'disgust' of the popular revolutionary leaders was general, and a full-scale revolt, with stirring agrarian overtones, seemed imminent.[201] And when the revolt came, it faithfully reproduced the pattern of 1910–11: the same leaders, places and tactics were again evident, observers noted 'the same frame of mind among the people' as a year before, and the cycle of rebellion, which reflected the agricultural calendar, was similar, rising through the winter to peak in the spring, and fall away in the summer.[202] And Madero and his local minions found themselves in precisely the same position as their Porfirian enemies of 1910, facing the same problems, employing (if with greater reluctance) the same remedies.

Yet the Maderistas' problems were, if anything, greater, for the revolution against Díaz had both raised popular expectations and created a crop of popular *cabecillas* in whom popular hopes were now vested: men often from the 'lower classes [who] have made use of their personal talents', who had risen to revolutionary prominence, and now 'enjoy[ed] a certain prestige' amongst the people. To pack these men home, condemning them once again to their 'miserable wages', was neither just nor politic. But in practice the writer (Emilio Madero) shared the same anxieties as Governors Castelazo or Pérez Rivera, when they confronted (respectively) Navarro and Gavira; in the Laguna, for example, Enrique Adame Macías was a 'man of ideas so subversive that nothing can be done with him'; so Emilio appealed to his brother to give the offending populist a prestigious job in Mexico City, which would remove him from the turbulent local scene.[203] But, granted both the current notions of political aptitude, and the intense competition for office among the civilian Maderistas, the best such plebeian leaders could expect in 1911 was a commission in the *rurales*. And, by the end of that year, many of the northern rebels had indeed been drafted into the *rurales*, often with their *gente* of 1910–11. Sixto Ugalde now commanded 279 men in southern Coahuila/ Zacatecas; Jesús Agustín Castro 336 in the Laguna; Gertrudis Sánchez 152 in the Laguna/Durango region; Orestes Pereyra 302 in Durango/northern Zacatecas; Pascual Orozco 214 in Chihuahua.[204] All told, the total number of *rurales* in the country had quadrupled since the days of Díaz, and, in the intensely revolutionary territory that stretched in a wide arc from western Chihuahua, down through Durango and the Laguna to northern Zacetecas, there were deployed some 1,200 rurales, most of them ex-rebels, commanded by ex-rebel *cabecillas*. Such a concentration was unique, and telling evidence of the strength of the revolution in north-central Mexico (elsewhere in the Republic, though rebels received similar commissions – Rafael Tapia in Veracruz, Salvador Escalante in Michoacan – many of the old Porfirian *rurales* survived;

and many more rebels who would gladly have settled for a local commission were disappointed).[205]

Thus the north, where the revolution had proceeded faster and farther, now contained a large, para-revolutionary military force, which was to play a crucial – if ambivalent – role through 1911–13. Some of these new rural commanders stayed loyal to the Madero regime: Gertrudis Sánchez fought loyally in the north, and later in Guerrero; Jesús Agustín Castro showed a similar respect for constituted authority. But in these cases, loyalty was often demonstrated in service far from the *patria chica*, and the loyalists were precisely those leaders – such as Castro – who were most readily mobile, and least attached to the *patria chica*, and to the local, rural interests which went with it.[206] In 1911, such men were a small minority: the great bulk of the ex-revolutionary *rurales* were staunch parochials, who therefore made poor policemen, and whose efforts were frequently counter-productive. Even if the *jefe* remained loyal, it was not certain that his men (over whom he exercised a strong but conditional authority) would do the same: Sixto Ugalde loyally undertook to quit the Laguna and campaign elsewhere, but his men disliked garrison service in the bleak, coal-mining towns of north-eastern Coahuila and, when the opportunity arose, they forsook their chief, rebelled, and returned to the fray in the Laguna, now under the leadership of the redoubtable Benjamín Argumedo.[207] But more usually, *jefe* and *gente* trod the path of rebellion together: the classic case, that of Orozco, will be considered in a moment.

The tense, revealing relationship between the Madero regime and the ex-rebels turned *rurales* is exemplified in the career of Calixto Contreras, one of the key Laguna *cabecillas*. A bitter and troublesome enemy of Governor Alonso y Patiño, Contreras was coaxed into government service when Emiliano Sarabia replaced Alonso y Patiño early in 1912. At the head of his 'several thousand' Ocuila Indians, Contreras was now set to police his own district around Cuencamé, which had been 'the principal trouble source up to the present time'. It seemed a shrewd move, since Contreras was known to be 'very much dissatisfied with the attitude of the government towards the allotment of certain lands which the Ocuila Indians had taken possession of near Cuencamé', and it was feared that he would imminently rebel.[208] By delegating power to the local populists – by matching *de jure* with *de facto* authority – Sarabia certainly showed a degree of prescience, for peace would eventually be brought to Mexico by means of such mechanisms. But in 1912 it was an untypical policy, espoused only reluctantly under the harsh pressure of circumstances. For, unless carefully controlled (and in 1912 such control was almost impossible) it threatened a return to the old, political patchwork of local *cacicazgo* and *caudillaje*, and an abrogation of the centralised, authoritarian state which Díaz had created. And this was anathema to the Maderista civilians, who favoured a liberalisation of Díaz's state, not a regression to mid-nineteenth-century localism and barbarism. In Mexico as in Argentina, Sarmiento and Facundo stood poles apart.

The experience of the Laguna brought home the lesson. For a short time, the Contreras regime conferred a semblance of peace upon eastern Durango. But the character of the regime, and the secret of its stability, were plain to see:[209]

> [Contreras] visits all the leaders of the different robber [sic] bands, with nearly all of whom he is on excellent terms, and says, 'boys, the time is not yet ripe for trouble; I am entrusted with pacifying this part of the state and I ask you as a personal favor to lie low; you need not surrender your horses and arms as you may have to use them later on; await my signal'.

Similarly, in the mountainous west of the state, a kind of order could be achieved only by co-opting rebels like Orestes Pereyra and the Arrieta brothers, who agreed to continue in official service.[210] But to critical observers – like the manager of the Velardeña smelter – such a policy simply legitimised the actions of local brigands; the appointment of Contreras 'did not look good to us as we do not trust him, or any of his men, who are the same men who have been robbing us'.[211] For these revolutionaries turned *rurales* displayed the defects of their virtues. The very familiarity with the local terrain and local trouble-makers which made them potentially effective policemen all too often lured them back to the path of rebellion – or, at best, led them to connive at the rebellions of others. Contreras maintained his amicable relations with the 'robbers' of the Laguna; and there were constant fears that he would re-cross the narrow divide between conditional submission and outright opposition to the government. Conservative plotters, well aware of the political ambivalence of the ex-Maderista irregulars, sought to win some over to a common – if anomalous – alliance against the Madero regime; Conrado Antuna was allegedly offered 50,000 pesos to lead his 500 men in revolt but (though his service to the government was less than enthusiastic on other occasions) Antuna denounced the plotters, who were arrested. In Chihuahua, a couple of months later, the same strategy proved more successful.[212] And more generally, the ex-revolutionary *rurales* had a poor record of loyalty and efficiency in the line of duty. By early 1912, many of the *rurales* in north-eastern Durango had defected and 'none . . . can be trusted in a pinch'; the removal of Federal troops from Durango left the city in the hands of police and *rurales* who were reckoned to be 'almost worthless for defensive purposes' since, in the event of a rebel attack, 'they would make common cause with the invaders'; while in October, government forces (they included Conrado Antuna) abandoned Rodeo during an attack, enabling Gregorio Sánchez and El Indio Mariano to capture the town with (it was reported) dire results for the local girls.[213] By this time, the state governor dared not send *rural* detachments into the countryside 'for fear that they might only serve to aggravate the conditions which they were sent out to correct'.[214]

Thus, even when local leaders like Contreras or the Arrietas sided with the government, their adherence was strictly conditional, and based on local self-interest. They supported the Madero government, in other words, for the same reasons they had supported the Madero revolution: to secure local gains by way of agrarian reform, self-government, and the rectification of other Porfirian abuses, and they expected these gains to accrue promptly and permanently. Meanwhile, their civilian allies, playing the political game in the cities, could offer no more than gradual, legal reform, and they had no desire to govern by leave and through the mediation of illiterate rural bumpkins; this was not the decorous, liberal system they hoped would succeed the fall of Díaz. Both sides therefore temporised, each seeking to use the other, and neither had much faith in the alliance's durability; sooner or later, the arrangement collapsed – and it would continue to collapse until the civilians could stomach the promotion of plebeian, military leaders to high political office, and until the military forsook their parochial stance, came to terms with the national power structure, and learned to advance their claims within that structure, rather than against it with carbine and machete on the banks of the Nazas.[215] In the case of Durango, the honeymoon finally ended (after many preliminary sulks and recriminations) in the late summer of 1912 when, as usual, a gubernatorial election raised the political temperature and aggravated social conflicts. The triumph of Patoni, the official candidate, over Juan García, who enjoyed the support of many ex-Maderistas, gave fresh stimulus to social unrest; and the fortunate arrival of 350 Federal troops under General Blanquet provided the local regime with the muscle to enforce its will. Contreras and Domingo Arrieta – the revolutionary caciques of east and west Durango respectively – were arrested, charged with insubordination (and, in Contreras' case, with offences against property) and sent to Mexico City.[216] The government, now freed from the menace of Orozco's Chihuahuan revolt, resolved on outright repression, and relinquished the messy policy of co-optation.

That the policy of repression also failed must be attributed to the nature of the war being fought, and here we switch from the leadership of the popular movement to the rank-and-file and its objectives – a transition which involves serious problems of evidence and interpretation. Who were the Durango/Laguna rebels, and what were they fighting for? The reports of the American consul at Durango make it clear that the rebellions were extensive and essentially rural, displaying a marked dependence on country people and on the harvest cycle. By February 1912 the city of Durango was packed with *hacendados* and *rancheros*, their families and employees, who had fled the rural unrest, particularly severe in the Laguna region, where a summer drought had ruined the corn harvest and 'caused the labourers to join the ranks of the *revoltosos* and to adopt a program which calls for nothing further than plunder and loot', thereby creating a 'virtual state of anarchy'.[217] That the rebel rank-and-file comprised peons and villagers was evident during a lull in the fighting, which 'had the effect of causing some of the malcontents to desert the revolutionary ranks and again seek employment upon the haciendas which they had left'.[218] Meanwhile, in the northern part of the state, towards Inde and El Oro, rebellion was rife (as it had been in 1910–11); by the summer of 1912 these towns had been 'picked clean' by Argumedo and his force of over a thousand men; while on the borders of Zacatecas – where the harvest had also failed in 1911 – large rebel contingents roamed the country.[219] To the west, however, where the rains and the harvest were better, trouble was less widespread.[220] Nevertheless, a conservative estimate, made at midsummer 1912, put the total number of rebels in the state of Durango at some 3,500.[221]

The same observer, commenting on the rebels' aims, mixed a good deal of general denunciation of 'rapine', 'brigandage' and 'anarchy' with the more precise information that the rebels had 'drawn up a platform of principles among which the speedy redistribution of land and the protection of foreign lives and property are not the most important'.[222] In the Laguna, therefore, as in Mexico as a whole, the popular revolution was strongly agrarian, hardly xenophobic at all. Other observers concurred. A Maderista from Mapimí, collating 'many views ... chiefly from among the lower people', warned Madero that rapid demobilisation was alienating the rebel rank-and-file, and providing ample grounds for agitation. The soldiers 'see no practical result from the struggle in which they helped you: the land is not divided, not even the smallest communities' property, which the big proprietors seized from them, has been restored, the worker is not supported in his demands'; and even the horses acquired during the months of rebellion now had to be returned to their owners.[223] Similar advice, stressing the importance of agrarian reform in the Laguna, reached Madero from the Aguirre Benavides family.[224] As for the rebels themselves, they were less articulate, they formulated no coherent, extant plan (though some, like Macías, made it plain that 'they resented the fact that Zapata was being persecuted for the fact of wanting lands'),[225] but they displayed their agrarian concerns by direct action, and thus the Laguna revolts were punctuated by incidents of *de facto* agrarian reform and reprisal.

Contreras, as we have seen, continued his battle to recover Cuencamé's lands, even while he was on the government's payroll. When, following Contreras' arrest, Argumedo's forces attacked a government garrison at Cuencamé, 'many of the Indians of that vicinity were recognised among the attacking party'.[226] Attacks on haciendas and hacienda authorities were frequent, and went far beyond the immediate needs of foraging and petty extortion. In July 1912 there were 'numerous bands in the Laguna committing daily outrages on the plantations'; the landowners, facing a 'reign of terror', had congregated in the state capital.[227] Matters were not helped by the ambivalent attitude of the (ex-Maderista) *rurales* who, sent to police the countryside, sometimes made common cause with the insurgents and, on one hacienda, supported 'the obstreperous laborers who demanded, with menace of firearms, full pay for incompleted tasks'.[228] Repression failed. At the end of a traumatic year, at a time when the government had given up co-optation in favour of extermination, a horde of some 1,500 rebels, the combined forces of Argumedo, Cheche Campos, Luis Caro, El Indio Mariano and others, rampaged through the Laguna, pillaging haciendas, exacting reprisals, encouraging rebellion and jacquerie. At the Haciendas Carmen and Juan Pérez the buildings were blown up and burned, and four hacienda employees executed; at Saucillo (a huge property owned by Julio Curbelo of Durango) the employees fled but the book-keeper and *administrador* were caught and shot, along with the survivors of a force of twenty-seven field guards, stationed there to protect the property; then, 'the magnificent country residence of Senor Curbelo, which had been furnished in regal style and which contained many priceless old paintings' was blown up with dynamite.[229] At the Hacienda Cruces, part of the Tlahualilo estate, Cheche Campos and El Indio Mariano scattered the *rurales* garrison and fired the hacienda buildings; then, the manager reported,[230]

they summoned the people and informed them that the dominion of the hacienda and of the *extranjero* (that's me) was over, that no-one was to rescue a stick of wood from the burning under pain of death. Then, singling out the *mayordomos*, they made as if to shoot them, standing them up against a wall, but finally permitted them to flee in the darkness. They remained at Cruces, drinking and dancing until noon on the following day.

In the same region, the violent passage of the rebels prompted action on the part of the rural labourers. At the Santa Catalina Hacienda, where the *tienda de raya* was especially resented, 'the peons rose, sacked the store, and burned all the books, thereby destroying all evidence of their indebtedness'.[231] Thus, as the year drew to a close (and with it the allotted span of the Madero regime), the Laguna haciendas were still being subjected to raids and revolts; and John Reed, crossing the region eighteen months later, could still see the burnt-out shells of haciendas put to the torch by Cheche Campos and his colleagues.[232]

So intense was rebel activity at the end of 1912 – and so feeble the authorities' response – that small towns began to fall into revolutionary hands, and new victims were found, indicative of popular resentments. At San Lucas, the town's 'most prominent citizen', the ex-*jefe* Juan Villareal, was shot by Gregorio Sánchez' forces; at Peñón Blanco, another familiar trouble spot, El Indio Mariano sacked the Spanish-owned woollen factory; and, in one unusual episode, rebels sliced off the heads of sacred images in the church at Guatimape, on the Tepehuanes Railway.[233] But it was the big *hacendado* and his employees who bore the brunt. The onslaught was violent, destructive and sustained – indicative not only of popular resentments but also of the rebel leaders' decision to wage economic war on the regime and on the well-to-do.

Whatever agrarian reform took place within this context was inevitably chaotic, arbitrary and transient, leaving few or no records for the historian to review. Hacienda fields were certainly seized, and Cheche Campos, a mysterious figure whose dramatic end is better known than his obscure origins, clearly espoused a form of *de facto* agrarian reform (though it is difficult to assess whether political principle or the exigencies of recruiting provided the main incentive). Encamped with 1,500 men among the haciendas around Mapimí, Campos[234]

has ordered that the sharesmen [sic] and peons on all the ranches . . . continue with the harvesting of the crop, all of which they may retain for their own uses, or for sale. Thus on many ranches in that vicinity the corn harvest will be a total loss to the owner of the property, while Cheche Campos, by his magnanimous methods, has made many friends and obtained many recruits among the peons, rendering the pacification of that district more difficult.

But, whatever Campos' motives, it is clear that he enjoyed widespread popular support in his battle with the authorities and that this gave his campaigns the appearance of classic guerrilla warfare. As in 1910–11, the rebels were distinguished by their mobility, partly because they could draw on the local population (as at Cuencamé) to supplement their main force, partly because of their excellent mounts, 'the pick of all the best saddle animals in the country through which they pass'.[235] This (combined with 'their good news service, there usually being sympathisers among the peons on every ranch') enabled the rebels to strike when and where they pleased, while avoiding serious engagements with the Federals.[236] The latter, meanwhile, could expect little assistance from the rural population: eighty-two *rurales*, assured by the locals that there were no rebels in the neighbourhood, rode into the Hacienda Las Cruces and at once ran into a fierce assault, including a fusillade of dynamite bombs hurled from the huts of the peons; at Chalchihuites, forty *rurales* were lured into the town and wiped out by the rebels, while 1,000 assorted Federals and *rurales* dallied a matter of miles away.[237] The rebels thus dictated the tempo and location of the fighting, following 'the same tactics as [were] used last year', and the authorities' response, when it was not positively disastrous, was usually sluggish and devoid of initiative.[238] Furthermore, on occasions when the government turned the screw, the rebel host rapidly melted away, as the loose authority of the commander-in-chief (such as Campos, who controlled 1,500 at the end of 1912) lapsed, as the troops slipped back to hacienda and village, and as the *cabecillas* went to ground in their familiar bolt-holes: Gregorio Sánchez to his 'favorite hunting grounds' around Inde; Jorge Güereca to the San Juan Michis ranch, west of Chalchihuites, Caro and Argumedo to the region around San Miguel Mezquital, 'which point, on account of the very mountainous character of the country has been a favorite rendez-vous for these bands for several months past'. On occasions, these rebels – like the bandits they resembled – had urban contacts, and their havens assumed almost sybaritic qualities. At Pánuco de Corondoa (Dgo), the brothers Ortiz (Pedro, Luis and Ramón, all rebels and leading a 'large following of *sinverguencistas*') came and went, replenishing their supplies and enjoying urban comforts, since they were on familiar terms with the municipal boss, Luciano Sifuentes; Sifuentes was seen in their company in town, attending 'balls and orgies'.[239]

Despite its great superiority in arms, the government could mount only ineffectual campaigns. It could win pitched battles (or skirmishes which became pitched battles in the pages of the press, only to be deflated by hearsay and experience) but such victories never looked like extinguishing rural unrest. For the time being, the tide of popular insurgence ran strongly, and it would take many cumulative defeats and Pyrrhic victories before the tide began to ebb and the forces of law and order recovered the initiative. In 1912, these forces still faced insurmountable problems, indicative of the strength of popular rebellion. Government volunteers and irregulars were, as we have seen, notoriously unreliable; Federal officers disliked mounting costly and inglorious counter-insurgency campaigns in the interests of the incongenial Madero regime; and the Federal rank-and-file, while rarely displaying outright insubordination, were sullen and demoralised, as befitted conscript troops.[240] But, having abandoned its policy of conciliation and co-optation, the regime now saw repression as the only solution to the problems of the Laguna, and it was therefore driven into unmistakably Porfirian postures. After José Maciel had been caught and killed while raiding haciendas in the Pinos district of northern Durango, his and followers' bodies were didactically displayed in the streets of the state capital.[241] Efforts were made to raise local defence forces to supplement the Federal Army: the students of Durango were recruited into a 'corps of national defence' and began drilling; some rural communities attempted to man their own defences, one at least (Tejamen) with success.[242] As yet, however, such belligerent municipal self-help – a common feature of the later years of the Revolution – was rare.

The planters of the Laguna, on the other hand, soon began to experiment with private defence forces and field-guards. An 'independent corps of trustworthy men' was recruited and paid 1.50 pesos a day to protect the 1911 harvest, their job was to 'patrol the haciendas and ranches where many disorders have occurred'.[243] Again, in 1912, the *administradores* of the Laguna recruited men to police the estates, a peon caught without an official pass was liable to arrest and 'if the circumstances appear at all suspicious [he is] summarily dealt with'.[244] And repression increased late in 1912. After a rebel host had been scattered (though hardly defeated) at Chalchihuites, Federal troops were pumped into the district with orders 'to compel the peons on all the haciendas, under penalty of death, to restore all [the] plunder taken by them or given to them by the rebels (back) to the rightful owners.[245] At the same time, the state government was sounding out the Laguna planters with a view to securing two years taxes in advance, the necessary financial prerequisite for 'the sternest sort of measures', designed to crush 'all political and labour agitators'.[246] Though the sheer concentration of Federal troops could – as in January 1913 – force the rebels onto the defensive, there was no evidence to suggest that this was anything more than a temporary development.[247] And, in some respects, heavy-handed repression further stimulated the rebellion it was meant to crush. In the process, the policy of repression conferred greater power on the Federal Army, undermining the tenuous basis of legitimacy enjoyed by the Maderista civilians. The liberal hopes of the latter wilted in the torrid heat of civil war, while the conservatives (especially the officer corps) found increasing justification for the belief that Díaz's methods had been the only ones right and proper for Mexico. For them, liberal scruples and political restraints were irksome inhibitions. Some civilian Maderistas – like Governor Venustiano Carranza of Coahuila, whose state embraced part of the Laguna – grew alarmed at both the palpable failures and growing weakness of the Madero regime, and also the mounting power of the military. In January 1913 Carranza was 'enraged' to discover that the Federal commander of Torreón had ordered Coahuilan state troops into action at Pedriceña (in the state of Durango) and he promptly countermanded the order.[248] Such civil–military friction, the consequence of the growing contradictions within the Madero regime, was tending towards a violent resolution.

LOCAL POLITICS: (4) THE POPULAR CHALLENGE – OROZQUISMO

Nowhere, however, were the contradictions and problems of the Madero regime more saliently revealed than in the state which had made the biggest contribution to Madero's conquest of power, that of Chihuahua. Here, all the causes of disaffection already mentioned were abundant, and the very men and regions which had stood out in the revolution against Díaz now took the lead in opposition to Madero. This opposition, first verbal, then violent, coalesced in the Orozco rebellion, which dominated Chihuahua (and much of its neighbouring regions), reverberated throughout the Republic, and threatened to descend on Mexico City. It was the biggest, best organised and most overtly political of the anti-Madero movements and it had a decisive effect on the history of the Madero regime. Yet it shared the same roots and many of the same characteristics as the lesser popular revolts which proliferated throughout the country in these years.

By virtue of its pre-eminent role in the Maderista revolution, Chihuahua produced a large crop of *cabecillas* and a host of rebel troops – approaching 5,000, according to one careful estimate.[249] Meanwhile, the overthrow of Porfirian authorities and their replacement by political newcomers had proceeded farther and faster here than elsewhere. Among the *cabecillas*, Pascual Orozco had done as much as any one individual to topple Díaz, and he enjoyed a commensurate prestige, by no means confined to Chihuahua itself. Failed revolutionaries in the south wished that they, too, had succeeded like Orozco; to the liberal *Diario del Hogar*, Orozco was the 'soul of the Revolution'.[250] When the house of ex-Governor Mercado in Uruapán (Mich.) was converted into a barracks for Maderista troops, it became the Cuartel Pascual Orozco; when Maderistas in Tlaxcala baptised their new political clubs, Orozco's name outran in popularity those of all living candidates, Madero's included; such was the appeal of the *macho caudillo* over the civilian *político*.[251] And when Zapata drew up his rebellious Plan of Ayala in November 1911 he 'recognised as Chief of the Liberating Revolution ... the illustrious General Pascual Orozco' – even though Orozco was still, a loyal, if disillusioned employee of the Madero government.[252]

In Chihuahua, meanwhile, the governorship had passed to Abraham González, the 'portly and paternal' rancher who had mobilised the Maderista opposition in the state and – unlike most civilian Maderistas – participated with valour, if not with distinction, in the revolutionary campaigns.[253] But Orozco was the man of the hour; on entering the state capital at the head of 1,500 men he received 'a great ovation, which exceeded even that accorded Governor González'.[254] Orozco and his men had their tails up. They were no last-minute, band-waggon revolutionaries, they were the pioneers of the Madero revolt, who had defeated the Federal Army and they were, potentially, the determining factor in Chihuahua's political future. Already, at Juárez, Orozco and his lieutenants had made light of Madero's authority and now, with peace and demobilisation on the agenda, they were conscious that the revolution had been officially terminated while they were on top, and while unfinished business remained. A doctor who met Orozco in June 1911 was told:[255] 'if you get to talk to Señor Don Pancho Madero, kindly inform him that I still have four waggons of ammunition, some men, and a desire to give the Federals a whipping, if he so wishes and orders'. But there were to be no more whippings. The peace treaty 'returned the issue of change to the ... dimension of politics', in which dimension Orozco, though ambitious, was less adept; he remained a *guerrillero* uneasy with urban politics and, it was said, prone to manipulation by literate secretaries and advisers and, through them, by conservative interests.[256]

Like Gabriel Hernández at Pachuca, Orozco soon became the centre of considerable attention and cultivation. A mountain was named after him, commemorative 'Orozco spoons' were minted, women, it was said, freely offered themselves to him. Altogether, 'the vanity of the ex-muleteer was meticulously inflated'.[257] Most important, a mixed bunch of Porfirian conservatives and disgruntled ex-Maderistas combined to support Orozco's candidacy to the governorship, thus placing him in direct opposition to his erstwhile mentor, Abraham González.[258] But the alliance was premature: Orozco was ruled ineligible on the grounds that he was under thirty, and

González, like most of the 'official' candidates of 1911, skated home without real opposition, carrying on his coattails a collection of Maderista civilians.[259] These, though they gave 'an impression of earnestness and righteousness', were inexperienced and 'were for the most part . . . men little known in the state' – by definition, therefore, not prominent *cabecillas*.[260] Of the revolutionary military, only Maclovio Herrera, one of a powerful rebel clan, secured important political office, as mayor of Parral; Parral was to prove a bastion of loyalty to the regime in an otherwise disaffected state. Orozco's exclusion from politics was therefore typical. But as a free agent, he was a headache for the government; there was talk of an Orozco–Reyes flirtation and at a Reyista convention held in the capital in September 1911, a speaker heaped praise upon the Chihuahuan *cabecilla* eliciting cries of 'Viva Orozco!'.[261] A trip to Mexico City in October revealed both Orozco's abiding prestige and his taciturn manner, but it failed to produce the desired accord between government and subject.[262] For a time, Orozco was persuaded to serve as commander of *rurales* in Sinaloa (the usual ploy, which sought to purchase loyalty, while capitalising on irregular military expertise) but this lasted only a couple of months; in January 1912 he resigned, evidently disgruntled, and his chagrin was shared, it seems, throughout the north, where it was felt that 'the eminent services rendered to the country by the valiant General Pascual Orozco had been repaid with ingratitude'.[263]

Orozco's subsequent political convulsions and conduct responded to the complex situation developing in Chihuahua. Elected governor, Abraham González soon sought leave of absence to serve as minister of Gobernación in Madero's cabinet. Not only did this leave the executive in the hands of an obscure individual (Aurelio González), who lacked Abraham González's close ties with the revolutionary movement, it also invited comparison with Porfirian absentee rule (Creel had gone to serve as Foreign Minister), and complaints of continued Porfirian practice were reinforced by the 'imposition' of Pino Suárez at the expense of Vázquez Gómez.[264] Yet more important, the two distinct, dissatisfied groups – disillusioned ex-revolutionaries and fearful conservatives – whose alliance had been adumbrated in the Orozco gubernatorial candidacy, now marshalled their considerable forces with a view to armed rather than electoral opposition to the regime. So important was the outcome of this anomalous alliance, that the motives behind it merit closer analysis.

The widespread dissatisfaction of the ex-Maderista forces with the regime they had put in office, evident throughout the country, was particularly pronounced in Chihuahua. While the risks of a conservative coup could be discounted, observers thought, the danger of a renewed outbreak by the Maderista rebels of 1910–11 was very real: around Parral, for example, 'many of the Maderista troops are very much dissatisfied on account of not receiving what was promised them and . . . a counter-revolution would be popular among them'.[265] Late in 1911, this dissatisfaction produced a rash of minor revolts – labelled, for want of a better name, Vazquista – notably in the regions of western Chihuahua which had led the way precisely a year before.[266] In one, the ex-Maderista colonel Antonio Rojas 'pronounced' for Vázquez Gómez, claiming to support Orozco for the vice-presidency.[267] Disdaining the compliment, Orozco sent forces which crushed the uprising and arrested its leader. But the groundswell of rebellion could not be contained. By February 1912 the American consul at Chihuahua was 'astounded at [the] extent [of the] disaffection against [the] government'.[268] Now, the discontent crystallised in a major revolt: *rurales* at Juárez, protesting against the government's policy of mustering them out, rioted, 'discharged their fire-arms in the air and cheered for Zapata', then, as the mayor went to ground, they took control of the city and went through the usual procedures – deposing incumbent officials, opening the gaol, burning the judicial records. In an interview given to the American press, the leaders declared their support for Vázquez Gómez and alleged that Madero had reneged on the promises of the Plan of San Luis; in particular, 'the estates have not been divided, as had been planned, and the poor have received no benefit from the victory'.[269] At the same time, troops and political authorities at Casas Grandes declared for the rebellion without incurring local opposition.[270] Most serious of all, an attempt to demobilise *rurales* in the state capital led to an attack on the penitentiary, a two hour gun battle, and the release of the recently captured Rojas.[271]

Interim Governor (Aurelio) González was helpless. Rojas and over 400 dissidents threatened the state capital; not a man among the remaining *rurales* garrison could be trusted (emissaries from the Juárez rebels were at work among them); and 'a very large proportion of the inhabitants of the city and state were against the regime'.[272] Governor González tendered his resignation. The key figures in this critical situation were now Orozco, still nominally loyal to the government but under strong pressure to 'secede' to his old *compadres*, and Abraham González, who now hurried north from Mexico City, bearing (it was said) 300,000 pesos 'for distribution among the destitute of the state'.[273] Resuming the governorship, González dispatched loyalist forces – including 500 men under Pancho Villa – to combat the rebels. But, by late February, it was clear that the latter were gaining strength. Rojas had retired to his old stamping ground in the sierra; but the Casas Grandes rebels were heading towards Juárez in force, and the revolt had received the support of the state's lieutenant-governor, Braulio Hernández.[274] The seriousness of the situation was plain: 'we cannot disguise the fact', a railway manager commented, 'that the country is now facing a crisis much more acute than any ... created by the last revolution'.[275]

If, in terms of regions and personnel, this was a re-run of the 1910 revolution, the rebels now assumed a 'Vazquista' label. But, even more than Madero had been in 1910, Vázquez Gómez was a mere figurehead: as the rebellion spread, its titular leader remained in Texas, a target for Madero's taunts, and when he finally crossed to Mexico in May 1912, styling himself provisional president, the military leaders would have nothing to do with him.[276] Another would-be national *caudillo* had failed, and failed for want of the local, popular support which was the key to success in 1912. This was exemplified by the Casas Grandes rebellion, led by José Inés Salazar and Emilio Campa. Salazar was a native of the locality, an old contact of Orozco, and reputed by the Porfirian authorities to be 'ignorant . . . [and] of the lower class'.[277] His record of pre-1910 dissidence included membership of the PLM (he was one of the handful of Maderista leaders for whom such membership can be reasonably established) and Magonista influence was certainly at work in these border regions at the time.[278] But it would be wrong to appropriate such rebellions – whether in terms of their membership or their programme – for the PLM, for the latter was more the beneficiary than the instigator of current political discontent, and, as discontent crystallised into rebellion, Magonismo gave a certain radical colouring but no central, 'hegemonic' direction. Leaders like Salazar, who might enjoy PLM contacts, were essentially local revolutionaries of some standing, who behaved in the same manner as others lacking such contacts: a sympathiser (incidentally the brother of Ricardo Flores Magón) argued Salazar's loyalty to the Madero regime and backed his request – typical enough and hardly anarchist – for a police or military command in his home town of Casas Grandes.[279] When this was ignored, Salazar, like other *cabecillas*, expressed his resentment in rebellion.

This is not to attribute the anti-Madero revolts, however, to personal pique (even if such a factor was present). A strong collective commitment, reinforced by the events of 1910–11, underwrote such rebellions, and they often produced specific, coherent demands. Like Zapata, Salazar and his colleagues adopted the slogan 'Tierra y Libertad'; their initial plan of February 1912 denounced the 'despotic, dictatorial and tyrannical acts of President Madero', alleged that the Plan of San Luis had gone unfulfilled, and urged the establishment of genuine democracy. They also went out of their way to guarantee foreign interests in the country; popular radicalism, even under a veneer of Magonismo, did not imply economic nationalism or xenophobia.[280] Similar grievances were expressed by Braulio Hernández, ex-college teacher, Anti-Re-electionist journalist and Protestant convert, who was certainly no Magonista. Unusually for a middle-class activist, Hernández had played an important role in the 1910 revolution, serving as the 'brains behind the Madero revolutionists . . . in the mountains about Ojinaga'; like Almazán or Pedro de los Santos, he thus established a foothold in the popular camp, and was reckoned a man in whom 'the Mexican common people have placed their faith'.[281] He did not let them down. Appointed lieutenant-governor of Chihuahua, he grew impatient with Madero's failings, resigned in November 1911, and three months later came out in support of the revolution, leading a successful assault on Santa Eulalia and linking up with Salazar's and Campa's burgeoning army. His supporters, it was reported, consisted of several hundred 'sans-culottes [sic] from the ranches of eastern Chihuahua'.[282] Hernández also brought to bear his considerable qualities as a polemicist. In his manifesto of 4 February – the first to emerge from the chaotic, decentralised Chihuahua rebellion – he urged the overthrow of Madero and fulfilment of the Plan of San Luis; in conversation he denounced the peculation of the Madero family, who had tried to purchase his submission, and he explained that he had 'broken with his former friend and chief (Abraham González) . . . after the Governor went to Mexico City to mingle with the diplomats and leave his people to starve in Chihuahua'.[283] But, in addition to *ad hominem* polemics, Hernández espoused radical ideas, he was seen by some as a 'socialist', he preached and later practised agrarian reform, his men carried the slogan 'Tierra y Justicia' in their hats and claimed they were 'fighting for a distribution of the land of the country among the poor'.[284]

As popular revolt spread, Orozco prevaricated. Government and rebels alike claimed to enjoy his support (but, one cynic put it, 'the general opinion [is] that he is for "Pascual Orozco" first and always'). Quite likely – as in many such junctures of the revolution – genuine confusion outweighed cynical calculation and, in such instances, decisions were often precipitated by events. At the beginning of March, Salazar, Campa and Rojas entered Juárez (where government authority had been briefly restored following the mutiny); they imposed forced loans, seized the customs and the railways and, with the 'property owners and men of means' in hiding, they seemed to enjoy broad support in the town.[285] A planned advance on Chihuahua City was held up when pro-Madero railwaymen switched rolling stock to the American side of the border, but this did not prevent panic and crisis overtaking the state capital. Governor González seemed to have 'lost all influence with the masses [sic] of the people', well-orchestrated demonstrators took to the streets denouncing González and Madero, and on 2 March the governor was obliged to flee. Next day, when Pancho Villa – still loyal to the government – made a move against Chihuahua City, he was repulsed by Orozco himself. Thus Orozco declared his hand, and the curtain was raised on the Orozco–Villa vendetta, a violent sub-plot in the drama of the northern revolution. Three days later, Salazar, Campa and Hernández arrived at the head of 2,000 troops, hailing Orozco as their commander-in-chief, Orozco accepted, stating that the road to Mexico City now lay wide open, and the Orozquista rebellion (for it can now receive its official, historical label) was under way.[286]

The continuity between 1910 and 1912 was striking; the Orozquista revolt, especially at the outset, was in a sense a neo-Maderista rather than an anti-Maderista movement. When Salazar's army marched into Chihuahua City it was at once noted that 'quite a number of these [men] took part in the Madero revolt'.[287] Of the leading *cabecillas* of 1910, most went over to Orozco (several, of course, had preceded him); only José de la Cruz Sánchez – it appears

— remained loosely loyal to the government, Pancho Villa and the Herreras of Parral more aggressively so. Orozco did not exaggerate, therefore, when he boasted that by the end of March his rebellion 'encounters no opposition throughout the whole extension [of Chihuahua] save that of the highwayman Francisco Villa, on which point I congratulate myself'.[288] Madero agreed; after the revolt had been put down he opposed punitive measures on the grounds that they would make it 'necessary to try all the state of Chihuahua, for it cannot be doubted that it was a movement in which all the state took part'.[289]

Ideologically, however, Orozquismo both incorporated and went beyond Madero's original, liberal programme. The Plan Orozquista, published on 25 March, called for the removal of Madero and Pino Suárez and the enactment of familiar political reforms (freedom of expression, the abolition of the *jefaturas*, municipal autonomy), but it went further in advocating better wages and conditions for workers, suppression of the *tiendas de raya*, restrictions on child labour, nationalisation of the railways and of their labour force.[290] And it gave explicit recognition to the agrarian question as the problem requiring most immediate and effective action. Michael Meyer is, no doubt, correct to see the Plan as a 'highly significant' document, by virtue of these socio-economic provisions; and James Cockcroft in this instance rightly discerns the influence of the PLM in Orozco's programme.[291] But the Plan must be seen in context. First, comparisons with the Plan of San Luis are somewhat misleading, since the latter was a much shorter document (about half the length, discounting preambles) and concentrated on the mechanics of overthrowing Díaz; many Maderistas who rallied to the Plan looked beyond it, and were sympathetic to social reforms — which, though unmentioned, were by no means ruled out. This suggests, secondly, that the chief virtue of the Plan was less its inherent originality, than its codification — in a context of real political struggle — of ideas which, as Cockcroft admits, were already 'in the air'.[292] In this respect, it is dangerous to leap from textual similarity — between, for example, the Plan and the 1917 Constitution — to causal relationship: rather than one following the other, according to some crude genealogy of ideas, both sprang from a common pool of contemporary thought and practice. By the same token, the Plan should not be distorted by a too vigorous attempt to fit it within the presumed teleology of the Revolution as a whole. For Meyer, the Plan is 'ultra-nationalistic', 'anticipating the surge of nationalism that would soon sweep over Mexico'.[293] Leaving aside the question of whether such a 'surge' ever took place, it must be recognised that the nationalism of the Plan Orozquista was modest, conventional, and not directed against American economic interests in Mexico. Traces of anti-Americanism were evident in the denunciations of Madero — notably Madero's supposed complicity with Wall Street. But this represented the stock-in-trade not only of Mexican polemicists (of different political hues) but also of a good many Americans too; Wall Street was not synonymous with what the leading Orozquistas, Salazar and Campa, chose to call 'our sister republic' or 'sacred American soil'.[294] Nor did the Orozquistas display a strong or consistent hostility to American interests, which were well represented in the north; Orozco himself (who had worked conscientiously enough for American companies before the Revolution) had recently advocated American investment as a means to provide jobs; while the sole economic nationalist provision of the Plan (the nationalisation of the railways) implied a policy also preached by Madero, and even practised by Díaz.[295]

More generally – as Meyer certainly recognises – plans are not always a faithful guide to the character of a political movement. Some were no doubt drawn up to deceive, some – like the Plan of Tacubaya – incorporated fine phrases and radical ideas but had minimal political impact, while others – such as the Plan of San Luis – were eagerly taken up by thousands who had never read it, who had only a dim notion of its content, and who read their own objectives into its limited but malleable provisions.[296] Plans and ideological statements could be of great importance, but they must be analysed in terms of their social support and immediate political context. Initially, the radical, popular character of the Plan Orozquista matched the movement itself, staffed, as it was, by revolutionary veterans (many of *serrano* origin), who were committed to social reforms including the division of the large estates.[297] Thus Madero (being a man of principle) found it hard to credit stories that the Terrazas oligarchy might 'foment a revolt which in reality had to be one of socialist ideas', while Zapata, on the other side of the fence, was able to approve the Plan Orozquista virtually in its entirety – indeed, some conservatives regarded Orozquismo and Zapatismo as variants of a similar subversive tendency, typified by 'the despoliation of [the] landlords'.[298] *Chacun à son goût*: Molina Enríquez, with his all-purpose ethnic explanations, saw Orozquismo as a 'blind collision' between 'the mestizos, or at least, the Indian–mestizos' and the 'Criollos Señores'; the bitterly critical American consul at Chihuahua attributed the rebellion to 'a mingled desire for revenge, the manifestations of a semi-socialistic spirit, and . . . the lust for loot and lawlessness'.[299]

All were, in a sense, testimonies to the popular character of Orozquismo; to its mobilisation of the same groups – cowboys, smallholders, villagers, Indians, frontiersmen, bandits – as had rallied to the cause in 1910. Such men did not move in the enlightened, respectable, urban milieu of Madero and his kind. They came from a rougher, rural environment, were familiar with violence and vendetta, and did not readily stomach the prompt dismissal they received in 1911. Resentment against the civilians was compounded by contempt. Orozco, who had man-handled Madero at Juárez, 'had the contempt of his class for the dwarfish and scholarly' president; some of Madero's collaborators, like Giuseppe Garibaldi, seemed to Orozco a collection of 'dandies'.[300] Conversely, the educated civilians disdained Orozco's want of letters and culture.[301] It was not, therefore, a clear, ideological rejection of the Madero regime which (save in rare cases, like Braulio Hernández's) generated rebellion, nor was it a crude, self-interested desire for loot, as some historians as well as some contemporaries have suggested.[302] Rather, it was a general, yet localised and thus fragmentary, rejection of the new regime, of its unsympathetic, aloof personnel, of its (as yet) ineffectual policies, of its almost treasonable ingratitude to those who had risked all in 1910. *Serranos* like Salazar, Rojas and Orozco did not take kindly to the peremptory, pettifogging authority of the lawyers, doctors and editors who now held power, and they did not appreciate the merits of gradualism. They had overthrown Don Porfirio's regime – the regime under which most of them had lived since birth – why should they not overthrow Don Pancho's, which they had created in the first place?

But there was more to the Orozco rebellion than this. Like the planters of Morelos, Chihuahua's conservatives were staging a political revival and looking to the eventual overthrow of Madero – to which end the co-optation of revolutionary leaders (Figueroa in the south, Orozco in the north) promised benefits. At the moment of his triumph in 1911 (if not before), Orozco was subjected to a barrage of flattery; conservatives were active in his brief gubernatorial campaign; Reyista leaders had kind words for the caudillo of Chihuahua.[303] As 'Vazquista' revolts pullulated early in 1912, 'conservative spokesmen began to cultivate Orozco assiduously' and the awareness of potential financial backing from such quarters perhaps influenced Orozco's decision to join the rebels.[304] Certainly the American consul alleged financial assistance and believed that the rebellion was, from the outset, 'promoted by adherents of the old regime'; more concretely and reliably, he described how Antonio Cortazar – linked by political and family ties to Creel – incited demonstrations against the Maderista authorities, calling upon the services of 'boys and town loafers', and how, during the critical days while the Juárez rebels advanced south, tramcar employees could be seen on the streets of Chihuahua City offering drinks and free rides to those who would join the demonstrations against President Madero and Governor González.[305] Nor were there wanting intermediaries to convert the conservatives' and the ex-Maderistas' shared antipathy to the regime into a definite alliance, in which the former would provide the money, the latter the muscle. Initially, Orozco's ambitious, scheming secretary, José Córdova, was seen to perform such a role; as the rebellion got under way Gonzalo Enrile, an ex-Porfirian Post Office and Consular employee, became its treasurer, tax-gatherer and – as the consul put it, with his novelettish touch – 'the intermediary through whom the unseen and unknown powers behind the revolution hand out payment to the janizaries [sic] who are engaged to fight the battles'.[306]

Such conspiracy theories exercised – and still exercise – a powerful appeal, particularly in situations such as this where, it was alleged, 'bright and capable men' exploited the 'torpid and dull-witted Orozco'.[307] Often, however, the boot was on the other foot: popular and plebeian leaders called upon the services of scribes, secretaries and fixers without necessarily abdicating control of the movement which they had initiated; if there was exploitation, it went both ways.[308] This was abundantly clear in the case of Zapatismo and evident, to a lesser degree, in Orozquismo as well. As the rebellion spread, conservative connivance certainly became apparent, and was the subject of political gossip in Mexico City; significantly, the newly appointed 'rebel' Governor of Chihuahua was Dr Félix Gutiérrez, 'a man of fine education . . . well connected socially and . . . in sympathy by birth and education with the wealthy classes of the state'.[309] Historians have readily accepted accounts of conservative – especially Terracista – support, and even American backing for the rebellion.[310] Certainly, Juan Creel, who managed the Banco Minero in Chihuahua City, bought up 80,000 pesos of Orozquista bonds, without even troubling to plead *force majeure*; but his son, Creel lamented, was 'a victim of the ambience in which he lived', and there does not appear to have been a concerted attempt to back the revolt on the part of the Creel/Terrazas interests.[311] Luis Terrazas, the patriarch of the clan, denied any complicity, even in private correspondence with his son-in-law, while Creel himself, in Mexico City, appears to have been initially unaware and subsequently critical of the family's involvement locally.[312]

Though an anti-Madero alliance of 'left' and 'right' was thus assembled, it remained loose and conditional. The conservatives could not be sure of controlling their plebeian allies: 'the entire month of February [1912] was spent in getting control of the unruly elements that had given rise to the situation'; and, thereafter, the well-to-do could not ignore the 'socialist' pretensions of many of the Orozquistas – especially while Máximo Castillo was plundering and partitioning Terrazas estates in the Galeana district.[313] On the other hand, some of the more radical and clear-sighted rebels – notably Braulio Hernández and his men – grew increasingly 'discontented over the prominent part the members of the so-called "Científico" party are taking in the conduct of the revolution'.[314] In a public manifesto, Hernández rehearsed the evils of both the Madero regime and the Terrazas dynasty, admitting that there were 'some ambitious members of the old Científico party who are attempting to exercise some influence over Pascual Orozco'; this attempt, however, was bound to fail. But Hernández's optimism was misplaced. By mid-May, he had been 'eliminated' as a rebel commander, and his men distributed among other Orozquista detachments.[315]

If the conservatives' role in the rebellion was clear (without necessarily being dominant), their motives were not so immediately obvious. The landlords and businessmen of Chihuahua had been justifiably alarmed at the popular revolution of 1910–11, yet now some of them projected an alliance with the revolutionaries in opposition to a regime which, for all its constitutionalism, was socially conservative and concerned to restore peace and stability, not least by speedily demobilising the Liberating Army. But there were two basic divergences between the Maderistas and Chihuahuan elite. First, if they agreed on certain aims, they differed as to means. For Madero, responsible, representative government would ensure peace, for the old Porfiristas it would entail anarchy – and they were not entirely wrong. For Luis Terrazas, the moderate liberalism of the Plan of San Luis was the product of Madero's 'sick mind', and the cause of the present confusion.[316] Conservatives did not trust Madero to defend peace and property, however sincere his intentions; hence the myth of the 'iron hand' and the brief vogue for Reyes in 1911. Yet, in revolutionary Chihuahua, it was necessary to seek the 'iron hand' among the popular *cabecillas*, for – until the Federal Army could be persuaded to act – they were the only group capable of cajoling, disciplining, and, where necessary, repressing the rebel rank-and-file. Orozco was seen as 'the only person who has any control over the rabble which is following the cry of the new democracy'; it was said – no doubt hopefully by some, fearfully by others – that 'if the [Orozco] revolution succeeds, a more oppressive dictatorship will be set up than was known in the days of General Díaz'.[317] But this was not necessarily a coolly conceived and executed conservative strategy, it was more of a dangerous, even desperate gamble, forced upon the Chihuahuan elite by events. Though Orozco had been wooed for months, it was the advance on the capital of Campa, Salazar and Hernández (men of radical repute, leading tough *serrano* soldiers) which pushed the conservatives – as it also pushed Orozco – into a hastily concluded, ambiguous alliance. It was a bargain reminiscent of the Italian liberals' later co-optation of Mussolini and the fascists, but since, in this case, it presaged defeat rather than victory, it is impossible to say which party would have called the tune, or derived greater benefit from the arrangement.

The second factor distancing the conservatives from Madero was the reformist character of the state administration in Chihuahua. The essence of the Maderista programme was constitutional liberalism, but within the political framework thereby established, elected administrations enjoyed a range of autonomy. In some states, conservatism triumphed; in some, the Catholics dominated; and in a few, socially conscious Maderistas sought to enact genuine, evolutionary social reform: Cepeda in San Luis, Lizardi in Guanajuato, Alberto Fuentes in Aguascalientes and Abraham González in Chihuahua. González, in particular, sought to implement a classic progressive programme in the fields of education, fiscal reform and social moralisation.[318] Such policies not only redounded to the advantage and appealed to the sensibilities of the middle-class constituency on which Maderismo had been based; they also represented a real threat to the political and economic power of the old oligarchy. The sale of public land was suspended, incentives were provided for small business, and the land tax was revalued; González went further in proposing an upper ceiling on individual landholdings, the recovery of unpaid back taxes, and an official inquiry into the Banco Minero robbery (which threatened to implicate the Creel–Terrazas interests). Many of these reforms, it is true, did not materialise until later in 1912 – after the Orozco rebellion – and their radicalism may have been a response to conservative backing for Orozco. But fiscal reform was certainly in the air before the rebellion (apart from the immediate, local threat, Terrazas was apprised of recent precedents elsewhere, as in Guanajuato); and the threat of an inquiry into the Banco Minero case – paralleling similar exposures which were taking place in other states and municipalities – clearly alarmed the oligarchs.[319] Some, like the suave and diplomatic Enrique Creel, preferred to deflect the threat by covert lobbying.[320] But in Chihuahua itself, where the threat of both Maderista reformism and popular radicalism was more keenly felt, desperate remedies seemed appropriate; the anxious oligarchs looked to pluck the flower of safety from the nettle of popular revolt; extremes would combine against the centre, patrician and plebeian unite in joint opposition to middle-class reformism.

This political alignment was unique to Chihuahua. For it to occur, the three major political actors of the Madero period – the Porfirian oligarchs, the middle-class Maderistas and the popular movement – each had to display a certain autonomy and vigour. Only when such a balance of forces existed would the oligarchs contemplate an alliance with popular elements. With three such variables, many permutations were logically possible, though in fact only four real alternatives were apparent. In Sonora, for example, there was a genuine 'political renovation' which, as in Chihuahua, substituted Maderistas for Porfiristas, but, save for the insurgent Yaquis, there was no strong popular movement to which the deposed Porfiristas could turn for succour, and an alliance between General Torres and the Yaquis was unthinkable on both sides.[321] In Morelos and many central states, meanwhile, the reformists – never so strong – were mercilessly squeezed between powerful, contending extremes, and generally obliged to side with the conservatives for fear of social dissolution. In the states of the south, the entrenched oligarchy successfully beat off the weak challenges of both middle-class reformism and popular rebellion. Finally, the electoral politics of some states (better, some cities) displayed a polarisation between oligarchs and middle-class reformists, in the absence of any significant popular government.[322]

For the Chihuahuan pattern to evolve, reformism had to present a real threat to the status quo (without placating popular demands), and defenders of the status quo had to risk cultivating popular forces which – while they too challenged vested interests – seemed to be potential and powerful allies. But such social equations are not value-free. Political actors of this kind represented not only power but also class and ideological interest, and there is an evident explanatory problem in the alliance forged (however desperately or conditionally) between the revolutionary veterans of 1910 and the oligarchic rulers they had initially sought to overthrow. And this is by no means an isolated problem, since anomalous alliances and ideological inconsistencies tend to mount up as the Revolution progresses. Hence there is a *prima facie* case for explaining revolutionary behaviour in terms of shallow self-seeking, devoid of social or political significance, and for interpreting the Revolution (as many foreign diplomats and Mexican conservatives did) as a Hobbesian struggle for power and wealth. This is such an important, recurrent problem, touching the heart of the Revolution, that a pause for thought is necessary. The following brief section therefore introduces the notion of the 'logic of the Revolution', and further develops the distinction between *serrano* and agrarian revolt, taking Orozquismo and Zapatismo as examples, after which, the narrative of their combined action against the Madero regime, and the regime's response, can be resumed.

THE LOGIC OF THE REVOLUTION: *SERRANOS* AND *AGRARISTAS*

For historians sympathetic to Madero, like Valadés, the Orozquistas were out for plunder and a good time: why else would they turn against a reformist president (and, it might be added, a yet more reformist governor)?[323] But the reforms, though sufficiently impending to alarm the well-to-do (they, after all, read the press and the *Diario Oficial*), did not come fast enough to satisfy the masses. Nor were they necessarily the right reforms. It was the middle class – the small businessman, the *ranchero*, the liberal, *bien-pensant* professional – who stood to gain from González's policies, which were precisely those (fiscal, educational, moralising) ceaselessly advocated by the pre-1910 opposition press. Some, such as the puritanical campaigns against drink, gambling and vagrancy, were quite antithetical to the prevailing mores of rural, revolutionary Mexico.[324] Conversely, there were popular demands – for the break-up of haciendas, for regular employment (these two obviously linked) and, above all, for the relaxation of central political control – which were neglected or actively resisted. The consequent dissatisfaction was sometimes expressed in formal manifestos, but it could also take the form of personal commitment to Orozco, or some lesser *cabecilla*, and of *de facto* rejection of the remote, uncongenial civilians who now claimed authority over the popular movement. This was a clash not only of classes, but also of cultures: one that was urban, respectable, educated, national in outlook, self-consciously progressive and wedded to the idea of a rational–legal political authority based on free suffrage, the other predominantly rural, plebeian, illiterate, parochial in outlook, displaying (for all its radical programmes) backward-looking, nostalgic traits and a commitment to political authority that was local, personal, and traditional/charismatic.[325]

The latter were the fundamental characteristics of the popular movement, of which Orozquismo and, *a fortiori*, Zapatismo were members. But generalisations of this kind, if initially essential, suffer diminishing returns. As the careers of the Orozquistas illustrate, political affiliations became increasingly convoluted, expedient and resistant to analysis couched in such broad, sociological terms. For – and this point will recur frequently – as the Revolution unfolded it evolved a logic of its own, which cannot be precisely related to the social origins or ideologies of participant groups, of the kind we have already discussed. As different political solutions were attempted, as regimes (national and local) came and went, as battle was joined at all the different levels of conflict – ideological, regional, ethnic, class and clientelist – previously identified, so the various social actors departed from their original characterisations and – to varying extents – were taken over by the drama. We may revert to Tannenbaum's hydraulic metaphor: over time, the broad current of popular rebellion, which at its source flowed pure and fast, impelling the Revolution, was checked, dammed and diverted, sometimes driven underground, sometimes harnessed for the use of others, like a captive mill stream; thus, a once torrential river became like Matthew Arnold's 'shorn and parcell'd Oxus', a multitude of individual channels and pools, some agitated and fast-flowing, some stopped and stagnant. Broad tendencies, like tides, may affect the entire system, but the pilot who tries to steer his way through must increasingly take note of all the complex variations and interactions, which seem to defy generalisation.

As the historian delights to inform the sociologist, ostensibly minor, contingent events may have major, 'structural' consequences.[326] The Orozquistas' decision to rebel in 1912 determined not only their own future careers, but in many respects the career of the northern, popular revolution. Their rebellion and its ramifications illustrate on a grand scale what happened in numerous states and localities, as people reacted rapidly to shifting events which were beyond their control – and reacted often in an expedient, *ad hoc* fashion. Hence the once clear aims and commitments of revolutionaries became blurred, compromised or forgotten. The Revolution flowed on; or, according to Azuela's more violent metaphor, raged like a hurricane, sweeping along individuals like dried leaves.[327] Of course, such metaphors, however illustrative, are no more than metaphors: 'the Revolution' is an abstraction (whether it be the neat, almost providential abstraction of modern political myth, or the grim joke of cynical deities, as in Azuela's novels), and to invoke the 'logic of the Revolution' is not to go the way of teleology and meta-history. The 'logic of the Revolution' implies no *a priori* pattern, no grand Hegelian design; it suggests, rather, the whole complex of crises, events, options and opportunities which confronted participants and over which they felt themselves to have little control. There is nothing mystical about this and – granted adequate data – it is capable of rational analysis. But, as the years go by, analysis couched in broad social terms (the rise of urban Maderismo, the genesis of agrarian protest) must give way to narrower, more specific explanations: 'social history, the history of groups and groupings' gives way to 'traditional history . . . *l'histoire événementielle*'.[328]

Generalisations must now be framed at a lower level. They must concern themselves more with the behaviour of individuals (like Orozco) or smaller social groups (the Chihuahuan elite) than with that of large, aggregate social entities (the peasantry, the urban middle class). And this behaviour may depend critically on the vicissitudes of time and place. As the Revolution progressed, rural populists like the Arrietas found themselves running states, one-time political agitators, like Manuel Diéguez, commanded armies and exercised authority in towns, like Cananea, which had earlier thrilled or trembled at their agitation. In such cases, the motives which had first stimulated rebellion were now overlaid or superseded by fresh considerations, deriving from the Revolution itself. The agitator turned revolutionary general was not simply an armed tribune of the people; the transition implied new commitments and attitudes, of which the Revolution was a prolific source.[329] Indeed, the ultimate victors, inheritors and beneficiaries of the Revolution were precisely those men most moulded and conditioned by the revolutionary experience, who were the Revolution's creatures *par excellence*, and who in many cases lacked a significant pre-revolutionary past. And if the logic of the Revolution provides for the historian an increasingly vital dimension of explanation, it provided for the participants the ineluctable context of social action. In the case of Pascual Orozco, the decision to rebel against Madero – taken under the pressure of events in Chihuahua City in March 1912 – led by a tortuous but logical route to his feud with Villa, his alliance with Huerta, and his death in a running battle with Texas Rangers in the summer of 1915.

But, while recognising the growing importance of individual and contingent events and the decreasing utility of general, socio-economic explanations, the historian should not lose sight of such explanations: 'resounding events are often only . . . surface manifestations of these larger movements and explicable only in terms of them'.[330] In some cases, in fact, 'events' show a marked fidelity to their parent 'movements'; action follows a consistent ideology or practice; people – putting it crudely – behave as they might be expected to behave, granted certain prior allegiances. But even where this is not the case (and increasingly it is not) the very lack of consistency, the lack of 'fit' between allegiances and actions, requires some explanation. Inconsistency and opportunism should not be taken as given immutable traits of human (or, as many foreigners said, Mexican) nature: like their antitheses, they were conditioned by circumstances, and are capable of explanation. A comparison of Orozquismo and Zapatismo, the two pre-eminent popular movements which emerged from the Maderista coalition, and which caused most trouble for its successor regime, can be suggestive in this regard.

Though both Orozco and Zapata rebelled against Madero, out of a common disgust with the Madero regime, the character of their rebellions differed, and not simply in a random, contingent fashion. From 1911 to 1919, Zapata showed a dogged adherence to the ideals of agrarian reform and local self-government (the interdependence of which has already been mentioned). He was prepared – increasingly – to countenance bizarre alliances with city radicals, disaffected conservatives, anyone who shared his hostility to the enemy in Mexico City and who might aid the Zapatista cause. But in doing so, Zapata never compromised his essential aims, he never abdicated power within Morelos, and he always kept his allies at arm's length. It was this dour, suspicious, protective attitude, the product of communal solidarity and of a deep commitment to village society, culture and history, which guaranteed Zapata the loyalty of the *surianos* through years of bitter fighting. The same attitude was evident with other rural, populist leaders. But if it sustained local support, it could make them (in the eyes of outsiders) infuriating, intransigent partners, who displayed a peasant hostility to compromise; and, even where military alliances were struck, their intensely parochial commitment set narrow – some said cowardly or traitorous – limits to their sphere of operations.

Northern *serrano* leaders like Orozco and Villa were cast in a different mould. Like Zapata, they were rural populists, they mobilised a significant degree of support on the basis of agrarian demands, and a parochial indifference to national concerns characterised their movements too. But these common traits – the distinguishing features of the popular movement – were also offset by important differences. Though northern Mexico contained analogues of Zapatismo (and these were often key centres of rebellion, like Cuencamé), the forces of communal solidarity, village tradition and historical precedent, which pervaded the Mesa Central, were less powerful in the north, where spatial and social mobility were greater. If northerners in general displayed a more self-interested concern for goods, land and power – rather than an attachment to communal interests – this reflected the prevailing social mores of the region. Furthermore, northern *agrarismo* (whose importance should not be underestimated) often fitted within the structures of *serrano* revolt: that is, instead of pitting villagers against haciendas in a well-defined class struggle, capable of transforming rural society, it served to focus attention on the cacique's monopoly of land and power, the overthrow of which became the dominant *serrano* objective uniting different strata within the community. Thus, not only were *serrano* revolts typically 'polyclassist' – socially eclectic in their recruitment of local, anti-cacical elements – it was also the case that their programme or 'project' was more limited and less radically subversive. The overthrow of the cacique and his few minions, the recovery (in some cases) of alienated land, the installation of popular authorities: these victories were often soon accomplished, and *serrano* movements, lacking the ballast of strong communal loyalties or agrarian revindication, thereafter tended to veer rudderless and without direction, as compared with the straight course steered by the *surianos*. To put it another way: the moral economy which informed and guided Zapatista rebellion was present in the north only in a more fragmented, imperfect fashion.

As so often, inferences about the character of these movements must be drawn from the respective leaderships. Zapata stuck tightly to Morelos; when fighting ebbed he would return to Tlaltizapán, his new home and headquarters, where he could be seen with his *compadres*, sitting 'relaxed in the plaza, drinking, arguing about plucky cocks and frisky horses, discussing the rains and prices with farmers who joined them for a beer'.[331] Northern leaders – as befitted the more heterogeneous society whence they came – were a good deal less static and bucolic. After the success of the Madero revolution, Orozco acquired a range of business interests, involving mining, retailing and (his old profession) transport; Pancho Villa, whose previous entrepreneurial activity had been largely criminal, bought himself a slaughterhouse in Chihuahua City.[332] Their armies, too, carried a certain stamp of professionalism, which grew more marked as the years went by, and which enabled them to campaign on a more extensive scale – though not necessarily with greater ultimate success – than the Zapatistas. In part this military capacity reflected the strategic imperatives of the north (the terrain, the proximity of the US), but it also reflected the social base upon which the northern armies were built: one that was more mobile, occupationally hybrid, and independent of the agricultural cycle.

Northern leaders were, like Zapata, men of the people, they lacked the urban culture and sophistication of the civilian Maderistas (and later contestants for power), their personal tastes were, again like Zapata's, closer to the pushpin than to the poetry end of Bentham's felicific spectrum. But their chosen retirements – when the fighting abated or ended – were a good deal more grandiose, and uninhibited by any concern for communal egalitarianism. Tomás Urbina, for example, appropriated the Hacienda of Las Nieves in the middle of the revolution, and there set himself up in seigneurial style: Las Nieves, an American noted, 'belongs to General Urbina – people, houses, animals and immortal souls'.[333] So it was, or would have been, for many northern leaders: their goals were less either national power or the assertion of communal political and agrarian rights, than a confiscated hacienda, a convivial retirement in the company of veteran retainers, and the easy life of a successful ex-*condottiere* or Brazilian *coronel*. Urbina, striving for this goal a little prematurely, paid for his impatience with his life; but Villa enjoyed it, albeit briefly, at Canutillo in the early 1920s, as Saturnino Cedillo did at Palomas until the late 1930s.[334]

Such personal achievements did not necessarily represent betrayals of the popular support which had made them possible. Followers tolerated, applauded and sometimes benefited from their leaders' acquisition of power and property: the revolutionary magnate was not only a useful *patrón* and protector, he was also *muy hombre*, the estimable epitomy of *macho* values, and a source of some psychic satisfaction to his plebeian followers.[335] The attributes of the traditional hacendado – conspicuous consumption, authoritarian mien, and penchant for private violence – could be readily assumed by the *serrano caudillo*, and this was especially true in the north, where the landlord's military role was a not so distant memory, and where, in the absence of strong communal villages, mechanisms of equalisation did not inhibit gross disparities of wealth and power.[336] The traditional, seigneurial hacienda (once, though no longer, the formative institution of northern Mexican society) thus left its mark on the revolutionary movements of the north. And the assumption of such seigneurial attributes by revolutionary *caudillos* could fulfil as much as betray the expectations of their followers.

But, like the old-style *hacendados* they now emulated, these *caudillos* also had a great capacity for oppression. Lacking either an affective commitment to the village, or a sophisticated grasp of modern political practice, they had no compass to guide them through the stormy seas of revolution. Their careers often seemed to deteriorate into aimless violence and opportunism and, despite their impeccably popular origins, they could become the new scourges of the people, levying and press-ganging without regard for the civilian communities which had once supported them (a regard which Zapata, in contrast, never relinquished). Equally, they responded to conservative blandishments. In the absence of a generalised, clear-cut conflict between village and hacienda, alliances with *hacendados* (*some hacendados*) were tolerable. There were popular rebels, like Villa, who had collaborated with friendly landlords during their bandit days, and bandits, as we have noted, could make up into excellent policemen and foremen – the tranquillisers rather than the exponents of popular grievances. The political ambivalence of the bandit (even the 'social' bandit) was thus recreated in the form of the *serrano caudillo*.[337] Where such *caudillos* did not – like Urbina – supplant the *hacendado*, appropriating his estate and social pre-eminence, without changing the basic structures of rural society, it was possible for them to collaborate instead, offering protection in return for acceptance. Thus, after all, many of the old Porfirian caciques had established themselves during the civil wars of the nineteenth century.

This propensity for self-advancement, for political opportunism, and for cross-class alliances of apparently anomalous character, was a feature not simply of northern rebellion, but of *serrano* rebellion: that is, of movements deriving ultimately from resistance to centralising pressure, rather than from a fundamental agrarian polarisation. Northern *serranos* (by virtue of being both northern and *serrano*) merely exhibited it to the greatest degree. But, just as *agrarismo* flourished in some pockets of the north – at Cuencamé or in the Yaqui valley – so *serrano* traits and rebellions could also be found in the centre/south. These will receive fuller treatment at the end of this chapter.

Here, by way of contrast between the two popular paradigms, we shall briefly consider the Figueroa and Zapata revolts: movements which, despite their geographical proximity, responded to different causes and adopted different modes.

The Figueroa rebellion, centred on Huitzuco (Gro), displayed classic *serrano* features: it represented a reaction to continued Porfirian political impositions and sought 'a return of control over local affairs to the hands of local men, and an end to central interference in the state'.[338] 'The sons of the state', as Francisco, the intellectual of the movement put it, '[claimed] the place in politics which outsiders had usurped.'[339] Once this had been achieved by force of arms during the Maderista revolution, the Figueroas' objectives became harder to fathom. They espoused no agrarian programme: Francisco denied that an agrarian problem existed in Morelos, while Rómulo, a few years later, told local *agraristas* that 'if we want lands, we should buy them'.[340] But they had an appetite for power and, it has been suggested, they sought to recreate the old Alvarez *cacicazgo*, which had dominated Guerrero until the 1860s.[341] They could thus appear as potential allies for the embattled Morelos planters, somewhat as the Orozquistas did for the elite of Chihuahua: they possessed military muscle, they had no personal stake in Morelos, and they were hostile to Zapata's agrarian demands. Again, the flexibility and opportunism of *serrano* leadership were evident.

But hopes of mutual benefit were soon dashed – here, as in analogous cases. The Figueroas' military and political intrusion into Morelos offended not only the Zapatistas but also the middle-of-the-road civilian reformers, the rump of the old Leyvista party, who still believed in the possibility of peaceful, progressive change, and who resented the strong-arm methods of outsiders like Ambrosio Figueroa and Victoriano Huerta. Furthermore, with popular and agrarian upheaval affecting Guerrero too, Madero felt (rightly) that Ambrosio would serve better as an agent of repression in his home state, rather than in Morelos. So Ambrosio quit the governorship and was shunted back to Guerrero as military commander. Here, throughout 1912, he pursued a dual policy: ruthlessly combating rebellion in the name of the central government, while asserting the political dominance of his family and their clients in the manner of a traditional, aspiring cacique.[342] To the *agrarista* Jesús Salgado (one of Ambrosio's chief bugbears) the overthrow of the 'odious *cacicazgo*' of the Porfiriato had been achieved only so that the people now had to 'pay . . . homage to [Ambrosio Figueroa] as cacique of the state'.[343] The complaint was valid. The Figueroas, like other *serrano* caciques, sought to subvert the political, not the social order, they aimed to roll back the frontiers of the power-hungry, centralising Porfirian regime and replace it by a form of traditional *caciquismo*, run by themselves and their supporters. This implied a change not just of personnel, but also of political approach, and, like other *serrano* caciques, the Figueroas could count on a good deal of genuine popular support in pursuit of these objectives, even in default of a socio-economic programme. The resentments and 'moral outrage' which generated rebellion did not have to be of simply material origin.

The specificity of *serrano* rebellion is brought home by the fact that it clashed not only with Porfirian centralisation and Zapatista (or Salgadista) *agrarismo*, but also with Maderista liberalism. This clash was not at first so evident. *Serranos* and Maderistas could ally against Díaz, *serrano* caciques invoked liberty, self-government, and the Constitution of 1857; both sides were hostile to agrarian rebellion. In the case of the Figueroas, kinship was strengthened by the presence of Francisco Figueroa, who conformed to the image of a rural Maderista intellectual. But beyond a certain point the ways parted. *Serrano* movements were fundamentally rural, provincial, and retrospective, heirs of a long tradition, now revitalised by the centralising pressures of the Porfiriato; Maderismo was urban, progressive and cosmopolitan, a product of the burgeoning cities, of the educated middle class, of an articulate, universal ideology. If – to take this specific example – Madero dallied with the Figueroas, it was not out of sympathy with their *caciquista* ambitions or their somewhat primitive political methods, but rather out of a pragmatic recognition that the Figueroas could be more easily accommodated – for the time being at least – than Zapata and his fellow-*agraristas*. Figueroa was preferable to Zapata but, ultimately, there was little place for either in the new scheme of things which the urban Maderistas (and, later, their Constitutionalist successors) sought to introduce. Madero's concept of the rule of law, of impersonal, impartial political institutions, could not co-exist indefinitely with the arbitrary, personal power of *serrano* caciques, any more than with the rampant *agrarismo* of village populists. Thus, Madero cautiously reproved Figueroa for failing to observe 'legal requirements' in the summary execution of an opposition journalist, and politely – but vainly – instructed him to lead 500 men against the rebels in Chihuahua (instructions designed as much to get Figueroa out of Guerrero as into Chihuahua). [344] Winkling *serrano* caciques out of their *cacicazgos* was an irksome business. [345]

Despite their mutual antipathy, therefore, Zapata and the Figueroas shared certain traits which set them apart from the nationally-minded, progressive, urban groups who initiated (and later terminated) the revolutionary process: [346] 'the vision of Mexico held by Emiliano Zapata and his followers was very different from that of the ambitious *rancheros* of Huitzuco. And yet both represented traditionalist views of Mexico completely out of tune with the new era which the whirlwind of the Revolution swept in.' Though analytically valid, this somewhat anticipates the story. As of 1912, the Figueroas were lukewarm allies of Madero, while Zapata – soon to be seconded by Orozco – was in arms against his erstwhile leader. In facing these two celebrated rebels, the Madero regime confronted its biggest challenge, and in meeting it, it stored up fresh problems for the future. The logic of the Revolution pushed

Madero in directions he neither foresaw, nor wholly favoured. Nor were the rebellions themselves free and autonomous. They displayed, in particular, a marked interdependence: Zapata – in 1912, as again in 1913–14 and after 1915 – needed a northern ally, a second front in the north which would bleed the Federal Army and limit its activities in Morelos. Lesser *cabecillas* too felt a similar need, and their fortunes fluctuated according to those of the Chihuahua revolt. Though Orozquismo and Zapatismo (and other lesser movements) might respond to local concerns, and differ from each other in important respects, their fates intertwined and were determined by the regime's response to their cumulative – but hardly concerted – challenge.

ZAPATISMO AND REVOLUTION

Once inaugurated as constitutional president, Madero at once faced the vexed problem of Morelos, where the hawkish policies of de la Barra and Huerta had driven Zapata into outright rebellion.[347] A couple of weeks after the inauguration, Zapata met with key supporters in the hills near Villa de Ayala where, under the guidance of the local schoolmaster, Otilio Montaño, they drew up and signed the Plan of Ayala.[348] Published on 28 November 1911, the Plan was more than a denunciation of Madero and a call for agrarian reform; it was to be 'a veritable catholicon ... almost a Scripture', upon which the fundamentalist Zapatistas would never compromise, and it has since been hallowed as a sacred text in the Mexican people's exodus from Porfirian bondage into the promised land of the Revolution.[349] For all its later, radical connotations, the Plan – with its references to 'the immortal code of 1857', the 'immortal Juárez' and the 'revolutionary blood of Ayutla' – was steeped in the popular, folk liberalism of the nineteenth century. Madero's (liberal) Plan of San Luis was not therefore rejected, rather, it was appropriated ('the revolutionary junta of the state of Morelos makes the Plan of San Luis its own'), and it was held up as a tissue of fair but unfulfilled promises.[350] But the Plan also went beyond these. Its basic theme was indignation at Madero's sell-out of the revolution, 'gloriously ... initiated with the help of God and the people': Madero had 'left standing most of the governing powers and corrupted elements of oppression of the dictatorial government of Porfirio Díaz'; he had persecuted, gaoled and killed erstwhile revolutionary allies, and had 'tried with the brute force of bayonets ... to drown in blood the pueblos who ... demand from him the fulfillment of the revolution'.[351] In particular, the Plan denounced the imposition of Pino Suárez, and of state governors like Ambrosio Figueroa, 'the scourge and tyrant of the people of Morelos'.[352] The Plan is thus shot through with moral indignation; both preamble and provisions ring to the theme of the revolution betrayed.

Practically, the Plan combined the usual schedule of political revolution with longer term provisions which, in their precision and radicalism, went beyond the Plan of San Luis. In the first respect, the Zapatistas showed a characteristic hostility to compromise: the post-revolutionary political settlement would be the work of a revolutionary junta, there would be no provisional president, only a Chief of the Revolutionary Army (Pascual Orozco – or, if he declined, Zapata himself). The lessons of the *transacción* of May 1911 had been well learned. In the second respect, too, the Plan went beyond its predecessor. Not only would the illegally usurped lands of the villages be restored, as Madero had promised, in addition, one third of all rural 'monopolies' would be expropriated (though with prior indemnification), to provide land for the landless, and any 'landlords, científicos or bosses' who opposed the Plan would be liable for total expropriation.[353] Already, the polarising effect of the armed struggle had pushed agrarian (and other) demands beyond the lowest common denominators of 1910, and imparted a new militancy.[354] Yet the Ayala programme was still in some senses moderate (to put it another way, the process of Zapatista radicalisation still had a way to go): indemnification was stipulated and (save for enemies of the cause) expropriation was limited to a third of landlords' property. On paper, as in practice, therefore, the Zapatistas did not aim at a fundamental restructuring of rural society: 'like their fathers and grandfathers, the villagers and *rancheros* . . . remained traditionally tolerant about the pattern of life in Morelos: they would grant the hacienda its place. But they would also insist on their own place.'[355]

Thus, for all its radicalism – which would later become more marked and more schematic – the Zapatista movement was fundamentally defensive, backward-looking, and nostalgic; like other agrarian rebellions of the time, it represented 'a conservative reaction against economic and social changes that were proving detrimental to indigenous culture'.[356] Defence of that culture (using the word in its broadest sense) was central to Zapatismo; its guiding aim, inspiration, and organisational principle was the free association of landowning villages, a society which, though it might never have existed in its full perfection, was at least closer of attainment in the past than in the present. It was a communal movement, not simply in the narrow sense of demanding the restitution and protection of communal lands (whose importance varied from place to place anyway), but also because grievances, membership and objectives were constituted at the level of the community, rather than that of (say) occupational groups, formal political organisations, or even the 'rational' individuals who are said to populate some peasant villages.[357] But this implied no primitive (or progressive) communism: communal organisation – in both the broad, political and the narrower, tenurial sense – was compatible with individual usufruct, as well as a good deal of individual conflict; but, as already suggested, the bonds of the community were strong enough to contain these, especially when an external enemy loomed.[358] Hence Zapatismo displayed an enduring solidarity, a subordination of military to civilian

interests, and an avoidance of the excesses of *caudillismo* which marked other –
notably *serrano* – popular movements.[359]

Communal organisation was also compatible with the survival of the
hacienda. Landowning village and hacienda had existed in symbiosis for
centuries. But there was no place for the voracious plantation of Porfirian
Morelos, with its monopolistic claims to land, water and labour. And, as the
struggle proceeded, polarising the combatants, so the last vestiges of the old
collaboration faded; planter, foreman and cacique found no place in Zapatista
Morelos which organised itself along the lines of 'the utopia of a free association
of rural clans'.[360] In practice, this meant a form of rural anarchism. The
Zapatistas, according to Díaz Soto y Gama, sought[361] 'not socialisation, not
collectivisation. [Rather] free land, free plot. Free cultivation, free exploitation of the plot. Without foremen, without masters in the *ejido*, without
individual tyrannies exercised by the state or by the collectivity'. But this was
anarchism ignorant of Bakunin, nurtured in a long, distinctively Mexican
tradition, whose chief ideological discourse was one of popular, patriotic
liberalism.[362] The explicit anarchism which characterised a fringe of Mexican
radical thought since the 1870s was only detectable in the rhetoric of certain
Zapatista intellectuals and orators, none of whom were genuine veterans of the
movement; and even here it consorted with liberalism, socialism and *indigenismo*, displaying a promiscuous disregard for ideological consistency and an
incapacity to influence revolutionary events.[363] In many respects, Zapatismo
ran counter to this explicit anarchism, of the kind historically associated with
both Latin Europe and Latin America. 'Nowhere in the Plan [of Ayala]',
Womack observes, 'is there a reference to "peace" or "progress" or "democracy", the goals professed in other plans and pre-eminently the concerns of the
citified men of the day.'[364] Anti-clericalism had no place either; the Plan
invoked 'God's help', and the Zapatistas – like rural rebels in Sinaloa, Tepic,
the Laguna and elsewhere – carried the emblem of the Virgin of Guadalupe in
their banners and hat badges.[365] In addition, Zapatismo betrayed none of the
ascetic spirit, none of the concern for strict morality, sobriety, hard work and
self-improvement which characterised anarchist thought and practice, not
least in urban Mexico.[366] As one of Zapata's radical, 'citified' spokesmen later
commented, in some disgust, the movement had suffered from its leader's
excessive fondness for 'good horses, fighting cocks, flashy women, card games
and intoxicating liquors'; a fondness which, it may be presumed, endeared
Zapata to his rural followers more than it offended them.[367]

In terms of formal ideology, therefore, Millon is correct to dispute the
'anarchist' label which some scholars have accorded Zapatismo. But formal
ideology is often a false god. The 'radical petty-bourgeois philosophy' which
Millon, with his simple Marxist categories and crude textual exegesis,
attributes to Zapatismo, is partly a fiction (there was not much evidence of
Zapatista 'anti-imperialism') and partly a red herring (most of it also char-

acterised the Constitutionalists, who warred with the Zapatistas for years and established a regime scarcely congenial to Zapata and his followers).[368] As I shall later try to show, the promiscuous usage of the 'petty bourgeois' category is fraught with analytical dangers and confusions.[369] For, even if the class (sic?) can be identified in terms either of its relationship to the means of production or of its espousal of a distinctive liberal or 'Jacobin' ideology, the fact remains that it was grotesquely fractured along social, cultural and geographical lines (urban and rural petty bourgeoisies differed; within the latter – to take but one example – the *ranchero* class embraced a host of variations); and it was thus capable of interpreting an ostensibly shared ideology (liberalism) in radically different ways.[370] Maderista liberalism – which exerted a strong appeal to the urban petty bourgeoisie – looked to political innovations of a 'modern', 'progressive' type which, far from weakening the state, would place it on surer institutional foundations; reforms, meanwhile, would have to be mediated through this new, impersonal system and all would redound to the benefit of a dynamic, North American style capitalism. For the Zapatistas, liberal reform offered a means to village self-government, the necessary prerequisite of an agrarian reform which would be rapid, local, specific and not at all conducive to capitalist development of the countryside. Similar slogans and symbols were thus made to serve quite different political visions. The 1857 Constitution contained the promise of progressive liberal democracy, North American style or *à la française*; it also conjured up images of the old, popular guerrilla struggles against Maximilian and the conservatives – images in many respects incompatible with the ethos of a 'typical liberal state'.[371]

For it was in their contrasting attitudes towards the state that the Zapatistas and their urban enemies (Maderista, later Constitutionalist) most clearly differed, and that the basic ambivalence of liberalism (evident not just in Mexico) was most obviously revealed. The Zapatistas, as we shall see, spurned the state and made no sustained bid for national power, as their enemies did. Patriotic they were, but nationalist they were not (and the absence of nationalism, both political and economic, correlated with the absence of anti-clericalism).[372] In terms, therefore, of its practice and ethos – rather than of its assembled *obiter dicta* – Zapatismo displayed a close kinship with rural anarchism. Hence, beneath its many distinctively Mexican features it can be seen as part of a secular phenomenon, those rural movements of anarchistic inclination which sought to establish 'the peasant Utopia . . . the free village, untrammelled by tax-collectors, labor recruiters, large landowners, officials'.[373] Some, like the Makhnovschina of the Ukraine, were explicitly anarchist, but there were many more which pursued anarchist practice in default of a formal anarchist commitment – some, like Zapatismo, under the guise of an extreme, anti-state liberalism.[374] Thus, in its brief heyday, Zapatismo approached the Proudhonian ideal, a society marked not by the total dissolution of order and structure, but by the resurgence of small, local social units (families, clans, villages), enjoying self-government and linked in a loose, voluntary formation.[375]

It is worth establishing the aims and character of Zapatismo before proceeding to the history of its struggle, since the latter's outcome – the degree of success or failure – must be gauged against the participants' objectives. Arnaldo Córdova denies Zapatismo revolutionary status, arguing that revolutionaries cannot assume a parochial, retrospective stance, but must look forwards, to the seizure of state power and the implementation of a 'national project of development'.[376] Now 'revolution' and 'revolutionary' are what you make them. They can (and in this book sometimes do) refer to any armed movement directed against an established regime. But analysts have usually sought a more rigorous and specific definition, which often involves dichotomising 'revolution' and 'rebellion'. Thus Córdova – whose general picture of Zapatismo is convincing – looks for an attempted seizure of state power under the aegis of a forward-looking social and political programme. Some, such as Huntington, go even further, relegating many of Córdova's revolutions to the status of mere rebellions; for them, 'revolution' represents 'a rapid, fundamental and violent domestic change in the dominant values and myths of a society, in its political institutions, social structure, leadership and government activity and policies'.[377] There are not many of these in human history, and one suspects that some of the examples, conventionally assumed by political scientists like Huntington, might not pass this extreme definitional test when put under the historian's microscope. As this book – as well as studies of other 'great revolutions' – tends to suggest, there is often more Tocquevillean continuity to the phenomenon that at first meets the eye (or than the revolutionaries themselves would care to admit).[378]

All such definitions (and many more could be mentioned) have an arbitrary quality to them, and present particular problems. By ruling out parochial and – even more inexplicably – backward-looking political movements, Córdova denies revolutionary status not only to Zapatismo but also to the majority of the popular elements which fought between 1910 and 1920; the Mexican Revolution, according to this paradox, was the work of diverse, localised, backward-looking rebels, who were themselves *not* revolutionary. Huntington (who discusses the Mexican case, not too impressively) must limit his analysis to successful revolutions, for only with success can the 'fundamental ... domestic change', which is the hallmark of real revolution, take place. In both analyses, therefore, it is the final outcome which provides the revolutionary yardstick: Huntington's 'fundamental ... domestic change', Córdova's 'proyecto nacional de desarrollo y ... concepción del Estado'. There is, therefore, a strong teleological bias here: the past is appraised in terms of its contribution to and congruence with the future (which, thanks to hindsight, the historian knows about). Such an analysis also sits very comfortably alongside the dominant historiographical school of the Revolution: that of the revolutionary consensus, whereby all revolutionary participants – despite their ostensible conflicts – contribute in some measure to the grand, concluding and consum-mating synthesis.

True, the outcome of the conflict was a synthesis, but it was not one to which all participants contributed and subscribed. Zapatismo left its mark, but it cannot be said that Zapatista objectives, as outlined in this section, were ultimately achieved.[379] Still less did the *serranos* enjoy success commensurate with their efforts. The final synthesis, in other words, did not represent a consensus, so much as a victory: among the bitterly contesting groups (whose conflicts the consensus school plays down) some emerged as winners, some as losers. But there is no good reason for favouring the winners (as Córdova and *a fortiori* Huntington do), nor for ignoring Tawney's advice and 'dragging into prominence the forces which have triumphed and thrusting into the back-ground those which they have swallowed up'.[380] History (*pace* E. H. Carr) is not a success story.[381] And if the analysis is purged of teleological elements, there is every reason for according Zapatismo – and other popular rebellions – 'revolutionary' status. 'Revolution', as I have said, is what you make it; but, apart from the broad, simple meaning of an armed movement against an established regime, it generally implies a violent political conflict in which, at the very least, more than a governmental reshuffle is at stake. The *cuartelazos* of the age of Santa Anna were not revolutions. Thus, whether it is the 'dominant values and myths of society', the hegemony of a ruling class, or rival programmes of national development which are at stake, there is an assump-tion that the outcome matters in some fairly profound way.

For such a revolution to occur – or be attempted – two conditions have to be met (here I am interpolating my own working definition). First, a group or groups must be seeking power – by violent as well as other means – in order to implement policies in accord with a preferred vision of society (this would seem to correspond closely to what Skocpol calls the 'political-conflict approach', typified by Tilly's work).[382] Visions of society (or ideologies, if you prefer) are thus important and, as I have suggested elsewhere, are to be found among all groups and classes.[383] But the source of such visions (past, present or future), their content (reactionary, conservative, radical) and the practical chances of their implementation – though all these are of obvious *historical* importance – are not *definitionally* crucial; as Lawrence Stone put it, in an earlier quotation, nostalgic visions can challenge the status quo and fuel revolutions.[384] Indeed, the 'moral economy' approach suggests that such visions may be precisely those with most revolutionary potential. But to make a revolutionary contribution, any vision or ideology must be sufficiently cogent – inspiring to its supporters, horrifying to its enemies – to fulfill the second criterion of revolution: a high degree of genuine popular mobilisation. Peasants, for example, participated – as conscripts and cannon-fodder – in the *cuartelazos* of the nineteenth century, but these were not examples of genuine popular mobilisation. The latter can be said to occur only when the struggle for power, the struggle between rival visions of society, involves large groups acting not out of coercion but rather out of identification with particular, participating movements. In this respect we may, for a change, agree with Huntington: 'revolution is the extreme case of the explosion of political participation. Without this explosion there is no revolution.'[385] And for explosions of this kind (rare enough in world history) to occur, important issues must be at stake, capable of mobilising people on a grand scale and in the face of profound dangers.

'Mobilisation', in this sense, involves more than just military recruitment; it denotes all forms of mass participation, violent and non-violent, which influence the outcome of the struggle; its sheer extent and novelty are hallmarks of revolution – certainly of the Mexican Revolution. It is for this reason that popular perceptions of right and legitimacy – often neglected or denied – are so important, and analyses – whether specific or comparative – which display a 'statolatrous' scepticism concerning genuine popular movements (sometimes linked to assumptions of 'false consciousness') are so palpably wrong.[386] Leviathan may have ruled since the Revolution, curbing, co-opting and crushing such movements, but he did not rule – indeed, was more minnow than Leviathan – during the decade of armed conflict, when such movements briefly flourished. And prominent among them was Zapatismo, an exemplar of both popular mobilisation and powerful challenge to the Porfirian order. Like many fellow-rebels – like Tupac Amaru or Father Hidalgo – the Zapatistas were revolutionaries, even if they were not winners in the 'success story' of history.

At the end of 1911, too, Zapatismo was resurgent. This resurgence – coinciding, Governor Figueroa noted, with the end of the 'small farmers' harvests' – gave the rebels control of most of Morelos, confining the Federals to the major towns.[387] Now, Zapatismo acted as the nucleus of a widespread movement which included semi-independent rebel bands, 'social' bandits, and some outright brigands, which spread beyond Morelos into its neighbouring states; the sheer decentralisation of the guerrilla war made it seem 'less a revolt than a rural riot'.[388] Zapata himself controlled the south east of the state, Salazar and Neri the centre, de la O the north-west; José Trinidad Ruiz pushed up into the north east, into the state of Mexico, frequenting the towns where he had preached in the past (his text now ran: 'down with the monopolies of woods, lands and waters; down with financial extortion; down with Madero; long live General Zapata!'); to the south Jesús 'Tuerto' Morales crossed into Puebla, mopped up the villages around Chiautla and appeared to operate there with virtual impunity.[389]

The waves of revolt spread further, encouraged if not impelled by Zapatismo. By the spring of 1912 much of southern Puebla was overrun and railway communications were crippled.[390] Zapatistas from de la O's fief easily penetrated into Mexico state (the Federals failed to block the strategic gap at Zumpahuacán) and made incursions into Guerrero, where they were loosely allied to the local *agrarista*, Jésus Salgado.[391] In northern Oaxaca, too, where Angel Barrios, having rebelled on the day of Madero's inauguration, had been defeated and captured, his followers fought on under the leadership of Manuel Oseguera, their campaigns around Cuicatlán merging with Zapatismo, rather than with other Oaxaqueño movements. Though the local *jefes políticos* were loyal and active Maderistas, they could not suffocate the rebellion, which continued to cut communications between Puebla and Oaxaca through the spring and summer of 1912.[392] All these campaigns displayed similar characteristics (most fully researched in the case of Morelos). Here, as in Durango, Chihuahua or Sinaloa, the government surrendered control of the countryside to the rebels: in Mexico state, for example, a large Federal garrison sat in Toluca, refusing to defend strategic outlying areas.[393] And on occasions, the rebels could even threaten the cities: Cuernavaca nearly fell to de la O's 3,000 men in January; in March there were rumours that Tehuacán had fallen – rumours which strict government censorship merely amplified.[394]

In general, the rebels' shortage of ammunition and complete lack of artillery saved the cities. Small towns like Tepotzlán and Jojutla were captured in the spring 1912 offensives, but could not be held. In larger communities, like Cuernavaca, life was disturbed, but not threatened: people stayed indoors, the hotel business slumped, shops and saloons profiteered at the expense of the Federal soldiers.[395] But outside the towns it was a different story. The Federal troops were brought in from other states and were unfamiliar with the rough terrain. Moreover, they found the country people united against them, if not up in arms. The *rurales*, supposedly counter-insurgency specialists, were hamstrung by local opposition: at Santa Cruz, a major reported, the people of the pueblo 'refused to give me information, despite the fact that spies had been seen in the woods who assuredly came from that very village'; in fact, Santa Cruz, protected by deep *barrancas*, was the current headquarters of José Trinidad Ruiz, who could securely spend the night there with his men since the villagers were 'almost all armed and Zapatistas'.[396] In the wooded mountains around Ajusco, too, a tough-minded lieutenant-colonel recommended a purge of the authorities, since 'most of the villages are rotten (*gangrenados*) with Zapatista ideas, and bandits are living under the protection of the locals, which makes it extremely difficult to mount an effective campaign against them'.[397] Other commanders were beginning to think similarly impatient thoughts.

As Zapatista activity spread, the government resolved on tougher measures. In January 1912 Ambrosio Figueroa was sent to police Guerrero, martial law was declared in Morelos, Guerrero, Tlaxcala and parts of Puebla and Mexico state – a good indication of the extent of rebellion south of the capital. In the following month the frustrated Federal commander at Cuernavaca, repeatedly harassed by the forces of de la O, ordered the total destruction by fire and shell of de la O's village, Santa María; in which holocaust the rebel leader's young daughter died.[398] The experience of Santa María was soon to be generalised. For General Juvencio Robles was now appointed military commander in Morelos. Robles, a career soldier with experience of the Yaqui campaigns and of garrison service in Morelos during the political troubles of 1909, had a crude grasp of the situation: 'all Morelos', he told the press, '... is Zapatista and there's not a single inhabitant who doesn't believe in the false doctrines of the bandit Emiliano Zapata'; this, he believed, gave him *carte blanche* for a policy of thorough repression. Municipal presidents of doubtful loyalty were turfed out of office; suspects were shot without trial and hostages taken from the families of prominent rebels (Zapata's included); villagers were herded into 'concentration camps' supervised by the Army, after the policy of Valeriano Weyler in Cuba. With the 'civilian' population thus concentrated, Federal flying columns could scour the countryside, shooting at will; Madero further suggested that a swathe 200 metres wide be cut either side of the railway tracks, to flush the rebels out of the woods.[399] Free-fire zones and defoliation thus came to Morelos.

In pursuit of this policy, Nexpa, San Rafael, Ticuman and Los Hornos were burned; Villa de Ayala was partially destroyed; Coajumulco and Ocotepec, through which *arrieros* passed supplying the rebels, were raised to the ground. At the Zoquiac ranch, a 'haven of bandits' near Milpa Alta, where the inhabitants were known to aid the Zapatistas, the people were evicted from their dwellings and the latter – 'houses, huts and cabins' – were torn down. The victims were 'reconcentrated' at San Pablo Oxtotepec, where more arrests – of Zapatista shepherds – were made; yet still military observers noted 'a constant movement of muleteers carrying provisions into the woods'. And, less surprisingly, they reported that 'hostility against [our] forces is very marked and evident'.[400] Throughout, it was the villages and hamlets – the nuclei of the Zapatista movement – which bore the brunt; farmers, *arrieros*, shepherds were the victims. Some townspeople might show a sneaking sympathy with Zapata, but they stayed put and kept quiet, making 'fun of the professional soldiers behind their backs because they could never quite stamp out this guerrilla war'.[401] Gradually, respectable opinion in Morelos began to question the wisdom of such indiscriminate repression (though the Mexico City press – including the liberal *Diario del Hogar* – considered it a necessary unpleasantness).[402] The planters were caught in a bind. The army carefully refrained from attacks on plantation property, the peons' huts escaped the destruction that was visited upon village and ranch, but the peons themselves, who now began to follow the villagers into the conflict, received the same treatment – arbitrary arrests and summary executions in the old Porfirian style. And, try as they might, the army could not prevent the lush canefields from being turned into fields of battle.[403] On the other hand, the planters could hardly overlook the real threat which Zapatismo – especially the radicalised Zapatismo of 1912 – posed to their interests. There were frequent reminders of the agrarian issue which lay at the heart of the conflict: at the Hacienda San Pedro a corporal of the *rurales*, 'surprised twenty individuals working the fields and dividing them up among themselves without the order of the hacienda, for which they were arrested and put at the disposition of the Lieutenant-Colonel'.[404] The planters feared that, if the troubles continued Mexico would sink to 'a nation of the last order, a true Niggerdom'. But how to halt the troubles was another matter. General Robles offered a once-and-for-all solution, an application of the mythic 'iron hand'; he would serve as a local General Reyes. But repression – apart from its material consequences – was also a dangerous gamble, for it could radicalise and extend the rebellion; it was said of the people of Huitzilac, 'that they were not concerned with Zapata till the Federals came and burned their village' – and now they were keen Zapatistas.[405]

In the late spring, a combination of factors induced a new calm. A flurry of attacks against major towns had left the Zapatistas exhausted, low on ammunition, and without positive gains. They began to retreat to favoured havens in the mountains, to rest and regroup.[406] At the political level, voices of moderation began to overrule Robles, and fresh attempts at conciliation were made. Perhaps most important, the onset of the rains and the planting season encouraged quiescence: 'it was now the rainy season and time to plant, and many of the rebel soldiers went home to work in their fields'; and, no doubt, the political initiatives undertaken by old Governor Leyva and new Governor Naranjo benefited from the mood of pacificism which the rains instilled in all *morelenses*, from the planters down. In June, as the rains came, Robles was transferred out of the state, at least for the time being.[407]

For Madero and the central government there was an additional cogent reason for cutting their losses in Morelos in the spring of 1912: the rapid growth of the Orozco rebellion, which threatened to topple the regime itself. Orozco's influence was not confined to the north: as in 1910–11, his example encouraged rebellion elsewhere in the country and there could be little doubt that, just as continued Orozquista success would stimulate further revolts, so his rapid defeat would redound to the benefit of the regime nationally. That 'Pascual Orozco's victories [should] have given new life to the revolutionary movement' in northern states like Durango, which shared a common revolutionary history and personnel with Chihuahua, was no surprise; but the demonstration effect of Orozquismo went further. Zapata took heart from Orozco's success and hoped for material help from the north, as did the Zapatistas of Mexico state; rebels on the Isthmus called themselves Orozquistas and gave receipts for goods redeemable 'when Pascual Orozco is President'.[408] The outcome of the northern rebellion was eagerly awaited as far afield as

Tabasco, where further Orozquista victories were thought likely to encourage malcontents in what had hitherto been a fairly quiet region, and in parochial Oaxaca, where interest in national politics perked up with the possibility of the overthrow of the regime.[409] As in 1910–11, the fortunes of Mexico seemed to be centred on the 'storehouse of storms', Chihuahua.

THE REGIME'S RESPONSE

Here, once Orozco had declared for the rebellion in the first week of March, its progress was precipitate. In Chihuahua City, Juárez and elsewhere, public opinion was overwhelmingly for the rebels and against the government; the great majority of the ex-Maderista troops – numbering 3–4,000 and rising – had gone over to the revolution, and they confronted a Federal force numbering hundreds.[410] Only two pockets of irregular resistance remained: at Ojinaga, somewhat removed from the action, where Colonel José de la Cruz Sánchez caused surprise by resisting the Orozquista embrace, and at Parral, where Pancho Villa and 500 loyalists, backed by the local rebel hero Maclovio Herrera, stood alone against the swelling hosts of Orozco roundabout.[411] Villa's decision to stay loyal – which surprised some – had momentous consequences. It enabled him to emerge in later years as the pre-eminent Chihuahuan revolutionary, perhaps the greatest popular *caudillo* of the age. But, of course, Villa could not have known this; his decision, like so many, was an expedient response to immediate events. An old grudge (which antedated the fight at the gates of Chihuahua on 3 March) was said to lie between Villa and Orozco, and this was compounded by Villa's loyalty to his political mentor and 'close friend', Abraham González.[412] In part, therefore, his political loyalism was built upon the typical personal loyalism of the 'social bandit', which, for him, transcended class, ideological and other 'universal' allegiances. Clientelism ruled, and Villa's decision to support the government was an example less of shrewd political judgement than of a naive, personalist political ethic.

There was also an important – and typical – regional factor.[413] Villa was at Parral as the revolt gathered strength, it was to Parral he went when his opposition to Orozco was confirmed, and Parral was the last loyalist stronghold to fall to the rebels. Like Ojinaga to the north, Parral represented a locus of revolutionary support and activity distinct from the regions which generated Orozquismo – the classic *serrano* districts of Guerrero and Casas Grandes. Parral thus possessed its own network of anti-Díaz oppositionists, subversives and rebels; Villa, shortly before the revolution, had roamed and raided in this zone, supposedly with the connivance of oppositionist families like the Bacas, local *rancheros*, and one of this family (brother of a revolutionary pioneer who had died in November 1910) was said to enjoy a longstanding 'ascendancy' over Villa, which was exploited to secure his loyalty.[414] The Baca family were also old allies of Parral's most prominent rebel clan, the Herreras, and according to one (somewhat hagiographic) account, it was Maclovio Herrera who took the lead against Orozco (it will be remembered that he had received the mayoralty of the town), with Villa playing a dependent, even inglorious role.[415] Much to the benefit of his later career, it therefore seems, Villa was rather fortuitously co-opted for the regime, when most of his fellow-rebels of 1910 had turned against it.[416]

In the state capital, meanwhile, the rebels instituted martial law, and a tough, arbitrary but orderly regime. State bonds to the value of 1.2m. pesos were issued to finance the campaign (recruits were promised two pesos a day) and, when reluctance was shown in taking up this issue, forced loans were levied on the leading banks, manufacturers and merchants.[417] The military (or in some cases their appointees, like Enrile, who ran the loan assessment junta) controlled all political offices. Maderista supporters were arrested, Maderista newspapers closed or censored out of existence. Meanwhile, the Orozquista army was built up to honour Orozco's promise of a swift march on Mexico City. The offer of two pesos a day helped swell the army to some 8,000 in a few weeks; volunteers, it was said, had to be turned away. Since, though Orozco's cause was popular, the supply of arms and ammunition was deficient from the start, all private arms in Chihuahua were expropriated, mechanics were set to work manufacturing small, smooth-bore cannon, and Antonio Rojas busied himself crating up dynamite bombs, the ubiquitous, ersatz shells of northern guerrilla warfare.[418] Their control of several towns (and towns with some industrial capacity) gave the Orozquistas an advantage over the Zapatistas with regard to arms supply, but Orozco's army was bigger, more 'professional', and committed to open warfare, sometimes against entrenched garrisons of armoured trains; its military needs were therefore much greater than those of the *surianos*.

There remained the US – a close, abundant source of supply, if the Orozquistas could raise the cash. This, to an extent, they could do. But on 13 March a joint resolution of the American Congress empowered President Taft to cut off arms supplies to Mexico so long as 'conditions of domestic violence' obtained.[419] Only arms clearly destined for the constituted government would be allowed into Mexico. This decision (which, it should be noted, owed much to Lord Cowdray – so often depicted as a Porfirist ogre, bent on the defeat of Madero and the restoration of dictatorship) was a serious blow; and nothing Orozco did by way of despatching highly respectable agents to plead his case in Washington could alter it.[420] In response, the Orozquistas – who had so far shown no significant hostility to American interests – began to display those anti-American attitudes which some historians have mistakenly backdated to the inception, even the fundamental origin of the revolt.[421] Thereby, the Orozquistas conformed to a pattern which was repeated in later years with the Villistas: such movements were not inherently anti-American, but quite capable of anti-American statements and actions when US policy was construed as hostile. Revolutionary (as well as non-revolutionary) 'xenophobes' of this kind were made rather than born, and they were made by short term factors relating to US–Mexican relations, rather than by any grand process of social conditioning, foreign capitalist penetration, nationalist resentment and the like.[422]

In that the American decision to embargo arms to Orozco had important consequences, allegations of American 'interference' in the Revolution are morally legitimate, if historiographically rather futile. The US could not but 'interfere' one way or the other. A recognition of Orozquista belligerency – carrying with it a licence to import American arms – would also have constituted 'interference', and would have placed the northern rebels and the elected government on an equal footing. The fact is that in general, in 1912 as in 1910–11, the Taft administration adhered to a consistent, legalist line, observing the neutrality laws to the best of its ability, thereby favouring the central government (first Díaz, then Madero) at the expense of the rebels; not until 1913, with the onset of Woodrow Wilson, a fresh revolutionary confrontation in Mexico, and the diplomacy of the 'New Freedom', was this line abandoned. And while American policy told against Orozco in 1912, his failure cannot be premised on this single factor, for in 1910–11 and again in 1913–14 northern rebel movements proved that this obstacle could be overcome, if other domestic factors were advantageous. It was in Mexico, not in Washington or even on the border, that such civil wars were won and lost.

The American embargo would take effect over time. But at the outset the Orozquistas carried all before them. Within days of Orozco's defection Mexico City began to thrill to rumours of an impending attack from the north: able-bodied citizens came forward to defend the capital and a massive demonstration of pro-government supporters took to the streets pledging their allegiance and vilifying Orozco; the American Ambassador cabled a typically intemperate request to the State Department for a thousand rifles and million rounds to defend the embassy.[423] Distinguished members of the capital's elite met at the Casino Comercial to form a Committee for the Defence of the Constituted Government: representing Porfiristas and Maderistas, bankers, industrialists, *hacendados* and professionals, it indicated that Madero – for all his faults – was regarded more favourably than the rabble-rousing Pascual Orozco.[424] Meanwhile, the military response was swift. War Minister José González Salas – whose career to date had been largely confined to 'instructing swimming and swordsmanship at the Colegio Militar' – took leave from the Ministry to lead the northern campaign in person (it was said he had been goaded into this decision by the barbs of the opposition press).[425]

By mid-March González Salas had mobilised about 6,000 Federals at Torreón, and skirmishing had begun in the no-man's-land along the Chihuahua–Durango border. The Federal plan involved a three-prong advance, with the commander-in-chief leading the largest force along the Mexican Central Railway, which linked Torreón and the rebel headquarters at Jiménez. Traversing arid country, the main army reached Rellano, on the southern edge of the bleak and barren Bolsón de Mapimí – once a favourite haunt of Apache raiding parties. There on the afternoon of 23 March an Orozquista force of 800 under Emilio Campa surprised the Federals with devastating effect: a locomotive packed with explosives (*una máquina loca*, as such devices were called) was sent careering into the Federal vanguard, killing sixty outright, halting the advance, and sowing panic. The Federal reaction converted a setback into a defeat. González Salas, dismounting from the train, was badly wounded; soldiers of the 20th Battalion mutinied and shot two officers who tried to discipline them; the two Federal support columns under Aubert and Téllez failed to reach the scene before González Salas precipitately ordered a retreat to Torreón. En route, having contemplated the corpse of his chief-of-staff, slain by mutineers, the commander-in-chief took his own life.[426]

In purely military terms, the defeat was hardly disastrous, Federal casualties were about 300.[427] But the combination of ignominy and incompetence had a shattering effect on public opinion, despite the government's attempts to withhold or doctor the publication of news.[428] It was, after all, the first defeat of a Federal Army by rebels in open country during nearly three years of sporadic warfare. There was talk of the imminent fall of the government; both the American Ambassador and the Reyista ex-Governor of Coahuila, Miguel Cárdenas, anticipated such an outcome (Cárdenas was also scathing about González Salas: 'torpe en vida y torpe en muerte' was his obituary for the dead general – who nevertheless received a hero's funeral in Mexico City); at Saltillo, not far from the fighting, it was 'generally believed [that] the Federal cause [was] lost'.[429] General Aureliano Blanquet, who was also wounded in the action, echoed Cárdenas' criticism, though more philosophically: 'what could be expected?', he commented, 'we attacked in the German fashion and they fought us like Mexicans'.[430] Certainly Campa's tactics had been in the best tradition of Mexican guerrilla combat while the Federal debacle may be attributed – not to mimesis of Germany – but to the equally established Mexican tradition of forced military service, mutiny, and irresponsible officerdom. But the Federal Army was far from being a beaten force, indeed, the defeat at Rellano can be seen with hindsight as the beginning of a chain of events which was to augment the size and importance of the army beyond all precedent.

The Orozquistas' first task after Rellano was to mop up the remaining loyalist garrison at Parral. Here, Villa was running affairs much as Orozco ran the rest of Chihuahua: banks and business houses were mulcted (again, the Terrazas interests paid up, further complicating the question of their partisanship), and preparations were made to resist the inevitable Orozquista attack – which, when it came on the night of 1/2 April, was beaten off. But two days later the attackers returned in greater numbers (over 2,000 against Villa's 300) and Villa prudently withdrew. There followed 'the most dreadful night Parral has known' – a repeat, though less bloody, of the wild scenes witnessed after the fall of Torreón the previous year. Parral was thoroughly looted, first by the Orozquista troops, then by the city mob. Drink flowed freely, stubborn doors were blasted open, dynamite bombs were lobbed into patios. Though foreigners, who owned much of the town's business, suffered along with Mexican businessmen, the riot was not specifically xenophobic; in fact, many private Mexican residences were forcibly entered while 'with a few exceptions the houses of foreigners were not touched . . . [and] the General-in-Chief Inés Salazar . . . treated the Americans very well indeed'. The American owned and managed Parral and Durango Railroad, for example, suffered no damage and the workers (as was usually the case) stayed on the job, even after the shortage of banknotes compelled the company to institute payment in chits.[431]

Such an 'orgy of looting and dynamiting',[432] though exceptional, served to remind respectable people of the ever-present threat of mob action, which had been apparent during the revolutionary spring and summer of 1911 and which typically occurred immediately after the fall of a town, when victorious leaders – whether out of accident or design – encouraged instead of containing the mob's penchant for riot. Here, there was evidence of design. Parral had distinguished itself as a loyalist stronghold, its business houses had (under pressure) funded Villa's war chest, and 200 men of Emilio Campa's forces had died in the initial, abortive attack. When the Orozquistas entered, the manager of the town slaughterhouse and his brother, both 'very well-known Mexicans', were executed on the grounds that they were 'Villistas'. Some weight is thus added to the supposition that Parral represented a network of revolutionary clientelism separate from and hostile to that upon which Orozquismo was based.[433] Faced with overwhelming odds, Villa had headed south to the Laguna where, at Bermejillo, he met up with General Aubert's Federals, who had skilfully extricated themselves from trouble after Rellano.[434] But with the suicide of González Salas the Division of the North had no commander-in-chief, and this Madero soon remedied with the appointment of General Victoriano Huerta, who had led the Federals in their assault on Morelos in the summer of 1911. Now he was entrusted with an even more important assignment, possessed of better prospects of definitive success and advancement, as well as serious political implications. For in Huerta some now discerned the 'iron hand' which would end rebellion and institute a new Porfirian peace. And Huerta was particularly well suited to play this part and to pander to these hopes.

General Huerta was then in his late fifties, a stocky, bullet-headed individual, whose customary ill-humoured frown owed as much to bad eyesight as to a stern disposition.[435] The son of a mestizo *campesino* and a Huichol Indian mother (which, for some, explained both his stoic virtues and brutal vices) Huerta had joined the army at the age of fourteen, offering his services as secretary (he had acquired a basic literacy at a country school) to General Donato Guerra, as a military convoy passed through Colotlán (Jal.). With Guerra acting as his patron, Huerta graduated from the Military Academy and entered the Corps of Engineers. For thirty years his career progressed according to the familiar, unspectacular pattern of Porfirian professional soldiers: in Huerta's case, campaigns of internal repression interspersed with surveying and cartographical assignments; the reduction to neatness and order of the wild country and the wild people of Mexico. After an initial campaign in Tepic (1879), Huerta put down the rebellion of Canuto Neri in Guerrero (1893), participated in the endless war against the Yaqui (1900), returned to Guerrero to quell the revolt of Rafael del Castillo Calderón (1901) and waged his last pre-revolutionary campaign against the troublesome Maya of Yucatán (1901). Repeated experiences of repression – generally successful – seem to have reinforced Huerta's bloody and authoritarian streak.[436] At Mezcala (Gro, 1893) he showed a fondness for summary executions, even while an amnesty was in force; his campaign around Mochitlán (Gro, 1901) was marked by arbitrary shootings, deportations and liberal use of the *leva*.[437] If ruthless and contemptuous of criticism, Huerta was certainly brave, efficient, and tactically competent, all his campaigns (save the Yaqui war) met with success; the 'iron hand' was shown to work. Meanwhile, he acquired some useful contacts: with Reyes as early as 1879; with General Angel García Peña in the 1880s; with his 'sinister acquaintances', Dr Aureliano Urrutia, later his personal physician and Minister of Gobernación, during the campaigns in Guerrero.[438] In the early 1900s Huerta was drawn into the Reyista camp, supporting Don Bernardo against Limantour and the Científicos; when Díaz forced Reyes out of the War Ministry and back to Nuevo León in 1904 it is said that Huerta urged his *patrón* to mount a coup d'état.[439] But Reyes refused, and, as the Reyista star went into decline, Huerta's career seemed to enter its twilight. In 1907 he took leave of absence to work on engineering contracts at Monterrey (where Reyes' friendship counted); two years later, when Reyes left for Europe, Huerta set up in Mexico City, supporting his family on an army pension, supplemented by part-time teaching. A bland, sedentary retirement stretched before him, and the talent and ambition which had once marked him out – so it had seemed – for the Under-Secretaryship of War now suffered frustration.[440] Meanwhile, whether in retirement or on earlier, thirsty route marches through Guerrero or Yucatán, Huerta had developed a pronounced taste for hard liquor.

The Revolution changed all this (save the taste for hard liquor). In April 1911, as the Díaz regime tottered, Huerta was pulled out of retirement and appointed military commander in Guerrero, where he had gathered his bloody laurels in the past. But now the old repressive machine was seizing up, General Huerta received only 6% of his promised troops, and these had got no further than Cuernavaca when Díaz resigned; Huerta's chief role in 1910–11, therefore, was that of escorting the deposed dictator to Veracruz where (according to one dubious account) Díaz commented 'there is the man who will be able to control my people'.[441] Certainly, the Revolution brought a return to active service and swift preferment. De la Barra despatched Huerta to Morelos, where his single-minded pursuit of a military solution irritated Madero and drove Zapata to outright rebellion; since, in addition, Huerta's Reyista sympathies were well known, it was no surprise when Madero removed him from active service, and the bad relations between the two became a matter of public knowledge and discussion.[442] Now, five months later, at a moment of national crisis, the cabinet and the new War Minister, García Peña (one of Huerta's old cronies), prevailed upon the president to entrust the vital northern command to Huerta, despite Madero's own misgivings.[443]

Establishing his headquarters at Torreón, Huerta planned his campaign methodically, even ponderously. The army he inherited was a conglomerate: the Federal troops of Aubert, Téllez and Rábago, mauled at Rellano; irregular companies under the Madero brothers, Raul and Emilio; and Pancho Villa's forces, fresh from Parral, whose presence and reputation alarmed the citizens of Torreón. Morale was low, and many were ill-equipped and ill-trained.[444] In April, a wave of typhoid swept through the garrison, and mutinous tendencies surfaced again when 400 irregulars declared they would not fight against the Orozquistas – their caution or cowardice no doubt influenced by a reluctance to oppose their fellow-revolutionaries of 1910–11. Mistrustful of these irregular corps, Huerta reorganised the command structure of the army (meticulous organisation of tactics, logistics, even the minutiae of military equipment was one of Huerta's characteristics); he built up his artillery train, and used convict labour to dig new defences around Torreón; finally, in mid-May, he sallied forth, leading his troops north along the railway, bound for the site of González Salas' ignominious defeat of two months earlier.[445] Huerta's apparent procrastination – which some observers criticised – suggested a sound grasp of the situation. As the campaigns of 1914 were to reveal, Torreón was the strategic key to northern Mexico, through which any Chihuahuan army would have to pass on its way to Mexico City. Dug in here, with their superior artillery, the Federals could not be dislodged. Orozco, it was correctly predicted, would not risk his army against Torreón; the Sierra Madre barred expansion to the west; so, if the rebels were to maintain momentum now that all Chihuahua lay in their grasp (and this, for both military and political reasons, was vital) a move to the east, into Coahuila, was the only remaining option.[446]

So José Inés Salazar was sent into Coahuila, where he could count on limited support from local dissidents, some in the Burro mountains to the north, some in the southern marches of the state, Gertrudis Sánchez's old stamping ground.[447] This campaign, though a sideshow, revealed some interesting alignments in the present conflict and also established some reputations and relationships which were of importance for the future. In the face of Orozquista aggression, the Coahuilan state government drummed up volunteers; those ex-rebels of 1911 who had remained in service (like the 100 commanded by Eulalio Gutiérrez at Concepción del Oro) were now supplemented by hurriedly recruited irregulars, over 400 of whom were drilling in Saltillo by mid-April.[448] As usual, such irregulars proved unreliable, especially when they confronted forces of similar extraction, like the Orozquistas; 400 ordered to hold the Puerto del Carmen against Salazar refused and were arrested.[449] The payment of such state forces also became the subject of acrimonious dispute between state and Federation, governor and president (of which more anon).[450] In response to the Orozquista invasion, and the regime's appeal for support, some old Porfiristas prevaricated, but some – their dislike of Madero and Carranza overcome by their fear of Orozquista radicalism and rapine – rallied to the cause.[451] Alberto Guajardo, for example, one-time Porfirian *jefe*, and a major beneficiary of the dispossession of the Kikapoo Indians, captained a force of irregulars and proved one of the most successful of counter-insurgency commanders, as a result of which he received back his *jefatura*.[452] At the other extreme, the rural poor do not seem to have responded: at best indifferent to the regime, they may even have felt a certain sympathy with Orozquismo. Certainly the story of the Federal patrol which returned from the Burro mountains with five 'rebel' prisoners who 'declare[d] that they are farm labourers only' is reminiscent of Morelos.[453]

Hence the main burden of resistance fell upon the Maderista civilians, their clients, and loyalist irregulars. Madero's brothers, Raul and Emilio, undertook to combat Orozquismo in the Laguna, along with their close relative and friend Eugenio Aguirre Benavides; Governor Carranza hastened back from Mexico City and placed his brother, Jesús, in charge of the volunteers destined for Monclova; Captain Lorenzo Aguilar, of the Monterrey volunteers, executed by the rebels at Pedriceña, came from 'one of the best families in the republic' and was a first cousin of the President.[454] The civilian Maderistas – the respectable, propertied liberals of 1908–10 – were perforce having to overcome their distaste for organised violence and popular mobilisation. And, as they sought to defend the regime, their property, and their new political power, they established a certain identity of interest – not with the peasantry – but with the urban workers. The 2,000 demonstrators who protested their support for the government on the streets of Saltillo were middle-class or industrial workers: 'neither the wealthier class nor the peons participated. It was evident that the participants were those who would be most seriously affected in case of a continuance of the internal disturbances.'[455] In 1910–11 the coal mines of Coahuila had remained quiet, relatively untouched by revolution; now, in 1912, small contingents of miners were recruited into the Coahuilan state forces to fight against Orozco.[456] The congruence of interest between urban workers and middle class – a congruence part economic, part ideological – was thus displayed, even if it was as yet only dimly discerned and tentatively exploited by the respective parties.

But the Maderista civilians, however adept they were at demonstrating, propagandising and administering, were still indifferent performers when it came to insurgency – or, in this case, counter-insurgency. The Orozquista advance was therefore swift. The Coahuilan irregulars of Pablo González, Governor Carranza's chief lieutenant, were defeated by Salazar's rebel force in the first of many battles that González was to lose, as he established his reputation as 'the general who never won a victory'.[457] Cuatro Ciénegas, Carranza's home town, fell, Saltillo seemed threatened, and only the timely arrival of Trucy Aubert's Federals saved Monclova.[458] But now, in May, the Orozquista impetus was fading. The ammunition shortage was chronic; Orozco was making an 'all-out effort' to lure Federal troops into the rebellion, in order to secure their weapons; Marcelino Villareal was sent to Sonora to recruit and smuggle all he could across the Arizona border.[459] Political divisions were also apparent within the heterogeneous Orozquista coalition. Emilio Vázquez Gómez crossed from the US to claim his presidential inheritance and was sent packing, further evidence, some said, of mounting 'Científico' influence within the movement, deployed against the more doctrinaire radicals.[460]

Huerta's delay at Torreón thus served his interest, for, as he began to inch his way north, the rebels found themselves in a dilemma – needing a victory to maintain momentum, yet ill-prepared to face the Federals and their wily commander in open battle. On the plains of Conejos on 12 May, the Orozquistas suffered an initial defeat and pulled back to Escalón; ten days later a second, major engagement was fought at Rellano (scene of Orozquismo's greatest victory), where through afternoon and evening the superior Federal artillery pounded the Orozquistas into a shambles. Two hundred rebels were killed, and more wounded; horses and guns were lost; morale was shattered.[461] After a brief pause, Huerta resumed his inexorable progress north, repairing the bridges and track destroyed by the retreating rebels. The latter were now short of pay as well as ammunition, and 'disintegration' had begun.[462] Bands of Orozquistas deserted and drifted home to the western Chihuahuan villages whence they had come. Enrile, Orozco's financial agent, fled to El Paso, narrowly escaping an attempt on his life.[463] Orozco himself decided to turn and fight at Bachimba canyon, relying on a tactical variant of Campa's *máquina loca*: the railway track was mined with 100 lb. of dynamite at Consuelo, seven miles south of the Orozquista position, but the mine failed, destroying only one Federal coal car, and when battle was joined the result was a total rebel defeat.[464] By the end of May, with the civil government of Abraham González restored in Chihuahua City, Huerta was able to return to a relieved Mexico City, there to receive a hero's welcome and the rank of divisional general.[465]

As an organised political movement and a serious threat to the Madero government, Orozquismo was finished. But popular movements of this kind often flourished in defeat, just as they wilted in victory. They shook off political parasites; they renounced the shimmering mirage of national power; they drew in on themselves, renewing contact with the *patria chica* and their own local supporters and abandoned conventional campaigns for the more congenial business of rural guerrilla warfare. And, by the same token, the Federals lost the advantage which pitched battles conferred and again sank into the morass of counter-insurgency operations. Thus Orozquismo (like Villismo four years later) experienced a kind of lusty second childhood in the wake of defeat; symbolic of the transformation was the flight of Enrile, and the resumption of his old duties as Orozco's 'general factotum' by José Córdova, one-time country store clerk and village intellectual.[466] Meanwhile, the prevailing drift of men and leaders was westwards, into the mountains, where resistance was feasible and the fearsome Federal artillery could not penetrate; 'everything', an observer commented, 'points to guerrilla warfare in western Chihuahua'.[467] But the Orozquista diaspora went wider. Orozco himself, outrunning Federal pursuit, arrived at Juárez, headed east along the Rio Grande (possibly taking Cuchillo Parado and Ojinaga) and finally sought sanctuary in the US.[468] Argumedo, likewise evading capture, resumed his activities on the Durango/Zacatecas borders, as did Cheche Campos in the Laguna; Caraveo, still leading several hundred men, marched into Coahuila and harried Federal forces in the cattle country west of Múzquiz.[469]

But the largest fraction of the dissolved coalition – Campa, Salazar, Rojas and others – threaded their way through the Sierra Madre towards Sonora; a path which the *serranos* of Chihuahua took almost instinctively, in 1910, now in 1912, and later in 1915–16. This time, they had reasons to expect a welcome. Sonora – as already mentioned – had produced no indigenous variant of Orozquismo; the rebellious protests of disillusioned veterans had been few, feeble, and easily contained by the new state administration.[470] On the other hand, the deposed Porfirian elite (headed by Miguel Mascareñas, a landowner, banker and now political exile in Arizona, whose backers were said to include ex-Governors Torres and Cubillas, as well as several ex-Porfirian officials and editors – in short, 'the former "Científico" element of Sonora') now sought to co-opt the defeated rebels of Chihuahua, much as the Terracista elite had tried at the outset of the rebellion. Mascareñas assured Campa and Salazar that Sonora would welcome them as deliverers from the Maderista yoke. And Mascareñas' son (also Miguel) joined the Orozquista leaders as they crossed their homeland around Casas Grandes (where their maltreatment of the Mormon colonists initiated the great exodus back to the north) and penetrated the high passes of Bavispe and Dolores (passes which in winter would have been severe obstacles and which, even in summer, as an American asserted, perhaps with thoughts of Thermopylae uppermost in his mind, a mere hundred could hold against an army of 5,000).[471] But the Sonorans did not try to emulate the Spartans. For one thing, the Sonoran administration was jolted by the sudden death, from appendicitis, of the energetic vice-governor, Eugenio Gayou, whom some had seen as the 'mainstay' of the local regime.[472] In addition, the Sonoran state forces sent east into the mountains had little stomach for an alpine conflict, and thus the Orozquistas, emerging from familiar territory, were able to slip down from the mountains in small groups, largely unresisted. By August 1912 some two to three thousand were in Sonora, threatening key points: Alamos, Nacozari, Ures and Agua Prieta.[473]

But now the territorial imperative came into play. Faced with the Orozquista invasion from without (as well as Yaqui troubles from within), the state administration had encouraged the formation of local defence forces – a traditional feature of northern, frontier society.[474] But in addition it had also established a full-time, salaried volunteer force, a 'small army' of over 2,700 men, distinct from the Federals and at the orders of the Hermosillo government; among them was the 4th irregular battalion, recruited and led by the new mayor of Huatabampo, Alvaro Obregón.[475] Now, as the Orozquistas descended from the mountains, the government could appeal to the people's 'deep-rooted provincial disposition to fight only in their own backyard [*gallinero*], in order to defend their own village and the families of the combatants'.[476] Mascareñas' promises of welcome therefore proved hollow; in contrast to the situation in Chihuahua, an observer noted, 'the [Sonoran] government has [the great advantage] . . . that the people are loyal and the rebels get no recruits or very few'.[477] So the Orozquistas faced stiff resistance – proof that *serrano* rebellion was not exportable. Luis Fernández (alias Blas Orpinel) was repulsed by a local force at Alamos, Emilio Campa was similarly driven from Ures. The Orozquistas, finding they were mounting an invasion of hostile country, not conducting a popular guerrilla war, resorted to intimidation.[478] Rapidly, the offensive fragmented: Fernández headed for Sinaloa and further defeat; Campa, with his back to the torrid Altar desert, preferred to cross to the US; Salazar and Rojas were decisively beaten by Sonoran forces at the battle of San Joaquín on 20 September. By the autumn, therefore, the Orozquista threat had been conjured; Sonora was safe, and the state forces – particularly their young cavalry commander, Obregón – had collected the first of what were to be many laurels.[479]

Though defeated, Orozquismo was not entirely defunct. Remnants of the rebel army were scattered through the Chihuahua sierra where, around the turn of 1912–13, there was a noticeable recrudescence of guerrilla activity.[480] And most of the Orozquista leaders (and, one assumes, some of the rank-and-file) lived to fight again. Yet, even if they had never come back, their influence on the course of the Revolution had already been marked. They had thrown up the biggest challenge to the regime, epitomising the resentments of the 'betrayed' Maderista veterans, and exemplifying *serrano* readiness to ally with dubious, conservative allies. In doing so, they were militarily defeated, but they contributed mightily to the wreck of the Madero regime. For all armed opposition undermined the liberal basis of the government, forcing it to adopt neo-Porfirian repressive practices. In particular, the Orozquistas obliged Madero to drain the treasury, to expand the army, and to promote Victoriano Huerta to a dangerously exalted position. Under the pressure of the Orozco rebellion, Madero doubled the military payroll; this, in turn, necessitated a twenty million peso loan, which excited fierce debate in Congress, while filling the army required extensive use of the *leva*, an abuse which Madero had vociferously condemned.[481] Most important, the defeat of Orozco brought with it a politicisation of the army, and a militarisation of politics. The crushing of rebellion implied both phases of outright military rule (as in Sinaloa) or serious civil–military friction (as in Coahuila).

Friction of this kind was now evident at the highest level. Before accepting the northern command Huerta requested (and got) an assurance from the president that he would be given a free hand and would suffer no civilian interference (as he believed he had suffered in Morelos); in this, Huerta received 'the applause of the entire army'.[482] But Madero took a close, if amateurish, interest in the campaign, he chivvied Huerta for his supposed failure to hunt down the defeated Orozquistas, and his recommendations were construed by Huerta as civilian meddling, of the kind Madero had at the outset renounced.[483] Petty incidents aggravated the relationship. Madero counter-manded General Blanquet's order banning *soldaderas* (camp-followers) on the campaign, he corresponded with junior officers, criticising their seniors, and, in one famous case, Madero's brother intervened to prevent the execution of Pancho Villa, whom Huerta proposed to have shot for allegedly robbing civilians. All these incidents contained a common factor: the uneasy – or downright hostile – relations between Huerta's Federals and their recent revolutionary opponents, the Maderista irregulars. The latter were the prob-able victims of Blanquet's ban; Madero's correspondents were irregular officers like Luis Garfías, sent by the president to organise Coahuilan volunteer forces; and Villa, of course, was the leading revolutionary loyalist in Chihuahua.[484] These irregulars were often undisciplined and intractable (as befitted their popular, revolutionary origins); Huerta wanted to see them licked into shape and made obedient to his orders, as his ingrained military instinct required, rather than to the whim of wayward individual *jefes*; possibly he favoured their disbandment – or annihilation – altogether. Thus Madero's defence of the irregulars soured relations further, and when a Mexico City well-wisher sent Huerta a shipment of Madero lapel buttons, the general had them consigned to a rubbish bin.

On the other hand, Madero's impatience with Federal inactivity was in part justified. After their victory at Bachimba, an American observer, Federal cavalry officers watched through field-glasses as the Orozquistas straggled north, at the mercy of Federal pursuit. But the Federals did not stir: first, the same observer went on, because they showed a contemptuous disregard for Madero, second (an explanation more revealing of the observer's mentality than the army's) because 'the army itself . . . only typifies the weak efficiency of the race as a whole'.[485] The validity of the first explanation, however, soon became clear, indeed, a senior officer readily admitted that 'the Army had no love nor patience with the new regime . . . [and] General Huerta shared this attitude completely'.[486] Hence, the Army's performance was 'entirely perfunctory' and most of the mopping-up operations had to be conducted by the irregular volunteers, who displayed the necessary mobility and enthusiasm for such a task: José de la Luz Blanco in Chihuahua, Cándido Aguilar and Cesareo Castro in the Laguna.[487] By their efforts (which contrasted with what even a Federal general admitted was the 'apathy' of his fellow-officers) they naturally won Madero's applause, and, even after Orozco's definitive defeat, they remained a significant operational group, loyal to the regime, and capable of reacting to new developments and challenges. Irregular commanders like Aguilar, Castro, González and Obregón, would later play decisive roles in the unfolding Revolution.[488]

Some put a more sinister construction on the inactivity of the Federals: it indicated not just lukewarm feelings about the Madero regime, but positively treasonable thoughts, prompted by the new-found importance of the army. If they were to be the defenders of order and government, why not order and government of a congenial, conservative kind – a revived Porfiriato – rather than the sloppy, ambivalent liberalism of Madero? So the argument ran, and both its premise (the growing importance of the army) and its conclusion (that the army should have a direct political say) were plausible. There could be no doubt, Letcher wrote from Chihuahua,[489]

that the Army has a realising sense of its own importance as the sole element which stood between the Government and disintegration during the [Orozco] Revolution, and it is not unthinkable that it may wish to demand power in the country commensurate with the importance of the part it has played.

Certainly Huerta, as military commander in Chihuahua, added his political counsels to the debate over the policy to be adopted towards the defeated Orozquistas, opposing Governor González' hard-line policy, and advocating a form of clemency which was uncharacteristic, and suggestive of ulterior motives.[490] The dilatory pursuit, and now the advocacy of clemency, seemed to point to an understanding between Huerta and the rebels: perhaps an explicit deal, arranged through the Orozquista prisoner-of-war, David de la Fuente; alternatively, an implicit agreement, whereby Huerta acted 'so as to antagonise as little as possible the elements behind the revolution and thus prepare the way for winning their support to (himself)'.[491]

Rumour went further in attributing to Huerta a burning personal ambition to achieve the presidency (to which end he now angled for Orozquista sympathy). García Peña who, as Minister of War, had been instrumental in securing the northern command for Huerta, later claimed to have warned his protégé that he would have him shot 'if, when you get to the top of the army hierarchy, that crazy idea you've had since boyhood of being president should make you default on your duties'.[492] In this light, Huerta's vendetta against the Maderista irregulars was designed to remove them from the scene, prior to the removal of their patron and president Madero, hence the attempted execution of Villa and the decimation of the forces of Toribio Ortega at Bachimba – a 'mistake' which served Huerta's Machiavellian ends.[493] Such stories may have been concocted with hindsight. But even hindsight would not have suggested such infamies, had not Huerta soon proved that he was quite capable of committing them.[494]

In defeat as well as victory, therefore, the Orozco rebellion promoted the fortunes of the Federal Army in general, and of Victoriano Huerta in particular. But meanwhile, Orozco's defeat – like his earlier successes – had a multiplier effect throughout Mexico. The news of (second) Rellano had an impact far afield: in Sinaloa, in Mexico City, in Tabasco and Oaxaca; the regime now seemed safe, its opponents were disconcerted.[495] In Morelos, too, the news conspired with the planting season to produce a lull in the fighting, which gave the state's political moderates a last chance to seek a peaceful solution to local conflicts. In May local elections brought 'a fairly uniform crew of reformers' into the state legislature; in June General Robles was transferred from Morelos. The new state deputies were classic civilian Maderistas (or, in this case, Leyvistas), respectable, urban, middle-class people, chary of political violence; 'men of local standing, city folk [who] . . . owned no farms, managed no plantations . . . none [of whom] had taken an active part in the Maderista revolution'.[496] In the short time allowed them, these earnest reformers sought to translate their liberal creed into practical measures: they favoured direct elections and the abolition of the *jefaturas*; they passed tax reforms in the interests of small proprietors, urban and rural; they tried to boost the power of legislature against the executive, and to ensure that the latter was held by a local man.[497] A similar, classic liberal reformism was evident in their approach to the agrarian problem. They approved a 10% increase in hacienda taxes and the establishment of a state college of agriculture; one deputy proposed bringing hacienda markets into the public domain, which would 'redound to . . . the benefit of free trade' (a typical middle-class, commercial rejection of hacienda autarky).[498] Education, fiscal reform, and free trade were the mechanisms with which the Morelos liberals (like liberals elsewhere) would tackle the agrarian question. Expropriation, land distribution and *ejidal* conservation did not figure.

The contrast with the Plan of Ayala is manifest. Yet even this display of moderation and good will was enough (granted the rains, the defeat of Orozco and the removal of Robles) to instill a distinct political calm; an indication, it must be recognised, of the equivalent moderation of popular demands, the continued overlap of these with liberal reforms (for example, the abolition of the *jefaturas*) and the sheer aversion to fighting which the *surianos* – for all their lurid image – quite reasonably entertained. Though sporadic fighting continued, conciliatory appeals to the rebels had some effect. Zapatista recruitment fell away, Zapatista leaders felt it prudent to move out of Morelos, Zapata and de la O, reminiscing two years later, recalled this as the time when their confidence had been at its lowest ebb.[499] Thus, popular support for the cause – fierce and sustained during periods of heavy-handed repression – faltered during Morelos' brief interlude of reformism, an indication that Maderista liberalism had not yet squandered all its moral capital, that it retained some room for manoeuvre, some capacity for government. But the interlude was all too brief. A new state legislature, which took office in September 1912, was composed of different men, 'distinctly more conservative than their predecessors'.[500] They talked out or voted down the reform proposals hung over from the previous session, and seemed more concerned to deliver the *coup de grâce* to a declining Zapatismo. Hence, in the latter part of the year (the trend can be seen from October onwards) Zapatista fortunes rose again, and by the end of 1912 Morelos again constituted a major headache for the government.[501] Whether the Maderista liberals, given world enough and time, could have brought peace to Morelos is difficult to say; Womack does not rule out the possibility. But the fact is that the potential of the liberal, reformist policy was never fully explored; reform and conciliation were attempted but briefly and tentatively (though, it should be stressed, with some success), before being abandoned in favour of repression. The regime's response to popular rebellion – locally and nationally – thus implied a derogation of liberal principle, and a revival of both Porfirian methods and Porfirian interests. And if in some contexts (like Sinaloa) this produced a temporary Roman peace, in others (like Morelos) it further provoked and radicalised rebellion.

AGRARIAN PROTEST

The major rebellions which confronted the de la Barra and Madero administrations thus revealed a common feature: the central importance of ex-Maderista popular leaders and forces who turned against the regime they had helped create in 1910–11, and whose protest – be it *agrarista* or *serrano* – derived from those basic grievances which the Porfirian regime had suicidally stimulated. In this respect it was Madero and his government, not the popular rebels, who were the real 'counter-revolutionaries'. And it is wrong to lump these rebels – Zapata, Orozco, Navarro, Banderas, Contreras – along with the frankly conservative opponents of the regime (such as Reyes or Félix Díaz), whose revolts drew on Porfirian inspiration, counted on elite support, and failed to mobilise a genuine mass following.[502] It is also wrong to play down the importance of these rebellions. 'No warning . . . is necessary', Peter Calvert writes, 'against viewing [the internal history of the Madero administration] solely as a series of abortive revolts.'[503] Of course not; no-one would go that far. But if Calvert's statement is not to be taken literally (in which case it would be phatic), it must be suggestive, but wrong. For rebellion was the key factor which determined the character of the period, which exemplified the character of both the regime and the continuing social revolution, and which fundamentally affected the outcome of Madero's liberal experiment. But perhaps for 'rebellion' one should substitute 'popular protest': for, if the revolts mentioned so far posed the biggest military threat to the regime, they only represented the more advanced, organised and formal challenges; and behind them were a host of lesser movements, obscure, confused, inarticulate, which cumulatively worried the Madero regime into policies of clumsy repression (policies which belied its liberal *raison d'être* and which, by provoking a conservative reaction, indirectly led to its downfall).

These lesser movements varied greatly. They might be categorised by their size and significance, by the organisational form they assumed (organised rebellion, jacquerie, social banditry), or by the factors which stimulated them (agrarian dispossession, political impositions, regional rivalry). It is also possible to distinguish between movements obeying the pristine objectives of the 1910 revolution, and those reacting to events arising out of the Revolution (a distinction which will be shortly clarified). Finally, such movements may be analysed either individually and seriatim, or by means of generalisations drawn from different cases in different localities. The first approach, useful for a discussion of the major, organised rebellions (Zapata's, Orozco's) must now give way to the second, and the generalisations will be grouped under three headings – agrarian protest, banditry, and the second wave of *serranos*.

In one of the best images of the Mexican Revolution that has been put to paper, Tannenbaum likened it to 'a series of waves having more or less independent beginnings and independent objectives', sometimes fusing, sometimes separating, occasionally changing direction, constantly interacting with others, vanishing and then reappearing.[504] The aptness of this image should now become apparent. 1910–11 had witnessed a major outburst of popular mobilisation and protest (more profound and extensive than many accounts suggest); subsequent attempts to curtail this met with only modest success, and sometimes aggravated the very condition they were meant to correct; hence the plethora of 'neo-Maderista' rebellions already mentioned. But meantime, new movements got under way. Some were late starters: movements obeying the same causes as the pioneer rebellions of 1910–11, but which had been initially arrested for want of organisation, or because surveillance and repression were too tight; their development, in the course of 1911–12, indicated the continuing vitality of the popular movement. In addition, the 'logic of the Revolution' provoked new rebellious responses: the imposition of new officials goads a hitherto peaceful community to revolt; the relaxation of authority prompts families to renew feuds, bandits to step up their activities, peons to challenge the authority of the hacienda, *serranos* to plunder the plains; while official attempts at repression (notably by requiring mass conscription) provoke popular protest where hitherto it had been absent. Rebellions of this nature should not be dismissed as 'meaningless and useless' (which probably suggests that historians cannot fathom their meaning, rather than that they have none).[505] Nor should they be neglected on the grounds that they were not integral to 'the Revolution': for this presupposes an idea of 'the Revolution' as a clearly defined, consistent entity, as a kind of club, with approved, paid-up members inside, and blackballed cads outside. Rather, it was a complex, collective experience, to which many groups contributed in different ways and for different reasons. It therefore deserves a catholic analysis, which neither prejudges the issues, nor privileges certain groups at the expense of others.

The most significant popular agrarian revolt which fell outside the ambit of conventional politics – that is, which repudiated the nation state and its associated formal ideologies, lacked articulate plans or leaders and was readily identified as an apolitical caste war – was the Yaqui rebellion in Sonora. Sonora had experienced a real degree of political renovation as a result of the revolution, the demobilisation of its Maderista forces had proceeded relatively smoothly (lubricated, no doubt, by the high wages prevailing in the region) and there seemed to be a general desire for peace and work.[506] Further evidence of Sonoran stability and efficiency came with the defeat of the Orozquista invaders in 1912. The one blot on this peaceful political landscape was the Yaqui tribe. As in the past, they had been drawn into the white man's quarrel, some had fought for Díaz's Federals, some for Madero's rebels; now, the quarrel concluded, some remained in government employ (notably the forces of Luis Buli, veterans of such service) while others were promptly mustered out.[507] Like other rebels, the Yaquis demanded the price of their participation: 'the Yaquis claim that Madero offered them all the lands on the Yaqui River for their services and that they are going to have them and all Mexicans and Americans would have to leave'.[508] The old cry 'río libre y fuera blancos' thus acquired a new legitimacy, conferred by Madero himself.[509] In the summer of 1911 attempts to disarm Yaqui contingents provoked resistance; up to 1,000 Yaquis were said to be roaming the river valley, molesting *mestizo* towns (once the site of Yaqui communities) like Bacum and Cocorit. Cattle were being rustled, reports of a muleteer robbed or a hacienda raided generated panic and demands for troops; even the Yaqui peons on the Sonoran estates were infected with subversive ideas.[510]

The government resorted to the usual ambiguous policy of combined repression and conciliation, the first more sincerely prosecuted (Governor Maytorena, as he admitted himself, hoped to string along the Yaquis with

talks, prior to undertaking full-scale repression when the time was ripe).[511]
And in this he had the support of the Sonoran press, landowners and public
opinion generally.[512] The talks began; a delegation of Yaqui chiefs went to
Mexico City; Maderista spokesmen promised to repatriate 500 Yaqui deportees
from Quintana Roo and undertake a settlement of the land question.[513] But,
like the Zapatistas, the Yaquis saw no swift improvement, and the fighting
grew worse. The insurgents rustled and raided, the government sent additional
troops, *rurales* and Pima Indian recruits into the valley, and a regular guerrilla
war ensued.[514] In an otherwise peaceful, prosperous state (which the Sonorans
gratefully compared with the chaos reigning in neighbouring Sinaloa) the
Yaquis represented the one serious problem — a problem 'of much greater
importance than any that may arise from politics', and one that was no more
manageable for being familiar. It was, as one Sonoran put it, 'the rock where so
many come to grief . . . the great problem of Sonora and of the country'.[515]

The peace talks continued into the new year and finally collapsed in April.
By then the campaigns had assumed their old, familiar pattern. Despite their
numbers, the Federal forces failed to achieve sure control of the river valley: the
Yaquis (*broncos* and *mansos* together) were so numerous and dispersed that
rebels could easily melt into the population, so that it was 'impossible to tell
the bad ones from the good'. When pursued, the Yaquis hid their arms in the
countryside and took refuge in the towns, where work was usually available, or
they made for the sierra, where chiefs like Luis Espinosa could gather war
parties of 1,000 men, and where Federal operations were hampered by rough
country, an adverse climate (many of the Federals would have been lowland
conscripts) and poor logistics, not unconnected to the graft and peculation
prevalent among the Federal officers.[516] Thus for much of the summer the
initiative lay with the Yaquis and, as the authorities diverted troops to meet the
Orozquista threat, so the Indians established control over a chunk of territory
where the government's writ no longer ran and where the Yaquis 'do just as
they please'.[517] There were also fears — exaggerated but not altogether
groundless — that the Yaquis were in collusion with the Orozquistas; Orozquista (and 'Científico') agents were said to be bidding for Yaqui support in
return for the usual commitment 'to restore to them all their lands'; a proclamation 'on behalf of the Yaqui revolutionaries', embodying Zapata's Plan of
Ayala, circulated in the state, causing consternation.[518] But, like the feared
Yaqui–Magonista alliance of 1911, this came to nothing. After the manner of
other *agrarista* rebels, the Yaquis were single-minded in their objectives and
realistic in their appraisal of the situation. They would exploit circumstances,
support and then spurn allies, assume and discard superficial political labels.
Espinosa might style himself an Orozquista chief (as others had styled themselves Maderistas, and would later become Maytorenistas) but when the Orozquista push into Sonora was halted, it had little effect on the Yaquis, who
continued their local campaign with no less energy or success.[519]

In September – with Orozquismo a spent force – the Yaquis were daily raiding pueblos and haciendas in the valley, reaching even to the outskirts of the railway junction of Empalme, where they looted a Chinese store and killed a couple of policemen. This took them almost to the gates of Guaymas, but the port was thought to be safe, since 'it is said [that the Yaquis] never attack towns'; and for the time being, the rule held.[520] On the border, meanwhile, a party of Yaquis was caught smuggling arms near Nogales and Yaqui contingents in the Federal Army began to display mutinous tendencies, refusing orders they disliked.[521] It was now clear that Sonora faced the biggest Yaqui rebellion since 1908 and that the conflict showed no sign of resolution. As 1913 began, Yaqui bands roamed freely in the valley, local communities and ranchers undertook their own self-defence and the state government, free of the Orozquista threat, planned a major onslaught upon the recalcitrant Indians.[522] Then, events in Mexico City upset their schedule. Here, therefore, the narrative must be broken off, to be resumed later. But it is worth pausing briefly to consider why repression rather than conciliation characterised the Maderista authorities' policy towards their erstwhile Yaqui allies; why, that is, the Maderistas – like previous factions, liberal and federalist, conservative and imperialist – enlisted Yaqui support but refused to meet Yaqui demands.

Maderista policy on the question of agrarian reform – though mildly favourable in theory – was dilatory and over-cautious in practice.[523] Madero himself, true to character, urged conciliation of the Yaquis, he declared himself in favour of the return of deportees from the south east (as he had earlier in *La Sucesión Presidencial*), but neither the Yaquis nor their Sonoran opponents were much impressed by such presidential concern.[524] The room for compromise, earnestly sought by Madero in this as in other agrarian conflicts, simply did not exist; the Yaquis and the Sonorans, like other agrarian protagonists, were placed in a 'fundamental antithesis', in which one side's gain was the other's loss, and the central struggle over land and water was overlaid by rival claims to cultural/ethnic supremacy.[525] To the Sonorans, the Yaquis were 'impervious to civilisation' and ignorant of the rights of property (which the Sonorans took very seriously).[526] As much under Maderista liberalism as Porfirian dictatorship, therefore, Yaqui tribalism and agrarianism had no place: 'a great number of the inhabitants of Sonora', Madero was informed, 'maintain the firm belief that the state will only achieve peace by the extermination of the Yaquis'.[527] Compromise and peaceful acculturation, another Sonoran commented, were impossible: the Yaquis constituted 'an untameable race who, unfortunately, will have to be annihilated, at least those who live in the sierra and do not want to work. Their pretensions are so absurd that it would cost the government more to satisfy them than to reduce them to order by force.'[528]

As the history of Sonora's great neighbour to the north displayed, liberal government and capitalist development did not happily co-exist with independent and belligerent Indian populations. Thus there was general support when Governor Maytorena resolved on a policy of tough repression, justifying it on the grounds of the Yaquis' 'instinct for pillage and evil-doing', and propensity for breaking agreements on 'the most frivolous pretext[s]'.[529] But Maytorena was somewhat disingenuous. As a major landowner in the Yaqui Valley, who had employed Yaqui peons and trafficked in Yaqui prisoners, he was surely aware of the entrenched interests which ruled out any acceptable and lasting agreement. The good land claimed by the Yaquis had passed to white/mestizo farmers, and the government – by distributing *baldío* land – could provide for only one-third of the tribe (even assuming they would accept this munificence).[530] And the vested interests included not only powerful Maderista *políticos* like Maytorena, but also lesser men like Ernesto Meade Fierro, a loyal Maderista editor of San Pedro, who received the backing of the Department of Fomento in his claim to property 'in Sonora in the region of the Yaqui {River}', which was threatened by the activity of the 'locals'.[531] As in the case of Morelos, therefore, material interests (some of them impeccably Maderista) vetoed Madero's preferred policy of conciliation, and, in the end, like Pilate, Madero washed his hands of the matter. When Maytorena decided to take firm action, the central government concurred in the need for 'an active campaign, both political and military' which would achieve the definitive 'pacification of the Yaqui'.[532]

In its origins and fundamental character, the Yaqui rebellion closely resembled Zapatismo. Its forms were, of course, different: while the *surianos* were well integrated into the mestizo state, and fought their campaigns with an array of political and ideological – as well as physical – weapons (recruiting intellectuals, espousing a popular, liberal ideology, publishing articulate plans, eliciting some sympathy in the press), the Yaqui revolt was more mute, tribal, isolated and atavistic. The Zapatistas, for example, were ardent patriots; when American troops touched Mexican soil 'it made Zapata's blood boil', while the same incident left the Yaqui chiefs supremely indifferent.[533] Acculturation thus affected the manner in which common grievances were expressed. But, either way, both the Yaquis and the Zapatistas mounted powerful, broadly-based, sustained challenges to the political and agrarian status quo. In other cases, however, comparable agrarian conflict was more constricted, confined to a single valley, municipio, hacienda or village. Here, agrarian movements of the breadth and stamina of Zapatismo, or the Yaqui rebellion, could not develop. Instead, the outcome was sporadic, isolated revolt, short-lived jacquerie, or endemic but confused social banditry.

Phenomena of this kind were evident on the fringes of the best organised and coherent rebellions. The occupation of Jojutla (Mor.) by men of Trinidad Ruiz in August 1911 involved looting, attacks on Spaniards and settling of old local scores; Iñigo Noriega, the Spanish landlord responsible for the draining of Lake Chalco was forced to quit his Hacienda Zoquiapam for fear of reprisals;

and, with the decline of organised Zapatismo in the summer of 1912, bandits troubled the peace of Morelos.[534] All these incidents occurred within the general, geographical orbit of Zapatismo. And elsewhere in Mexico, such decentralised, 'unofficial' action was often the norm. It characterised, for example, the Huasteca region, on the eastern escarpment of the Sierra Madre Oriental. Here (or hereabouts) three inter-related areas of revolutionary activity can be identified, all falling within an area bounded by Tampico, Ciudad Victoria, Río Verde and Papantla: the Huasteca proper, an area of broken, tropical country, stretching from the valley of the Pánuco down into northern Veracruz; the Tamaulipas/San Luis borderlands, south of Ciudad Victoria; and the central region of San Luis, between Río Verde and Cd del Maiz.[535] The entire area possesses only a rough, analytical unity, but it was notable for its vigorous, if varied, rebel movements (which inter-acted with each other, not always amicably), and it contrasted with the relatively peaceful zones of highland San Luis, to the west, and Tamaulipas to the north.[536]

In such areas of decentralised rebellion, political labels meant little. Serious challenges to public order were often blamed upon 'bandits', such as those operating around Ocampo and Jaumave (Tamps.) and between Pánuco and Tantoyucán (Ver.) in the spring of 1911, when the Governor of San Luis admitted his inability to deal with 'brigandage . . . especially in the eastern part of the state'.[537] Ex-Maderistas of spring 1911, like Emilio Acosta, roamed the Pánuco district under a Reyista banner later in the year; yet he (and other supposed 'Reyistas') were 'not so much Reyistas . . . as . . . anti-Madero', and the failure of Reyes' own revolt in December did little to restrain them.[538] National affiliations changed; local activities went on. Early in 1912, following the example of Chihuahua, 'Vazquista' was the preferred label; 'Vazquistas' briefly took Río Verde, others took Ixhuatla and threatened Chicontepec, 500 were said to be active around Forlón.[539] Possibly more meaningful labels were derived from state politics. During the fierce Tamaulipas gubernatorial contest of early 1912, supporters of Medrano protested at the 'election' of the official candidate, Matías Guerra, adding to the turmoil around Xicontencatl; at the same time, as the 'Científico' Manuel Alegre put up for governor of Veracruz, it was anticipated that 'the "Indians" or natives of the interior intend to take matters into their own hands if Señor Alegre is declared elected' – which, as it turned out, he was not.[540] Granted the important consequences (not least the agrarian consequences) which flowed from the appointment of a conservative state governor – like Carreón in Morelos – or, conversely, but more rarely, of a radical – like Antonio Hidalgo in Tlaxcala – such a popular reaction was entirely plausible.[541]

All the more, local, municipal political conflicts elicited fierce partisanship, which could dissolve the control of the central government. The feuds and ambitions of Pedro de los Santos and his family have already been mentioned (with the proviso that their social significance remains murky); what is clear is that Huasteca communities with a long history of political and agrarian disaffection, and sometimes recent revolutionary participation, continued troublesome during the Madero period. Tancanhuitz had been the scene of violent feuds in the 1890s and 1900s; the same families contributed to fresh troubles in 1912.[542] Valles, Huehuetlán and Tampamolón were likewise affected. To the west, Río Verde, captured by Daniel Becerra in March 1912, had been the scene of the famous agrarian revolt of 1879.[543] The troubles at Papantla, where several hundred rebels were active in 1912, demanded Madero's attention: here, villagers were in dispute with the Hacienda La Isla, and the president urged a rapid settlement of their grievances 'since it is not the opportune time to antagonise the Indians'.[544] Tantoyucán was another known trouble-spot; while the Canton of Ozuluama, plagued with 'outright anarchy', also elicited presidential concern.[545] Further north, in the region around Chamal, San Dieguito, Ocampo and Forlón, American settlers found themselves victims of agrarian resentments and reprisals: an unusual example of genuine, popular anti-Americanism, of the kind so frequently alluded to in histories, so rarely found in practice. The victims, it should be stressed, were colonists who had settled in numbers (ninety families at Chamal); like the Mormons of Chihuahua, who also suffered persecution, they appropriated land without providing the jobs and higher wages which were often associated with American real estate investment; thus they conformed more to the model of the middling *ranchero* who – whether Mexican, Spanish, or in this case, American – could in the right circumstances figure as the target of popular agrarianism.[546] Being American was not, as I have argued, a guarantee of popular hostility, but, equally, it was not a guarantee against it. Hence at Chamal there were fires and robberies which the local authorities did nothing to investigate or prevent, 'not wish[ing] to antagonise the people', and the colonists resigned themselves to 'trying to raise a little cattle a little faster than they will steal them'.[547] Further south, at San Dieguito, an American was murdered by local 'bandits' and there were repeated threats that the Americans would be killed, run out of town, or suffer the seizure of their property.[548]

The agrarian element dimly discernible in several of these movements appeared unequivocally in the Cedillo revolt, around Cd del Maiz. The Cedillos were smallholders at Palomas, a *ranchería* recently carved out of the huge Angostura hacienda. By birth, education and income they stood far beneath the Potosino elite, but they were a family of some local status and substance (they owned land, reared cattle and goats, and ran a store) and, though placed above the lesser tenants, sharecroppers and peons of the region, this did more to qualify them for – rather than debar them from – the leadership of a popular, agrarian movement. They could therefore play a role similar to Zapata's, Orozco's, the Figueroas', or the *ranchero* revolutionaries' of Pisaflores.[549] During the late Porfiriato the fibre boom had encouraged local *hacendados* (like the politically powerful Espinosa y Cuevas family, owners of Angostura) to expand at the expense of local communities, provoking litigious conflict, and when the fibre market contracted in 1908–9 the *hacendados'* efforts to cut costs caused further disputes, not least with the Cedillos and the people of Palomas.[550] The fall of Díaz and triumph of Madero made no difference. The landowners pressed ahead with their claims (the Espinosa y Cuevas secured a favourable judgement under the new regime concerning a longstanding dispute with a *ranchero* community); following the demobilisation of the Liberating Army they blacklisted Maderista peons as 'agitators', refusing them employment, and they resisted sharecroppers who sought to sell their crops on the open market, rather than to the landlord, at fixed, inferior prices.[551] The Cedillos, however, employed 'Maderista' peons, and took the part of the aggrieved sharecroppers; when – at the *hacendados'* behest – *rurales* arrested fifty of the trouble-makers, hanging two and gaoling the rest, the Cedillos protested to Governor Cepeda, and Cepeda (one of the more progressive Maderista governors) had the prisoners released and the landlords reprimanded. Now, the familiar whispering campaign began: had not the Cedillos supported Madero's candidacy in 1910? Was not Palomas a nest of banditry? And the landlords turned the economic screw: the owner of Montebello, where the Cedillos pastured their cattle, raised the rent to prohibitive levels. On the other side of the social divide, meanwhile, the Cedillos enhanced their reputations as champions of the common people. When, in September 1912, some sixty sharecroppers of the San Rafael and Montebello estates resolved to take up arms – machetes and cudgels – to press their grievances, they approached the Cedillos, requesting their leadership. In reply, the family urged patience; but when the local *jefe político* took steps to arrest them, they decided to act first.

In a joint move with other local rebels – involving attacks on Tula (Tamps.) and Río Verde – the Cedillos captured Cd de Maiz. From the start their agrarian concerns were evident: during their brief occupation of the town, the Plan of Ayala was solemnly read out to the assembled *campesinos*; and later, particularly through their alliance with the revolutionary *maestro* Alberto Carrera Torres, these concerns were further codified and translated into action.[552] Initially, the struggle was uphill. Cd del Maiz could not be held. Shifting to the traditionally troubled region around Río Verde, the Cedillos took to guerrilla warfare, robbing the Tampico–San Luis train of 80,000 pesos, part of which was distributed Robin Hood style to the poor peasants of the district, and part used for the purchase of arms in the US. It was as he returned home from the border in January 1913 that Saturnino Cedillo (who had already acquired a reputation for audacity and cunning) was arrested and gaoled, but his brothers fought on, capitalising on their local support in San Luis and, soon, the vicissitudes of national politics gave this incipient agrarian revolt further opportunity and encouragement.[553]

If the Cedillos captained the most organised, explicitly agrarian (and later extensive) revolt in the Huasteca/San Luis region, thus emulating Zapata, the general conditions of upheaval also displayed parallels with Morelos. 'Anarchy' and 'apolitical banditry' were common descriptions, mobility and decentralised guerrilla organisation were again apparent. 'The organising strength in this section', it was reported, 'seems limited to the raising of bands of 20 to 50 men in a neighbourhood; as they leave one locality they gain new recruits and lose others who return to their homes'; the rebels could thus threaten haciendas and villages, but not major towns, and they scattered in the face of well-armed Federal detachments.[554] A certain freelance individualism characterised these operations: José Cordero raided the Hacienda Ganahl (a favourite target throughout the Revolution) 'on account of a personal grudge'; in December 1911 Ponciano Navarro's band were bold enough to spring their captured colleagues from San Luis gaol in a 'wholesale gaol delivery'.[555] Such incidents illustrated the weakness of the authorities, compared with the halcyon days of the Pax Porfiriana. But they took their toll. Rebel leaders (and, one must assume, their followers) faced a high mortality. Ponciano Navarro, though 'brave and resourceful' was killed in battle at Tancanhuitz, Daniel Becerra, the Río Verde rebel, fell into government hands in March 1912, Saturnino Cedillo narrowly escaped execution in 1913.[556] Particularly in the absence of a more structured, centralised rebel organisation, these losses had a serious effect: by the summer of 1912, with the demonstration effect of Orozquismo fading and with Governor Cepeda judiciously combining repression with conciliation it seemed that the authorities were beginning to dominate the situation.[557] Thus, although 1913 opened to fresh outbreaks, there were signs in San Luis, as in Morelos and other parts of the country, that the popular revolution was on the defensive, and that the Madero regime (far from descending into anarchy, as its critics alleged) was stronger, albeit more cynical and unloved, now than before.

But if the arrests, executions and petty victories of the government met with some success and curbed organised rebellion, they could not resolve the social tensions which often underlay rebellion, and which also provoked other forms of popular protest. And these challenged and eroded not only political authority, but also the bedrock of rural society, the hacienda system. The latter's dissolution (initially evident more in changing social relations than in the physical division or destruction of the great estates) was to be a long, gradual, cumulative process. The years 1911–13 witnessed only the start, and there were still in these years many haciendas which remained unaffected and capable of returning handsome profits.[558] But the process of challenge and erosion had begun, and while – unlike the later, official agrarian reform – it cannot be quantified, and must be illustrated by 'soft', impressionistic evidence, there is no reason for it to be ignored or underestimated on that account. Indeed, it may be time that the tyranny of numbers (especially pretty dubious numbers) was expunged from Mexican agrarian history.

However, to appease the enthusiastically numerate, let us note at the outset that rural San Luis was dominated by the hacienda; 82% of the population lived within hacienda boundaries.[559] This in itself suggests why rebellions in the state were often fragmentary and short-lived; they had to exist (especially outside the Huasteca, where the dominance of the large estate was less marked) within the interstices of the hacienda system, lacking a supportive network of free villages. But the hacienda was also under threat from within. Hacienda peons rarely took the lead in rural revolt, but it was clear that the rebels – be they dispossessed villagers or *rancheros*, populist political aspirants, or social bandits – could count on a degree of peon support or sympathy, which obliged the authorities to crack down on 'the lower classes who aid the bandits and rebels'.[560] The source of this support was also clear. During rebel raids on haciendas, it was noted, 'those employers who have treated agricultural labor with most severity have been the worst hit'. The Cedillos were responsible for shooting the owner of Angostura; rebels under Lázaro Gómez, who captured Wadley in northern San Luis, 'called, by name, for certain administrators who were reputed to be harsh with employees . . . for the purpose of executing them'.[561] Contemporary observation confirms Bazant's view that, long before large-scale territorial division began, the hacienda was already 'the chief target of the revolutionary movement' in San Luis, and that hacienda peons – who had suffered falling real wages and who were by no means indifferent to the appeal of the *reparto* – now contributed to the revolutionary onslaught.[562] 'So far as concerns the San Luis district', a shrewd observer wrote in September 1912:[563]

the whole revolutionary activity of the past two years is considered primarily as an attempt on the part of the laborers and especially the farm laborers to better their conditions . . . Rebel leaders have resorted to plantation labor for recruits, certain to find discontent there . . . [and] local violence has been directed chiefly against property and only incidentally against [the] government . . . Hence the discontent is local and economic, and the danger spots are usually where there are large numbers of agricultural laborers.

A dramatic illustration of this occurred at the Sierra Prieta hacienda, twenty-five miles north-west of the state capital.[564] Here, Luis Toranzo, an authoritarian landowner of the old school, employed a thousand men: they received 25c. a day (about average for central Mexico) but were paid in scrip, redeemable at the hacienda store, where prices were high; in addition, Don Luis 'also considered himself entitled to services from the families of laborers without additional payments'. When, in the agitated atmosphere of early 1912, the peons grew emboldened and made complaints about their pay and conditions, Toranzo reacted by cutting wages from 25c. to 18c. The resident administrator prudently declined to implement the change and resigned; no replacement could be found (local candidates no doubt being aware of the peons' mood) until a young Spaniard, Elías Alvarez – probably one of those young men on the make, fresh from Europe – agreed to take up the challenge. He cut wages as instructed and within a few days had a strike on his hands. Labour relations at Sierra Prieta were about on a level with Zola's Le Voreux, and the outcome was similar:

some forty of the peons refused to work and asked [for] an interview with the administrator. He refused to talk to the men and punished the spokesman. The same day they gathered around the office and forced the young Spanish administrator to the door, where he was killed by some forty knife thrusts, one from each peon. The plantation is now paying 25c. per day and has a guard of armed men to protect the administrator. The peons are admitted to the office only one at a time, and any one of them who complains is beaten by the guards.

Thus here, as at the Carpizo plantation in Tabasco, the workers' attempts to press their claims were resisted, and the hacienda's tight system of social control was enhanced. But victories of this kind had a Pyrrhic quality about them. At Sierra Prieta the old wage rates were restored, and, more generally, repression could not halt (and indeed was itself a symptom of) more subtle changes that were taking place. Labour was becoming more mobile and vocal in its demands. Efficiency, Potosino businessmen complained, had fallen 20% since the 1910 revolution. In the cities, where labour organisation was more advanced, some workers' demands had been met and the more progressive employers were experimenting with piece rates, apparently with success.[565] The present climate thus accelerated the shift from 'paternalist' compulsion to financial incentive, which was already under way. And though the great mass of rural labour remained unorganised and subject to traditional work discipline, *hacendados* could not insulate their estates against the twin contagions of revolutionary violence and urban example. The first might be vigorously resisted, the latter's gradual, enervating effects had no known antidote. In one case, an entrepreneur who established a large woollen factory on – and in combination with – his estate in San Luis, was obliged to shift the factory to the town, 'finding it was impracticable to operate a factory and a plantation together at widely varying rates of pay'.[566] Already, in 1912, in advance of any effective legislation on the subject, some landowners began to phase out their *tiendas de raya*, preferring to rely on a simple cash nexus to secure and retain labour. The sheer political and social instability of 1910–13 thus prompted change in Mexican rural society, not so much by initiating reformist legislation (though we will note that some transpired), but rather by weakening established authority and compelling those in power to take note of popular demands and – to the extent that these could not be easily repressed – to accommodate them within a more flexible system.

Changes of this kind – gradual, unspectacular, but crucial – can only be seen over time and they must await analysis at the end of Volume II. For the moment, it was the more virulent form of revolutionary contagion which claimed attention and alarmed the well-to-do: the attacks on the hacienda system by rebels, bandits and insurgent peons. Even in periods of quiet, the knowledge that the revolution had put arms in the hands of the poor caused anxiety: in March 1912 'there is constant fear of the lower-class people who continue in an expectant and dissatisfied attitude'; in August, 'there is fear of the lower classes, rumors and plots and undertainty of [sic] the future'.[567] With business depressed and fears of rebel attacks fathering rumours and false alarms, the well-to-do felt increasingly apprehensive and critical of the Madero government.[568] And the elite's response to popular unrest became a key factor in the political alignments of the Madero regime. First – taking the example of San Luis – the elite acted. Landlords solicited (and got) extra forces to police their estates, businessmen met to discuss common action 'against possible mob violence', and 'some of the better class of young citizens' began organising a voluntary militia in the state capital.[569] It is clear therefore that the Potosino elite (especially the landed elite) felt seriously threatened; that the threat they perceived (if sometimes exaggerated) was real enough and that it emanated not from the Madero regime, which was committed to the suppression of popular disorder and which projected no radical reform to the detriment of the landed interest, but rather from the cháotic but powerful popular movement which Madero had unwittingly unleashed. Though 'in this state', it was noted, 'there is little probability of any effort being made to confiscate or to deprive the owner of his land', nevertheless a piecemeal erosion of 'the economic, social and political power which ownership has heretofore bestowed' seemed likely.[570] Though innocent, the administration did not escape fierce criticism. For the well-to-do, the current unrest afford further evidence of the chronic delinquency of the Mexican plebs, which only traditional, authoritarian government could check. Madero's flirtation with democracy had begun the process of degeneration, his demagogy had incited popular violence; now his weakness and incapacity prevented a solution. Thus, with the rural populace abetting rebellion, the elite retreated into sullen opposition; both locally and nationally the Madero regime found itself generally unpopular, sniped at from both sides, teetering on the narrow (and narrowing) base afforded by those sections of the urban middle and working class who remained faithful to their old Maderismo.

The endemic rural unrest which affected San Luis and the Huasteca was now a common feature of the countryside. Oaxaca, for example, is sometimes depicted as an oasis of peace and order within the desert of revolution (it was an image Oaxaqueño leaders liked to cultivate, not wholly disinterestedly). A more recent analysis contrasts the 'non-revolutionary' peasants of Oaxaca with the firebrands of Morelos.[571] While there is obviously something in this, nevertheless the extent of popular rebellion in Oaxaca has been under-estimated, and its character somewhat misconceived. The 1910–11 revolution had produced several important uprisings in the state: that of Angel Barrios, for example, or of Gabriel Solís and Francisco Ruíz, who entered Nochixtlán with 1,000 men in May 1911; while, amid the agitation, agrarian ideas circulated, at least 'in the inland section [where] the Indians have the idea that [Madero] will divide up the land, for which they will not have to pay', and where people entertained 'visions of less taxes'.[572] The political settlement of 1911 was bitterly contested, giving rise to further revolts: that of Angel Barrios, already mentioned, and of 'Che' Gómez and the men of the Sierra Juárez, both of which will figure shortly. These movements displayed clear political aims, leadership and organisation. But on their fringes – or even quite separate – there were fragmentary local protests, often of an agrarian character, which are easily overlooked.

When, for example, Barrios and his Cuicatlán rebels resisted demobilisation, some of his command drifted home to their villages, their heads filled with bold ideas of reform. One such group returned to Atatlauca, Jayacatlán and Boca de los Ríos, villages subject to the *cabecera* of Etla, north of the state capital; they came home, it was said, 'full of the intention of dividing up the Hacienda (of Concepción)', which lay in their district.[573] Concepción (complete with its pending local dispute) had been bought by a British planter, Woodhouse, just six years before, in a complicated transaction which reserved certain lands 'of the extinct village of Zoquiapam' to the communities mentioned above. But the villagers alleged that Woodhouse had overstepped his rights, burning the thatched huts of two of their number (Isidro Sánchez and Mateo López) and illegally retaining the old church bell of Zoquiapam on his estate. In the turbulent atmosphere of 1911, the returning rebels sought revenge, rustling the hacienda's cattle and even making an attempt on the *hacendado*'s life (the attackers included Santiago and López). Woodhouse resisted, a regular skirmish ensued, and police finally came and arrested eleven of the culprits. But, as they were being taken to gaol at Etla, a party of sympathisers, led by the Jayacatlán schoolaster, David Aguilar, freed the prisoners, returned in force to Concepción, beat up Woodhouse and (with a nice touch of irony) deposited him in Etla gaol. Soon released, Woodhouse campaigned to get his assailants punished, but in vain. 'The populace', he complained, 'have taken charge of Etla and the surrounding district and have intimidated the judge.' Indeed, authority at all levels seemed either rotten or inept. When the mayor of Atatlauca was ordered to make the arrests, Angel Barrios countermanded the order (the culprits had, after all, served in his command); the *jefe político* at Etla, Febronio Gómez, was another ex-Maderista, who sympathised with Woodhouse's enemies, and, at the top, the state governor was 'powerless or afraid to act'. Again, we note the interdependence of 'political' and 'agrarian' issues, and the key importance of the changes in local government wrought by the Maderista revolution.[574] As a result, David Aguilar and his cronies were still at large at the end of 1911, robbing the hacienda and 'threatening to kill [Woodhouse's] administrator in order that they may proceed to divide up his property . . . among themselves'. By now,

Woodhouse himself had fled, but, we may note, as a peculiar coda to this otherwise familiar confrontation, that Mrs Woodhouse remained, unmolested, 'as, by her charities, she has much endeared herself to the Indians'.

South of the city of Oaxaca, too, in the valley of the Atoyac River, a more serious and extensive agrarian movement developed, in a region where (unusual for Oaxaca) the regime of the commercial hacienda dominated. Fighting broke out in the spring of 1912, affecting the countryside from Zaachila (only fifteen miles from Oaxaca) down river to Ejutla.[575] 'The trouble', an observer noted, 'seems to be on account of the natives not getting land, which under the Madero administration they were promised. The outbreak is directed against several large haciendas.'[576] Details are hard to come by. The movement had the characteristics of a jacquerie: haciendas and ranches were sacked, cattle were rustled, the rebels were 'not well organised . . . and poorly armed'.[577] In time, the rebels grew bolder, 'robbing haciendas in all parts of the valley'; there were fears that the two main concentrations, at Zaachila and Ejutla, might unite in a formidable coalition; for there were reckoned to be 'a very large number of discontents [sic]' around Zaachila, while 1,700 men attacked Ejutla in May, robbing the railway station of goods and money.[578] In fact, this represented the high point of the troubles; fresh troops were brought into Oaxaca, and the state's attention was claimed by rebel movements elsewhere, and of a different kind. In the absence of further details, deeper analysis is impossible, but it is worth noting that it was in the Atoyac Valley, and especially around Zaachila, that Oaxaqueño agrarianism made most impact in the 1920s.[579]

Neighbouring Guerrero was even more severely affected by rural discontent. In 1911, the state had witnessed outbreaks like that at Ometepec; Ometepec and the Costa Chica remained agitated, with Liborio Reyna, the village lawyer and rabble-rouser of April 1911 now (December 1911) reckoned to be the guiding spirit behind the, 'bandits who now call themselves Reyistas', who plagued the region.[580] Again, in October 1912, only a providential cyclone saved Ometepec when it was at the mercy of 300 rebels under Abraham García; and, we shall note, the persistent agrarian conflicts of this zone (in which despoiled, usually 'Indian' villagers were pitted against mestizo *rancheros*) were once more superficially redefined in terms of national factional labels in 1914–15.[581] Meanwhile, the state as a whole became a labyrinth of confused conflict between rebel and government forces. In April 1912, the latter (the bulk of them ex-Maderistas commanded by Ambrosio Figueroa at Huitzuco, or Tomás Gómez on the Costa Grande) numbered some 3,000; their opponents, comprising a congeries of different commands and *guerrillas*, were considerably more numerous – 3,000 were reckoned to be operating solely in the Mina and Río Grande districts, north of Iguala, on the borders of Mexico state and Michoacán. These were nominal Zapatistas, captained by Salgado, Basave, and a clutch of lesser *cabecillas*. Salgado, the most powerful, commanded 1,000, exercising a loose hegemony in this region, which the central government had refused to legitimise; late in 1912 they were reinforced by 300 well-armed 'Zapatistas' who invaded Guerrero from the east under Almazán.[582] If sympathetic to Zapata, and sharing his agrarian commitment, these chiefs were not as yet formally linked to the Ayala movement; their 'Zapatismo' denoted simply a popular rejection of the Madero regime. Indeed, it was generally the case that 'the great majority of the people of this state are Zapatistas. It is not to be inferred from this that they are all bad [sic] but that they are in sympathy with the movement against the Madero government.'[583]

Meanwhile, the Costa Grande, the Pacific coast north of Acapulco, fell under the sway of Julián Radilla, who had served under Silvestre Mariscal in 1911, and now came into his own as his old commander languished in Acapulco gaol, his revolutionary career temporarily eclipsed. Radilla, like so many veterans of 1911, rebelled against the government, quixotically calling himself an Orozquista well after Orozco's definitive defeat.[584] This did not impede his progress: 'aided by the populace' he captured Aguas Blancas, Atoyac and Tecpán; again, at Coyuca de Benítez, his forces were 'aided by the inhabitants' in their attack. As in Chihuahua and the Laguna, Radilla encountered greatest opposition from a fellow ex-Maderista, who remained a loyalist irregular, Tomás Gómez; but loyalism did not suit Gómez's forces, which experienced heavy losses and desertions. An additional factor, also reminiscence of Chihuahua, ensured Radilla's success: a tacit agreement with the Federal commander at Acapulco, Colonel Gallardo, who allowed Radilla to overrun the Costa Grande, abandoned Gómez and his irregulars to defeat, and even warned Radilla of the approach of Federal troops, despatched against him by presidential command.[585] Thus, the Federals avoided a costly campaign in the interior, and allowed Radilla's and Gómez's ragged forces to butcher one another, leaving Colonel Gallardo – like General Huerta – a *tertius gaudens*. And the logic of the Revolution, in its local application, encouraged Radilla to dally with the Federals, thus keeping them out of his patch, and enabling him to maintain his parochial supremacy.

The scale of upheaval and of the challenge to authority could not be doubted, but – particularly in the light of anomalous alliances like Radilla's – the violence often seemed self-seeking or downright purposeless. Conditions in the hinterland of Acapulco were 'very bad'; government forces were insufficient and ill-coordinated (for reasons partly touched upon); and the collapse of authority created a[586]

situation . . . which facilitates the paying off of old scores and grudges. Some petty leader or 'bad man' . . . raises a company to take a town, in reality to kill some enemy. There is a fight, the village may be taken, sacked or burned; or the hacienda may be despoiled, and it is all credited to 'the revolution'.

If this description seems to trivialise a great social revolution – reducing it to acts of petty vandalism and vendetta – it must nevertheless be recognised that the revolution was built upon these foundations: upon acts of popular violence perpetrated against landlords and officers, caciques and officials; and violence which, though it was often channelled through organised revolutionary armies, also broke out in countless local incidents, which are no less important for being obscure. We may see through a glass darkly, but we can be sure that there was a lot going on the other side. Such was the case in Guerrero. Salgado's activities in the north, for example, fed upon and in turn sustained a crude, popular agrarianism. He had recruited his thousand or so men 'offering the Indians to divide up the lands when the revolt triumphs'; the promise of land, the beleaguered state governor agreed, 'was the bait he used to attract a following for his thankless work'.[587] Whether or not the implication of Salgado's deviousness was valid, the fact was that the 'hordes', once recruited, could not be counted on to obey orders; rather, they did as they pleased and Salgado himself could not 'control the agitation which he has caused among the ignorant masses concerning the despoliation of lands'.[588] Around Iguala the Zapatista, Pablo Barrera, raided landlords and merchants and urged the people (though they needed little urging) to withhold payment of rents.[589] Hacienda administrators, like Rosendo Duarte of San Vicente, on the Guerrero/Michoacán border near Cutzamala, complained of their properties being ransacked, and threats being made against their person; at Santa Fe, near Taxco, an American plantation manager reported a condition of anarchy, with government 'weak and vacillating', railway stations abandoned, and all the local planters and their employers (save the intrepid correspondent) fled to the towns.[590] The local people, he went on, were running amok: 'in this fine sugar district they are burning the cane, taking the stock, robbing and killing the Spaniards' (sugar and Spaniards, it should be noted, were an infallible recipe for popular violence). The manager had his own problems: 'the Indians want my land', he complained, 'and think if they do away with me all they have to do is take the place'; he blamed Madero for running a feeble government and for having 'promised to divide the lands which of course he cannot do'. His removal, when it came, was not as violent as was to be expected, especially at a time when, by his own account, haciendas were being destroyed and managers murdered; rather, the local magistrate ('a Nigger Indian judge') sent a posse ('a drunken band of twenty-nine') to arrest him on an alleged ('trumped up') charge of rustling; after which he spent a month in gaol before representations in high places ('four or five senators and about eight congressmen') secured his release. As in the case of Woodhouse in Oaxaca, agrarian revindication was not gratuitously violent, and was in fact mediated through the new, popular, local authorities. Or, as the victim himself put it: 'the Indian and the peon is on top and it's sure —, and getting worse all the time'.

Across the Balsas in Michoacán, similar conditions were reported. While the eastern part of the state, bordering Guanajuato, was afflicted by banditry, the western part, heavily Indian and agricultural, witnessed sporadic agrarian outbreaks. As in other states of central Mexico, observers contrasted this endemic, decentralised upheaval with the more coherent, 'political' revolt led by Orozco in the north:[591]

> while in the north there is a more or less organised revolution . . . here the danger, which is a constant one, comes from the absolute lack of law, or, rather, of the enforcement of the same, combined with the Indian element and the resultant acts of revenge or of pure savagery.

As for the motives behind these troubles, the same observer continued, 'these Indians either have or imagine they have a grievance . . . on account of lands which they consider they have been robbed of'. The consequent outbreaks (some examples of which have already been given for Michoacán) had the sudden, isolated, inconclusive character of jacqueries. Pichátaro, for example, was one of many Michoacán communities whose inhabitants had suffered from the intrusion of lumber companies into their locality:[592] 'for some time past they had been incensed against the foreigners who exploited the forests belonging to the community of the natives of Pichátaro because, in their opinion, they had appropriated the aforesaid forests which by rights belonged to the indigenous inhabitants'. During a fiesta (here, as in pre-industrial Europe, fairs and carnivals were often the occasions of popular outbursts), as the villagers enjoyed music, fireworks and plenty of drink, their feelings were translated into action: led by Francisco Sánchez (the only villager who possessed a gun – his position in the community is unfortunately not recorded), they marched up to the company manager's house, 'intoxicated with rage, incited by the seditious cries of Sánchez and breathing hatred'.[593] They demanded and received money, then, as a squabble started and led to firing, they killed the manager. Order was soon restored through the intervention of Maderista troops under Martín Castrejón who, like Añorve on the Costa Chica, or Ambrosio Figueroa in Morelos, had no time for agrarian rebels, his own revolutionary allegiance notwithstanding. Castrejón at once constituted a court martial which, by nine votes to two, voted for the summary execution of the two alleged assassins. And the sentence was carried out without delay and without fuss; for the two prisoners, both day labourers of Pichátaro and old men by peon standards, were 'dumbfounded by the terrible nature of the punishment which awaited them and raised no objection or protest whatsoever'. Peace reigned at Pichátaro.

Such swift repression, which was the norm, appeared to work, in the short term at least. The passivity of the two prisoners was shared, it seems, by their colleagues, for Pichátaro does not feature again, at least not in this account of the Revolution. But in another, better researched case, a comparable incident can be placed within a broader context. The people of Naranja, also in

Michoacán and also victims of agrarian commercialisation, took note of revolutionary ideas and examples which filtered into their pueblo between 1910 and 1912. But until the latter year, nothing happened. Life went on much as usual; the mestizo sharecroppers and hired labourers of the Cantabria Hacienda continued to frequent the village, getting drunk at the (mestizo) Torres' cantina, firing their pistols and chasing the local women.[594] One Saturday in 1912, while a dozen mestizos were roistering, a villager tolled the church bell, summoning a crowd of Naranjeños, who surrounded the 'besotted intruders', laid six of them out with well-aimed sling-stones, and proceeded to lance them with fish-spears. It is indicative of the state of local research that the outcome of this dramatic incident is unknown (at least, Friedrich gives no details). Certainly the villagers did not – probably could not – follow up their violent action, which thus remained an isolated event, divorced from any organised rebellious protest. The Spanish landlords, their mestizo 'trusties' and clerical allies managed to retain control in the region for years to come. But the event of 1912 lived on in village memory, and the nucleus of radical *agraristas* who began to agitate during and after the Revolution was drawn from amongst those who had participated in the 'bloody happenings' of that year.[595] Events of this kind were spatially as well as temporally isolated. In the neighbouring pueblos of Tiríndaro and Tarejero, too, the years after 1911 saw the beginnings of agrarian organisation and of incipient, violent confrontation between villagers and landlords; while Cherán, which lay 'in the centre of the agrarian movement in Michoacán' (indeed, in the middle of the triangle formed by Naranja, Paracho and Pichátaro, the three cases mentioned here), there was no *agrarismo*, no organisation, and no violent confrontation.[596] This dual isolation (which contrasts with the spatial solidarity and temporal continuity of Morelos *agrarismo*) enabled the landlords of the region to retain the whip-hand. Trouble-makers were persecuted, assassinated, driven to the sanctuary of the sierras or of revolutionary armies elsewhere. But this very landlord repression revealed that the old system of social control and old assumptions of legitimacy were irretrievably ruptured; and though repression might succeed in the short-term, during the decade of revolution, it also served to encourage a more organised, more militant, and ultimately more successful popular, agrarian opposition.[597] The parochial jacquerie paved the way to the regional peasant league.

BANDITRY: THE BAJÍO AND POINTS SOUTH

Rural movements could thus assume different guises. They might be broadly based and coherent, like Zapatismo, or isolated and apparently ephemeral, like the jacqueries which affected parts of Oaxaca, Guerrero and Michoacán. But the great majority had in common the fact that they derived from and depended upon the surviving free villages for their existence: for it was the villages' conflicts with landlords and caciques which fuelled the revolution, their moral and physical resources which sustained it. Tannenbaum's forty-year-old assertion that 'these villages ultimately made the social revolution in self-defense' is still broadly valid, despite a good deal of recent criticism.[598] Equally, Tannenbaum's figures indicating the numerical strength of free villages in different states display a rough but convincing positive correlation with states notable for their organised revolutionary contribution: Morelos, Puebla, Tlaxcala, for example.[599] Conversely, in states where the hacienda dominated rural society (San Luis, for example, particularly its western half; or the states beyond the Isthmus, which will be mentioned shortly) rural rebellion could not be sustained, or even initiated, and rural protest was largely confined to brief, sporadic outbreaks of violence.

But there was an alternative form of protest suited to regions where the hacienda dominated and the free village was weak: banditry. According to one pioneer study (undertaken before banditry became academically fashionable) the social and topographical factors conducive to banditry (which in this analysis are derived from Andalusía) are as follows: large estates, often owned by absentee landlords; underpopulated expanses, poor in communications; few villages, a concentration of population in the towns, and a large rural proletariat (as against peasantry).[600] Certainly those regions of revolutionary Mexico most afflicted by banditry – as compared with other forms of rural violence – tended to fit this description: notably the Bajío, the Isthmus, and beyond. But before this hypothesis can be investigated, a couple of conceptual problems must be cleared up: what was banditry? And what is banditry?

The first question relates to contemporary usage, and asks how contemporaries (overwhelmingly the literate, respectable contemporaries who referred to the phenomenon in reports, speeches, articles) applied the label. They applied it, as most people would, to a form of collective, basically rural 'crime' ('crime' in the sense of contravening the formal law of the land, irrespective of popular perceptions); but, in the context of social revolution, they did so ambiguously, without clarifying the distinction between bandits and rebels. Thus Zacatecas was 'literally overrun with bands of revolutionary brigands [sic]' in April 1912; in Durango, the Federals were pursuing 'quasi-revolutionary brigands'; *rurales* campaigning in Morelos and Puebla used 'Zapatista', 'bandit', and 'rebel' almost interchangeably, and the local planters were similarly undiscriminating.[601] A distinction was only (though not invariably) invoked, when it was recognised that a 'rebel' espoused a political programme – which a 'bandit' did not. Thus, as already mentioned, de la Barra and others distinguished between Madero's 'political' revolution of 1910–11 – which claimed national power, issued a plan and was led by men just conceivable as national leaders – and the 'brigand bands' of Puebla and Morelos. The Morelos planters agreed, alleging that the state was now 'revert[ing] to what was the normal condition . . . in the state of Morelos in the old days, brigandage'; 'as General Zapata has no known political plan', the governor of Puebla asserted, 'those who are bemused enough to follow him must be considered as mere bandits'.[602] All this antedated the Plan of Ayala (though not other Zapatista statements of a clearly 'political' character). Yet even after the Plan there were plenty – like Generals Huerta and Robles – who continued to qualify Zapatismo as banditry and to act accordingly.[603]

Madero, too, followed similar criteria and reached similar conclusions. At the start of 1913, he told the American Chargé, he was prepared to amnesty 'all those who were like Orozco or Félix Díaz, fighting for what they considered patriotic motives, but for those who were common criminals, like Cheche Campos, he felt there should be no mercy'.[604] Campos, of course, had recently belonged to the grand Orozquista coalition; the case suggests that the rebel/bandit distinction depended upon a fairly subjective evaluation of an individual's motives, sincerity, sophistication and respectability (within which, the promulgation of a formal Plan was significant, but not definitive proof either way). Orozquismo, it is interesting to note, veered from bandit to revolutionary status and back again, depending on the time, the place and the observer. To the American consul some way off at Nuevo Laredo, the initial revolt of March 1912 was 'entirely without cause or principle . . . being backed by . . . bandits who are ready to cry "viva" for anybody so that they can have an excuse to pillage towns and ranches'; his colleague at Torreón (not necessarily more perspicacious, but witnessing the movement at first hand) emphatically disagreed: 'it is ridiculous for anyone to call this anything but a revolution, there are some bands that are bandits, but the large force that is surrounding this place is composed of revolutionists and are [sic] offering serious resistance to the Federal forces'.[605] And, while Madero and his colleagues had no doubt that Orozco was mounting a full-scale 'political' revolt in the spring of 1912, the Orozquista forces, following their defeat, became variously 'rebels', 'bandits' or 'gangs' (*gavillas*) once again.[606]

It is clear from these examples that contemporary usage, while following certain rough criteria, is hardly adequate for historical explanation. Popular movements like Zapatismo were often termed 'banditry', as were many lesser movements which, however localised or inarticulate, displayed evident political objectives. There are prima-facie reasons, therefore, for looking at every reported case of 'banditry' with a view to converting it to political status. But that is not to say that there were no professional bandits, whose political claims were threadbare. Here, as we approach the question of historical (or even 'scientific') usage, we encounter the 'social bandit': the bandit who, while following the familiar *modus operandi* of the trade, represents a form of popular protest, directed against landlords and officials, dependent on peasant support, and working to the advantage (material and/or psychic) of the common people.[607] But the social bandit's career within Academe has somewhat paralleled his life under the greenwood tree. Introduced by

Professor Hobsbawm, he was initially welcomed, even feted, and he put in many appearances in academic company; but then (inevitably, after such uncritical acceptance) some academics grew leery, and the recent trend – especially among experts – has been to qualify, de-emphasise and even deny his role.[608] One recent study depicts the Mexican bandit less as Robin Hood than Henry Ford: 'the business of Mexican bandits was business. These were not the justice-seeking, precapitalist peasant bandits whom Eric Hobsbawm describes. The only thing the Mexican brigands seemed to protest was their exclusion from rewarding sectors of the social system.'[609] The social bandit, it seems, has been shown the door.

From our perspective, the dismissal is premature. Hobsbawm (and, *a fortiori*, some of his disciples) were no doubt too promiscuous in their attribution of 'social' characteristics to bandits through the ages. But in the context of the Mexican Revolution it cannot be doubted that forms of social banditry existed. Indeed, one problem is to distinguish between social banditry on the one hand and other forms of localised, inarticulate rural protest (of the kind referred to by contemporaries as banditry) on the other. The *modus operandi* was substantially similar; and, to the extent that bandits emerged from the peasantry and had 'no ideas other than those of the peasantry . . . of which they form part', they shared a similar ideology, loosely termed 'traditional'.[610] Even the most hardened professionals, by continuing bandit activities during the revolution, acquired 'social' characteristics; for, during the Mexican as during the French Revolution, 'banditry was never purely criminal; it always took on political overtones'.[611] The crucial question, therefore, was not so much one of size, *modus operandi*, or political sophistication, but rather of popular support; for it was popular support which gave bandits their 'social' function, which assimilated them (often indistinguishably) to rural protest movements more generally, and which set them apart from their professional colleagues.

Such a criterion is analytically clear, faithful to the original concept, and historically relevant. But it is not easy to apply. When the people of Sayula (Jal.) complained of being threatened by 'gangs of bandits' who had taken to the activity 'owing to the revolution . . . with the sole aim of committing crimes against honourable *vecinos*'; when a worthy citizen in the same state alleged that 'among the revolutionary forces were mixed . . . elements of disorder who tried to defend their pillaging with the banner of the revolution'; then the implication of 'anti-social' banditry is clear.[612] But, since 'social' banditry describes not an inherent characteristic so much as a relationship (between bandit and rural population), it is not possible to take even such clear statements at face value. Their validity must depend upon the vantage point of the observer. When the mayor of Totoloapam (Mex.) organised volunteers to defend the town against (what he called) bandits styling themselves revolutionaries, did he enjoy widespread popular support (i.e., were the bandits

bandits *tout court?*) or was he striving to contain a form of genuine popular protest?[613] It is often impossible to judge the validity of such reports, without considerable additional information. Sometimes, presumptions may be made, one way or the other. There is no doubt that bandits operated in Morelos, particularly in the later years of the Revolution; that they were distinct from the Zapatistas; and that Zapata took steps to extirpate them.[614] When the *bona fide* Zapatista, Trinidad Rojas, had two bandits executed and their bodies displayed on the streets of Amecameca, it may be presumed that these were bandits with scant 'social' credentials.[615] Conversely, the whole gamut of repressive policies employed by Ambrosio Figueroa in Guerrero 'in order to put an end to the banditry which has so boldly confronted the legitimate government' included a good many popular rebels among its victims.[616] Scepticism is also in order when Americans reported 'bands of roving bandits . . . bent merely on pillage and plunder' infesting Sinaloa; or 'abounding' in the foggy Ajusco mountains south of the capital; or plaguing Tepic, the Huasteca, or Michoacán (which was said to contain 3,000 bandits in the summer of 1912).[617] It was not that these reports were wantonly fictitious (they were often revealing, and later borne out by events); but rather that they misrepresented an actual, important phenomenon.

The defining characteristic of social banditry was, therefore, relational, not inherent. As such, it was mutable, and it could change without the activities of the bandit(s) necessarily changing. For, just as pre-revolutionary, professional banditry, overtaken, swallowed up, and thus politicised by the popular revolution, thereby acquired 'social' attributes, so too social banditry could be professionalised (or 'de-socialised') as the revolution ebbed, leaving it stranded without the popular support and sympathy which maintained and defined it. Or, a variant on this theme, successful social bandits broke out of their local (and 'social') confines and appeared elsewhere not as avenging Robin Hoods but rapacious Salvatore Giulianos. Either way, spatial and temporal change brought a change in the bandits' relation to rural society: the social bandit of 1911 became the terrorist of 1917; the social bandit of one valley crossed the mountains and terrorised another. Important though it is, this qualification need not detain us further here. For, in the early years of the Revolution, as the popular movement gathered strength, such changes were rare: suitably 'social' bandits could – like the rural rebels they so closely resembled – count on sustained popular support; and, as yet, few aspired to break out of their parochial confines and risk forfeiting this support. Later, we shall note, such changes came thick and fast, in response to the logic of the Revolution: veritable bandit armies terrorised the countryside and, as erstwhile sympathisers found they had now become victims, so forms of local, communal self-defence (attempted, occasionally and without much success, in the early years) now became both ubiquitous and effective.[618]

During the Madero years, however, social banditry – distinguished by the popular sympathy it elicited – was endemic in some regions. Popular rural protest in the Bajío, for example, lacked the political expression and organisational cohesion which Orozquismo and (even its critics often had to admit) Zapatismo possessed; and this reflected the social and geographical matrix in which it developed – one of open plains, populous towns, numerous haciendas and ranchos, but few traditional villages.[619] Here, banditry was not so much an alternative to popular rural rebellion, as a suitably modified variant thereof. In 1911, Cándido Navarro's forces had scoured the countryside, raiding haciendas, alarming the authorities by their speed of movement, and penetrating even to the gates of the towns. But they had failed to build a military or administrative framework which could secure their gains, or seriously challenge the existing authorities. Hence the latter made a sustained recovery after the fall of Díaz. Rebel forces were demobilised, troublesome *cabecillas* were removed, new Maderista authorities were undermined.[620] By the spring of 1912 only two veterans of the Maderista revolution were still in arms against the government; but their meagre forces were greatly outnumbered by the alleged 'bandits' who now posed the greater threat to order and government.[621]

The distinction carried some practical weight, at least in the eyes of the volunteers recruited to defend the city of Guanajuato, who cautiously agreed that they would resist any bandit attacks 'if . . . they, the volunteers, had the advantage in numbers, but, on the other hand, if the attacking party were revolutionists they would make no resistance whatsoever' (a condition governing the recruitment of volunteers in other states too).[622] Nevertheless, there was a marked continuity between the revolution of 1910/11 and the banditry of 1911/12/13, with regard to men, location and method. Again, it was the south and west of the state of Guanajuato which was most affected; Cándido Navarro's old patch around Silao and Comanjillo was particularly troubled, and his old supporters were believed to be responsible for the trouble.[623] The *modus operandi* was again one of fleet mobility, which enabled the bandits to operate almost at will in the countryside, from Celaya westwards into Michoacán, even provoking fears among the inhabitants of Jalisco that the hordes of Guanajuato were 'casting longing eyes in the direction of this rich district'.[624] And locally the bandits could count on a good deal of popular support, as we shall see.

Haciendas, their owners and managers, afforded the chief targets – and raids were clearly designed, not simply to replenish supplies, but also to exact reprisals. The owner of the Guarichos Hacienda (who came of a 'very prominent family') was killed even after he had handed over the keys of the property to the bandits, inviting them to take what they wanted; the managers of the Hacienda Román Rivera Nieto and the Rancho de Cuchicuato, both near Irapuato, were murdered; Spanish *administradores* were once again mortal victims at Abasolo and Puruándiro (the latter a notorious trouble spot).[625] Nor were these wanton attacks, randomly conceived. Targets were selected. The *jefe político* of Valle de Santiago set off in pursuit of a 'gang of bandits' on the Guanajuato/Michoacán border: 'my attention', he reported,[626]

was drawn to the fact that the band of wrong-doers passed by the small ranches, where they did no harm, while they did do harm at the Hacienda de Pantoja . . . I learned from reports given me that the Spaniards who manage this hacienda, along with its *administrador*, are hated by the poor of the district, and this ill-will is well borne out by the way they burned the hacienda books, the office documents . . . destroyed various pieces of furniture, shot and stole things and were about to burn down the whole place but refrained on the plea of an employee.

In this case, the inhabitants of Pantoja, who had 'made common cause' with the bandits, were duly arrested, their pathetic booty (chiefly 'a vast number of straw hats') was recovered, and they were sent to the city to face justice. This pattern, already familiar from other examples, appears to have been common in the Bajío. A core of full-time bandits – perhaps as many as 200 – was aided and abetted by local people, who participated in attacks and robberies and then returned (if they were allowed) to their agricultural employment. Of the gang which attacked the Spanish-owned Hacienda La Bolsa, for example, it was reckoned that 'many . . . chiefly those on foot, are inhabitants of the ranches of that district: so that, when scattered, they lose themselves among the little *rancherías*'.[627] It was even suggested that the 'full-time' bandits themselves were peons: 'men who in the day-time are presumably honest laborers but who, at night, form themselves into small bands and rob all the nearby haciendas, killing anyone who opposes them'. By these methods, the bandits could mobilise large forces suddenly, and maintain – it was reckoned – several thousand armed men in opposition to the government.[628]

Even where the peons did not arm themselves with their 'knives and machetes' and join in the fighting, they nevertheless lent the bandits their support. 'Throughout this entire district', the American consul reported from Guanajuato, 'it would seem that the peons on the ranches are ardent sympathisers with the bandits and are working in with them either directly or indirectly in giving them money and provisions.'[629] Since there is little evidence of either intimidation or communal resistance to banditry (as there was to be in later years), it must be presumed that this sympathy was largely genuine. And the bandits certainly cultivated it. In a neat – though less macabre – parody of official practice, they marched Federal prisoners overland with them, 'exhibit[ing] [them] . . . at all the small ranches in order to enthuse the peons to join them against the government'.[630] In some cases, this sympathy extended some way up the social hierarchy. The ranchers of La Magdalena, including the influential Marciano Nieto, were said to provide a haven for bandits; Puruándiro was so riddled with bandit influence that the local authorities liberated (or did not dare hold?) bandit prisoners arrested in that region.[631] It may be that *rancheros* organised and captained some bandit groups, mobilising local peons much as the Cedillos did at Palomas; there is certainly evidence of *ranchero* banditry in the Bajío in later years.[632] What is not clear is the motivation behind this collusion. Only detailed, micro-historical research will reveal if these early *ranchero* bandits nursed political or agrarian grievances; if they were Vanderwood's petty entrepreneurs; or if, in the face of rebellious peons, they decided if they could not beat them they would join them.

Irrespective of motivation, banditry became extensive and ingenious. Haciendas were the principal but not the sole targets. Attacks on trains – a feature of Porfirian banditry – were common, and increasingly daring, with the line linking Irapuato, Silao, León and points north being worst affected. Trains were halted, robbed, in one case derailed; train crews were shot or belaboured with the flats of machetes; two high-ranking state officials were, in one instance, stripped of their belongings and beaten up, the bandits making off with the mailbags they accompanied. One bandit/rebel, having captured locomotive No. 789 south of Aguascalientes, opened the throttle and sent it steaming down the line (empty); it careered for thirty miles across northern Jalisco – providentially avoiding other traffic – and came to a halt beyond Encarnación.[633] This was not simply mindless vandalism. While it is unlikely that the bandits of the Bajío shared that popular antipathy to the railway and all its works which characterised certain rural communities, nevertheless their activities had a tactical pay-off (over and above the loot they collected).[634] Train crews and repair gangs were understandably reluctant to enter the region; unless better protection were afforded, the Superintendent of the National Railways told the Governor of Guanajuato, services in the western part of the state would be curtailed. This raised the spectre of stoppages in the mines, mass unemployment, and further, dramatic recruitment for the bandits. The governor had no choice but to increase railway garrisons and escorts, thereby denuding other districts of troops, while further straining the state's already precarious finances.[635]

These fears illustrated an important negative point: the bandits did not depend on the mining camps for their recruits. While the mines and smelters continued to work, it was felt, the men would stay put. The presumption (by no means confined to Guanajuato) was generally valid. *Pace* Guerra, mining no more sustained social banditry than it did popular rebellion. Occasionally, mines (like La Luz) were molested by bandit gangs; but there were many more which continued operations, despite bandit activity in the vicinity, and without their labour force being leached away. Perhaps banditry was not quite the glittering career it has recently been cracked up to be. But if the mines (and, incidentally, the Americans associated with these and another business in the state) emerged largely unscathed, virtually every ranch in the environs of Silao had, by the late summer of 1912, suffered from bandit attacks.[636] Indeed, even the towns were not safe. Here, the sheer mobility and bravado of the Bajío bandits enabled them to pull off coups which more cautious peasant rebels either did not dare attempt, or did not consider worth attempting. Nor did they confine their attention to small communities like Jarapitio or Calderones (both near Guanajuato, in the second of which the *cura*, yanking the bell-rope in his room, alerted the villagers and frightened off the raiders – though not before they had 'shot the plastering around the bell full of holes'). The bandits also penetrated major towns like Silao, through which a *gavilla* rode in March 1912, passing within a hundred yards of a Federal barracks and shouting 'Viva Zapata!'; like Lagos de Moreno, entered by Pérez Castro a month later, or Irapuato, where a hundred bandits, attempting to break open the city gaol, were finally repulsed by local volunteers, with seven innocent citizens dying in the consequent panic.[637] A similar gaol-break was anticipated in the state capital in May: already, dynamite bombs had been tossed into the city barracks; and Pedro Pesqueira, Cándido Navarro's old lieutenant, was believed to be luring the Federals into the countryside so that others could pounce on the gaol, where political prisoners (including one prominent local bandit) were noticed going to bed fully dressed, ready for their imminent departure.[638] Such fears aggravated existing tension. The Bajío towns had experienced or narrowly avoided serious riots in 1911; now, in Guanajuato at least, 'quite bitter feeling was manifested by the lower elements against the present government'; the Independence celebrations there were marred by crowd disorders and police repression.[639] It was quite plausible – and not at all paranoid – for the well-to-do to recall the events of 1911, note the mood of 1912, and fear that bandit attacks might trigger popular violence in the cities, as they did in the countryside.[640]

In the towns and cities, therefore, the elite (and not just the elite) were much more fearful of banditry than they were deviously supportive (a point to which we shall return, and which tends to corroborate the 'social' character of such banditry). As proof and consequence of this fear, several volunteer corps were established in the towns and cities of the Bajío in 1912. Forty of 'the better middle class' formed a militia at Irapuato; a prominent citizen of Guanajuato recruited 110 men 'who are all working in the different stores, banks and mining companies'.[641] Such volunteers came, therefore, from the very urban, commercial interests threatened by the continuation of banditry and rural rebellion; they represented an urban – as well as a propertied – reaction to the disorders in the countryside, which seemed likely to engulf them. The rich and influential took the lead (at Moroleón it was the wealthy – the *clase adinerada* – who urged resistance to Pantoja's bandits and initiated a local defence force) but they could usually count on some support from urban workers, who had an important stake in the maintenance of peace, order, trade and employment.[642] The fifty volunteers led by the *jefe político* of Valle de Santiago in his fruitless pursuit of bandits 'were for the most part artisans', and they were keen recruits, not sullen conscripts.[643] Unfortunately, neither they nor their well-to-do sponsors made up into effective counter-insurgency forces. The Guanajuato militia, as we have seen, hedged its commitment with cautious qualifications; the Irapuato volunteers repulsed bandit attackers, but at the cost of innocent lives; at Silao, the *jefe* could not drum up enough support. At best, such forces provided static auxiliaries for the army; they rarely ventured outside the towns and when – like the Valle de Santiago posse – they did, it transpired that 'being artisans, they lack[ed] the powers of resistance of soldiers' and proved no match for the bandits, who were of rural stock.[644] The lesson of 1910–11 was rammed home again: the countryside was the home of rebellion, and urban man found it hard, even impossible, to make the transition to guerrilla (or counter-guerrilla) combat. 'Assuredly', as Gabriel Gavira admitted, forty years before Guevara, 'the effort city man (as I was) has to make in these situations is much greater than that of the man of the countryside, accustomed to live outdoors, and always on horseback.'[645] Meanwhile, the cost of raising and maintaining these local forces placed an intolerable strain on the state's finances: by the end of 1912, Guanajuato was two million pesos in debt, and seeking to place a loan on the New York market to cover the deficit.[646] For all its 'apolitical' character, the banditry of the Bajío had a telling effect on both the political and economic life of the region it afflicted.

The same was true of the tropical south: the extensive region stretching from the state of Veracruz through the Isthmus to the south east, where, again in the relative absence of a strong, independent peasantry, organised rural rebellion was rare, but alternative forms of protest flourished. Indeed, the diversity of this zone affords further, varied evidence of the ecology of popular protest already suggested. In the northern and upland parts of Veracruz, for example, organised rebellion paralleled and often merged with the insurgency of the central plateau. Local troubles erupted at Tantoyucán, Ozuluama and Papantla; the Madero revolution had elicited armed responses around Córdoba and Orizaba (led by Gavira, Tapia and Aguilar), at Altotonga (Bertrani and others) and west of Coatepec (Manuel López).[647] Here, the prevalence of villages and hamlets, combined with a significant level of agrarian conflict, gave the rebels purchase. It is suggestive that the revolutionaries of 1911 almost all headed west, towards the Puebla sierra, rather than east into the lowlands; those who attempted an eastern offensive (as Colmenares Ríos did) were disappointed; and the political torpor of the *tierra caliente*, evident at the outset, continued through 1911–13, as we shall note.[648] In the southern part of the state, the Acayucán/Los Tuxtlas region stood out as the principal exception: here, in a 'land of unprecedented fertility', coffee and tobacco had prospered since the 1880s, giving rise to agrarian conflicts, provoking an Indian revolt in 1883, and facilitating both PLM rebellion and social banditry in the 1900s.[649] In 1911 the canton of Acayucán was a good deal more agitated than the rest of the south. As in 1906, the Sierra de Soteapán and its hard-pressed Indian population provided refuge for rebel forces, which gathered strength before liberating Sayula, Jaltipán, Texistepec, Oluta and finally Acayucán itself, which fell to 650 rebels in June.[650]

A similar pattern was evident in 1912. In the upland country, rebellion built on the revolutionary legacy of the previous year: Gavira rebelled (without success) in the canton of Misantla; Tapia went east and supported Governor Hidalgo of Tlaxcala in his running battle with local conservatives; Bertrani and others joined a Vazquista revolt which 'took on alarming proportions' around Teziutlán in February. And again, towards the end of the year, observers detected 'a revolutionary plot . . . ramified over [the] mesa country of Puebla and Veracruz'.[651] All these challenges to authority were checked. But, in the wake of defeat, banditry (so-called) continued. Bandits harassed the Mexican Railway, frightening the Spanish businessmen of Córdoba; they were active around Teziutlán, where they counted on the connivance of some local authorities; eighty entered Coatepec, in the rich coffee country, and freed their captured colleagues (and a good many other prisoners) from the town gaol.[652] In consequence the government did not win friends when it despatched Veracruzano forces to fight in Morelos, even though 'marauders are still present and active in many parts of the state'.[653]

In the tropical lowlands, meanwhile, where organised rebellion was at a discount, banditry became the primary form of protest. Through the spring and summer of 1912 there were 'alarming reports' of bandit raids and Indian marauding; bandits operated within a few miles of the port of Veracruz, scorning the slothful Federal garrison there.[654] To the south, the marshy plains of Tierra Blanca were 'infested' with banditry; Panuncio Martínez extorted from the plantations of Tezonapa (and continued to charge a regular retainer even after the government had bribed him into a temporary surrender).[655] But the worst affected region lay along the rivers which drained into the Gulf between Cosamaloapán and the Isthmus: around Chinameca, where Tomás Hernández (a self-styled Orozquista) launched murderous raids from his base on the Coscopa plantation; further inland, at Playa Vicente, Achotal, Santa Rosa and Sochiapa, where small towns and plantations had been hacked out of the flood-prone forests, bandits came and went with apparent impunity.[656] In some cases, bandits and planters achieved a sort of symbiosis. Panuncio Martínez's long local career (involving repeated amnesties, relapses and changes of political affiliation) was based on a working relationship with the Tezonapa planters. Bandits of this kind were not necessarily beloved of the landlords; but at least they were tolerated parasites, which, like the viruses of endemic disease, did not kill off their hosts, might fight off other, more virulent parasites, and were in some cases even preferable to the antidote of government intervention. But even this relatively benign parasitism could, over time, sap the vital forces of the plantation system. Much more enervating, of course, was social banditry. Late in the summer of 1912 an unusual calm prevailed around San Juan Evangelista, in the heart of southern bandit country. But one contingent maintained a relentless activity; for, a planter explained, it

seems to be a local affair ... they do not go out of a certain neighbourhood and [it] is caused by the local government having taken away the lands from them to the big Hacienda de Corral Nuevo ... [hence] for years there has been trouble there and I expect there always will be unless the government kills them all off or gives them back the land they claim.[657]

Upriver, at Playa Vicente and Tatahuicapa, bandits were busy booting out incumbent officials and installing their own appointees; at Playa Vicente their leader (who was noted for his orderly conduct) was made mayor; at Tatahuicapa, where a similar change was effected, 'unquestionably the brigands received aid and comfort from some of the local people of this pueblo'.[658]

Thus, although organised, 'political' rebellion was largely absent, and at least some of the endemic banditry was distinctly 'unsocial' and supportive of the status quo, nevertheless the cumulative effect of these scattered challenges to the government was serious. For all their displays of activity, the authorities were 'apparently powerless. Depredations may be expected and do occur most [sic] any time throughout [the] state.'[659] The Federals, as usual, showed little enthusiasm for campaigning in the countryside, and below-strength garrisons even allowed the bandits to approach and sometimes enter towns and cities. Amnesties, though common, were no more efficacious in curtailing banditry: they cost money, they compromised the reputation of the government, and they were short-term solutions – for recidivism among amnestied bandits was exceptionally high.[660] Meanwhile, planters began to detect a change of mood among local people, particularly among their own peons. There was 'an independent feeling among the people' of Tierra Blanca, where taxes were refused, and the government took no action in reply; at San Gabriel 'generally there is a feeling of unrest and discontent among the working classes'.[661] Such observations are sadly vague. But in once case, the practical implications of banditry and unrest were made clearer. The Indian village of Oluta, close by Acayucán, had figured in the revolutionary itinerary of Pedro Carbajal back in 1911. The usual procedures had been followed, with new officials acceptable to the people being installed.[662] But Oluta happened to be the main source of labour for a plantation at Tezonapa, whose manager would annually attend the village fiesta in mid-June and secure contract labour for the rest of the year. Now, in 1912, the regular routine threatened to break down: following the revolutionary events of the previous year, the district had fallen prey to bandits, notably the local thug (as he was regarded), Antonio Pavón Gallegos, and the more businesslike Panuncio Martínez. Yet the government had been forced to reduce the local garrison and, in June 1912, seemed likely to reduce it further. The plantation manager was aghast: while protesting that 'we are well-known and have the complete confidence of the indigenes [sic] . . . [for] just and humane treatment has invariably characterised our relations with them', nevertheless he feared that if 'this source of terror' (the local garrison) were removed, it would mean an end to the smooth functioning of labour recruitment. No troops, no peons. The abstraction of 'extra-economic coercion' here appears clothed in flesh.[663]

The failure of authority could, of course, bring disruption of a more violent kind. The American manager of the Esmeralda plantation, also in the Acayucán district, had his throat cut by 'three or four natives'; and, though the ringleader was arrested, it was not thought that much could be done to guarantee life and property, the local authorities being 'badly crippled'.[664] Furthermore, this was only the beginning. In the years to come complaints of lawlessness, violence and unrest proliferated; regions like Los Tuxtlas became famous for their 'notorious intrigues . . . endless tales of injustice . . . hair-raising stories of murder, assaults and ambushes'.[665] And this violence fed on itself, as landlords took their own reprisals against bandits, social bandits and agrarian protestors. Already, in 1912, the planters were yearning for repression: 'a good whipping would do these people a lot of good', commented one; 'the sunrise greeting against the adobe wall', counselled another, 'has a wonderfully deterring effect'.[666] Locally and nationally the lobby for repression grew more vocal.

As the focus shifts away from the central plateau towards the Isthmus and the south east, so the popular challenge to the hacienda – and to authority more generally – becomes weaker, but by no means negligible. In this respect the state of Tabasco marks something of a watershed: the western districts mirror southern Veracruz, while the east anticipates the relative calm of Campeche and Yucatán; and the division is further suggestive of the revolutionary ecology which we hypothesise here. Revolutionary activity in 1911 had displayed two main concentrations; a primary one which stretched from Chontalpa and the headwaters of the Grijalva River through the municipalities of Huimanguillo and Cárdenas to the coast at Paraiso; and a secondary one represented by the Chiapaneco enclave which contained Reforma and Pichucalco, and which – in terms of revolutionary geography – belonged as much to Tabasco as Chiapas. In contrast, the less populous regions of eastern Tabasco, where the Grijalva and Usumacinta flowed into the Gulf, were correspondingly quiet, for reasons which will be suggested shortly. Though, as we have noted, agrarian disputes played their part in the western zone, the generation of revolt obeyed other motives and reflected the nature of rural society: one that was characterised by a scattered, shifting and relatively low population (the chief concentrations being along the river banks), by the absence of stable villages, and by the co-existence of numerous small *rancherías* alongside banana and cacao plantations. It was, too, a region where observers later commented on 'the frequent homicides which take place in these exceedingly

diffuse, individualistic communities'.[667] Such a society had more in common
with the Bajío than with Morelos; but it displayed an even greater kinship
with the Brazilian *sertão*, where violence (not least banditry) flourished amid
the fluid, anomic communities of the north-eastern frontier.[668]

Thus, after the conclusion of the Madero revolution, raids and feuds
continued; Maderista veterans feared (and suffered) reprisals from adherents of
the old regime; planters found that the 'absolute lack of guarantees' made it
difficult to police their estates and recruit labour.[669] During the 1912
troubles, the same *municipios* were again prominent. Huimanguillo and
Cárdenas were 'the centres of almost all the revolutionary movements in this
state'; the former, in particular, was the chief 'foco de revolucionarios', and the
unrest there was considered 'endemic'. Early in 1913, renewed outbreaks were
anticipated in Huimanguillo, Cárdenas and Paraiso.[670] And the same towns
and villages were visited by bandit/rebels: Jalpa, Pichucalco, Reforma and
Teapa, 'places remote from the centre and eternally threatened by elements of
disorder'.[671] But, especially with the news of Orozco's defeat, these troubles
remained sporadic and isolated, and showed no signs of gelling into an
organised rebellion.[672] Despite his unpopularity, and his alleged failure to
fulfil political promises (for example, with respect to agrarian reform), the
state governor remained in control of the situation; in May 1912 he even sent
some locally recruited *rurales* to serve in Chihuahua against Orozco, a move
which may have indicated confidence, but which exacerbated his unpopularity.[673] But while the small bands of insurgents could not mount a serious,
sustained challenge to the regime, they could pull off sudden, sometimes
spectacular, coups, of a kind which had but rarely disfigured the Pax
Porfiriana.[674] At Jalpa, the *jefe político* and three police were killed by bandits,
who made a point of attacking state and Federal offices, leaving the rest of the
community unmolested.[675] About the same time, the bandit Pedro Padilla
made a daring raid on the port of Frontera, where he robbed the business and
customs houses, hijacked a launch and, having waited for the stevedores to coal
the vessel, 'gracefully waved his hat to the gasping crowd, saying "Adios
población simpática" and ordered the steamer to proceed at full speed down
the river to the Gulf of Mexico'.[676] And on the same day, a 'Tabascan faction'
attacked Pichucalco, initiating an invasion of Chiapas which, though well-
equipped, proved unsuccessful.[677]

Padilla (reputedly a 'small landowner' himself) was said to be in the pay of
old Porfirians, like ex-Governor Policarpo Valenzuela, who sought to discredit
the local Maderista regime.[678] Certainly landlords and *políticos* allied with
bandits (the *jefe* at Frontera was in cahoots with Padilla; at a higher level, as we
have seen, the Chihuahuan elite flirted with Orozquismo); and bandits were
not averse to such alliances. But it would be wrong to categorise all bandits as
mercenaries and lackeys, to strip them of all 'social' characteristics, and equally
wrong to attribute all the banditry of 1912 to Porfirian machinations, as has

been done.[679] It is inconceivable that, as a general rule, 'landed men aided and abetted bandits by whose followers the estates of those same proprietors were overrun'; this would have been a *politique du pire* beyond even the most crazy revolutionaries, let alone conservative admirers of the Pax Porfiriana.[680] On the contrary, there was a general recognition that the plantation system and its supportive authorites were facing a serious challenge which – though still contained – could not be ignored. And, as in the north, the traditional instruments of control were now often worse than useless. *Rurales* under the command of the 'habitual inebriate' and ex-rebel Pedro Sánchez Magallanes drank, brawled and feuded at Paraiso. *Rurales* were responsible for attacking two of Policarpo Valenzuela's plantations in March 1912, smashing doors, desks, strongboxes and furniture.[681] A 'self-styled major' (whether *rural* or rebel is not clear) attacked Pichucalco in July, while a peace-keeping force sent to the same town in November (when 'slight disorders' were reported there) got drunk, mutinied and shot one of their officers.[682] Not surprisingly, the state governor was relieved to see the back of these forces: the 'famous 45th Rural Corps' sailed from Frontera (probably bound for Chihuahua) with the poetic young governor praying 'to Heaven that other climes . . . might discipline them and make them truly worthy of their noble calling'.[683] Regular Federal troops were more reliable, but the small garrisons stationed in the threatened towns – Frontera, Huimanguillo, San Juan Bautista – 'were hardly sufficient to maintain order in these places'. Hence there were demands for more troops, for the replacement of the governor by a more energetic executive, and even for the establishment of military rule.[684]

Such demands, highly significant for the future, indicated the anxiety of the planters in these zones. But the incidence of rebellion and banditry in the south was patchy; some planters continued unscathed and relatively un-worried; and any hypothetical ecology of revolution must try to take into account regions of quiescence as well as regions of revolt. 'An explanation based only on cases where something happened', Tilly reminds us, 'is quite likely to attribute importance to conditions which are actually quite common in cases where nothing happened.'[685] And there certainly were regions where 'nothing happened', where, in other words, either the legitimacy of the old order survived, or repression curbed potential protest. Looking down from the highlands near Teziutlán to the tropical lowlands of Veracruz, as they stretched from Misantla to the coast at Nautla, an observer anticipated 'absolutely no danger of any revolutionary movement from those people living below here in the "hot country"'; for, compared with the local highlanders, 'the people there are altogether of a different type . . . and have no time to mingle in politics and as a general rule are ardent supporters of the constituted government'.[686] It was a vague, sweeping generalisation, but it was borne out by events. The sierra, as we have noted, was far more productive of sustained rebellion. In contrast, the coffee planters of Misantla (unlike those of southern

Veracruz) maintained their paternalistic authority largely intact; the region gave no support to Gavira's rebellion in the spring of 1912; and, when revolt finally came to Misantla, a couple of years later, it came at the behest of the landlords themselves, who fought to defend their pre-eminence and property.[687]

Similar distinctions were made in the southern part of the state, where the troubles around Los Tuxtlas compared with the calm prevailing along the Papaloapán River, 'in the rubber districts where . . . the Americans are going right along . . . harvesting their rubber and clearing some more land'; here, the contagion of rebellion, imported from outside, was resisted: 'the peones make good wages, from a peso a day up, and among this class it is difficult to find adherents to any political or revolutionary movement'.[688] Assuming such reports to be trustworthy (and there was no good reason why their authors should have tried deliberately to mislead) they afford further evidence of both the peon's resistance to revolutionary appeals, and the American employer's proclivity (in certain circumstances) to secure labour by means of cash incentives, thereby further reinforcing that resistance. The 'certain circumstances' may be hypothesised as those in which the new plantations appeared as welcome sources of employment, capable of recruiting voluntary labour, rather than as agents of agrarian expropriation; indeed, 'many small farmers' were reported as being active in this region, presumably unaffected by the rubber interests, save in that those interests provided jobs and, perhaps, markets.[689] But a stability born of legitimacy – of a genuine absence of conflict – should be distinguished from a stability imposed by repression, even if such a distinction is not easily established empirically. The troubles of western Tabasco, recently mentioned, contrasted with the peace and order prevailing in the eastern municipalities, which marched with Campeche and Chiapas: Jonuta, Montecristo, Balancán, Tenosique and Macuspana (municipalities whose experience of rebel activity was confined to occasional, precipitate flights to the sanctuary of Guatemala).[690] While the region contained peasant communities with disputed claims to land (such as Jonuta), these were islands within a sea of virgin country and newly established, foreign-owned plantations, engaged in the export of tropical fruit or timber.[691] Here, the evidence points more to a stability born of control and repression, and Francisco Múgica, later governor of Tabasco, was not guilty of rampant hyperbole in describing, 'the Indians of the state . . . [as] the most enslaved among all the inhabitants of the Republic'.[692] Here, debt-peonage of an oppressive form flourished, even, it seems, on American plantations; and it was particularly severe in the upland *monterías* where – as the novels of B. Traven suggest – 'the workers . . . [were] treated like slaves from time immemorial'.[693] The absence of reports of rebellion or even banditry in this zone may reflect the poverty of sources as much as the quiescence of the peons.

But it cannot be doubted that, pending the arrival of revolutionary forces from outside, the control of the plantocracy remained formidable, and free from serious challenge.

The same was broadly true of the rest of the south east, particularly the state of Yucatán. Here, the brief storm of 1910–11 had been weathered at the price of a few modest political changes. In Chiapas, it is true, a more serious political crisis supervened, and this in turn facilitated a degree of social unrest, as bandits raided and peons fled from their estates.[694] But the social order remained unchanged, and in most respects unchallenged. In Yucatán, henequen production was unaffected and exports from Progreso grew throughout the Madero period.[695] In Chiapas the 1912 coffee harvest was brought in as usual.[696] And the old abuses continued: Yaqui deportees still languished on the plantations of Yucatán and Campeche; Spanish foremen in the *monterías* of Chiapas still beat their peons, while the owners traded them like slaves.[697] The peons' efforts to improve their lot were few and unsuccessful. In most cases, a careful observer in Yucatán noted: 'lost on the estates, ignorant of Spanish, without the least idea of the political organisation of the land where they live, and under the close vigilance of the *administradores*, who are also the municipal authorities of the haciendas, [the Indians] cannot voice complaints when they are abused'.[698] As a result, complaints and modest attempts at reform emanated more from middle-class, Maderista *ladinos* than from the Indians themselves (who, said one such Maderista, were themselves chiefly to blame for getting 'hooked' in the first place). But neither the publicity of abuses nor – in the case of Chiapas – the passing of legislation designed to curb them (legislation for which there were ineffectual Porfirian precedents) made much difference to the Indians' plight, or to the planters' business.[699] Indeed, not only did the Chiapas landlords kit out their own rural defence forces; they could also count on the support of the new, Maderista, reformist regime. The *jefe* at Tapachula, for example, 'continued to make good his promises to assist the planters in every possible way and owners and managers report greater attempts to afford them assistance in managing their field hands than they have experienced for some time'.[700] Meanwhile, the erosion of peonage owed more to the market than to political reformism. In Yucatán, planters 'of more advanced ideas' (as well as bankers who had acquired control of some estates) were making 'modest efforts' to substitute free for peon labour, on the grounds that the former was more profitable; similar trends were discerned in Tabasco, too, at least in regions (such as the hinterland of Frontera) where the demand for labour was keener.[701] Before long, an imported political radicalism would second and accelerate the inexorable effects of the market. But for the moment the plantation and plantocracy of the south east survived, still secure, but in more straitened circumstances than in the past.

PRO PATRIA CHICA MORI

At an earlier stage, a fundamental distinction was made between the agrarian and *serrano* rebellions. The first was premised on the recovery of land (*ejidal* and/or freehold) which had gravitated into the hands of *hacendados* or caciques; it was represented by movements of great stamina and conviction (Zapata's, the Cedillos', Calixto Contreras', the Yaqui Indians'), as well as numerous lesser, local protests; all, despite their ethnic and organisational differences, responded to common grievances. *Serrano* rebellions reasserted local autonomy: they sought self-government, and freedom from taxation, conscription and political impositions; they could mobilise entire communities, creating broad, 'polyclassist' movements which – for all their military aptitude – often proved politically ambivalent and opportunistic. Such categories, of course, are ideal types; and their particular characteristics were not mutually exclusive in practice. Some *serrano* movements (such as those of western Chihuahua) had clear agrarian elements, though these did not dominate the movement as in Morelos. Yet more generally, agrarian rebels shared the *serranos'* desire for self-government and autonomy – though these did not represent ends in themselves so much as means towards their overriding agrarian goal. But certainly, in *serrano* Chihuahua and agrarian Morelos alike, it was the 'landlords, the rich ... the bureaucrats and politicians who needed the government; in the villages they had no need, they governed themselves'.[702] Both movements, furthermore, were quintessentially popular, and represented broad, collective, voluntary protests against key features of Porfirian Mexico: the commercialisation and concentration of agriculture on the one hand, the construction of a strong, centralised state on the other.

The pioneer *serrano* movements of the revolution – notably those of Chihuahua – assumed a radical guise, since their prime target (the Creel–Terrazas oligarchy) was so integral a feature of the Porfirian establishment. Over time, however, both the radical and the popular character of *serrano* rebellion could fade. *Serrano* leaders readily contented themselves with a revived *caciquismo* of the old style: one that was more personal, local and probably more sensitive to its subjects' interests than the new, centralising *caciquismo* of the Porfiriato; one that resisted rather than furthered political integration into the nation state; but one which remained fundamentally hierarchical and undemocratic, and which envisaged no major social restructuring. The Figueroas, for example, sought to evict Díaz's imposed caciques, the agents of centralisation, and to recreate the old Alvarez *cacicazgo* of the mid-nineteenth century; the Orozcos (father and son) perhaps entertained similar hopes, acting in the old tradition of the 'Papagochi party' which had controlled the district of Guerrero back in the 1880s.[703] Meanwhile, even as these pioneer movements began to display something of their innate conservatism, new generations of *serrano* rebels were born: those of 1911–13 (whom we shall consider here), those of 1913–14, and of 1914–20 (a particularly numerous and lusty generation), who will figure later in the book. All were popular, in that they enjoyed genuine, voluntary support among the mass of the people; and all revealed the fundamental *serrano* attachment to the *patria chica* and hostility to outside interference. But social radicalism – and the related agrarianism which affected some early *serrano* rebellions – were almost entirely absent, and many of these movements appeared to adopt formally conservative or anti-revolutionary programmes. Why, then, should they be assimilated to the (revolutionary) popular movement? Were they not (as is usually said of the Felicistas of 1914–20) outright reactionaries; or, at best (like the Oaxaqueño *serranos*), rather feeble, 'non-revolutionary' rebels, unworthy of direct comparison with (say) Zapata?[704]

First, it should be made clear, such movements differed from Zapatismo, just as the more radical, pioneer, *serrano* rebellions differed from Zapatismo. But it would be presumptuous to assume that, in the relative absence of agrarian confrontation and its related class conflict, popular rebellions were necessarily more feeble, or somehow of secondary importance. It may be a matter for regret, but popular forces clearly mobilised – with enthusiasm and alacrity – behind local *serrano* caciques, even landlords, and fought doggedly under their leadership. Though class divisions were thereby blurred, and class consciousness was correspondingly dulled, these movements were both extensive and important and, as such, they merit historical analysis. Furthermore, the fact that, in many cases, they were not coeval with the Revolution, but developed in response to the 'logic of the Revolution' in subsequent years, is no reason for neglect; since the ultimately victorious revolutionary coalition (which perforce cannot be neglected) was a comparable late-comer, with no pretensions to veteran status. But the strongest argument for assimilating *serrano* movements of different generations and ostensibly different political complexions lies in the common character of their enemies (again, despite generational and political differences). The pioneer *serranos* of 1910–11 fought against Díaz (in this and all other examples the rider 'and his local minions' must be added); those of 1911–13 against Madero; in 1913–14, Huerta was the target; after 1914 the emerging Constitutionalist/Carrancista regime. The nature of the particular enemy of course had a bearing on the formal ideology and platform of each rebellion. Opponents of Díaz necessarily sounded more radical than opponents of Carranza: in some cases they were, but often they were not; thus, divergent political statements could mask a basic continuity of revolutionary practice. The similarities uniting movements like those of de la Rocha (1911), Gómez (1911), Lucas (1913), Meixueiro (1914) and Fernández Ruiz (1915), are more noteworthy than the differences which separated them. The *mapache* rebels of Chiapas (1915), though led by the *hacendado* Fernández Ruiz in opposition to the 'revolutionary' regime, 'rebelled to defend their *patria chica* from abusive outsiders'; and in doing so they counted on extensive local and popular support.[705] The second wave of *serrano* revolts, similarly directed against the 'revolutionary' regime of Madero, was precisely comparable. And this continuity could be achieved – notwithstanding more superficial political differences – by virtue of the continuity of the state, be it Porfirian, Maderista, Huertista or Carrancista. In Mexico as in France 'a new power was created by the Revolution or, rather, grew up almost automatically out of the havoc wrought by it'.[706] National revolutionary elites proved as greedy for power as their Porfirian predecessors (the great exception was the Villista elite which, as we shall see, retained enough of its popular *serrano* character to squander the chance of taking national power) and, as a result, they constantly provoked *serrano* resistance, just as the Porfirians had. The continuity of the centralising state ensured the continuity of *serrano* revolt. That the stimulus to revolt might be 'conservative' (Porfirian or Huertista) in some cases, 'revolutionary' (Maderista or Carrancista) in others, was not without political significance, but it did not affect the fundamental character of the *serrano* response.

The second wave of *serrano* rebellions, directed against Madero's regimes, derived from longstanding grievances (as did most popular rebellions); but they were stimulated by two more immediate factors – the current relaxation of authority and the bitterly contested allocation of power and patronage which followed the fall of Díaz. The first enabled old feuds and resentments, repressed or conciliated by the dictator, to come to the surface; the second aggravated them further, or in some cases created new issues of contention between political centre and political periphery. These may be seen at all levels of political society, but this analysis will begin at the lowest (and most conjectural) level, and proceed upwards. The Madero revolution had embraced and further stimulated a host of local conflicts which pitted community against community (rather than, say, class against class). Often, however, what appears at first sight to be an inter-communal struggle, devoid of 'economic' or 'class' significance, reflecting simply the traditional antagonisms of the locality, may change its character on closer inspection. The attack of the people of Igualapa and Huehuetán on Ometepec was no mere inter-communal feud, practised by comparable communities (of the kind which proliferated in Morelos or the sierras of Oaxaca); Ometepec was a mestizo settlement, which had usurped the communal lands of the Indians of Igualapa and Huehuetán. Close by, the struggle between Jamiltepec and Poza Verde displayed a similar class dimension; or, to put it differently, horizontal divisions underlay the ostensibly vertical divisions between the warring communities.[707] Similarly, when the Yaquis descended from the mountains to raid the river valley, they were not engaged in the traditional struggle of *serranos* against plainsmen (as occurred in the central region of Oaxaca); they were fighting to recover their recently lost tribal lands.

Battles between village and village, region and region, could thus derive from fundamental agrarian conflicts, in which one actor played the role of the engrossing landlord. But, even allowing for imperfect knowledge, which may serve to conceal such underlying relationships, this was often not the case. Village conflicts were common enough in pre-revolutionary Morelos, but after 1911 they were submerged in the joint struggle against the planters: 'people from traditionally rival places like Santa María and Huitzilac had died defending each other, which bound the survivors in a close sympathy'.[708] Elsewhere, in the absence of agrarian, class polarisation (of the kind which made the *surianos* sink their old rivalries), feuds still flourished. Sometimes, they seemed to lack any contemporary rationale; they were generations old (some, in Oaxaca, could be traced back to the pre-Columbian epoch); they had become fixed data in the collective memory and mentality of certain communities.[709] The men of Ixtepeji, it seems, fought with their neighbours because it had always been done (and, if comparable examples from Europe are anything to go by, it does not even follow that any distant, anterior, economic antagonism first generated the feud; it may trace back to relatively minor, 'conjunctural' events).[710] But between these two extremes (the feud-for-itself, and the feud as surrogate for agrarian class conflict) there lay a broad middle ground, within which *serrano* movements, great and small, were to be located. In other words, inter-communal and inter-regional conflicts reflected a basically *political* rationale, which was conditional upon the growth of the state (especially the Porfirian state), and the inequities and abuses which this encouraged.[711] The resulting rebellions were typically 'polyclassist', did not obey fundamentally economic motives, and were primarily concerned to slough off the thickening integument of state power.

The Madero revolution unleashed numerous petty local squabbles of this kind. Atlacomulca (Mex.), liberated by López Jiménez, sought to free itself from the political and fiscal dominance of El Oro, which the officials of El Oro struggled to prevent.[712] In Puebla (again, following a local liberation) Tehuizingo tussled with Tuzantlán: which was to be a *municipio*, which a mere ranch? Which was to control the local archives (over which fighting had started)?[713] The people of the Chiapas port of Mazatán (which 'does not bear a particularly good reputation and is credited with harbouring a turbulent class not met with in the agricultural districts further inland') nursed grievances against the authorities in the local *cabecera*, Tapachula; in June 1912, led by an aggrieved ex-official, they marched on Tapachula intending, it was said, 'to kill the *jefe* and to wreak vengeance on certain prominent families and to loot the National and Oriental Banks'.[714] If true, the intent was not fulfilled. The Tapachula *jefe* kitted out a volunteer force; six of the Mazatán 'bandits' were captured, and the rest turned back in disarray; the Tapachula forces marched down to the coast, occupied the refractory village at daybreak, and made further arrests. As with many such incidents, it remains a historical fragment, a vivid chip from a lost mosaic. Though there is circumstantial evidence of economic resentments here (Mazatán was a declining port, as well as a turbulent community)[715] this cannot justify an explanation of the conflict couched in terms of class: pending further research, it must be seen for what it ostensibly was – a collective protest by one community against the political dominance of an unpopular *cabecera*.

Analogous conflicts at the state and regional level are a little easier to unravel. In the same state of Chiapas, the rival metropolises of San Cristóbal and Tuxtla Gutiérrez contested for primacy. The old colonial town of San Cristóbal, cynosure of the Chamula Indian economy and seat of the local bishop, had been superseded as state capital by Tuxtla in 1892; subsequent attempts to reverse this decision had failed, and it was from Tuxtla that the energetic, modernising Rabasa clique built up their impressive array of political and economic power.[716] Tuxtla enjoyed the support of the progressive planners of the central lowlands and Soconusco, while San Cristóbal could count on the sympathy of regions like Comitán and Pichucalco, which resented Tuxtleco/Rabasista centralisation (and which, further accentuating the division, clung more doggedly to the institution of debt peonage); San Cristóbal also counted on the vocal championship of the bishop.[717] Economic issues were clearly at stake, but they formed only part of a broader, regional polarisation, which transcended class and mobilised both elites and masses on both sides of the geographical divide. In all these respects the San Cristóbal faction, steeped in nostalgic particularism, conformed to the *serrano* pattern: they 'could not see beyond the highlands and the glory their local society had once possessed. They wanted to repeal the changes of the past twenty years.'[718]

There was scant military activity in Chiapas during the Madero revolution and the Rabasista clique clung to power.[719] Even the appointment of a new interim governor merely confirmed (in Cristobalense eyes) 'the continuation of [a] ferocious *caciquismo*'.[720] But in the ensuing period of elections, appointments and rumours of plots, the two factions (each claiming Maderista credentials) coalesced, mobilised and squared up to each other: on the one hand the Tuxtla interests (the 'camarilla Tuxtleca', 'Científicos', or 'Porfirio-Reyistas de Tuxtla' as their enemies called them); on the other, the 'outs' of San Cristóbal, branded as benighted, clerical rabble-rousers by the incumbent elite.[721] An incipient Cristobalense revolt was checked in July 1911, and the summer was spent in politico-electoral conflict in which the Tuxtleca interest triumphed. In response, Juan Espinosa Torres marshalled the forces of San Cristóbal: Chamula Indians were recruited and garrisons were established in the highlands; a horde of 8,000 was thereby created (so his enemies alleged), including 'Kuriki, Chamula and Lacandón, giants and pygmies', and their mobilisation threatened a 'caste war', as in the late 1860s.[722] In order to achieve this following, it was said, the Cristobalense leaders had relied not only on the appeal of the bishop, but also on promises of land distribution and exemption from taxes.[723] And the characteristic patterns of popular revolt were followed as the 'Chamula hordes' captured Ixtapa, killing the local officials, and as the people of Acalá rose up, evicting the resident cacique and his minions, 'destroying the houses which they had acquired with the work and blood of the poor'.[724] There were soon fears that 'a spread of agitation or revolutionary movement might reach the agricultural workers and endanger the gathering of the coffee crop' in the Soconusco district; but the *cafetal* workers in fact proved indifferent to the lure of *serrano* rebellion.[725] For this was clearly the character of the San Cristóbal movement. Its enemies termed it a 'caste war', since it mobilised genuine, extensive popular (Indian) support; they also blamed Científico machinations (just as everyone was now 'Maderista', so all enemies were now 'Científico') since well-to-do landlords and clerics were involved.[726] Such an ostensibly inconsistent categorisation was possible since this, like many serrano movements, combined both landed elite and (in this case Indian) peasantry in a 'polyclassist', parochial opposition to political centralisation. Economic issues were not irrelevant to such a movement, but the proffered solution was conceived in political terms, such that it permitted a broad alliance of landlord and peasant, mestizo and Indian, posed no threat to agrarian social structures, and focussed its hostility on Tuxtleco centralisation.

As it turned out, even this threat was parried. Backed by the Federal government, the Tuxtla faction recruited its own forces (the 'Sons of Tuxtla') and defeated the rebels in a pitched battle at Chiapa de Corzo in October 1911.[727] Negotiations began and the Cristobalenses were obliged to acquiesce in the status quo.[728] Their forces were disbanded, and some Indian recruits were sent home with their ears severed, to mark them forever as rebels against established authority.[729] A 'fragile truce' ensued; but there were fears, late in 1911 and again in 1912, that the old quarrel would revive.[730] And, after 1915, it did, though with a characteristic change in official terminology.

Meanwhile, two broadly comparable rebellions developed in Oaxaca: one on the Pacific side of the Isthmus, centred on Juchitán; the other in the Oaxaca highlands, north of the state capital. Both were extensive, setting both state and Federal governments major problems; both derived from (Indian) peasant rejection of political centralisation (now imposed by a 'revolutionary' regime); and both drew their leadership from traditional local elites. Juchitán (population 8,000), standing on a broad dusty road some ten miles from the Pacific, had given its name to a branch of the Zapotec tribe, renowned 'as the most ferocious, untameable fighters in Mexico [as regards] . . . the defense of their own rights against petty tyrants'.[731] The Juchitecos had rebelled against Bourbon enlightened despotism in the eighteenth century, against colonial rule in the early nineteench, against Maximilian and the French in the mid nineteenth. Throughout these vicissitudes, Juchitán faced the opposition of nearby Tehuantepec, a more conservative clerical town, the seat of government, the abode of white landlords, and the hereditary enemy of Juchitán.

Local partisanship was indicated – with Byzantine commitment – by the shibboleth of colour: red for liberal Juchitán, green for conservative Tehuantepec. Any attempt to conciliate the reds and the greens – 'of whose terrible hate for one another you have no conception', an official lamented in 1913 – was doomed to frustration; Juchitecos, fighting in faraway Yucatán in 1915 refused to wear green insignia since 'back home in their own country they belonged to the red faction; [hence] it was treason to their own to wear [a] green ribbon'.[732] The chromatic distinction was still evident as late as the 1930s (though now chiefly in fiesta decorations and women's fashions).[733]

Typically, the two communities polarised during the liberal feuds of the 1870s. Juchitán stayed loyal to Juárez, and Díaz's younger brother Félix ('Chato', 'Pug-nose', Díaz), serving as Governor of Oaxaca, appointed a reliable crony as political boss there, in the hope that he would keep the refractory Indians in line. For neither the first nor the last time, the Juchitecos rebelled against such an imposition and hounded Díaz's appointee from the Isthmus; Chato marched down to the coast with a strong army and captured the town; properties were looted, prisoners executed and (worst of all) the Juchiteco patron saint, San Vicente, was carried off (or, according to another account, put to the torch).[734] A few years later, however, when Porfirio Díaz rebelled against Juárez, the Juchitecos had the satisfaction of abetting his defeat; and, when Chato Díaz made for the Pacific coast in the hope of a get-away, he was 'caught in the burning sand-dunes of Chacalapa and lynched to cries of "Viva San Vicente!"'.[735] Personal feelings therefore conspired with *raison d'état* in leading Díaz, as president, to curb Juchiteco independence. When the Juchitecos rebelled in protest against the proposed Isthmian railway, Díaz personally commanded an expedition against them; Juchitán was besieged for over a month; and, when the town fell, he exiled the rebels' women and razed the forests where the warriors concealed themselves.[736] Repression, aided by cholera, famine and earthquake, brought a kind of peace to the Isthmus. The Isthmian railway, as it conferred prosperity on Salina Cruz, brought economic decline to Juchitán and Tehuantepec (this economic factor may have aggravated Juchiteco provincialism; but it certainly did not engender it); but while Tehuantepec, ruled by the formidable *cacica* Juana C. Romero, enjoyed the favour of Díaz, Juchitán's official reputation was evidenced in the build-up of San Jerónimo Ixtepec, close by, as one of the biggest garrison towns in Porfirian Mexico.[737]

During the Madero revolution, this south-eastern sector of Oaxaca remained quiet. In May 1911, however, both Tehuantepec and Juchitán ousted their incumbent officials and installed popular replacements by means of the then fashionable political riot; these did not involve rural mobilisation or guerrilla warfare; and the installation of José F. Gómez ('Che' Gómez) as mayor of Juchitán gratified Juchiteco particularism.[738] But, with the establishment of the new regime, Benito Juárez Maza was elected Governor of

Oaxaca. Juárez Maza inherited his father's truculence, but displayed it in pursuit of petty ends rather than great crusades; even Madero (no harsh critic, and initially well-disposed towards Juárez) believed he lacked the abilities to be state governor.[739] Once in power, Juárez shuffled the pack, promoting friends and allies, seeking to rivet the control of the 'centre' (Oaxaca City) on a state that was large, fissiparous, and agitated; in doing so, it was rumoured, he followed the guidance of an old Porfirista *político*, Heliodoro Díaz Quintas.[740] After an affray in the streets of Tehuantepec, Juárez deposed the new *jefe politíco*, Santibáñez, and appointed a Porfirista, Carlos Woolrich; fighting broke out between the two factions, Woolrich was killed, and Santibáñez consigned to gaol.[741] And now, more seriously, Juárez also challenged the authority of 'Che' Gómez, the mayor of Juchitán and chief champion of Juchiteco provincialism.

Gómez appears in the pages of Casasola, a squat, fat mestizo, standing in a dusty Isthmian street, a revolver stuck in his bulging waistband, his eyes askance, avoiding the camera.[742] His family had been traditionally powerful in Juchitán, vying with rivals (like the Leóns) for local office; as a lawyer, popular among the troublesome Juchitecos and less than 'addicted' to Díaz, he had been kept on the move during the Porfiriato, receiving judicial posts anywhere but on the Isthmus. But the Revolution brought an opportunity for him to assert his local, cacical ambitions. Carried to power by mob acclaim in May 1911, he was confirmed as local boss by Madero, and he at once set about constructing an administration packed with 'relatives and devotees', a revived version (his enemies alleged) of the *partido gomista* which had dominated the region during the rebellious 1880s.[743] Again, *serrano* protest was couched in terms of nostalgic particularism, political *revanche*, and opposition to the agents of centralisation, both state and Federal. And again (note the comparison with the Figueroas) *serrano* caciques preferred the old methods to the new niceties of liberal democracy. Enemies (like the León family) were persecuted, the opposition press was silenced, there were alleged assassinations; having used force to assume the *jefatura*, Gómez, it was said, was now organising his supporters throughout the Isthmus with a view to rebellion.[744]

Whatever the truth of these stories, Governor Juárez resolved to root out the *cacicazgo chegomista*, and he chose as his instrument Enrique León, whom he appointed *jefe político* in Gómez' place. León, said a state deputy, was a known reactionary; more important, he was disliked in Juchitán, where his father had feuded with Gregorio Gómez, Che's father; he was known to be Che's 'irreconcilable enemy'. Though lacking local support, he enjoyed the friendship of the Federal general commanding at San Jerónimo, Telésforo Merodio, who had himself clashed with Gómez back in the 1890s.[745] All the ingredients of *serrano* protest were therefore present. When León arrived at the head of 200 Federal troops, Gómez refused to hand over the *jefatura*, and the people resisted.[746] A thousand or so Juchitecos surrounded the barracks and municipal palace, besieging the soldiers; it was noted that 'the Gómez forces . . . seem to comprehend the populace generally', and they drew on reinforcements from nearly a score of Juchiteco villages to the east of the town. For three days they controlled Juchitán: a small Federal relief force was wiped out trying to relieve the beleaguered garrison; and, as was customary in such moments of popular insurgence, a tax-collector and magistrate were killed.[747] On the fifth day Federal cavalry and light artillery managed to fight their way in and Gómez and his forces retired to the east, to the sanctuary of the Juchiteco villages. All told, Gómez was reckoned to command some 5,000 men, and only Juchitán, Tehuantepec and San Jerónimo remained in Federal hands, though precariously so.

According to the glib formulae of the time, Gómez was a 'Vazquista' rebel.[748] But (even more than usual) such a national label was meaningless. The rebels' overriding aim was the old one of self-government, independent of Mexico City or (all the more) Oaxaca: Gómez's favourite slogan was: 'while we depend on Oaxaca we are lost'; and, as for his followers, 'it is claimed that as far as the poor people are concerned, the trouble is purely local. They want to have more say in the governing of their own little pueblos'.[749] It was a dream similar to that of Morelos, even if the element of agrarian revindication was largely absent (the Juchitecos were *campesinos*, in the main, and there were instances of local land seizure, but the revolt was not fundamentally agrarian).[750] And the strong emphasis on local autonomy enabled critics to charge Gómez with secessionist ambitions: he aimed (they alleged) at the creation of an Isthmian state, independent of the Mexican Federation.[751] The absence of powerful agrarian grievances did not make the rebellion any less popular or vigorous. By the end of 1911 it constituted the biggest armed movement in the country, bar Zapatismo, and the newly inaugurated President felt compelled to intervene. A deputation of Veracruzano rebels – Gavira, Jara and Aguilar – was sent to parley with Gómez, and it was agreed that Aguilar should serve as *jefe* at Juchitán, pending a settlement. And, no doubt, a settlement of some sort was feasible: *serrano* protest was easier to conciliate than rampant agrarianism. But Governor Juárez saw Madero's intervention as an infringement of Oaxaca's rights and dignity; and (Oaxaca being notoriously touchy about its state's rights) the governor received ample support in the legislature, especially from representatives of the sierra and Oaxaca City. As Madero regarded Zapata, so Juárez regarded Gómez: a criminal trouble-maker, whose rabble of a following needed to be taught a lesson.

Accordingly, Governor Juárez refused to parley with the Juchiteco rebels, and governor and president, state and Federation, found themselves at loggerheads.[752] When Madero gave Gómez a safe-conduct to come to Mexico City for talks, Juárez issued a warrant for his arrest. Heading inland across the Isthmus, Gómez was arrested at Rincón Antonio: a Federal escort was despatched to collect the prisoner, but, before it arrived, Gómez was removed from the town gaol and gunned down in the nearby village of Santa María Petapa. Accounts of the killing differ. The official, Oaxaqueño version was that, as Gómez was being removed from the gaol for fear of a lynch-mob, prisoner and escort were attacked by persons unknown: 'no-one knows who did the deed'. In Mexico City, family enmities were blamed; it was another *tierra caliente* vendetta. Yet, it was pointed out, none of the police escort had been injured, while Gómez's corpse was found to have fifty-two gunshot wounds. Hence the unofficial (and probably correct) version: that the state government, fearing that the Federal escort would whisk Gómez to relative safety in Mexico City, had him done to death; that it was a 'put-up job', a neat variation on the old *ley fuga*.[753] A recent historian, indeed, refers to 'Juárez Maza's skillful {sic} application of *Ley Fuga* ... [which] brought the Gómez adventure to a conclusion'.[754] Notwithstanding the striking empathy with Porfirian political mores evident here, the comment is not entirely valid. The Juchitecos, it is true, took no immediate action (they had already shown a certain apprehension at Gómez's parleying with the Federal government: 'you order and we obey', they had allegedly told their cacique, 'but if you trick us you do not escape'); some 2,500 even accepted Governor Juárez's offer of an amnesty.[755] But the rebellion did not end with Gómez's death, and Juchiteco amnesties were somewhat like Yaqui truces: many rebels, it was believed, had taken to the hills after the fighting at Juchitán in November, in order to recuperate and gather strength.[756]

In the new year, therefore, the rebellion revived. By March 1912 some 2,000 were under arms, controlling the country between Juchitán and Reforma, raiding the Panamerican Railway, effectively cutting Chiapas off from the rest of Mexico. As in the Yaqui wars, the rebels dominated the countryside, mopping up the smaller towns and villages, confining the Federals to the beleaguered cities and hazardous railway lines; and they did not repeat their mistake of November 1911 by contesting Federal control of key centres like Juchitán itself. Meanwhile, the miasma of rebellion drifted from the hot lowlands of the Isthmus to the temperate Chiapas highlands, infecting the migrant Juchiteco workers on the coffee estates. On one *cafetal*, drunken Indians brawled with local workers and, when the German manager intervened, they attacked him with rocks and machetes. Two were killed in the affray and twenty-three arrested; what is more, a gloomy planter reported, the cry 'Viva Zapata!' was heard on the Indians' lips.[757]

The rebellion – and its associated troubles – continued until midsummer 1912. By then, four factors conspired to curtail its activity. Repression brought the death of some Juchiteco leaders, the surrender of others.[758] Orozco's defeat in the north had its effects in Oaxaca, as elsewhere. But there were two more important and proximate factors: the death of Governor Juárez, the first begetter of all these troubles, in April; and the exigencies of the 1912 planting season. Even more than in other parts of Mexico here, on the dry

Isthmus, the imperative of the summer rains was compelling. Thus, by late July, 'the great majority of the country people are devoting themselves to putting in their crops'; and, it was thought, 'the necessity of getting crops planted and cultivated has probably been the most potent factor in causing the people to become pacific'.[759] So, with Juárez dead, and the Juchiteco rebels 'returned to their farms', the Chegomista revolt came to a close – though there were fears, later in the year, that peace would only last 'until the end of January [1913] when the last of the crops of the small farmers will be harvested', and *serrano* pretensions might be revived.[760] Early in the new year, however, a major, national upheaval undercut any such predictions.

The Juchiteco revolt provided a further reminder of the Juchitecos' fierce commitment to self-government (albeit self-government under the aegis of traditional caciques, who were far from being model, Maderista liberals); it seriously challenged the state government and alarmed the Federal administration. There does not appear to have been a clear economic dimension to the conflict. Agrarian claims were scarcely mentioned. Perhaps the political impositions of Oaxaca City implied heavier taxation, or diverted the spoils of office away from native Juchitecos, but there is little to suggest that such rational cost-accounting determined the rebels' behaviour (certainly not that of the rank-and-file). On the whole, the Juchitecos were prosperous and progressive, in their limited way: they ran much of the coastal trade below Tehuantepec; their head town boasted electric light before most others in the region; they showed a desire and often an ability to 'get on', whether through commerce, education or the law.[761] Unlike the Zapatistas (or the Yaquis) they did not face a mortal challenge to their basic way of life. Perhaps this helps account for the greater tenacity over time of the Zapatistas and Yaquis. But it would be wrong to underestimate the strength of Juchiteco provincialism, or its capacity to inspire a dogged defence of the *patria chica* (even in default of 'economic' grievances). The crucial difference between the two movements, *serrano* and agrarian, lay less in the strength of initial motivation, or the superior 'revolutionary' status of *agrarismo*, than in the contrasting reactions of government, which could more easily tolerate – at least for a time – a degree of Juchiteco independence than it could a display of Zapatista agrarianism, with all its obvious implications for property and the social order. Ultimately, of course, Juchiteco independence would also have to be terminated, whether by force or co-option (as the rebel rank-and-file, with their evident suspicion of Che Gómez's negotiations, perhaps feared); indeed, though the Juchitecos could not know it, the forces of oppressive centralisation would spring back all the more alive and vital after their period of enforced quiescence.

Oaxaca has sometimes been categorised as a state unacquainted with revolution (at least prior to 1914). Yet, while the Juchitecos rose in arms, the followers of Barrios and Oseguera were active around Cuicatlán; agrarian revolt affected the valley of Oaxaca itself; and banditry plagued the Gulf side of the Isthmus. If this were not enough, the men of the Sierra Juárez, the brooding range north of the state capital, now also rose in revolt. Their revolt paralleled the troubles on the Isthmus and was, in a sense, their legacy; for, in accordance with the tortuous logic of the Revolution, and the class, regional and clientelist rivalries which informed it, the price of suppressing a rebellion in the coastal lowlands was a rebellion in the mountains. Again, the historical roots went deep. The Mixtecs of the Sierra Juárez farmed their own lands or worked in the small, primitive mines which dotted the region. Political control was in the hands of mestizo caciques like the Hernández and Meixueiro families, who held land, mining interests and 'elected' office and who – in the absence of polarising agrarian conflicts – exercised a paternalistic, traditional authority over their clients. Lic. Guillermo Meixueiro litigated on the Indians' behalf (defending Lachatao's claims to communal land, for example), provided employment in his mines, and, when necessary, led his men out to battle. It had been the 'improvised, ill-disciplined and badly armed' *serranos* from around Ixtlán, raised by the Hernández and Meixueiro families, which won the first victories which brought Díaz to power in 1876. And in return, Díaz (who had himself served as *jefe político* at Ixtlán) favoured the *serrano* caciques and their clients, allowing their political enclave to survive.[762]

A generation later, when the Revolution came, the same families and villages were soon prominent, and memories of the 1870s came flooding back.[763] Like the Juchiteco revolt, therefore, the Sierra revolts of 1912 and 1914 were strongly atavistic: they followed old precedents – not in the calculating, posturing way of revolutionary intellectuals, Mexican or French – but out of innate, historical compulsion; for the rebels of the Sierra, as for the Juchitecos, the Revolution was but another episode in a saga of ancient conflicts. These conflicts, furthermore, while they pitted Sierra against valley, also pitted village against village; and they flared up anew when the Pax Porfiriana (which in Oaxaca had brought an attenuation of old feuds, not a sharp polarisation of social classes) came to an end in 1911. Thus, *serrano* revolt did not represent a concerted response to Madero's call to arms. On the contrary, it grew cumulatively and chaotically out of the political instability of 1911–12, reaching its apogee after 1914; its adherents fluctuated and were riven by internal feuds; but it clearly depended upon the hostility of the *serranos* to the valley, and above all to the City of Oaxaca, a hostility which was warmly reciprocated.[764]

In 1911, Governor Juárez sought to recruit the men of the Sierra which bore his name in order to bolster his control of the state. Already, his gubernatorial predecessor and close adviser, Díaz Quintas, had secured the support of Pedro León of Ixtepeji (whose followers had just ransacked a textile factory at Xía) and had laid out funds 'to arm the sierra'.[765] Altogether, Juárez recruited three companies of *serranos* (from Ixtepeji, Yavesía, Lachatao and other villages) who, though they took no part in the Juchiteco campaign (it is unlikely they would have consented to such far-flung operations), were engaged in 'peace-keeping' in the Valley of Oaxaca and, in one case, were responsible for the massacre of civilians at Tlalixtac de Cabrera.[766] At the end of 1911 two of the *serrano* companies were disbanded; and in April 1912, with the sudden death of their sponsor, Governor Juárez, the remaining forces of Pedro León were also demobilised and allowed to drift home, returning to the mountains – like so many demobilised rebels – bearing their arms.[767] But they were not ready to return to their quiet life amid the pine forests of the Sierra: there was talk (almost certainly ill-founded) that Governor Juárez had been poisoned, in which case his shade cried out for vengeance; more plausibly, the *serranos* feared official reprisals for their wild conduct at Tlalixtlac.[768]

Already, it seems, there was disaffection in the Sierra. The caciques Hernández and Meixueiro, old allies of Díaz, were known to be unhappy with Madero; they were thought to have planned armed resistance in the summer of 1911; there were rumours of revolt even before Pedro León's demobilised troops returned, bringing a supply of arms.[769] At any rate, León's arrival precipitated rebellion. Aided by local villagers, the demobilised *serranos* raised a force of two to three thousand and descended to the valley again, scattering the *rurales* sent against them, encamping on the northern outskirts of the City of Oaxaca in mid-May 1912.[770] As the revolt progressed, so the role of León's Ixtepejanos (who comprised the nucleus of the first *serrano* company) came to predominate, to the chagrin of many of their fellows. The 1912 revolt did not, therefore, unite the entire Sierra. But, as the rebels laid siege to Oaxaca, it was clear that 'the *serranos* [were] . . . recognised as the ancient enemies of the town people' and, indeed, of the valley people more generally; for they attacked and occupied the same villages their fathers had in 1876 – Huayapán, San Felipe de Agua, Tlalixtlac, even as far up-valley as Etla.[771] And in the city, fear of the *serranos* was so great and apparently universal that the authorities were prepared to distribute 1,700 rifles among the townspeople, confident that they would be pointed towards the hills without, rather than the rulers within. Such confidence was unusual in revolutionary Mexico. But it indicated the strength of regional loyalties which cut across class (economic) affiliation. No doubt the city of Oaxaca's centralising claims had an economic dimension: it was the merchant community which was most vociferous in calling for a prompt reconquest of the Sierra.[772] But commercial (or fiscal) exploitation alone cannot explain the *serranos*' bitter opposition to the city. The poor of the city, the villagers of the valley, gave the *serranos* no support: for both sides, the battle-lines were drawn by commitments to region, family, cacique and an ill-defined but powerful folk memory; and these commitments cannot be reduced to some prior economic rationale. Misguidedly or not, both sides believed it was decorous to die for the *patria chica*.

Like *serrano* rebels elsewhere, those of Oaxaca were doughty fighters. Their long-range hunting rifles picked off defenders at up to 1,000 yards, and casualties were far heavier among the townspeople than the besiegers. But the arrival of 500 Federal reinforcements – even if they came on 'very poor horses [and with] a large number [of] small boys, all in bad condition' – saved the city from capture.[773] The familiar stalemate ensued. Such static warfare was not to the *serranos'* liking. At the end of May, stung – though far from defeated – by Federal sallies and short of ammunition, they decamped to the hills, chastising villages, like their old bugbear Tlalixtlac, which had failed to lend them support.[774] The natural ebb and flow of urban–rural, government–rebel conflict now asserted itself. Having driven off the *serranos*, the authorities sought to follow up their victory. Fresh troops, equipped with rapid-fire field guns, were pushed into the foothills, aiming 'to teach the *serranos* a lesson'.[775] Pedro León, caught by hostile villagers, was handed over to a firing squad at Ixtlán; and Madero, following these grim events in Mexico City, and clearly sympathetic to the city-based forces of order and civilisation, applauded their successes and the 'well-deserved punishment suffered by [the *serrano*] *cabecilla*', and looked forward to the rapid termination of the revolt.[776]

Such confidence was misplaced. Predictably enough, the tide turned and the *serranos*, back on home ground near Ixtepeji and now led by Pedro León's son (of the same name), inflicted a serious defeat on the Federals, killing some 200 and confining the remainder in Ixtlán. There were now reckoned to be 5,000 rebels in the Sierra (though not all armed) and a potential 15,000 more.[777] Perhaps this was an exaggeration, but it indicated the seriousness of the threat, as seen from the valley, and suggested that the rebellion counted on more than simply Ixtepejano support. Additional government forces were sent into the mountains, led by Colonel Celso Vega who, only recently, had been fighting Magonistas and American filibusters in Baja California. They met with no conspicuous success.[778] By September, the *serranos* were again moving into the valley, sacking Etla, brushing close by Oaxaca. Again, they were repulsed from the state capital, unable to withstand the barrage of Federal artillery and rifle fire (though it took 200 shells and 40,000 rounds to kill 50 *serranos*, most of them shrapnel victims).[779] But if the City of Oaxaca was saved, the rebels still prowled the valley at will. Frustrated, the Federal commander did what came easiest: he selected a nearby village (San Felipe de Agua), which had been briefly occupied by the *serrano* forces, and summarily executed thirty-nine civilians for alleged 'complicity'. The bodies of the innocent victims were left in a heap, on the streets, the military authorities, after the manner of Creon, forbidding a decent burial.[780] Rough treatment was meted out to other villages through which the *serranos* had passed, and the pro-government volunteers of Tlalixtlac, having helped evict the *serranos* from Huayapán, proceeded to burn the village to the ground.[781] Thus regional and personal vendettas were kept alive and virulent; and, as the conflict persisted, Ixtepeji became a depopulated wasteland.[782] By the end of 1912, energies were temporarily spent. Thanks largely to the *serranos'* efforts the state treasury was empty and the administration was running a 75% monthly deficit.[783] But bankruptcy was a sure ally of peace: no further expeditions were equipped for the Sierra, and Oaxaca enjoyed a moment's calm. As for the *serranos*, 'who have long boasted that they have never been conquered', they were still entitled to make the boast; and they lived to fight another day, against different enemies, but again in defence of their stubborn independence.[784]

THE IMPLICATIONS OF PROTEST

Throughout this chapter, the focus had been fixed on the countryside: on the various forms of rural revolt and protest unleashed by the Madero revolution, combated, contained, but never quelled by the Madero regime. Such was the social context in which Madero's liberal experiment (the theme of the following chapter) had to be conducted: one characterised by military revolt (chiefly by disgruntled veterans of 1910), by peasant jacquerie, peon unrest, banditry and provincial insurrection. Each had their distinctive leaders, locations and causes; but all attested to the weakening of authority, and to the alarming, agitated 'state of mind prevailing in a great part of the country', in Evaristo Madero's words.[785] These currents of rural protest welled up from the mass of peons, *campesinos* and *serranos* – who, to the well-to-do of the cities, seemed alien, uncivilised, barbarous and threatening, like the 'sullen people, half-devil and half-child' ruled by Kipling's proconsuls. And, as the dykes of authority and deference crumbled, it seemed that the tide might flood the cities themselves: the giants and pygmies of the Chiapas highlands (to take one lurid example) would carouse in the smart streets of Tuxtla Gutiérrez, rather as Prince Charles Edward's highlanders had in the streets of Edinburgh.

Certainly, as the tide of rural protest rose, it began to lap at the gates of the cities, where governors, officials, intellectuals, foreigners and landlords (the old absentees now supplemented by a rush of new refugees) surveyed the ferment in the countryside with mounting alarm. Oaxaca was twice besieged; Cuernavaca and Tehuacán were believed to be threatened; the Yaquis raided the outskirts of Empalme and Guaymas. The Laguna towns (not for the first or last time) became islands of order and government in a sea of rural rebellion. Acapulco was no better placed: refugees flocked in, business stagnated, bullion piled up in the vaults of the city banks, offering an additional incentive to the rural hordes. Any depletion of the Federal garrison – as when troops were sent to protect the Rothschild plantation at the mouth of the Balsas – further tightened the screw of collective panic.[786] There were, long after the conclusion of the Peace Treaty, eruptions of violence within the towns themselves; the ouster of officials at Juchitán and Mazatán; the repeated gaol-breaks, attempted, and sometimes carried out, with the help of rebel/ bandits – at Chihuahua, San Luis, Guanajuato, Irapuato and Coatepec. Bandit raids carried rural trouble-makers into the heart of Guanajuato, Silao, Frontera

and elsewhere. Meanwhile, the fears and susceptibilities of the urban population were played on by the press, with its stories of Zapatista and other
atrocities; and rumours of rural barbarities spiced street corner conversation,
adding to the atmosphere of anxiety.

These threats and fears were supplemented by those indigenous to the city.
The nascent labour unions – though weak, largely ineffectual, and, by most
standards, moderate in their aims – offered a new challenge to employers.
And, certainly more serious, there was the perennial fear of the city mob. In
the Bajío towns, scene of the worst riots of 1911, the spectre of mass
unemployment conjured visions of mayhem; fears of 'mob violence' and
looting were endemic at Durango and San Luis; they troubled Mexico City,
hitherto largely immune from violent upheaval. At the port of Mazatlán
merchants were taking out insurance policies with British companies, to cover
themselves in the event of pillage.[787] In particular, it was feared that rebel
attacks would trigger off riots: the apprehension that 'a large percentage of the
population . . . would rise to aid an attacking party and would join in looting
the town', though voiced at Acapulco, was not confined to that community.[788] Such anxieties were not without foundation. Few cities fell to rebel
forces in the Madero period, but two of the largest to do so – Cd Juárez and
Parral – provided reminders of what could happen in such circumstances.[789]

To the well-to-do, the literate and the propertied, it seemed that authority
had wilted, that Don Porfirio's patient work of pacification had been undone.
The common people – of city and countryside alike – displayed an unwonted
independence; they threw out unpopular authorities, they got involved in
electoral conflict, they gave aid and comfort to rebels and bandits. Loyalty to
village, *patria chica* and popular cacique supplanted deference to landlord and
jefe político. Meanwhile, the traditional instruments of Porfirian social control
proved blunt and ineffective. The myth of the *rurales* was further deflated:
packed with ex-Maderista veterans, *rural* detachments were often as much a
liability as an asset, mutinying, defecting and looting where they should have
been keeping the peace.[790] What reliable police or *rurales* there were found
themselves intolerably stretched and forced to leave large tracts of country
unprotected and at the mercy of rebels or bandits.[791] In response, those with
property to protect sometimes went freelance. The planters of Morelos and the
Laguna deployed armed field-guards (not, it seems, with much success); the
wealthy Spanish merchant houses of Acapulco hired a local thug, Victorio
Salinas, at 1,000 pesos a month (plus his 100 men at 1.25 pesos a day), to
patrol the streets of the city by night and to guard their warehouses.[792] If, in
1912, such freelance operations did not achieve much, they indicated the
prevailing mood and established precedents for later more extensive action. In
general, however, these threatened elites displayed a strange supine indifference (a point which will be further analysed in volume II). *Hacendados* resorted
to successful self-defence precisely in those regions (like the highlands of

Chiapas) where the agrarian threat was weak, and where an enduring legitimacy gave them the capacity for action; where the threat was more severe – in Morelos, the Laguna, and numerous regions of central Mexico – landlord legitimacy was spent, and landlord self-defence was largely impossible. Anxious owners of property therefore looked to the Federal Army to guarantee their interests, and this the army did, in the cities if not throughout the countryside, though at the price of mounting military expenditure and ambition.

The civil authority also found its legitimacy undermined, and its capacity for repression impaired. Officials did not forget the treatment their kind had received during the Madero revolution, and they faced regular reminders in the course of 1912. Where they survived, in areas of popular protest, they often did so by keeping a low profile, by taking account of popular attitudes and sanctions to an extent unknown during the Porfiriato. Hence the constant complaints of authorities failing to take decisive action, 'not wishing to antagonise the people' (Tamps.), of their being 'weak and vacillating' (Gro), 'apparently powerless' (Ver.), 'powerless or afraid to act' (Oax.). In Tepic, 'the authorities make little more than a burlesque of themselves. Everyone knows they fear "the people"'; in many cases they were seen to connive at banditry.[793] Respectable politicians and aspirants to office now had to take note of popular pressures, even of rival popular candidates – like Navarro in Guanajuato, Gavira in Veracruz. Generally, such candidates failed: the criteria of political respectability, and the capacity to rig elections, were only gradually being undermined (more of this in the next chaptere). But popular candidacies generated instability, and could lead to outright rebellions, like Gavira's. Just occasionally, popular candidates might attain high office (as Antonio Hidalgo did in Tlaxcala) and enact reforms. Though the consequent measures of tax equalisation and political renovation were less than revolutionary, they were enough to alarm an elite long cosseted by Porfirian conservatism; and, in the case of Chihuahua, moderate reforms stampeded some of the old elite into an anomalous alliance with Orozco.

But more worrying, to propertied and political elites alike, were the *ad hoc*, anarchic, popular attempts at 'reform', particularly those of an agrarian character. These involved retributive attacks on harsh managers and overseers, the seizure and division of hacienda fields, the recovery of common rights to waters, forests and pastures. They were incited – so landlords, businessmen and officials lamented – by demagogues preaching 'socialistic' or 'semi-socialistic' doctrines, or by disgruntled revolutionary soldiers who returned to village and hacienda, their heads full of crazy, subversive ideas of *reparto* and revenge. More generally, the holders of power and property lamented the bold independence of mind, the rejection of reassuring Porfirian norms, which now characterised the common people, of the countryside at least. 'Anarchy' prevailed in the Culiacán Valley, or in the Canton of Ozuluama; 'the rabble . . .

dominates Sinaloa' and could only be held in check by the uncouth *cabecilla* Juan Banderas, just as Orozco alone, it was thought, could restrain the 'rabble' of Chihuahua. In Guerrero, 'the Indian and the peon is on top'; Chiapas faced a 'caste war'; Zapatismo threatened to plunge not just Morelos but all Mexico into a 'true Niggerdom'. Sometimes these fears were greatly exaggerated; sometimes officials, like the *jefe político* of Zacatlán (Pue.), exercised a devious imagination, 'citing revolts which have not happened . . . in order to depose decent and honourable officials, intimidate peaceful citizens, and impose [his own] candidates as municipal presidents'.[794] But the very resort to such ploys indicated the mood of the times, for in Don Porfirio's day officials more often erred on the side of confidence and complacency. And in many cases the fears and anxieties, if written up in emotive terms, nevertheless reflected a genuine alarm on the part of elites who felt truly threatened.

The response of these threatened elites was – as has been suggested – ineffectual, certainly in those regions where the threat was pronounced. And, in default of action, they often relied on rhetorical consolation, criticising Madero while advocating, in Pavlovian fashion, authoritarian and repressive solutions. Mexico's problems were seen to stem from racial and economic backwardness; they could only be tackled (and probably not solved) by strong government on Porfirian lines. Madero, with his 'sick mind' and sloppy liberalism, merely encouraged chaos. His removal would make way for Mexico's natural, appropriate regime, that of the 'iron hand'. Some saw the embodiment of the 'iron hand' in Reyes; then, after Reyes' debacle, in de la Barra, or Huerta; locally, adherents to the faith sought salvation in military rule, as practised in Morelos or Sinaloa, or advocated in Tabasco. The suitability of the individual candidates scarcely mattered (hence the subsequent vogue for Félix Díaz); like all myths, that of the 'iron hand' depended on faith rather than reason; and it was maintained by the mouthing of empty litanies, formalised prayers for 'good whipping[s]' to chastise Mexico's plebeian sinners. It was translated into action in Juvencio Robles' Morelos campaigns; in the Sonorans' resolution to proceed with 'the extermination of the Yaquis'; in the Chihuahuan conservatives' hopes of establishing 'a more oppressive dictatorship . . . than was known in the days of General Díaz'. Some even began to look to the US to provide the 'iron hand'.[795] So strong was the myth that many Maderistas, and even Madero himself, in some measure fell under its spell; and adherents were not usually disabused of their faith by its failures in practice, notably in Morelos. Hence, far from weakening, it went from strength to strength, finally achieving its greatest mass conversions, its loudest paeans, and its supreme apotheosis, in the Huerta regime of 1913–14.

Madero's position in all this was unenviable. As the well-to-do – including many of his old, urban, middle-class supporters – turned against him, as he faced the armed opposition of one-time popular allies as well as fresh plebeian adversaries, so he found himself marooned on a shrinking political isthmus.

On both sides the waters rose, and the narrow spit of sand on which the president and his loyal supporters clustered grew ever more cramped, shifting and treacherous, a poor foundation for the new, liberal Mexico they hoped to build. Modest reforms, which would not satisfy the radicals and populists, raised in conservative eyes the spectre of class war and social dissolution. The great coalition of 1911 had fragmented, the Maderista bandwagon had ground to a halt. Madero, once the conquering hero, was now a figure of fun. Yet, in strictly realistic terms, Madero's position was not so hopeless. It was inevitable and perhaps healthy that the febrile enthusiasm of summer 1911 soon dissipated. Even before his inauguration in November, it was clear that the fiesta was over, and Madero would have to prove his capacity to govern, and in highly straitened circumstances. Major crises afflicted the regime through 1912, but these were weathered; Orozco was defeated, Zapata was contained, along with dozens of lesser popular challenges; by the late summer of 1912, political observers detected a new stability, a new confidence. This was gained at a steep price: the sheer financial cost of repression, the much greater political cost of resorting to Porfirian methods and reneging on many of the promises (implicit as well as explicit) of the 1910 revolution. The pro's and con's of this exchange may be debated; they will figure more prominently in the next chapter.

But it cannot be denied or ignored that, despite these severe tests, the Madero regime had survived. Though the turn of 1912–13 witnessed, if anything, a resurgence of popular revolt, the latter did not attain the high levels of spring 1912; the regime which the military overthrew in February 1913 was no terminal case. And this reflected an obvious but important fact about the struggles being fought out in revolutionary Mexico: popular protest was fundamentally rural in origin, and popular forces were unwilling or unable to seize power in the cities. They could dominate the countryside, undermine the hacienda system, embarrass the government, induce panic among towns-people. But however powerful and alarming they might be (and, in general, their strength has probably been underestimated by historians), these forces did not seriously threaten to seize state power and supplant the national government. Of the popular rebels of 1912, only those of Chihuahua – the most organised and experienced – captured major towns: Chihuahua City, Juárez, Parral. The Laguna towns had been surrounded, but none had fallen. Zapata had not repeated his costly assault on Cuautla; the Guerrero rebels never attacked Acapulco, despite its depleted garrison; the Bajío towns had suffered raids, but no threat of occupation. The old adage that the Yaquis 'never attack towns' still held good. This was not simply a question of military hardware, important though that was. True, Federal artillery made an enormous difference, repelling the *serranos* from Oaxaca, decimating the Orozquistas ('it is useless for us to attempt to stand against Huerta's cannon', Orozco lamented); sieges and pitched battles also placed an intolerable strain on the inferior small arms and scant ammunition of rural rebels.[796] Few of the 1912 rebel movements could therefore consider exchanging the mobility of rural guerrilla war for the static siege or defence of urban centres. But it was also the case that few really wanted to. While this reluctance became clearer in later years, when the capture of cities was more feasible, it was apparent as early as 1912. Rural rebels, *serrano* and agrarista, displayed a certain indifference to the city and its accumulations of power and wealth: they were chiefly concerned to dominate their own patch, to lop off – rather than to appropriate – the tentacles of political and economic power which stretched from city to countryside. As regards this power, the Zapatistas, for example, 'did not wish to enter into it, but to dissolve it: they were fighting for the decentralisation of power, to render it all-pervasive like the guerrilla war'.[797]

Only when the popular rebellions acquired unusual scale, organisation and political ambition (as Orozquismo did) was the capture of cities – and all that this entailed – both feasible and desirable. But in the process, there was a real danger that the popular movement would lose its soul – to political fixers, intellectuals, fellow-travellers and opportunists, those aware of and greedy for the power and wealth which lay in the cities. Already, therefore, a paradox was evident at the heart of the popular movement: while it remained true to its basic principles and progenitors (as, for example, Zapatismo did), it avoided the contamination of the cities; but thereby it deprived itself of the chance to take power, it allowed the regime to limp along, and it confined its own activities to the rural hinterland. Nor, it might be noted in passing, was there any remote hope that the urban proletariat would perform a 'vanguard' role, providing the urban leadership and initiative which the peasantry lacked. The urban workers were too weak, too 'economist' in their aims, and, above all, too closely identified with government and employer to play any such role: they were, in many respects, an integral part of that urban, capitalist, administrative structure which the rural revolution chose to ignore, to dismantle, but never to appropriate. Those who mourn the failure of proletariat and peasantry to come together in revolutionary solidarity engage in counter-factual self-delusion: neither the social structures nor the historical conjuncture (borrowing terms the mourners may approve) were conducive to such an alliance.

Rural rebellion and unrest could therefore reach epidemic proportions while, as a result of the peasantry's self-denying ordinance (and the Federals' monopoly of artillery), the cities remained securely in the hands of the government and its allied urban interests: merchants, businessmen, landlords, officials, generals, prelates. These, the leaders of the 'political nation', could survive the rural challenge, but at the cost of bitter internal dissension and of the surrender of their traditional control over the villages, estates and mountains of the hinterland. And, during the Madero presidency, this elite dissension swelled, pending the day when these leaders would revoke the surrender, resume the offensive, and, like their distant Spanish forebears, mount a gradual, bloody *reconquista* of their lost patrimony.

6

The Madero regime:
(2) The liberal experiment

CENTRAL GOVERNMENT

Maderismo, successful on the battlefield in 1911, failed in the political arena in 1911–13. The old Porfirian system had been knocked sideways, but no viable alternative could be found. Some compared the period with the 1870s, when Díaz had come to power on a liberal platform, and begun to fashion the Pax Porfiriana out of the endemic unrest; some therefore concluded that a new Díaz was now required to turn the trick again. Certainly there were striking, if superficial parallels: a new president come to power by the sword; banditry and rural protest; provincial rebellion in the sierras.[1] But, as Díaz's own nephew pointed out to the American press, circumstances were in many respects radically different, and lessons could not easily be drawn.[2] Above all, the situation differed in two crucial aspects. First, forty years of Porfirian peace and progress had augmented, rather than decreased, the tensions (in particular the class and regional tensions) in Mexican society, at the same time as they had eroded some of the traditional forms of social control; hence the plethora of popular rebellions already mentioned. Second, Madero was pledged to democratise Mexican government: the old Porfirian methods – whereby the Pax Porfiriana had been fashioned, even in defiance of initial Porfirian promises – were to be abjured; repression, bribery, *caciquismo* were to be extirpated. Only by reneging on his basic programme could Madero restore order along Porfirian lines (even assuming that were possible). Instead, he and his *coreligionarios* were committed to reforms which went against a political grain that had grown and hardened over decades; and they set out to fulfil this commitment during times of profound social ferment.[3]

The essence of the Maderista programme was constitutional liberalism. Once constitutional procedures had been set in motion (free and fair elections, division of powers, judicial independence) then other problems, including social problems which Madero regarded as pressing, could be resolved in a peaceful, consensual manner. 'The revolution of San Luis', as Madero told the people of Huichipán (Hgo) in June 1912, 'took place to recover our liberty, because liberty, by itself, will resolve all problems ... once the people can elect their representatives to Congress, their legitimate representatives will enact all the laws necessary for the growth and prosperity of the Republic'.[4] Under the device of *Sufragio Efectivo, No Re-elección*, the government had to create consensus, which meant not only instituting free and fair elections, but also cajoling the country into participating in them and observing the new rules of the game. As much as anything else, the new regime had to be exhortatory, propagandist and proselytising. Unless it could win the hearts and minds of men, it would fail.

Towards his political enemies, therefore, Madero displayed an un-Porfirian tolerance. Already, by virtue of the Juárez Treaty and the de la Barra *interinato*, members of the old regime dominated the national legislature and the supreme court; the first remained in being until congressional elections were held in the summer of 1912, and Madero declined to interfere with the judicial arm.[5] Towards the burgeoning Catholic Party Madero was benignly tolerant; high-ranking members of the Federal Army were wooed; and towards disaffected elements whom Madero thought simply misguided (rather than congenitally hostile) he displayed that magnanimity which many construed as weakness or political naiveté. Almazán was pardoned because, Madero believed, he had 'reflected and understood his fault' (he soon rebelled again); *cabecillas* like Gabriel Gavira were amnestied, to the acute embarrassment of state authorities.[6] Conservative dissidents also benefited from Madero's conciliatory approach. When Abraham González returned to the governorship from which he had been hounded by the Orozquista rebels and their Terracista allies, he was bombarded with presidential letters urging clemency; he was to 'open his arms to all and forget their faults'; in particular, he was to 'contrive to win over the upper classes, who are the ones who most complain about [him]'. Political émigrés, from Chihuahua and elsewhere, would be allowed back into the country if they agreed to abstain from politics, but their inalienable right to vote could not be stripped from them.[7] Such magnanimity, it should be noted, was reserved for respectable dissidents, members of the 'political nation' who – whether of the 'left', like Almazán or Pedro de los Santos, or of the 'right', like Félix Díaz and the Terracistas – might be redeemed and reinserted into the constitutional system. Popular dissidents ('bandits' like Cheche Campos, agrarian rebels like Zapata or the Yaqui Indians) were neither ripe for redemption, nor deserving of such indulgence.[8]

Towards the press – at once the mould and mouthpiece of city opinion – Madero was conscientiously liberal. With the fall of Díaz, press freedom was readily conceded; there was a sudden efflorescence of dailies, periodicals, magazines and broadsheets; cartoonists were no longer afraid to sign their pictorial lampoons. Most of these publications were fiercely political and polemical, linked to parties (as *El País* and *La Nación* were to the Catholics) or to factions, like the famous anti-Madero 'Quadrilateral' of conservative deputies.[9] As his enemies came to realise that Madero's offer of press freedom was genuine, they moved onto the attack. Hence, particularly in Mexico City, the press began to criticise Madero, often in bitter, scurrilous and obscene terms; for the first time in Mexican history, the literate public enjoyed the spectacle not only of a free press, but also of a press mercilessly lampooning the head of state.[10] Papers like *El Mañana* – 'the most insolent of the opposition press' – jeered at Madero's short stature, his youth, his taste for dancing, his eccentric beliefs (spiritualism and homeopathic medicine), his lack of *machismo*. The president had botched the swearing-in ceremony; he had cried at the funeral of Justo Sierra; he had demeaned himself by riding in an airplane and embracing a bullfighter in public.[11] The Madero family, too, were attacked, for alleged graft and nepotism; mildly risqué jokes were made about the President's wife.[12] Prominent Maderistas also suffered: Abraham González was portrayed as a country bumpkin, while attention was drawn not only to Pino Suárez's 'imposition' as vice-president, but also to his long nose and indifferent poems.[13] Throughout, the capital's press pandered to *capitalino* prejudices – against the new political elite from the provinces (chiefly the north), the money-grubbing Maderos and their gauche, provincial hangers-on. The women of the Madero entourage, for example, seemed 'unsophisticated and prudish' compared to Mexico City high society and its 'liberally powdered women of social prominence'; cosmopolitan, Europhile (and conservative) Mexico City disdained the ingenuous, somewhat Americanised *arrivistes* from the northern frontier.[14] Thus, after the hysterical welcome of June 1911, the capital – as reflected in its press – lapsed into a smug, carping hostility towards the new regime.

In the face of the press barrage, Madero was stoical, confiding to friends that he never read the papers or, if he did, never believed them; his own 'sincere convictions' held him back from placing controls on the press.[15] Perhaps, in a country of high illiteracy, Madero's disdain for the fourth estate was justified, and, certainly, the impact of press criticism – as measured by Mexico City society and the press itself – was exaggerated.[16] But by February 1912, with revolt under way in Chihuahua, and with the press publishing divergent, unreliable and speculative reports on the matter, presidential patience began to wear thin and the administration began to consider counter-measures.[17] The next month, as the crisis peaked, a seemingly care-worn and nervous president convened the Mexico City editors, rebuked them for their hostile and inaccurate reporting, appealed to their patriotism, and reminded them of the article of the Penal Code which forbade actions causing public alarm.[18] After the Federal defeat at Rellano, censorship was imposed (the closure of *El Heraldo Mexicano* almost provoked a riot) and the public became dependent on bland, uninformative, official hand-outs. In capital and provinces alike the dearth of news stimulated resentment and rumour.[19] Later in 1912 Madero returned to the question, appealing to Congress to pass a 'liberal law' that would halt press abuses without infringing basic freedoms, but the session ended without legislative action.[20]

Government curbs on the press, though roundly denounced by conservatives, were in fact short-lived, and did not subvert the essential and unprecedented liberty of expression enjoyed during the Madero period.[21] But the regime was also accused of using informal methods – of Porfirian provenance – in order to control the press. In *Nueva Era* the administration had the once bold, oppositionist paper of the past, now converted into a bland, official organ: its circulation (somewhat less than 10,000) was respectable, but its attempts to 'reflate' Madero's image, after it had been 'steam-rollered' by public opinion, do not appear to have been successful.[22] According to several accounts, the government – through Gustavo Madero – sought to buy a slice of the press to supplement *Nueva Era: El Diario* was rescued from oblivion at the end of 1911, the prestigious *El Imparcial*, with its seasoned Porfirian hacks, was acquired a year later.[23] But, during a period of press freedom and political effervescence, government control was the kiss of death. *Imparcial*'s circulation dropped by a quarter within days of its becoming 'official', and advertisers began to cry off. The literate, urban population (many of them hostile to or disillusioned with Maderismo) simply preferred the lurid, scurrilous and informative (if unreliably informative) opposition press to the anodyne official publications. The latter could only flourish in a climate of more rigid censorship and control, which Madero – despite the urgings of some of his supporters – was not prepared to countenance.[24] Meanwhile, the administration's often quite legitimate attempts to influence opinion through the press were construed as lapses into Porfirian malpractice. Here, as in the even more important area of electoral politics, the fine distinction between legitimate influence and illicit pressure was hard to draw in a society undergoing transition from *caciquista* inertia to democratic participation.

The most extreme – but also the most conjectural – form of illicit pressure was that of the *Porra*, a band of city thugs allegedly hired by Gustavo Madero, the boss of the PCP, and the chief political broker of the Maderista administration, in order to intimidate electors, rival political candidates and the opposition press. In January 1912 *porristas*, led by a self-styled law student, demonstrated against anti-Madero newspapers like *Multicolor* and *El Mañana*, eliciting a counter-demonstration and violent conflict; the Catholic editor of *El País* was assaulted and there was an alleged attempt to set fire to the offices of *El Imparcial*.[25] The truth of all this is impossible to establish. But there was certainly a hawkish element within Maderismo which fretted at Madero's liberal scruples, and which advocated fighting fire with fire. It was not entirely coincidental, therefore, that Gustavo Madero, chief of the hawks, became the butt of these allegations of violence and illegality. Whether valid or not, they besmirched the liberal reputation of the regime and ensured that, when the time came for political scores to be settled, Gustavo Madero, '*Ojo Parado*', figured high on the list of potential victims.[26]

The problem of deploying legitimate influence without falling into Porfirian malpractice was all the more acute in the matter of elections; and the electoral process was, after all, at the very heart of Maderista political philosophy. Here again, in his dealings with the political nation and the electoral squabbles in which its members participated, Madero strove to maintain a position of liberal tolerance; for such squabbles were only to be expected in the nursery of democracy. Thus, in dozens of states, on dozens of occasions, governors and *jefes* were ordered to allow free and fair elections: special instructions were issued to the Governor of Chiapas to extend guarantees to the Catholic Party during elections in Tonalá; the military commander at Guadalajara was to guarantee the state legislature so that it could 'deliberate in complete liberty' regarding the convocation of local elections.[27] And Madero went further in rejecting traditional political practice, in the interests of an abstract, impersonal democracy. He subscribed to the novel and unpopular idea that, when it came to making local political appointments, outsiders were preferable to natives; and, while Díaz like the Spanish crown had pursued this policy (selectively and pragmatically) in order to reinforce the power of the 'centre' *vis-à-vis* the states, Madero did so in the idealistic belief that outsiders, lacking local clients and enemies, would govern in a spirit of detached impartiality, for the good of all.[28] Such a policy at once incurred the hostility of the provinces against the 'centre' (as it had in the days of Díaz or the Bourbons – no matter that the rationale had changed); it conflicted with the strong local preference for an *hijo del país* – a local man – to enjoy power; and it threatened the ancient accretions of local power built up by families through bonds of blood, *compadrazgo* and clientelism. In this, as in many other respects, Madero's notional *pays légal* accorded ill with the historic *pays réel* he had to govern; fitting the two together was a messy, Procrustean job.

The sheer frequency of Madero's instructions guaranteeing fair elections attests to his sincerity; but it also attests to the scale of the problem. The switch from a system of executive dictatorship and local *caciquismo* to one based on the impersonal norms of constitutional democracy could not be achieved by presidential fiat. Ingrained political habits died hard, and Madero, in his sincere attempts to make the new politics work, was driven back to the old methods, was obliged to compromise with ugly political reality, in the hope thereby of effecting some gradual, permanent change. Inevitably, such apparent backsliding brought howls of protest from disillusioned liberals and disingenuous conservatives. It has often been debated how far a liberal society may curtail some of its liberal freedoms in order to secure its essential survival. Madero's dilemma was similar, but more acute, and one more often debated in the context of socialism than of liberalism: how far could basic principles be compromised in the *creation* (not the maintenance) of a society in which those principles prevailed? This dilemma lay at the heart of the liberal experiment of 1911–13.

A major problem was the continued survival in positions of authority of veteran Porfiristas, wedded to the old politics, sceptical or downright hostile to the new. The changes effected at local level in 1911 were, as we have seen, partial and varied: enough to mark a break with the old regime, to raise fears and hopes, but insufficient to produce a complete renovation of authority on Maderista lines. The state legislatures which adjudicated disputed elections were – pending their own renewal – still Porfirista; in states like Veracruz the old legislature remained in power until the end of 1912. Many pueblos were in the same position as Zaragoza (Coa.) where, liberals lamented, the old 'Científico gang', Porfiristas and freemasons to a man, clung to power through 1912–13, despite popular opposition and their known sympathy for Oroz-quismo. The gang included the police chief, postmaster, judge and public notary (the latter the 'intellectual'of the clique); the 'eternal', irremovable secretary of the town council; two successive municipal presidents (the first elected by claiming a spurious liberal affiliation in 1911, the second winning a rigged election in 1912); and a handful of well-to-do *comerciantes* and *cantineros*, whose services (by way of transport and hospitality) helped ensure such electoral victories.[29] It was not that Zaragoza was afflicted by political inertia: the revolution and new regime had, it seems, made for livelier local politics; but the old caciques had managed to make the necessary adjustments and thus to survive.

Furthermore, even where bona fide Maderistas were installed in office – as state governors, for example – it was quite possible for their concern for law, order and stability to override liberal commitments to free government, thereby ensuring an *immobilisme* of men and methods alike. Governor Guada-lupe González of Zacatecas was a genuine Maderista – an Anti-Re-electionist candidate in 1910, a representative of Madero at the 1911 peace talks – yet his regime was one of standpat conservatism: 'he made absolutely no change, no dismissals among those in public office' in the state; the entire Porfirian judiciary remained intact.[30] Governors like Patiño, in Durango, even encour-aged the return of Porfirian officials in the interests of 'the smooth progress of the administration'.[31] It was not surprising that Madero lamented the 'great difficulties' he encountered in seeking to 'implant effective suffrage in Mexico . . . one of the most serious [being] that the very government functionaries themselves even forget their duties'; to correct which, 'energetic measures' – within the law – were frequently necessary.[32] Local complaints were even more common than presidential exhortations. The *jefes* of Coyuca de Catalán, Taxco and Tlapa were actively supporting the gubernatorial campaign of Alarcón in Guerrero; the *jefe* of Tehuacán (a Liberal Club president alleged) had violated the law to impose congenial authorities at San Gabriel Chilac (the *jefe* denied it); armed men intimidated voters at Valles, in the troubled Huasteca, so that, being 'fearful, they did not approach to cast their votes'.[33] In Hidalgo, *jefes* and tax-collectors were said to be backing Ramón Rosales for governor; while Rosales complained that the incumbent governor and *jefe* at Actopán were obstructing his efforts.[34] There were similar complaints from Puebla, where the governor allegedly sought to impose his chosen successor, 'using the same methods as were used during the dictatorship'.[35]

These repeated infractions of 'free suffrage' (for, while some reports were no doubt exaggerated or concocted, many must have been true) stemmed from scepticism as much as cynicism. With good reason, people did not believe that old traditions would die overnight; they anticipated pressure from the 'centre'; they took it for granted that the bonds of clientelism and realities of power would count for more than the disinterested totting up of citizens' votes. This – as well as other features of Maderista democracy – was exemplified in the Veracruz gubernatorial election of 1912. Of the nine candidates, six were serious contenders: all came from the upper echelons of society (the most popular, plebeian Maderista, Gabriel Gavira, was languishing in San Juan de Ulúa gaol); and all, in their different ways, conducted their campaigns by informal means – bribery, fixing, the quest for official endorsement – rather than by the formal and open methods of democracy.[36] Manuel Alegre, though a Maderista journalist, was backed by the still powerful Dehesa interests in the state; Hilario Rodríguez Malpica, a naval officer and chief of the presidential general staff, could count on a Maderista clique which enjoyed ready access to the president; Tomás Braniff, a Mexico City millionaire, also had his supporters in high places, including Gustavo Madero and Vice-President Pino Suárez.[37] Most of them appreciated the popularity of Gavira and sent delegations to secure – by bribery or persuasion – the prisoner's endorsement. To general surprise, Gavira delivered his coveted endorsement in favour of Antonio Pérez Rivera, an *hacendado* with Catholic support, but a candidate whom Gavira considered 'honest and independent' and the least of several evils.[38] Meanwhile, the attempts of different candidates to suborn the incumbent governor led to his removal; several *jefes políticos* committed abuses and were dismissed; and Madero, hoping first for a peaceful contest and second for the election of a sympathetic governor in this politically powerful state, was increasingly dragged into the conflict, to the detriment of his presidential prestige.[39] The Braniff candidacy in particular presented problems. It was not just that he lavished his family fortune on the campaign, that he counted on the corrupt support of *jefes* at Misantla and Orizaba, and that he dragooned his peons and foreign employees to vote on his behalf; in addition, he thought it necessary to approach the president, to inquire, respectfully, if he was 'persona grata' with the administration, and to promise that, if elected, he would 'march in perfect harmony with the centre'.[40] Several times Braniff solicited Madero's endorsement, to their mutual frustration and disgust: Braniff could not credit Madero's protestations of neutrality, and Madero was appalled to 'hear from him the idea that, to be elected governor, it was all a question of money'; to which the president retorted that 'the governments of the states were not up for sale, and that he did not have money enough to buy the votes of all the worthy sons of Veracruz.[41] When Braniff finally ran, still without official support and spending freely, he put it about that Madero had attempted to suborn him, and 'an unseemly public controversy' ensued.[42] In fact, far from throwing the weight of the 'centre' behind a favoured candidate, Madero swayed this way and that, leaning first towards Rodríguez Malpica, then Alegre, finally Pérez Rivera. In circumstances of great confusion (which is reflected in the historical accounts), and amid reports of official abuse and mob pressure, the legislature adjudged Pérez Rivera to have won the election.[43]

Such electoral problems were endemic. Candidates considered it essential to sound out presidential preferences, and Madero had constantly to repeat assurances that he sought only a free and fair election, that all candidates were 'persons highly acceptable to me'.[44] But, of course, not all candidates were highly or equally acceptable and, as a practical reformer (which he had been since his first excursions into politics in Coahuila), Madero wanted to get results, and not just to maintain, virginally intact, an immaculate but irrelevant dogma. It was important to get fellow-Maderistas and liberals into the state-houses, to secure a sympathetic National Congress, to win majorities for proposed legislation; that, after all, was what constitutional democracy was all about, and it commanded a good deal of presidential attention, both overt and behind the scenes.[45] At election time, therefore, while Madero strove to ensure fair procedures, he strove also to get his supporters elected. But this distinction – between the executive as a party-political figure, engaged in electoral conflict, and the executive as an impartial agency, safeguarding the rules of the conflict – was unfamiliar in Mexico, as in any system of artificial democracy; and, in the absence of precedents, guidelines, and the appropriate 'political culture', not only did Madero unwittingly connive at – and his supporters certainly practise – electoral corruption, but also most people readily believed this to be the case, acted on that assumption themselves, and judged the liberal experiment accordingly.

Just as Maderistas might expect jobs in the bureaucracy, or a helping hand with pending litigation, so they could count on executive support in elections. Governors were given clear instructions concerning favoured candidates: in Zacatecas, the Potosino student Ernesto Barrios Collantes had done a lot for the cause; the Governor of San Luis was urged to help four Maderistas in view of the 'necessity that these persons come here [Mexico City] to Congress'; a senator from the same state was asked to stand down in favour of another, a member of a prominent landed family, who, Madero explained, 'with the knowledge he has of the Senate and his intimacy with every one of the Senators of the old regime, who at present form a majority . . . could help me . . . in a more effective way than you could'.[46] With Pérez Rivera elected governor in Veracruz, Madero bent his efforts to ensure a majority of sympathetic deputies in the state congress; only thereby could justice be done to the 'opinion of the Veracruzano people, clearly manifested in the elections . . . in which they designated Pérez Rivera governor by an overwhelming majority'.[47] Maderista contacts in Torreón (which were extensive) were exploited to get Rafael Hernández, then Minister of Fomento, elected to Congress.[48]

While friends were rewarded, enemies were punished, or, at least, gently obstructed. The Governor of Morelos was rebuked for backing the congressional candidacy of Nemesio García Naranjo (the editor of *El Debate* and an outspoken critic of the government): while 'under the new regime of effective suffrage' every citizen had the right to participate and no-one – not even 'our worst enemies' – should be debarred, nevertheless it was quite wrong to 'smooth the path and lend support to those who patently refuse their willing co-operation in the solution of the problems which our country faces'.[49] Guillermo Pous, also from the stable of *El Debate*, was similarly blackballed in the Veracruz gubernatorial contest. And some of Madero's electoral interventions carried the stamp of *realpolitik*. The president – not always the naive dreamer he is sometimes depicted – struck alliances with powerful vested interests whose support was desirable, even if their political antecedents were dubious. A gubernatorial election in Puebla produced the familiar tangle and consequent revolt by the defeated candidate, Agustín del Pozo (a local landowner and belated revolutionary of 1911). Del Pozo took to the sierra and declared himself rightful governor at Tetela, in the heart of the country controlled by the Indian cacique, Juan Francisco Lucas. Lucas was no Maderista, but he had supported the Madero regime (as he had every regime which respected his local interests) and his son Abraham had just been elected deputy for the district, 'thanks to the influence which [Lucas] has in those parts'. But it now seemed likely that the state legislature would reject Abraham Lucas' credentials and nullify the election: such a move, Madero wrote pointedly to the state governor, would be 'impolitic and inconvenient' at a time when Lucas' support for the government, which had not wavered through 1911–12, had to be guaranteed in the face of the del Pozo rebellion.[50]

Here, it would seem, expedience overcame principle. But it is not easy to determine whether Madero's sins – in this respect – were few and venial, or many, cardinal and sufficient to invalidate the 'new regime of effective suffrage' he claimed to favour. Presidential recommendations to state governors, such as those sent to Maytorena in Sonora, suggesting 'the convenience of Sr Eduardo Ruíz being elected for the district of Hermosillo and Major Emilio López Figueroa, the present Inspector-General of Police, for Alamos, persons who . . . will be as welcome to you as they are to me', are clearly open to different interpretations, which cannot be resolved by textual analysis.[51] Maybe Madero deserves the benefit of the doubt in many such cases. His benign optimism is well attested: the president 'had posted a deaf and blind sentry at the gateway of life to cry "All's well", and there were times when he would hear no other voice'.[52] And there were certainly cases where principle overcame experience. Andrés Farías' election, by fraudulent means, as mayor of Torreón was overturned since, Madero instructed, 'although Andrés Farías is a worthy citizen and a good friend of ours in every respect, it is not fitting that on any account the will of the people should be frustrated'.[53] But, powerful though the presidency was, Madero's own views were only part of the story. Presidential recommendations (such as those issued to Maytorena) could be variously interpreted, and thus lead to abuse where none was intended. To some of his supporters, Madero's liberal conscience was a tiresome burden, his concern for constitutional niceties seemed pernickety, naive and even dangerous. Some, like Governor Carranza, grew impatient at the president's conduct of affairs; others, like Gustavo Madero, perhaps took matters into their own hands, and deployed the *Porra* against Reyistas in 1911, and Catholics in 1912.[54]

For all Madero's protestations and efforts, therefore, electoral abuse continued, and the promise of the new politics was not wholly fulfilled. But this was hardly surprising. What the historian of the liberal experiment – like the historian of so many episodes – must try to answer are questions of degree, though questions to which neat, quantitative answers are impossible: how fair and free were the elections of the Madero period? How far did they break with Porfirian precedent, inculcate new attitudes, encourage participation, and achieve a renovation of the political elite? And what patterns of electoral and party behaviour emerged in the short time permitted? We cannot hope for the supposed precision of modern psephology. But we can hazard answers which shed light on the character of the Madero regime, on its capacity to deliver the liberal goods promised in 1910. And, while national generalisations can be attempted, it is more revealing to turn to the provinces and observe the divergent patterns of political behaviour which they exemplified.

VOTERS, PARTIES AND BOSSES

Nationally, the experience of continued manipulation and corruption bred disillusionment. Popular faith in the new politics – perhaps never very strong – flagged and failed. As early as July 1911, earnest Maderistas were anticipating major problems in the establishment of 'effective suffrage': granted the 'condition of semi-anarchy' in the country, the people's 'lack of civic education', and the pressing electoral schedule, it was feared that 'the action of the local authority will be decisive in determining the outcome of the ballot'.[55] The presidential election of autumn 1911, though fairer than any predecessor, was strangely quiet, more an exercise in acclamation than in political choice.[56] The 'imposition' of Pino Suárez as vice-president was then followed by alleged 'impositions' in gubernatorial and other elections throughout 1911–12. At the end of June 1912 the whole country voted for the Twenty-sixth National Congress according to a new, more democratic method of direct election.[57] Eight parties fielded candidates, the most important being the government's PCP and the opposition (Catholic) PCN: the Maderistas and their allies won a bare majority in the Chamber of Deputies, but not in the Senate, and a significant number of outspoken critics of the administration were elected.[58] For some, the government's failure to manufacture a solid working majority indicated the absence of official pressure: a cynically undemocratic regime would not have allowed the 'Quadrilateral' to take their seats in Congress and begin their assaults on the administration.[59] This was true enough, but the outcome was quite compatible with a significant degree of manipulation – particularly manipulation which was ineffective or which worked to the advantage of anti-government as well as government candidates.

The Catholics, winning twenty-three seats, claimed to have deserved a hundred, the rest having been stripped from them by official fraud; Ramón Prida mentions 'tremendous [electoral] atrocities' being committed.[60] These claims may well err in the other direction. Recent, revisionist historians – keen to debunk 'revolutionary' orthodoxy – are perhaps a little too ready to accept Catholic claims at face value. The Catholic *El País* applauded the 'liberty of suffrage' evident on election day in June 1912; Maderistas – like Madero himself, or Alberto Pani – were benignly tolerant of Catholic political activity and success; and, to the extent that there were abuses, the Catholics were not wholly innocent themselves.[61] But two points do emerge with some clarity from the welter of claims, counter-claims and hypotheses. First, the electoral system was clearly freer than in the days of Díaz, and this encouraged a degree of participation and party organisation that was unprecedented. The 'time-honored Díaz system of "tagging" a Congress into office' could no longer be strictly followed; the election campaign of summer 1912 was 'a novelty for the younger generation, for those who grew up in an age in which liberty of suffrage was absolutely non-existent'.[62] Apart from fulfilling – at least partially – the Maderista promise of free elections, this also made possible a partial renovation of the national political elite, which had been one of Maderismo's implicit promises to the aspiring urban middle-class and upper-class 'outs'. 'No re-election', even on a limited scale, implied a breakdown of the old, self-perpetuating political monopolies of the Porfiriato, a more rapid circulation of elites, and more 'jobs for the boys'. In Díaz's time, over two-thirds of the political elite enjoyed 're-election'; almost 70% of Díaz's final administration (1910–11) had held office in the preceding one. Under Madero this index of *continuismo* fell to a third (and some of these were survivors, not of the Porfirian epoch, but of the de la Barra *interinato*).[63]

But the second point to emerge was the perceptible decline in enthusiasm, and growth of cynicism, concerning the electoral process. Even though the

initial presidential election had been indirect, observers saw it to be more open
and enthusiastic than subsequent polls. Turn-out in the June 1912 congressional elections was reckoned to be less than 10% outside the Federal District.
The congressional poll was 'not quite of that open order which had distinguished the Madero presidential election'.[64] Taken together, these two points
suggest that, while Maderista democracy represented a notable advance (in
terms of electoral freedom and participation) on its artificial Porfirian predecessor, it still had a long way to go, and it was possibly heading in the wrong
direction anyway; at any rate, there is little evidence of gradual, linear
progression towards fuller, freer democracy during the years of the liberal
experiment. Instead of being coaxed and educated into fulfilling their
democratic duties, many citizens simply grew disillusioned and apathetic.
Others threw themselves into the enlivened politics of the days with enthusiasm, and in ways which will shortly be described. But in neither case was the
result particularly favourable to the kind of classic, liberal democracy advocated by Madero and his pioneer reformist colleagues. Apathy, for them, was
anathema; but so too was electoral violence or political bossism. Yet it was
these latter phenomena which, all too often, took the place of apathy: mass
participation in politics, and genuine conflict over the choice of men and
measures, tended to be conducted through new clientelist organisations, far
removed from the developed constitutional models Madero sought to emulate,
and quite prepared to resort to graft and even intimidation. It must be stressed
that this did not mean a simple regression to Porfirian practice. The *apertura* of
1910–11, the collapse of long-standing authority, the mass participation
brought about by the revolution – these were crucial changes which could not
be undone. Even where Porfirian caciques survived (as they often did: at
Zaragoza, for example) they did so on somewhat different and uncertain terms
compared with the past. Meanwhile, new forms of authority, representation
and mediation had to be found. Some yearned for the 'iron hand', a Porfirio
redivivus. Some still believed that liberal democracy, on European lines, could
be established. Over time, both were proved wrong: political solutions,
evolving piecemeal, led to neither a neo-Porfirian nor yet a classically liberal
order. Although in 1911–13 this halting – in many respects classically
dialectical – progress towards a new order was underway, its drift and eventual
outcome were still unforeseen. Hence contemporaries still couched political
judgements in the old categories. When the brief euphoria of 1911 evaporated
and dogged political battle was joined, involving force, fraud, corruption, but
also some real popular participation and party mobilisation, this was too
readily dismissed as a descent into anarchy and a derogation of Madero's liberal
ideals. Conservatives sneered or cried 'havoc!'; disillusioned liberals turned
away in disgust, or fear. Neither perceived that this was also a time when new
forms of authority and participation were gestating, and that these represented
neither the rebirth of the narrow authoritarianism of the Porfirian past, nor the

incarnation of Madero's liberal hopes. Rather, they were something else again, a third alternative, neither Porfirian nor Maderista, conceived in and characteristic of a 'developing', agrarian society, undergoing the pangs of social revolution.

Thus, where contemporaries saw chaos, conflict and failure, the historian can also see new initiatives, a heuristic political practice and pointers to the future. Already, as they sought new solutions (often on the basis of unrealistic philosophies), the political nation of 1911–13 followed recognisable paths and left clear tracks. Often, this took them up blind alleys or into dark corners from which there was no return. But they also tried new routes forward, and cut paths that would later be broadened, lengthened and tarmacked to take the tread of millions. Like the patterns of rural revolt, these are best mapped locally. It is possible to exemplify regions where the 'new politics' took hold: where parties flourished and elections were sufficiently free and popular to have a real significance; conversely, there were those in which force, corruption, fixing and apathy still predominated. Among the former, it is also possible to distinguish between those where the new politics were conducted *comme il faut* (peacefully and consensually), and those where electoral freedom and political mobilisation brought fierce confrontation and violence. Finally, divergent patterns of political conflict can be discerned: on the one hand, a 'sectarian' polarisation between liberals and Catholics, on the other a polarisation by classes, rich against poor, employers against workers.

Generally, elections were more free and genuine (though not necessarily quiet and orderly) in states which had been relatively unaffected by armed revolution. Again, therefore, we note a clear dysjunction between armed revolt (a rural phenomenon, strong in particular states) and liberal reform (a feature of urban life, and of different states and regions). And it was particularly in such militarily quiescent states that the Catholic Party (PCN) did conspicuously well. One such was Aguascalientes. Here was a state lacking an acute agrarian problem and consequent rural unrest: 'Aguascalientes', an observer noted, from the vantage point of 1917, 'has never taken a very active part in the revolution, owing to the fact that there are no enormous holdings of land, as in most other states, and consequently the people have not had that incentive, the partition of the land.' The city of Aguascalientes itself was smart and prosperous; though it contained a large population of skilled workers (railway and smelter employees), it had something of a clerical reputation.[65] This seemed to be a recipe for peaceful electoral participation. The state elected its first governor by free suffrage in the summer of 1911; the next year, elections to Congress passed off quietly, with the Catholic slate being elected; and the Catholics triumphed again in the municipal elections later in the year.[66] Though Governor Fuentes (chosen during the Maderista boom of 1911) backed the liberal ticket, there were few infractions of the law and the Catholics suffered little discrimination. When the Catholic Eduardo Correa won his congressional seat he received a graceful letter of congratulation from his defeated liberal opponent (and ex-college friend) Alberto Pani.[67] This was politics as men like Madero and Pani had hoped: peaceful, legal, decorous and democractic. And, in such a context, the Catholics showed the spirit of *ralliement* and participated in the workings of the liberal state, to their own advantage.

Liberal hopes were also borne out at Monterrey. The city's 'peace and tranquillity were notorious'; its inhabitants (workers included) were disposed to participate in the new politics, and too busy making and selling things to let elections disrupt the city's economic well-being.[68] A conservative ex-governor of Nuevo León was returned to the state-house (now under a Maderista label); both his election and that of the state legislature were reckoned to be free and honest; and 'a greater number of citizens participated in both of these elections than has ever been known in this part of the country before'. In one local election in Monterrey, six candidates shared over six thousand votes between them: 'obviously', Ross comments, 'it had been a very real election'.[69] In Sonora too the elections for vice-governor and the state legislature appear to have been reasonably genuine and open, helping to further the rapid turnover of political personnel which the state experienced.[70] In these – somewhat untypical – cases, drawn from regions of relatively high literacy and economic development, yet low incidence of popular revolutionary participation, the Madero regime seemed to fulfil some of its self-proclaimed objectives. Liberal reforms were effected without social upheaval; there was a significant renovation of the political elite; elections produced legitimate winners and graceful losers.

Other regions of 'non-revolutionary' character, however, underwent a marked transition from military quiescence to political agitation. Jalisco offers one example (which bears comparison with its neighbour Aguascalientes); the port of Tampico and its hinterland another, which may be contrasted with Monterrey. Here, the new politics broke out of their consensual framework, producing bitterly contested – if sometimes rigged – elections, widespread politicisation (not necessarily of a model, democratic kind), and sporadic violence and revolt. Neither politics Porfirian-style, nor yet politics as promised by Madero and partially realised in Aguascalientes and Monterrey, these examples pointed the way to new forms of organisation, blending Porfirian *caciquismo* and Maderista democracy into a synthesis quite distinct from its two historical progenitors. This was particularly the case in Tampico, where politics assumed a class dimension and the workers and their unions began to play a major role in electoral conflict.

Jalisco remained quiet during and after the Madero revolution. 'The symptoms of revolt', an American noted in September 1912,' . . . have never been really serious and now make but little stir.'[71] One local Maderista had to make his way to Chihuahua in order to participate in 1911: at home, he complained, revolt was largely unknown, since 'in this state . . . property is divided up, and the owners of ranches and haciendas undertake the pursuit of rebels themselves and the people are by nature very patient'.[72] But if Jalisco eschewed rebellion, it was not against political agitation and involvement. Indeed, the presence of a liberal in the National Palace tended to revive the state's tradition of clericalism, conservatism, and suspicion of the 'centre'. In the course of 1911 the PCN acquired 'huge importance' in the state; de la Barra won a large majority in opposition to Pino Suárez; and the Catholics swept the board in the elections to the state Congress. Late in 1912 it was reckoned that the PCN outnumbered the liberals in Jalisco by four to one.[73] This created problems for the state governor, Alberto Robles Gil, a nominal liberal, who clung to power, deliberately postponing a gubernatorial election in the sure knowledge that a Catholic would win.[74] As Madero sought to hasten the overdue election, political divisions became more pronounced: 'the strife between liberals and clericals [was] bitter'; there was talk of a Catholic revolt; and an active Guadalajara press whipped up partisan feelings.[75] Sectarian conflict was complicated by regional rivalry. When Madero ran out of patience and tried to remove the governor, local hackles rose; though Robles Gil was scarcely popular, the people of Guadalajara turned out onto the streets to protest (as they had to greet Reyes and mob Corral in 1909), and Madero had to pause.[76] Rumours now flew that Robles Gil would impose a liberal successor by force. In fact, he was forced to capitulate: when elections were held the Catholic candidate, López Portillo y Rojas, won by a two to one margin over the combined opposition; and, despite talk of further upheavals and even armed resistance by disgruntled liberals, he assumed power peacefully.[77]

If Mexico as a whole was now a laboratory of Maderista liberalism, so Jalisco, ruled by a Catholic legislature and (ultimately) a Catholic governor, 'became a testing ground for the Catholic program of Social Action'.[78] Legislative encouragement was given to the creation of labour unions, co-operatives, mutual aid societies and family farms. Catholic unions began to develop; a branch of the National League of Catholic Students was set up in Guadalajara; and it was in the same city that the idea of a national, Catholic youth organisation was first seriously taken up.[79] In all this there was clear evidence that Catholic opinion was being mobilised, not just in an electoral, party-political fashion, but across a wide range of social groups and activities; and that, at least in certain quarters, Catholics displayed a lively social conscience and an eagerness to grapple with social questions in a constructive, 'progressive' fashion. If Jalisco was the best example of this, it was not the only one. A Catholic/liberal division marked the political life of many states in central and west-central Mexico: the PCN won the governorship of Zacatecas and dominated the legislatures of seven states, including Michoacán, Guanajuato, Mexico and Puebla; it provided the mayors of Puebla and Toluca. There were also near misses: in Michoacán, Dr Miguel Silva's Partido Liberal (a classically Maderista party of professionals and small businessmen) defeated a strong Catholic challenge for the governorship; in Puebla, too, the Catholic candidate was narrowly beaten; and in both cases the Catholics alleged government rigging, as they had done after the congressional polls too.[80]

Such allegations, though no doubt partially true, should not be taken at face value. If the Puebla gubernatorial election was rigged against the Catholics, it was rigged locally, and against the wishes of the president, who was all for a fair contest and had no objection to the PCN candidate.[81] Madero clearly welcomed the emergence of a kind of two party system (Catholic and liberal); he encouraged Catholic political involvement, echoing the exhortations of the episcopate. Catholic and liberal politicisation thus marched hand in hand, and even did so with a certain camaraderie. Madero urged respect for the PCN, the bishops preached respect for constituted authority. While there was sometimes bitter conflict at election time; while the government sometimes discriminated against the Catholics; and while die-hard anti-clerical liberals still entertained a profound suspicion of the Catholics and all their works; nevertheless there could be no doubt that Díaz's old policy of Church–state detente was being continued, perhaps more rapidly and on surer foundations. The Church no longer grudgingly tolerated the liberal state: it now participated in its workings, emulating and sometimes outdoing its secular political rivals.[82] This detente received striking publicity at the end of 1912 when the Minister of Gobernación conferred with the Papal Delegate to secure 'the influence of the clergy to achieve the pacification of the country' – which was duly promised.[83]

The Minister's appeal not only afforded another example of Maderista *realpolitik*; it also illustrated another facet of Catholic influence which should not be overlooked. Alongside detente there was also conflict, which harked back to the old, primordial division between liberal and conservative, anti-clerical and clerical.[84] The Catholics of 1911–13 were not (as some accounts tend to suggest) all eager democrats and sincere social reformers. The PCN might deny being the heir to the clerical conservatives of the nineteenth century, but liberal allegations to that effect were not wholly paranoid, and the party was clearly able to count on the influences of the bishops and (more important) the parish priests in drumming up political support, particularly at election time. The power of the *cura* was well-known, especially in the countryside; it had been evident during the presidential election of 1911; it was explicitly recognised by the government in its appeal to the Papal Delegate, who had been approached not for spiritual consolation or divine intercession 'but [rather in the sense of] pointing out to him the advisability of recommending the priests of the rural districts to use their influence with the peasant and labouring classes in the fight to stamp out brigandage'.[85] Such influence, which the government hoped to deploy in the interests of pacification, could also supply the fuel in a Catholic political machine. And it was by no means the case that such influences, or such a machine, would work for democracy and reform. Though there were progressive, even 'Maderista', priests, there were also many – and I suspect more – who inclined to conservatism, even reaction, who were cast in the same mould as Azuela's Father Jeremiah. And, if *The Bosses* gives an accurate picture of Catholic politicking in a Jalisco town, it is clear that the PCN depended on the votes of clients – peons, textile workers, bank clerks – mobilised by local caciques.[86]

The political Catholicism of 1911–13, therefore, was – like the Church itself – a divided entity. The 'old Church', the 'willing handmaiden of reaction', was still strong and influential, through the agency of priests and bishops who aligned with vested interests and saw the PCN (if they accepted its role at all) as a *caciquista* device to maintain those interests. The clearest proof of the strength of this constituency came with the Huerta regime of 1913–14.[87] Meanwhile, 'the new Church ... caught up in the winds of change of *Rerum Novarum* was on its way to becoming an instrument for social reform' and it took advantage of the new freedom inaugurated by Madero to compete with the liberals on their own terms.[88] The events of 1913, however, aborted this development: parallel democratisation, liberal and Catholic, was halted, to be resumed later in radically altered circumstances. Thus Mexico did not evolve towards a bipolar, liberal–Catholic political system, involving a strong Christian Democratic Party, as seemed quite probable during 1911–13. Democratisation stopped and the emerging consensus dissolved. Church and state, Catholic and liberal once again veered apart, their distancing and mutual hostility reaching unprecedented proportions in the wake of the Revolution. But like many aspects of the 'late' Revolution, this had not been signalled early on, in Madero's time; the 'late' Revolution, in its anti-clericalism as in its economic nationalism, was less a logical culmination, than a new departure.

The 'sectarian' pattern of politics was most evident in the Mexican heartland: central and west-central Mexico. In regions where the Church was weaker, and the urban working class stronger, a form of class-based politics emerged. The best example of this was the oil port of Tampico. Like Jalisco, the state of Tamaulipas had remained on the margin of the Madero revolution: Anti-Re-electionism had made little impact, and Reyes was popular; the state's scant contribution to the 1910 Revolution made people fear that Tamaulipas would be cold-shouldered by the new president.[89] But if there had been little armed revolt, there had been trouble enough in Tampico, where the port and oil-workers, concentrated in the proletarian suburb of Doña Cecilia, had acquired a reputation for subversion; and, when political activity got under way in the summer of 1911, these workers played an important role. Tampico was thus a clear case of a general phenomenon: once political conflict was transferred from the battle-field to the polling booth the urban working class – whose revolutionary contribution had been negligible – assumed far greater prominence. As city dwellers, enjoying higher standards of literacy than the peasants, the urban workers stood on the fringes of the political nation; they could react (and contribute) to the spate of printed political comment which was evident in 1911–13; and, as we shall go on to note, they were now organising and striking on an unprecedented scale.[90] And these characteristics were especially marked among the classic proletarians, concentrated in the new (usually foreign-owned) industries, and in the burgeoning commercial/industrial towns. 'The workers of the big cities', a knowledgeable observer commented, 'live in days of emancipation, and the authority of the representatives of dogma – be it official, religious or social – does not exercise such decisive influence over them as over the *peonaje*.'[91] The city workers were, in a sense, *disponible*, ripe for mobilisation; but they were not, therefore, inert, malleable victims; on the contrary, with the Revolution they displayed 'a very marked tendency to associate', both politically and economically.[92]

To the political nation, the workers represented both a threat and an opportunity. The threat lay in some autonomous working-class movement – whether the disorganised rioting of May 1911, or the militant syndicalism preached by a handful of agitators. But the opportunity was also there to recruit urban labour as an ally in the new politics of the period: to follow and extend the precedents set by Porfirians like Dehesa and Landa y Escandón, and mobilise the workers as voters and demonstrators (roles which were now at a premium). Unlike the insurgent peasantry, the urban workers – including the organised urban workers – seemed reasonable, often moderate, and certainly capable of maintaining a dialogue with upper and middle-class *políticos*: they shared an urban milieu; they could present a common front against rural barbarism and superstition; and they had a joint vested interest in the continued running of the urban economy, now jeopardised by revolt in the countryside. The workers' demands for higher wages, even union recognition, while distasteful to the more 'paternalistic' employers, did not imply the same threat to the status quo as some of the peasant demands for Land and Liberty. They could be haggled over, even grudgingly and occasionally met; strikes could be broken (as much by the reserve of available labour as by outright repression); and physical resistance, within the towns, could easily be contained. Altogether, the urban worker was a safer, more congenial, and more cost-effective ally (or client) than the dour, refractory, unreasonable *campesino*.[93]

For their part, the urban workers pressed their claims for political participation in 1911–13, as they had in 1909–10. Simultaneously, they organised unions and struck for better pay and conditions. No doubt these activities had a mutually reinforcing effect (not least at the level of organisation). But on the whole the political and economic struggles remained distinct, as they had in the past. Of course, a *político* elected with working-class support might look favourably upon economic demands, and might even apply pressure upon management (though this was hardly a common occurrence in 1911–13). But there was no doubt that the workers were playing the client role: they sought concessions from sympathetic *políticos*; they did not attempt to install working-class representatives in high political office. No more did they use the strike as a political weapon: industrial action served 'economist' ends, while political participation was characterised by voting, demonstrating and propagandising. And in playing their client role, the workers displayed the same pragmatism as they had in the past: they would reward friends and punish enemies regardless of formal political labels.

This was evident in the turbulent political life of Tampico in 1911–13. Immediately upon the fall of Díaz, conservative elements got together to nominate a congenial candidate for governor; the local Maderistas also began organising their forces, looking to recruit the workers who had shown something of their power and militancy in May. The 'lower class' was generally reckoned to be Maderista, and a prominent local lawyer and Maderista activist, Alberto Aragón, built up a clientele in Doña Cecilia (where, it was said, he owned some gambling dens), expressing support for strikes at the Waters Pierce refinery and on the waterfront. But he was not alone: observers noted how 'politicians interested in controlling the coming elections wished to place the laboring classes under obligations to them by helping them obtain an increase in wages'.[94] In the autumn, a protracted campaign for the state governorship got under way. Two main candidates emerged: García Medrano, a lawyer, said to be a Reyista, strong in northern Tamaulipas; and Francisco Legorreta, a Maderista, whose support lay in the south, and whose supporters (his opponent sneered) consisted of 'half a dozen professors, half a dozen relatives, and a hundred suckers (*engañados*)'.[95] Both candidates made a serious bid for the Tampiqueño workers. Legorreta visited the port in October 1911 and was met by a band and 'a number of members of the local labor unions'; García Medrano, notwithstanding his Reyista leanings, forged an alliance with the powerful stevedores union (or, strictly, with its militant leader, Samuel Kelly); on visiting Tampico and attempting to speak from a balcony, García Medrano was howled down by the Legorretista *porra*, and fighting broke out.[96]

The campaign continued, brisk and passionate, until – almost on the eve of polling – Legorreta suddenly died (there were rumours of poison), and the Maderistas switched to Matías Guerra, who had previously served as interim governor. At Tampico, the supporters of García Medrano alleged that the municipal secretary planned to rig the vote in the city hall, and he was prevailed upon to quit; in the state capital, Cd Victoria, Guerra's partisans gave out that they would physically prevent García Medrano crossing the threshhold of the state palace, if he were 'elected'. The count (and whatever else went on behind closed doors) lasted for days, before Guerra was finally declared the winner, in the face of strenuous protests and at least one rebellion. Already, García Medrano's faction, with the dockers prominent, had taken to the streets of Tampico, complaining of electoral abuses; they were dispersed, and the dockers' leader, Kelly, was arrested. Soldiers patrolled the streets and the Chamber of Commerce, recalling the fracas of May 1911, asked the Federal government to send 500 additional troops. In the usual way the city people talked apprehensively of rural hicks and hoodlums who seemed to be invading Tampico, in anticipation of riot and pillage (the Spaniards, typically, were the most anxious).[97]

With the question of the governorship settled – albeit to the dissatisfaction of many – Tampico politics did not go to sleep. In March 1912, as the Orozco revolt progressed, Maderista city councillors mounted a 'peace' demonstration, in which the workers marched to affirm their support for the government.[98] Meanwhile, President Taft's mobilisation on the border provoked resentment and fears of American intervention. In this context, the dockers' union sponsored a vigorous anti-American campaign, conducted in the press, in posters, even in threatening letters (some of a particularly lewd kind). The consul and the wives of American residents were advised (in so many words) to leave Tampico, and an anti-American uprising was promised for 16 March.[99] Such threats were scarcely original: there had been a nation-wide scare of this kind in 1906 which, though it passed into the collective folklore of the American colony, had come to nothing, merely emphasising the shallowness of 'Yankeephobia', as measured by actual, violent events.[100] So, too, in Tampico in 1912. The Mexican gunboat *Bravo* trained its searchlight on the city during the night of March 16th, which passed quietly. Revolts and pogroms were not the preferred tactics of the Tampico workers. Even their rhetorical nationalism bears closer inspection. Though it coincided with the Taft mobilisation – and thus chimed in with a broader, national protest, indicative of the workers' place within the political nation – it also obeyed other motives. There may have been elements of economic confrontation, in that the dockers' chief bugbears were the labour contractors, who controlled dock work, and these at least included American interests.[101] But it was also the case that, since the beginning of 1912, two American lawyers, newly arrived at Tampico, had poached much of the legal business ('which is very large on account of the oil business') hitherto monopolised by Mexican attorneys. Lic. Parra, the bright young attorney of the stevedores' union, was now said to be orchestrating the anti-American campaign in response. If true, the incident points once again to the middle-class, professional origin of most of these nationalist campaigns; as well as to the middle-class, professional tutelage which influenced, if it did not dominate, the nascent trade unions.[102]

Meanwhile, the political pattern established early in 1912 continued throughout the year. Hardly had Governor Guerra taken office than the state was plunged into 'a warm political campaign' for congressional elections. [103] The Maderista lawyer Alberto Aragón reappeared as a candidate in Tampico, again backed by the workers: it was said that the authorities did not dare curtail his agitation at the refineries because 'they did not want to antagonise the laboring element' – another example of the sad decline of authority since the days of Díaz. [104] The campaign was marked by the usual broadsheets and polemics, rich in personal invective: Aragón was a property swindler and racketeer; he was living in sin; most heinous of all, he had plagiarised his doctoral dissertation. [105] And again, at the end of the year, the city's municipal elections produced a similar line-up: two candidates 'who represented the better element and educated class', and two 'who represented the stevedores and peon class'. After a close election a commission had to be empowered to recount the votes; the matter was still pending when the Madero regime fell. [106]

The evident politicisation of the Tampiqueño workers, which indelibly marked the political life of both the city and the state, in part reflected the general politicisation of the Mexican working class, which will be mentioned presently. But it was also an extreme case, deriving from special circumstances. First, political and economic organisation tended to proceed in tandem, and port workers throughout the country were among the first to take advantage of the new freedom conceded by the Madero regime: at Tampico, Progreso, Veracruz, Mazatlán, Acapulco. [107] At Tampico – as at Veracruz – the dockers sought to bargain directly with the big import/export houses, rather than through middlemen; to this end they needed a strong union, which could resist blacklegging; and the union leadership at once saw the utility of political alliances (of a pragmatic kind) in the furtherance of these aims. And ports, like Tampico or Acapulco, were particularly receptive to news, ideas and examples transmitted from Europe or North America. [108] But probably even more important was the economic environment. Tampico was a boom port where the supply of work, whether on the docks or in the oil fields, gave the workers a stronger bargaining position vis-à-vis employers than was the case in many industries (textiles would offer a clear contrast). By certain objective standards the Tampico workers were weak, poor and exploited; but compared with most of their compatriots the Tampiqueños seemed 'very prosperous and contented'; 'the labourers have continuous work and their wages are above those paid in other parts of Mexico (and there appears to be no idea of revolution)'. [109] Thus, at Tampico, on the railways, in some of the bigger, corporate mining enterprises like Cananea, it was the better off, 'modern', sometimes skilled or semi-skilled proletariat which pioneered labour unions and led the working-class breakthrough into political participation. But the Tampico workers were probably well aware that the boom conditions, and the associated demand for labour, were not immutable; the bubble might burst, as it had in 1907–8. Even in 1911, as the asphalting of the streets of Tampico (which had boosted the demand for labour) neared completion, fears of unemployment rose, and the 170 Bahamian blacks, brought in to work on the project, became the object of deep hostility on the part of Mexican workers.[110] Later in the year, as political uncertainty grew, business faltered, and 1,000 men were allegedly laid off.[111] The local economy soon picked up again in 1912; but the predicament of workers in boom towns like Tampico – or perhaps Torreón – encouraged a degree of militancy, and a collective desire to consolidate the gains of the good years (through unionisation and political alliance) against the day when the lean years began.

Tampico represented an extreme case of a general phenomenon: a parallel, usually distinct, mobilisation of the working class in both 'economistic' and political organisations. Unionisation and strike activity will be considered separately in a moment; here, it is the political thrust of the working class which demands attention. Like the old Anti-Re-electionist Party, the newly formed PCP of 1911 included a significant working-class element; of some dozen PCP clubs established in the city of Puebla, the 'Martyrs of Río Blanco' claimed 200 members, the Union of Freightworkers a little less; similar affiliates were to be found at Orizaba, Durango, Guadalajara and elsewhere.[112] Despite their impeccably proletarian names, however, clubs of this kind often enjoyed a varied membership. At Múzquiz (Coa.) the Club Obreros Libres Juan Antonio de la Fuente had as president a well-placed local merchant and veteran Maderista; mutualist societies in general often had a significant proportion of artisans and white-collar workers among their members.[113] Middle-class participation (and sometimes leadership) in such organisations further illustrated the urban solidarity and pragmatic alliance-building which characterised the working-class movement.

At election time, the urban workers (industrial and artisan) showed a much greater disposition to turn out and vote than either the peons or the city lumpenproletariat (the marginals, beggars and vagrants). The congressional election of June 1912 was quiet and orderly, reported an American who toured the polling booths of the capital; but, he went on, 'while I saw many well-dressed men, seemingly of the professional class, and those of the labouring class, I did not see any of the lower or "pelado" class voting'.[114] There was a high turn-out among the miners of Cananea during state elections in Sonora; while the presidential primary returns from San Pablo (Ags.) also suggest a high rate of participation among workers, illiterate as well as literate.[115] In Tlaxcala, as already noted, the ex-railway and textile worker Antonio Hidalgo won the governorship on the strength of a working-class (and peasant) vote. The Tlaxcala elite were alarmed both by his radical (allegedly 'socialist') programme, and by the implications of his election: 'there can be no doubt that Sr Hidalgo, being bound up with the [textile] operatives, since they were the ones who gave him their vote, will not be able to keep them in check, and they will pose a constant threat to the *hacendados* [and] industrialists'.[116] In response, the elite lobbied Mexico City and organised a Liga de Agricultores to contest subsequent elections in the conservative interest. Though popular candidates triumphed in both the gubernatorial and congressional elections, the Liga cobbled together a majority in the state legislature, which blocked the new governor's appointment, provoking a constitutional crisis. Government offices in Tlaxcala were invaded by the people; two governors came and went, and the elections were annulled; before new ones could be held and the crisis resolved, the Madero government fell from power.[117] Quite clearly, the political mobilisation of the Tlaxcalan workers had been real enough and the local elite – though they survived – did so by virtue of a rearguard political action, fought according to the new rules of the game.

Taking Mexico as a whole, however, these areas of significant popular politicisation (as measured in electoral terms) were exceptions, though important ones. More often, elections were subject to constraints and abuses or, even if they were not, popular interest seemed low, indicating the 'dead weight of political practice which the new regime inevitably inherited' from the old.[118] For some rural communities, this was the first time in their history that they had voted, hence elections were strange, novel events; yet even in worldly wise Mexico City it was apathy – more than official pressure – which most contributed to a low turnout.[119] And, over time, there was probably a decline in electoral participation (though not necessarily of politicisation more broadly defined), as the euphoria of 1911 evaporated and a certain disillusionment with the new politics became evident. Particularly in areas of continued revolutionary activity, elections failed to convince. In Durango, for example, the official candidate for governor, Carlos Patoni, triumphed over the popular candidate, Juan García, in suspicious circumstances: Patoni, 17,213 votes; García, 8,623; spoiled ballots, 10,033. Not surprisingly there were protests and threats of rebellion. But with Campos and Argumedo loose in the countryside, with Arrieta and Contreras but recently arrested, and with a garrison of 700 troops in the city, no-one attempted an armed protest.[120] There were similar frauds in the troubled Laguna towns: Julio Madero wrote to his brother of the 'general discontent . . . in the whole Laguna region, since in many places the municipal elections have been rigged [*falseadas*], so that some authorities are as bad as or worse than those of Porfirian times'.[121] In Sinaloa, also affected by rural insurgence, the official candidate, Riveros, won an anodyne election for the governorship.[122]

It is particularly interesting that municipal elections – now conducted with electoral registers, polling booths and all the regular (and irregular) paraphernalia of democracy, rather than by mob acclamation in the plaza, as in May 1911 – now aroused far less enthusiasm. The election of the mayor and town council in San Luis 'evoked little interest' and, when 'it was officially announced that the most palpable frauds had been practised and the mayor was deposed, the news created no interest or comment'. [123] In Tabasco, local elections were conducted in peace and quiet and 'as a rule the state administration candidates were elected by large majorities'; in June 1912 the election of a city council at Veracruz proved 'ineffective for want of voters'. [124] Outside the cities, the apathy and irrelevance of many elections were even more pronounced. In the free villages, of course, a brand of informal democracy, ensuring a choice of officials that was 'free, serious, and respected', had long flourished where it was permitted; such democracy – traditional, personal, and particularistic – lay at the heart of Zapatismo. [125] But there was no guarantee that villagers would wish to change the old ways for the new, accepting formal, rational–legal procedures and authorities in place of older, traditional forms. The ballot-slips, parties and hustings of the new politics appeared as yet more alien, urban incursions into their preferred but threatened way of life.

A fortiori, villagers under the heel of cacique and landlord, or peons resident on the great estates, could expect little from the democratic innovations which (in theory) would lead to their emancipation. Poor, illiterate, 'subject to what we might call the iron bonds of landlord boss-rule' (a rule often bolstered by the influence of the *cura*), the peon and dependent villager were likely to have their experience of the new politics confined to that of voting (if they voted at all) according to the *patrón*'s instructions. [126] In Oaxaca, Benito Juárez Maza was elected on the strength of the *serrano* vote, marshalled by the mountain caciques; in Jalisco (if Azuela is to be credited) the PCN could count on a bloc client vote. [127] The landlords of Tlaxcala, facing a strong popular challenge, used similar methods, at least in regions where their authority was unimpaired: Manuel Sánchez Gavito, running for deputy on the Liga (*hacendado*) ticket, harvested a big vote from the Calpulalpán district, where his estates lay, and where his support was 'essentially agricultural [representing an] imposition on the peons of the field'. [128] Braniff, running for governor in Veracruz, collected votes from 'his peons, *gachupín* employees and various subjects of the Kaiser', so it was alleged; while at Paso del Macho, in the same state, the conservative Club Perseverancia (uniting 'members of the old regime . . . people with capital . . . speculators and concessionaires in the pulque and meat monopolies') brought gangs of peons (including many out-of-state migrants) into town at election time, billeted them in appropriate houses or pool halls, and showed them how to fill in their ballot slips in favour of the Club's candidates. All this because the members 'did not approve of the appointment of authorities indifferent to their personal designs'; in which respect they were successful, as all the old Porfirian office-holders were, thanks to these methods, returned to power in the municipality. [129]

If such procedures were more common and effective in the traditional, hacienda-dominated states of central Mexico, they were not unknown in the more progressive north either. Labour might be more free and mobile, the Church less influential, but men of property and position could still swing elections by other than strictly legitimate means. Sonora, for example, witnessed serious political campaigns and elections which, if imperfect, were not at all travesties of public opinion.[130] But here, too, the expansion of political participation was accompanied by a good deal of fixing and corruption. From a comparative perspective, this was hardly surprising. In no country were the constitutional practices admired by Madero and his fellow-reformers rapidly implanted: they grew up gradually, often developing out of earlier 'corrupt' practices, associated with 'artificial' or 'limited' democracy and characterised by boss-rule, networks of patronage and machine politics. It might even be argued that such practices could be functional to the subsequent development of genuine mass democracy, in that they helped integrate marginal, illiterate and immigrant groups into the national polity. Eatanswill and the Duke of Newcastle's rotten boroughs played a part (and a not wholly negative part) in the development of British parliamentary democracy, just as Tammany Hall helped assimilate America's immigrant masses. Had it not been for the Radical machine in Argentina, or the *grandi elettori* of Giolitti's Italy, would the mass movements of Peronism or the Italian Communist Party have been possible? In time, of course, corrupt practices could bar the way to fuller democracy (acting analogously to the feudal remnants which, in the Marxist scheme, inhibit the maturation of capitalism). But, just as feudalism fathered capitalism, so artificial sired genuine democracy.

Sonora is interesting in this respect, since politics here combined a genuine expansion of participation with palpable (yet perhaps functional) manipulation; and, though no-one could have known it at the time, Sonora was to provide the principal model for the politics of post-revolutionary Mexico. Several of the post-revolutionary elite therefore cut their teeth – so far as practical politics were concerned – during Sonora's liberal experiment. They thus witnessed Maytorena's sweeping victory as governor, and Gayou's bitterly and at times dirtily fought campaign against Morales in the vice-gubernatorial election. The latter was scarcely publicised in the rural hinterland of Hermosillo, where 'the illiterate peons and ranchers ... have never witnessed or appreciated the worth of an act like voting'; yet this same district returned a suspiciously high (and, as it turned out, crucial) vote for Gayou, who won.[131] When Alvaro Obregón contested and won his first democratic election, for the municipal presidency of Huatabampo, he counted on several assets, apart from his undoubted intrinsic merit: 'gangs of peons' were brought in from outside the electoral district by friendly *hacendados* (some were under age, and some voted twice); the Mayo Indian 'Governor', Chito Cruz, induced his tribal followers to vote; the local garrison and officials (not least the candidate's brother, then the interim municipal president) lent their support.[132] Obregón's victory was not the arbitrary imposition of a Porfirian oligarch; his campaign involved genuine participation, propaganda, and vote-winning. Public opinion was by no means ignored, but neither was it the sole, sacred arbiter of the outcome. If this was the nursery of democracy (and Obregón went on to win the 1920 presidential election), it taught a form of democracy which, though more ample and responsive than the Porfirian travesty, did not measure up to the ideal of rigorously legal, impartial constitutional liberalism espoused by Madero.

Behind these accounts of rigged elections, of a dragooned or apathetic electorate, there lurks an apparent paradox. The question of free elections had been central to the politicking of 1909–10, and to the revolution of 1910–11. It was not an irrelevant question: elections could control political appointments, and political appointments could control taxation, agrarian policy, labour legislation and so on. It clearly mattered to people who was to serve as governor, *jefe político*, or municipal president, and this had been borne out by the reformist protest of the late Porfiriato, by the published revolutionary grievances of 1910–11, and by the prolific local insurrections of 1911. If men were prepared to organise and orate, to fight and riot about free elections, why did they seem indifferent when the elections finally happened? As Roque Estrada put in, a few years later: thousands of Mexicans participated in a long and bloody struggle when called to 'the reconquest of their sacred liberties', yet 'with the enemy beaten and mastered, with the way clear of obstacles, the number of these same keen combatants who cast their votes barely reaches 40%'.[133] The paradox is even sharper since, we have argued, electoral participation was often highest in 'non-revolutionary' states (like Aguascalientes) and classes (like the urban workers) and lowest among the revolutionary vanguard, whether this be viewed socially or geographically.

In general terms, the paradox may be easily explained. The original promise of free elections exercised a powerful, effective appeal by virtue of its breadth and flexibility: its capacity to elicit a response from different social groups, by appealing to certain basic aspirations, with slogans like '*Sufragio Efectivo, No Re-elección*' serving, it might be said, as code-words, differently interpreted by different people according to these aspirations. The Maderista programme and philosophy were thus variably conjugated: for some, they implied a progressive, up-to-the-minute polity, well-governed, hard-working and prosperous; for some, a political housecleaning and overdue access to power; for some, a reassertion of old, heroic, liberal values; for some, agrarian restitution and/or village autonomy. And, unlike, say, nationalism, which also claimed a broad, aggregative appeal, that of Maderismo was potent and genuine, since it seemed to have relevance for specific, acute grievances, in a way that nationalism did not.

In retrospect the optimism, even the self-delusion, with which Madero's promises were taken up may seem naive; but the rapid politicisation of 1909–10, the sudden, startling success of the revolution, and the overthrow of a seemingly permanent dictatorship all bred a mood of euphoria. These were times when 'a benign spirit was abroad'; when hopes were high, optimism prevailed, and men believed that they 'should see the people having a strong hand / in framing their own laws whence better days / to all Mankind'.[134] But which laws? What kind of regime would free suffrage create? To these questions, different groups gave different answers. To the supporters and beneficiaries of the Porfirian system, the answer was easy: free elections meant anarchy, economic collapse, the undoing of all Porfirio Díaz's patient work; the dogmatic certainty – and the practical worthlessness – of their answer became clear in the wake of Madero's fall. To many others, almost certainly a majority, the promise of 'a real vote and no boss rule' exercised a real appeal, at least at the outset. But it was an appeal which depended on the translation of general, abstract principles into concrete, local realities. The 'boss' was a flesh-and-blood figure – cacique, *jefe político*, state governor – and the elections would usher in specific, desired changes. 'Everyone wanted to see the Plan of San Luis Potosí put into effect', a 'man of the common people' told an American in Acapulco; and, when asked what the Plan implied,

he readily explained that it meant no more than the correction of old abuses, the opportunity for the people to choose and elect their own governors and deputies and other officials at honest elections; that they wanted the right to select 'un hijo del país' (a son of the state) as governor; that they wanted to know how their public funds were expended; they wanted to establish schools, etc.[135]

Here, then, was a reiteration of the kinds of grievances (particularly those of urban origin) which had been evident in the opposition press of the 1900s, in political manifestos both before and after the 1910 revolution, and in many local political conflicts. And though, under Madero, some were partially met, many were not: arbitrary authorities and political abuses continued, elections were still fixed, scandals were covered up. Such failings were cited by disgruntled Maderistas, some of whom took to rebellion again; and, in more cynical fashion, by Porfiristas, whose consciences could hardly have been clear in these respects. Together, they helped erode the once massive moral capital of the new regime. Expecting speedy redress, people now experienced swift disillusionment. They were not prepared to await the slow maturation of constitutional democracy (which, for some high-minded Maderista thinkers, was an end in itself), but looked rather to immediate, practical solutions, and these were slow in coming. They were particularly slow in the realm of agrarian reform. Rebels like Zapata sought a rapid, specific, if sometimes modest reform: a reassertion of village rights to particular lands, protection from engrossing landlords, and a degree of political autonomy. To the extent that free elections (within the state and municipality especially) furthered these aims they were welcomed and fought for; to the extent that they merely brought a new, power-hungry, city-based elite into office (an elite not much more tolerant of either agrarian *reivindicación* or political decentralisation than its Porfirian predecessor), they seemed a hollow sham. Zapatistas – and other popular rebels – were not prepared to sacrifice their immediate, local objectives in the interests of some grand, abstract, national design: the construction of a constitutional regime that would place Mexico alongside the progressive, democratic states of Europe and North America. The grand abstractions – 'liberty', 'democracy', 'progress' – meant a lot to the educated, middle-class Maderistas of the cities, but much less to the *pelados*, peons and *campesinos*, for whom free elections were (as for the radical Chartists of nineteenth-century Britain) a 'knife and fork question'. 'Ideas are imperishable, eternal', declared Don Timoteo, the fictional yet archetypal small town Maderista of Azuela's *The Bosses*; yet the masses' grasp of these fine abstractions was poor.[136] 'Progress', Womack reminds us, does not figure in the Plan of Ayala.[137] 'We are fighting for *libertad*', a northern rebel told John Reed; 'what do you mean by *libertad*?', Reed countered; '*Libertad* is when I can *do what I want*' came the reply.[138] 'What, *amigo*, is this *democracia* for which all are shouting?', one 'white-pyjamad peasant' asked of another, as Madero's carriage swept by, 'why, it must be the lady who accompanies him', replied his companion, pointing to Madero's wife.[139]

Patronising and possibly apocryphal though they are, these exchanges illustrate something of the gulf which separated two distinct discourses: that of the city and that of the countryside; of the educated and of the illiterate; of the 'great' and the 'little' traditions. It was not that the peasants and the poor lacked the intellectual capacity for handling abstractions (after all, most still believed in God); rather, they were understandably ignorant or distrustful of the grand, literate abstractions (such as 'Progress') in whose name they had been plundered in the past and would be plundered again in the future. General principles like those of Maderista liberalism could only maintain their initial appeal if they were translated into the political vernacular, and rendered intelligible in immediate, concrete terms. In seeking practical benefits rather than abstract promises, the Mexican peasantry behaved like any other peasantry, for whom the luxury of such promises was ruled out by the exigencies of their social position.[140] Agrarianism, too, could be framed in general, rhetorical terms: yet Zapatismo (whose popular appeal no-one doubts) depended on specific, local and immediate reform to win adherents. Hence Zapatista veterans, even after decades of post-revolutionary political socialisation, still recall the struggles of 1910–20 in highly individual terms:

their accounts are simple and concrete. Everyday names and trivia figure in them . . . their conversations are rich and replete with details which, to the ears of the devout listener, sound heresy, by virtue of their apparent insignificance . . . there is never an ideological statement, an explicit reference to their principles and demands.[141]

Within Zapatismo, therefore, rhetorical abstractions were at a discount; proper rather than generic names populated Zapatista discourse; and ideology, often mute and implicit, 'was expressed in congruent actions, which radically transformed reality'. [142] Here, as in most popular movements, loyalty was given to a personal *jefe*, rather than to an abstract cause; agrarian reform was local and specific, based on historical precedent, and confirmed by the authority of the *jefe*. [143] It would be wrong to infer from the absence of explicit ideology an equivalent absence of political principle, or to categorise Zapatismo and other popular movements (as certain oral historians, working from individual recollections, have tended to do) as a somewhat aimless, anomic expression of individual inclinations. [144] The *raison d'être* of a popular movement cannot be reconstructed simply – or even primarily – from the reminiscences of its veteran survivors; the historian must take into account yet transcend such individual accounts, matching them with the collective experiences and macro-social trends of which the individuals may have been only dimly aware.

Concerned with the local and the concrete, suspicious or ignorant of grand abstractions, the mass of the Mexican people were not captivated by the prospect of building democracy *per se*. They could only be won over (and had, briefly, been won over in 1910–11) if the grand design implied some fairly rapid, tangible benefits. It was therefore imperative that the Maderistas make a reality of their philosophy of liberal politics and social conciliation. [145] Elections alone could not achieve this; indeed, the liberal politics encouraged by the regime made for social conflict rather than cohesion. The Porfirian alternative – repression – was no better, and created more problems than it solved, at least so long as the tide of popular protest ran strongly. Neither a narrow liberalism nor a narrow authoritarianism would work. A viable regime would have to put down roots into the soil whence popular rebellion sprang; it would have to meet, or at least deflect, popular demands, promote or co-opt popular leaders; instead of (or perhaps as well as) repressing the popular movement, it would have to establish its ideological hegemony over it. If the promise of free elections had stirred a genuine but short-lived popular response in 1910–11, creating a sudden, strange alliance between city liberals and rural populists, it was now up to the Maderista rulers of Mexico to cement the alliance and translate their constitutional liberalism into practical measures which, by responding to popular demands, would bind the people to the emergent liberal state. Social reforms – in the areas of land and labour, for example – would be complementary, not antithetical, to the institution of free elections.

REFORM: LAND AND LABOUR

It is a commonplace, though a valid one, that Madero and his colleagues were essentially concerned with political reform, in the narrow sense. Not that Madero himself ever denied the importance of social and economic problems: his correspondence and publications reveal a clear advocacy of land distribution and an awareness of working-class grievances (he had, after all, been one of the most progressive and enlightened of northern Mexico's entrepreneurs).[146] But he did not regard the direct solution of these problems as the prime task of his regime. The task was to secure decent representative government, whereby particular groups could press their claims and seek reform through the constitutional channels; such was the advice given by Madero to workers and peasants alike.[147] The middle class, too, the backbone of the old Anti-Re-electionist Party, could advocate its favoured, 'social' policies: tax equalisation, public works, education, and the elimination of those vices – drink, dirt, gambling, bloodsports, prostitution – which weighed as heavily on respectable consciences as on the national economy.[148] But in all these respects the government's duty was to respond to legitimate pressure; it did not have to take a lead with positive measures of social engineering. The Maderista state was to be a passive state, following Porfirian precedent: budgetary priorities remained the same, with *per capita* expenditure rising only marginally, and 'administrative' costs (those devoted to the basic running of the state machinery) still absorbing over 70% of the total.[149]

The passivity of the state may be illustrated in the fields of agrarian and labour reform: two areas of policy which were later to become synonymous with 'the' Mexican Revolution. In each case, however, it is necessary to distinguish between official action – legal, governmental, and codified – and unofficial, *de facto* reform, undertaken by interested parties on their own behalf. As regards agrarian reform, for example, by far the greater of the changes enacted during 1910–20 were of the second kind: they were localised, popular and technically illegal, occurring in defiance of – rather than in response to – official policy. Efforts at land recovery and redistribution figured in the Revolution from its very inception; authorities, Porfirian and Maderista, strove to counter them; the 'return to normalcy' measures undertaken by the *interinato* in the early summer of 1911 involved a guillotine on all illicit, *de facto*, agrarian reform. Madero was adamant that reform would thereafter have to come legally and gradually; as the people of Huichapán (Hgo) were told in 1912 the conquest of (political) liberty was the overriding revolutionary goal and popular need, next to which,

all other needs [such as the agrarian problem] were pale in comparison . . . It has been maintained that the object of the San Luis revolution was to resolve the agrarian problem; that is not correct; the revolution . . . was to recover our liberty, for liberty, alone, will of itself resolve all problems.[150]

Granted liberty, the people could send their elected representatives to Congress, where they could legislate for the common good regarding the agrarian and other problems. The Mexico City press was likewise disabused of the idea that the 1910 revolution had promised 'the division of the great estates [and] their distribution among the proletariat'; such promises had never been made, Madero asserted, and therefore they could not have gone unfulfilled, as some alleged.[151] Article 3 of the Plan of San Luis, the source of these misinterpretations, merely provided for the revision of arbitrary, immoral land dispossessions; and, under the terms of the Juárez Treaty ('so advantageous to the nation'), Porfirian legal judgements were declared legal and binding.[152] All complaints would therefore have to proceed through the courts and there could be no *de facto reivindicaciones* or *reparto*. It was not that Madero was anything but favourable to the growth and protection of small-holdings (*la pequeña propiedad*); 'but that does not mean that one proceeds to despoil any landlord of his properties ... it is one thing to create small-holdings by means of constant effort, another to divide up the great estates, which I have never thought to do, and never offered in any of my speeches or proclamations'.[153] Outright confiscation was not to be considered, the government lacked the funds for massive purchases, and no loan could be raised for such an end. Thus, if the state declined to play a direct role, if *de jure* expropriation was to be ruled out (and *de facto* expropriation was to be restricted), there remained only the distribution of public lands (*baldíos*) or the free play of the market to provide land for the landless. But after the great Porfirian hand-out, cultivable public land was scarcely to be had, while the market had historically worked to the detriment of villager and smallholder and to the advantage of landlord and cacique.[154]

Like Madero, most prominent Maderistas followed their liberal predecessors in advocating a division of landed wealth that would create a prosperous smallholding class, conducive to peace, stability and constitutional government, yet they had few precise or practical ideas as to how this might be achieved.[155] The PCP platform of August 1911 buried its agrarian proposals under a heap of familiar political promises (no re-election, respect for the Constitution, suppression of the *jefaturas*, a free press, judicial independence, better education, and the inevitable campaign against drink); and what proposals there were went no further than the establishment of agricultural colonies and 'small agricultural interests', fairer taxation, and a vague commitment to 'combat all monopolies and special privileges'. Speakers like Bordes Mangel had no doubt that small and large agrarian interests could co-exist and prosper together.[156] Gubernatorial and other candidates usually included some passing reference to the protection and development of agriculture (especially *la pequeña propiedad*), but there was no hint of structural reform.[157] And some still harped exclusively on the old themes of effective suffrage, the *jefaturas*, tax reform and suchlike.[158] Even those Maderistas seen by some as more radical (like Pino Suárez) denied government an active, interventionist role in the solution of the agrarian problem: 'understanding and encouragement', rather than direct action, would ameliorate the situation.[159]

A good deal of Maderista agrarian policy (to the extent that there was a policy) was therefore cast in the old nineteenth-century mould. Like the gubernatorial candidate Manuel Villaseñor, most Maderistas believed that the conversion of communal *ejidal* land into private plots should continue. Nor was this at all surprising, given not only their liberal, *laissez-faire* philosophy, but also – in cases like the Figueroas of Huitzuco, or Nicolás Flores and the Pisaflores revolutionaries – their own family background as *rancheros*, and beneficiaries of the *desamortización* laws. [160] But continued *desamortización* also benefited landlord and cacique at the expense of the landholding village, and would do so even if the Maderista commitment to end force and fraud was honoured; for it was less force and fraud than the inexorable operations of the market within a radically unequal rural society which brought about agrarian polarisation and protest. Nevertheless, the break-up of communal land went on, and *baldíos* were alienated much as they had been under Díaz. [161] Nor was there any guarantee that, under the new regime, the courts would show any more favour to villages engaged in protracted legal disputes with haciendas. [162] National innovations in the agrarian field were, in typically Maderista fashion, well-intentioned but ineffective. Minister of Fomento, Rafael Hernández, headed a National Agrarian Commission ('composed of distinguished agriculturalists, lawyers, engineers and bankers') to report on the question, but its members were no more radical than Hernández himself, one of Madero's conservative north-eastern relatives. [163] Like some enlightened Porfirian predecessors, the Commission showed a concern for progressive agriculture (better communications, stock, irrigation and technical education); it favoured the continued dissolution of the *ejidos* and the sale of *baldíos*; it looked to the provision of mortgages and the establishment of a corps of trained agronomists. The problem, as the Commission conceived it, lay in the technique rather than the structure of production. And the solution did not lie directly with the government: [164] 'the basic philosophy was that land should be made available to those who had the resources and the ambition to work it and make it pay; there were to be no gifts, nor was the government to sustain a financial loss from the program'. As in the old days, however, plans for reform tended to favour the powerful. With the expectation of government purchase of surplus land, values rose further, and *hacendados'* offers of sale were – predictably enough – confined to inferior property. [165] At national level, therefore, Maderista policy represented no more than a refurbished liberalism, in which the traditional attachment to property and market principles was supplemented by an enlightened (but often impractical and contradictory) concern for social justice. It is hardly surprising that this failed to satisfy either agrarian rebels in the field, or the handful of radical commentators who favoured more rapid, drastic, illiberal measures to resolve the problem. [166]

But the situation was highly fluid: it could not fail to be given the scope and incidence of agrarian rebellion during Madero's presidency. New ideas were filtering through, even among the Maderista rulers of Mexico. Some state governors, for example, diverged from the national norm, and displayed either a greater awareness of past mistakes, or a greater commitment to immediate reform. In Chihuahua, Abraham González halted the alienation of public land; Governor Guillén of Chiapas repealed the Ejidal Law which provided for the parcelisation of communal holdings.[167] Antonio Hidalgo's programme in Tlaxcala combined conventional Maderista reforms with more radical measures, including 'the expropriation, in the public interest, of rural property, agricultural colonies thereby to be established to the benefit of the people'.[168] It is not clear how far this was implemented: the political deadlock in the state ruled out a coherent legislative programme, and (not least because of this proposal) Hidalgo was soon locked in a mortal struggle with the Tlaxcalan old guard. But the governor's stance certainly encouraged peasant organisation and politicisation, as reformist 'propaganda was spread . . . by way of the market system, through pedlars and rural teachers, and landless labourers were advised about their civil rights and the illegal status of debt peonage'.[169]

The Tlaxcalan reforms were, by contemporary standards, far-reaching. But they embraced two measures which appeared regularly in other Maderista administrations: the regulation (or even elimination) of debt peonage, and the equalisation of rural taxation. The Maderistas – with their predominantly urban, commercial–professional, and often northern origins – held no brief for debt peonage. Not only was it harsh and immoral; it was also retrograde and inefficient. Free wage labour would not only prove more productive, but would also redound to the benefit of the domestic market.[170] It was therefore thoroughly in accord with Maderista philosophy to further the dissolution of debt peonage, abetting a process that in some – though only some – regions was already proceeding. In Chiapas (a state where peonage was fading in some districts, but flourishing in others) Governor Guillén's Ley de Sirvientes of 1912 afforded rural workers extensive protection: all contracts were to be written and filed with the local authorities; maximum hours and pensions for the disabled were laid down; the advance of wages and accumulation of debt – though permitted – were not to be heritable, and were to be closely regulated.[171] Like many Maderista proposals, however, this reform was fine on paper, but all too fallible in practice. Precarious state administrations lacking a strong base of social support could hardly challenge the entrenched interests of the southern planters. A radical reform of the peonage system, as the governor of neighbouring Campeche observed, would require 'no little abnegation and some sacrifices on the part of the noble members of the worthy company of hacendados': as the diffident, deferential tone indicated, Maderista administrations were not likely to compel landlord compliance with reform in cases (which were common enough) where voluntary compliance was refused.[172] In most states, therefore, the practical achievements of Maderista reforms in this area were scanty. Even in Chiapas, where formal reform went farthest, the very agency established to monitor labour recruitment and eliminate abuses 'quickly became . . . a corrupt and abusive agency itself'.[173] Good intentions were not enough: a successful assault on debt peonage required – in addition to benign reforms – a deliberate political attack on the planter class, and its instruments of control and domination.

In the realm of fiscal reform (a constant theme of pre-1910 progressives) Maderista administrations had more success. Here, they were impelled not only by the demands of their middle-class constituents and the glaring inequity of outdated cadastral rolls, but also by the need to boost government revenue, as budgetary problems and deficits mounted.[174] With this in mind, they were prepared to risk the displeasure and opposition of the landlord interest. Thus, in Chihuahua, Governor González instituted a tax reform 'blatantly favourable to the middle-class businessman and small farmer', at the expense of big landowners and companies: hence, in part, the Chihuahuan elite's dalliance with Orozco.[175] Similar reformist objectives were entertained by the 'law-abiding revolutionaries' of Morelos, although their fiscal revaluation was modest in comparison.[176] And tax revaluation became a major issue in several states of the Bajío, a region where agrarian rebellion was relatively feeble, but where a large smallholding class stood to benefit from such reforms, and where Maderista office-holders faced a strong challenge from Catholic political aspirants. Governor Loyola of Querétaro, striving to balance the state budget at a time when inflation was afflicting the poor, decreed a tax reform shifting the burden onto the 'well-to-do classes', and further urged a cut in the tariff on imported grain, which would stimulate competition, lower prices, and encourage 'a division of the big properties, since . . . large-scale agriculture would not [then] be the coveted business it is now'.[177] But, a true liberal, Loyola would not go beyond tariff and tax measures: there could be no expropriation, and, as regards the shrinking real income of the poor, 'it does not depend on the Government to increase wages in proportion to prices'. In Guanajuato, Governor Lizardi increased the taxable value of landed property between five- and ten-fold, to bring it into line with market prices: to the *rancheros* of the state the reform was 'most welcome'; but the León Chamber of Commerce, representing the big landowners, advised its members to pay up to double the old rates, but no more. In the ensuing confrontation, Madero backed up the governor against the landed interest.[178] And the president similarly endorsed the fiscal reforms of Governor Alberto Fuentes of Aguascalientes. Fuentes – a 'socialist' or 'anarchist' to his conservative opponents – espoused a thorough-going Maderista programme (bullfights were banned and clients of the old regime – down to the boss of the city slaughterhouse – were removed); his tax revaluation (which Madero termed a 'thoroughly equitable' measure) provoked a fierce political battle, in which the governor counted on both presidential and popular support to overcome the opposition of a hostile state legislature.[179]

Policies of agrarian fiscal reform were therefore common enough; and Madero came round to the view that a general tax revision should be undertaken throughout the entire Federation.[180] If, from the landlords' point of view, this was a matter of concern, it was still not a profound threat: their political representatives (and these would seem to have included the Catholic Party, certainly in Aguascalientes) showed formidable powers of resistance; and the reformers almost unanimously shrank from expropriation and other forms of direct government intervention in the land market.[181] But while the practical effects of official Maderista agrarian reform were – as all agree – exiguous, there was nevertheless a growing debate over the agrarian question, as the political nation was forced to come to terms with the unrest affecting the countryside. And, belatedly, the debate began to produce some more radical answers. Luis Cabrera, something of a bell-wether of progressive, 'revolutionary' thinking, experienced a conversion to agrarian reform (just as he had earlier from Reyismo to Maderismo; he would later discover economic nationalism). In December 1912, as deputy for that southern section of the Federal District which knew Zapatismo first hand, he made a celebrated speech in defence of the *ejido*, the traditional form of communal village land tenure. Questioning the official policy of peace before reform, he argued that only reform could bring peace, and that reform could no longer continue along classic, liberal lines. The survival of village lands throughout the colonial period, he pointed out, was due to their corporate character: liberal legislation, by destroying corporate tenure, had opened the door to a massive transfer of land from village to hacienda and cacique. Furthermore, this transfer had been entirely legal in some 90% of cases, and the Maderista policy (enunciated in the Plan of San Luis) of rectifying only illegal land seizures would barely scratch the surface of the problem.[182] It was time, Cabrera believed, to ditch inappropriate policies, derived from alien models, and to base reform on 'the personal and local knowledge of our country and its needs'.[183] Corporate tradition remained strong, certainly on the densely populated Central Plateau, and the government, instead of shredding it with a liberal scalpel, should conserve it in the interests of rural peace and justice. *Ejidos* should be reconstituted and given legal identity; land grants should be to collectivities rather than to individuals. Perhaps Cabrera did not espouse this solution passionately (he still regarded private property as fundamental, and the *ejido* more as a necessary concession to Mexico's rural backwardness) but his conversion was nonetheless significant.

Cabrera's defence of the *ejido* came in the twilight of the Madero regime and had no practical results; indeed, he had just been passed over for the post of Minister of Fomento (in which capacity he could have made a start on the policy he advocated) and was about to leave the country.[184] Though he had his supporters among the more radical Maderistas, Cabrera did not find favour with Madero, who regarded his proposal as 'very dangerous' and who did not 'believe that there existed an agrarian problem of such a nature in Mexico' (or so Cabrera himself related).[185] Manuel Bonilla, who took the Fomento portfolio, showed more urgency than some of his predecessors, but no inclination to sponsor the reconstruction of the *ejido*.[186] Cabrera's ideas thus remained on paper, and events soon overtook the slow march of official agrarian reform. But the shift away from classic, liberal notions of private property and individual ownership towards communal concepts derived from Mexico's past and requiring for their implementation both active government intervention and the infringement of property rights, was one of great moment: it pointed the way forward and, above all, it gave recognition to the fundamentally agrarian character of the popular revolution. Cabrera himself had been no agrarian firebrand in 1910 (or even 1911); but by the end of 1912 he had undergone a 'marked ideological evolution', which brought him to the conclusion that the condition of the rural masses was the crucial question facing Mexico's rulers, and that many other questions were ancillary to it.[187] While some *políticos* continued to deny that an 'agrarian question' existed (de la Barra was still one of them in 1916), and while others clung to liberal remedies which often aggravated the condition they were supposed to treat, at least some members of the educated, civilian, political elite were now taking note of popular, agrarian agitation, recognising that it derived from tangible problems rather than innate waywardness, and proposing new, radical solutions to deal with the situation. 'Official' agrarian reform began to veer closer to the 'unofficial' reform which had been taking place since 1910.

Whereas educated opinion reacted only slowly – and official policy hardly at all – to the popular demands embodied in dozens of peasant revolts, the regime's attitude to urban labour, which had played a marginal role in the political violence of 1910–13, was more benign and actively reformist. Just as the civilian Maderistas (who had not done the fighting) collected the spoils in 1911, so urban labour (which had not fought either) did relatively well out of the new regime. This happened because urban labour (or, an important qualification, the organised sector thereof) proved capable of operating within the new constitutional order. The urban workers voted and joined parties; their political support was courted. At the same time, with the workers showing 'a very marked tendency to associate', nascent trade unions were able to improve their organisation, voice their demands, and win occasional, limited gains.[188] Most of this Madero approved and encouraged: self-help, political involvement, the pursuit of betterment through peaceful, moderate means, were all commendable virtues in the new political context – just as land seizures, banditry and violence were irredeemable vices. Despite their obvious and important differences the middle and working classes of the cities shared not only common interests, but also a measure of common ideology: to a significant extent they thought and acted alike, and differently from the *campesinado*.[189]

The urban working class made a negligible contribution to the success of the 1910–11 revolution.[190] But even before Madero's triumph, there was evidence of greater activity on the part of labour unions, in anticipation of concessions from either the faltering Díaz administration or the impending new regime. The Puerto México dockers struck late in March; the Orizaba textile operatives (of whom much had been expected, in vain, in November 1910) went on strike – peacefully – in April; and in the same month the United Railways of Yucatán workers struck for better hours and wages, demands which the company were prepared partially to meet.[191] Then, throughout the summer of 1911, the land seizures and jacqueries occasioned by the lapse of authority in the countryside were paralleled by repeated strikes in the cities, the ports and the mining camps.[192] The northern states and the Gulf ports appear to have been the worst hit; while to the south (Oaxaca) and west (Jalisco) business was, as yet, unaffected.[193] The incidence of strikes correlated in large measure with the weakening of authority produced by the revolution, and with the presence of certain occupational groups which were in the van of working-class organisation: the miners and smelter workers, the railwaymen, and the dockers. Thus, in Coahuila, the coal mines (pro-revolutionary in 1910, and heavily unionised by contemporary standards) faced shutdowns in June 1911; Santa Eulalia and lesser mines in Chihuahua were struck, as were *potosino* mines at La Paz, Matehuala and Charcas; Mazapil (Zac.), Cananea (Sra) and the mining camps of Aguascalientes were also affected.[194] So too were smelters at Torreón, Wadley (SLP), Monterrey and Aguascalientes. In addition to the Yucatán incident, mentioned above, there were strikes at the Tehuantepec National terminal at Salina Cruz, in the Aguascalientes railway shops (where skilled Mexican labour overhauled rolling stock) and among the railwaymen – though not, it seems, the textile operatives – of the state of Puebla. Dockers rivalled the miners as the most prolific strikers: at Tampico and Veracruz, whence the example spread to Frontera (though this was an 'insignificant' emulation of stoppages further up the Gulf coast) and (once again) at Puerto México. At Manzanillo, on the west coast, a stevedores' strike on the railway wharf was, like the Frontera incident, attributed to the demonstration effect of strikes elsewhere; and, soon, the Acapulco dockers joined the action.[195] Factory operatives do not appear to have been particularly active during the efflorescence of strikes in the summer of 1911: apart from Orizaba, there were strikes in the factories of Chihuahua, in a *potosino* nail factory, in the rubber and soap plants of Torreón; much of the industrial heartland, however, remained relatively quiet. More conspicuous were two other urban groups: public utility workers and (for want of a better term) artisans. Tram workers struck in Chihuahua City (where the telephone company was also affected) and in the Federal capital; light and power workers struck in Torreón. Bakers refused to bake in Mexico City and Mazatlán; and in the latter case they were joined by shoemakers, barbers and shop clerks. Later in the year, at Torreón, carpenters and masons were prominent among the 2,000 workers who struck in support of an eight hour day.[196]

Strikes were particularly newsworthy in the summer of 1911 since they coincided with the more general unrest, and were seen as part of a widespread decline of authority and rapid growth of plebeian pretensions. The miners of Concepción del Oro were reckoned to display 'restless and impertinent behaviour'; at Torreón the spate of strikes coincided with signs of ominous popular uppishness; at Durango, in July, it was observed that 'more strikes have taken place in the last two months than in all the history of the district'.[197] The concentration of strike activity was thus rightly seen as a response to the current relaxation of authority; at times, even, it depended on the deliberate connivance of new, shaky authorities seeking working-class support. Strikes, in other words, were a product of the revolution, not *vice versa*, and strikers were taking advantage of a situation they had done nothing to bring about, save in those cases where there had been proletarian support for the Anti-Re-electionists (and this, at best, represented an indirect contribution), or where – rarer still – urban workers had shouldered arms against Díaz. The strike against the Mazapil Co., for example, responded to long-standing economic grievances; this and other strikes in the region 'would not have occurred except for the condition of political unrest' prevailing.[198] Often, it was observed, the authorities were reluctant to take tough action, along Porfirian lines, either because they feared the workers' resistance (as at Cananea) or because they were too busy cultivating the working class vote (at Tampico, Chihuahua and Torreón).[199]

After the rapid succession of strikes in the summer of 1911 the situation grew calmer. The decline in strike activity derived from factors both internal and external to the labour movement itself. Within the young, weak and inexperienced trade unions, the militancy of mid-1911 tended to dissipate: this militancy was in a sense the industrial equivalent of the political optimism of the time, which soon gave way to greater realism, even pessimism. According to some (not altogether trustworthy) accounts, strikes had been undertaken in a cavalier spirit: because repression had been eased, because there was a strike in the next port up the coast, because strikes were now in fashion. Some of the workers' demands were said to be 'trifling and evidenced more a desire to exercise a new privilege than to gain any particular advantage'.[200] No doubt this goes too far; but there was probably a sense in which the workers were testing their powers in the new, uncertain conditions following the fall of Díaz, and doing so in optimistic, experimental fashion. The outcome, however, was rarely favourable, and the result was often disillusionment. At Aguascalientes, for example,

the strikes we have had here seem to have only discredited the revolutionary party for in most of the strikes the strikers gained very little of anything and the poor people learned that the revolutionaries were not Gods ... In most every case the strikers appealed to the authorities to help them out. The authorities used all their influence to smooth matters over but didn't accomplish much in the way of getting the demands of the strikers [met].[201]

But, equally, in towns where the strikers made some gains the disruption was brief, most disputes 'were settled to the satisfaction of all parties concerned' and there was a rapid return to work.[202] As in the political sphere, the freedom and mild euphoria of the early summer gave way to a more realistic appraisal of the situation, which brought home the need for solid patient organisation if gains were to be consolidated or advanced. The unions' organisation was, as yet, largely embryonic, their membership low, their funds almost non-existent. Unemployment was still a spectre, and there is evidence that the onset of winter discouraged militancy, especially in the chilly mining camps of the north. At Cananea, certainly, winter was conducive to industrial peace, which was expected to last 'till warmer weather' returned: the season cycle therefore acted upon peasant and proletarian unrest in a contrary rhythm (though its imperatives were of course less categorical in the case of the urban workers, especially those of the coastal lowlands).[203]

Militancy was also affected by external factors, chiefly the revival of political authority with the *interinato* and the inauguration of Madero as president. Though strikes continued throughout 1911–12 – with the usual pacemakers; the miners of Cananea, the Orizaba textile operatives, the railwaymen – they were now more sporadic and the authorities were less rattled. Hence the threat – and occasionally the use – of repression became more frequent. During the *interinato* blood was shed when troops were deployed against the Mexico City tram workers and the miners of El Oro; troops likewise opened fire on textile workers in the capital and in Querétaro, and were sent to cow the troublesome miners in the Coahuila coalfields, where the (Maderista) authorities ordered the arrest of the union leaders.[204] Later in the year, with Madero installed in the National Palace, troops were concentrated in the Laguna towns during a massive strike involving some 10,000 workers; troops were despatched to Cananea in November 1911 and again in February and December 1912; while the Puebla textile bosses were still in the habit of calling for the *rurales* when they feared disorderly industrial disputes.[205] Not that the despatch of troops was *per se* sinister or repressive (from the workers' point of view). Strikes produced violence (which even radicals like Francisco Múgica deplored) and it was not necessarily the strikers so much as the urban *canaille* which sometimes posed the threat. During the big Torreón strike of November 1911, for example, stories circulated of 'thousands of peons and women coming in from the ranches with baskets, *serapes* and other things in which to carry away the loot', which they anticipated.[206] For the mob (which was socially distinct from employed, organised labour) strikes conjured visions of pillage and mayhem, much as the revolution had in 1910–11. Nevertheless, the despatch of troops, especially when it coincided with the arrest of working-class 'ring-leaders' (as in the mines of Coahuila) or 'agitators' (among the Manzanillo railwaymen), smacked of Porfirian practice and created another odious parallel between the old and new regimes, which radicals could seize upon, and which Madero – for all his evident solicitude for urban labour – could not entirely disclaim.[207]

With regard to the aims, organisation and methods of labour agitation in 1911–13 it is broadly valid to say that they were 'economist' and apolitical. The embryonic Mexican unions thus followed the classic pattern described by Lenin: acquiring 'trade union consciousness' and struggling for economic gains, without posing a serious ideological or political threat to the regime. It was for this reason that (unlike the peasantry) they could often be accommodated rather than repressed.[208] But 'economist' aims, it should be stressed, did not represent a soft option in the context of 1911–13. Attempts at unionisation, claims for union recognition, specific demands for better pay, hours and conditions were often bitterly resisted by employers who regarded such developments as outrageous infringements of managerial prerogatives and who sought to maintain the rigid 'paternalism' which characterised many industries.[209]

Thus, while many – probably the majority – of disputes concerned pay and hours, a significant number derived from the intransigence of management, and took the form not of strikes but of lock-outs. This was particularly the case in the textile industry (as in 1906). When workers at the Santa Rosalía factory at Tepeji del Río (Hgo) asked for a half-day off on the festival of San Juan, the manager resolved to shut the plant for a week, 'it not being possible to work without discipline'; within a week, he believed, the workers would return penniless and suitably chastened.[210] A similar request from workers at a Puebla factory (this time for a holiday in commemoration of the local revolutionary martyr, Aquiles Serdán) received similar treatment, with the manager closing the plant for eight days, then re-hiring only approved employees (and not the 'agitators').[211] When operatives at La Concepción (Atencingo, Pue.) struck in protest at the alleged beating of a worker, the company closed the mill for an indefinite period 'while due order does not obtain'.[212] In matters great and small, therefore, managers jealously defended their prerogatives against the presumptuous unions: at La Trinidad (Tlax.) they enforced a ban on food and cigarettes in the factory; in the Aguascalientes railway shops they sacked a union organiser (for being a union organiser); at the Río Hondo textile mill (D.F.) they urged operatives not to recognise the new Department of Labour representative, maintaining 'that in their house only their orders should prevail'.[213] And in defence of their prerogatives companies were prepared to declare lock-outs, to ignore government rulings, and to slither out of agreements previously made with workers' leaders.[214]

Such were the barriers of 'paternalism' against which even the most modest demands might collide. In general, these barriers were stronger in the textile industry than in the big Anglo-American corporations. But the climate of labour relations throughout industry was such that even the cautious, economist demands which were the norm in 1911–13 seemed bold, perhaps radical, compared with the past. Pay and hours were the crucial questions at the Monterrey smelter, the Salina Cruz railway terminal, in the mines of Cananea and on the wharves of Puerto México; the Frontera stevedores won a pay rise after a day's stoppage; the big Laguna strike was for an eight-hour day, while the Yucatán railwaymen were conceded a nine in place of a ten-hour day.[215] This concentration on pay and hours did not mean that the urban workers were apolitical; on the contrary, they participated in parties and elections and, in some cases, such as Tampico, played a major role in the new politics. But they did not resort to the strike (or other forms of 'direct action') to achieve political ends, to bring down the government, or to foment revolution. Strikes were not revolutionary. Rather, they were called to secure betterment, in a gradual, evolutionary fashion; and there was an added incentive during the Madero period in that inflation forced down real wages, compelling the workers to take defensive action. Strikes often looked to the maintenance of threatened standards, rather than the conquest of new benefits. And, to the extent that the 'economic' and 'political' struggles meshed at all, it was the former which predominated: that is, while the strike was rarely used as a political weapon, political involvement could sometimes serve economic ends, in a calculating, pragmatic fashion.[216]

In certain instances there were also more specific objectives, especially where the better organised unions were concerned. The railwaymen continued their campaign against American dominance of skilled jobs; they organised 'in order to achieve the Mexicanisation of the National Railways, which objective should be the ideal of every patriot'.[217] Since the policy of Mexicanisation – begun by Díaz – continued under Madero, it was now the American employees who protested, struck and, in April 1912, quit their jobs. The railways did not grind to a halt; Mexicans replaced the American strikers; the Mexicanisation of the work force was largely achieved.[218] At Cananea, too, Mexicanisation was a familiar demand, along with calls for union recognition and an end to the company bonus system; at Tampico, as we have seen, the labour contractors' control of jobs on the waterfront provided a specific stimulus to working-class organisation in the port. In these three cases, there was a degree of anti-foreign sentiment, directed against the American overseers and skilled workers on the railways and at Cananea, and against foreign labour contractors (not to mention the West Indian labourers). But, far from typifying a general anti-Americanism or 'xenophobia', these cases were in fact unusual, standing in contrast to the general pattern. Firms of all nationality were struck in the course of 1911–13: American mines (Cananea), British smelters (Wadley), French factories (Orizaba), as well as numerous Mexican and Spanish-owned and/or managed enterprises. But rarely was the issue of foreign ownership at stake: save in the cases just mentioned (where conflicts had arisen more *within* the labour force, than against foreign ownership *per se*) no popular economic nationalism infused working-class thought or action. At Chihuahua, for example, 'the question of nationality . . . does not appear to have figured in the grievances of the strikers'; at Torreón, likewise the site of many foreign enterprises, strikers attended *en masse* a demonstration given 'in favor of the foreigners', which the American consul gratefully witnessed.[219]

In fact, there were many companies in which clientelist relations prevailed and where the workers, keen to maintain jobs in the relatively well-paid export sector, had little time for strikes and co-operated in keeping the business running through difficult times. At Nacozari, near Cananea, where the mine management switched from machine to hand drills in order to maintain high employment, 'the feeling among the people at the present time [April 1912] is against any revolution, as they wish to be given an opportunity to continue at work'.[220] Similarly, at the American Smelters Securities Co. plant at Velard-eña (Dgo), the work force cursed the bandits (possibly Orozquistas) whose depredations in the area meant that the company had to pay wages in chits rather than cash: 'the *gente* were very much worked up against any bandits as they say that they are the cause of our paying in *boletas*. [But there is] not a murmur against the company', since the company could alone provide jobs and sustenance.[221] So, too, at Parral, where the upheaval of the Orozco rebellion forced many, particularly the smaller, enterprises to close down, the Parral and Durango Railroad continued operations, perforce paying their workers in credit notes for want of cash: nevertheless 'all the men without exception have agreed to stay on'.[222] Such displays of working-class clientel-ism must be set against the fewer, though more publicised, cases of 'xenopho-bia' – cases which themselves, on closer inspection, often prove to have been exaggerated, and linked more to politico-diplomatic events than to funda-mental economic grievances.

Since the chief objective of most urban workers was to maintain their jobs and, where possible, achieve modest economic gains, they were usually hostile to political violence, which threatened to upset the economy and throw them into the ranks of the unemployed. Not only did they therefore shrink from armed rebellion; they also came out in support of the constituted government, displaying again some of the docility and clientelism that was apparent in their relations with (certain) employers. To the urban workers' affiliation to specific political factions (evident, for example, at Tampico) must therefore be added a more general, 'supra-factional' adherence to the regime, whatever its char-acter; for it was the task of the regime to provide peace, and thus economic stability and high employment, the workers' chief desiderata. Some regimes, of course, were preferable to others; nevertheless, there was a sense in which Mexico's urban workers, like Italy's industrialists, were 'government support-ers by definition'.[223] Thus, workers' groups were often to be seen parading their support for the regime, frequently in alliance with urban middle-class elements: city interests pulled together in common opposition to rural rebellion, the identity of material interests paralleling a broader cultural affinity.[224] This was particularly evident during the critical weeks of March 1912, when the Orozco rebellion threatened to plunge the country into renewed civil war. At Saltillo, 2,000 men including 'the labourers of the various industrial enterprises' marched on the governor's palace in an orderly demonstration of loyalty; at the same time Monterrey witnessed a 'patriotic demonstration . . . among the business and working people for the upholding of the constituted government'; banners carried through the streets called for 'peace, prosperity and patriotism'. So, too, in Mexico City demonstrators paraded the slogan: 'the workers are with the supreme government'; and representative of the capital's 'working men' were sent to parley with Vázquez Gómez in the US, in the capacity of 'peace delegates'.[225] Even in Chihuahua itself, at the height of the Orozco revolt, the workers of the state capital showed little of the revolutionary enthusiasm of the *serranos* and country people: rather, there was 'a certain strong sentiment among the working classes for the established government, or rather for *an* established government, as against the irregular governments brought into being by revolution'.[226]

In addition to such political gestures, there were signs of an interesting new development: the recruitment of urban workers into military formations, for the defence of the regime. The coal-miners of Coahuila – militant enough in the pursuit of their economist aims – were willing to shoulder arms in support of Madero's government; the artisans of Santiago del Valle (Gto) manned the town's posse, though not to great effect.[227] In June 1911, Madero received an offer of the formation of a 'railwaymens battalion or regiment' which, it was said, would be invaluable in sustaining the new regime and obviating the problems which Díaz had faced in 1910–11 on account of the railway workers' non-cooperation.[228] The idea (which Limantour had earlier floated) was translated into practice with the creation of a volunteer corps of railway workers in March 1912.[229] Many similar offers were made, though not usually followed up. At the time, late in 1911, when fears of Reyista plots were strongest, fifty Cananea workers offered their services to the government.[230] In 1912, Angel Flores (a Mazatlán stevedore, and later a prominent revolutionary general) volunteered to combat banditry in Sinaloa, along with eighty of his colleagues; the miners of Etzatlán (Jal.) likewise offered to police their district.[231] Thus the belated, somewhat tentative involvement of the urban workers in the armed revolution came not by way of 'spontaneous', autonomous movements, analogous to the popular movements of the countryside, but rather by way of official recruitment, under the aegis of the established government, and with a view to pacification rather than subversion. The government stood not only for peace and stability, which the workers favoured, but also for political power, to which workers' leaders looked – much as aspiring candidates like Braniff did – for sympathy and support, in return for services rendered. These might be political (the demonstrations and delegations) or military. Either way, they represented a working-class commitment to the 'centre'. Thus the Madero period saw the gradual evolution of an alliance – albeit an unequal alliance – between the city-based government and the city-based labour movement: political detente, even military collaboration, proceeded alongside the separate and distinct battle for union recognition and economic gains. In later years, both the detente and the collaboration would proceed farther and faster.

The moderation and clientelism of the labour movement reflected its inherent weaknesses. In an overwhelmingly rural society, the urban workers were a minority, and a divided minority. To the extent that they were organised at all, many belonged to mutualist societies rather than combative unions – indeed, mutualism represented an important but often neglected feature of the labour movement during the revolutionary period. Coahuila, for example, boasted sixty-seven mutualist societies, twenty of them in Saltillo, the rest scattered in towns throughout the state; in Nuevo León, Monterrey alone had 34.[232] In supposed hotbeds of radicalism like Cananea, mutualist societies provided a form of (relatively) stable, consistent organisation underlying the more volatile and factious workers' groups whose strikes and political activism caught the headlines.[233] But all proletarian associations, whatever their complexion, worked under major handicaps. Years of Porfirian growth had stunted their growth, so that leadership and experience were in short supply; hence, at the national level, the disproportionate role played by foreign activists, notably Spaniards like Eloy Armenta, Pedro Junco, Amadeo Ferrés and others.[234] In the provinces, leadership was home-grown, and both membership and resources were in short supply. While the bigger mines and ports produced vigorous unions, the smaller industrial/commercial centres were often isolated and vulnerable to domination by an authoritarian employer, or by a business elite like the Spanish merchants of Acapulco. As for the classic proletariat – the factory workers of Mexico City, Orizaba, Puebla and lesser industrial communities – they constituted a minority within the urban working class and suffered from their own specific handicaps. Many (for example in the Mexico City cigarette factories) were women, less amenable to unionisation; while in the textile industry, the biggest concentration of proletarian labour, problems of over-production made it all too tempting for the management to resort to lock-outs in order to break the unions. Indeed, the general condition of the labour market placed the bosses in a powerful position *vis-à-vis* their employees. Many strikes were successfully broken, or allowed to fizzle out: railway navvies were brought into Manzanillo to break the dockers' strike there; when American *enganchadores* recruiting contract labourers at Acapulco faced wage demands they simply moved further down the coast to get their quota of 'brown meat' for the *cafetales* of Central America.[235] Some management ploys verged on the cynical. During the Aguascalientes railway strike the employers threatened to restore American personnel to the posts which they had recently quit.[236] And in Veracruz, during the difficult days of July 1911, the Chamber of Commerce, in agreement with the military commander and *jefe político*, conceded large pay rises (50–100%), 'taking such measures subsequently as might present themselves in order to reduce the demands of the men to a moderate figure'. The strategy appears to have worked.[237]

Thus, as we turn (as we must) to certain better known examples of ideological sophistication or practical militancy, it must be recognised at the outset that these were exceptional cases within a labour movement that was weak, disorganised and fragmented. Four topics require attention: first, the question of national (or would-be national) labour organisations; then, three major geographical concentrations of proletarian power: Orizaba, and the textile industry more generally, Torreón, which witnessed some major strikes, and Cananea. Orizaba and Cananea in particular deserve mention, since they have been seen as important contributors to the Revolution, in both the 'precursor' phase and after.

In the new freedom conceded by the Madero regime, labour unions began to come together in regional and national associations. As early as July 1911, in the coal-fields of Coahuila, the nucleus of the Unión Minera Mexicana was formed; by 1912 it claimed sixteen affiliates. The workers of Torreón established the Confederación del Trabajo, the textile workers the Comité Central de Obreros, while the bakers of Veracruz launched the Confederación de Sindicatos Obreros, which claimed national status.[238] The greater press freedom also permitted the publication of numerous workers' papers and periodicals, some of them strongly critical of the government. Most important and outspoken of the workers' organisations of the Madero period was the Casa del Obrero Mundial (House of the World Worker), established in September 1912. The Casa grew out of a Mexico City anarchist group, which had strong support among the tailors and printers of the capital: it was characterised by a cosmopolitan leadership, a garbled ideology, redolent of European anarcho-syndicalism, and a strong emphasis on the principles of self-help, education and enlightenment which historically appealed to the better-off artisans. Its aims included the dissemination of these principles, and the organisation, on a national basis, of the Mexican labour movement.[239] By 1913, it could claim to have achieved some co-ordination of the Mexico City workers, and to have played a part in over seventy strikes. Perhaps more important, it provided a forum and training ground for a generation of labour leaders, polemicists and agitators. But by fomenting strikes and preaching class war, it contravened Maderista principles of industrial harmony and conciliation: Casa and Department of Labour were soon battling for the hearts and minds of the workers; and the official *Nueva Era* replied to outspoken Casa press criticism in similar fashion. And freedom was not absolute. In the summer of 1912 the government had arrested certain anarchist leaders and deported Juan Francisco Moncaleano, one of the leading Mexico City radicals.[240] The Casa itself appears to have survived (the sources are strangely contradictory here); but it is clear that during its brief co-existence with the Madero regime relations deteriorated, as they were bound to, granted the incompatibility of official labour policy and Casa philosophy. It fell to later regimes to decide how the growing challenge of the Casa should be met, and whether by peaceful competition, co-option, or repression.

At Orizaba, scene of the 1907 affray, a strong military presence deterred any revolutionary impulse in 1910–11. But late in April 1911, at the turn of the year 1911–12, and again in the summer of 1912, the textile factories faced major stoppages, as unionisation increased and employers dug in to resist; it was a story, wrote a partisan observer, of 'strike after strike at short intervals and always under the most unreasonable pretexts', and factories in Mexico City and elsewhere were also affected.[241] It was chiefly in response to these problems in the textile industry that the government set up the Department of Labour, within the Ministry of Fomento, as an agency to collect data, provide advice on questions of employment, and arbitrate in industrial disputes. The last was its key function: in government eyes 'the Department [was] a tool for handling strikes'.[242] The initiative, it is worth noting, came from de la Barra (another indication of 'conservative' awareness of the labour problem – de la Barra denied that an equivalent agrarian problem existed); but it was under Madero that the Department was established, with a staff of twelve, under the leadership of Antonio Ramos Pedrueza, a lawyer, ex-Porfirian congressman, and political moderate who, though he had some familiarity with mutualist associations, was far from being a radical spokesman of the rights of labour.[243] The Department soon began to play an active, conciliatory role in labour relations: it sent inspectors to monitor wage agreements; it assisted mutualist societies, providing funds, officers, or furniture; above all, it worked to harmonise the interests of labour and capital, to the benefit of industrial peace and production. It thus epitomised the Maderista concern for social cohesion, for stable economic development, and for 'progress' – all concerns with which enlightened Porfiristas could also sympathise.

But employers of the traditional type – who abounded, especially in the textile industry – resented the intervention of the Labour Department in their domains. And they did so notwithstanding that Ramos Pedrueza and his staff had the interests of the industry at heart, being aware – as individual managers often were not – of the global problems of industrial relations and of the need for rationalisation of both production and employment. For the Department officials never deviated from their belief in a free market, capitalist system, and their cultivation of workers' groups, their exercises in arbitration and inspection, were designed to develop and strengthen the system, drawing on foreign models; they had no time for proletarian 'malcontents and agitators'.[244] In a sense, they were trying to save the industrialists (of the traditional type) from themselves; to bring sense to those who, more Porfirian than Don Porfirio, clung to the old, authoritarian ways, who believed that 'management alone had the right to determine what was good for the worker', who threatened that 'if the worker did not change his attitude, sooner or later management would teach him a lesson he would never forget'.[245] Díaz himself had come to question this dangerous philosophy, seeing that it could propel the workers into the camp of radicals, syndicalists and socialists. And (though he did not live to see it) the example of Tsarist Russia confirmed his judgement.

Now, pursuing the same line of thought, de la Barra and Madero favoured a degree of state intervention in the interests of peace, conciliation and production. Neither, of course, were social subversives, and the strategy they adopted had many parallels in both Europe and Latin America.[246] In Ramos Pedrueza, too, they found a willing instrument, for in the short time and with the scant budget allowed him, he showed a canny grasp of the state's capacity to control and manipulate the new labour unions, thereby deflecting them away from more radical groups such as the Casa. He helped the textile workers set up their Comité Central de Obreros, establishing it as a semi-official association which could dampen militancy and resolve strikes; the Department could count on the Comité 'to stop agitation' in the mills. Department representatives were more generally used to 'calm their companions', as Ramos Pedrueza reassured alarmed industrialists; some of the latter began to see the utility of such official sponsorship and set about organising 'yellow' unions in opposition to the radicals.[247] Soon, as already suggested, the Department and the Casa began their conflict for the allegiance of the urban working class; a conflict between rival conceptions of working-class mobilisation, one 'moderate', state sponsored and thus dependent, the other more militant and autonomous.

The textile industry was the chief, though by no means the only, battleground of these competing ideologies. Late in 1911 the Orizaba operatives, backed by workers in Puebla and Tlaxcala, undertook a strike in support of better wages and a ten-hour day; most mills were closed, and management, anticipating 'tumultuous demonstrations and violent outbursts', requested the presence of fifty mounted police to guarantee order.[248] Anxious to settle the dispute without resorting to such overtly Porfirian methods, the Ministry of Fomento (acting on presidential instructions) convened a meeting of mill-owners at which various reforms were suggested and discussed, the Ministry putting the workers' case by proxy.[249] After much debate the owners grudgingly conceded a ten-hour day and some modest pay increases; but proposals for minimum and uniform wages, for control of female and child labour and for a closed shop were all thrown out. Furthermore, many bosses –

like the management of the Veracruz Terminal Co. – had no intention of honouring the agreement anyway: hours and wages remained as before, union members were sacked. Meanwhile, the workers pressed ahead with unionisation, encouraged by the government, which admitted the Comité Central de Obreros to a standing committee on the textile industry. By the summer of 1912, the workers' disillusionment became manifest in another wave of strikes, to which the government responded by calling a second textile convention.[250]

This was a classic Maderista exercise: well-intentioned, prolix, and productive of fine paper solutions which could not be translated into practice. The workers – through the Comité – now had a voice, and the Department of Labour provided a 'neutral' arbiter: after a month's discussion an agreement was reached: a 'charter of freedom for the Mexican laborer' (according to one historian); a 'timid blueprint for labor reform' (according to another).[251] Timidity was certainly evident in the convention's refusal to regularise and raise wages throughout the industry, or to recognise the right of workers to join unions. But the workers made many gains, at least on paper: a minimum wage of 1.25 pesos a day, maximum hours, fixed overtime rates, legal holidays, a ban on child labour, company stores, and payment in *vales*, regulation of fines and of the conduct of foremen. Equally – and no less in accord with Maderista thinking – the workers were reminded of their obligations as regards discipline, attendance and productivity. Here was something for everyone: indeed, in the fertile minds of the Department officials, the deal was conceived as self-financing, since the shortening of the working day would cut output, mitigate the problem of over-production, and push up prices, benefiting all within the textile industry (though not, of course, the consumer). And, in fact, this appears to have happened, further aided by a government commitment to cut the 1893 textile tax.[252]

The great drawback of the agreement lay less in its content than its implementation. Some textile workers, disappointed at the failure to raise wages, struck at once, albeit briefly and unsuccessfully. Threatened, in some cases, with eviction from company houses, they soon went back to work; though 'many were singled out and refused further employment'. Despite government pressure, the companies maintained this hard line, and an official scheme to offer redundant workers plots of public land in Chiapas (a typical piece of benign but useless charity) came to nothing.[253] In many other respects the employers reneged on the agreement and ignored government rebukes. Department of Labour inspectors, touring the country in the latter part of 1912, found that child labour was still rife, that wages, hitherto in excess of 1.25 pesos, had been cut to the minimum (as if it were a maximum), and that the whole agreement had in some cases been formally denounced. Nor did they find much trace of the schools and medical services recommended in July. Sometimes, it should be noted, the refusal to countenance reform and the rejection of official intervention characterised the workers as well as the bosses. At a textile factory in León, where the work force was 90% female, an *obrera* told the visiting inspector that here 'we like the manager a great deal, as he performs many services for us . . . and we don't want the new [wage] rates, since we can keep ourselves very well with what we earn already.'[254] Whether fear or 'false consciousness' determined such a response, it was significant nonetheless. Elsewhere, the textile workers might be less docile and deferential: resentment at the non-fulfilment of the July agreement smouldered and flared up in sporadic strikes; but there was no repeat, during the remainder of the Madero period, of the near-general strike which had afflicted the industry at the end of 1911. At Orizaba, the sizeable garrison of 1910 was whittled down to a mere twenty-five, indicating that the labour question – from the point of view of public order – was no longer so acute. As a social and political question, however, it remained pending, absorbing the attention of ministers and officials, and awaiting some viable solution.[255]

The efflorescence of labour activity at Torreón produced a similarly indecisive result, broadly unfavourable to the workers. At the height of summer 1911 there had been a spate of strikes: at the Continental Mexican Rubber Co., the Torreón smelter, the Laguna Soap Co. (of Gómez Palacio) and on the city trams. These were 'settled to the satisfaction of all parties concerned' after brief stoppages; the workers made some gains or, at least, felt they had; and they were keen to get back to work.[256] Calm prevailed until November when, perhaps because they had come to realise that the 'gains' of the summer were largely illusory, the workers of Torreón struck again, chiefly demanding an eight-hour day. Some 2,000 workers began the protest, shutting down the rubber company; they were joined by carpenters, masons and other labourers who spilled onto the streets, marching, chanting, and alarming respectable inhabitants.[257] Within days the strikers numbered 8,000 and the movement seemed to be assuming 'all the characteristics of a general strike'; it spread to Gómez Palacio and Mapimí, where 3,000 miners at the Peñoles Co. threatened to walk out. In Torreón itself, rife with rumours of a Reyista plot, there were fears of renewed riots, on the lines of May 1911; the well-to-do began to leave, citizens were 'panic-stricken' at reports of an impending Federal evacuation, and there was an influx of rough-looking country people, eager for the looting to start.[258]

The outcome hardly did justice to the fears of the Laguna elite, still less to the hopes of the *pelados*. In the face of local pressure, troop movements out of Torreón were cancelled, and a strong garrison was retained. Soldiers were sent to Peñoles and the mines continued working. Some of the strikers were promised an eight-hour day; but the big companies, such as the smelter and the soap and rubber factories, refused to make the concession and their employees 'were compelled to return to work under the old conditions'.[259] Thereafter, labour troubles abated. No doubt the workers grew more aware of the problems they faced in taking strike action, and of the need for better, more patient organisation. But, in addition, economic factors now conspired against them. Rural rebellion, endemic in the Laguna, throttled business and created mass unemployment: by March 1912 there were 6,000 men redundant in the city, as factories and merchant houses closed down or curtailed their activities; the Peñoles mine, it was felt, would soon shut down – for want of supplies and cash, not because of the miners' militancy. Food prices rose and in mid-March, during the worst of the rebel blockade (for this, in effect, was what it was), mobs roamed the city demanding food. Such conditions militated against successful unionisation; indeed, one effect of the hardship was to convert the workers' bold antipathy to the authorities into a kind of enforced dependence. Torreón's workers showed no sympathy for the rural rebels: it was as much as the Federals could do to prevent rebel prisoners being lynched by the mob. Rural rebellion meant lost jobs and destitution, a bitter sequel to the high hopes of 1911; hence there could be no grand alliance between peasant and proletarian. Indeed, it was observed, 'the common people [of the city] are now with the government', since the government alone could crush the rebellion, guaranteeing subsistence in the short term, prosperity in the long term.[260] The contrast apparent in the evolution of the labour movement in Tampico and Torreón (both of which had been in the forefront of 1911) thus derived in large measure from their respective locations and relations with the countryside. Tampico was spared proximate, disruptive rebellions: the oil boom provided abundant jobs and gave the town a secure, insulated economy, concentrated in the narrow span between the well-heads and the off-shore tankers. Blessed with a buoyant economy, the Tampico working class could press their claims, both politically and economically. At Torreón, economic collapse undercut the labour movement at a crucial time, forcing it into the arms of the government: a loose alliance of urban classes and interests emerged, based on shared hostility to the rural menace, and this could not but inhibit the growth of strong, independent labour unions. In any given region (it might be tentatively generalised) the power of the organised proletariat varied in inverse proportion to the power of the insurgent peasantry.[261]

There is, finally, the celebrated case of Cananea. Its celebrity stemmed from the famous events of 1906, which historians have rather too readily assimilated to the catch-all 'Precursor Movement'.[262] But, as already suggested, Cananea was highly untypical of the Mexican labour movement; and its links to the Revolution were both more tenuous and more complex than often supposed. It was a massive, newly created mining community, isolated from the rest of Mexico (and thus paying higher wages), familiar with American unionism, and profoundly affected by the dual nationality of the work force. In 1910, with the onset of the revolution, Cananea was just emerging from a period of transition: the company had been rationalised and was again paying its way;

the ratio of American to Mexican employees had fallen from 35:65 to 7:93, and the promotion of Mexicans to technical, skilled jobs had accelerated.[263] These developments by no means removed all the workers' grievances, nor did they allay management's fears of a repeat of 1906; but they indicated that both sides could strive for a *modus vivendi* in the interests of jobs and production. Hence, in part, there was no upsurge of revolutionary militancy. The rebel leader Juan Cabral (once a cashier at Cananea, and well regarded by the company) entered the town peacefully in May 1911; new municipal authorities were named, including several protagonists of the 1906 strike; and the company started paying taxes to the *de facto* revolutionary regime, cementing their necessary politico-fiscal relationship.[264] Trouble soon started, but when it did it was the Maderista troops, rather than the miners who were the chief culprits. True, the miners took advantage of the new atmosphere of political freedom: labour agitation revived and by June the company was presented with a set of familiar demands, which included the eight-hour day and an end to the system of bonus payments.[265] A radical newspaper, *La Verdad*, espoused the miners' cause and acquired a large readership. But it was the troops, not the miners (and each group pursued their distinct aims and tactics), who presented the real threat. While the workers devoured *La Verdad* and held late night fiestas and speeches in the plaza, the Maderista garrison – like so many others – resisted demobilisation, defied their officers, rioted, released prisoners from the gaol, and demanded an immediate pay rise.[266] This, the worst situation the company had to face in 1911, was settled as the officers recovered control, confined their troops to barracks, and – probably thanks to a timely Federal subsidy – paid off their fractious followers.[267] Throughout, the mines continued to work flat out.

The remainder of the *interinato* was quiet.[268] In November, about the time of Madero's inauguration, the arrest of a prominent 'labor agitator . . . caused some little excitement among the workmen'; but Cananea now had a more reliable garrison and, under the watchful eye of the prefect, Benajamín Hill, the 'presence of the troops prevented any outbreaks and the men are now apparently satisfied with present conditions'.[269] The miners' (alleged) Magonista sympathies were not translated into action and, when the rebel Isidro Escabosa prowled the nearby Ajo mountains, hoping for recruits from the mining camps, he was disappointed.[270] The year 1912 started quietly, save for a sudden, strange outburst when a group of miners attacked a police station, looted some stores, and took to the hills, supposedly crying 'Viva Zapata!'. The causes of this incident cannot be fathomed (neither Aguirre nor Aguilar even mention it); yet it appears to have been isolated, for within a month the town was denuded of troops and no fears were expressed in consequence.[271] A little to the south, Nacozari was benefiting from its ability to supply jobs to a population keen for work, and there is no evidence that Cananea was not in a similar position. This did not, of course, rule out industrial conflict. In July

1912 the miners threatened a strike, protesting as much against the surveillance and harassment which Prefect Hill visited upon the union, as against the faults of abuses of the company, important though these were.[272] With Orozquismo threatening the state, the authorities were not disposed to be lenient, but a combination of resolve and conciliation averted trouble.

Finally, at the end of the year, the miners were ready to present a comprehensive, revised set of demands to the company: the replacement of all American by Mexican foremen, a 20% rise, a one-hour shorter day-shift, and recognition of the union.[273] When the company rejected all these demands a strike was called, in which initially about 1,000 and later some 1,500–1,750 workers participated – approaching half the Mexican labour force. The Prefect, ordered by Hermosillo to prevent the strike, was backed by over 300 Federals and 60 police; a further 1,000 troops were within a day and a half of Cananea; there was no doubt that the authorities held the whip-hand. When the strikers demonstrated on the streets, police with rifles at the ready dispersed them and fifty men were arrested, without bloodshed.[274] After three days of continued tension the weather turned cold (winters at Cananea were bleak and windy) and half the strikers returned to work: the arguments of the married men, it was said, prevailed over the greater militancy of the bachelors (a division within the work force for which parallels can be found elsewhere).[275] Furthermore, the company now agreed to meet certain of the workers' demands and, by Christmas, the strike was settled and all the men were back at work. Indeed, one of the arrested strike leaders was released from gaol at Hermosillo and was back in Cananea by January.[276]

Thus, during two years of unprecedented – though far from complete – freedom at Cananea there was one major strike and one minor uprising (the latter of little significance); and, despite management fears, the mines worked uninterruptedly. Military pressure – brought to bear as much at the behest of the Maderista state authorities as of the company itself – clearly inhibited the miners' militancy, but there appeared to be little stomach for a prolonged strike in any case. The workers sought limited gains, and were (to varying extents) aware of the risks of strike action. And modest gains were made, without the cost – in lives and gaol sentences – of 1906: it was significant that the leaders of the 1912 strike expressly ruled out the use of violence.[277] Conversely, though the authorities showed they could be tough (and there were not wanting those who favoured even greater toughness), the mistakes of 1906 were not repeated, and both politicians and management showed rather more finesse in their handling of labour relations. Finally, there is little to suggest that Cananea stood in the mainstream of revolutionary history in 1910–13. As regards their aims, tactics, and achievements, the miners were far removed from the rural rebels of Morelos, Chihuahua, or the Languna, and it was the latter who overthrew Díaz, posed the main threat to Madero, and stamped their character on the Madero period. The miners, like the urban workers more generally, took advantage of 'revolutionary' conditions which they had done little to bring about; their economist aims and gradual, peaceful tactics represented no fundamental threat to either company or regime, and could be partially tolerated. If Cananea boasted the most militant proletariat in revolutionary Mexico, the boast was more a comment on the moderation of the Mexican proletariat than on the militancy of Cananea.

When confronted with renewed labour agitation in centres such as Orizaba, Torreón or Cananea, the Madero regime initially took a classic, liberal line. The state would provide the necessary pre-conditions – political freedom and representative democracy – for the workers to organise, unionise and press their claims legally and peacefully. Madero did not rule out the formation of unions ('powerful associations which might enable you, united, to defend your rights'), nor did he discount the possibility of reformist legislation designed to help the working class ('laws whose object is to improve the workers' lot and raise his material, intellectual and moral level').[278] Both, after all, were quite compatible with the kind of advanced, twentieth-century liberalism which Madero took as his model. But Madero's commitments in this respect were necessarily vague and abstract; for it was not the job of the state to anticipate the demands of the labour movement or a proletarian electorate; in politics as in economics, self-help was the key to progress. Thus, just as he ruled out any rapid, *de facto* agrarian reform, so too in the field of labour relations Madero warned the workers against placing their faith in a paternalist state, rather than their own independent efforts.[279] Most Maderistas took the same line. Madero's famous declaration at Orizaba ('it does not depend on the state to raise wages or cut hours') was echoed by Governor Loyola ('it does not depend on the government to increase wages in proportion to prices'). Ramos Pedruza, at the Labour Department, stressed his respect for property and the laws of the market; Federico González Garza, an enlightened, progressive governor of the Federal District, ordered the arrest of workers in 1912, warning demonstrators that, 'Mexico does not need socialism; here there are no problems between labour and capital.'[280]

Thus, while the Maderista regime was tolerant of orderly strikes, conducted in a 'moderate attitude', and sought in such cases to uphold the 'freedom . . . to associate and hold peaceful demonstrations', it was quite prepared to use force or the threat of force to deal with strikes it felt to be subversive, violent, or threatening to property.[281] As incidents at Cananea, Torreón and elsewhere indicated, this was often enough. But it soon became clear that, in practice, these two policies – a complete 'hands-off', or old-style repression – were inadequate to meet the needs of the situation. Just as, in the political sphere, either thoroughly free or thoroughly fixed elections presented major problems (the first being seen as leading to anarchy, the second to Porfirian reaction), so, too, in the field of labour relations a *via media* had to be found between the extremes; principles of social justice had to be balanced against the rights of property and the imperatives of production. For this to happen, labour relations could not be left to the arbitrary collision of bosses and unions – especially not old-style authoritarian bosses and new-style radical unions. It was particularly worrying to the Department of Labour that the boldest, most outspoken workers tended to dominate union leadership, at the expense of the most educated or competent; 'it is therefore an urgent necessity', the Department concluded, 'to acquire an understanding of the workers' associations, pointing out to them the course they ought to take'. [282] And Madero, facing a level of industrial unrest unknown during the Porfiriato, fully agreed. 'The practice of striking for the most futile and insignificant pretext', he complained to the leader of the Veracruz dockers, 'is highly inconvenient'; notwithstanding its sympathy for the workers' cause, the government was thereby gravely embarrassed and could not achieve 'the administrative progress which I have in mind to improve all your lots'; 'for this reason', Madero concluded, 'I urge you to influence your colleagues and the other unions . . . with whom you have relations, so that these many strikes may cease'. [283]

By the end of his presidential period, therefore, Madero had clearly shifted away from a *laissez-faire*, non-interventionist position. Groups like the Veracruz dockers were urged to take their grievances to the Department of Labour or even 'if it is necessary to me, and I will help you'. The 'centre' could not remain aloof (Díaz had come to the same conclusion) and a groping, grudging interventionism came to characterise Maderista labour policy. And, just as the regime sought to guide the nascent labour movement (in the direction of collaboration rather than conflict with management) so, too, there was a work of education to be done with many employees, especially the textile bosses of central Mexico. At its most coherent (which was not very coherent) this interventionist policy could be seen in the creation of the Department of Labour, and in the belated moves towards more comprehensive labour legislation, which the fall of the regime aborted. [284] But it was also evident in sundry lesser items of government patronage designed, at least partly, to mollify and cajole the labour movement: Gustavo Madero's pressure on industrialists to ban child labour; the president's offer of premises to the Mutualist Society of Railway Clerks and Telegraphists; the administration's scheme to provide locked-out textile workers with forty acres and a mule (or their rough equivalent) in Chiapas. [285] All this may not have added up to much, and the material gains of the workers under Madero may have been strictly limited. [286] Certainly more strikes were lost than won. But equally certainly the administration showed an awareness of labour's grievances and a readiness (derivative of many and mixed motives) to correct them. Indeed, there were not wanting critics within the Maderista camp – like Cabrera – who contrasted the regime's solicitude for urban labour with its indifference to rural grievances. [287]

Yet more important, and aside from the question of positive government policy, it is clear that the Madero period witnessed a degree of freedom for working class organisations that was unprecedented. Though there was repression, it was less thorough and consistent than in the days of Díaz; and, won or lost, strikes were held on a scale greater than ever before, providing the workers with valuable cumulative experience. A radical press flourished, and there were moves towards state and national labour confederations; 1 May 1912 saw the first May Day celebrations in Mexican history.[288] And observers (not least employers) noticed the growth of a new mood among the working class. The rigid 'paternalism' which often characterised labour relations was beginning to crack, and the workers displayed less submission. In San Luis, as we have noted, there were various indicators of labour's new-found freedom and mobility: wages were higher, *tiendas de raya* were losing ground, the railways were switching to an all-Mexican labour force; one local smelter closed because management could not hire labour at pre-revolutionary rates, and refused to increase the rate. Workers, it was said, 'show independence and irregularity in labor'; efficiency was reckoned to have dropped by 20%.[289] Elsewhere there were other straws in the wind. Workers demanded extra holidays for which there was no precedent and, employers argued, no justification: for the festival of San Juan or the anniversary of the death of Aquiles Serdán.[290] The Veracruz dockers demanded not only a wage increase and a cut in hours but also union control of the supply of labour, and the dismissal of four officials of the Terminal Co. including the superintendent.[291] The dockers of Manzanillo were no better: when the Mexican gunboat *Guerrero* put into the port to coal in December 1912 the crew refused to do the job (which was significant in itself) and the local stevedores demanded 50% overtime for doing the work.[292] Even the middle-class students of the National School of Jurisprudence acquired the habit, striking in protest at the new system of assessment introduced by Luis Cabrera.[293]

Such things had not happened in Don Porfirio's day – or, if they had, they had been speedily punished. In the city, as in the countryside, the employers noted, denounced (and perhaps sometimes exaggerated) this new spirit of insubordination, this Mexican equivalent of the *buntarstvo which* animated the workers of revolutionary Petrograd.[294] 'One lamentable effect of the last two years of revolt and overthrow of constituted power', an observer commented, 'is the example it has offered in cases of minor discontent. Whenever six persons of like mind are gathered together they do not hesitate to demand . . . the immediate dismissal of any superior from factory boss to governor.'[295] Conversely, the working class was not blind to the gains – some more intangible than material – which had been made as a result of the Madero revolution and regime. Real wages may not have shot up, but the climate of industrial relations had perceptibly changed. Rightly or wrongly (and more rightly, I suspect, than some historians have suggested) the workers felt they had a stake in the new regime. Never was this more clearly evidenced than at the time of Madero's fall, when the delight of the bosses was matched by the regret and resentment of their employees, who saw their recent advances jeopardised. In the Laguna, to take but one example, 'the common people, especially the mechanic [sic] class exhibit, verbally, indignation and declare that the people will not submit to a new dictatorship'.[296] This was, perhaps, the most fitting working-class epitaph that could be placed on the grave of the Madero regime.

MORALS AND MONEY

Madero's sins of omission in the fields of agrarian and labour reform were hardly surprising, given the pedigree of Maderismo. Only forces external to the original movement (the rash of strikes and rural rebellions) gradually compelled some deviation from pristine, *laissez-faire* liberalism, and this deviation never proceeded far or fast enough to arrive at lasting solutions. But, over and above the simple, central principle of 'effective suffrage, no re-election', there were other reforms dear to the hearts of the Maderistas, which, though in retrospect they may seem quaint, even irrelevant, do not deserve the neglect which is usually shown them – especially since they retained their appeal long after the fall of Madero: education, public works (the *mejoras materiales* beloved of nineteenth-century liberals) and, above all, the reform of public morals through the elimination of alcoholism, gambling, vagrancy and squalor.[297] These formed an important part of every Maderista programme from 1909 through to 1913. Madero stressed the uplifting role of education and the degenerative effects of pulque.[298] The PCP programme of 1911 pledged the party to improve education (pt V), to assist the working class by 'combating alcoholism and gambling' (pt VI), and to further the development of mining, industry, agriculture and commerce (pt VII).[299] Candidates to local office concentrated on the same points. Manuel Villaseñor, running for Congress in Guanajuato, promised his opposition to vagrancy, alcoholism, and gambling, and his support for education (by means of scholarships and teacher-training schemes) and useful public works – road, railways, and irrigation.[300] Even radical Maderistas, like Antonio Hidalgo of Tlaxcala, combined their agrarian proposals with familiar provisions: for improved education and roads, orphanages and old people's homes, and anti-drink and anti-gambling legislation.[301]

These concerns – and particularly the concern for education and public morals – were central to the Revolution, even if in retrospect they have been de-emphasised in favour of agrarian and labour reform. They may be seen as part of a broader 'developmentalist' ideology which infused progressive, literate thought and which was to prove exceptionally powerful in the later stages of the Revolution (1915–20 and after), now allied to anti-clericalism.[302] Furthermore, though it is the Maderistas who now demand attention, these concerns were by no means a Maderista monopoly: they were evident in the late Porfirian press, in the debates of the Catholic Congresses of the 1900s, and among many enlightened Porfiristas too.[303] Perhaps more surprisingly, they also figured in the discourse of the urban working class, notably the serious self-improving artisanate of the big cities.[304] To its critics, however, the Porfirian regime had too often paid lip-service to these ideals, which in practice had been sacrificed in the interests of *caciquismo* and corruption. Drink, crime and prostitution therefore flourished; and 'the ignorance of the masses [remained] a national calamity', the necessary foundation of Díaz's forty-year tyranny.[305] The Maderistas now had the chance to match theory and practice.

In fact, little was accomplished. To the extent that they were feasible at all, such reforms required time, since – according to Maderista philosophy – they depended on individual conversion and self-help, which would make for a population that was literate, industrious, public-spirited and (in both the literal and figurative sense) sober. It was not easy for the state – least of all a liberal, *laissez-faire* state – to compel such conversions. Madero might dislike bullfights and denounce the poisonous effects of pulque, but he would not take high-handed executive action to ban such popular vices.[306] Some Maderistas were tougher-minded, prepared to challenge both the tastes of the populace and the powerful vested interests which gratified them. A ban on bullfights was imposed at Aguascalientes (but later lifted).[307] Governor González of Chihuahua, concerned to strengthen the 'moral fibre' of his people (especially those lured to the fleshpots of Juárez), campaigned against saloons and gambling houses, vagrancy and the observation of San Lunes: in Mexico as elsewhere these were seen as closely related problems.[308] Calles, cleaning up Agua Prieta in his new role as police chief, banned drink during the Independence celebrations – a move which reflected not simply a prudent concern for public order but also a profound Puritan sensibility. Underlings were sacked, at Agua Prieta, for lack of 'discipline and morality', for displaying 'deeply rooted, perverse habits' (an example, perhaps, of the zeal of the convert).[309] In many of these cases, however, the desire for clean towns and clean citizens was frustrated. Reformist governors like González had to contend with the enmity of vested interests, the obstruction of (fellow-Maderista) minions, like José de la Luz Blanco, and the example of (fellow-Maderista) governors, like Cepeda of San Luis, who tolerated or even encouraged the vices which the reformers abhorred.[310] Here, as in other respects, Maderismo willed the end but not the means; in later years, however, the same end would be pursued by men, like Calles himself, who were prepared to take more drastic (though not necessarily more effective) measures.

The same was true of education. Despite the rhetorical emphasis, in practical terms 'relatively little was accomplished': maybe fifty new rural schools were established; shoes, clothes and canteens were provided for the schoolchildren of the Federal District; a couple of agricultural and industrial schools were set up.[311] As regards the total educational budget, which might serve as an indicator of the regime's commitment, authorities differ. Ross mentions a budget appropriation of twelve million pesos – a 50% increase on Porfirian budgets – but Wilkie places Porfirian and Maderista educational spending on a par, at about 7% of total expenditure.[312] Granted the unreliability of much of this data, it is probably not worth pursuing fanciful mathematical comparisons. Certainly Madero inaugurated no decisive changes in educational policy: 'no new philosophy or concept of education' flowered, no real attempts were made to bring literacy and enlightenment to the masses.[313] Even if Ross's figures are accepted, the increase in the educational budget partly represented a continued, long-term trend, whereby educational spending had risen through the 1900s. Nor is this surprising, given not only the Porfiristas' commitment to education (of a certain kind, for certain people), but also the continuity evident in respect of policy (e.g., the creation of a national primary school system) and of policy discussion (e.g., successive National Congresses of Primary Education).[314] Perhaps the emphasis on rural schools and the plans for more appropriate rural education initiated by Pino Suárez late in 1912 showed the drift of policy; but, like so many Maderista measures, these came too late to make their mark, or even to achieve conceptual clarity.[315]

One obvious constraint, which inhibited Maderista reform, was that of finance. The acquisition of land for distribution, the provision of rural credit, the improvement of education, all had budgetary implications. So, too, did the public works which the regime (again following Porfirian precedent) was keen to carry through. Nationally, the government sought to repair the ravages which the railways had suffered in 1910–11, to build new lines, and to rationalise the administration of the system. This involved, among other things, the purchase of Lord Cowdray's Tehuantepec National Railway interest, and the continuation of port improvements at Salina Cruz and Puerto México. Frontera, too, was to benefit from dredging, in accordance with an electoral promise made by Madero in 1911; and there were plans for the electrification of central Mexico.[316] But lack of funds as well as lack of time frustrated these projects. Negotiations with Cowdray dragged on, delayed by political crises and financial uncertainty; in seeking a loan for the Tehuantepec purchase the administration came to blows with Congress; and the deal, though nearing completion, was still pending when Madero fell.[317] Locally, the financial squeeze was even more acute. Capital projects, dear to the hearts of progressive Maderista governors, had to be shelved: Governor Guillén's scheme for a Chiapas road network required Federal funds which were not forthcoming; Castillo Brito of Campeche envisaged a 'series of major, indispensable material works which my government proposed to realise', including a gaol and industrial school, a ferry service to El Carmen, the paving of the city of Campeche and a new highway, 'Calzada 20 de noviembre de 1910'; but these too necessitated Federal funds which were not to be had.[318]

Some governors did not dare to dream of new vote-winning projects; they were too busy trying to meet day-to-day needs. If, in the relatively untroubled south, expansion seemed feasible (Castillo Brito justified his request for Federal funds on the grounds of the Campechanos' 'implacable hatred of anything which hints at revolt or treason'), elsewhere retrenchment was the order of the day. By the end of 1912 Guanajuato was 2m. pesos in debt, largely because of expenditure on state troops, and was trying to raise a loan on the New York market; at San Luis, where the projected 1913 budget was three times that of 1910, the administration owed the Light and Power Co. for a year's street lighting (and the city therefore faced an imminent black-out); only by selling off three public buildings could Governor Cepeda avert bankruptcy.[319] The Oaxaca state government, running a monthly deficit of 30,000 pesos, sought a loan from the Federal administration; but, while Madero was prepared to allocate 2m. pesos to pay the interest on various state bonds, in order to protect Mexico's credit, he could do no more to bolster the states' teetering finances.[320] Increasingly, the president found himself caught between a critical, budget-conscious Congress, and state governors avid for Federal funds – whether for public works, interest payments or, as in the case of Sonora and Coahuila, the maintenance of state military forces. Madero could not satisfy both. The governors grumbled: Maytorena and Carranza met to grumble *à deux*, and it is possible that they went further, considering more drastic action to curb what they saw as Madero's folly.[321] Congress, meanwhile, asked to approve a 100m. pesos loan in January 1913, prevaricated, cut the figure to 40m. and then deadlocked the bill in the Senate. This was the situation when, as one commentator put it, 'on the 9th of February [1913], the table was overturned, the lights extinguished, and the game was ended'.[322]

If several of the more troubled states faced financial crises, the position of the national treasury was less serious. Here, however, accounts differ. Certainly there were times when government finance looked shaky: in the spring of 1912, at the time of the Orozco revolt, and again in October when the congressional opposition drummed up a 'national bankruptcy scare'.[323] Such 'grave problems of finance' could provide a possible alibi for Maderista failures; yet on the other hand some Maderista apologists have argued that government finance was sound, thrifty, and a credit to the regime.[324] Much depends on the yardstick of comparison used. Compared with the late Porfiriato the Madero period showed some worrying reversions to earlier financial history. There were, as we shall note, increased military costs. On a few occasions, pay failed to reach the troops. Congress (chiefly for political reasons) refused to co-operate in authorising loans; and for the first time in years, Mexico's foreign credit became a matter of serious official concern. The manager of the National Railways found it harder to renew his railway notes; Lord Cowdray feared a slump in Mexican stocks; and his agents in Mexico had trouble transacting business with the government because of political crisis and financial uncertainty.[325] As has been seen, Madero salvaged certain state loans, and it was said that the sudden – and unpopular – despatch of troops from Acapulco to the Rothschild plantation at the mouth of the Balsas obeyed similar financial – rather than military – exigencies.[326] Direct foreign investment, too, was frightened off.[327]

If all this seemed like a further fall from Porfirian grace, the underlying reality of government finance – reflecting, as it did, the revenue-bearing capacity of the 'real' economy – was not so bleak. Revenue exceeded expenditure in 1910–11 and again in 1911–12 (though the size of the 1911–12 surplus depended on a cut in expenditure rather than an increase in revenue).[328] Customs revenue increased in the second half of 1912 compared with 1911, reflecting a sustained level of foreign trade: imports remained level throughout 1909–13, but exports went up, generating a healthy surplus on visible trade.[329] Thus the peso remained firm and 'all the Federal Government's obligations with respect to the Public Debt were religiously complied with in the fiscal year 1912–13'.[330] Clearly, the revolution had not yet undermined the Mexican economy. The old staple of silver mining maintained output; gold production fell, but that of copper rose.[331] By regions as well as sectors the impact of the Revolution varied, such that decline in some quarters was offset by prosperity elsewhere. Trade across the northern border might suffer, but this was more than counterbalanced by the sustained commerce of the Gulf ports. Local reports confirmed this chequered pattern: business remained depressed in San Luis throughout 1912, contributing to Governor Cepeda's mounting financial problems; the Laguna cotton estates were ravaged, and most of the mines of Durango were forced to close for long periods.[332] Yet even in the more troubled regions, business showed great ingenuity and stamina, keeping going despite adverse circumstances, and reaching deals with rebel or bandit forces in order to maintain production. That they could do so (to the relief of their employees) afforded further evidence of the marginal position of foreign interests *vis-à-vis* the Revolution: closures were brought about by transport or financial breakdowns, occasioned by the fighting; they were not forced by hostile revolutionary action, still less by any policies of economic nationalism emanating from the Madero regime.[333]

And, conversely, there were many regions where the effects of revolution were limited or transient. In Yucatán and the south east generally plantation exports still flourished.[334] At Salina Cruz the port works kept men busy night and day, and the Tehuantepec Railway, the object of Cowdray's lengthy negotiations with the government, effected 'a tremendous transportation across the Isthmus'.[335] While the hinterland might be troubled by rebellion, ports like Tampico and Manzanillo prospered (facilitating the militancy of the stevedores); the Federal capital and, as usual, Monterrey still did good business.[336] Perhaps the best example of the economy's resilience was given by Coahuila. Troubled by Orozquista incursions and the cut-off of supplies – notably guayule – from Viesca and points west, the state entered the economic doldrums in the spring of 1912. But with the defeat of Orozco in the summer, business revived: the mines had managed to continue operations and 'an abnormally large amount of exports' to the US was noted; by mid-July, 'travelling salesmen, summer tourists and those seeking cooler summer climates' began to throng the hotels of Saltillo.[337] We shall later have occasion to contrast the condition of the north-eastern economy in 1911–12 – when setbacks were overcome – with that of 1913–14, which witnessed the start of an inexorable economic decline.[338]

The economy and the government finances which rested upon it were therefore basically sound in 1911–13, albeit subject to greater strains and alarms than in the days of Díaz. The damage done by the revolution was, so far, limited and reparable: the Maderista economy was much closer, in character and appearance, to its Porfirian predecessor than to the run-down, ricketty structure of 1914–18 – years of rampant inflation, fiscal chaos, unemployment, hunger, disease, and destitution. It is therefore hard to accept the argument that the political failure of Maderismo stemmed from financial problems: lack of funds neither undermined the regime nor barred the way to radical new policies (save in the important, negative sense that solvency encouraged moderation, in the interests of continued solvency while, as later experiences showed, bankruptcy could foster radicalism: *va banque* was a more attractive ploy when there was nothing left in the bank). Unlike some of his successors, then, Madero was not driven to desperate, seemingly radical, solutions. But nor yet was he shackled by debt. The failure of the regime to come up with more radical polices depended on internal, political, rather than external, financial constraints. The Maderistas, in other words, willed their own fate by cleaving to men and policies which could neither secure peace nor bring about that 'uplift of the poor' which Madero at least sincerely desired.[339] But the 'failure' of Maderismo, so often alleged, has also often been misconstrued. The character of that failure demands careful analysis, which will set the scene for the regime's final debacle.

THE LIBERAL APOSTASY

In matters such as these, it is easy to be wise after the event, but foolish to impose ahistorical prejudices upon past regimes. Commentators are fond of pointing out where Madero (or Kerensky, or Allende) went wrong, how they should have espoused this or that policy. Such counter-factual hypotheses are not in themselves illicit, and they may be useful; but they can also be entirely spurious and misleading, and it is vital that analysts of the counter-factual clarify what is at issue in their formulations. Two kinds of hypothesis may be attempted. One permits any counter-factual proposition, however massively inconceivable or 'ahistorical'; it is – properly understood – less a 'might-have-been' supposition than a reformulation of an old question by counter-factual means. Robert Fogel's celebrated analysis of an American economy without railways represents a novel way of asking the question 'how did the railways contribute to American economic development?'.[340] In the case of Mexico, it can be fruitful to hypothesise about the country's development in the absence of the Revolution – not out of reactionary whimsy or a naive, accidentalist view of history – but in order to point up the effects of the Revolution, to note where it reinforced or departed from pre-revolutionary trends, and to avoid the old error of *post hoc ergo propter hoc* (a besetting sin of post-revolutionary historiography). This is a useful but purely logical exercise, which does not commit the framer of the counter-factual hypothesis to the belief that things *could* really have turned out that way, with a few minor changes. In effect, it consists of the artificial abstraction of an important variable, the better thereby to understand its causal role; it does not involve the arbitrary imposition of ahistorical preferences of a normative kind (e.g., that America would have been better off without railways, or Mexico without a Revolution).

Counter-factual hypotheses concerning Madero, however, are often both inconceivable and heavily normative. It is useless to speculate about the sweeping social reform Madero might (and commonly should) have implemented; futile to blame him and his administration for not building socialism in Mexico. In this respect, Gladstone or Gambetta would be no less culpable, yet for some reason European leaders are less often subjected to this bizarre form of criticism.[341] Given the character of both Maderismo and Mexico, sweeping social reform was inconceivable (so, too, was the worker–peasant alliance, another counter-factual favourite).[342] Equally, certain other developments were entirely conceivable: Madero's respect for the large estates, the 'economism' of the nascent trade unions. Speculation which ignores these inexorable constraints is ahistorical and also lacks the heuristic value of, say, Fogel's railway hypothesis (which is concerned with the analysis of a particular, real variable, rather than the advocacy of various, hypothetical alternatives).

But there is a different species of counter-factual hypothesis which the historian should attempt, which is also non-normative, but which precisely rules out the 'inconceivable' and strives to remain within the bounds of plausibility. For the philosopher, perhaps, all events are equally determined and in a sense inevitable, be they social revolutions or the result of this year's Derby. But the historian must recognise degrees of inevitability: some events are, to use the fashionable jargon, 'over-determined', others are 'accidental', not in the sense of having no cause, but in the sense that an alternative outcome was well within the bounds of possibility. This second type of event generally concerns individual (as against collective) phenomena, but that is not to say that it is always historically irrelevant. Madero could have been killed at the battle of Casas Grandes in March 1911, instead he was wounded; Bernardo Reyes could have been wounded in the Zócalo in February 1913, instead he was killed. Both outcomes were important, but neither had the inevitability of Madero's rejection of agrarian expropriation, or the unions' of revolutionary radicalism. In the field of policy, too, where human wills and decisions (rather than Federal marksmanship and the laws of ballistics) determined the outcome, there were degrees of the inevitable, and thus possible alternative outcomes. There was no question of a Maderista regime expropriating the landlords, but there was a growing debate on the agrarian problem which produced different policy responses. In other areas, too, Maderista policy reflected governmental divisions and debates, and it is from among these – rather than a shopping list of the world's political philosophies – that must be taken the alternatives which *might* have afforded the regime greater success and stability. To the extent that such viable alternative policies existed, were advocated, but rejected, they stand as an indictment of the regime, of its shortsightedness and incapacity; if they cannot be found, however, the failure of Maderismo takes on the appearance of Greek tragedy, in which the actors are ineluctably drawn towards a fate which no human wit, virtue or contrivance can prevent.

In the realms of labour and agrarian reform (where counter-factual speculation has been most vigorous and imaginative) Maderista thinking underwent gradual evolution, but there was more consensus than conflict over Maderista policy in these areas, and there is little evidence that a coherent, radical alternative was rejected in favour of the tepid reformism which prevailed. On other questions, however, there was real debate within the Maderista camp, and genuine, feasible alternatives to government policy were propounded. But these questions were political rather than socio-economic, and it was in the political arena that alternatives emerged which can form the basis of plausible counter-factual hypothesis, and thus of legitimate criticism of the regime.

Popular rebels, we have noted, received less tolerant treatment than dissidents within the political nation. So far as the latter were concerned, the regime hoped for conversion and collaboration within the new politics: thus Almazán, or fellow middle-class dissidents like Pedro de los Santos, could expect greater magnanimity than Zapata or the Yaquis. Furthermore, the political nation still included a large Porfirian constituency, to whom this same charity was extended. Over this question, however, there was real debate in the Maderista camp. At the outset, many Maderistas (especially the younger, military Maderistas) objected to the survival and promotion of Porfiristas under the new regime.[343] Later, even their more senior civilian colleagues began to mouth the same sentiments. In January 1913 the Bloque Renovador, the eighty or so staunchly Maderista national deputies, presented a lengthy petition to the president outlining their criticisms of the regime. It did not touch upon 'socio-economic' questions; rather, it rehearsed the political failures of the government and urged political remedies. Too many Porfiristas remained in high office, obstructing the regime; the opposition press had been permitted to poison public opinion; the Bloque Renovador, though working in the interests of the administration, was ignored, rebuffed and ridiculed by Ministers and their officials. The judiciary, in particular, was riddled with Porfiristas and must be urgently reformed. The Ministry of Gobernación permitted a situation, in many states, where 'neither the *jefes políticos* nor the municipal officials are loyal to yourself, or to the cause of the Revolution'; it was necessary, therefore, to 'modify the present political psychology of these states', and this was a 'life or death' question, demanding a political effort that 'must be daily, indefatigable, determined, diligent, stubborn, tenacious, until it constitutes a real political obsession'. In short, the Renovadores concluded, the power of the government and the prestige of the revolutionary cause had suffered because 'the Revolution has not governed with the Revolution'; 'only with the revolutionaries in power can the cause of the Revolution forge ahead'.[344]

Here was a call not only for the promotion of one's own, but also for the proscription of one's enemy. And many other Maderistas harped on this theme. Roque Estrada and Alfredo Robles Domínguez had warned against excessive compromise with the old regime back in 1911.[345] Governors like Cepeda, Carranza, and Maytorena were much exercised by the problem late in 1912.[346] Vice-President Pino Suárez ('smoking a fine Vuelta Abajo cigar and with a glass of Chartreuse in his hand') confided to a sympathetic diplomat that the government faced a critical situation: 'the policy of detente [*acercamiento*] with the aristocracy [sic] . . . is casting us into the abyss. At the moment we are not exactly a Científico government, but still less are we a popular government'; in such a predicament

only a change of methods will avert catastrophe; the change is under way, and the government will retreat from the precipice. An energetic hand, a determined, definite, unswerving political leadership are all that the country's agitated condition requires.[347]

By 1912, therefore, a belief was growing — particularly among some top Maderistas — that the regime had to undertake more radical measures, at least in the political sphere. Above all, this meant the elimination of old centres of Porfirian power and the promotion of loyal Maderistas to high office. And it implied hawkish policies of purge and proscription, an end to the policy of conciliation, and a surrender of the comforting belief that all Mexicans, Porfirians included, could be clasped in the embrace of the new politics. Though this might involve some derogation of liberal principle, it did not run counter to fundamental Maderista assumptions — in the way that, say, agrarian expropriation did. Furthermore, it could be justified in terms of the original Maderista commitment to oust the (political) old regime and break down longstanding political monopolies.

This new, hawkish Maderismo was thus seen as politically necessary, and both ideologically and practically feasible. Gustavo Madero, who was prominent among the Maderista hawks, took active steps in this direction, organising the Maderista deputies in Congress (and perhaps the *Porra* on the streets), warning his brother against the machinations of the opposition.[348] Some alleged that he went even further, drawing up lists of enemies to be eliminated when the confrontation finally came.[349] Locally, too, the political renovation begun in 1911 could be furthered. If, in many states (such as Jalisco), the *jefatura* system still gave rise to abuses and complaints, there were Maderista governors like Riveros (Sin.), who removed several incumbent *jefes*, or Cepeda (San Luis), who abolished the institution altogether – a highly popular move.[350] In Coahuila and Sonora, Maderista governors jealously preserved the state irregular forces which, though they provoked wrangles with the 'centre', also conferred a certain independence of the Federal Army.[351]

Clearly, Maderista rulers could have gone much further in their attacks on the old guard; they could have called upon the countervailing power of rival groups – veterans of the Liberating Army, the Renovadores, even labour unions and peasant forces. Given suitable government sponsorship, this need not have been a recipe for anarchy (witness developments after 1915). But, while some Maderistas moved in this direction, the prevailing tenor of the regime was insufficiently altered. Some Maderistas, fearful of the popular movement, succumbed to conservative blandishments; for them, the policy and personnel of the old regime provided a shield against further rebellion and upheaval; their embrace of the Porfirian 'aristocracy' (to use Pino Suárez's phrase) was positive, even enthusiastic. But there were others – of whom Madero himself was the classic example – who retained a sincere belief in the new politics, who regretted – while they could not prevent – the continuance of old abuses, and who clung to the principle of conciliation and patient conversion. They had no time for political purges, press manipulation, the *Porra*, the wholesale reconstitution of the civil service and local government, or the build-up of irregular forces which rivalled – and therefore antagonised – the Federal Army. For them, the still powerful survivors of the old regime awaited redemption, not annihilation. Hence, Madero was magnanimous in his treatment of conservative rebels like Reyes and Félix Díaz; indeed, the question of Félix Díaz's fate after his abortive coup of 1912 provided something of a litmus test of the relative attitudes and strengths of the Maderista hawks and doves.[352]

Similarly, Madero too readily discounted reports of military disaffection and treason and, when the Renovadores pressed him to take tough measures, to eliminate Porfirian elements and 'govern with the Revolution', he politely listened, then brushed aside their fears. One such exchange took place while Madero and Pani rode down the Paseo de la Reforma in the presidential limousine; as the car swept through the gates of the National Palace, to the applause of some by-standers, the president turned to Pani and 'closing our argument with a lapidary comment, exclaimed: "There is nothing to fear while the people applaud me".'[353] Such confidence, evident throughout Madero's term of office, became increasingly misplaced as time went by.[354] But, despite the Vice-President's assurance (to the Cuban Minister) that new, tough policies were in the offing, there was little practical evidence of such a development: hawkish Maderismo was discussed more than it was implemented. Towards the end of 1912, indeed, Madero seemed to have acquired renewed political zest and confidence, and this, far from impelling the president towards the tougher policies favoured by the Renovadores, encouraged him to revert to his natural, facile optimism.[355] It was significant that, just as Cabrera, the leading spokesman for official agrarianism, was leaving Mexico City early in 1913, so, too, Gustavo Madero, the doyen of the Maderista hawks, was scheduled to make an official visit to Japan: in his own words (according to a source whose validity is hard to assess), 'I can accomplish nothing here but discredit for myself. Let them run things their own way.'[356]

Here then, lay the Maderistas' – and, in particular, Madero's – chief sins of omission: not their failure to implement (say) sweeping agrarian reform, but their reluctance to adopt policies which were currently debated, feasible, and capable of placing the administration on a firmer footing. To the extent that this limited, counter-factual proposition (of the plausible kind) is accepted, then the regime must carry some responsibility for its own demise. Yet more clearly, it is possible to identify the regime's sins of commission – the positive corollaries of these negative failures, either perpetrated by the Maderistas, or allowed to be perpetrated under Maderista auspices. And there was nothing inevitable (or 'over-determined') about these either. For, along with the wholesale survival of Porfirian elements, the regime permitted – and in many cases eagerly practised – a wide range of Porfirian abuses, which indelibly stained its liberal reputation and undermined its popularity and legitimacy. While the regime's neglect of sweeping social reform need not be wondered at (it was in a sense 'inevitable'), the liberals' apostasy in resorting to – or allowing – so many Porfirian malpractices was another matter: often cynical and gratuitous, it was also short-sighted and ultimately disastrous for its perpetrators.

Many of the administration's departures from liberal principle were venial sins, if sins at all: occasional infringements of electoral freedom (the problems of interpretation have been alluded to), the deference shown to established *cacicazgos*, like Lucas' in the Puebla sierra.[357] More serious were the curbs on the press imposed in March 1912, or the more prolonged suspension of constitutional guarantees – which permitted summary, military justice against 'bandits' and subversives – in something like one-third of the Republic.[358] These were, of course, capable of justification in terms of the liberal argument, whereby elements of liberal freedom may be curtailed in order to maintain the general fabric of liberalism; this, in many respects, was the philosophical rationale of the Maderista hawks. But such an argument was open to much debate, easy abuse, and widespread misinterpretation. The suspension of guarantees, for example, 'even though it may have been justified, was intensely unpopular as a manifestation of tyranny seriously at odds with the fundamental philosophy of the revolution'.[359] Official surveillance of labour unions, the arrest of labour 'agitators', and the suppression of strikes also smacked of Porfirian practice – even if these were less common (relative to the incidence of strikes) after 1910, and also – sometimes – capable of liberal justification. Here again, leading Maderistas differed in their attitudes: the acting governor of Sonora, seduced by Porfirian precedent, favoured sending the ringleaders of the Cananea strikers to the plantations of Quintana Roo; but softer counsels, more in keeping with the official tone of the new regime, overruled him.[360]

But it was above all in the treatment of rural rebellions that reversions to Porfirian practice were most striking. These occurred in the provinces, where the control of the president and the national executive was weaker, and their victims were generally rural hicks and hoodlums who, it was thought, deserved no better. In Morelos, to take the prime example, General Robles' 1912 campaign was marked by arbitrary shootings, the burning of villages, and the 'concentration' of the civilian population. Madero regretted and warned other commanders against emulating these brutal methods: the burning of Santa María, he pointed out, had earned the regime the costly hostility of Genovevo de la O.[361] Equally, Madero deplored the murder, by means of the *ley fuga*, of Che Gómez in Oaxaca. But there was an element of Pilate's hand-washing in such protestations, as there must be whenever liberals deplore the illiberal, brutalising effects of wars whose ultimate objectives they nevertheless endorse. If Madero willed the end result (the extirpation of rebellion and establishment of peace on his own terms) he could hardly display an over-scrupulous conscience about the means employed. Thus his attitude to the Morelos campaign was either disingenuous or naive, as was his advice to General Blanquet:

benign measures with the inhabitants are always preferable, for if they are sympathisers with Zapatismo, treating them well will make them friends of the government; on the other hand, it is justifiable to show extreme rigour to those who are found with arms in their hands.[362]

Furthermore, such advice was largely ineffectual. Federal commanders, well versed in such punitive campaigns, continued in the same manner, even if some were less sanguinary than Juvencio Robles; the summary justice and arbitrary executions went on, despite the prickings of Madero's conscience (and partly legitimised by the government's own suspension of guarantees). In Morelos the failure of reform brought a resumption of hostilities, with General Felipe Angeles (the great liberal of the Federal Army) 'bombarding and burning suspect villages and executing captives en masse' – albeit with somewhat more discrimination than either Huerta or Robles.[363]

Elsewhere, the story was often similar. In Oaxaca, the campaign against the rebellious *serranos* produced 'many tales of much killing of suspects in different districts'; rebels caught in the Mazapil region of San Luis were shot out of hand and denied prisoner-of-war status.[364] In the same state, Brigadier-General Manuel Rivera prided himself on the prevailing tranquillity: strikers at the La Paz mines had been 'reduced', and a potential strike at the smelter 'avoided'; escapees from the state penitentiary had been recaptured and rebels put to flight at Río Verde and Santa María del Rio; seventy-eight prisoners had been despatched to Mexico City and two new cavalry corps established. 'I therefore have the pleasure', he concluded, 'of presenting this zone as the most tranquil, thanks to the tactic of killing in the cradle all uprisings which threaten to disturb public order.'[365] This was certainly the path to swift promotion under the old regime; but it hardly carried the hallmark of the new, liberal politics. Nor were such attitudes the monopoly of Federal officers and old Porfiristas. Brigadier-General Rivera claimed to enjoy the full support of Governor Cepeda; in Sonora, the Yaqui war was prosecuted by a Maderista state government in much the same manner as the Yaqui wars of old; while from the Laguna Emilio Madero complained to his brother of the 'many individuals who proliferate among the haciendas and ranches without work . . . [and who] are the very ones who daily join the ranks of the bandit gangs', advising that they be deported to Yucatan or Morelos, there to serve in the army, and requesting orders 'authorising me to send to Mexico City, with this end in view, however many thousand of such individuals' as might be necessary.[366]

Other characteristically Porfirian touches reappeared. Despite Madero's regret at the demise of Che Gómez, the *ley fuga* lived on. In Tabasco the troublesome opposition editor José Gurdiel Hernández was several times committed to gaol and finally shot by a police escort 'while trying to escape'. The killing occurred deep in the interior of the state, and Tabasqueños observed that Gurdiel and his fellow-prisoners had been manacled and tied to their horses prior to the 'escape'.[367] Another tiresome *tinterillo*, Salustio Carrasco Núñez, was summarily executed by Ambrosio Figueroa in Guerrero: not because he had taken up arms (Figueroa admitted) but because he had denounced the government in the Iguala press, daily predicting and advocating rebellion, and praising Zapata; and because Figueroa himself was 'resolved to make peace in this state at the cost of however much blood may be necessary'.[368] Madero, sympathising with these motives, regretted that Figueroa had exceeded legality; but his protest was polite and feeble.[369] And for every such incident consummated and brought to light, there must have been others which remained covert, or which were projected but not carried out. The Mexican consul at Douglas, Arizona, sniffing out a conspiracy against the government in Sonora, urged the arrest of Plutarco Elías Calles, Agua Prieta's police chief, along with others, who should be sent to Mexico City 'in order to make them talk by whatever methods are possible or to apply the *ley fuga* on account of their disloyalty'.[370] But Governor Maytorena vouched for Calles' innocence, and the Agua Prieta police chief survived: a matter of no small consequence for later Mexican history.

In addition to the *ley fuga*, the grim practice of displaying rebel corpses in public places (first noted in November 1910) was now revived: it was followed in Durango (where the bodies of José Maciel and his gang were laid out in the city streets); in Silao (where Jesús Armendares' corpse was placed on a cot 'as an object lesson'); and it enabled photographers to snap the gory pictures of serried rows of bodies which appear in Casasola.[371] An alternative means of disposing of rebel/bandit prisoners, without adding to the content of the crowded, insecure penitentiaries, was to enrol them in the army. This, too, was standard Porfirian practice. But its reintroduction, on a grander scale and at a time of endemic rebellion, carried obvious dangers, which even the diffusion of prisoners, or their despatch to distant, unfamiliar regions could not entirely overcome. The 150 'recruits' (said to be prisoners-of-war) who arrived at Ensenada late in 1912, or the 200 'so-called Zapatistas, a lot of half-naked savages' who disembarked at Mazatlán for military service in Tepic, were hardly likely to make up into fine soldiers, and they added to the army's already general problems of desertion and indiscipline.[372]

Such desperate recruiting reflected not only the problem of surplus prisoners, but also that of filling the ranks of the Federal Army. Since Madero — and, with greater enthusiasm, many of his subordinates — sought a military solution to Mexico's crisis, success hinged upon the increase and improvement of the army as an instrument of repression. And it was in this respect that the Madero regime came most to resemble its predecessor; that the liberal apostasy was most flagrant. In the summer of 1911, after the fall of Díaz, the Federal Army stood at about 15,000.[373] Subsequently, numbers rose. Early in 1912 the press talked of 24,000 men being under arms, and supporters of the government were advocating dramatic increases: Carlos Madero regarded 50,000 as a minimum.[374] For once, action soon followed. In March 1912, confronting Orozco's revolt, the executive proposed to Congress an increase to 60,000 and Ernesto Madero, interviewed by the American press, said that 70,000 would be achieved and that recruiting was already under way.[375] But what sort of recruiting? Filling the notional ranks was a constant problem, even when recruits were offered bounties and regular wages; whereas the life of a *rural* offered certain attractions — to the young, the unemployed, the footloose ex-rebel or the small-time grafter — a career in the Federal Army enticed no-one. Ambrosio Figueroa rejected out of hand the idea of merging the *rurales* into the regular army: 'such a measure would be impolitic and inopportune, since no *rural* would want to enter the Federal ranks, and they would be disgusted by the ingratitude with which their services were [thus] rewarded'.[376] Hence, the sight of officers drumming up recruits – without conspicuous success – became commonplace in the major cities, especially in the spring of 1912.[377]

Alternatives to voluntary enlistment therefore had to be found. Opposed to the 'immoral methods of recruitment' employed by Díaz (notably the *leva*), and disenchanted with his wayward ex-revolutionary irregulars, Madero opted for a system of compulsory military service, with recruits chosen impartially by lot thoughout the country. For – and here again presidential naiveté stands out – such a system could alone guarantee 'a completely healthy contingent of vigorous young men, of much superior morality to those who were recruited under the old system'; indeed, such a system could furnish an army like that of Republican France, inculcating sober patriotism and disciplining the 'national character'.[378] Again, however, these alien if attractive ideas could not take root in Mexican soil. Talk of conscription – and its subsequent implementation in 1912 – generated rumours of mass revolts, protests from earnest Maderistas (who saw this as a departure from the earlier commitment to a volunteer army), and warnings from state governors that men would quit the country or, worse, join the rebels rather than be conscripted.[379] As it was, there seems to have been little marked reaction to the introduction of compulsory military service: probably because, in fulfilling their quotas, states fell back on the old, strong-arm methods (which, though unpopular, were at least familiar), and ignored the new, impartial mechanism of the lottery. Certainly this was the case at Tlacotepec and San Juan Tilapa where, the inhabitants complained, the required system had not been used, poor men with large families had – against all the rules – been taken for military service, and (Madero himself suspected) the iniquitous *leva* had been at work.[380] Conscription by lot, like democratic elections and civil rights, thus took on a phantasmagoric existence when transported to Mexico City from Europe (where, to be sure, there were abuses too); beneath such shimmering, insubstantial forms, the old Mexican realities prevailed, and there was little Madero could do about them.

So the press-gang continued in business. Perhaps the American Ambassador's report of the government's 'unlawful practices in the matter of impressment in the army' cannot carry much weight; but the Chargé d'Affaires, generally more reliable, noted how, in June 1912, 'every man arrested in this vicinity [of Mexico City] on drunkenness or disorderly conduct [charges] is being forced into the army and sent to the front', at the rate of fifty a day.[381] Convicts were drafted out of the gaols of the major cities, like Mexico City's Belem; down in Veracruz they could be seen arriving from the capital and from the cities of the central plateau, like military debt-peons in the service of the state.[382] Popular fears of the press-gang – which still remained vigorous – were thus revived, particularly in response to incidents like that which occurred in the summer of 1912 when common labourers heading north from San Luis (possibly they were *braceros* making for the border) were hauled off their trains and put into uniform.[383] The government also fell back on that old source, Indian manpower. Yaquis, Mayos, Pimas and Pápagos were recruited in Sonora, and plans were made to send 500 Oaxaqueño *serranos* (just recently in revolt) to fight in Chihuahua, thereby releasing loyal Coahuilan troops for service in Morelos.[384] Even down to the complex geographical disposition (designed to keep troops in strange territory, unencumbered by local sympathies), such plans were redolent of Porfirian government. And the resulting contingents were odd, makeshift and inefficient: Colonel Rivera, taking command of a detachment in Sonora, found that he led 200 Mayo Indians, 75 Pima, 86 ex-convicts (from Belem), 70 old Federal regulars, and a rump of so-called volunteers, 'petty offenders and worthless characters, who have been drafted into the army from various towns in the state'.[385] Hence, in large measure, the torpor and inefficiency of the army in combatting rural rebellion. Desertions were common: they were running at the rate of five to ten a day among the Ojinaga garrison (admittedly a precarious post) in May 1912; and a deserter was responsible for leading 2,000 men in an attack on Rosario (Sin.) in the same month.[386] Federal officers were understandably inhibited by the character of the troops they commanded: some, leading a dissolute and sullen rabble, 'dare[d] not trust themselves in the mountains with their own men'.[387]

The chief alternative to the draft and the *leva* was the recruitment of genuine volunteer forces which could supplement the Federal Army. These assumed many forms; but, taken together, they represented a sizeable military establishment, which made a significant contribution to the militarisation of Mexico under Madero. Two groups enjoyed a certain Maderista legitimacy. First, there were the veterans of 1910–11, the military Maderistas who, unlike many of their kind, opted to serve the government as *rurales* or irregulars. While some proved useful and reliable (operating, it should be noted, away from their home states: Sánchez in Guerrero, for instance, or Aguilar in the Laguna), many others were sources of trouble and anxiety, refractory in their conduct, doubtful in their loyalty: Gabriel Hernández in Hidalgo, Banderas in Sinaloa, Contreras in the Laguna.[388] Nor was this surprising, in that they still represented popular forces and interests, at odds with much of Maderista policy. The handful of loyalists, however, were among Madero's staunchest supporters, as the events of 1913 were to reveal.

The same was true of the state forces called into existence – chiefly in the northern states of Sonora and Coahuila – to combat rebellion. These were also 'Maderista', in that they defended the constituted government: but their loyalty was to the state as much as to the Federation (and to state governor as much as to national president); and, although there was a degree of overlap between the two groups, they were Maderistas of a different stripe from the veterans of 1910–11. The nature of this difference – between the veterans of 1910 and the new, state forces of 1912, between, for example, Villa and Contreras on the one hand, Obregón and González on the other – is a complex question, important for any interpretation of the Revolution, and one which will be tackled in greater detail later.[389] Here, it is sufficient to note that while the 1910 veterans captained genuinely popular guerrillas, in a 'spontaneous' revolt against Díaz, the state forces created by Governors Maytorena and Carranza, chiefly to resist Orozquismo, were 'official', in some senses 'mercenary', and constructed from the top down. They were salaried, well-organised, disciplined and generally efficient, fit to serve as the guardians of order and government in opposition to disaffected popular rebels such as Orozco. The Sonoran forces, which constituted a 'small army', approaching 3,000 men, were not homogenous: they comprised Maderista veterans, a few Federals, some forced recruits, Indians, and genuine, mercenary volunteers. But they were knitted together by the cash and authority of the Sonoran state government, a 'constituted bureaucratic power'; they did not therefore represent a 'large scale popular mobilisation'; and 'pay, rather than political partisanship, ideological conviction, or loyalty to one *jefe*, was the motor behind these initial revolutionary militias in Sonora'.[390] In that they depended on pay, the Sonoran forces resembled the Federals. But at least the Sonorans were honestly mercenary (and, perhaps, able to count on a genuine regional loyalty to the state itself), and they did not need to resort to extensive forced recruitment, after the manner of the Federals. As a result their forces were man for man more effective than the Federals; and they were superior to the rough-and-ready popular hosts of 1910–11, if not by virtue of morale, then certainly by virtue of discipline, co-ordination and logistical back-up. They may be seen, in effect, as a synthesis of the popular and Porfirian methods of making war and, as such, they represented the military equivalent of a new political synthesis emerging in these northern states.[391]

Both the veteran irregulars and the state forces were, in their different ways, 'Maderista'. But during the Madero period Mexico saw the proliferation of other volunteer and mercenary groups which, though lacking 'Maderista' credentials, contributed to the militarisation of society. Indeed, as more men – Federals, *rurales*, volunteers, mercenaries, rebels, bandits – came under arms, and as organised violence became more commonplace, so liberal dreams of a peaceful, consensual, civilian society necessarily receded, and the military establishment (in its various guises) assumed pre-eminent importance. The pure milk of liberalism soured in the heat of battle; and, as in Great Britain two years later, 'war and the conduct of war threatened to eliminate liberalism as a coherent political position'.[392] Yet Madero – a forthright critic of praetorianism – and many of his colleagues not only permitted but in many instances also encouraged this process of militarisation.[393] And observers were not slow to point out this derogation of liberal principle and return to Porfirian practice. Cartoonists depicted the Madero family exhuming the recently interred body of 'Dictatorship', retailing gramophone records entitled 'Tyranny and Dictatorship', or building a mountain of corpses ('Juvencio Robles' Morelos campaign') which dwarfed the pile left by Díaz.[394] Conservative critics were often hypocritical in this respect (given the chance – which they were in 1913 – conservatives proved to be more uninhibitedly ruthless than Madero had ever been); yet there is no doubt that they had a point when they denounced Maderista militarisation and repression. Vera Estañol perhaps exaggerated, but did not entirely mislead, when he argued that by the end of 1912 public opinion had turned against Madero, that many of his old revolutionary supporters were now in rebellion against him, and that 'Madero [now] counted solely on those resources which the organised power of the state gave him'.[395] To the extent that 'moral ascendancy' (Vera Estañol's phrase) had given way to 'bayonets and violence', that – putting it differently – coercion rather than legitimacy underpinned Maderismo, the regime may be said to have reneged on one of its philosophical fundamentals.

The liberal apostasy was clearest in those instances where the regime – in the interests of pacification – welcomed the collaboration of old practitioners of the Pax Porfiriana. The Federal officer corps, the obvious example, will be considered separately in a moment. But they were not alone. Old *rural* commanders survived and prospered: Cruz Guerrero, now (in 1912) in his forty-third year of service; Luis Medina Barrón who, as a major, had commanded the Cananea repression of 1906, and now, as a Lieutenant-Colonel, campaigned against the Zapatistas in Morelos; Emilio Kosterlisky, also a veteran of Cananea, who came out of retirement to serve again in Sonora, instilling a 'feeling of confidence' in the region around Nogales.[396] Bernardo Reyes himself, one of the great architects of the Pax Porfiriana, against whose militarist tendencies Madero had fulminated in 1909, was not only allowed back to Mexico but was also offered the Ministry of War, in the interests of stability and conciliation, and to the disgust of many Maderistas.[397] Critics further alleged that Madero secured the services of disgraced members of the old regime like ex-General José Delgado and the ex-police chief of the Federal District, Antonio Villavicencio.[398] And there is ample evidence of Porfiristas and Reyistas recovering power through their command of local military forces. At Saltillo, Cayetano Ramos (a landowner, known Reyista, suspected plotter and brother-in-law of ex-Governor Cárdenas) became *jefe de las armas*, commanding 375 men; subsequently, General Manuel Velázquez, 'an army man of the old regime and a great Porfirista', was sent to Saltillo to 'consolidate military operations and bring the state organisation under direct Federal supervision' – which meant usurping control of Governor Carranza's irregulars, subordinating Maderistas to Federals, and antagonising the governor.[399] No better was the government's dalliance with some of the 'last-minute' revolutionaries who had sprung out of the ground in the spring and summer of 1911. Miguel Arriaga, for example, the Porfirian cacique of the Puebla sierra, who had 'rebelled' in 1911, feuded with Gabriel Hernández, and defied the Federal administration, was now cast as a potential ally: Gustavo Madero urged that overtures be made to Arriaga and his men (numbering 1,000) with a view to using them as volunteers in the campaign against Zapata.[400]

Opportunist rebellions, like those of Arriaga, or Soto and García in Guanajuato, represented local, defensive reactions to the revolutionary upheaval of 1911.[401] And, since the upheaval continued into 1912 and 1913, such freelance activity continued, tending to increase in scope and importance; it was ultimately to reach its apogee in the Felicista movement of 1916–20.[402] Thus, in town and countryside, there sprouted defence forces, vigilantes, private police and *guardias blancas*, all further contributions to the militarisation of Mexico, and to the military costs which, directly or indirectly, the economy had to bear. Such forces constituted the mirror-image of the rebel hordes, bandits and disorderly elements whom they sought to combat; and, just as the forces of 'disorder' can, with some difficulty, be divided into the true revolutionaries and social bandits on the one hand, the apolitical, 'unsocial' thugs on the other, so, too, the forces of local defence fell into two categories, the one representing (roughly) a class reaction on the part of threatened landlords, property-owners and Porfiristas, the other the collective response of entire communities, largely transcending class and sectional differences. Genuine revolution and social banditry – being challenges to the status quo – elicited the first; professional thuggery stimulated the second.

It is therefore a comment on the character of the revolution in these years that the first category considerably outweighed the second (later, the balance would shift). Rebels and social bandits could still count on a fund of popular support which ruled out broadly based, collective resistance. However, there were exceptions, when communities voluntarily and collectively mobilised to resist bandit–rebels, who were seen either as professional villains, or as unwanted revolutionary interlopers. In Chiapas, the Tapachula volunteers repulsed the 'turbulent' Mazatecos who sought to attack their town. In the Bajío, officials raised posses among the townspeople to resist bandits (these may have been 'social' bandits from a rural perspective but in this, as in so much, town and country saw things differently). When the Orozquistas – and the Yaquis – threatened Sonora in 1912, the state government relied not only on forced recruitment or the mercenary instincts of Obregón's forces, but also on the voluntary efforts of pueblos like Santa Cruz (Magdalena) or the villages of the Sonora River valley. *Hacendados*, it is true, provided men, money and horses; but the forces thereby created had a genuinely voluntary, even popular character: 'nobody obliged us to take up arms', declared the Santa Cruz soldiers, 'but we have offered our services to the constituted government of our own free will'.[403] The inhabitants of the sierras of northern Durango – clustered in remote mining towns – were also tenacious in their own self-defence: Guanaceví several times beat off bandit attacks; 70 rebels were repulsed by the people of Tejamen (which had no garrison); when Cieneguilla was attacked by 200 Orozquistas the town's merchants holed up in the pits and tunnels of the Inde Gold Mining Co. and opened fire on the raiders, forcing them to flee.[404] In these cases there is no suggestion of popular sympathy or support for the attackers; and this is quite plausible, granted that the region had suffered heavily through two years of warfare, that Federal defences were inadequate, and that local livelihood depended on continued mining pro-duction, which these upheavals threatened. Communities therefore pioneered a form of collective self-defence which was to flourish in later years, notably in western Durango, but also more generally throughout the country.

But in 1912, such efforts were exceptional. More often, local resistance clearly responded to the interests and initiative of the well-to-do, and lacked popular support. Some examples have already been mentioned: the predomin-antly middle and upper-class forces recruited to repulse bandits and deter rioters in several major cities (San Luis, Silao, Irapuato, Durango); the vigilantes hired by the Acapulco merchants; the field guards deployed by the planters of Morelos and the Laguna. At Colima, too, 300 men were raised as a 'volunteer corps . . . to defend the city . . . from bandits'; three or four 'merchants and *hacendados*' were behind the scheme and one *hacendado* alone provided one hundred men and mounts. Manzanillo, close by, soon had an equivalent force, and the elites of the two towns co-operated in the organi-sation of a mounted corps of forty-eight men whose task it was to patrol country roads and estates and to 'arrest fugitives from justice, disturbers of [the] peace and agitators'.[405] Some schemes verged on the grandiose: in February 1912 the 'well-to-do citizens' of Durango agreed to raise 250,000 pesos to pay for extra state *rurales*, and in the following month the 'best citizens' convened and decided to form a citizens militia costing 3,200 pesos a month.[406] On a smaller scale, individual *hacendados* followed the example set by the García Pimentel family, who kitted out fifty field guards for their Morelos estate: the redoubtable Señora Eucaria Apresa recruited one hundred men to resist the Zapatistas of Guerrero; a platoon of 'Xico volunteers' was formed to defend Iñigo Noriega's Veracruz hacienda.[407]

The government's attitude to these measures was one of toleration, even encouragement: the Laguna forces, for example, received both the blessing and the active support of the administration.[408] What is not clear is the degree of success they achieved. In the cities, the corps of young clerks, students, professionals and dandies were hardly put to the test (save during occasional, daring bandit raids, when they did not win many laurels). It was the Federal Army, scattered in the towns and cities of the Republic, which provided the ultimate guarantee against both rural incursions and internal upheavals. In the countryside, where the Federals were thin on the ground – or even non-existent – there was more scope and necessity for freelance military formations. Here, their success was mixed. They could tip the balance against emerging or chaotic popular movements, successfully insulating regions from agrarian rebellion, at least for the time being: Eucaria Apresa claimed to have secured the surrender – after negotiation – of two troublesome local *cabecillas*; around Naranja and Tiríndaro (Mich.) the employment of 'roving firing squad[s]' by the local landlords enabled them to repress a nascent agrarianism for years.[409] But, as already noted, landlord self-help was least effective in those areas where rebellion was strongest and landlord legitimacy weakest: coercion (Skocpol might note) required a degree of prior legitimacy. In Morelos, the García Pimentel recruits achieved little, and their fellow-planters ignored their example, preferring to sit out the struggle in the security of Mexico City.[410] In the Laguna, too, it was the Federal Army rather than the new plantation guards, who bore the brunt of the fighting, and on whom the resolution of the conflict rested. The same lesson was rammed home in 1913–14.[411]

Freelance forces could thus supplement the Federals and could achieve some limited success in minor theatres of the civil war; but even this depended on the Federals containing the area of conflict, preventing its ramification, and winning the battles which really mattered. By the same token, while the growth of private armies constituted a serious anomaly within Madero's would-be liberal, civilian polity, it was the increased power and importance of the Federal Army which was most significant, and most threatening to the Maderista experiment in constitutional rule. Díaz's had not been a military regime: the army had been numerically small (and getting smaller), the officer corps had been politically docile, and a civilian, cacical authority – vested in the president and his oligarchic collaborators – had prevailed. Furthermore, revolts had been seen not to work. The 1910 revolution changed all that. Thereafter, the 'centre' was in crisis; the civilian oligarchs were much weakened; the deference and docility born of a generation of peace had evaporated.[412] The product of revolution, the new regime was itself liable to revolutionary overthrow. Of the several pillars that had sustained Díaz, only the Federal Army remained intact, and Madero's regime, though philosophically further removed from militarism than even Díaz's, nevertheless conceded the army greater influence and greater resources than in the past. And the army, less respectful of Madero than it had been of Díaz, soon became aware of its enlarged role, and of the new regime's incongruous reliance on Federal bayonets.

The army emerged from the 1911 revolution larger than in the last days of the Díaz regime; and, if chastened by defeat, it could plead – with more justification than the Reichswehr of 1918 – that it had been stabbed in the back, sold out by the politicians. In no sense had it been whipped: no major battles had been lost; of the cities of the Republic only Juárez had been taken by the rebels *a fuerza y sangre*. Madero pandered to the army's pride by adopting an overtly generous attitude towards it. No opportunity was missed publicly to praise the army's virtues, and, in all Madero's *política de conciliación,* no Porfirian group was more earnestly conciliated than the army. The 'National Army' (to be distinguished from the Maderista 'Liberating Army') was enjoined to share in the rejoicing of 1911: the dictatorship, not the army, had been defeated by the revolution; the aspirations of army and people were as one and 'an army like our own is a guarantee of republican institutions'.[413] President de la Barra distributed medals to Federal officers; the Minister of Gobernación (the supposedly radical Vázquez Gómez) praised the 'tight discipline and incorruptible morality' of the army, which now constituted 'one of the most sure and powerful elements' for the defence of the Revolution; and the War Ministry asked governors to submit recommended decorations and promotions 'with which to reward the soldiers of the Federal Army, to strengthen further, if possible, its manifest love of the country'.[414] This assiduous cultivation continued well after the summer of 1911. Visiting Monterrey in October, Madero reviewed military detachments, eulogised the army, and received a rousing 'Viva!' in return.[415] And the irresponsibility of the Mexico City press (particularly its reporting of Federal mutinies which, Madero said, had never happened) was contrasted with the rectitude of the army: 'of everything left to us by General Díaz, it is the finest, the most admirable; its loyalty to the government, its selflessness are moving'.[416]

All this, of course, was for public consumption (though some believed Madero really meant it).[417] Behind the scenes, however, Madero took pains to win over this admirable, loyal, and selfless army. As his astute brother Emilio advised him, recommending some recognition for Colonel Prisciliano Cortés, who had defended Torreón in 1911,[418]

it would be convenient to attract him to our side; not because I fear a counter-revolution among the Federal troops; but [because] it is always useful that the officers of the Army start to appreciate your influence in politics, so that you may acquire some ascendancy over them.

And the president showed himself to be sensitive to the susceptibilities of such high-ranking officers. General Gerónimo Treviño, the Porfirian veteran commanding in the north east, was not to be offended: his public decisions – Governor Carranza was warned – were to be respected; and his private interests (the Babia estate) were to be protected.[419] Victoriano Huerta was another object of presidential solicitude. Notwithstanding the disastrous results of Huerta's campaign in Morelos, Madero brought him out of semi-retirement and offered him the command against Orozco; subsequently, the president indulged Huerta's sulky humour, praising his achievements, sympathising with his problems and promising him promotion. After the defeat of Orozco the promised promotion (to Divisional General) was forthcoming; Maderista eulogies inflated the general's ego; and a big Mexico City sewage concession was pushed his way by Alberto Pani, following the administration's 'insistent recommendations that [Huerta] be somehow or other done a favour'.[420] Other generals benefited too: Trucy Aubert received a house; Aureliano Blanquet, hospitalised after the Chihuahua campaign, was visited by Madero, who personally conferred his promotion to general, along with a bejewelled gold watch.[421]

But apart from – and even more important than – this cultivation of the officer corps, the regime also accorded the army great and growing authority in the country. Clearly, the initial decision to retain the Federal Army in being, while demobilising the Liberating Army, was crucial. This meant that the anomalous situation of summer 1911 – which had produced several Federal–Maderista clashes – was resolved in favour of the Federals, who would henceforth enjoy a near-monopoly of the state's monopoly of legitimate violence. Virtually no Maderista veterans were rewarded with places in the Federal ranks.[422] And where Maderistas remained (legally) under arms – as *rurales* or local irregulars – they generally came under Federal command, and Federal commanders strove not only to keep them in their place, but even to demobilise them in the surest possible way, by getting them killed.[423] Meanwhile, the scope and intensity of the 1911–13 campaigns gave the army unprecedented powers. Generals like Huerta, Juvencio Robles, or Ojeda (in Sinaloa) eclipsed the civil power; and there were not wanting those – in other, troubled states – who saw military government and martial law as the answer to local problems.[424] Conversely, there were states like Coahuila or Guanajuato where the civil authorities grew resentful at military pretensions, and friction developed.[425] By 1913 the Federal Army was both more powerful and more politicised than it had been under Díaz.

This process of militarisation had obvious financial implications. So far as possible, Madero sought to provide the army with the wherewithal for victory. But this was costly. Rather surprisingly, Wilkie's budgetary analysis suggests that the military share of government expenditure remained steady as between 1910–11 and 1911–12 (more credibly, the administration projected a cut, which could not be achieved).[426] If this is correct, it means that Madero defeated Orozco, combated Zapata, the Juchitecos, the Yaquis and many lesser rebels, and tripled the military payroll, while maintaining much the same budget as Díaz. Over the longer term, however, the figures accord better with the historical evidence. As between 1910–11 and 1912–13 the military share of expenditure rose from 20.4% to 25.8% – that is, from 7 to 10 pesos (1950 prices) per capita.[427] This increase was confined by Ernesto Madero who, addressing Congress at the end of 1912, put current (1912–13) military expenditure at 30m. pesos, or 26% of government expenditure; the estimated expenditure for 1913–14 was 40m., or 31%.[428] By then – even on official figures – the liberal Madero administration would have been spending well over twice as much on the military as its Porfirian predecessor.[429]

Such a trend was inevitable, given not only the increase in the army establishment from less than 20,000 (1910) to 70,000 (1912), but also the Federal subsidies flowing to state forces, such as those of Coahuila and Sonora.[430] And Madero did not stint on weaponry: 1,500 Mausers were sent to Ambrosio Figueroa (even though the president was somewhat sceptical of the 1,680 active troops whom Figueroa claimed); and Colonel Reynaldo Díaz, campaigning in the same state, was promised an armoured car, as soon as the consignment arrived from Europe.[431] Though, as already noted, government finances never collapsed, this military build-up created strains and problems. Madero found himself retreating on commitments made to hard-pressed states: 1,000 men promised to Governor González in Chihuahua at the end of 1912 could not be sent for want of funds.[432] Even more serious, the sort of events unknown for a generation began to recur: Federal troops advancing against rebels in Durango stopped at Rodeo and refused to go further until the back pay they were owed was paid to them.[433] By the end of 1912 it was reckoned that the government had sufficient cash to meet the army's wages bill only until the middle of January.[434] Such fears and incidents – even if partly exaggerated – showed that the growing military burden was readily perceived: by worried *políticos*, self-important generals, unpaid troops, luckless conscripts, critical radicals, and alert government creditors. And if, of all this varied crowd, it was the rank-and-file who (along with the rebels) constituted the chief victims of militarisation, it was the generals who most pondered the significance of this trend, and the direction in which it might be leading.

THE TWILIGHT OF MADERISMO

In the latter part of 1912 a series of new challenges to the regime developed, with the expanded Federal Army playing a crucial role. These new challenges, coupled with the longstanding problems of Morelos, Chihuahua and elsewhere, made the autumn and winter of 1912/13 – the twilight of Maderismo – a tense and uncertain time; and, before the new year was very old, they conspired to bring the liberal experiment to a bloody end.

But this was no inevitable denouement; still less was the regime's history one of progressive deterioration. The defeat of Orozco in the summer of 1912, the eclipse of Zapata during Morelos' reformist interlude, and the 'demonstration effect' of these events, coming at the most active period of the agricultural year, helped to bring a period of relative peace during the summer months. Orozco's challenge to the regime was spent (though mopping-up operations would be long and messy); in Morelos, this was the time when 'Zapata and de la O would [later] recall . . . they had been most uncertain about ultimately winning'.[435] If Oaxaca was threatened by the *serranos*, the Isthmus was quiet (save for sporadic banditry), the Juchitecos had returned to their fields for planting, and the Panamerican Railway was running efficiently – or, at least, as efficiently as it ever did.[436] Banditry troubled parts of Veracruz and the Bajío, but organised rebel movements were played out; San Luis enjoyed 'extreme quiet', outside the Huasteca; states like Aguascalientes and Sonora were, as usual, peaceful, though the Yaquis continued to give rise to anxiety.[437] Ojeda's military government had brought a form of peace to Sinaloa, where the revolution, once so intense, had 'apparently ended'; though it was recognised that this political calm continued with the rains and many anticipated a renewed outbreak in mid-winter.[438] The north east, meanwhile, was getting back to business: Monterrey and Saltillo were prospering and even Chihuahua – notwithstanding continued operations against the Orozquista remnants – experienced an economic upswing.[439] In Mexico City, where the threat of Orozco had rallied support for the government, both commercial and political confidence had revived by the summer: 'public opinion is very optimistic and it is thought that the revolution has ended'; Americans in the capital believed that Madero 'had got his second wind'.[440]

This did not mean that the popular revolution was over. It meant that the only serious, revolutionary challenge for national power – Orozquismo – had been defeated; that the regime still stood, four-square, on the bases of city, army, railway and revenue; and that while these bases remained it would endure, sometimes shaken, but nevertheless secure. However, the bases themselves were not impervious to the popular threat. Madero's fall was thus brought about by a combination of direct popular challenge, and the indirect effects of this challenge upon the political nation, notably the Federal Army. For 1912, like 1911, witnessed a decline in revolutionary activity during the summer, only to be followed by a recrudescence in the autumn. As a perceptive critic of the regime argued, addressing the Chamber of Deputies in October 1912, the causes which had generated the Revolution were still extant; hence,[441]

that revolution is still afoot; the present government thought that throwing a blanket over it would bring it to an end for good; but then that blanket began to move and it turned out that all those seeds most deep in our society were under the blanket and beginning to break out.

So it turned out in the last quarter of the year. The extirpation of Orozquismo proved much harder than anticipated: partly because of the movement's revival in decentralised, guerrilla form (a return to its old *serrano* origins), partly because of the slothful, perhaps treasonable, attitude of the Federal Army. By December, it was reported, 'the remnants of Orozco's army are undoubtedly showing more evidence of concerted action' and, despite a stream of exhortatory and advisory letters from Madero to his northern commanders, the campaigns dragged on, a constant drain on government finances and, Madero

believed, a potential threat to good relations with the US.[442] Rebels like
Salazar still roamed with impunity in the countryside; Federal commanders
continued to quarrel among themselves and display what the President termed
'criminal apathy'.[443] So commands were shuffled about, tactical instructions
were issued concerning the use of flying columns or the necessity of blocking
the rebels' bolt-holes in the sierra.[444] Such interference, however warranted
by Federal inactivity, further soured Madero's relations with the officer corps.
And similar exhortations were sent to the southern command – Generals
Blanquet, Angeles, Riveroll – who were combating a resurgent Zapatismo.
Here, with the failure of Morelos' reformists, Zapata's fortunes picked up and
his revolt came to display a more sophisticated organisation. Plantations were
levied on a regular weekly basis; and, if they did not pay up, the cane fields
were burnt to the ground. The cost of the campaigns was thus shifted from the
pueblos to the plantations and, as the latter were forced to halt production,
peons and casual workers were thrown into the arms of the rebels. Zapatista
leaders like de la O and Mendoza, whose forces had declined to 100 or 150 at
the end of the summer, commanded between 500 and 1,000 at the beginning
of 1913. The rebels could thus mount more ambitious, co-ordinated campaigns against the Federals, while still displaying an 'astonishing mobility'.[445]

No less serious – indeed, probably most alarming of all – was the
deteriorating situation in Durango and the Laguna, noted from September
onwards.[446] By the autumn the rebels had free run of the countryside from
south-west Coahuila through Durango to Zacatecas: Cheche Campos (and
others) terrorised the plantations of the region; the mountain trails to the
mines of western Durango were perilous; and the state government, desperate
for funds and unable to rely on Federal subsidies, seemed incapable of coping
with the situation.[447] In October 1912 Gregorio Sánchez sacked Rodeo, Luis
Caro routed the garrison at Chalchihuites, Campos attacked Mapimí, and local
Indians seconded Argumedo's assault on Cuencamé.[448] The next month,
rurales mutinied and ran amok at Cruces; in December, with 'a great revival of
revolutionary activity in all parts of the state (of Durango)', Peñón Blanco, San
Lucas and San Juan del Río were all raided, and the rebels raised extra recruits
by promising the imminent sack of the state capital. Only a constant infusion
of Federal reinforcements prevented further deterioration.[449]

While these chronic ulcers festered, there were many lesser symptoms of the
country's still febrile condition. In Coahuila, the detritus of Orozquismo
dotted the north: rebels haunted the Burro Mountains and billeted themselves
on General Treviño's La Babia Hacienda, south-west of Múzquiz; in October
1912 the aspect of the Coahuilan countryside was bleak, marked by 'the almost
complete abandonment of the haciendas and farms'. Landlords gathered what
crops they could and made for the cities (where prosperity was more evident),
leaving caretakers in charge, their peons unemployed and a prey to rebel

recruiting sergeants.[450] A diffuse, generalised discontent was evident throughout much of the remainder of the country, even the deep south, where the governor of Tabasco lamented the 'disintegration' of society, and the government of Chiapas was 'in crisis'.[451] Disaffected *cabecillas* might be picked off: the arrest of the 'very dangerous' Saturnino Cedillo (whose forces had taken Cd del Maiz in November) promised greater peace in San Luis; but this was at once offset by fears of a revolt by young Gabriel Hernández in the Huasteca Hidalguense.[452] Meanwhile, electoral battles – some clearly derived from class conflict – produced a regular crop of protests and rebellions. Agustín del Pozo, having lost the gubernatorial contest in Puebla, denounced the official 'imposition', took to the sierra, and proclaimed himself governor at Xochia-pulco, in the heart of a notoriously fractious, ungovernable region; in Tlaxcala, 'an army of several thousand peasants and workers' occupied government offices to prevent a conservative governor taking power.[453] The inauguration of Governor Lizardi in Guanajuato provoked riots in which – to cries of 'Viva Porfirio Díaz!' and 'Muera Lizardi!' – the 'peon element' was dispersed by cavalry with drawn swords, and retaliated with rocks and knives; two were killed in this reminder of the riotous tendencies of the Bajío towns.[454]

By the turn of the year, therefore, the hopes raised in the summer were – if not dashed – at least set back: 'in the final months of 1912 the progressive weakening to which Madero's government seemed condemned visibly acceler-ated'; such, at least, was the impression of one loyal Maderista.[455] True, no rebel movement (save Orozco's, and that only briefly) seriously threatened the overthrow of the national government. But that was because the rebels' objectives were primarily local and rural. *Serrano* rebels, by definition, sought to dismantle rather than to capture the government. Thus, the government's control of city and garrison town, railway and commercial revenue, was largely conceded, and on these bases the government could survive. But, collectively and cumulatively, popular rebellions could bleed a regime, sap its resolve and legitimacy and drain its finances, thereby encouraging and enabling other forces (those more ambitious for national power) to deliver the *coup de grâce*. And this is what happened in 1913.

So far, the great bulk of the revolutionary action against the Madero regime came from what may be loosely termed the 'left'. It drew upon disaffected Maderista soldiers, populist *cabecillas*, agrarian rebels, social bandits; and these, while they were not 'left-wing' in the sense of espousing an articulate, radical ideology (a few Magonistas did, but many more were God-fearing Catholics, patriotic, nostalgic, and traditional in sentiment), they nonetheless were overwhelmingly popular and plebeian, and they posed a grave threat to established authority and propertied interests. Wherever they may be placed on some – possibly inappropriate – political spectrum, they may be legiti-mately regarded as 'revolutionary'.[456] Their objections to Madero were two-fold: that he allowed too much of status quo to remain, or to revive; and that his moves in the direction of reform (for Madero was no standpat conservative) were too tardy, too modest, or simply not the ones they wished to see.

Clearly, such rebels differed from conservative interests who favoured the Porfirian status quo ante, and who opposed even Madero's political reformism. Threats from this quarter – from the 'right' – were sparse and much less serious. The most notable, prior to the autumn of 1912, was the Reyes fiasco, which effectively quashed hopes of a national, Reyista counter-revolution. More ambiguous and also more dangerous had been conservative backing for Orozco; but this, too, had failed.[457] Fears of local counter-revolutions were recurrent: Próspero Cahuantzi, long-time cacique of Tlaxcala, was supposedly gathering forces at his hacienda, preparing for a comeback, as early as June 1911; Policarpo Valenzuela resigned as Governor of Tabasco (it was said), having furtively stockpiled arms on his properties, and he remained a focus of conservative/Reyista plots in the state; Policarpo Rueda, of Chiapas, was said to nurture similar plans.[458] Some of these conspiracies, I suspect, existed largely in the minds of jittery Maderistas, and were woven out of newspaper speculation and saloon-bar gossip. In practical terms, conservative plots did not get far: few got as far as the battle-field which, in 1911–12, as in 1910–11, remained the preserve of popular forces. Landlords might – with varying degrees of success – take local, defensive action against rebels and bandits, but they did not, as a rule, participate in armed rebellions or plot to overthrow the government.[459]

Nor was this surprising. While there was plenty for the conservatives to carp about in the Mexico City press, the Madero regime in fact gave them relatively little seriously to complain – and therefore to revolt – about. After the frightening events of April–May 1911, when popular revolt reached a climax, the government – initially that of de la Barra, one of the conservatives' darlings – regained the upper hand. All the policies which offended the rebel rank-and-file (the rapid demobilisation, the return of Porfirian officials, the curtailment of *de facto* and the absence of *de jure* agrarian reform) were balm to the conservatives, soothing their frayed nerves. With men like Hernández, Calero and Ernesto Madero in the cabinet, with governorships entrusted to the likes of Carreón and Carranza, Maytorena and López Portillo y Rojas, with the old generals in charge of a burgeoning Federal Army, there was little point in chancing a revolt whose chances of success were slim. The conservatives were not positively happy with the regime; they were worried by some of the more actively reformist governors (González in Chihuahua, Fuentes in Aguascalientes, Hidalgo in Tlaxcala); but there were many more safe and practical ways of countering them than by armed revolt – conservatives, with their money, education, contacts and clients, were able to play the new politics to their own advantage. Only in the exceptional circumstances of Chihuahua did some conservatives think it worth allying with the rabble in common opposition to

Maderista reformism.[460] More generally, Maderista reforms (such as tax revaluation) might prick, but they did not mortally wound, and the lower classes still presented the chief threat to order and property.

There is little evidence, therefore, of a close correlation between Maderista reformism and conservative counter-revolution. The conservatives of Aguascalientes, though hostile to Fuentes' reforms, did not figure in anti-government plots and rebellions. Conversely, Veracruz, governed by a succession of conservative Maderistas, produced or attracted a series of plots and rebellions. Perhaps the closest to a typical situation was that of San Luis where, by the latter part of 1912, the entire population (office-holders excepted) was 'indifferent [to] and suspicious' of the Madero regime; where the lower classes, once keen Maderistas, felt disappointed, 'alarmed and alienated' by the forced recruiting taking place; where the upper class, who had 'never adhered to the Madero government', objected to proposed tax reforms and sniped at the Cepeda administration, but confined their opposition to sullen, peaceful, political protest, eschewing armed revolt (they were not that sort of people), restrained by their 'fear of the lower classes', whose new temper and recent acquisition of arms made them a greater threat than in the past.[461] It does not seem likely, therefore, that conservative hostility to Madero derived primarily from Maderista reformism, actual or potential. That was a secondary consideration, and one that could not provoke serious conservative counter-revolution. In many respects the conservatives understood and sympathised with Madero's chief preoccupation (the restoration of peace) and they went along with many of his policies in this regard (it might be truer to say that he went along with theirs). While popular rebellion continued, order was the chief desideratum; until order was established, reforms – notably agrarian reform – had to be postponed;[462] on this fundamental syllogism conservatives and (civilian) Maderistas broadly agreed, and the bonds uniting them were thus stronger than the forces which divided. The radical implications of free elections (the old shibboleth of Maderismo) were now less evident than in the days of direct democracy in May 1911: two years of 'effective suffrage and no re-election' had not filled state-houses and legislatures with wild radicals; the new-found freedom of organised labour was closely circumscribed. Perhaps more worrying to conservatives than the regime's tepid reformism was the growth of a new, steelier Maderismo, epitomised by Gustavo Madero, which promised to root out recalcitrant opponents and 'govern with the Revolution'. But this had made little progress by the end of 1912, at which point its influence in government circles was arguably declining. Objectively, it did not seriously threaten conservative interests; but the conservatives themselves might have seen things differently. It was no mere coincidence that Gustavo Madero figured as the conservatives' *bête noire* of 1912 and sacrificial victim of 1913.

The main divergence between Madero and his conservative critics concerned persons and attitudes more than fundamental policies. On the practical issues of the day they could agree: Mexico needed a bigger army, intensive campaigns should be waged against rebels, bandits and agitators, the army should be deployed against land seizures and strikes which threatened public order. The liberal apostasy made such agreement possible. But the conservatives could not visualise Madero successfully carrying through such policies: they liked the music but loathed the conductor. Madero was not, in their eyes, the iron man who would save the country and them. Up to a point, they were right. Though Madero implemented repressive policies, he did so with a certain pained reluctance and, on occasions, he wavered in their implementation: he had been pushed into a military solution of Zapatismo when his own inclination had been to negotiate; he allowed liberal sentiment to influence his treatment of the press, and of revolutionary recidivists like Almazán. Above all, he was no *macho*. He was a small, quirky, provincial businessman who had never worn gold braid, and who had fulminated against militarism. To the elite of Mexico City, the cream of the old Porfiristas, he was a gauche *norteño*.[463] To generals like Huerta – however fast he promoted them, however generously he praised them and provided them with men, Mausers, and armoured cars – he was a meddlesome civilian, not one of their own. Hence their antipathy to Madero arose less from their fears of what he was doing, or would do, than from their conviction that they and their kind could do it better and faster. They had graduated in the school of Porfirian repression; they would not be inhibited by liberal scruples. Thus, although Madero undertook many of the repressive policies advocated by conservatives – and many, even in 1911–13, could be seen to fail – the myth of the iron hand daily acquired new adherents, since its failures could be put down to Madero's own deficiencies and incompetence. In a shameful spectacle, the new president negotiated with the 'imbecile bandit' Zapata, when 'the reward Zapata has earned with his ceaseless crimes is to be hung like a Bulgarian bandit, or shot like a dog' – this was the view of two irate Guanajuato landowners; and it was a view which filtered through to supposedly informed, international opinion, prompting the *New York Times* leader-writer, for example, to assert that Díaz would have suppressed Zapata 'in a fortnight', while Madero, by his weakness, had incurred a long and costly guerrilla war.[464] Madero's character thus served as a spurious alibi for the failure of repressive policies which the conservatives confidently advocated, which the regime more hesitantly applied, but which events were to reveal as fundamentally misconceived.

The key institution within the conservative, Porfirian camp was the Federal Army; and it was the generals who felt most keenly the ambivalence inherent in Maderista policy. Why should they perform the spadework of repression in the name of an effete, interfering, civilian regime with which they had little sympathy? It was not that they disliked the spadework, or feared that Madero's vague reformism would be translated into radical policy; rather, they felt that those who did the work should both call the tune and collect the spoils (local examples have been given).[465] A military take-over was necessary, many believed, less to forestall revolution than to carry through, with greater expedition, the counter-revolution which had begun in 1911, and which Madero had continued, albeit with certain misgivings. A coup would not wrench the government into drastic new forms, it would rationalise what was already happening, it would streamline (and somewhat militarise) the administration, it would create a happy symmetry between real (military) and formal (civilian) power in the country. This was an argument which appealed to simple, soldierly minds, uncluttered with political niceties (minds like Victoriano Huerta's); and it appealed particularly to generals who had witnessed a rapid growth in the size and importance of their army. In this respect, Madero's encouragement of military expansion – and thus military ambition – was suicidal as well as hypocritical. For the army alone could bring down the regime. Popular rebellions stopped at the city gates. The civilian, conservative constituency (landlords, businessmen, professionals, prelates) might carp at the administration, opposing it on the hustings, in the press, from the pulpit and in the legislatures; but such groups had neither the will nor the capacity to overthrow it. This, the Federal Army alone could do, as the events of 1912–13 revealed. The removal of Madero was attempted, by conservative conspiracy, in October 1912; the army stayed loyal and the plot failed. Four months later, the army took the lead, and the revolt was successful. These two, related episodes formed the last act of Madero's tragedy.

After sailing into exile, Porfirio Díaz made it clear he did not intend returning to Mexico, or getting involved in Mexican politics, and he appears to have stuck by this resolution.[466] His son, Porfirito, similarly abstained from politics. The Porfirian mantle was therefore inherited by the dictator's nephew, Félix Díaz, son of Félix ('Chato') Díaz, whom the Juchitecos had done to death 'in the burning sand dunes of Chacalapa' in 1871.[467] Then, Félix Díaz *hijo* was still a toddler; forty years later, when his uncle fell from power, he was a dapper brigadier, Federal deputy for Oaxaca, and recently chief of police in the capital. Díaz was not tarred with the Científico brush; he was a political *compadre* of Governor Teodoro Dehesa of Veracruz, and thus stood within that stream of Porfirian conservatism which, particularly in the army, was critical of Limantour and sympathetic to Reyes. The revolution did not bring political extinction: Díaz was offered – but declined – the honourable but remote office of Governor of Baja California (Norte); he contested the Oaxaca governorship, losing to Benito Juárez Maza in September 1911; and he remained a serving officer until August of the following year.[468] He made no secret of his dislike of the Madero regime. Democracy was fine, he thought, but ambitious agitators took advantage of it, inciting the people, incurring the risk of 'outright anarchy'; the anti-Madero revolts, though reprehensible, were only to be expected, since the 1910 revolution 'had served only the personal, self-centred aggrandisement of one family [the Maderos] and their hangers-on, thus leaving unfulfilled all the many promises they had made'; Madero himself was a hapless, impractical dreamer. Díaz's own political nostrums were vague but characteristically conservative: to the people of Oaxaca he promised educational improvements and economic development, justice, the management of affairs by practical men, a repudiation of 'dreams and . . . Utopias', and, above all, 'order and peace'.[469]

From early on, Félix Díaz's name was associated with supposed plots and rebellions. At the time of Madero's inauguration there were rumours that Díaz would pronounce in Veracruz (the story proved accurate, though highly premature); in the late summer of 1912 the rumours flew again, associating him with revolts in Veracruz and Oaxaca, the two states where he might be expected to gather most support.[470] Veracruz was then agitated by a disputed gubernatorial election (the result had been kept under wraps for weeks); in Oaxaca, the *serrano* caciques Meixueiro and Hernández were known sympathisers of Díaz and the Porfirian cause. Federal generals, similarly sympathetic, also came under suspicion and one old veteran, Higinio Aguilar, rose in revolt in Puebla in September.[471] Félix Díaz's own expected pronouncement came in mid-October at the port of Veracruz: the garrison (of 1,000 men) went over to him without fighting, the city officials remained in office, and the Federal commander at Orizaba, Colonel Díaz Ordaz, marched down to the coast with 200 men to join the rebellion.[472] There were ripples of revolt elsewhere along the Gulf: Guillermo Pous, a failed candidate in the recent Veracruz gubernatorial election, led a revolt at Tlacolalpán; rebels, styling themselves Felicistas, raided in the Zongólica district; Colonel Ortega y Rivera captained a band of ex-Federals in the canton of Ozuluama, a known trouble spot, and a supposed fief of Díaz's old crony, Dehesa.[473] Although the Felicista movement was not, therefore, confined to the port of Veracruz alone, it made little impact outside the immediate hinterland: rumours of revolt at Guadalajara, Pachuca, Tampico and elsewhere proved unfounded.[474]

Once in control of Veracruz, Díaz issued the customary manifesto: he berated the cruelty, corruption and ineptitude of Madero and his '*numerosísma familia*'; he promised peace with justice through the medium of fair elections; and he stressed two basic themes – the re-establishment of peace and the restoration of the honour of the army (though quite what the latter implied, apart from a bid for Federal support, it is not clear).[475] In contrast to Orozco's Plan, there were no social or economic provisions and even the political commitments were vague – a good deal vaguer than those of Madero's Plan of San Luis. The day when all plans (including those of conservative authorship) would pay deference to agrarian and labour reform had not yet arrived – though it was not so far off. Félix Díaz's *pronunciamiento* – in style, pomposity, and even location – was in the old, nineteenth-century tradition of Santa Anna.

Meanwhile, if military support was lacking there was a broadly favourable response to the revolt among the upper and middle classes throughout Mexico. Since the failure of Reyes there had been a dearth of strong men and iron hands; now a new candidate had appeared, and one bearing the correct surname. Mexico City, conservative and Porfirian to the core, remained quiet, but there was no concealing the sympathy for Díaz and the 'talk of many other *pronunciamientos*' which it encouraged. At Durango, the news of the coup was 'received with great rejoicing', chiefly among the 'better classes', who now eagerly awaited news of the fall of Madero; at Torreón, Federal officers toasted Díaz and, throughout the army, *'felices días'* became a popular greeting; at Saltillo in the north and Salina Cruz in the south, sentiment – especially that of the army – was with Díaz (though no doubt opinion differed a few miles away at Juchitán).[476] Up the coast from Veracruz itself, the port of Tampico 'apparently pleasantly anticipates capture by [a] gunboat which is expected from Veracruz' (Tampico was disappointed, since the gunboats remained loyal); while in Oaxaca, the most thoroughly Porfirista of cities, the conservative press welcomed the news, army officers wore pictures of Díaz in their lapels, and Díaz's supporters planned a demonstration against the government – but were prevented. It was feared that the state governor, Bolaños Cacho, was in league with the high-ranking officers who favoured Díaz, and there were similar doubts about the governors of Yucatán and Campeche.[477]

There were exceptions to this generally favourable reaction on the part of the 'better elements'. Catholic Guadalajara was unmoved by the coup (geographical and ideological distance both, no doubt, played their part); while at Monterrey, 'the most common expression concerning the situation of the Mexican businessmen [here] is "we care not who occupies the presidential chair, if we can only have peace and business and prosperity"', which, it was felt, the Díaz rebellion was unlikely to bring.[478] But the crucial fact, throughout the country, was that the army declined to act, notwithstanding its Felicista sympathies; indeed, at Oaxaca it was the commanding general who banned the proposed Felicista demonstration. Here and there a few suspect officers were arrested and – it was generally believed – Madero dug deep into government coffers to secure the loyalty of other waverers.[479] And if the army would not act, the conservative civilians would not and could not go it alone. *Attentisme* became the order of the day. All eyes were focussed on Veracruz: had Díaz pulled off some bold stroke the army might have departed from its position of political non-involvement; but, as it was, his torpid inactivity reinforced his supporters' caution. He held Veracruz, but the naval gunboats in the harbour stayed loyal; and troops under General Joaquín Beltrán were ordered down from Orizaba to invest the port. For five days a stalemate ensued. Beltrán hesitated to attack, waiting at La Tejería: if he, too, was a prey to the prevailing *attentisme*, he at least had the excuse of digging in and desiring to avoid a bombardment of the port, with possible diplomatic consequences.[480] Indeed, with elements of the 21st Regiment in both camps, and with Beltrán being Díaz's godfather, the outcome of any engagement was unpredictable.

Meanwhile, in the port itself – from which the townspeople could see the Federals massing in the hills – fresh food ran out and eggs reached 15c. apiece; Díaz spent his time writing fond letters to Beltrán, appealing to him to join the revolt 'for the good of the homeland'; he did not, it seems, spend much time preparing the defences of the port which, both Beltrán and the German Military Attaché noted, were inept.[481] Since Díaz's immobility convinced waverers that now was not the time to rise up, the continued delay served the government rather than the rebel interest. Finally, early on the morning of 23 October, Beltrán mounted an attack through the undefended railway yards. Stories of treachery soon became current: that the Federals advanced under cover of a white flag; that Beltrán reached a deal with Díaz, agreeing to join the rebellion for a fee of 200,000 pesos, and then double-crossed him. Though plausible, such explanations are not necessary to account for the fall of the city. The defenders were easily rolled back and by mid-morning the Federals controlled the port. Total casualties were some fifty dead and wounded, most on the rebel side. Díaz himself was captured; Colonel Díaz Ordaz fought his way out to the south and remained in arms against the government; the bulk of the rebel forces, however, readily surrendered in the hope of rejoining the army. Meanwhile, the customs house reopened, and the business life of the port resumed; the dockers' union collaborated with the White Cross in tending the wounded; and on the streets government orators lauded Madero and the gallant Federal Army.

In the provinces the summary collapse of the Felicista revolt produced disappointment, just as its inception had generated hope. The news was 'received with anything but joy' at Durango; there was disappointment in Veracruz itself; at Saltillo people were 'stunned at the unwontedly quick action of the government in suppressing the Díaz movement' – it seemed as if Díaz and Madero had got their roles reversed.[482] No doubt, too, the implicit contrast was with the Orozquista, Zapatista and other revolts which had dragged on, defying the swift suppression which had been inflicted on the Felicistas. But, in this case, observers failed to compare like with like. Popular, rural revolts might avoid the cities, but, like old buried tree roots, they were notoriously hard to unearth and eliminate; urban insurrections of the kind attempted by Díaz in 1912 (or Aquiles Serdán in 1910) could be lopped off like the upper branches, so long as the army remained loyal and the rebel commander did not push out into a friendly countryside (which Díaz, of course, had not done).[483]

His failure by no means punctured the myth of the iron hand, which still remained powerful. But it impaired his personal prestige (while it did not terminate his political career) and ensured that he no longer topped the list of potential saviours of the country. And, if his supporters were disappointed in

October 1912, their reaction was mixed, complex, and indicative of the conservative mentality of the time. They would have liked a swift, surgical coup, to rid the country of the inept Madero and to install a second Díaz in the presidency; but when this palpably failed they – being men of property and substance – were relieved that the revolt had not led to another prolonged, cancerous guerrilla war: 'in a sense the public is glad that the revolution has failed. To be more correct, the public is glad that the revolution failed so quickly if it could not succeed. There is a general feeling of regret that it did not succeed as quickly as it failed.'[484] In other words, short of a total, sudden victory, the next best thing Félix Díaz could achieve was a total, sudden defeat. In this respect, at least, he did not entirely let his supporters down. And there was a moral to the story conservatives would have done well to ponder. Their reaction to Díaz's debacle was quite logical: the quick, painless establishment of a neo-Porfirian regime was certainly preferable to Madero's continuance in office; but, even more certainly, Madero's continuance in office was preferable to a runaway civil war, which would greatly augment the threats to property, status, and power. Any attempt to establish – by violence – such a neo-Porfirian regime was therefore a gamble, in which the potential gains (the elimination of Maderismo) had to be set against the potential losses – which, in the event of renewed civil war and popular revolution, could prove incalculable. In betting terms, the conservatives were laying the odds: incurring a heavy risk for a more modest gain. Such a gamble was rational only if the military could oust Madero, and oust him quickly, neatly, and without spurring serious, popular resistance. It demanded unshakeable confidence in the capacity of the iron hand. But this the conservatives seemed to possess.

After their capture, Díaz and his chief lieutenants were court-martialled at Veracruz, many of them (Díaz included) receiving death sentences. There were protests in Mexico City; a deputation of 'leading ladies' of the capital begged Madero to show clemency; Díaz's lawyers appealed to the Supreme Court for a stay of execution on the grounds that he had resigned his commission and therefore was not subject to a court-martial.[485] The matter became a test case of the struggle between Maderista hawks and doves. The hawks – like Madero's private secretary Elías de los Ríos – regretted that 'the sword of law does not fall at once on the guilty with all its rigour'; one favoured faking a cut in telegraph communications (easily attributable to the Zapatistas) which would prevent the Supreme Court stopping the execution.[486] But Madero would countenance no departure from legality. Execution was stayed, the appeal was considered, and late in January 1913, Díaz was brought under guard to the Federal District penitentiary in Mexico City. This, as it turned out, was what Díaz's supporters (who were already at work on another, more elaborate plot) had hoped.[487]

The defeat of Félix Díaz was a fillip for the hard-pressed administration. On hearing of the revolt, Madero was said to have welcomed it as a means of finally extinguishing Porfirismo; and after its collapse, the President – and several of his colleagues – radiated confidence, predicting peace and progress from now on.[488] Old Porfiristas, like Enrique Creel, agreed that the regime was now more secure: 'it is now thought that nothing will interrupt the progress of Sr Madero's administration, and that he will finish his [presidential] term without new revolutions'.[489] Those who remained loyal in the face of temptation (like the Veracruz naval commander, Captain Manuel Azueta) received commendation; while tough-minded Maderistas took pains to find out which office-holders had wavered in the days of crisis.[490] But, though the administration's confidence revived, talk of further troubles and conspiracies continued. There were persistent rumours of another coup in Veracruz, scheduled for early 1913, and involving 'very wealthy persons [who] . . . are spending a great deal of money to further their plans'.[491] In addition, a favourite old rumour resurfaced, suggesting that certain northern state governors were concerting to overthrow the regime. There had been similar talk at the end of the summer of 1912, implicating Venustiano Carranza; now, both the rumours and the circumstantial evidence were more substantial.[492]

Carranza had never been a devout Maderista: originally a partisan of Reyes, he had served as a senator and provisional state governor of Coahuila under Díaz, flirting with the opposition in 1909 when the 'centre' opposed his gubernatorial candidacy.[493] When the Madero revolution began Carranza remained inactive, displaying a 'very circumspect' attitude, ignoring Madero's letters, which urged fuller commitment.[494] In January 1911, having incurred the suspicion of the authorities, Carranza crossed to the US: the Porfirian regime (and quite possibly Madero too) remained unsure of his exact motives and loyalties.[495] When Madero crossed to join the revolution, Carranza stayed in San Antonio, holding fund-raising meetings and – it was said – keeping in touch with his old mentor Bernardo Reyes.[496] In May, with the revolution triumphant, he arrived at Cd Juárez for the peace negotiations, where he allegedly argued for tougher terms, and briefly served as War Minister in Madero's temporary 'cabinet'.[497] Disappointed at not receiving the Gobernación portfolio (so one account went), Carranza consoled himself by becoming Governor of Coahuila, thereby satisfying an ancient ambition.[498]

Though political allies and fellow-Coahuilans, Carranza and Madero were never close.[499] And as governor and president respectively, they continued to have their difficulties, which centred upon the volunteer troops raised in Coahuila to resist the Orozquistas. Madero believed that these should be under Federal control, even officered by Federal appointees; Carranza argued the utility of local forces, commanded by an ex-revolutionary or 'someone of prestige' in the locality.[500] A compromise was reached, but by September 1912 the same 'irritating difficulty' (Madero's phrase) cropped up again, as Carranza and local Federal commanders feuded: orders and counter-orders flew, some Coahuilan irregulars virtually mutinied, and in one incident shots

were fired and a man was killed. Meanwhile, as the Federation continued to
foot the bill for Carranza's state troops, there were rumours that the payroll was
padded with the names of dead soldiers.[501] In December 1912 Carranza
visited Mexico City in search of a settlement, but he returned to Coahuila at
the end of the month without satisfaction. Though the governor was permitted to retain a small force under Francisco Coss in Coahuila, the bulk of the
state troops, led by Pablo González and paid by the central government, would
operate – under Federal direction – in Chihuahua and Durango. By the end of
January 1913, Carranza's local army had thus been slimmed or dissipated.[502]

It was in the wake of this decision that Carranza convened a meeting of
northern governors – under the guise of a hunting party – on his estate at
Ciénega del Toro.[503] Cepeda of San Luis attended in person, González
(Chihuahua), Fuentes (Aguascalientes) and Maytorena (Sonora) sent representatives. The motives behind this meeting have been more discussed than
clarified. What is clear is that all five governors were facing acute problems
(some of a common character), and that they shared certain 'hawkish'
attitudes. Several were at loggerheads with the 'centre': Carranza and Maytorena over the question of state troops; González over his brusque treatment of
the Chihuahuan elite; Cepeda over the vexed politics of the Huasteca. In each
case, they felt that Madero was meddling, naively and dangerously, in state
matters. Like many Maderista governors, all five faced conservative opposition
within their states, Fuentes and González being most afflicted: both had
pioneered land-tax regulations which offended local landlords. In the light of
these circumstances all five may be seen as 'radical' Maderistas – not so much in
terms of thorough, reformist measures (though this was true of Fuentes,
González, and perhaps Cepeda),[504] but rather of their espousal of a hardheaded
realpolitik. Carranza and Maytorena wanted to maintain their state forces under
arms; González and Cepeda favoured a hard line against rebels and malcontents
in their respective states; all took exception to Madero's excessive faith in
conciliation. They therefore represented at provincial level the hawkish
Maderismo of which Gustavo Madero was the chief national exponent.

This community of interest helps explain why the Ciénega del Toro meeting
took place but it does not establish the precise plans which were discussed.
Critics of Carranza and his allies argue that they were feeling their way towards
rebellion (hence Carranza's concern to maintain the Coahuilan forces under his
own personal control). But this case (much of it based on the conservative press
of 1913–14) is overdone: the available evidence does not warrant – though,
equally, it by no means excludes – the conclusion that Carranza was on the
point of rebelling against Madero early in 1913.[505] Defenders of Carranza –
much more numerous – argue that the meeting was designed to stiffen
Maderista resolve in the face of conservative threats (like the Díaz revolt, just
stifled); Carranza's dogged retention of the Coahuilan irregulars showed his
shrewd concern for revolutionary self-defence.[506] Here, as in the critical view,

there is a kernel of truth. As a Maderista hawk, Carranza believed that Madero was too soft and conciliatory; he felt happier with a loyal, local army at his back. There is no justification either for positing an imminent anti-Madero revolt, or for investing Carranza with superlative virtues: Cato's fortitude, Cicero's public spirit, and Cassandra's prescience. Hagiographers who depict Carranza as the guardian of 'the Revolution', combating both Porfirian reaction and Maderista naiveté, err in several respects: they neglect Carranza's own Porfirista and Reyista connections; they accept too readily his supposed opposition to the Juárez Treaty and his alleged revolutionary intransigence; they infer that both his maintenance of irregular forces and his participation at Ciénega del Toro responded to high-minded 'revolutionary' concerns, rather than to more immediate considerations of political advantage.[507] Above all, they (usually tacitly) assume a clear 'revolutionary' interest, which could be discerned and furthered by exceptional citizens like Carranza. There was no such interest: the Revolution one and indivisible was the creation of later politicians and polemicists. At the time, several revolutionary interests were in conflict: what was good for one (say, Madero's) was not necessarily good for another (say, Zapata's); Carranza, at best, defended the sectional interests of Maderista *políticos* who, after two years' enjoyment of power, felt themselves threatened by conservative opposition, abetted by Madero's own complaisance. There are no grounds for extracting and reifying this particular sectional interest as that of *the* Revolution: to do so is to produce an Hegelian caricature of history.

It is easy to see why Carranza's politics have – with the aid of hindsight – received privileged treatment. Whatever his motives, the Governor of Coahuila was to play a crucial role in the years to come. In the immediate context of 1912–13, his activities added to the prevailing political uncertainty and speculation.[508] More important, even if they did not presage an anti-Madero rebellion, they afforded him a measure of politico-military independence which was denied most state governors. Like Maytorena, he had retained – largely at Federal expense – a force of loyal troops who, even when hived off to Federal command, stayed loyal to their local *patrón*. He was not mortgaged to the Federal Army. In addition, he had established a loose alliance with like-thinking governors, the provincial Maderista hawks. Carranza thus enjoyed options which most state governors lacked, and which enabled him to play a prominent role in 1913: his jealously husbanded irregulars, united with Maytorena's, would form the nucleus of the Constitutionalist Army and carry him to the presidency. If, therefore, they had been cast as the agents of Madero's overthrow, as some have alleged, they were ultimately to serve as his posthumous avengers.

At the time, however, fears of a Carrancista revolt – though not discounted – were subsumed into a more general, pervasive belief that, soon, something would happen to end the uncertainty, topple Madero, and inaugurate a new regime. Here, practical plans for subversion blended with vague hopes of counter-revolution. In Sinaloa, an observer noted 'rumors of impending revolutionary outbreaks which do not materialise, and a general feeling of expectation'; at Saltillo, where political pessimism ruled and the press harped on the theme of intrigue in high places, the messianic belief in the iron hand revived – the belief 'that at a critical and psychological moment a leader will arise and overthrow the present administration'.[509] Such hopes were not misplaced: for, even then, an 'army intrigue of gigantic proportions' was being concocted in Mexico City.[510] This plot was four months gestating: its conception lay back in October 1912, even before Félix Díaz's abortive *pronunciamiento*, and its preparation spanned almost all that conspiratorial winter. Inevitably, rumours and warnings leaked out, but Madero consistently discounted them.[511] The alleged 'soul of the conspiracy' was General Manuel Mondragón, a Felicista, career soldier, and profiteer, who was joined by Cecilio Ocón, a prominent Mexico City businessman, and General Gregorio Ruiz, an old, corpulent veteran of the French Intervention.[512] From the start, the plan they hatched involved a coup in the capital, which had so far escaped its revolutionary baptism by fire; and from October they signed up recruits – supporters of Félix Díaz, disappointed by the Veracruz fiasco, Reyistas (including Reyes' son, Rodolfo, a Federal deputy), and disaffected members of the military. They faced a problem in that the two main figureheads of the conservative opposition were now in gaol: Reyes in the military prison of Santiago Tlatelolco, Díaz (after January 1913) in the Federal District penitentiary.[513] But it was not difficult for the plotters to gain access to the prisoners (Mexican gaols, though harsh enough for the *pelados* who were their main customers, usually provided a genial service for wealthier, prestigious inmates – as even some revolutionaries found); thus Reyes and Díaz were able to participate in both the early planning – and later the execution – of the coup.

Of the many overtures Ocón and Mondragón made to potential recruits, perhaps the most important was that directed to General Victoriano Huerta, made at the recommendation of Huerta's old *patrón*, Reyes.[514] Huerta, convalescing after eye surgery, was told of the plot; but, to the surprise of the plotters, he declined to join them. Equally, he made no attempt to denounce them. Huerta's refusal, as his biographer points out, conflicts with the common assertion that Huerta was a committed party well before the outbreak of the revolt; but, as he also indicates, it did not derive from any new-found affection for Madero. Rather, after his successes and promotion during the northern campaign, Huerta was reluctant to play a subordinate role in any conspiracy. He was not averse to overthrowing Madero, but he preferred that it should be accomplished with Victoriano Huerta giving – or at least jointly giving – the orders; and, at present, Huerta could not compete with the Reyes/Díaz duumvirate. As the plotters proceeded, therefore, Huerta bided his time, and he was still on the side-lines when – after various hitches and postponements – the revolt broke out in Mexico City in the early hours of 9 February 1913.[515]

The plan was for a classic urban coup and seizure of government. It would follow Malaparte's model and accomplish what Madero had hoped – but failed – to achieve in November 1910; and, this time, the rebels had the inestimable advantage of regular army support. Nevertheless, Mondragón's plans misfired: not, as it turned out, disastrously for the plotters, but badly enough to turn Mexico City into a battle-ground for the next ten days. Hence this critical period acquired its familiar title: La Decena Trágica. The Tragic Ten Days began when Mondragón raised some 700 troops in revolt and proceeded first to free Reyes from the Military Prison (dawn had not yet risen over the sleeping city, but Reyes was dressed and ready to go), then to liberate Díaz from the Penitentiary (Díaz, uncertain of the precise schedule was caught shaving: smart *señorito* that he was, he completed his toilet before joining the rebellion).[516] Meanwhile, another detachment, mostly cadets, was sent to occupy the National Palace, the seat of presidential government (though not the residence of the head of state: this was Chapultepec Castle, where Madero first received news of the events taking place downtown). It was assumed that the cadets had completed their mission.

At 7 a.m., therefore, the main body of the rebels, led by Reyes and Díaz, approached the National Palace where 'the gates were to be swung wide for them and General Reyes was to be shown at once to the presidential quarter', from which he would address the nation, denouncing Madero and declaring himself provisional president.[517] Fat General Ruiz was sent ahead to investigate and disappeared into a door of the Palace. Reassured, Reyes advanced across the Zócalo. As he approached the Palace, a demand for his surrender rang out and, almost at once, a fusillade hit the advancing column. For some ten minutes the Zócalo became a battle-field: Reyes was shot dead along with 400 others, many of them civilian bystanders. In a quandary, Díaz collected his mauled troops and retreated westwards, easily capturing and establishing his headquarters in the Ciudadela, the old city arsenal about a mile and a half from the Palace.[518] The cause of this – for the rebels – disastrous turn of events soon became clear. The Tlalpán cadets, numbering some 200, had indeed taken the National Palace according to plan, capturing Gustavo Madero and the Minister of War, García Peña; but loyalist forces under General Lauro Villar, swift to react to the situation, had recovered the building, liberated the prisoners, and in turn arrested their captors. Hence as Reyes and Díaz advanced from the north, Villar had prepared the Palace's defences, placing riflemen on the roof, mortars and machine-guns in the gateways; and he had personally welcomed General Ruiz with drawn pistol when the old man marched unsuspectingly through the door.

Meanwhile, at Chapultepec, Madero was told the news and, with a small escort, he rode on horseback down Reforma, pressed about by cheering spectators.[519] Even this short trip did not lack incident. As Madero approached the Zócalo – with the sounds of battle echoing down Avenida Juárez – a policeman standing close by was hit by a bullet, and the presidential party stepped inside the Daguerre Photo shop, to take cover while the main battle resolved itself. And – less dramatic but more significant – close by the Alameda, General Victoriano Huerta met the party and, offering his services to the threatened administration, took his place alongside the president. It is not known whether Huerta's appearance was premeditated or coincidental.[520] Once the rebels had retired to the west, Madero proceeded across the square, now strewn with the corpses of men and horses, and into the National Palace (still accompanied by Huerta). Inside, it became clear that the initial government victory had not been cheap. In particular, General Villar, commander of the loyalist forces in the city, had been seriously wounded and a successor had to be found. Competent, trustworthy and accessible generals were in short supply; so, on the advice of War Minister García Peña (who for the second time favoured his old protégé) Huerta was given this crucial command.[521]

Díaz and Madero, rebel and president, faced each other across downtown Mexico City. The rebels, numbering some 1,500, dug in, occupied buildings, and placed artillery in the deserted streets around the Ciudadela. For a couple of days a fragile peace ensued. Both sides had hopes of reinforcements: Díaz anticipated help from General Blanquet, commanding at Toluca; Madero, summoning troops from the provinces, slipped out to Cuernavaca (a bold move, with Zapata still active) and conferred with General Angeles. Together, they returned to the capital with over a thousand men, adding to the detachments of *rurales* which had come from the north.[522] In the National Palace, meanwhile, General Ruiz was summarily executed, along with fifteen cadets: whatever the source of this contentious order, it was Huerta who carried it out (perhaps as an earnest of his loyalty to the government), and, Meyer notes, it marked the start of a new brutality in the treatment of respectable prisoners (the less respectable had never enjoyed much clemency).[523] On the morning of 11 February, government forces opened the attack on the Ciudadela with a massive artillery barrage (to which the rebels replied in kind) followed by waves of infantry; there were over 500 casualties, including many civilians. This set the pattern for the following four days. In successive attacks government troops dislodged the rebels from strategic buildings – the 6th precinct police station, the church of Campo Florido, the YMCA – but the Ciudadela itself remained apparently impregnable.

For the citizens of Mexico City, hitherto an island of peace and civilisation in a sea of civil war, this was a novel, frightening experience. So far, the capital had been spared the afflictions of the provinces: it had lived the good life, even managing to ignore the Zapatistas close by in the mountains.[524] The Decena

Trágica changed all that. Shells were lobbed across the city centre, machine-gun fire raked chic residential and commercial streets. The lamp-posts leaned, and festoons of telegraph wire draped themselves across deserted plazas. Rubble and corpses strewed the streets, and between them dodged 'Buen Tono' vans, commandeered from the cigarette company, acting as makeshift ambulances. Initially, crowds of people had witnessed the battle in the Zócalo, and the president's procession down from Chapultepec; pro-government mobs (Gustavo Madero's *Porra?*) had tried to sack the premises of four anti-Madero newspapers. But, as civilian casualties rose, prudent citizens kept off the streets, save during lulls in the fighting when they could be seen, filing out of the belligerent zones, carrying mattresses on their backs. Stray shells and grenades were not the only problem. Fresh food became scarce, prices shot up, and some people – it was later said – dined on dog or cat. The provisioning of the troops also presented problems, which private charity had to help solve; yet, throughout, the embattled rebels in the Ciudadela did not want for beer, nor their officers for champagne – an illustration of the good contacts they enjoyed in the city. The corpses which accumulated in the streets, menacing public health, were carted out to the plains of Balbuena and incinerated; some, however, were soused in petrol and burnt where they lay, their twitching limbs and noxious smell creating an indelible impression on observers.[525] And if this were not enough, a rebel shell breached the wall of Belem prison and, 'in a mad scramble', prisoners fled, were shot, were recaptured, or managed to escape, to join either the rebels, or the parties of looters who took advantage of the chaos. Finally, to the fear of the mob (which foreign diplomats felt most acutely) was added fear of Zapatista incursions: rumours flew round that the hordes of Morelos had taken Tacubaya, or that Genovevo de la O had been seen, severed heads swinging from his saddle-bow, as he rode up from San Angel into the city.[526]

Had the Decena Trágica been resolved purely militarily, the government must surely have won. Loyalist forces outnumbered the rebels; the Cuidadela – no longer the fortress it once was – could have been effectively blockaded and/or reduced by artillery.[527] Madero's optimism never deserted him: had not General Sóstenes Rocha, back in 1871, reduced a rebellious – and, as it happened, a Porfirista – garrison there, in a matter of hours, to the advantage of Madero's liberal predecessor Juárez? But, behind the scenes, forces were working for a non-military solution. The Federal Army did not fancy tearing itself apart in a protracted struggle. Within two days of his appointment by Madero, Huerta was in touch with rebel spokesmen, discussing a possible deal; as yet, however, Huerta was not satisfied with the prospective pickings, and so he prevaricated. It was in his interest, meanwhile, to spin out the conflict: General Blanquet, arriving at the city outskirts with reinforcements, was ordered to wait; the Felicistas were allowed to replenish their supplies (hence the champagne and beer); the artillery commander shelling the

Ciudadela took pains not to breach the vulnerable walls. And, most cynically of all, Huerta ordered loyalist *rurales* into suicidal assaults down Calle Balderas, which was commanded by rebel machine-guns.[528]

Political and diplomatic moves were also afoot. Now, the American Ambassador, Henry Lane Wilson came to play a prominent part. Wilson ranks high in the demonology of the Revolution: in the post-revolutionary murals he figures along with the greenly syphilitic Cortés and the squinting, bespectacled Huerta, among the leading villains of Mexican history. And it is not difficult to see why. From the strictly historical point of view, Wilson's role is of interest in that it marks one of three unequivocal cases of direct American interference in the course of the Revolution.[529] By and large, this influence (as compared with the more general, pervasive influence associated with American investment, immigration, or cultural penetration) has been exaggerated: America's capacity to shape events south of the Río Grande, whether by political machinations or outright military intervention, was extremely limited. But Ambassador Wilson, playing something of a freelance role, was an exception which deserves some attention.

Wilson had taken up his post in Mexico in 1910, after service in Chile and Belgium.[530] He was a short, stooping man, whose eyes peered out from beneath bushy brows, and whose taste for hard liquor was well-known. Wilson's attitude to Madero was not (as some have suggested) hostile *ab initio*.[531] In fact, he was 'greatly pleased' with the composition of the original Madero cabinet, and he predicted, with both gratification and foresight, that, as president, Madero would be 'compelled by the force of circumstances to more and more revert to the system implanted by General Díaz'.[532] But in the course of 1912 Wilson grew disillusioned and his reports became increasingly critical, inaccurate, and derivative of the *Mexican Herald*, Mexico City's English language newspaper, which was strongly anti-Madero. By January 1913, when the Ambassador was filing, almost verbatim, lurid press stories as 'plain narratives of fact', even the State Department woke up to the fact, but their mild rebuke brought a fierce ambassadorial reaction.[533] By now, Wilson's reports combined extreme pessimism with strong personal criticism of Madero.[534] And, with the rebellion in Mexico City, Wilson cast himself (and, it seems, was cast by others) as a leading actor in the drama. On the day of the coup a Felicista spokesman visited the Ambassador, urging him to press for Madero's resignation in order to avoid bloodshed; gripped by the image of the peacemaker, Wilson cabled Washington and requested either that 'firm, drastic and perhaps menacing' instructions be issued to the Mexican leaders (on both sides) or that he be given discretionary powers to negotiate a peace settlement between them.[535] The justification for such interference was the threat to foreign lives and property, as well as general considerations of humanity. In this regard, Wilson could claim a neutral stance. But the 'information' contained in his reports on the Decena Trágica revealed, from the outset, a clear sympathy for the rebels.[536]

Taft and the State Department, resolutely opposed to physical intervention in Mexico, had no desire to risk such threats and bluff, even if they, too, were seduced by the name of Díaz and the prospect of a neo-Porfirian peace which it conjured up; Porfirista sentiment in the US administration was not therefore translated into American support for the Porfirista cause.[537] In Washington, on this occasion, the Big Stick had been put aside. But the rarefied air of Mexico City did not induce diplomatic docility: like his British counterpart, Sir Lionel Carden, in 1913–14, Wilson chose to disregard metropolitan restraint and go it alone. Rounding up the British, Spanish and German Ministers (as Ambassador, Wilson was doyen of the Diplomatic Corps) he first led deputations to Madero and Díaz, protesting against the continued hostilities and threatening American intervention; then, in the small hours of 15 February he convened the same three diplomats and, 'nervous, pale and with exotic gestures told [them] for the hundredth time that Madero was crazy, a fool, a lunatic, who could and should be declared incompetent to sit in the [presidential] office'.[538] Having discussed the matter till 3 a.m., the diplomats agreed that the Spanish Minister should convey this unpalatable message (suitably dressed up as 'an appeal to the President's feeling of patriotism') to the Madero himself. The Minister – a veteran of the Peking siege, and a figure curiously Quixotic in appearance, with greying beard, bald head, and sunken, lugubrious eyes – set off to inform Madero that his resignation 'would simplify the situation and lead the way to peace': this, Wilson later maintained, was no unwarranted interference in Mexican domestic affairs, but a humanitarian measure, designed to speed an inevitable outcome.[539] Madero did not see it that way, was understandably indignant and cabled Taft, protesting at the threat of American intervention; Taft, in turn, was understandably perplexed, and replied that no such intervention was considered.[540] One effect of this interchange, however, was an 'intervention scare' (the first of several), which radiated out from Mexico City into the provinces, producing a spate of anti-American press reports and political declarations. Not much came of this: Americans were not molested, and the scare soon passed. Like other groups which later attempted the same ploy, the Maderistas found that nationalist agitation, which they hoped would underwrite their shaky position, paid poor dividends.[541]

Meanwhile, Mexican *políticos* were getting in on the act. The Foreign Minister, Pedro Lascuraín, called on Ambassador Wilson 'profoundly impressed with . . . the threatening attitude of [the US] government and intimated in confidence that he thought the President ought to resign'.[542] Lascuraín, a conservative lawyer with no Maderista convictions, convened a delegation of Senators, who followed the Spanish Minister to the Palace, bearing a similar message which called for Madero's resignation; other

Senators visited Huerta and General Blanquet, newly arrived with reinforcements on the outskirts of the city.[543] These overtures had no effect on Madero (though he was persuaded to declare a twenty-four-hour armistice) but they helped Huerta make up his mind. For, by the evening of 16 February, Meyer believes, Huerta had decided to throw in his lot with the rebels, and he sent Ambassador Wilson a message to this effect, promising the removal of Madero 'at any moment'. But Huerta was in a delicate position, plotting a coup at Madero's right hand, while waging a phony – but bloody – war against his fellow-plotters; and, but for Madero's trustfulness, all might have been lost. When, for example, Madero learned that supplies were being allowed into the Ciudadela, Huerta ingeniously argued that this served to concentrate the rebels ready for the *coup de grâce*; and when reports came in of Huerta's dealings with Félix Díaz, Madero brushed them aside. Not all the administration were so trusting. Gustavo Madero, true to character, repeatedly urged his brother to sack Huerta. Finally, on the evening of 17 February, Gustavo arrested Huerta at pistol-point. But the president, having questioned Huerta carefully and heard his protestations of loyalty, ordered his release, returned his gun, and upbraided Gustavo for his 'impulsive' action.[544] Huerta was free to spring the trap the next day.

The morning of the eighteenth was quieter; only sporadic volleys disturbed the city. Another party of Senators visited the Palace; after conferring with Huerta, they reiterated their request for Madero's resignation; and – in a scene of consummate black farce – the president refused, calling on Huerta to outline his forthcoming plan of attack, which would reassure the doubting Senators. Huerta, who counted on senatorial backing for his impending coup, was thus presented as the regime's gilt-edged asset. All, save Madero, must have gagged on the stench of treachery. And soon Madero's innocence, too, was at an end. Shortly before lunch (which Huerta was taking, with Gustavo Madero and others, at the fashionable Gambrinus Restaurant) a platoon of soldiers from Blanquet's 29th Battalion confronted Madero in a salon of the National Palace. As their commander announced that he was arresting Madero in the names of Generals Huerta and Blanquet, two presidential aides went for their guns, there was an exchange of fire, and men on both sides fell. Madero, 'brave to the point of temerity', urged the troops to cease firing and rushed from the room. But as he emerged onto the patio below he met Blanquet, pistol in hand, who demanded his surrender. Men of the 29th thronged the patio: there could be no resistance and no escape. Over at the Gambrinus, Huerta excused himself from the table and phoned the palace, confirming the success of the coup. Shortly after, troops came and arrested Gustavo Madero. By 2 p.m. the cathedral bells were ringing out the news that peace had been restored, and people were reemerging onto the streets. The Madero regime had ended, as Ambassador Wilson had already reported to Washington some two hours before the event.[545]

The regime had been *de facto* terminated; it remained to liquidate it *de jure* and establish its successor. But this presented major problems. Huerta and Díaz had been in touch during the Decena Trágica (notably through the mediation of Enrique Cepeda) but the terms of the deal they reached remain uncertain.[546] It seems probable, however, that the taste of success, and the promises of senatorial support, emboldened Huerta to overstep the original terms. His defection, after all, had been the crucial turning point; and, with Reyes out of the way, he could now claim a certain pre-eminence. Having communicated to the American government that, with the support of the army, he had overthrown Madero, and that 'from now on peace and prosperity will reign', he put out a broadsheet, later reproduced in the press, stating that he, Victoriano Huerta, had assumed the executive power.[547] This arrogation of authority threatened the accord with Díaz, who fancied his own presidential claims, and there were even fears that fighting might break out again. On the evening of that eventful day, therefore, Ambassador Wilson invited the two principals, Díaz and Huerta, to confer in the American Embassy. The chief point at issue was the provisional presidency: Díaz favoured a political light-weight, Luis Méndez, who would serve as a stopgap executive; Huerta favoured Huerta. Encouraged by Wilson, Díaz gave in and, by the terms of the 'Pact of the Embassy', Huerta assumed the provisional presidency. Agreement was also reached on the composition of the cabinet, and on the distribution of political prisoners, who became pieces in the Díaz–Huerta power struggle. Madero and Pino Suárez, the major pieces, Huerta jealously retained. Gustavo Madero and Adolfo Bassó, Superintendent of the National Palace, the minor pieces, were handed over to the Felicistas in the Ciudadela.[548] Thus Ambassador Wilson, having played his part in the downfall of the Madero regime, similarly helped to construct its successor.

With the new regime drawn up on paper, the old had to be eliminated, by force and fraud. Huerta's top priority was a written resignation from Madero and Pino Suárez, which would grant him the security of a 'legal' succession. Pressed by Congressmen and generals, president and vice-president finally agreed to submit resignations on certain conditions: that the political status quo in the states would be respected (a major condition); that Maderistas would not be persecuted under the new regime; that Madero, Pino Suárez and their families would be permitted to leave Mexico, with a diplomatic escort.[549] In theory, their resignations would remain in neutral hands until the prisoners had safely quit Mexican territory. In fact, once signed, they were promptly presented to the Chamber of Deputies and, after some discussion, overwhelmingly accepted. Why was this? Madero's enemies in Congress naturally did not put up a fight. Nor, however, did his supporters (save five, who bravely voted against acceptance). Resistance, they were later to argue, would only have jeopardised Madero's life. To Lascuraín, in fact, Huerta had supposedly sworn on his scapulary medallion that the prisoners would come to no harm; so Lascuraín played out his inglorious role, being sworn in as president at 10.24 p.m., appointing Huerta Minister of Gobernación, and resigning at 11.20. According to the terms of the Constitution, therefore, Huerta became president.[550] In the space of an hour, late on 19 February 1913, Mexico had three presidents; and, with the appointment of the third, the boyhood ambitions of the Indian from Ocotlán were finally realised.[551]

Constitutional niceties having been observed, the dissolution of the old regime could now proceed apace, and by other means. Indeed, it had already begun. Before going to sleep that night – in the company of Pino Suárez and the Cuban Minister, Manuel Márquez Sterling, guarantor of the prisoners' safety – Madero inquired after his brother Gustavo. He had asked before, and the answers had been evasive. In fact, Gustavo was already dead, having been delivered up to the carousing Felicistas in the Ciudadela where, on the night of 18 February, the mob had set upon him, gouged out his one good eye, beat, stabbed, and shot him to death. His fellow-prisoner, Bassó, was killed shortly after.[552] The character of the new regime was forming. When, next day, it was announced that the train scheduled to take Madero and his companions to Veracruz had been cancelled (on the grounds that a rescue might be attempted), suspicions grew; from the sanctuary of the Japanese Legation, Madero's family pleaded that the prisoners be spared; freemasons and diplomats interceded on their behalf with President Huerta. But, despite State Department instructions to warn against 'cruel treatment of the ex-president', Ambassador Wilson refused to convene the Diplomatic Corps in order to make representations to Huerta; Wilson was more concerned to secure international recognition for the regime which – to his unconcealed delight – he had helped establish.[553]

As for the new rulers' precise intentions, these remain obscure, and the subject of controversy.[554] But the chronology of events is clear enough. On the afternoon of 22 February, Huerta and his new cabinet attended a party at the American Embassy, commemorating Washington's birthday; here the British Chargé met the president and found him, 'true to his reputation, half-drunk'.[555] After sinking several brandies, Huerta left, with his cabinet. Later that evening, Madero and Pino Suárez were collected from the National Palace and driven in two hired cars to the Federal District penitentiary.[556] General Blanquet and Cecilio Ocón (one of the original conspirators) supervised the arrangements, and Major Francisco Cárdenas, one of those swaggering *rural* officers who captivated lady tourists, commanded the prisoners' escort.[557] They drove to the penitentiary and stopped by a side gate. The prison lights were doused. Cárdenas ordered Madero out and, with a parting insult, shot him in the back of the neck, with a .38. Pino Suárez received the same treatment. More rounds were pumped into the bodies and into the two cars, so that the government could announce that the prisoners had died when Maderistas sought to liberate them. It was a variation on the old *ley fuga*, and no-one believed it.[558]

The question of the ultimate responsibility for the murders – which came to assume great political significance – cannot be finally resolved (until, perhaps, Major Cárdenas' diary, lodged in the Guatemalan Foreign Ministry Archives, is opened to historians).[559] Beyond the immediate circle of assassins – Cárdenas, Blanquet, Ocón – the guilt of Díaz or Huerta is strongly implied by circumstantial evidence, though not absolutely certain.[560] It is perhaps not all that important. What is incontrovertible is that the repercussions of these murders echoed down the halls of revolutionary history. Madero's death erased the memory of his failings, and established him as the martyred Apostle of Democracy, in whose name multitudes could unite in a crusade of vengeance. The posthumous legend thus proved more potent as a symbol of revolution than the living president.[561] A day or two before his death, during the long and uncertain hours of custody, Pino Suárez had written to a friend: 'will they have the stupidity to kill us? You know, they would gain nothing, for we would be greater in death than we are today in life . . .'[562] Pino Suárez was right: in striving to quell the revolution and achieve peace, Huerta was dogged – like some Shakespearian usurper – by the bloody legacy of these murders.

Notes

1 Porfirian Mexico

1 Lauro Villar to León de la Barra, 23 Jan. 1912, ALB carpeta 3.
2 Henry Baerlein, *Mexico, The Land of Unrest* (London, 1914), p. 219; Tower to Grey, 31 Dec. 1910, FO 371/1149, 1574.
3 Salvador Novo, *Cocina Mexicana o historia gastronómica de la Ciudad de México* (Mexico, 1967), pp. 136–7.
4 Moisés González Navarro, *Historia moderna de México: El Porfiriato, la vida social* (Mexico, 1970), p. 396; Fernando Horcasitas, *De Porfirio Díaz a Zapata. Memoria Nahuatl de Milpa Alta* (Mexico, 1974), pp. 91–9; *El Correo de Chihuahua* (henceforth *El Correo*), 18, 20 Sept. 1910.
5 Luis González y González, *Pueblo en Vilo. Microhistoria de San José de Gracia* (Mexico, 1972), p. 114.
6 Cf. the bizarre typology in Samuel P. Huntington, *Political Order in Changing Societies* (New Haven and London, 1971), p. 272.
7 Vitold de Szyszlo, *Dix milles kilomètres à travers le Méxique* (Paris, 1913), p. 176.
8 Francisco López Cámara, *La estructura económica y social de México en la epoca de la reforma* (Mexico, 1967), p. 5.
9 Anselmo Marino Flores, 'Indian Population and Its Identification', in *Handbook of Middle American Indians*, VI (ed. Manning Nash, Austin, 1967), p. 13.
10 Moisés González Navarro, 'El mestizaje mexicano en el período nacional', *Revista Mexicana de Sociología*, XXX (1968), pp. 35–40.
11 Cf. Andrés Molina Enríquez, *Los grandes problemas nacionales* (Mexico, 1909), pp. 227–8; Antonio García Cubas, *Mexico, its Trade, Industry and Resources* (Mexico, 1893), p. 25; Oscar Lewis, *Pedro Martínez: A Mexican Peasant and his Family* (London, 1969), p. 28; see also Julio de la Fuente, 'Ethnic Relationships', in *Handbook of Middle American Indians*, VI, pp. 432–5.
12 Alan Knight, 'Intellectuals in the Mexican Revolution', paper given to the Sixth Congress of Mexican and US Historians, Chicago, Sept. 1981.
13 Baerlein, *Mexico*, p. 123; Frederick Starr, *In Indian Mexico, A Narrative of Travel and Labor* (Chicago, 1908), p. 85; Rosa King, *Tempest Over Mexico* (Boston, 1935), p. 25; Lespinasse, Frontera, to State Department, 21 Mar. 1911, SD 812.00/1175 (subsequent references to this archive will indicate only the source, the destination of reports in all cases being the US Department of State).
14 Miguel Covarrubias, *Mexico South, The Isthmus of Tehuantepec*, (Mexico, 1946), pp. 245–305; Starr, *In Indian Mexico*, pp. 131–2, 396–7.
15 Anon. Letter, Mexico City, to Woodrow Wilson, 25 Mar. 1914, WWP, series 2, box 103.
16 Ralph L. Beals, 'Acculturation', in *Handbook of Middle American Indians*, VI, p. 463.

17 John M. Tutino, 'Hacienda Social Relations in the Chalco Region in the Era of Independence', *Hispanic American Historical Review*, LV (1975), p. 525.
18 François Chevalier, *Land and Society in Colonial Mexico. The Great Hacienda* (Berkeley and Los Angeles, 1970), p. 77; de Szyszlo, *Dix milles kilomètres*, p. 214.
19 Oscar Lewis, *Life in a Mexican Village: Tepoztlán Restudied* (Urbana, 1963), pp. xxiii–xxiv.
20 Covarrubias, *Mexico South*, p. 245.
21 *Ibid.*, pp. 50–1; Oscar Schmieder, *The Settlements of the Tzapotec and Mije Indians* (Berkeley, 1930), pp. 22–7; Salomon Nahmad, *Los mixes* (Mexico, 1965), pp. 39–40.
22 Alicia Hernández Chávez, 'La defensa de los finqueros en Chiapas, 1914–20', *Historia Mexicana*, XXVIII (1979), pp. 346–7; Carnahan, Aire Libre, 11 Sept. 1913, SD 812.00/9223; Luis Cabrera in Jesús Silva Herzog, ed., *La Cuestión de la tierra* (4 vols., Mexico, 1961), II, p. 307.
23 Frank Tannenbaum, 'La Revolución agraria mexicana', *Problemas Industriales y Agricolas de México*, IV (1952), p. 29.
24 *Ibid.*; Manning Nash, 'Indian Economies', in *Handbook of Middle American Indians*, VI, p. 88–90; Carl Lumholtz, *Unknown Mexico* (2 vols., London, 1903), I, pp. 119–20, 198, 503.
25 González Navarro, *Vida social*, pp. 249–59; Hostetter, Hermosillo, 15 Aug. 1914, SD 812.00/13099.
26 Gilbert M. Joseph, 'Revolution from Without: the Mexican Revolution in Yucatán, 1915–24' (Yale Ph.D. diss., 1978), p. 118; Barbara Luise Margolies, *Princes of the Earth. Subcultural Diversity in a Mexican Municipality* (Washington, 1975), pp. ix, 156.
27 Eric Wolf, *Sons of the Shaking Earth* (Chicago and London, 1972), pp. 233–47; Roger D. Hansen, *The Politics of Mexican Development* (Baltimore, 1971), pp. 141–5.
28 González Navarro, *Vida social*, p. 35.
29 Hans Gadow, *Through Southern Mexico: Being an Account of the Travels of a Naturalist* (London and New York, 1908), pp. 214–17; Dolores Huerta to Robles Domínguez, 27 May 1911, AARD 24/6; Lumholtz, *Unknown Mexico*, I, p. 225.
30 Gadow, *Through Southern Mexico*, pp. 173, 457.
31 E.g., Charles R. Berry, *The Reform in Oaxaca, 1856–76: A Microhistory of the Liberal Revolution* (Lincoln, 1981), pp. 22–4.
32 John Womack Jr, *Zapata and the Mexican Revolution* (New York, 1970), p. 225; Robert Redfield, *A Village That Chose Progress: Chan Kom Revisited* (Chicago and London, 1970), pp. 8–21; Schmieder, *Tzapotec and Mije*, pp. 13, 23; Nahmad, *Los Mixes*, p. 40; Michael Kearney, *The Winds of Ixtepeji: World View and Society in a Zapotec Town* (New York, 1972), p. 33.
33 Eric R. Wolf, 'Levels of Communal Relations' in *Handbook of Middle American Indians*, VI, p. 304.
34 Nash, 'Indian Economies', pp. 98–9; Wolf, *Sons*, pp. 217–28.
35 Margolies, *Princes*, p. 62.
36 Joel S. Migdal, *Peasants, Politics and Revolution* (Princeton, 1974), pp. 66–84.
37 H. B. C. Pollard, *A Busy Time in Mexico* (London, 1913), p. 73.
38 Cf. Richard N. Adams, 'Nationalization', in *Handbook of Middle American Indians*, VI, p. 476; T. G. Powell, 'Mexican Intellectuals and the Indian Question, 1876–1911', *Hispanic American Historical Review*, XLVIII (1968), pp. 19–36; William D. Raat, 'Los intelectuales, el positivismo y la cuestión indígena', *Historia Mexicana*, XX (1971), pp. 412–27.
39 Greene, Tokyo, to Grey, 31 Dec. 1913, FO 371/2025, 3300.
40 Rosa E. King, *Tempest*, p. 34; Petrie to Quai d'Orsay, 26 Aug. 1910, AAE, Mex., Pol. Int. N.S., II, n. 97.
41 Tower to Grey, 31 Dec. 1910, FO 371/1149, 1574.
42 González Navarro, *Vida social*, pp. 134–66; Raat, 'Los intelectuales', p. 421.

43 Charming Arnold and Frederick J. T. Frost, *The American Egypt: A Record of Travel in Yucatan* (New York, 1909), p. 324; Baerlein, *Mexico*, pp. 161–2; King, *Tempest*, p. 31.

44 Charles C. Cumberland, 'The Sonora Chinese and the Mexican Revolution', *Hispanic American Historical Review*, XL 2 (1960), pp. 191–211.

45 Lewis, *Pedro Martínez*, pp. 129–30; Lewis, *Tepoztlán*, pp. 51, 54, 93–5.

46 *Ibid.*, p. 95; Starr, *In Indian Mexico*, pp. 56–61, 245.

47 *Ibid.*, p. 131; Lumholtz, *Unknown Mexico*, I, p. 183.

48 Margolies, *Princes*, p. 145; Lumholtz, *Unknown Mexico*, I, p. 203.

49 Starr, *In Indian Mexico*, p. 100.

50 See pp. 23, 57–8.

51 Paul Friedrich, *Agrarian Revolt in a Mexican Village* (Englewood Cliffs, 1970), pp. 8–9, 42–4, 50; Frank Tannenbaum, *Peace By Revolution: Mexico After 1910* (New York and London, 1966), p. 29; Leticia Reina, *Las rebeliones campesinas en Mexico (1819–1906)* (Mexico, 1980), pp. 353, 358.

52 Gonzalo Aguirre Beltrán, *Regiones de refugio* (Mexico, 1967), pp. 110, 125.

53 Starr, *In Indian Mexico*, pp. 99–100, 220–6, 249; Tannenbaum, *Peace*, p. 29.

54 Hence mercantile concern to reconquer the sierra in 1912; Lawton, Oaxaca, 8 Aug. 1912, SD. 812.00/6632; Mario Gill, 'Los Escudero de Acapulco', *Historia Mexicana*, III (1953), pp. 291–308; Ian Jacobs, *Ranchero Revolt: The Mexican Revolution in Guerrero* (Austin, 1982), p. 124.

55 Reina, *Rebeliones Campesinas*, p. 37.

56 Carleton Beals, *Mexican Maze* (Philadelphia and London, 1931), p. 46.

57 Womack, *Zapata*, pp. 102, 142; petition of twenty-one Americans, Mexico City, 27 Sept. 1913, SD 812.00/10312.

58 Edith O'Shaughnessy, *A Diplomat's Wife in Mexico* (New York, 1916), p. 179.

59 González Navarro, *Vida social*, p. 358; report of Governor Maytorena to the Twenty-third Sonoran state legislature, 23 Sept. 1912, SS r.9. Cf. José Fernandez Rojas, *De Porfirio Díaz a Victoriano Huerta, 1910–13* (Mexico, 1913), p. 214, on the Zapatistas' 'morbid appetite for pillage'.

60 See pp. 115–16ff.

61 Louis Lejeune, *Terres mexicaines* (Mexico and Paris, 1912), p. 94; Florence C. and Robert H. Lister, *Chihuahua, Storehouse of Storms* (Albuquerque, 1966), p. 159.

62 Lejeune, *Terres Mexicaines*, p. 261.

63 Patrick O'Hea, *Reminiscences of the Mexican Revolution* (Mexico, 1966), pp. 57–8.

64 Lister, *Chihuahua*, pp. 163–8; Charles H. Harrison, *A Mexican Family Empire: the Latifundio of the Sánchez Navarros 1765–1867* (Austin, 1975); Héctor Aguilar Camín, 'The Relevant Tradition: Sonoran Leaders in the Revolution', in D.A. Brading ed., *Caudillo and Peasant in the Mexican Revolution* (Cambridge, 1980), pp. 106–7.

65 Barry Carr, 'Las peculiaridades del Norte Mexicano, 1880–1927: ensayo de interpretación', *Historia Mexicana*, XXII (1973), pp. 320–46; Friedrich Katz, *La servidumbre agraria en México en la epoca Porfiriana* (Mexico, 1980), pp. 42–8.

66 Alfonso Dollero, *México al Día* (Mexico, 1911), pp. 227, 254.

67 François Chevalier, 'Conservateurs et libéraux au Méxique: essai de sociologie et géographie politiques, de l'indépendance à l'intervention française', *Cahiers d'Histoire Mondiale*, VIII 3 (1964), pp. 457–74.

68 González Navarro, *Vida social*, p. 18.

69 Lejeune, *Terres Mexicaines*, p. 261; cf. Fernando Rosenzweig, 'El desarrollo económico de México de 1877 a 1911', *Trimestre Económico*, XXXII (1965), pp. 419–21.

70 D. A. Brading, *Haciendas and Ranchos in the Mexican Bajío León 1700–1860* (Cambridge, 1978); George M. McBride, *The Land Systems of Mexico* (New York, 1923), pp. 98–9.

71 Percy F. Martin, *Mexico of the Twentieth Century* (2 vols., London, 1907), II, pp. 64–5; De

Szyszlo, *Dix milles kilomètres*, pp. 245–8; H. Bourgeois to Quai d'Orsay, 18 July 1912, AAE, Méxique, Affaires Commerciales, I, B/28/1, n. 9.

72 Gadow, *Through Southern Mexico*, p. 421.

73 Lawton, Oaxaca, 19 Sept. 1912, SD 812.00/5121.

74 Brickwood, Tapachula, n.d., Aug. 1911, SD 812.00/2346; Starr, *In Indian Mexico*, pp. 49–51; Nelson Reed, *The Caste War of Yucatán* (Stanford, 1964) pp. 26–7, 85, 105.

75 Gadow, *Through Southern Mexico*, pp. 29–30.

76 *Ibid.*, p. 34ff.; C. Reginald Enock, *Mexico* (London, 1909), pp. 322–7; Howard F. Cline, 'The Henequen Episode in Yucatán', *Inter-American Economic Affairs*, II (1948), pp. 30–51.

77 Gadow, *Through Southern Mexico*, p. 176.

78 De Szyszlo, *Dix milles kilomètres*, p. 89.

79 Gadow, *Through Southern Mexico*, pp. 117, 383.

80 Report from state government of Guerrero to Carranza, n.d. (Oct.) 1915, AJD, r.1.

81 Katz, *Servidumbre agraria*, p. 29; Friedrich, *Agrarian Revolt*, p. 46; Moisés T. de la Peña, *El Pueblo y su tierra: mito y realidad de la reforma agraria en México* (Mexico, 1964), p. 124.

82 John Kenneth Turner, *Barbarous Mexico* (Chicago, 1910).

83 Tannenbaum, 'Revolución agraria', p. 36.

84 Daniel Cosío Villegas, *Historia moderna de Mexico, el Porfiriato, la vida política interior*, parte segunda (Mexico, 1972), p. 693.

85 *Ibid.*, p. 67.

86 José Fuentes Mares, *Y México se refugió en el desierto* (Mexico, 1954), pp. 181–233; Harold D. Sims, 'Espejo de caciques: los Terrazas de Chihuahua', *Historia Mexicana*, XVIII (1969), pp. 379–99.

87 Baerlein, *Mexico*, pp. 18, 166–80; Joseph, 'Revolution from Without', pp. 68–113.

88 Baerlein, *Mexico*, p. 170.

89 James. D. Cockcroft, *Intellectual Precursors of the Mexican Revolution, 1900–1913* (Austin and London, 1976), p. 21; Francisco Almada, *Diccionario de historia, geografía y biografía sonorenses* (Chihuahua, 1952), p. 683.

90 Brickwood, Tapachula, 19 Mar. 1911, SD 812.00/1412.

91 Atenedoro Gámez, *Monografía histórica sobre la génesis de la revolución en el estado de Puebla* (Mexico, 1960), pp. 9–14; Alfonso Francisco Ramírez, *Historia de la revolución en Oaxaca* (Mexico, 1970), p. 29. The speaker was the great orator Jesús Urueta.

92 Cosío Villegas, *Vida política*, pp. 444–9.

93 E. V. Niemeyer, *El General Bernardo Reyes* (Monterrey, 1966), p. 32ff; Andrés Montemayor Hernández, *Historia de Monterrey* (Monterrey, 1971), pp. 272–3.

94 Cosío Villegas, *Vida política*, p. 426; Moisés Ochoa Campos, *Historia del Estado de Guerrero* (Mexico, 1968), pp. 277–9.

95 Cosío Villegas, *Vida política*, p. 769; Carleton Beals, *Porfirio Díaz, Dictator of Mexico* (Philadelphia, 1932), p. 289.

96 Cosío Villegas, *Vida política*, pp. 122, 425–6.

97 Beals, *Porfirio Díaz*, p. 286; Francisco Bulnes, *El verdadero Díaz y la revolución* (Mexico, 1967), p. 296; Edwin Lieuwen, *Mexican Militarism: the Political Rise and Fall of the Revolutionary Army* (Albuquerque, 1968), p. 4.

98 Bulnes, *El Verdadero Díaz*, pp. 292–7; Jorge Vera Estañol, *La revolución Mexicana. Orígines y resultados* (Mexico, 1957), p. 51, n. 2.

99 Niemeyer, *Reyes*, pp. 23–4; Michael C. Meyer, *Huerta. A Political Portrait* (Lincoln, 1972), pp. 9–14.

100 Heriberto Frías, *Tomóchic. Episodios de la Campaña de Chihuahua* (Mexico, 1968; first published 1894).

101 Jorge Alberto Lozoya, *El ejército mexicano 1911–65* (Mexico, 1970), pp. 30–1; W. Schiff, 'German Military Penetration into Mexico during the late Díaz Period', *Hispanic American Historical Review*, XXXIX (1959), pp. 568–79.

102 Lt. Col. Petrie to Quai d'Orsay, 26 August 1910, AAE, Mex., Pol. Int., N.S. II, n. 97.

103 Gadow, *Through Southern Mexico*, pp. 177, 361.

104 De Szyszlo, *Dix milles kilomètres*, p. 263; Womack, *Zapata*, pp. 62–3; Pastor Rouaix, *Diccionario geográfico, histórico, y biográfico del estado de Durango* (Mexico, 1946), pp. 101–2.

105 Robert E. Quirk, *The Mexican Revolution and the Catholic Church, 1910–29* (Bloomington, 1973), pp. 11–2.

106 Cosío Villegas, *Vida política*, pp. 512–3; Karl Schmitt, 'The Díaz Conciliation Policy on State and Local Levels 1876–1911', *Hispanic American Historical Review*, XL (1960), pp. 182–204.

107 Adrian Lyttelton, *The Seizure of Power. Fascism in Italy, 1919–29* (London, 1973), pp. 7–8.

108 Thomas Beaumont Hohler, *Diplomatic Petrel* (London, 1942), p. 173; Alan Knight, 'Nationalism, Xenophobia and Revolution: the Place of Foreigners and Foreign Interests in Mexico, 1910–15' (Oxford D.Phil., diss. 1974), pp. 99–103.

109 De Szyszlo, *Dix milles kilomètres*, p. 32.

110 Lumholtz, *Unknown Mexico*, I, pp. 5–6; Paul J. Vanderwood, *Disorder and Progress. Bandits, Police and Mexican Development* (Lincoln and London, 1981), p. 116.

111 Starr, *In Indian Mexico*, p. 247.

112 The critic was Luis Cabrera. Isidro Fabela, ed., *Documentos históricos de la revolución mexicana: revolución y régimen maderista* (5 vols., Mexico, 1964/5), I, p. 1. (Henceforth: DHRM, RRM).

113 Beals, *Porfirio Díaz*, pp. 273, 290; Cosío Villegas, *Vida política*, p. 445.

114 Graham, Durango, 19 Apr. 1911, FO 371/1147, 17946.

115 Baerlein, *Mexico*, p. 124.

116 Cosío Villegas, *Vida política*, pp. 683–5; José Yves Limantour, *Apuntes sobre mi vida pública* (Mexico, 1965), pp. 136–7.

117 Cosío Villegas, *Vida política*, pp. 648–70, 841, quoting Juan Sánchez Azcona.

118 Leopoldo Zea, *Apogeo y decadencia del Positivismo en México* (Mexico, 1944), pp. 210–4; cf. William D. Raat, *El Positivismo durante el Porfiriato (1876–1910)* (Mexico, 1975), pp. 114–42.

119 Madero to Díaz, 15 May 1910, in Fabela, DHRM, RRM, I, p. 49; José Yves Limantour, *Apuntes sobre mi vida pública* (Mexico, 1965) p. 149; Jesús Luna, *La carrera pública de Don Ramón Corral* (Mexico, 1975), pp. 84–97.

120 Adolfo Gilly, *La revolución interrumpida, México 1910–1920: Una guerra campesina por la tierra y el poder* (Mexico, 1971), pp. 43, 334–9; B. T. Rudenko, 'México en vísperas de la revolución democrático-burguesa de 1910–17', in B. T. Rudenko, *et al.*, *La revolución mexicana. Cuatro estudios soviéticos* (Mexico, 1978), pp. 19, 83–5; Juan Felipe Leal, 'El estado y el bloque en poder en México: 1867–1914', *Historia Mexicana*, XXIII (1973–4) pp. 716–21.

121 Luis Nicolau D'Olwer, 'Las inversiones extranjeras' in D. Cosío Villegas, ed., *Historia moderna de Mexico. El Porfiriato. La vida económica* (2 vols., Mexico, 1965) II, p. 1161.

122 José Luis Ceceña Gámez, 'La penetración extranjera y los grupos de poder en el México Porfirista', *Problemas de Desarrollo*, I (1969) pp. 76–8.

123 D'Olwer, 'Inversiones extranjeras', pp. 1171–2; González Navarro, *Vida social*, p. 157; Alfonso María y Campos, 'The Científicos and the Gold Standard', Cambridge seminar paper, 1975.

124 Robert F. Smith, *The United States and Revolutionary Nationalism in Mexico, 1916–1932* (Chicago, 1972), pp. 8–12; Marvin D. Bernstein, *The Mexican Mining Industry, 1890–1950; A Study of the Interaction of Politics, Economics and Technology* (Albany, 1965), pp. 79–82; John H. Coatsworth, *El impacto económico de los ferrocarriles en el Poririato* (2 vols., Mexico, 1976), I, pp. 57–61.

125 González Navarro, *Vida social*, pp. 52–134, 416–28, 564–94; Carmen Sáez, 'Ideology and Politics in Mexico, 1879–1904. Aspects of Científico Theory and Practice' (Oxford D. Phil.,

diss. 1980), pp. 275–6, 295; Josefina Vázquez de Knauth, *Nacionalismo y educación en México* (Mexico, 1970), pp. 81–91.

126 See vol. 2 ch. 3.

127 Judging by the repeated invocation of 'progress', condemnation of 'those who impede progress', and advocacy of education, sobriety and hard work (the 'virtue of great peoples'): see, e.g., *Nueva Era* (Parral, Chih.), 8 Mar., 8, 24 June, 18 Oct., 2, 16, 23 Dec. 1906; *jefe político*, Juárez, to Creel, 29 June 1908, STA, box 28.

128 Clark W. Reynolds, *The Mexican Economy, Twentieth-Century Structure and Growth* (Yale, 1970), p. 21.

129 Limantour, *Apuntes*, pp. 49–63, 174–5; Peralta Zamora in Cosío Villegas, *Vida Económica*, II, pp. 887–972, especially pp. 951–9.

130 Cosío Villegas, *Vida política*, p. 859.

131 Blas Sobrino to Robles Domínguez, 1 June 1911, AARD 15/72; John Rutherford, *Mexican Society During the Revolution: A Literary Approach* (Oxford, 1971), pp. 191–2.

132 Lawton, Oaxaca, 3 Apr. 1911, SD 812.00/1300; Limantour, *Apuntes*, p. 178.

133 Cosío Villegas, *Vida política*, p. 854.

134 Henry Lane Wilson, Mexico City, 20 March 1911, SD 812.00/1027.

135 Moisés Ochoa Campos, *La revolución mexicana, sus causas políticas* (2 vols., Mexico, 1968), II, pp. 215–32; Cosío Villegas, *Vida política*, p. 853.

136 Francisco R. Almada, *La revolución en el estado de Chihuahua* (2 vols., Mexico, 1964), I, pp. 24–5; cf. Pastor Rouaix, *Diccionario geográfico, histórico, y biográfico de Durango*, p. 136; Héctor Aguilar Camín, *La revolución Sonorense* (Mexico, INAH, 1975), pp. 97–8.

137 Ochoa Campos, *Causas políticas*, II, pp. 229–32; Lewis, *Tepoztlán*, pp. 94, 230.

138 Baerlein, *Mexico*, p. 168; Starr, *In Indian Mexico*, p. 78.

139 *El Correo*, 14 May, 21 Sept. 1909.

140 See below, pp. 117, 122, 125. Even if the local boss was a decent enough fellow, it was later recalled, 'he always had to be on the side of the rich'; Simón Márquez Camarena, interviewed by María Isabel Souza, 1973, PHO 1/113, p. 12.

141 Lowell L. Blaisdell, *The Desert Revolution, Baja California 1911* (Madison 1962), p. 37; Womack, *Zapata*, p. 40.

142 Gadow, *Through Southern Mexico*, pp. 246, 278; Womack, *Zapata*, pp. 32–3.

143 *El Diario del Hogar*, 9 Oct. 1910.

144 Baerlein, *Mexico*, pp. 120–1.

145 *El Correo*, 7 July 1910; cf. the same paper's report of 10 Sept. 1909, on the management's veto of the establishment of a political club at Dolores.

146 John Hays Hammond, *Autobiography of John Hays Hammond* (2 vols., New York, 1935), I, p. 118; Alfred Tischendorf, *Great Britain and Mexico in the Era of Porfirio Díaz* (Durham, 1961), pp. 73–4. On the 'collaborating elite', see Ronald Robinson, 'Non-European Foundations of European Imperialism' in Roger Owen and Bob Sutcliffe, *Studies in the Theory of Imperialism* (London, 1972), p. 120.

147 David M. Pletcher, *Rails, Mines and Progress. Seven American Pioneers in Mexico 1867–1911* (Ithaca, 1958), pp. 203–4; Rodney D. Anderson, *Outcasts in their own land. Mexican Industrial Workers 1906–1911* (Dekalb, 1976), pp. 105–9, 130–3, 155, 159.

148 Bernstein, *Mexican Mining Industry*, p. 91.

149 *El Correo*, 3 July 1910.

150 Harry Arthur Buick, *The Gringoes of Tepehuanes* (London, 1967), pp. 94–5.

151 Gadow, *Through Southern Mexico*, pp. 155–6; Ramírez, *Oaxaca*, p. 24.

152 Cesareo Ortiz and others to Gobernación, 16 July 1911, AG 898.

153 *El Correo*, 7 July, 5 Oct., 1910.

154 See below, pp. 110, 113, 120, 123, 222.

155 Gill, 'Los Escudero de Acapulco', pp. 291–308; Pangburn, Acapulco, 4 Apr. 1911, SD 812.00/1366.

156 *El Correo*, 26 July 1910; R. Sandels, 'Antecedentes de la revolución en Chihuahua', *Historia Mexicana*, XXIV (1975), p. 398; Aguilar, 'La Revolución Sonorense', pp. 98–105.

157 Margarito Vázquez, Cuajimalpa, to Gobernación, 10 July 1911, AG 898.

158 Vanderwood, *Disorder and Progress*, p. 86; Ochoa Campos, *Causas políticas*, II, p. 216.

159 Womack, *Zapata*, p. 32; Niemeyer, *Reyes*, p. 77.

160 Cosío Villegas, *Vida Política*, p. 427, quoting *El Diario del Hogar*.

161 Graham, Durango, 19 Apr. 1911, FO 371/1147, 17946; *Diario del Hogar*, 6 Oct. 1910; J. Trinidad Cervantes to Madero, 4 July 1911, AG 898; Vanderwood. *Disorder and Progress*, pp. 154–5; Rodrigo González to Madero, 9 Nov. 1911, AG (CRCFM); Rutino Zamora and Manuel Herrera to Robles Domínguez, 27, 30 May 1911, AARD 11/22, 11/43.

162 Baerlein, *Mexico*, pp. 93–4.

163 Aguilar, 'La revolución Sonorense', pp. 99, 101; Miller, Tampico, 22 Mar. 1911, SD 812.00/1196; Charles Macomb Flandrau, *Viva Mexico!* (New York and London, 1921), p. 68; *El Correo*, 25 Mar. 1909, 24 June 1910.

164 Baerlein, *Mexico*, p. 93; Brickwood, Tapachula, 19 Mar. 1911, SD 812.00/1412.

165 Womach, *Zapata*, pp. 38, 40; *El Correo*, 9 Nov. 1909, 4, 8, Mar. 1911.

166 Baerlein, *Mexico*, p. 37; Flandrau, *Viva Mexico!*, p. 71.

167 *El Correo*, 2 Apr. 1909.

168 Aguilar, 'La revolución Sonorense', pp. 100–1.

169 Flandrau, *Viva Mexico!*, p. 71; Brickwood, Tapachula, 19 Mar. 1911, SD 812.00/1412; Ochoa Campos, *Guerrero*, p. 280.

170 Turner, *Barbarous Mexico*, pp. 73, 76; Aureliano Tenorio to Robles Domínguez, 5 June 1911, AARD 7/54; see also Baerlein, *Mexico*, p. 87.

171 Katz, *Servidumbre agraria*, p. 31; Turner, *Barbarous Mexico*, p. 85. Pochutla is unflatteringly described by Aldous Huxley, *Beyond the Mexique Bay*, (London, 1955), p. 162.

172 Rutherford, *Mexican Society*, p. 153.

173 Lewis, *Pedro Martínez*, pp. 129–30.

174 Gracey, Progreso, 15 Jan. 1914, Germon, Progreso, 20 Aug. 1914, SD 812.00/10658, 13125. Cf. Baerlein, *Mexico*, p. 20 on another 'sensuous despotism'.

175 Vanderwood, *Disorder and Progress*, p. 153; Baerlein, *Mexico*, p. 91.

176 Womack, *Zapata*, p. 38; Aureliano Tenorio to Robles Domínguez 10 June 1911, AARD 7/54.

177 Aguilar, 'La revolución Sonorense', p. 104; *El Correo*, 8, 30 Mar. 1911; Almada, *La revolución en el estado de Chihuahua*, I, p. 81.

178 Gustavo Casasola, *Historia gráfica de la revolución mexicana* (5 vols., Mexico, 1967), I, p. 221; Rutino Zamora to Robles Domínguez, 27 May 1911, AARD 11/22.

179 Schmucker, Ensenada, 2 Apr., Simpich, Ensenada, 19 July 1911, SD 812.00/1312, 2241; cf. Baerlein, *Mexico*, pp. 203–4 on official profiteering from smallpox.

180 *El Correo*, 8, 9, 21, 26 July 1910.

181 Salvador Alvarado, *La reconstrucción de México. Un mensaje a los pueblos de América* (2 vols., Mexico, 1919), I, pp. 11–13.

182 Womack, *Zapata*, p. 40.

183 *El Correo*, 20, 22 July 1910.

184 Such as Jesús González Garza, the 'Tiger of Velardeña'; Vanderwood, *Disorder and Progress*, pp. 154–5.

185 Miller, Tampico, 22 Mar. 1911, SD 812.00/1196.

186 *El Correo*, 7 Aug. 1910.

187 Casasola, *Historia gráfica*, I, p. 221.

188 *Ibid.*; Cosío Villegas, *Vida política*, pp. 683–8; Baerlein, *Mexico*, pp. 202–5.

189 Cosío Villegas, *Vida política*, pp. 664, 698–700.

190 *Ibid.*, pp. 864–5; Cockcroft, *Intellectual Precursors*, pp. 101, 120–1, 128; see also the abundant correspondence in the Terrazas Archive.

191 Baerlein, *Mexico*, p. 44; Thompson, Mérida, 19 Mar. 1911, SD 812.00/1260; Pierce, Mérida, 1 May 1911, FO 371/1147, 20161.

192 *El Correo*, 14 Aug. 1909.

193 Leone Moats, *Thunder in their Veins*, (London, 1933), pp. 50–1; Mrs Alec Tweedie, *Porfirio Díaz, Seven Times President of Mexico* (London, 1906), p. 278; Gadow, *Through Southern Mexico*, pp. 337–8.

194 Paul J. Vanderwood, 'Los Rurales: producto de una necessidad social', *Historia Mexicana*, XXII (1972), pp. 36–7, 40; Vanderwood, *Disorder and Progress*, pp. 107–9.

195 Reports in AG 653.

196 Casasola, *Historia gráfica*, I, p. 215; Vanderwood, *Disorder and Progress*, p. 102.

197 *Ibid.*, p. 130; De Szyszlo, *Dix milles kilomètres*, p. 251.

198 Vanderwood, *Disorder and Progress*, p. 110–8.

199 Juan Jiménez to Gobernación, 20 July 1910, AG 908.

200 Vanderwood, *Disorder and Progress*, pp. 125–9 for further examples.

201 Gadow, *Through Southern Mexico*, p. 338.

202 Bulnes, *El verdadero Díaz*, pp. 356–9; Armando María y Campos, *Múgica, Crónica Biográfica* (Mexico, 1939), p. 33.

203 Ochoa Campos, *Causas política*, II, p. 137.

204 Cosío Villegas, *Vida política*, pp. 683–4; Gadow, *Through Southern Mexico*, p. 252.

205 Madero to Evaristo Madero, 20 July 1909, AFM r. 9; Madero to Miguel Silva quoted in Cockcroft, *Intellectual Precursors*, p. 159.

206 See Huntington, *Political Order*, pp. 275, 316.

207 Barrington Moore Jr, *Social Origins of Dictatorship and Democracy. Lord and Peasant in the Making of the Modern World* (London, 1969), p. 442.

2 The opposition

1 Cosío Villegas, *Vida política*, pp. 640–7.

2 *Ibid.*, pp. 648–70; Ochoa Campos, *Causas políticas*, II, pp. 130–1.

3 Alfonso Taracena, *Venustiano Carranza* (Mexico, 1963), pp. 12–13; Niemeyer, *Reyes*, pp. 80–2.

4 Cosío Villegas, *Vida política*, p. 444.

5 *Ibid.*, pp. 442, 449, 451; Jesús Romero Flores, *Historia de la revolución en Michoacán* (Mexico, 1964), p. 53; Niemeyer, *Reyes*, pp. 114–25.

6 Ian Jacobs, 'Aspects of the History of the Mexican Revolution in the State of Guerrero up to 1940' (Cambridge D.Phil. diss., 1977), p. 116.

7 Cosío Villegas, *Vida política*, pp. 108–9, 439–40; Aguilar, *Revolución Sonorense*, p. 74.

8 Rouaix, *Diccionario*, p. 60; Jacobs, 'Aspects', pp. 116, 190.

9 Frans J. Schryer, *The Rancheros of Pisaflores. The History of a Peasant Bourgeoisie in Twentieth-Century Mexico* (Toronto, 1980), pp. 30–1, 70–1.

10 Buick, *Gringoes of Tepehuanes*, p. 112.

11 Cosío Villegas, *Vida política*, p. 633; Francisco I. Madero, *La sucesión presidencial en 1910* (San Pedro, 1908), pp. 7–8.

12 Cosío Villegas, *Vida política*, pp. 247–8, 567–8; Anderson, *Outcasts*, p. 178; Ron Tyler, ed., *Posada's Mexico* (Washington, 1979), pp. 103–4.

13 Baerlein, *Mexico*, p. 16.

14 Ernest Gruening, *Mexico and its Heritage* (New York, 1928), p. 57.

15 Cosío Villegas, *Vida política*, p. 743.

16 *Ibid.*, pp. 631–2; González, *Pueblo en Vilo*, pp. 98–9, 103.

17 Quirk, *The Mexican Revolution and the Catholic Church*, pp. 17–19; Anderson, *Outcasts*, pp. 126, 183–90.

18 Baerlein, *Mexico*, pp. 15–16; González, *Pueblo en Vilo*, p. 99; Womack, *Zapata*, p. 417.

19 Cosío Villegas, *Vida política*, p. 647.

20 González Navarro, *Vida social*, p. 20; Rosenzweig, 'El desarrollo económico', p. 478.

21 González Navarro, *Vida social*, p. 24; Alejandra Moreno Toscano, 'Cambios en los patrones de urbanización en México, 1810–1910', *Historia Mexicana*, XXII (1972), pp. 179–87.

22 Aguilar, *La revolución Sonorense*, pp. 85, 91–2; O'Hea, *Reminiscences*, pp. 57–8.

23 Rosenzweig, 'Desarrollo económico', p. 419.

24 Keith A. Davies, 'Tendencias demográficas urbanas durante el siglo XIX en México', *Historia Mexicana*, XXI (1972), pp. 481–537.

25 González Navarro, *Vida social*, p. 681,

26 *Ibid.*, pp. 531–2.

27 In the thirty years after 1878 the number of primary schools rose from 5,194 to 12,068, the public school population from 141,000 to 659,000: González Navarro, *Vida social*, pp. 599–600; Vázquez de Knauth, *Nacionalismo*, p. 86.

28 Alejandra Moreno Toscano, 'El paisaje rural y las ciudades: dos perspectivas de la geografía histórica', *Historia Mexicana*, XXI (1971), pp. 259–64; González Navarro, *Vida social*, pp. 651–2, 681, 690.

29 Mario Cerutti, 'Patricio Milmo, empresario regiomontano del siglo XIX', in Ciro F. S. Cardoso, ed., *Formación y desarrollo de la burguesía en México siglo XIX* (Mexico, 1978), p. 235.

30 Montemayor Hernández, *Historia de Monterrey*, pp. 262–4, 276–81; Roberto C. Hernández Elizondo, 'Comercio e industria textil en Nuevo León, 1852–1890' and Cerutti, 'Patricio Milmo', both in Cardoso, pp. 231–86; Dollero, *México al Día*, pp. 227.

31 Dollero, *México al Día*, pp. 221–3; Martin, *Mexico of the Twentieth Century*, II, p. 83; Lister, *Chihuahua*, pp. 172–3; J. Figueroa Domenech, *Guía general descriptiva de la república mexicana* (2 vols., Barcelona, 1899), II, pp. 96–108.

32 Aguilar, *La revolución sonorense*, pp. 62–8; Figueroa Domenech, *Guía general descriptiva*, II, pp. 557–65; De Szyszlo, *Dix milles kilomètres*, pp. 285–6.

33 Jacobs, 'Aspects', pp. 55–62, 122–3; Schryer, *Rancheros of Pisaflores*, pp. 28–36.

34 González, *Pueblo en Vilo*, pp. 95–109.

35 See vol. 2 ch. 2.

36 González Navarro, *Vida social*, pp. 383, 386; José E. Iturriaga, *La estructura social y cultural de México* (Mexico, 1951), p. 34ff.; Arnaldo Córdova, *La ideología de la revolución mexicana. La formación del nuevo régimen* (Mexico, 1973), pp. 17–18. For 'dual' analyses, cf. Cockcroft, *Intellectual Precursors*, pp. 34, 216; Rutherford, *Mexican Society*, pp. 300–2.

37 Charles A. Hale, *Mexican Liberalism in the Age of Mora, 1821–1853* (New Haven, 1968), pp. 95–6, 123, 223–4; Madero, *Sucesión presidencial*, p. 296; Amado Escobar to Nemesio Tejeda, 14 Oct. 1906, STA, box 26.

38 Donald B. Keesing, 'Structural Change Early in Development: Mexico's Changing Industrial and Occupational Structure from 1895–1950', *Journal of Economic History*, XXIX (1969), pp. 716–38.

39 Iturriaga, *Estructura social*, pp. 34–89; Nathan Whetten, 'The Rise of a Middle Class in Mexico', in Theo R. Crevenna, ed., *La clase media en México y Cuba* (Washington, 1950), pp. 1–29 is of limited use.

40 Joseph, 'Revolution from without', p. 140.

41 Holms, Guadalajara, 11 Apr. 1911, FO 371/1147/16692.

42 Baerlein, *Mexico*, pp. 129–30; Hamilton Fyfe, *The Real Mexico* (London, 1914), p. 3, quoting a coffee planter.

43 On the Creelman interview: Jesus Silva Herzog, *Breve historia de la revolución mexicana* (2 vols., Mexico, 1969), I, p. 112.

44 Romana Falcón, 'Los orígenes populares de la revolución de 1910? El caso de San Luis Potosí', *Historia Mexicana* XXIX (1979), p. 198.

45 Cockcroft, *Intellectual Precursors*, p. 91.

46 *Ibid.*, pp. 64–7, 86–7, 93–4; Ramírez, *Oaxaca*, pp. 15–16.

47 Cockcroft, *Intellectual Precursors*, p. 95, quoting Enrique Flores Magón (1934).

48 Cosío Villegas, *Vida política*, pp. 691–2.

49 *Ibid.*, pp. 693–4; Cockcroft, *Intellectual Precursors*, pp. 100–5.

50 *Ibid.*, pp. 117–20, 123.

51 *Ibid.*, pp. 130–3; Cosío Villegas, *Vida política*, pp. 700–3; Silva Herzog, *Breve historia*, I, pp. 76–107.

52 Cockcroft, *Intellectual Precursors*, p. 155.

53 Casío Villega, *Vida política*, p. 630.

54 *Ibid.*, pp. 689–91.

55 *Ibid.*, p. 695.

56 *Ibid.*, pp. 753–61; Limantour, *Apuntes*, p. 156.

57 Madero to Crescencio Villareal Márquez, 17 Aug. 1906 in Fabela, DHRM, *Actividades Políticas y Revolucionarias de los Hermanos Flores Magón*, pp. 73–5; cf. Jesús to Ricardo Flores Magón, 26 Sept. 1905, STA, box 26.

58 Rodolfo Valles (*jefe político*, Parral) to Creel, 20 October 1906, STA, box 26.

59 Dollero, *México al Día*, pp. 248–9; Lefaivre, Mexico City, to Quai d'Orsay, 7 July 1909, AAE, Mex., Pol. Int. I, n. 52.

60 Madero to Villareal (n. 57); Antonio Balboa to Antonio I. Villareal, 25 July 1906, STA, box 26.

61 Ignacio Gutiérrez Gómez to Manuel Mestre Ghigliazzi, 30 May 1910, in Manuel González Calzada, *Historia de la revolución mexicana en Tabasco* (Mexico, 1972), pp. 55–6.

62 Silva Herzog, *Breve Historia*, I, pp. 108–18.

63 Cosío Villegas, *Vida política*, pp. 716–7; Stanley R. Ross, *Francisco I. Madero. Apostle of Mexican Democracy* (New York, 1955), pp. 46–7; Charles C. Cumberland, *Mexican Revolution, Genesis Under Madero* (Austin, 1952), pp. 47–8.

64 Limantour, *Apuntes*, p. 157 suggests the third.

65 Cosío Villegas, *Vida Política*, pp. 768–75; Niemeyer, *Reyes*, p. 151.

66 Vera Estañol, *Revolución Mexicana*, p. 95.

67 Cumberland, *Genesis*, p. 48.

68 This account follows Niemeyer, *Reyes*.

69 *Ibid.*, pp. 114–24.

70 *Ibid.*, pp. 103–5; Taracena, *Carranza*, p. 14, reckons there were 15,000 reservists in Mexico City alone.

71 Niemeyer, *Reyes*, pp. 105–7; Cosío Villegas, *Vida política*, pp. 612–26.

72 *Ibid.*, p. 773.

73 Niemeyer, *Reyes*, p. 149.

74 Ross, *Madero*, p. 67; Cosío Villegas, *Vida política*, p. 787.

75 Cosío Villegas, *Vida Política*, pp. 784–5; Juan Sánchez Azcona, *Apuntes para la historia de la revolución mexicana* (Mexico, 1961), pp. 59–61.

76 Cumberland, *Genesis*, pp. 52–3; Ross, *Madero*, p. 66; Cockcroft, *Intellectual Precursors*, p. 164.

77 Miguel Ahumada (Governor of Jalisco) to Corral, 3 Feb. 1909, ARC carpeta 1.

78 Sanchez Azcona, *Apuntes*, pp. 72–3; Niemeyer, *Reyes*, pp. 164–6.

79 *Ibid.*, p. 155.

80 *Ibid.*, pp. 144, 160.

81 Miguel Ahumada (Governor of Jalisco) to Corral, 3 Feb., 24 May, 1 June 1909, ARC carpetas 1, 2.

82 Niemeyer, *Reyes*, p. 162, quoting *México Nuevo*.

83 *Ibid.*, p. 163; Lefaivre to Quai D'Orsay, 12 August 1909, AAE, Méx., Pol. Int., I, n. 61; Magill, Guadalajara, 20 Mar. 1911, SD 812.00/126.

84 Niemeyer, *Reyes*, pp. 161–2; Cosío Villegas, *Vida política*, pp. 809, 824.

85 Niemeyer, *Reyes*, p. 161; Gamez, *Puebla*, pp. 15–16; General Mariano Ruiz (*jefe político* Tepic) to Díaz, 17 June 1909, ARC carpeta 2; Hector R. Olea, *Breve historia de la revolución en Sinaloa* (Mexico, 1964), p. 38.

86 McCarthy, Alamos, 13 May 1911, SD 812.00/2044; Martin, *Mexico of the Twentieth Century*, II, pp. 38–9; and note Cosío Villegas, *Vida política*, p. 613.

87 *Ibid.*, pp. 811–13, 817.

88 Manuel J. Aguirre, *Cananea* (Mexico, 1958), pp. 172–3; Madero to Miguel Sánchez Adame, 30 July 1909, AFM r.9.

89 Alberto J. Pani, *Apuntes autobiográficos* (Mexico, 1951), p. 65.

90 Aguilar, *La revolución Sonorense*, pp. 70–1, 76, 78.

91 Rouaix, *Diccionario*, p. 60; Muñoz Arístegui (Governor of Yucatán) to Corral, 11 May 1909, ARC carpeta 2; Edmundo Bolio, *Yucatán en la dictadura y la revolución* (Mexico, 1967), pp. 22–35.

92 Lefaivre to Quai D'Orsay, 6 July 1909, AAE, Méx., Pol. Int., I, n. 45.

93 Brickwood, Tapachula, 19 Mar. 1911, SD 812.00/1412.

94 Limantour, *Apuntes*, p. 158.

95 On this phenomenon: Cosío Villegas, *Vida política*, p. 665; *El Correo*, 3 Apr. 1910, which described the 'obligatory' attendance of workers from the Aguascalientes railway workshops at Re-electionist rallies.

96 Cosío Villegas, *Vida política*, pp. 799, 831–2, 871.

97 *Ibid.*, pp. 803, 824–5, 831.

98 *Ibid.*, pp. 586; Sánchez Azcona, *Apuntes*, p. 100; Anderson, *Outcasts*, pp. 244–54.

99 Cosío Villegas, *Vida política*, pp. 813–4, 837, 863.

100 *Ibid.*, pp. 817, 824–5; Niemeyer, *Reyes*, pp. 167–8.

101 Cosío Villegas, *Vida política*, p. 825.

102 Niemeyer, *Reyes*, p. 168; Cumberland, *Genesis*, pp. 83–4.

103 Niemeyer, *Reyes*, pp. 170–1.

104 *Ibid.*, pp. 119, 171; cf. Womack, *Zapata*, p. 57.

105 Ross, *Madero*, p. 4; José C. Valadés, *Imaginación y realidad de Francisco I. Madero* (2 vols., Mexico, 1960), I, p. 25.

106 Dollero, *México al Día*, p. 219; Hanna, Monterrey, 8 June 1910, SD 812.00/322; Ross, pp. 3, 53.

107 Ross, *Madero*, pp. 6–12; Valadés, *Imaginación*, I, pp. 30–54, 81–2.

108 Ross, *Madero*, pp. 8–9, 12–13; see also Sánchez Azcona, *Apuntes*, pp. 12, 14.

109 Madero, *Sucesión presidencial*, pp. 9–10.

110 Dollero, *México al Día*, pp. 253–4; Valadés, *Imaginación*, I, p. 96.

111 Valadés, *Imaginación*, I, p. 98; cf. Madero to Fernando Iglesias Calderón, n.d., in Fabela, DHRM, RRM, pp. 13–15.

112 Valadés, *Imaginación*, I, pp. 98–103; Ross, *Madero*, p. 36.

113 Ross, *Madero*, pp. 36–9.

114 Madero to Villareal (n. 57); Cosío Villegas, *Vida política*, p. 883.

115 Madero to Villareal (n. 57); Madero, 'El Partido Nacional Antireeleccionista y la próxima lucha electoral', Mar. 1910, in Fabela, DHRM, RRM, p. 37.

116 Ross, *Madero*, p. 40, 43, 45; Valadés, *Imaginación*, I, pp. 117–8.

117 Cosío Villegas, *Vida política*, p. 872–3; Córdova, *Ideología*, p. 97–8.

118 Madero, *La sucesión presidencial*, pp. 145, 164, 209, 224–5, 236–8.

119 *Ibid.*, pp. 185–208; for comments, see Ross, *Madero*, pp. 57–64; Cosío Villegas, *Vida política*, pp. 875–81; Córdova, *La ideología*, pp. 99–108.

120 Madero, *La sucesión presidencial*, pp. 1–3, 17.

121 *Ibid.*, pp. 14, 21; Madero, 'El Partido Nacional Antireeleccionista', in Fabela, DHRM, RRM, I, pp. 33, 35.

122 Madero, *La sucesión presidencial*, pp. 13, 330; Cosío Villegas, *Vida política*, p. 881; Sánchez Azcona, *Apuntes*, p. 25.

123 Madero to Sánchez Azcona, 23 July 1909, and to E. Salido Muñoz, 31 July 1909, AFM, r.9.

124 Cosío Villegas, *Vida política*, pp. 870–2, 882.

125 Reyes to Díaz, 14 Aug. 1905, in Niemeyer, *Reyes*, p. 131; Evaristo Madero to Madero, 22 Nov. 1909, in Valadés, *Imaginación*, I, pp. 272–3.

126 De Szyszlo, *Dix milles kilomètres*, p. 52; Cosío Villegas, *Vida política*, pp. 887–8.

127 Gámez, *Puebla*, pp. 61–2.

128 Córdova, *La ideología*, p. 106, argues that Reyes' support came principally from the Porfirian upper class; hence Madero became 'the spokesman of social groups which Reyismo shunned'. This cannot be sustained.

129 Madero to Gustavo Madero, 26 July 1909, and to Félix Palavicini, 4 Aug. 1909, AFM r.9.

130 Ross, *Madero*, p. 82.

131 Niemeyer, *Reyes*, pp. 170, 174.

132 Ross, *Madero*, pp. 73, 89, 91; María y Campos, *Múgica*, pp. 28–30, 39; Gámez, *Puebla*, pp. 27–8.

133 Governor Ahumada to Corral, 8 Feb. 1910, ARC carpeta 3.

134 Madero to Palavicini, 23 July 1909 to J. Hermosillo, 29 July 1909, to Emilio Vázquez Gómez, 2 Aug. 1909, to Francisco Naranjo, 4 Aug. 1909, AFM r.9.

135 Ross, *Madero*, pp. 12, 84; Madero to Emilio Vázquez Gómez, 21 July 1909, to José María Pino Suárez, 15 Aug. 1909, AFM r.9.

136 Cosío Villegas, *Vida política*, pp. 741, 816.

137 Madero to Gustavo Madero, 20, 26 July 1909, AFM r.9; Ross, pp. 82, 90; *El Correo*, 18 Jan. 1910.

138 Ross, pp. 88–90; Madero to Heriberto Frías, 27 July 1909, AFM r.8; Olea, pp. 14–17; Aguilar, *La revolución Sonorense*, pp. 82–3, 110–11.

139 Madero to Mata, 10 Aug. 1909, AFM r.9.

140 AFM r.9.

141 Alberto Morales Jiménez, *Hombres de la revolución mexicana* (Mexico, 1960), pp. 85–9; *El País*, 13, 18, 24 Nov. 1910; Robles Domínguez to Madero, 20 Nov. 1912, AFM r.19.

142 Cockcroft, *Intellectual Precursors*, pp. 45–6, 57.

143 *El País*, 18 Nov. 1910.

144 Ramírez, *Oaxaca*, pp. 18–19; Everardo Cruz, 'Los precursores de la revolución', *El Universal*, 19 June 1953.

145 Madero to Mata (n. 139). For additional examples of Maderista personnel, see Aguilar, *La revolución Sonorense*, pp. 66–7; Jacobs, 'Aspects', pp. 117, 122.

146 Governor Muñoz Arístegui to Corral, 21 Sept. 1909, ARC carpeta 2.

147 Gregorio Alarcón to Robles Domínguez, 5 June 1911, AARD 15/112. Other examples are taken from this and the Madero archive.

148 Anderson, *Outcasts*, pp. 254–67.

149 Silvestre Dorador, *Mi prisión, la defensa social, y la verdad del caso* (Mexico, 1916), p. 2; Gabriel Gavira, *General de Brigada Gabriel Gavira. Su actuación político-militar revolucionaria* (Mexico, 1933), p. 6; Tyler, *Posada's Mexico*, p. 72; Madero, *La sucesión presidencial*, p. 241.

150 Cosío Villegas, *Vida política*, p. 867; Gámez, *Puebla*, pp. 22–3.

151 Gavira, *Actuación*, pp. 7–8; Rafael Tapia, *Mi participación revolucionaria* (Veracruz, 1967), pp. xvi–xviii; L. J. Nunn, Veracruz, 29 Apr. 1911, FO 371/1147, 18523, makes Tapia a 'bankrupt' saddler – like some later historians, contemporary observers were perhaps too ready to attribute political opposition to poverty rather than to principle.

152 Anderson, *Outcasts*, pp. 257–8; and below, pp. 137–40.

153 Cockcroft, *Intellectual Precursors*, pp. 43–4; Ramón Eduardo Ruiz, *The Great Rebellion: Mexico 1905–1924* (New York, 1980), pp. 48, 120–1.
154 Madero, *La sucesión presidencial*, p. 16; Francisco Madero Sr to Madero, n.d. (1908), in Fabela, DHRM, RRM, p. 16.
155 Cockcroft, *Intellectual Precursors*, p. 43; Joseph, 'Revolution from without', p. 113; Ruiz, *Great Rebellion*, pp. 37–8. See also below, pp. 120–1, 227, 299–300, 421–2.
156 In stressing latent functions, the proponents of these economic hypotheses not only fall into the pit of economic reductionism, there to join the Marxists of a former age; they also fall prey to the snares of functionalism, and must recognise the close – but, one imagines, distasteful – company of Parsons, Merton *et al.*
157 According to the figures compiled by Enrique Pérez López and reproduced in *La economía mexicana en cifras* (Mexico, Nacional Financiera, 1978), p. 23.
158 Ian Jacobs, 'Rancheros of Guerrero: the Figueroa brothers and the revolution', in Brading, ed., *Caudillo and Peasant*, p. 83; Madero, 'El Partido Anti-reeleccionista' in Fabela, DHRM, RRM, I, p. 28; note also the speech of Federico González Garza in the same volume, pp. 54–7 – pure politics.
159 Cockcroft, *Intellectual Precursors*, pp. 40–1; Ruiz, *Great Rebellion*, pp. 50–2. Bulnes' assertion that 70% of the middle class lived off the government in 1911 is nonsense: it would imply government dependents of nearly one million, at a time when total government expenditure was barely 100m. pesos. As regards the outright penury of middle-class *empleados*, furthermore, Bulnes is ambivalent: see *El verdadero Díaz*, pp. 42–3, 250–3.
160 Cockcroft, *Intellectual Precursors*, pp. 45–6, 57; Ruiz, *Great Rebellion*, pp. 107–9.
161 Ted Robert Gurr, *Why Men Rebel* (Princeton, 1970) is the main exponent.
162 Cockcroft, *Intellectual Precursors*, p. 45.
163 *Ibid.*; Edward Shils, *The Intellectuals and the Powers and Other Essays*, (Chicago, 1972), pp. 372–423.
164 Cockcroft, *Intellectual Precursors*, p. 44.
165 Lenin, quoted by V. G. Kiernan, *Marxism and Imperialism* (London, 1974), p. 38.
166 De Szyszlo, *Dix milles kilomètres*, p. 31.
167 Cockcroft, *Intellectual Precursors*, p. 45.
168 Cabrera to Filómena Mata, 11 Nov. 1910, in *El País*, 13 Nov. 1910; Vera Estañol, *Revolución mexicana*, pp. 209–10; Cosío Villegas, *Vida política*, p. 745.
169 William K. Meyers, 'Politics, Vested Rights and Economic Growth in Porfirian Mexico: the Company Tlahualilo in the Comarca Lagunera, 1885–1911', *Hispanic American Historical Review*, LVII (1977), pp. 425–54.
170 Felix F. Palavicini, *Mi vida revolucionaria* (Mexico, 1937).
171 Cosío Villegas, *Vida política*, pp. 747–8.
172 Cockcroft, *Intellectual Precursors*, p. 82; Morales Jiménez, *Hombres de la revolución mexicana*, pp. 282–3.
173 Cockcroft, *Intellectual Precursors*, pp. 23, 39. Assertions to this effect are legion: see, e.g., Frederick C. Turner, *The Dynamic of Mexican Nationalism* (Chapel Hill, 1968), pp. 54–6; J. F. Rippy, *The United States and Mexico* (New York, 1934), p. 322; M. S. Alperovich and B. T. Rudenko, *La revolución mexicana de 1910–1917 y la política de los Estados Unidos* (Mexico, 1960), pp. 203, 237; Myra Wilkins, *The Emergence of the Multinational Enterprise* (Cambridge, 1970), pp. 25–8.
174 Knight, 'Nationalism', pp. 84–105.
175 *Ibid.*, pp. 119–41.
176 Cockcroft, *Intellectual Precursors*, pp. 23–5.
177 Knight, 'Nationalism', pp. 76–8, 120–3.
178 Maderistas – like Madero, or Braulio Hernández – denounced the evils of the company town; but this did not imply a repudiation of foreign investment, or a policy of 'Mexico for

the Mexicans'. Opposition organs welcomed fresh infusions of foreign capital: cf. *El Correo*, 11 May 1909, 27 Aug. 1910; González Navarro, *Vida social*, p. 380.

179 Maria y Campos, *Múgica*, pp. 12–16, 23–4.

180 Maria y Campos, *Múgica*, pp. 23, 33; Anderson, *Outcasts*, p. 178, on the case of Sánchez Azcona. Madero threatened to be 'the cause of [his] father's ruin', on account of his politics: Francisco Madero Sr to Madero, n.d. (1908), in Fabela, DHRM, RRM, p. 16.

181 Pipino González to Ricardo Flores Magón, 8 Mar. 1902, STA, box 26. Madero uses a similar sepulchral metaphor, invoking the ghosts of 'our fathers of 1810 and 1857', in Madero to Fernando Iglesias Calderón, n.d. (1908), in Fabela, DHRM, RRM, p. 15.

182 Córdova, *La ideología*, pp. 87–8; cf. Laurens Ballard Perry, 'Modelo liberal y la política práctica en la república restaurada, 1867–76', *Historia Mexicana*, XXIII (1973–4), pp. 646–99, on the liberal reality.

183 Anderson, *Outcasts*, pp. 322–3; Gavira, *Actuación*, p. 15.

184 Jacobs, 'Aspects', p. 139; Niemeyer, *Reyes*, p. 160; Maria y Campos, *Múgica*, pp. 22–3; John Reed, *Insurgent Mexico* (New York, 1969), p. 66; Manuel González Ramírez, *Manifiestos políticos 1892–1912* (Mexico, 1957), pp. 173–6.

185 Note the political opposition of established liberal families like the Alvarez of Guerrero, the Sánchez Magallanes of Tabasco: c/o USS Yorktown, Acapulco, 19 Mar. 1911, Lespinasse, Frontera, 8 Apr. 1911, SD 812.00/1238, 1405 on propaganda and education; Agular, 'The relevant tradition', p. 280, n. 42; Knight, 'Intellectuals'.

186 Madero, *La sucesión presidencial*, pp. 1–3; Salvador Alvarado, *Actuación revolucionaria del General Salvador Alvarado en Yucatán* (Mexico, 1955), p. 21; Narciso Bassols, *El pensamiento político de Alvaro Obregón* (Mexico, 1976), pp. 122–7.

187 O'Shaughnessy, *A Diplomat's Wife*, p. 9; Ross, *Madero*, p. 7.

188 For evidence of the correlation between Protestantism and progressive politics: US Senate, *Investigation of Mexican Affairs, Report and Hearings before a Subcommittee of the Committee on Foreign Relations* (2 vols. Washington, 1920), testimony of S. G. Inman, pp. 9–10 (henceforth: '*Fall Report*'); S. G. Inman, 'Notes on a Tour', SGIA, box 11; Knight, 'Intellectuals'; Jean A. Meyer, *The Cristero Rebellion. The Mexican People between Church and State, 1926–1929* (Cambridge, 1976), pp. 24–7; John A. Britton, 'Moisés Sáenz: nacionalista mexicano', *Historia Mexicana*, XXII (1972), p. 78.

189 Quoted by Cordova, *La ideología*, pp. 106–7.

190 *El Correo*, 29 June 1910; cf. Alvarado, *Reconstrucción*, I, p. 33.

191 R. E. Robinson and J. A. Gallagher with Alice Denny, *Africa and the Victorians. The Official Mind of Imperialism* (London, 1961), pp. 1–4.

192 Alvarado, *Reconstrucción*, I, pp. 32.

193 Valadés, *Imaginación*, I, p. 22; Reed, *Insurgent Mexico*, p. 160; William H. Beezley, *Insurgent Governor: Abraham González and the Mexican Revolution in Chihuahua* (Lincoln, 1973), p. 15.

194 Almada, *Diccionario*, pp. 125, 457; Luis Aguirre Benavides, *De Francisco I. Madero a Francisco Villa* (Mexico, 1966), p. 13; see n. 188 above.

195 A correlation between Catholicism, conservatism and anti-Americanism is suggested in Knight, 'Nationalism', pp. 207–8, 258–64.

196 Womack, *Zapata*, p. 55.

197 *El Diario del Hogar*, 23 May 1911.

198 Taracena, *Carranza*, pp. 23–7; Cosío Villegas, *Vida política*, p. 475; Voetter, Saltillo, 18 Mar. 1911, SD 812.00/1060; Ross, *Madero*, pp. 76–7, seems confused.

199 Olea, *Sinaloa*, pp. 13–8; Valadés, *Imaginación*, II, pp. 14–8; Sánchez Azcona, *Apuntes*, p. 105.

200 Bolio, *Yucatán*, pp. 57, 69; Joseph, 'Revolution From Without', pp. 73–91.

201 Baerlein, *Mexico*, pp. 24, 110–14.

202 *Ibid.*, pp. 212–14; Bolio, *Yucatán*, pp. 31–47.

203 Womack, *Zapata*, pp. 14–15.
204 *Ibid.*, pp. 22–3.
205 *Ibid.*, pp. 20, 27–30.
206 Ross, *Madero*, pp. 88–91; Cumberland, *Genesis*, pp. 92–3.
207 *Ibid.*, p. 85; E. Arenas to Carranza, 1 Oct. 1915, AVC.
208 Ross, *Madero*, pp. 96–7; Cumberland, *Genesis*, pp. 102–3; Ellsworth, Cd Porfirio Díaz, 3 Nov. 1910, SD 812.00/414.
209 Cumberland, *Genesis*, pp. 101–2; Ross, *Madero*, p. 99; Madero, 'El Partido Antirreleccionista' in Fabela, DHRM, RRM, I, p. 37.
210 Ross, *Madero*, p. 100; Cumberland, *Genesis*, p. 96.
211 *Ibid.*, p. 107.
212 Madero, 'El Partido Antirreleccionista', in Fabela, DHRM, RRM, I, pp. 36–8; cf. Jerry W. Knudson, 'When did Francisco I. Madero decide on revolution?' *Americas*, xxx (1974), pp. 529–34.
213 Sánchez Azcona, *Apuntes*, pp. 77–80; Ross, *Madero*, p. 98.
214 Cumberland, *Genesis*, pp. 108–9.
215 Madero to Díaz, 26 May 1910, in Sánchez Azcona, *Apuntes*, pp. 44–6.
216 Cumberland, *Genesis*, p. 109; Manuel González Ramírez, *La revolución social de México: las ideas, la violencia* (Mexico, 1960), p. 193; Anderson, *Outcasts*, p. 275; Bolío, *Yucatán*, pp. 49–56.
217 Luis Liceaga, *Félix Díaz* (Mexico, 1958), p. 33.
218 Cosío Villegas, *Vida política*, p. 893; Madero to Díaz, 15 June 1910, in Sánchez Azcona, pp. 38–41; Ross, *Madero*, p. 107.
219 Ellsworth, Cd. Porfirio Díaz, 1 Aug. 1910, SD 812.00/340.
220 Sánchez Azcona, *Apuntes*, pp. 88–90; *El Correo*, 3, 7, 8, 14 July 1910.
221 Ross, *Madero*, pp. 110–11; Cumberland, *Genesis*, pp. 115–16.
222 Gustavo Madero to Madero, 27 Aug. 1910, in Cumberland, *Genesis*, p. 116n.
223 *El País*, 13 Nov. 1910; cf. Cosío Villegas, *Vida política*, p. 745.
224 *Ibid.*, p. 747.
225 Ross, *Madero*, p. 108; Gavira, *Actuación*, p. 24.
226 Madero, *La sucesión presidencial*, pp. 277, 330; Amado Escobar to Nemesio Tejeda, 14 Oct. 1906, STA, box 26.
227 Hohler, *Diplomatic Petrel*, p. 172; James Creelman, *Díaz Master of Mexico* (New York, 1911), p. 417; S. G. Inman to A. R. Atwater, 19 Nov. 1910, SGIA, box 11.
228 Bonney, San Luis, 4 Apl. 1911, SD 812.00/1291.
229 Baerlein, *Mexico*, pp. 112–13.
230 Cumberland, *Genesis*, p. 117, citing Roque Estrada.
231 *Ibid.*, p. 120; Ellsworth, Cd Porfirio Díaz, 8 Oct. 1910, SD 812.00/351.
232 Silva Herzog, *Breve Historia*, I, p. 137.
233 Madero to Maytorena, 26 Oct. 1910; to Eduardo Maurer, 1 Nov. 1910, AFM r. 18; Ross, p. 120; Cumberland, *Genesis*, pp. 122–3.
234 Madero to Manuel Madero, 7 Nov. 1910, AFM r. 18.

3 Popular protest

1 For the derivation of 'social revolutionary' characteristics from mass participation, see below, pp. 314–15.
2 Cf. Huntington, *Political Order*, p. 268; John Rutherford, *Mexican Society During the Revolution: A Literary Approach* (Oxford, 1971), pp. 27, 314.
3 O'Hea, *Reminiscences*, p. 13.
4 Friedrich, *Agrarian Revolt*, p. 1.
5 Moisés Ochoa Campos, *La revolución mexicana, sus causas sociales* (Mexico, 1967).

6 Alperovich and Rudenko, *Revolución mexicana*, pp. 122, 203, 237; Charles C. Cumberland, *Mexico: The Struggle for Modernity* (Oxford, 1968), p. 307.

7 Rutherford, *Mexican Society*, pp. 221–2; Robert A. White, S. J., 'Mexico: the Zapata movement and the Revolution' in Henry A. Landsberger, ed., *Latin American Peasant Movements* (Cornell, 1969), p. 115; Adolfo Gilly, 'La guerra de clases y la revolución mexicana' in Gilly *et al.*, *Interpretaciones de la revolución mexicana* (Mexico, 3rd edn, 1980), pp. 30, 39–40.

8 Eric J. Hobsbawm, 'Peasants and Politics', *Journal of Peasant Studies*, 1 (1973), p. 10. I take it that Hobsbawm is not simply venturing the platitudinous observation that less than an outright majority of Mexico's peasants shouldered arms in 1910–20; he is commenting on the social composition of the revolutionary forces, and de-emphasising the contribution of the peasantry.

9 Meyer, *The Cristero Rebellion*, and the same author's *La Cristiada: La guerra de los cristeros* (3 vols., Mexico, 2nd edn, 1974).

10 Hohler, Mexico City, 30 May 1911, FO 371/1148, 23276.

11 Tannenbaum, 'Revolución agraria', *Peace*, and Gruening, *Mexico and its Heritage*. Perhaps the most plausible critique of the old agrarian/populist thesis has been made by Brading, 'Introduction: National politics and the populist tradition', in Brading, ed., *Caudillo and Peasant*, pp. 9–16.

12 El Colegio de México, *Estadísticas económicas del Porfiriato* (Mexico, 1956), p. 28. I am taking communities with a population greater than 5,000 to be towns. González Navarro, *Vida social*, p. 39, takes 4,000 as the urban/rural dividing line.

13 *Mexican Year Book* (Los Angeles, 1922), pp. 340–4.

14 Friedrich Katz, 'Labor Conditions on Haciendas in Porfirian Mexico: Some Trends and Tendencies', *Hispanic American Historical Review*, LIV (1974), p. 1.

15 *Ibid.*; and Katz, *Servidumbre agraria*, p. 13.

16 García Cubas, *Mexico, its Trade, Industry and Resources*, p. 283; Fernando González Roa, *El problema ferrocarrilero* (Mexico, 1919), p. 30; John H. Coatsworth, *El impacto económico de los ferrocarriles*, I, pp. 45–53.

17 Molina Enríquez, *Grandes problemas nacionales* (1909), p. 291.

18 Coatsworth, *El impacto económico de los ferrocarriles*, I, pp. 123–4, 129, 147–8, Cumberland, *Modernity*, p. 221.

19 Coello Salazar in Cosío Villegas, *Vida económica*, II, pp. 732, 776; De Szyszlo, *Dix milles kilomètres*, p. 192.

20 Pollard, *A Busy Time in Mexico*, p. 43; Gadow, *Through Southern Mexico*, p. 272; Harry L. Foster, *A Gringo in Mañana-Land* (London, 1924), p. 31 on Standard Oil cans again.

21 Nava Oteo and D'Olwer in Cosío Villegas, *Vida económica*, I, p. 179, II, p. 1161; Rosenzweig, 'El desarrollo económico', pp. 424–5; Reynolds, *The Mexican Economy*, p. 21.

22 Rosenzweig in Cosío Villegas, *Vida económica*, II, pp. 635–8, 689–94.

23 Bernstein, *Mexican Mining Industry*, pp. 41–91; Rosenzweig in Cosío Villegas, *Vida económica*, pp. 660–88.

24 Lorenzo Meyer, *México y Estados Unidos en el conflicto petrolero* (Mexico, 1968), p. 19.

25 Cossio Silva in Cosío Villegas, *Vida económica*, I, pp. 3–5.

26 Rosenzweig in Cosío Villegas, *Vida económica*, II, pp. 640, 669, 673, 683. The question of staple food production is open to debate: see p. 129.

27 Jeffery M. Paige, *Agrarian Revolution: Social Movements and Export Agriculture in the Underdeveloped World* (New York, 1978), pp. 1–2.

28 Ezio Cusi, *Memorias de un colono* (Mexico, 1969), pp. 28, 37.

29 Lewis, *Tepoztlán*, p. xxv; Womack, *Zapata*, p. 42.

30 Dudley Ankerson, 'The Cedillos and the Revolution in the State of San Luis Potosí, 1890–1938' (unpublished Cambridge Ph.D. diss. 1981), ch. 1, pp. 6–8.

31 *Ibid.*, p. 9; Jacobs, 'Aspects', pp. 29, 55–63; Schryer, *Rancheros of Pisaflores*, pp. 28, 34–5.

32 González, *Pueblo en Vilo*, p. 105.

33 *Ibid.*, p. 101.

34 D. A. Brading, *Miners and Merchants in Bourbon Mexico 1763–1810* (Cambridge, 1971), pp. 211–19.

35 Robert Brenner, 'The Origins of Capitalist Development: a Critique of Neo-Smithian Marxism', *New Left Review*, CIV, July–Aug. 1977, p. 91.

36 Nathan Whetten, *Rural Mexico*, p. 81 and *passim*; see also McBride, *Land Systems of Mexico*, pp. 25–81, 103–38.

37 Magnus Mörner, 'La hacienda Hispanoamericana: examen de las investigaciones y debates recientes' in *Haciendas, latifundios y plantaciones en América Latina* (Mexico, 3rd edn, 1979), p. 28, citing Ewald.

38 Francois Chevalier, *Land and Society*, especially pp. 153–78.

39 *Ibid.*, pp. 206, 310–11; William B. Taylor, *Landlord and Peasant in Colonial Oaxaca* (Stanford, 1972), p. 197.

40 Tutino, 'Hacienda Social Relations', pp. 518–25; David Goodman and Michael Redclift, *From Peasant to Proletarian Capitalist Development and Agrarian Transition* (Oxford, 1981), pp. 62–3, reviews the literature.

41 Mörner, 'La hacienda hispanoamericana', pp. 35–7; Brading, *Miners*, p. 216; and cf. Arnold Bauer, *Chilean Rural Society* (Cambridge, 1975), pp. 49–50.

42 Brading, *Haciendas*, p. 12 and *passim*; Enrique Florescano, *Precios del maíz y crisis agrícolas en México (1708–1810)* (Mexico, 1969), pp. 88–97; Harrison, *A Mexican Family Empire*, pp. 253, 313.

43 Mörner, 'La hacienda hispanoamericana', p. 29; and, in the same volume, Enrique Semo y Gloria Pedrero, 'La vida en una hacienda-aserradero mexicana a principios del siglo XIX', p. 303.

44 Chevalier, *Land and Society*, p. 176; Harrison, *A Mexican Family Empire*, pp. 5–6.

45 See Rodney Hilton, 'Introduction' in Hilton, *et al.*, *The Transition from Feudalism to Capitalism* (London, 1978), p. 30.

46 A. G. Frank, *Capitalism and Underdevelopment in Latin America* (New York, 1967); and the same author's *Mexican Agriculture 1521–1630: Transformation of the Mode of Production* (Cambridge, 1979); I. Wallerstein, *The Modern World System: Capitalist Agriculture and the Origins of the European World Economy in the Sixteenth Century* (New York, 1974).

47 Cf. Cockcroft, *Intellectual Precursors*, pp. xiii–xvi, 29–30.

48 Ernesto Laclau, 'Feudalism and Capitalism in Latin America' in Laclau, *Politics and Ideology in Marxist Theory* (London, 1977), pp. 15–50.

49 Reyna, p. 24; Roger Bartra, 'Peasants and Political power in Mexico: a theorerical approach', *Latin American Perspectives*, V, 1975, p. 125–9.

50 *Ibid.*, p. 139; Laclau, 'Feudalism and Capitalism', p. 42; and, for a general statement of the position, John G. Taylor, *From Modernizatiion to Modes of Production* (London, 1979).

51 Cf. Mörner, 'La hacienda hispanoamericana', pp. 42–3; Bauer, *Chilean Rural Society*, p. 12.

52 Bartra, 'Peasants and Political Power in Mexico: a theoretical approach', *Latin American Perspectives*, V (1975), pp. 129–44, makes an interesting attempt; cf. Taylor, *From Modernization*, pp. 226–75; and John Gledhill, 'Agrarian Change and the Articulation of Forms [sic] of Production: the case of the Mexican Bajío', *Bulletin of Latin American Research*, I, 1981, pp. 63–80; Schryer, *Rancheros of Pisaflores*, p. 49, talks mysteriously of a complex articulation at local level, in turn determined by 'the larger social and economic system'. Perhaps the clearest and most constructive attempt to 'operationalise' the theory is Norman Long, 'Structural dependency, modes of production and economic brokerage in rural Peru', in Ivar Oxaal *et al.*, eds., *Beyond the Sociology of Development Economy and Society in Latin America and Africa* (London, 1975), pp. 265–79.

53 Daniel Chirot, 'The Growth of the Market and Service Labor Systems in Agriculture', *Journal of Social History*, VII, 1974–5, p. 76.

54 The Rankean quotation does not imply a belief in Rankean, value-free history. The acceptance of a degree of subjectivity, however, does not necessarily cast the historian adrift in a relativist sea, where all interpretations/theories are equally valid (and invalid) – as E. H. Carr comes close to suggesting. Degrees of objectivity are possible, and objective data/ criteria exist against which different interpretations may be judged: see Talcott Parsons, 'Weber's Methodology of Social Science' in Max Weber, *The Theory of Social and Economic Organization* (New York, 1969), pp. 9–10.

55 Frank, *Capitalism and Underdevelopment*, p. 27ff.

56 Laclau, 'Feudalism and Capitalism', p. 30; Bartra, 'Peasants', p. 127; see also Geoffrey Kay, *Development and Underdevelopment: A Marxist Analysis* (London, 1977), pp. 96–156.

57 Arnold Bauer, *Chilean Rural Society*, pp. 62–82; 'Introduction: patterns of agrarian capitalism in Latin America', in K. Duncan and I. Rutledge, eds., *Land and Labour in Latin America* (Cambridge, 1977), pp. 4–5.

58 Max Weber, *The Protestant Ethic and the Spirit of Capitalism* (London, 1974), pp. 53–7, 67–9.

59 See pp. 57–8, 69–70.

60 Weber, *Protestant Ethic*, p. 68; cf. Christopher Hill, 'Protestantism and the Rise of Capitalism' in *Change and Continuity in Seventeenth-Century England* (London, 1974), pp. 99–100.

61 Jan Bazant, *Alienation of Church Wealth in Mexico: Social and Economic Aspects of the Liberal Revolution 1856–1875* (Cambridge, 1971), pp. 288–90.

62 Schryer, *Rancheros of Pisaflores*, p. 7; cf. Polly Hill, *Studies in Rural Capitalism in West Africa* (Cambridge, 1970).

63 Katz, 'Labor conditions', p. 4 (I am compressing two of Katz's categories).

64 *Ibid.*, p. 27; David Ronfeldt, *Atencingo: The Politics of Agrarian Struggle in a Mexican Ejido* (Stanford, 1973), p. 8.

65 Wolf, *Sons*, pp. 208–10; Wistano Luis Orozco in Silva Herzog, *La cuestión*, I, p. 217; Gadow, *Through Southern Mexico*, p. 80.

66 It may be argued how important such bonds had been in earlier times, and investigation would no doubt reveal major regional differences; however, the fact of their decline seems clear.

67 Ankerson, 'The Cedillos', (diss.) ch. 1, p. 5; Margolies, *Princes*, p. 30; Katz, *Servidumbre agraria*, p. 48; Fuentes Mares, *Y México se refugió*, p. 244; Womack, *Zapata*, p. 42.

68 Katz, *Servidumbre agraria*, pp. 18–19.

69 See the excellent article by Arnold Bauer, 'Rural Workers in Spanish America: Problems of Peonage and Oppression', *Hispanic American Historical Review*, LIX, pp. 34–63, plus comments, pp. 478–89.

70 Katz, *Servidumbre agraria*, pp. 37–42; Moisés González Navarro, 'El trabajo forzoso en México, 1821–1917', *Historia Mexicana*, XXVII (1977–8), pp. 588–615; Simón Márquez Camarena interviewed by María Isabel Souza, 1973, PHO I/113, p. 24; *El Correo*, 26 February 1910 on the 'odious system of debt peons' in the Laguna; miners, too, were secured on an *enganche* basis.

71 Luis Cabrera in Silva Herzog, *La cuestión*, I, p. 296; cf. Gruening, *Mexico and its Heritage*, pp. 137–8.

72 Katz, *Servidumbre agraria*, pp. 37–40 and the report of Refugio Galindo (1905) in the same volume, pp. 83–103; though the information concerning the abolition of debts at Tochatlaco (pp. 40, 100) does not square with the hacienda records, which still indicate significant levels of indebtedness on the eve of the Revolution: the explanation is given by Marco Bellingeri, 'L'economia del latifondo in Messico. L'hacienda San Antonio Tochatlaco dal 1880 al 1920', *Annali della Fondazione Luigi Einaudi*, Torino, 1976, pp. 380, 407.

73 Jan Bazant, 'Peones, arrendatarios y aparceros: 1868–1904', *Historia Mexicana* XXIV (1974–5), pp. 94–121; Arturo Warman, *Y venimos a contradecir: Los campesinos de Morelos y el*

estado nacional (Mexico, 1976), pp. 67–8; Katz, 'Labor conditions', pp. 9–10; Zacarías Escobedo Girón, interviewed by Ximena Sepulveda Otaiza, 1973, PHO 1/129, p. 2, on the privileged *acasillados* on a Zacatecas hacienda, for which see also Harry E. Cross, 'Living Standards in Rural Nineteenth-Century Mexico: Zacatecas 1820–80', *Journal of Latin American Studies*, x, 1978, pp. 1–19, and Governor of Zacatecas to Trabajo, 12 September 1916, Trabajo 31/3/5, which indicate the continuity of economic privilege.

74 Warman, *Y venimos a contradecir*, pp. 67, 70, 72.

75 *Ibid.*, p. 73; Margolies, *Princes*, p. 26; Katz, *Servidumbre agraria*, pp. 31, 39, 95; O'Hea, *Reminiscences*, p. 33.

76 Report of J. M. Duane, Tlahualilo, 17 June 1896, MCETA, parcel 5; and, on the topic of peon passivity, Katz, *Servidumbre agraria*, p. 21 and the same author's *The Secret War in Mexico. Europe, The United States and the Mexican Revolution* (Chicago, 1981), p. 11.

77 Galindo report, in Katz, *Servidumbre agraria*, pp. 83–103. On drink, see pp. 23, 40, 74, 443–4.

78 Katz, *Servidumbre agraria*, pp. 39, 115; Simón Márquez Camarena interviewed by María Isabel Souza, 1973, PHO 1/113, pp. 18–19; Lewis, *Pedro Martínez*, p. 73. Many examples of revolutionary retribution, visited upon harsh overseers and unpopular shopkeepers, will be noted later.

79 Knight, 'Nationalism', pp. 178–99, 301–9.

80 Bazant, 'Peones', p. 94.

81 Juan Martínez Alier, *Haciendas, Plantations and Collective Farms: Agrarian Class Societies – Cuba and Peru* (London, 1977), pp. 15–16. For the 'orthodox' view, see E. J. Hobsbawm, 'Peasants and Rural Migrants in Politics' in Claudio Véliz, ed., *The Politics of Conformity in Latin America* (Oxford, 1967), p. 56.

82 The comparison is most fully drawn – with Chile as the principal Latin American example – by Cristóbal Kay, 'Comparative Development of the European Manorial System and the Latin American Hacienda System', (Ph.D. diss., Sussex, 1971, unpublished), pp. 174, 179–85 and *passim*.

83 Katz, *Servidumbre agraria*, pp. 25–33.

84 Bauer, 'Rural Workers', pp. 36–7, 62.

85 Enrique Rau (German vice-consul, San Cristóbal) to Governor of Chiapas, 27 Sept. 1915, AJD, r.3.

86 Cf. Bauer, 'Rural Workers', pp. 53–8; Weber, *Protestant Ethic*, pp. 59–60.

87 González Navarro, *Vida social*, pp. 168–72; Katz, *Servidumbre agraria*, p. 26.

88 Turner, *Barbarous Mexico*, pp. 13–33, 67–111; Joseph, 'Revolution From Without', pp. 119–29; Nevin O. Winter, *Mexico and Her People of Today* (London, 1913), pp. 188–91; Baerlein, *Mexico*, pp. 145–66, 178–89; Madero, *Sucesión presidencial*, pp. 191–3, 238 and to M. Mestre Ghigliazzi, 25 July 1912, AFM r.12.

89 Gruening, *Mexico and its Heritage*, p. 139; R. Hernández to A. Pérez Rivera, 7 Dec. 1912, AG 889.

90 González Navarro, 'Trabajo forzoso', p. 599; Katz, *Servidumbre agraria*, p. 48.

91 Baerlein, *Mexico*, pp. 148–9; cf. Gruening, *Mexico and its Heritage*, p. 138; Joseph, 'Revolution from Without', p. 124.

92 McGoogan, Progreso, 19 Mar. 1911, SD 812.00/1084; Katz, *Servidumbre agraria*, p. 32.

93 Eugene Genovese, *Roll Jordan Roll, The World the Slaves Made* (New York, 1974), pp. 587–91. On the quiescence of the southern peons: Katz, *Secret War*, p. 11; Walter L. Goldfrank, 'Inequality and Revolution in Rural Mexico', *Social and Economic Studies*, xxv, December 1976, pp. 401–2.

94 Stanley Elkins, *Slaverey: A Problem in American Institutional and Intellectual Life* (Chicago, 1959).

95 See pp. 226–7.

96 González Navarro, 'Trabajo forzoso', pp. 599–601; Katz, *Servidumbre agraria*, pp. 59, 100.

97 González Navarro, 'Trabajo forzoso', p. 603; Katz, *Servidumbre agraria*, p. 59; Ruiz, *Great Rebellion*, p. 98; Jorge Flores D., 'La vida rural en Yucatán en 1914', *Historia Mexicana*, x, 1960–1, p. 479.

98 Heather Fowler Salamini, *Agrarian Radicalism in Veracruz 1920–38* (Lincoln, 1978), pp. 7–8; Henry H. Harper, *A Journey in South-eastern Mexico* (New York, 1910), p. 61.

99 Katz, 'Labor Conditions', pp. 4–5; Katz, *Servidumbre agraria*, pp. 29, 78–9; among the sugar, coffee and rubber plantations of the Zongólica district of Veracruz the ratio of 'fixed' to 'harvest' peons was usually in the order of 1:5, sometimes as high as 1:8 or 9: see report of agricultural production, 1911, AZ f.74, r.9.

100 González Navarro, *Vida social*, p. 233; Vanderwood, *Disorder and Progress*, pp. 80–1.

101 Report on agricultural production, 1911, AZ f.74, r.9

102 Friedrich, *Agrarian Revolt*, p. 46.

103 Henri Favre, 'The Dynamics of Indian Peasant Society and Migration to Coastal Plantations in Peru', in Duncan and Rutledge, *Land and Labour*, pp. 253–67.

104 Margolies, *Princes*, p. 30; Katz, *Servidumbre agraria*, p. 44; Octavio Paz, 'El latifundismo en el Norte', *Crisol*, July 1931, on the Moncada family of Durango.

105 Katz, *Servidumbre agraria*, p. 44.

106 Katz, 'Labor Conditions', p. 4; Bazant, 'Peones', pp. 99–103; Margolies, *Princes*, p. 28.

107 Dollero, *México al Día*, pp. 211, 214; Katz, 'Labor Conditions', pp. 34–6.

108 The Potosino hacendado José Encarnación Ipiña reported workers heading north to the US in 'droves' in 1906: Ankerson, 'Cedillos' (diss.), ch. 1, p. 23. See also Ruiz, *Great Rebellion*, p. 85; F. González Roa, *El aspecto agrario de la revolución mexicana* (Mexico, 1919), p. 197; Mario T. García, *Desert Immigrants: The Mexicans of El Paso 1880–1920* (Yale, 1981), pp. 34–5, 244.

109 Warman, *Y venimos a contradecir*, pp. 55–6.

110 De Szyszlo, *Dix mille kilomètres*, pp. 244, 257, 286; Huxley, *Beyond the Mexique Bay*, p. 163.

111 Jacobs, 'Aspects', p. 79.

112 Katz, *Servidumbre agraria*, pp. 35, 51, 104; Ruiz, *Great Rebellion*, p. 81; Ankerson, 'Cedillos' (diss.) ch. 1, p. 24.

113 Brading, *Haciendas and Ranchos*, pp. 12, 206.

114 *Ibid.*, pp. 10, 205–6.

115 Margolies, *Princes*, p. 34.

116 Ankerson, 'Cedillos' (diss.) ch. 1, p. 24; Katz, *Servidumbre agraria*, p. 36; Julián Malo Juvera cited in Marte R. Gómez, *La Reforma agraria en las filas villistas* (Mexico, 1966), pp. 234–8; Tannenbaum, 'Revolución agraria', p. 51.

117 O'Hea, *Reminiscences*, pp. 31–2.

118 González Navarro, *Vida social*, p. 234.

119 Katz, 'Labor Conditions', p. 10.

120 O'Hea, *Reminiscences*, p. 32.

121 Jacobs, 'Aspects', p. 79ff.

122 Barrington Moore, *Social Origins*, p. 434; and Maurice Dobb, 'From Feudalism to Capitalism', in Hilton *et al.*, *Transition*, pp. 165–6, for an 'orthodox' statement.

123 Ankerson, 'Cedillos' (diss.) ch. 1, p. 20; Womack, *Zapata*, pp. 50–2; Jacobs, 'Aspects', pp. 57–63; Schryer, *Rancheros of Pisaflores*, pp. 63–5.

124 Warman, *Y venimos a contradecir*, pp. 55–7; Margolies, pp. 21–2; Ankerson, 'Cedillos' (diss.), ch. 1, pp. 23–4; cf. Enrique Florescano, *Precios de maíz y crisis agrícolas en México (1708–1810)*, (Mexico, 1969), pp. 182–95, and Gruening, *Mexico*, p. 132, on the continued importance of hacienda staple production.

125 Cf. Barrington Moore, *Social Origins*, pp. 434–7.

126 González Roa, *Aspecto agrario*, pp. 98–9, citing Lauro Viadas; Molina Enríquez, *Grandes problemas nacionales*, pp. 224–5; Coatsworth, *El Impacto económico de los ferrocarriles*, II, pp. 8–24.

127 González Roa, *Aspecto agrario*, p. 200.

128 Cossio Silva, 'La agricultura', in *Vida económica*, pp. 5, 19, 21; cf. p. 129 below.

129 Ruiz, *Great Rebellion*, p. 97; Bulnes, *El Verdadero Díaz*, p. 236; Ankerson, 'Cedillos' (diss.), ch. 1, pp. 25–6.

130 Alvarado, *Reconstrucción*, pp. 181–8; Reina, *Rebeliones campesinas*, pp. 33, 72, 92, 117, 123, 127.

131 González Roa, *Aspecto agrario*, pp. 90–4.

132 *Ibid.*; Mariano Ruiz, *jefe político* Tepic to Gobernación, 13 July 1910, AG Tepic, 1910–11, 17/9.

133 González Roa, *Aspecto agrario*, p. 92; Wistano Luis Orozco in Silva Herzog, *La cuestión de la tierra*, I, p. 219.

134 Rosenzweig, 'Moneda y bancos' in Cosío Villegas, *Vida económica*, pp. 847–8.

135 H. Bourgeois to Quai d'Orsay, 11 Aug. 1912, AAE, Méxique Affaires Commerciales, I, B/28/1 no. 10.

136 Rosenzweig, 'Moneda y bancos' in Cosío Villegas, *Vida económica*, p. 858; de Szyszlo, *Dix milles kilomètres*, pp. 280–1; González Roa, *Aspecto agrario*, pp. 104–6.

137 Womack, *Zapata*, p. 51; González Navarro, *Vida social*, pp. 393, 400–3; Flandrau, *Viva Mexico!*, pp. 130–1; de Szyszlo, *Dix milles kilomètres*, p. 194.

138 Womack, *Zapata*, p. 49; Margolies, *Princes*, pp. 19–20; Ankerson, 'Cedillos' (diss.), ch. 1, p. 8.

139 Warman, *Y venimos a contradecir*, p. 58.

140 Anon. letter, Culiacán, 1 Apr. 1911, SD 812.00/1249.

141 Rosenzweig, 'Moneda y bancos', in Cosío Villegas, *Vida económica*, pp. 856–7; Cockcroft, *Intellectual Precursors*, p. 36; Ruiz, *Great Rebellion*, pp. 128–30.

142 The planters of Yucatán, e.g., were hard hit, and were disposed to dabble in opposition politics; they did not, however, lend their support to armed revolution. *Hacendados* who did – Madero, Maytorena, or Señora Eucaria Apreza of Chilapa, Guerrero – were known oppositionists of years standing, members of 'out' families, or die-hard liberals; they were not recent converts to revolution, motivated by economic resentments.

143 González Navarro, 'Trabajo forzoso', pp. 602–2.

144 *Ibid.*, pp. 595–6 and González Navarro, *Vida social*, p. 235; at San Pedro (Chih.) the chief of police moved on migrant miners who had been unemployed for three days or more (a policy which many of the inhabitants approved): *El Correo*, 22 Feb. 1910.

145 Cf. Basil Davidson, *Africa in Modern History: the Search for a New Society* (Harmondsworth, 1978), pp. 106–113; J. Forbes Munro, *Africa and the International Economy, 1800–1960* (London, 1976), pp. 104, 110–11, 140–1.

146 Reina, *Rebeliones campesinas*, pp. 20–2; Jacobs, 'Aspects', pp. 45–6.

147 McBride, *Land Systems of Mexico*, pp. 73–4; Gonzáles Roa, *Aspecto agrario*, pp. 128–33.

148 González Navarro, *Vida social*, p. 203; Jacobs, 'Aspects', pp. 45–7, which notes the continuation of this policy until the very eve of the Revolution.

149 Gruening, p. 128; *El Correo*, 29 Apr. 1909; Anderson, c/o USS Yorktown, Acapulco, 19 Mar. 1911, SD 812.00/1238; Ankerson, 'Cedillos' (diss.), ch. 1, p. 20.

150 Whetten, *Rural Mexico*, p. 98.

151 González Navarro, *Vida social*, pp. 188, 196; McBride, *Land Systems of Mexico*, p. 75.

152 González Navarro, *Vida social*, p. 198 indicates the rise in value of *terrenos baldíos* during the Porfiriato: from 1.50 to 17 pesos a hectare in Tlaxcala, 2 to 27 pesos in Morelos, 50c to 7 pesos in Tabasco, 12c to 4 pesos in Coahuila, Sonora and Chihuahua.

153 Taylor, *Landlord and Peasant*, p. 199; Ruiz, *Great Rebellion*, pp. 73, 96–8.

154 González Roa, *Aspecto agrario*, p. 7.

155 Tannenbaum, 'Revolución agraria', pp. 23–6.

156 *Ibid.*, p. 33.

157 Pastor Rouaix, *Génesis de los artículos 27 y 123 de la constitución política de 1917* (Mexico, 1959), pp. 52–3; Octavio Paz, 'El latifundismo en el norte' *Crisol*, julio 1931.

158 Tannenbaum, *Peace*, pp. 192–3.

159 Womack, *Zapata*, p. 44; Warman, *Y venimos a contradecir*, pp. 53–4; Tannenbaum, 'Revolución agraria', p. 33.

160 *Ibid.*, p. 35.

161 Lucio Mendieta y Núñez, *El problema agrario de México* (Mexico, 1966), p. 150, citing Rouaix; J. G. Nava to Carranza, 15 Dec. 1915, AVC.

162 Manuel Gamio, *Introduction, Synthesis and Conclusion of the Work: The Population of the Valley of Teotihuacan, Mexico* (Mexico, 1922), pp. xiv–v; Luis Cabrera, cited in Silva Herzog, *La cuestión de la tierra*, II, p. 290.

163 McBride, *Land Systems of Mexico*, pp. 139–47.

164 Wistano Luiz Orozco in Silva Herzog, *La cuestión de la tierra*, I, pp. 207–11.

165 On the operations of the *tienda de raya*: González Navarro, *Vida social*, p. 219; Margolies, *Princes*, p. 30; Ankerson, 'Cedillos' (diss.), ch. 1, pp. 22–3.

166 Bonney, San Luis, 4 Apr. 1911, SD 812.00/1291; Baerlein, pp. 178–9.

167 Wistano Luis Orozco in Silva Herzog, *La cuestión de la tierra*, I, p. 218. Landlords could influence politics; but, it should also be noted, the accumulation of land could bolster political power (e.g., by creating new, dependent clienteles). Hacienda expansion could thus serve political, as well as 'economic' or 'psychological' ends: cf. Jacobs, 'Aspects', p. 88. Analyses which stress the importance of status and prestige in hacienda expansion risk not only underestimating economic rationale (within the imperfect market of latifundismo), but also neglecting such political considerations. Cf. Molina Enríquez, *Grandes problemas nacionales* (1978), p. 162; and Edith Boorstein Couturier, 'Modernización y tradición en una hacienda, San Juan Hueyapam 1902–1911' *Historia Mexicana*, XVIII, 1968, pp. 35–40.

168 Keys, Rosario, 29 May 1915, SD 812.00/15246.

169 See below, pp. 352, 361–3.

170 Schryer, *Rancheros of Pisaflores*, p. 7ff; Jacobs, 'Aspects', pp. 55, 58.

171 Tannenbaum, 'Revolución agraria', p. 32; Schmieder, p. 25; Nahmad, *Los mixes*, pp. 36, 40; Starr, *Indian Mexico*, p. 180.

172 De Szyszlo, *Dix milles kilomètres*, p. 68; cf. Lawton, Oaxaca, July 1911, SD 812.00/241.

173 Dollero, *México al Día*, p. 229.

174 De la Peña, *El pueblo y su tierra*, p. 286.

175 Luisa Beatriz Rojas Nieto, *La destrucción de la hacienda en Aguascalientes 1910–1931* (Mexico, INAH, 1976), p. 28; and below, pp. 400–1.

176 McBride, *Land Systems of Mexico*, pp. 91–5; González Navarro, *Vida social*, p. 211 on the definition.

177 Schryer, *Rancheros of Pisaflores*, pp. 7, 28–9; Jacobs, 'Aspects', pp. 54, 80; McBride, *Land Systems of Mexico*, pp. 97–100; Gruening, p. 125.

178 Jacobs, 'Aspects', pp. 122–3 and 'Rancheros', pp. 83–4; Aguilar, 'The Relevant Tradition', pp. 118–9; McBride, *Land Systems of Mexico*, pp. 87–8, 101; Schryer, *Rancheros of Pisaflores*, p. 7 on manners.

179 McBride, *Land Systems of Mexico*, p. 87.

180 Meyer, *Cristero Rebellion*, pp. 85, 92, 186; Jacobs, 'Aspects', p. 126; Schryer, *Rancheros of Pisaflores*, p. 70

181 McBride, *Land Systems of Mexico*, p. 102. A similar attitude may be distilled from González, *Pueblo en Vilo*.

182 Jacobs, 'Aspects', pp. 140–2, 'Rancheros', p. 84. It follows that simple generalisations about '*ranchero*' behaviour, which assume constancy and homogeneity where they do not exist, are mistaken: cf. Ruiz, *Great Rebellion*, p. 77.

183 Examples of hacienda social and ideological control abound: see Flores, 'La vida rural',

p. 477, on paternalistic supervision in Yucatán; de la Peña, *El pueblo y su tierra*, pp. 321–2, on hacienda elimination of peon independence; for an example of which, see Zacarías Escobedo Girón, interviewed by Ximena Sepúlveda Otaiza, PHO 1/129.

184 Ruiz, *Great Rebellion*, pp. 96–7.
185 González Navarro, *Vida social*, p. 218.
186 Katz, 'Labor Conditions', p. 24; Baerlein, *Mexico*, p. 165.
187 Ruiz, *Great Rebellion*, p. 82.
188 *Ibid.*, pp. 96–9.
189 Brading, *Haciendas and Ranchos*, p. 206. In San Luis, Ankerson notes, 'suggestions that large estates should be divided into small farms in order to absorb surplus labour and relieve social tension were ignored; and even those who put forward such proposals did not practise them': 'Cedillos' (diss.), ch. 1, pp. 23–4.
190 Barrington Moore, *Social Origins*, pp. 434, 438, 442.
191 Bazant, 'Peones', p. 121; Margolies, *Princes*, p. 28; González Roa, *Aspecto agrario*, p. 97.
192 'Verdammte Bedürfnislosigkeit', in the words of 'an embittered German trader': Stuart Chase, *Mexico: A Study of Two Americas* (New York, 1931), p. 313. Twenty years before Chase wrote it was even truer.
193 Anderson, *Outcasts*, pp. 29–31, 251.
194 Bonney, San Luis, 2 Nov. 1912, SD 812.00/5446.
195 Womack, *Zapata*, p. 10. Cf. Ruiz, *Great Rebellion*, p. 120, which stresses (and in my view exaggerates) the role of the 1907 depression as the 'watershed of the rebellion'.
196 V. I. Lenin, 'The Agrarian Policy of Social Democracy in the First Russian Revolution, 1905–7' in *Collected Works* (Moscow, 1962), XIII, pp. 241–3, 422.
197 Schryer, *Rancheros of Pisaflores*, pp. 34, 40, 50–8.
198 Reed, *Caste War*, pp. 47–8.
199 *Ibid.*, p. 48.
200 Mario Gill, 'Mochis, fruto de un sueño imperialista', *Historia Mexicana*, V (1955), pp. 303–20.
201 *Ibid.*; c/o US Navy, Topolobampo, 30 June 1915, SD 812.00/15653.
202 Hobsbawm, 'Peasants and Rural Migrants', p. 56.
203 González Navarro, *Vida social*, pp. 205–7; cf. Chevalier, *Land and Society*, pp. 142, 189–90.
204 See Donald J. Fraser, 'La política de desamortización en las comunidades indígenas, 1856–72', *Historia Mexicana*, XXI (1971–2), pp. 615–52; González Navarro, *Vida social*, p. 207.
205 Ronfeldt, *Atencingo*, pp. 7–8.
206 Cf. Schryer, *Rancheros of Pisaflores*, pp. 26–36 and José de Jesús Montoya Briones, 'Estructura de poder y desarrollo social en la Sierra de Hidalgo', *América Indígena*, XXVII (1978), p. 600; Rafael Vega Sánchez to Carranza, 23 Dec. 1916, AVC; *El Demócrata*, 12 Dec. 1915.
207 Raymond Th. J. Buve, 'Peasant Movements, Caudillos and Land Reform during the Revolution (1910–17) in Tlaxcala, Mexico', *Boletín de Estudios Latino-Americanos y del Caribe*, XVIII (1975), pp. 122–8; Governor A. Machorro to Carranza, 6 May 1916, AVC.
208 Gadow, pp. 5–6; González Navarro, *Vida social*, pp. 189, 206–7.
209 Gadow, *Through Southern Mexico*, pp. 5–6; Friedrich, *Agrarian Revolt*, pp. 5–45.
210 *Ibid.*, p. 43.
211 Cf. Rutherford, *Mexican Society*, pp. 221–2; Ruiz, *Great Rebellion*, pp. 7, 75; White, 'The Zapata Movement', p. 115.
212 A point made by Sotelo Inclán: see María Alba Pastor, *Aspectos del movimiento agrario sureño* (Mexico, DEAS, 1975), p. 5.
213 Womack, *Zapata*, pp. 42, 50.
214 *Ibid.*, p. 46.

215 Coatsworth, *El Impacto económico de los ferrocarriles*, II, pp. 41–76, 136–44; and the same author's 'Railroads, Landholding and Agrarian Protest in the Early Porfiriato', *Hispanic American Historical Review*, LIV (1974), pp. 48–71.

216 Apart from Michoacán and the sierras of Chihuahua, Mexico state also suffered from the railways' – and to an extent the mines' – demand for timber: see Margolies, *Princes*, pp. 21–2, José Martín and others to Carranza from the Acambay district, 2 May 1916, AV.

217 Marcos V. Méndez to Gobernación, 30 July 1911, AG 14, Relaciones con los Estados (Mich.); cf. J. L. García Mora, 'El conflicto agrario-religioso en la Sierra Tarasca', *América Indígena*, XXXVI (1976), p. 118; Antonio Díaz Soto y Gama, 'La revolución agraria en Michoacán', *El Universal*, 22 July 1953.

218 E. Michot to M. Armand Delille, 15 Sept. 1911, Gobernación 14, Relaciones con los Estados (Mich.); Mauricio Pérez, Acuitzeramo, to Gobernación, 23 Feb. 1913, AG57/3; Francisco Herrero, Los Reyes Ecuandereo, to Carranza, 18 Aug. 1916, AVC.

219 Jacobs, 'Aspects', pp. 52, 69.

220 Nahmad, *Los Mixes*, pp. 40–2 and below, pp. 113, 346–7.

221 George M. Foster, *A Primitive Mexican Economy* (Seattle and London, 1942), pp. 14, 109; C. D. Padua, *Movimiento revolucionario – 1906 en Veracruz* (Cuernavaca, 1936), p. 5; Canada, Veracruz, 12, 17 Apr. 1912, SD 812.00/3583, 3631; Lespinasse, Frontera, 18 May 1911, 29 Feb. 1912, SD 812.00/2016, 3233.

222 Vanderwood, *Disorder and Progress*, p. 90; Reina, *Las rebeliones campesinas* p. 359; De la Peña, *El pueblo y su tierra*, p. 294.

223 Guy Stresser Péan, 'Problèmes agraires de la Huasteca ou région de Tampico', in *Les Problèmes Agraires des Amériques Latines* (Paris, 1967), p. 202; Reina, *Las rebeliones campesinas*, pp. 18–19, 341–9.

224 *Ibid.*, pp. 271–8, 356; Ankerson, 'Cedilles' (diss.) ch. 1, p. 14.

225 Reina, *Las rebeliones campesinas*, p. 15.

226 Martin, *Mexico of the Twentieth Century*, II, p. 139; Dollero, *México al Día*, p. 180; Stresser Péan, 'Problèmes agraires', p. 204; Figueroa Domenech, *Guía general descriptiva*, II, p. 548.

227 Dollero, *México al Día*, pp. 171–80; Cossío Silva, 'La agricultura', in Cosío Villegas, *Vida económica*, pp. 52, 65; Ankerson, 'Cedillos' (diss.), ch. 1, p. 16.

228 Heather Fowler Salamini, 'Caciquismo and the Mexican Revolution: the Case of Manuel Peláez', paper presented to the Sixth Conference of Mexican and US Historians, Chicago, Sept. 1981; verbal exchanges with the author and with Dudley Ankerson.

229 Charles W. Hamilton, *Early Days. Oil Tales of Mexico* (Houston, 1966), pp. 68, 82–3; de la Peña, *El pueblo y su tierra*, p. 289; González Navarro, *Vida social*, pp. 242–3; Miller, Tampico, 6 Sept. 1910, SD 812.00/342; Donald F. Stevens, 'Agrarian Policy and Instability in Porfirian Mexico', *Americas*, XXXIX (1982), pp. 153–66, shows how economic trends defied even presidential concern.

230 Bonney, San Luis, 16 Oct. 1912, SD 812.00/5310; Ankerson, 'Cedillos' (diss.), ch. 3, pp. 3, 10.

231 Fowler, 'Caciquismo', and vol. 2 ch. 3.

232 Ankerson, 'Cedillos' (diss.) ch. 1, pp. 17–20.

233 Dudley Ankerson, 'Saturnino Cedillo: a Traditional Caudillo in San Luis Potosí' in Brading, *Caudillo and Peasant*, pp. 141–2; Eugenio Martínez Núñez, *La revolución en el estado de San Luis Potosí* (Mexico, 1964), p. 32.

234 J. G. Nava to Carranza 1, 15 Dec. 1915, AVC; cf. the defence of Gogorrón as a progressive, innovative estate in Miguel Angel Quevedo, 'Algunas consideraciones sobre nuestro problema agrario' in Silva Herzog, *La cuestión de la tierra*, IV, p. 281.

235 Andrés Segura and others to Gobernación, 6 Mar. 1913, AG65/18.

236 While the bulk of the land distributed in freehold under Díaz consisted of grants of *terrenos*

baldíos in the north and south of the country, some three-quarters of the land titles issued related to communal fields which had been 'fractioned' or denounced; though the area was less, the social consequences were plainly greater. For figures see González Navarro, *Vida social*, pp. 196–7; Whetten, *Rural Mexico*, p. 86; González Roa, *Aspecto agrario*, p. 83.

237 See below, pp. 118–22.
238 Ross, p. 3; *El Correo*, 30 Oct. 1909, 12 Mar., 12 May 1910.
239 Dollero, *Mexico al Día*, pp. 212, 219, 246, 251; O'Hea, *Reminiscences*, p. 41.
240 Graham, Durango, 15 Feb., 27 Apr. 1911, FO 371/1146, 8191, 1147, 17956; O'Hea, p. 16; Rouaix, *Diccionario*, pp. 101–2, 113.
241 J. Trinidad Cervantes to Madero, 4 July 1911, AG898; *El Diario del Hogar*, 6 Oct. 1910.
242 Zacarías Escobedo Girón interviewed by Ximena Sepúlveda Otaiza, PHO 1/129, p. 35.
243 Mariano Ruiz, *jefe político*, Tepic to Gobernación, 14 Mar., 4 Apr. 1911, AG Tepic 1910–11, 17/31.
244 *Jefe político*, Tepic, to Gobernación, 27 Oct. 1916, AG81/21.
245 Olea, *Breve historia*, p. 40.
246 Enrique Rojas and 120 *indígenas comuneros* to Madero, 19 July 1911, AFM r.21.
247 The main sources on the Yaquis are: Alfonso Fabila, *Las tribus Yaquis de Sonora: su cultura y anhelada autodeterminación* (Mexico, 1940); Evelyn Hu-Dehart, 'Development and Rural Rebellion: Pacification of the Yaquis in the Late Porfiriato', *Hispanic American Historical Review* LIV (1974), pp. 72–93; and Aguilar, *La Revolucion Sonorense*.
248 Fabila, *Las tribus Yaquis*, pp. 81–100.
249 González Navarro, *Vida social*, p. 250.
250 Fabila, *Las tribus Yaquis*, p. 103; Hu-Dehart, 'Development and rural rebellion', pp. 76–7.
251 Aguilar, *La revolución Sonorense*, pp. 34–7; González Navarro, *Vida social*, p. 253; de Szyszlo, *Dix milles kilomètres*, p. 296.
252 De Szyszlo, *Dix milles kilomètres*, p. 297; US Army border reports, Nogales, 15 May 1915, SD 812.00/15074. On the chickpea boom of the 1900s: Manuel Bonilla, 'Apuntes Para El Estudio del Problema Agrario', in Silva Herzog, *La cuestión de la tierra*, III, pp. 261–2.
253 González Navarro, *Vida social*, pp. 255–6, 258–9; Vice-Governor Alberto Cubillas to Corral, 28 Sept. 1909, ARC c.1; de Szyszlo, *Dix milles kilomètres*, p. 296.
254 Aguilar, *La revolución sonorense*, pp. 49, 55; Turner, *Barbarous Mexico*, pp. 16–17.
255 González Navarro, *Vida social*, pp. 257–8; Aguilar, *La revolución Sonorense*, p. 55.
256 *Ibid.*, pp. 56–60; Hu-Dehart, 'Development and rural rebellion', pp. 87–90.
257 Jacobs, 'Aspects', pp. 49–50.
258 *Ibid.*, pp. 50–1.
259 *Ibid.*, p. 42.
260 *Ibid.*, p. 56; Lewis, *Tepoztlán*, p. 115.
261 E. J. García, Amatengo (Oax.) to Gobernación, 29 November 1911, AG Correspondencia Con Don Francisco I. Madero, 1911.
262 Cf. Jacobs, 'Aspects', pp. 13, 52–3, 67, 74, 79, where the author, advancing abundant evidence of *ranchero* prosperity and of the predominance of tenancy over sharecropping, peonage or village farming, seems at pains to refute the old agrarian/populist interpretation of Tannenbaum; in fact, the evidence (which also reveals a measure of classic village/hacienda conflict too) is perfectly consonant with an amended agrarian/populist interpretation, in which the role of the *ranchero* is recognised (in the ambivalent form I suggest) and, above all, the process of agrarian development, concentration and stratification evident during the Porfiriato is seen as crucial in the gestation of the popular revolution.
263 Darío Atristaín, *Notas de un ranchero* (Mexico, 1917) is the principal source; see vol. 2 ch. 2.

264 AARD, 12/22, 29, 35 and *expediente* 27 *passim*; and below, p. 221–2.

265 Stresser-Péan, 'Problèmes agraires', p. 207; de la Fuente in *Handbook of Middle American Indians*, VI, pp. 440–2; Tannenbaum, *Peace*, p. 29.

266 Warman, *Y venimos a contradecir*, pp. 65–6; Ankerson, 'Cedillos' (diss.) ch. I, p. 12; Margolies, *Princes*, pp. 17, 32.

267 Lucio Mendieta y Núñez, *Efectos sociales de la reforma agraria en tres comunidades ejidales de la república Mexicana* (Mexico, 1960), pp. 210–40.

268 Morales Jiménez, *Hombres de la revolución*, p. 87; Graham, Durango, 15 Feb. 1911, FO 371/1146, 8191; Linda B. Hall, 'Alvaro Obregón and the agrarian movement 1912–20', in Brading, ed., *Caudillo and Peasant*, pp. 125, 129; similar alliances were forged in the Huasteca.

269 Schryer, *Rancheros of Pisaflores*, p. 7; and vol. 2 ch. 3.

270 Womack, *Zapata*, pp. 14–16, 37.

271 Schryer, *Rancheros of Pisaflores*, pp. 5–9, which concludes with the observation that the official party of the Revolution, 'represented to a great extent the patronage structure, the political tactics and the traditions associated with the Mexican peasant bourgeoisie'.

272 Knight, 'Peasant and Caudillo', pp. 27–8.

273 Aguilar, 'The Relevant Tradition', p. 106; Friedrich Katz, *Secret War*, pp. 13, 18–20; cf. Alistair Hennessy, *The Frontier in Latin American History* (London, 1978), pp. 110–21; Silvinio R. Duncan Baretta and John Markoff, 'Civilization and Barbarism: Cattle Frontiers in Latin America', *Comparative Studies in Society and History*, XX (1978), pp. 587–620.

274 I present this as my own working definition, without wishing to broach the whole, contentious and often sterile question of 'peasant-ness'. Cf. Henry A. Landsberger, 'Peasant Unrest: Themes and Variations', in Henry A. Landsberger, ed., *Rural Protest: Peasant Movements and Social Change* (London, 1974), pp. 6–18.

275 As Le Roy Ladurie comments, apropos of village resistance to tithing, 'the sheep-farmers and shepherd (sc. of the Pyrenees) constituted a world apart and would not be ridden over roughshod': Emmanuel Le Roy Ladurie, *Montaillou: Cathars and Catholics in a French Village 1294–1324* (London, 1980), pp. 17–20, 23.

276 Eric R. Wolf, 'On Peasant Rebellions' in Teodor Shanin, ed., *Peasants and Peasant Societies* (London, 1971), p. 269, cf. Migdal, *Peasants*, p. 26.

277 R. Waterbury, 'Non-revolutionary Peasants: Oaxaca Compared to Morelos, in the Mexican Revolution', *Comparative Studies in Society and History*, XVII (1975), p. 451; Katz, *Secret War*, p. 8.

278 Reed, *Caste War*, pp. 120–1; 159ff.; Reina, *Rebeliones campesinas*, p. 355.

279 Reina, *Rebeliones campesinas*, *passim*; Jean Meyer, *Problemas campesinas y revueltas agrarias 1821–1910* (Mexico, 1973).

280 Francisco Almada, *La rebelión de Tomochi* (Mexico, 1938); pp. 15–23, 37–41; Plácido Chávez Calderón, *La defensa de Tomochi* (Mexico, 1964), pp. 9–15.

281 Reina, *Rebeliones campesinas*, p. 37, introduces a category of 'rebellions for communal autonomy' within her five-fold typology and gives abundant examples, which are of great value. There are, however, certain problems with the typology and, in this particular case, I see no reason for confining such autonomist rebellions to Indian communities, or for equating them with 'caste wars'. Both the motives and the modes of such rebellions (for example, their ability to mobilise all strata within the community) were exhibited by non-Indian movements as well. To repeat an earlier point: ethnic (or 'caste') allegiances, while not unimportant, should not be raised to the primary level of analytical distinction. Hence my preference for a category (*serrano*) which transcends ethnicity.

282 Charles R. Berry, *The Reform in Oaxaca, 1856–76: A Microhistory of the Liberal Revolution* (Lincoln, 1981), pp. 131–4; Hernández Chávez, 'La defensa'; and below, pp. 372–3.

283 Beezley, *Insurgent Governor*, pp. 2–18; Covarrubias, *Mexico South*, pp. 160–1, 219, 226–45.

284 Knight, 'Peasant and Caudillo', pp. 57–8.

285 Lister, *Chihuahua*, pp. 41–3, 163–7, 183, 207.

286 *Ibid.*, pp. 164, 207; Fuentes Mares, *Y México se refugió*, pp. 150–1.

287 Aguilar, 'Relevant Tradition', pp. 94–8, 106–9.

288 Fuentes Mares, *Y México se refugió*, pp. 145–54; Beezley, *Insurgent Governor*, pp. 17–18; Harris, *A Mexican Family Empire*, pp. 128–37, 193–8, 287–9.

289 Hilton, 'Introduction', p. 30.

290 Katz, *Secret War*, pp. 8, 38.

291 Cf. Barrington Moore, *Social Origins*, pp. 469–71, for a general statement of this argument, to which the same author returns in *Injustice: The Social Bases of Obedience and Revolt* (London, 1978), pp. 40–3.

292 Lumholtz, *Unknown Mexico*, I, p. 413. The detrimental effect of the new railways was noted in many, minor respects: accidents, deaths, curtailments of rights of way, plundering of woods and other resources for the construction of the track; it may be presumed that these immediate consequences (as compared with the yet more important, indirect results, such as rising land values and expanding market opportunities) were particularly keenly felt in more remote, 'under-governed' regions. See Vanderwood, *Disorder and Progress*, p. 94 and Aguilar, *Revolución Sonorense*, pp. 93–6.

293 Pletcher, *Rails*, pp. 183–217.

294 Lister, *Chihuahua*, pp. 176–9; Edwards, Juárez, 13 Aug. 1912, SD 812.00/4651 provides a useful map.

295 *El Correo*, 25 July, 19 Aug. 1909, 21, 28 Apr. 1910; 1, 24 July 1909.

296 *Ibid.*, 9, 10, 16, 24 Mar. 1910; 29 Apr. 1909.

297 *Ibid.*, 7, 8 June 1910.

298 *Ibid.*, 29 Mar. 1910.

299 Almada, *Tomochi*, pp. 21–2; Chávez Calderón, *La defensa de Tomochi*, pp. 10–15; *El Diario del Hogar*, 28 Sept., 1 Nov. 1892. All concur that political, rather than religious, motives were paramount; that the rebels rose in opposition to the local authorities, not out of messianic fervour.

300 See Héctor Olea to Luis Terrazas, 28 Aug. 1899, 18 Aug. 1903, 15 Feb. 1904 and undated (1899) petition of inhabitants of Bachíniva to Terrazas, STA, box 26; and Ximena Sepúlveda Otaiza, *La revolución en Bachíniva* (Mexico, DEAS, 1975).

301 *El Correo*, 30 Apr. 1910.

302 *Ibid.*, 18 May, 8 June 1909.

303 *Ibid.*, 4, 24 Aug. 1909; Lumholtz, I, pp. 119–20, 135, 180–3, 194–8.

304 Tomas Urbina to Gobernación, 31 July 1911, AG legajo 898; I. Thord-Grey, *Gringo Rebel* (Coral Gables, 1960), pp. 89–91, 100, 234.

305 Michael C. Meyer, *Mexican Rebel: Pascual Orozco and the Mexican Revolution* (Lincoln, 1967), p. 9.

306 The 'progressivism' of the Creel/Terrazas oligarchy (and of Enrique Creel in particular) has already been mentioned and is of particular importance: it underlines the point that *serrano* rebellion represented a popular reaction *not* to an archaic tyranny, but rather to a new, expanding, 'modernising' regime. It is for this reason that it is legitimate to regard later *serrano* rebellions (directed against *revolutionary* centralisers) as belonging to the same generic type.

307 Cf. Mark Wasserman, 'Oligarquía e intereses extranjeros en Chihuahua durante el Porfiriato', *Historia Mexicana*, XXII (1972–3), pp. 279–319.

308 Almada, *Tomochi*, p. 17ff.; Beezley, *Insurgent Governor*, pp. 9–10.

309 *La Nueva Era* (Parral), 24 June, 21, 25, 28 Oct., 2 Dec. 1906.

310 In addition to many other alleged abuses, the Terrazas family was thought to have connived at or even participated in the celebrated robbery of their own bank, the Banco Minero, in 1908. See Beezley, *Insurgent Governor*, pp. 80–1, 110–1, and Robert L. Sandels, 'Silvestre Terrazas and the Old Regime in Chihuahua', *Americas*, XXVIII (1971), pp. 201–4.

311 *El Correo*, 18 Mar. 1909.

312 *Ibid.*, 4 Mar. 1911.

313 *Ibid.*

314 *Ibid.*, 9 Nov. 1909, 8, 30 Mar. 1911.

315 *Ibid.*, 20 Mar. 1909; Katz, *Secret War*, p. 38. San Andrés was also a centre of longstanding disputes over land: *La Nueva Era*, 8 July 1906.

316 *El Correo*, 6 Apr. 1909.

317 Francisco Mateus, Casas Grandes, to Alberto Terrazas, 7, 9 Dec. 1910, STA, box 28; Katz, *Secret War*, p. 38; and see below, pp. 176–7, 180.

318 Almada, *Tomochi*, pp. 86–7.

319 Knight, 'Peasant and Caudillo', p. 35; and cf. Reina, p. 37. The point will be developed more fully later.

320 Olea, *Breve historia*, p. 84; Aguilar, *Revolución Sonorense*, pp. 114–5.

321 Dye, Nogales, 31 July 1912, Alger, Mazatlán, 2 Apr. 1911, SD 812.00/4566,/1250; A. Cisneros to Gobernación, 18 June 1908 and *passim* in AG 653 (reports of Second Rural Corps, Tepic). On the historical antecedents; Vanderwood, *Disorder and Progress*, pp. 64–5, 98–100; Nicole Girón, *Heraclio Bernal: bandolero, cacique o precursor de la revolución?* (Mexico, 1976); Jean Meyer, 'El Reino de Lozada en Tepic (1856–1873). El montonero quien se estableció por su cuenta', paper submitted to the Cambridge conference on Peasant and Caudillo in the Mexican Revolution, Apr. 1977.

322 Martín Luis Guzmán, *Memorias de Pancho Villa* (Mexico, 1964), pp. 9–10; Aguirre Benavides, *De Francisco I. Madero*, p. 84; Gabriel García Cantú, *Utopías mexicanas* (Mexico, 1963), pp. 80–1.

323 Vanderwood, *Disorder and Progress*, pp. 14–15, 56, 96.

324 *Ibid.*, p. 56.

325 Cf. the critique of the concept of 'social banditry' and its indiscriminate use by Anton Blok, 'The Peasant and the Brigand: Social Banditry Reconsidered', *Comparative Studies in Society and History*, XIV (1972), pp. 494–503.

326 As Vanderwood's own evidence often suggests: see *Disorder and Progress*, p. 96 (Jesús Arriaga), p. 101 (Santana Rodríguez Palafox); also Guzmán, *Memorias*, pp. 9–14 and Hernán Rosales, 'El romanticismo de Santañón', *Todo*, 4 Nov. 1943.

327 E. J. Hobsbawm, *Primitive Rebels Studies in Archaic Forms of Social Movement in the 19th and 20th Centuries* (Manchester, 1974), pp. 13–29, and the same author's *Bandits* (London, 1972). Both Blok and Vanderwood are critical of this approach (see n. 323, 325).

328 See pp. 353–4.

329 *El País*, 16 Oct. 1910. Cf. Vanderwood, *Disorder and Progress*, pp. 8–9, and John Gresham Chapman, *La construcción del ferrocarril mexicano (1837–1880)* (Mexico, 1975), pp. 147–8, 153–6, 166.

330 Gadow, *Through Southern Mexico*, 410–7.

331 Pollard, *A Busy Time in Mexico*, pp. 30–1.

332 Juan Tavera, 5th Rural Corps, Pijijiapam, to Gobernación, 29 May 1908, AG 653.

333 Hammond, *Autobiography*, I, p. 130.

334 Frías, *Tomóchic*, p. 13, which is borne out by Almada, *Tomochi*, pp. 93–4.

335 Reed, *Insurgent Mexico*, p. 53; Rouaix, *Diccionario*, p. 473; Hostetter, Hermosillo, 9 Mar. 1911, SD 812.00/984; Aguilar, *Revolución Sonorense*, pp. 133, 143.

336 Rodolfo Valle, *jefe político*, Parral, to Governor Sánchez, 8 Oct. 1910, STA, box 28.

337 Hobsbawm, *Bandits*, pp. 24–9, 98–109.

338 Guzmán, *Memorias*, pp. 19–29.
339 Report of *Visitador político* Luis Puente, Acaponeta, to Gobernación, 11 July 1907, AG, Tepic 1907–8.
340 Lumholtz, *Unknown Mexico*, I, pp. 410–2 (evidence dating from the 1890s).
341 Aguilar, 'Relevant Tradition', p. 106.
342 Santos Rascón and others, Temosáchic, to Fomento, 31 Mar. 1910, in *El Correo*, 30 Apr. 1910.
343 Letcher, Chihuahua, 8 Aug. 1911, SD 812.00/2346; Baerlein, p. 230.
344 Lejeune, *Terres Mexicaines*, p. 99.
345 Aguilar, 'The Relevant Tradition', p. 106.
346 *El Correo*, 7, 8 June 1910; 21 Nov. 1909.
347 Vanderwood, *Disorder and Progress*, p. 91; Almada, *Tomochi*, p. 25; Berry, *Reform in Oaxaca*, pp. 124, 132–5.
348 Covarrubías, *Mexico South*, pp. 159–60; Gavira, *Actuación*, pp. 115, 119, 128, 130.
349 Anon. to Ricardo Flores Magón, 9 July 1906, STA box 26, concerning an arms cache hidden for twenty years in the Sierra Alta de Hidalgo.
350 Frías, *Tomóchic*, p. 5; Lawton, Oaxaca, 31 May 1912, SD 812.00/4172.
351 The research of Bazant and others suggests not only a growth of wage labour on Porfirian haciendas, but also a progressive 'monetisation' of other forms of remuneration, according to the imperatives of the market. Thus, just as debt could act as a monetary incentive, rather than as a 'pre-capitalist', semi-servile bond, so other 'pre-capitalist' rewards (food rations, rights to land and other tenants' perquisites) fluctuated in response to market conditions. Even on the most rigorously 'traditional' hacienda peons were only partially, not wholly, insulated from the (generally detrimental) effects of the market. See Bauer, 'Rural workers', pp. 45, 47.
352 See, e.g., Wilbert E. Moore, *Industrialization and Labor: Social Aspects of Economic Development* (Cornell, 1951), p. 280, concerning the Atlixco textile industry.
353 L. Wirth, 'Urbanism as a way of life', *American Journal of Sociology*, XLIV (1938), pp. 1–24.
354 Cf. Philip Abrams, 'Towns and economic growth: some theories and problems', in P. Abrams and E. A. Wrigley eds., *Towns in Societies: Essays in Economic History and Historical Sociology* (Cambridge, 1979), pp. 9–34.
355 See vol. 2 ch. 2.
356 Cockcroft, *Intellectual Precursors*, pp. 47–8; Ruiz, *Great Rebellion*, p. 68; José Mancisidor, *Historia de la revolución mexicana* (Mexico, 1971), pp. 60–73.
357 White, 'The Zapata movement', pp. 120–1, following Tannenbaum.
358 Rosenzweig, 'El desarrollo económico, p. 444; Anderson, *Outcasts*, pp. 39, 46–7; Reynolds, *Mexican Economy*, pp. 23–5; *Estadísticas económicas*, p. 46.
359 The Mexican population grew by 35% between 1877 and 1895, by 20% between 1895 and 1910. Though the rate of growth had therefore slowed, probably as a result of falling living standards, the labour market of the 1900s was still absorbing the generation of the late 1880s and 1890s: see González Navarro, *Vida social*, p. 19; Anderson, *Outcasts*, p. 67.
360 *Estadísticas económicas*, pp. 148–51; Anderson, *Outcasts*, pp. 58, 62.
361 González Roa, *El aspecto agrario*, p. 165.
362 Anderson, *Outcasts*, pp. 55, 64.
363 *Ibid.*, p. 64; and cf. above, p. 102.
364 John H. Coatsworth, 'Anotaciones sobre la produccion de alimentos durante el Porfiriato', *Historia Mexicana*, XXVI (1976), pp. 167–87.
365 *Ibid.*, pp. 183–5.
366 Anderson, *Outcasts*, pp. 199–200; Ruiz, *Great Rebellion*, pp. 61, 125–6.
367 Dollero, *México al Día*, p. 124. At Jiménez, in the summer of 1908 '(religious) holidays seemed desultory, on account of the oft-mentioned crisis': *El Correo*, 7 Aug. 1909.

368 Cossio Silva, 'La Agricultura', in Cosío Villegas, *Vida económica*, pp. 19–22; Katz, 'Labor conditions', p. 36; Ankerson, 'Cedillos' (diss.), ch. 1, pp. 24–5; *El Correo*, 27 Oct. 1909.

369

Value (in 1900 pesos):	Agric. Exports	Mineral Prod.	Value Added Mfg Industry	Federal Income
1905–6	52m.	189m.	191m.	102m.
1906–7	54m.	186m.	210m.	114m.
1907–8	58m.	213m.	206m.	112m.
1908–9	63m.	232m.	188m.	99m.
1909–10	67m.	237m.	198m.	106m.
1910–11	71m.	270m.	205m.	111m.

Source: Estadísticas económicas, pp. 61, 105, 135, 199.

370 *El Correo*, 23 Jan. 1910, on conditions at Guadalupe y Calvo, 22 Feb. 1910, on the police round-up of unemployed vagrants at Minas de San Pedro.

371 *Ibid.*, 24 Sept., 30 Oct. 1909, 18 Jan, 4 Mar. 1910; Mariano Ruiz, *jefe político* Tepic to Gobernación, 13 July 1910, AG Tepic 1910–11, 17/9.

372 Gurr, *Why Men Rebel*; and James C. Davies, 'Towards a theory of revolution', *American Sociological Review*, XXVII (1962), pp. 5–18 would seem to have had some direct or indirect influence; the validity of such general hypotheses is briefly considered in the final section of this chapter.

373 Ankerson, 'Cedillos' (diss.), ch. 1, especially pp. 25–6.

374 Anderson, *Outcasts*, p. 224; and note the table, p. 333.

375 Knight, 'Nationalism', pp. 91, 324–6.

376 *Mexican Year Book*, 1922, pp. 341–2; Anderson, *Outcasts*, pp. 39, 46–50.

377 *Ibid.*, p. 349.

378 Dollero, *México al Día*, pp. 125, 144; de Szyszlo, *Dix milles kilomètres*, p. 229; Rosenzweig in Cosío Villegas, *Vida económica*, I, p. 348.

379 Anderson, *Outcasts*, pp. 46–7; Gadow, p. 32, comments on the decline of artisanal weaving at Orizaba.

380 Anderson, *Outcasts*, pp. 39–40.

381 Esquivel Obregón (a native of Guanajuato) in Silva Herzog, *La cuestión de la tierra*, II, p. 132; Wistano Luis Orozco in the same, I, p. 213; Vanderwood, *Disorder and Progress*, p. 109.

382 Rosenzweig in Cosío Villegas, *Vida económica*, I, pp. 320–2; Womack, *Zapata*, p. 81; O'Hea, *Reminiscences*, p. 16.

383 Anderson, *Outcasts*, p. 49; note also Madero, *Sucesión presidencial*, p. 241.

384 Gavira, *Actuación*, pp. 5–9; Gavira's group included the Orizaba saddler Rafael Tapia, for whom see Tapia, *Mi participación*, p. xi; Nunn, Veracruz, 29 Apr. 1911, FO 371/1147, 18523.

385 A study of strikes during the Porfiriato reveals the prominence of miners, railwaymen, textile and cigarette factory operatives, tram workers and bakers (all, save the last, proletarian rather than artisanal groups): see González Navarro, *Vida social*, pp. 298–360, especially p. 358, and pp. 351–2 on the weakness of mutualism. Ochoa Campos, *Causas sociales*, pp. 279–87 presents a checklist of strikes which is corroborative.

386 Cf. E. P. Thompson, *The Making of the English Working Class* (Harmondsworth, 1972), p. 346.

387 Below, pp. 209–14.

388 Hobsbawm, *Primitive Rebels*, pp. 108–125; G. Rudé, *The Crowd in History 1730–1848* (New York, 1964).

389 Charles Tilly, Louise Tilly and Richard Tilly, *The Rebellious Century 1830–1930* (Cambridge, 1975), pp. 48–56, 252–4.

390 Some might cavil at this equation of violence with Revolution, and thus the subsumption of a variety of violent phenomena under the 'revolutionary' heading (to the exclusion of other phenomena); the point is taken up below, pp. 214, 313–15.

391 Anderson, *Outcasts*, pp. 23–6, 92, 101.

392 On the growth of the textile industry, see also Rosenzweig in Cosío Villegas, *Vida económica*, I, p. 434; Moore, *Industrialization*, p. 280; de Szyszlo, *Dix mille kilomètres*, pp. 170–1.

393 *Ibid.*; Martin, *Mexico of the Twentieth Century*, p. 256; Gonazález Navarro, *Vida social*, p. 330.

394 Cf. above, pp. 85, 90, 114.

395 Anderson, *Outcasts*, pp. 95, 308; and p. 139 on factory regulations.

396 *Ibid.*, pp. 60–1, 75–8, 95–6, 109; Moore, *Industralization*, pp. 280–2; de Szyszlo, p. 286; and Katz, *Servidumbre agraria*, pp. 114–5 on the operations of the (Spanish-owned) *tiendas de raya* of the Federal District.

397 Moore, *Industrialization*, pp. 280–2; Buve, 'Peasant Movements', pp. 123, 126–8. Anderson, *Outcasts*, pp. 308–9, hypothesises that the higher proportion of ex-campesinos among the Veracruz textile workers – compared with those of Puebla or the Federal District – imparted greater militancy.

398 Reginald E. Zelnik, 'The Peasant and the Factory' in Wayne S. Vucinich, ed., *The Peasant in Nineteenth-Century Russia* (Stanford, 1968), pp. 158, 186–90.

399 Anderson, *Outcasts*, pp. 77, 309; on popular Hispanophobia in general, Knight, 'Nationalism', pp. 301–9. As the thoughtful and perceptive American consul at San Luis pointed out, while anti-Americanism 'emanates from the upper classes [and] ... is found in newspapers, public meetings, clubs and writings', anti-Spanish feeling 'emanates from the lower classes; it is the result of experience in the relation of master and servant ... The Spaniard has been a hard master and the working classes realise it'. Hispanophobia was therefore plebeian, inarticulate, and potentially violent. On the other hand, 'the American has been a reasonable and fair employer [and] the working classes realise this': Bonney, San Luis, 28 May 1913, SD 812.00/7790.

400 Anderson, *Outcasts*, pp. 69–70, 186.

401 *Ibid.*, p. 26; Rosenzweig, in Cosío Villegas, *Vida económica*, pp. 318, 342.

402 Anderson, *Outcasts*, pp. 30, 62, 138.

403 *Ibid.*, p. 102 on profits; cf. Mólina Enríquez, *Grandes problemas nacionales* (1908), p. 227–36.

404 Cf. Cockcroft, *Intellectual Precursors*, pp. 47–8; Ochoa Campos, *Causas sociales*, pp. 286–7; Ruiz, *Great Rebellion*, pp. 69–72.

405 Anderson, *Outcasts*, p. 78ff.

406 *Ibid.*, pp. 103–4; González Navarro, *Vida social*, pp. 322ff.

407 Anderson, *Outcasts*, pp. 108–9, 142.

408 *Ibid.*, pp. 140, 144–5.

409 *Ibid.*, pp. 146–7.

410 *Ibid.*, pp. 106–7.

411 *Ibid.*, p. 121, and the same author's 'Crisis laboral', pp. 524–9; González Navarro, *Vida social*, pp. 326–7.

412 Anderson, *Outcasts*, p. 151; González Navarro, *Vida social*, pp. 331–2.

413 Anderson, *Outcasts*, pp. 154–64.

414 *Ibid.*, pp. 167–9; González Navarro, *Vida social*, p. 333.

415 Anderson, *Outcasts*, p. 156.

416 *Ibid.*, pp. 168, 170, 176; Vanderwood, *Disorder and Progress*, p. 152; and below, pp. 209–13.

417 González Navarro, *Vida social*, pp. 336–8; Anderson, *Outcasts*, pp. 194, 199–201; Gavira, *Actuación*, p. 9.

418 V. I. Lenin, *What Is To Be Done? Burning Questions Of Our Movement* (New York, 1929), p. 54ff.

419 My own somewhat loose translation. Cf. Rodney D. Anderson, 'Mexican Workers and the Politics of Revolution', *Hispanic American Historical Review*, LIV (1974), p. 95.

420 *Ibid.*, p. 100–4; Anderson, *Outcasts*, p. 202–4.

421 *Ibid.*, pp. 72–4, 195–6.

422 Anderson, 'Mexican Workers', p. 99.

423 Gavira, *Actuación*, pp. 15–16. Note the interesting parallel with the emergent British working-class movement of the late eighteenth century, which similarly espoused the 'rhetoric of constitutionalism': Thompson, *Making of the English Working Class*, pp. 85–97.

424 Anderson, 'La crisis laboral', p. 228.

425 Anderson, *Outcasts*, pp. 324–5. The patriotic/liberal association was particularly potent in stimulating anti-Spanish feeling: here, contemporary social resentments conspired with resonant historical myths, which were reinforced by national, secular fiestas (e.g., 15/16 Sept.). The same could not be said of anti-Americanism (though it often is): not only were contemporary resentments less widespread (see n. 399); the mythical associations were also more ambiguous – the US, after all, had favoured both the Independence movement and the Reforma.

426 Anderson, 'Mexican Workers', p. 99.

427 Montemayor Hernández, *Historia de Monterrey*, pp. 291–3; Niemeyer, *Reyes*, pp. 136–8; Anderson, *Outcasts*, pp. 244–9.

428 *Ibid.*, pp. 255–65.

429 *Ibid.*, p. 261; Córdova, *La ideologia*, p. 110.

430 Lefaivre to Quai d'Orsay, 20 June 1910, AAE Méx., Pol. Int., N.S. II, n.50.

431 Buve, 'Peasant Movements', p. 129; Anderson, *Outcasts*, p. 290.

432 As regards contribution to the armed revolution, the 'hyphenated' worker–peasant was more prominent than the classic proletarian: Tlaxcala and the Federal District may be taken as polar examples. The point made in n. 390 is also relevent here, however.

433 Anderson *Outcasts*, pp. 123–4; Ruiz, *Great Rebellion*, pp. 58, 64.

434 Anderson, *Outcasts*, pp. 124–5; Gavira, *Actuación*, pp. 9, 13, 17.

435 Anderson, *Outcasts*, pp. 230–1, 289; Gavira, *Actuación*, pp. 7–9. During the Centennial celebrations at Chihuahua, the *jefe político* presided over the activities of Comité Patriótica Mutualista: *El Correo*, 15 Sept 1910.

436 Cosío Villegas, *Vida política*, pp. 802, 815–6; Anderson, *Outcasts*, pp. 225, 249–50.

437 *Ibid.*, pp. 225, 232–3; Gavira, *Actuación*, p. 14; *El Correo*, 26 July 1910; the doctoral research of A. L. Morgan, on Porfirian Mexico City, illuminates Landa y Escandón's role.

438 Anderson, *Outcasts*, pp. 129, 234–5, 246.

439 S. Montemayor, *jefe político*, Cd Juárez, to Governor Sánchez, 16 Apr. 1907, STA box 28.

440 Brian Loveman, *Struggle in the Countryside. Politics and Rural Labor in Chile, 1919–1973* (Bloomington, 1976), pp. 24, 60–3, 113; Shepard Forman, *The Brazilian Peasantry* (New York, 1975), pp. 142–3, 168–72.

441 Anderson, *Outcasts*, pp. 230–1.

442 *Ibid.*, p. 233.

443 *Ibid.*, pp. 230, 246, 250.

444 The 1910 census gives figures of 79,000 miners and 16,000 smelter operatives. These figures do not appear to have been rising: in 1898 there were 89,000 mining employees. See *Mexican Year Book*, 1922, p. 342; *Estadísticas económicas*, p. 131.

445 Dollero, *México al Día*, pp. 309–10; cf. Gadow, *Through Southern Mexico*, p. 333 on the proliferation of small mines in Guerrero.

446 González Navarro, *Vida social*, pp. 313, 341. Anderson, *Outcasts*, p. 338, lists only seventeen mining strikes between 1865–1905 and eight between 1906–11; further local research would no doubt reveal many more.

447 Pletcher, *Rails*, p. 203; Knight, 'Nationalism', pp. 87, 324–6. Clientelist control was maintained positively by the higher wages and perks provided by some companies, especially the larger foreign ones, and negatively by the growing surplus labour supply, which placed a premium upon secure employment and inhibited militancy.

448 Bernstein, *Mexican Mining Industry*, pp. 50–6; Gadow, *Through Southern Mexico*, pp. 333–4; and Buick, *Gringoes of Tepehuanes*, passim, for a graphic if embroidered tale of family mining. Such enterprises, 'insignificant in size, representing the venturesome type of American pioneer', constituted 'the greater part' of US mining interests in Mexico: *Mexican Year Book*, 1922, p. 274.

449 Tannenbaum, 'Revolución agraria', p. 36; Almada, *Tomochi*, p. 21; Lumholtz, *Unknown Mexico*, I, p. 127.

450 *Fall Report*, testimony of N. O. Bagge, p. 1429. Cf. Guzmán, *Memorias*, pp. 29, 38–9 and (if it can be believed) Percy N. Furber, *I Took Chances From Windjammers to Jets* (Leicester, 1954), p. 109.

451 *El Correo*, 9, 23 Jan. 1910.

452 At Cananea (Apr. 1906) over 40% of the Mexican employees worked only a three-day week; only 20% worked a full month, compared with 70% of the non-Mexican employees. See auditor's report, SS, r.9.

453 See p. 149. So seductive is the appeal of Cananea that it regularly appears in the *curriculum revolutionis* of General Juan José Ríos, who was never there.

454 Cf. F.-X. Guerra, 'La Révolution Mexicaine: d'abord une révolution minière?', *Annales, E.S.C.*, XXXVI (1981), pp. 785–814; and, for a critique of this and other aspects of Guerra's thesis, Alan Knight, 'La Révolution Mexicaine: révolution minière ou révolution serrano?', *Annales, E.S.C.*, XXXVIII (1983), pp. 449–59.

455 *El Correo*, 11 May 1909, 23 Jan., 17 July 1910; Ruiz, *Great Rebellion*, pp. 125–6.

456 E.g., Beezley, *Insurgent Governor*, pp. 45, 48. Not only would demands for the maintenance of full employment have been anachronistic; they would also have been wildly Utopian, for the regime's capacity to offset the effects of international recession was exiguous, as Madero, *La sucesión presidencial*, pp. 227–8, recognised.

457 *El Correo*, 13 Oct. 1909.

458 See pp. 429–30.

459 Cf. Moore, *Injustice*, pp. 186, 199, 253, 273.

460 Bernstein, *Mexican Mining Industry*, pp. 87–91; *El Correo*, 25 Jan., 10 Feb. 1910 (*tiendas de raya* and venereal diseases respectively); Anderson, *Outcasts*, pp. 323–4.

461 'Entre el gremio ferrocarrilero no hay analfabetos [sic]': José Gutiérrez to Madero, 12 June 1911, AFM r.20.

462 Pletcher, *Rails*, pp. 205, 233; Buick, *Gringoes of Tepehuanes*, p. 64.

463 Cf. Dollero, *México al Día*, pp. 305–6 on Mapimí; Dye Nogales, 23 Feb. 1911, SD 812.00/861 on Cananea.

464 *El Correo*, 27 Aug. 1910, quoting Braulio Hernández.

465 See Nava Oteo in Cosío Villegas, *Vida económica*, pp. 252–4 on miners' wage rates; Fall Report, pp. 128–30, testimony of S. G. Inman, and note Inman to Harlan, 5 June 1911, SGIA, box 12, on the 'model mining camp' of Las Esperanzas.

466 Lister, *Chihuahua*, p. 181; Anderson, *Outcasts*, p. 87.

467 F. Sisniega to F. de Pedro, 23 Sept. 1900, STA (Sisniega letterbooks), r.7.

468 Knight, 'Nationalism', pp. 78–9, 85, 247–50, 264–8, 308–9, 321–6.

469 See below, pp. 212–13.

470 S. Ramírez to Madero, 21 Sept. 1911, AFM r.9; Hohler to Grey, 13 March 1911, FO 371/1146, 11453.

471 Cf. Hobsbawm, *Primitive Rebels*, pp. 1–3, 124–5. Such terms are loaded: their significance is given fuller treatment below, pp. 150, 160.

472 Ruiz, *Great Rebellion*, pp. 69–72, 112; Mancisidor, *Historia de la revolución mexicana*, pp. 62-73.

473 Aguilar, *Revolución Sonorense*, pp. 117–8; de Szyszlo, *Dix milles kilomètres*, pp. 305–6.

474 Aguirre, *Cananea*, pp. 50–1; Pletcher, *Rails*, p. 238. An American critic of Greene blamed him for overpaying his Mexican workers: Anderson, *Outcasts*, p. 110.

475 Governor Izábal of Sonora, addressing the Cananea workers, justified the pay differentials on the grounds that American whores cost more: Aguilar, *Revolución Sonorense*, p. 130. As for the railways, strikes in 1906, 1908 and 1909 prompted the government to push through the 'Mexicanisation' of the work force; this in turn provoked a strike by American employees. See Anderson, *Outcasts*, pp. 117–9, 214–5, 235–40; Letcher, Chihuahua, 11 Apr. 1911, SD 812.00/1429.

476 Pletcher, *Rails*, pp. 220–9; Bernstein, *Mexican Mining Industry*, pp. 56–8.

477 Anderson, *Outcasts*, pp. 114–5.

478 *Ibid.*; and cf. the description of PLM activists at Parral in Rodolfo Valles, *jefe político*, to Creel, 24 Oct. 1906 (and related correspondence) STA, box 26.

479 Aguirre, *Cananea*, pp. 71–150; Anderson, *Outcasts*, pp. 110–14; Aguilar, *Revolución Sonorense*, pp. 127–30.

480 Pletcher, *Rails*, p. 251; Anderson, *Outcasts*, p. 116, n.46.

481 *Ibid.*, p. 116.

482 *Ibid.*, p. 117.

483 Madero, *La sucesión presidencial*, pp. 207–8, 249; Anderson, *Outcasts*, pp. 112–4.

484 Aguilar, *Revolución Sonorense*, p. 93.

485 Anderson, *Outcasts*, pp. 112–13, 176; González Navarro, *Vida social*, pp. 807–11.

486 Loveman, *Struggle in the Countryside*, pp. 24, 60.

487 Pletcher, *Rails*, pp. 229, 255; Aguirre, pp. 156, 173.

488 Bernstein, *Mexican Mining Industry*, p. 59; Aguilar, *Revolución Sonorense*, p. 131.

489 Pletcher, *Rails*, p. 257. Relevant events are described later.

490 Montague, Cananea, 26 Feb. 1915, SD 812.00/14863; Pletcher, *Rails*, p. 257; Nava Oteo in Cosío Villegas, *Vida Económica*, p. 190.

491 US Army border reports, Nogales, 8 Mar. 1916, SD 812.00/17592; and Knight, 'Nationalism', pp. 77–9, on the comparable attitudes of other ex-employees of Cananea.

492 Madero to Sánchez Adame, 30 July 1909, AFM r.9; Aguirre, *Cananea*, pp. 172–3.

493 Aguilar, *Revolución Sonorense*, pp. 175–6.

494 Tillys, *Rebellious Century*, pp. 51–2, 249. Needless to say, we are here dealing with ideal types: accentuations, not reflections of reality.

495 I use the terms 'modern' and, in a moment, 'traditional', without necessarily condoning all the intellectual barbarities that have been committed in their name (by the same token, I use terms like 'class' and 'capitalism'). In this instance, the theoretical eclecticism is justified since, even many Marxists would concur, the growth of ('modern') capitalism has been matched by the growth of ('modern') working-class organisations, particularly characterised by unionisation, political reformism, and participation within state organs: what Thompson has called the 'imbrication of working-class organisations in the status quo': E. P. Thompson, 'The Peculiarities of the English', in *The Poverty of Theory and Other Essays* (London, 1978), p. 71.

496 Tillys, *Rebellious Century*, pp. 51–2, 249; cf. Warman, *Y venimos a contradecir*, p. 129 on the essentially 'defensive' nature of the Zapatista revolt.

497 Katz, *The Secret War*, argues the importance of these exogenous factors, though in my view, exaggerates them; cf. Walter L. Goldfrank, 'Theories of Revolution and Revolution without Theory', *Theory and Society*, VII (1979), pp. 135–65, especially pp. 148–51, who merely asserts them.

498 *Ibid.*, p. 150.

499 Abundance, of course, is as much the work of man as of nature; in the cases considered here, shortage or surplus depended on law, tenurial arrangements, political structures and other 'man-made' factors, as well as resource endowment.

500 Thomas H. Holloway, 'The coffee *colono* of Sao Paulo, Brazil: migration and mobility, 1880–1930', in Duncan and Rutledge, *Land and Labour*, pp. 301–21.

501 'Introduction', in Duncan and Rutledge, *Land and Labour*, p. 14.

502 Paige, *Agrarian Revolution*, p. 127ff.; Bauer, 'Rural Workers' and, in the same volume, Loveman's critique and Bauer's reply.

503 Bauer, *Chilean Rural Society*, pp. 51–6, 159–70.

504 Benjamin, 'Passages to Leviathan: Chiapas and the Mexican State, 1891–1947' (Michigan State University, Ph.D. diss., 1981), pp. 88–9, 103–4, 152–3.

505 Bazant, 'Peones', pp. 111–12; Warman, *Y venimos a contradecir*, p. 67; and Cristóbal Kay, 'The development of the Chilean *hacienda* system, 1850–1973', in Duncan and Rutledge, *Land and Labour*, pp. 104–113.

506 Goldfrank, 'Theories of Revolution', p. 154, dimly perceives these two modes (which is not difficult, in the light of Wolf's work), but then attempts the impossible by conflating them. For Goldfrank 'capitalist penetration' and 'relative autonomy from supervision' are independent variables, hence they can co-exist: the 'relatively autonomous' peasantry, it must be presumed, invite 'capitalist penetration' and then protest about it afterwards; only conniving *campesinos* suffer agrarian rape. It is the logic of the more unreconstructed elements of the English judiciary.

507 Paige, *Agrarian Revolution*, pp. 5–7 for a useful summary.

508 Cf. Mao on the 'owner–peasants' ('by owner–peasants Comrade Mao . . . means the middle peasants'), who are 'petty bourgeois' and hence politically ambivalent, and Eric Wolf's 'middle peasants', who constitute a 'pivotal grouping' for rebellion; the divergent behaviour of Stinchcombe's 'family tenants' and 'family smallholders' further complicates the picture. See Mao Tse-Tung, 'Analysis of the Classes in Chinese Society', in *Selected Works of Mao Tse-Tung* (Peking, 1967), vol. I, pp. 15–16, 20, and 'Report on an Investigation of the Peasant Movement in Hunan', same volume, pp. 30–4; Wolf, 'On Peasant Rebellions', pp. 269–70; Arthur L. Stinchcombe, 'Agricultural Enterprise and Rural Class Relations', *American Journal of Sociology*, LXVII (1961–2), pp. 165–76. On the role of the rural proletariat, cf. Hobsbawm, 'Peasants and Rural Migrants', p. 56; Aníbal Quijano Obregón, 'Contemporary Peasant Movements', in Seymour Martin Lipset and Aldo Solari, eds., *Elites in Latin America* (Oxford, 1970), pp. 308–9; and Paige, *Agrarian Revolution*, pp. 48–66.

509 Philip Corrigan, 'On the Politics of Production: A Comment on "Peasants and Politics" by Eric Hobsbawm', *Journal of Peasant Studies*, II (1973), p. 345. Hamza Alavi, 'Peasant Classes and Primordial Loyalties', *Journal of Peasant Studies*, I (1973), observes that the 'ascription of absolute characteristics to any group, regardless of historical context, is alien to the Marxist method'; or, indeed, to any reputable method.

510 This point has already been suggested (along with others of less cogency) by Arne Disch, 'Peasants and Revolts', *Theory and Society*, VII (1979), p. 249.

511 Meyer, *Problemas campesinos*, pp. 9–19.

512 Above, p. 111.

513 Tilly, *Rebellious Century*, p. 50; Roland Mousnier, *Peasant Uprisings in Seventeenth-Century France, Russia and China* (London, 1971), pp. 308–9, 329.

514 Meyer, *Problemas campesinos*, pp. 19–20.

515 *Ibid.*, pp. 10, 66; Reina, *Rebeliones campesinas*, pp. 33, 117, 127, 245, 423. Opposition to tribute figured prominently among the grievances of Hidalgo's rebels too: Hugh M. Hamill, *The Hidalgo Revolt: Prelude to Mexican Independence* (Gainesville, 1966), pp. 123, 136.

516 Buve, 'Peasant Movements', pp. 112, 119.

517 Cf. Rodney Hilton, *Bond Men Made Free: Medieval Peasant Movements and the English Rising of 1381* (London, 1973); James C. Scott, *The Moral Economy of the Peasant: Rebellion and Subsistence in Southeast Asia* (New Haven, 1976).

518 The *alcabala* (internal customs) sometimes figured among popular, fiscal grievances; so, too, in the early part of the nineteenth century, did the tithe and church baptismal and marriage fees. State support for tithe collection, however, was abolished in the 1830s, the *alcabala* in the 1890s. By the turn of the century, these grievances were largely a thing of the past. See Meyer, *Problemas Campesinas*, p. 12; Reina, *Rebeliones campesinas*, p. 236; Reed, *Caste War*, p. 23; Berry, *The Reform in Oaxaca*, p. 24.

519 Berry, *The Reform in Oaxaca*, p. 128; Benjamin, 'Passages', pp. 46–8, 278.

520 Above, pp. 120–1.

521 Wolf, *Peasant Wars*, pp. 15–17, 280–1.

522 Paige, *Agrarian Revolution*, p. 23; Huntington, *Political Order*, pp. 289–9; Brading, *Haciendas and Ranchos*, p. 10.

523 Paige, *Agrarian Revolution*, pp. 40–5.

524 Cf. Paige, *Agrarian Revolution*, pp. 40–5, Stinchcombe, 'Agricultural Enterprise', pp. 168–9: both static, homogenous models.

525 Cf. Taylor, *From Modernization*, pp. 221–2; and, for a vigorous critique (from a different perspective) of the 'ghostly pas de deux' of the modes of production, and 'the attempted Parsonianization of Marxism', see Aidan Foster-Carter, 'The Modes of Production Controversy', *New Left Review*, CVII (1978), pp. 51–2, 61.

526 Rosa Luxemburg, *The Accumulation of Capital* (London, 1971), p. 416.

527 Wolf, *Peasant Wars of the Twentieth Century* (London, 1973), pp. 51–69; Maureen Perrie, 'The Russian Peasant Movement of 1905–7', *Past and Present*, LVII (1972), pp. 123–55.

528 Bauer, *Chilean Rural Society*, pp. 56, 166–70.

529 Paige, *Agrarian Revolution*, pp. 155–6; Peter Kláren, 'The Social and Economic Consequences of Modernization in the Peruvian Sugar Industry, 1870–1930' and Magnus Morner, 'Latin American "Landlords" and "Peasants" and the Outer World During the National Period', in Duncan and Rutledge, *Land and Labour*, pp. 231–40, 468.

530 Henri Favre, 'The Dynamics of Indian Peasant Society and Migration to Coastal Plantations in Central Peru', in Duncan and Rutledge, *Land and Labour*, pp. 253–67; Joseph E. Grimes, 'Huichol Economics', *América Indígena*, XXI (1961), p. 304.

531 Scott, *Moral Economy*, p. 212.

532 Martínez Alier, *Haciendas*, pp. 67–71; Norman Long and Bryan R. Roberts, eds., *Peasant Cooperation and Capitalist Expansion in Central Peru* (Austin, 1978), pp. 13, 58, 85, 213–14 (these references culled from the introduction and articles by Carlos Samaniego, Julian Laite and David Winder).

533 Favre, 'Dynamics', pp. 253–4, 265–6; and the same author's 'Le Travail saisonnier des chamula', *Cahiers de l'Institut des Hautes Etudes de l'Amérique Latine*, VII (1965), pp. 63–134.

534 William E. Carter, 'Revolution and the Agrarian sector', in James M. Malloy and Richard S. Thorn, *Beyond the Revolution Bolivia Since 1952* (Pittsburgh, 1971), pp. 241–2.

535 Cf. Scott, *Moral Economy*, pp. 41–2.

536 Womack, *Zapata*, p. 204; Canada, Veracruz, 4 Sept. 1913, SD 812.00/8851; border report, Nogales, 15 May; H. Sibbett, memo., 6 Oct. 1915; SD 812.00/15074, 16843.

537 Gavin A. Smith and Pedro Cano H., 'Some Factors Contributing to Peasant Land Occupations in Peru: the Example of Huasicancha, 1963–1968', in Long and Roberts, *Peasant Cooperation*, p. 188.

538 Scott, *Moral Economy*, pp. vii, 2–34, 157–91.

539 *Ibid.*, p. 9.

540 Edward C. Bamfield, *The Moral Basis of a Backward Society* (New York, 1967), pp. 9–10ff.; Hinton quoted by Samuel L. Popkin, *The Rational Peasant: The Political Economy of Rural*

Society in Vietnam (Berkeley, 1979), p. 251; Alan MacFarlane, *The Origins of English Individualism. Family, Property and Social Transition* (Oxford, 1978).

541 George Foster, 'Peasant Society and the Image of the Limited Good', *American Anthropologist*, LXVII (1965), pp. 293–315; Oscar Lewis, *The Children of Sánchez: Autobiography of a Mexican Family* (Harmondsworth, 1970), pp. xxiv–xxviii.

542 Paige, *Agrarian Revolution*, pp. 32, 35.

543 Tillys, *Rebellious Century*, p. 42: and cf. Hobsbawm, 'Peasants and Politics', p. 7.

544 Peter Cuy, 'A Watershed in Mexican Rural History: some thoughts on the reconciliation of conflicting interpretations', *Journal of Latin American Studies*, III (1971), pp. 39–57.

545 Roger Price, *An Economic History of Modern France, 1730–1914* (London, 1980), pp. 67–71; Karl Marx, 'Peasantry as a Class', in Shanin, ed., *Peasants*, pp. 229–37; James M. Malloy, 'Revolutionary Politics' in Malloy and Thorn, *Beyond the Revolution*, pp. 125–8, 142–50.

546 Tillys, *Rebellious Century*, pp. 49–52.

547 Knight, 'Intellectuals'.

548 Knight, 'Peasant and Caudillo', p. 44.

549 Moore, *Social Origins*, pp. 186, 203; Theda Skocpol, *States and Social Revolutions: A Comparative Analysis of France, Russia and China* (Cambridge, 1980), pp. 151–3, 239, 241 is more ambivalent (or confused).

550 Hobsbawm, *Primitive Rebels*, p. 147 and 'Peasants and Politics'; though note his reply to Corrigan in *Journal of Peasant Studies*, II (1973), p. 351. See also Quijano Obregón, 'Contemporary Peasant Movements', p. 303.

551 Popkin, *Rational Peasant*, p. 256.

552 Knight, 'Intellectuals'.

553 *Ibid.* On the recurrent role of parish priests in nineteenth-century popular revolts see Meyer, *Problemas Campesinos*, pp. 9, 14, 24, 35–6, 219; Reina, *Rebeliones campesinas*, pp. 30, 63, 247.

554 Thompson, *Making of the English Working Class*, pp. 430–1: and Hobsbawm, *Primitive Rebels*, pp. 148–9.

555 Scott, *Moral Economy*, pp. 173–4; Martínez Alier stresses the same point, *Haciendas*, p. 17. The parochialism, 'inward orientation' or 'self-limiting' character of peasant protest are all familiar themes (e.g., Migdal, *Peasants*, pp. 46–50, 248–9; Wolf, 'Peasant Rebellions', p. 272). But such attributes (and their corollary, the absence of 'universal' values or affiliations) are not incompatible with a strong identity of class: for peasants as for workers 'class consciousness . . . present when workers see their common lot as uniting them into a single social organism with a uniform class position and destiny, can also be particularistic': Reginald E. Zelnik, 'Passivity and Protest in Germany and Russia: Barrington Moore's 'Conception of Working-Class Responses to Injustice', *Journal of Social History*, XV (1981–2), pp. 485–512.

556 Lawrence Stone, 'The English Revolution', in Robert Foster and Jack P. Greene, *Preconditions of Revolution in Early Modern Europe* (Baltimore, 1970, pp. 59–60; cf. Hobsbawm, 'Peasants and politics', p. 12.

557 Below, pp. 313–15.

558 Quijano Obregón, 'Contemporary Peasant Movements', p. 303, refers to the 'barely discernible objectives or intangible ends' of 'pre-political' peasant revolt (though the case of Mexico is arbitrarily excluded from these generalisations); for Mousnier, *Peasant Uprisings*, p. 321, the 'spontaneity' of peasant revolt makes it 'a sort of reflex action' – peasants are to Mousnier what pigeons are to Skinner.

559 John M. Hart, 'Agrarian Precursors of the Mexican Revolution: the Development of an Ideology', *Americas*, XXIX (1972–3), pp. 135, 144–5.

560 Or (even worse) those which were confined to 'irrational pillaging and rioting': *ibid.*, pp. 132, 139.

561 Reina, *Rebeliones campesinas*, pp. 337–40: 300–2; 223–7; note also Negrete's revolt in the Sierra Gorda, 1877–81; *ibid.*, pp. 313–21.

562 Variations in ideological sophistication or simplicity may in turn relate to the ethnic composition of rebellions – even where common socio-economic factors generated protest. The Indian revolts and 'caste wars' of the south (Yucatán, 1847–53; Chiapas, 1869) adopted more religious, messianic, and atavistic forms; while the (mestizo) *campesino* rebellions of the Sierra Gorda (1844–7, 1877–81) were secular, and coloured by 'socialism': Reina, *Rebeliones campesinas*, pp. 45–57, 380–416 and fn. 561 above. We would agree with Migdal, *Peasants*, p. 212, that 'it is fruitless to begin one's investigation of peasant organizational support with the content of the programs and ideology of those they have followed'.

563 Cf. Scott, *Moral Economy*, pp. 10–11; Moore, *Injustice*, p. 24; Migdal, *Peasants*, pp. 229, 246; Emmanuel Le Roy Ladurie, *The Peasants of Languedoc* (Urbana, 1974), pp. 192, 198–200, 266–9.

564 Cf. E. P. Thompson, 'The Moral Economy of the English Crowd of the Eighteenth Century', *Past and Present*, L (1971), pp. 76–136.

565 Reina, *Rebeliones campesinas*, p. 71; cf. Hart, 'Agrarian Precursors', p. 135.

566 Reina, *Rebeliones campesinas*, p. 65.

567 C. S. L. Davies, 'Peasant Revolt in France and England: a Comparison', *Agricultural History Review*, XXI (1973), p. 133.

568 Cf. Judith Friedlander, 'The Socialization of the Cargo System: an Example from Post-Revolutionary Mexico', *Latin American Research Review*, XVI (1981), pp. 132–43.

569 Laclau, 'Fascism and Ideology' in *Politics and Ideology*, pp. 97–8.

570 For a trenchant critique of Althusserian idealism and a re-emphasis of the need for a two-way 'dialogue between social being and social consciousness' see E. P. Thompson, *The Poverty of Theory*, especially pp. 196–201.

571 See pp. 21, 68–9, 138–9.

572 There are interesting European parallels. Jaime Torras, *Liberalismo y rebeldía campesina 1820–1823* (Barcelona, 1976), p. 23, notes the ambiguity in the language of peasant protest in Catalonia, the result of borrowings from the 'dominant ideology'; Thompson, *Making of the English Working Class*, pp. 84–97ff., shows the debt popular radicalism owed to the 'rhetoric' of liberty and constitutionalism.

573 The point has been made often enough: Tillys, *Rebellious Century*, p. 282; Thompson, 'Peculiarities of the English', p. 69.

574 J. H. Hexter, 'A New Framework for Social History', in *Reappraisals in History* (London, 1963), p. 14.

575 Knight, 'Intellectuals'.

576 Aside from the relatively recent, enervating influence of Althusserian idealism, the study of the Revolution has often in the past been vitiated by a kind of vapid *Ideengeschichte* which, as the Sixth Conference of Mexican and US Historians at Chicago, 1981, revealed, is not wholly extinct.

577 Tillys, *Rebellious Century*, pp. 42, 243. The contingent element in the ideology of popular protest is well illustrated by Thompson's analysis of Methodism, which preached submissiveness, yet was capable of abetting protest; so, too (*mutatis mutandis*) with Mexican liberalism. 'No ideology', Thompson points out, 'is wholly absorbed by its adherents; it breaks down in practice in a thousand ways under the criticism of impulse and of experience': *Making of the English Working Class*, pp. 431, 437. What is not clear (and cannot be clarified here) is the process whereby popular ideology is created: by the brutal imposition of the 'Great' upon the 'Little' Tradition? By more subtle forms of cultural osmosis? By the crystallisation of earlier folk beliefs and practices? George Rudé, *Ideology and Popular Protest* (London, 1980), pp. 27–37, touches on this problem, but does not progress far.

578 Moore, *Injustice*, pp. 90, 93, 97ff.

579 Scott, *Moral Economy*, p. iv.

580 Thompson, *Making of the English Working Class*, p. 222; Scott, *Moral Economy*, p. vii, Tillys, *Rebellious Century*, p. 293, argue the same point.

581 White, 'Zapata movement', pp. 120–1 (following Tannenbaum); Ruiz, *Great Rebellion*, 91, 120–35.

582 'It is this moral heritage that, in peasant revolts, selects certain targets rather than others, certain forms rather than others, and that makes possible a collective (though rarely coordinated) action born of moral outrage': Scott, *Moral Economy*, p. 167. Examples of both targets and forms will follow later.

583 Neither Popkin's 'rational peasant', nor his critique of 'moral economists', is particularly convincing; the second, it seems to me, involves a caricature of the 'moral economy' hypothesis. And it is precisely in times of revolt that 'rationality' (conceived in terms of an individualist political economy) is at a discount: for individuals now face great risks in pursuit of some notional public good. Recruits cannot be bought like floating voters, or revolutions sold like Republican presidents. Cf. Popkin, *Rational Peasant*, pp. ix, 17–28, 259–60, and Migdal, *Peasants*, pp. 237–41, who is similarly enamoured of this variant of exchange theory.

584 Moore, *Injustice*, pp. 23–4, 89, 440ff.

585 Skocpol, *States and Social Revolutions*, p. 32.

586 *Ibid.*, pp. xii, 16.

587 Scott, *Moral Economy*, p. 170. I take this to correspond to Weber's distinction between 'power' and 'legitimate authority': see *Social and Economic Organization*, pp. 152, 324–5.

588 David Hume, 'Of the First Principles of Government', in *Essays Moral, Political, and Literary* (Oxford, 1963), p. 29.

589 Gurr, *Why Men Rebel*, pp. 46–50.

590 Moore, *Injustice*, pp. 22, 26.

591 Scott, *Moral Economy*, pp. 4, 6, 9: John Iliffe, 'The Effects of the Maji Maji Rebellion of 1905–1906 on German Occupation Policy in East Africa', in Prosser Gifford and Wm Roger Louis, eds., *Britain and Germany in Africa Imperial Rivalry and Colonial Rule* (New Haven, 1967), pp. 560–1. In early modern France it was precisely the tax-collector 'whose demands … implied no reciprocity' who stimulated peasant revolt: Le Roy Ladurie, *Peasants of Languedoc*, p. 269.

592 Reed, *Caste War*, p. 48.

593 'It was not only the threat of physical enslavement, but an attack on their religious and moral standards, on the only way of life they knew or could accept' which drove the Maya to rebel: *ibid*, pp. 48–9. I am therefore using 'status' not in some specific (Weberian or other) sense, but as shorthand for a complex of attributes, economic, moral and psychological.

594 Of course, not all were: for some, the transition was partial, or only potential; it is nevertheless valid to see this transition as central to the process of revolt. On the significance – economic and psychological – of the villager/peon threshold, in Mexico and elsewhere, see Scott, *Moral Economy*, p. 39; Warman, *Y venimos a contradecir*, pp. 86–7; and Shepard Forman, *The Brazilian Peasantry* (New York, 1975), p. 190.

595 Note Weber's analysis of peasants and farm labourers in eastern Germany, where 'the peasant with very little land would rather starve than accept a job and work for someone else'; evidence, Weber thought, of 'the tremendous and purely psychological magic of "freedom"'. See Reinhard Bendix, *Max Weber, An Intellectual Portrait* (Cambridge, 1962), pp. 22–3.

596 Above, p. 121.

597 Womack, *Zapata*, pp. 39–41, 52–3, 63.

598 Above, pp. 8, 9, 112.

599 Rom Harré, *Social Being: A Theory for Social Psychology* (Oxford, 1979).

600 Lewis, *Pedro Martínez*, pp. 76, 129–30; Zacarías Escobedo Girón interviewed by Ximena Sepúlveda Otaiza, PHO 1/129, pp. 1–3.

601 Warman, *Y venimos a contradecir*, p. 74.

602 Anderson, *Outcasts*, pp. 59–61, 73–4, 76–7.

603 Moore, *Injustice*, pp. 233–68, comparing the Ruhr coal-miners and metal-workers.

604 Below, pp. 221–2, 225–6.

605 Margolies, *Princes*, pp. 22–35.

606 Cf. Christopher Hill, *The World Turned Upside Down: Radical Ideas During the English Revolution* (Harmondsworth, 1975); Le Roy Ladurie, *Peasants of Languedoc*, pp. 194–6, 208, 301.

607 Vol. 2 ch. 2.

608 For references and comments on the 'natural history' school (Edwards, Brinton, Pettee) see Skocpol, *States and Social Revolutions*, pp. 33, 37.

609 'The age of revolutions has passed into history and, even when the present Dictator dies another will come along and matters will continue the same': Amado Escobar (PLM supporter, Torreón) to Nemesio Tejeda, 14 Oct. 1906, STA, box 26; 'I consider general revolution to be out of the question, as does public opinion and the press', the German envoy Karl Bunz observed in 1910: Katz, *Secret War*, p. 3.

610 Goldfrank (partly influenced, it would seem, by Skocpol) is keen to detect exogenous factors: 'Theories of Revolution', pp. 148–51. As for Skocpol herself, the insistence on 'international and world-historical contexts' may have some validity in the main cases she considers (France, Russia, China), but the attempt to involve Mexico, though theoretically logical, is mistaken, and must cast a doubt on the entire theoretical construct: see Skocpol, *States and Social Revolutions*, pp. 19–24, 288–9.

4 The Madero Revolution

1 Anderson, *Outcasts*, p. 283; cf. *El Diario del Hogar*, 9 Oct. 1892.

2 Wilson, Mexico City, 10, 11, 15 Nov.; Miller, Tampico, 16 Nov. 1910, SD 812.00/365, 385, 450;/451. For what it is worth, Díaz also blamed political dissidents, so Wilson reported.

3 Wilson, Mexico City, 10 Nov. (twice), 19 Nov.; Magill, Guadalajara, 15 Nov. 1910, SD 812.00/360, 385, 390; /438. When the Piedras Negras consulate was attacked the town's four policemen were busy in a brothel a mile from the city centre, whether out of design or lust is not clear: Ellsworth, C.P.D., 11 Nov. 1910, SD 812.00/386.

4 Lawton, Oaxaca, in Wilson, Mexico City, 15 Nov. 1910, SD 812.00/450.

5 Knight, 'Nationalism', pp. 211–301, especially pp. 250, 267.

6 Shanklin and Wilson, Mexico City, 9, 10 Nov.; Magill, Guadalajara, 15 Nov. 1910, SD 812.00/356, 385; /438.

7 Hostetter, Hermosillo, 13 Nov., Hanna, Monterrey, 14 Nov. 1910, SD 812.00/397, 376; fears that Cananea might erupt proved groundless, while Saltillo remained quiet and Chihuahua City witnessed one orderly demonstration: Dye, Nogales, 25 Nov., Goetter, Saltillo, 14 Nov., Keena, Chihuahua, 13 Nov. 1910, SD 812.00/522, 437, 367.

8 Bonney, San Luis, 14 Nov. 1910, SD 812.00/396.

9 Magill, Guadalajara, 15 Nov., Bonney, San Luis, 14 Nov., Wilson, Mexico City, 10 Nov. 1910, SD 812.00/438, 396, 385.

10 Miller, Tampico, 6 Sept. 1910, SD 812.00/342; Hernan Rosales, 'El romanticismo revolucionario de Santañón', *Todo*, 4 Nov. 1943; Anderson, *Outcasts*, p. 275.

11 Ross, *Madero*, pp. 122–3; José Vasconcelos, *Ulíses Criollo* (Mexico, 1964), p. 257; Anderson, *Outcasts*, p. 286.

12 Casasola, *Historia gráfica*, I, p. 221.

13 Lombardo Toledano in James Wilkie, *Mexico visto en el Siglo XX* (Mexico, 1969), p. 237.

14 *El País*, 17, 18 Nov. 1910.

15 Serratos to Madero, 7 Nov. 1912, AFM, r.22.

16 *El País*, 20, 22, 25 Nov. 1910; Nunn, Veracruz, 29 Apr. 1911, FO 371/1147, 18523; Anderson, *Outcasts*, p. 284.

17 Lefaivre to Quai d'Orsay, 24 Nov. 1910, Méx., Pol. Int., NS. II; see also Gavira, *Actuación*, pp. 28–9.

18 Colmenares Ríos to Robles Domínguez, 13 June 1911, AARD 25/218.

19 Martínez to Madero, 1 Sept. 1911, AFM, r.19; note also the experience of Sebastian Ortiz, described in A. Tenorio to Robles Domínguez, 5 June 1911, AARD 7/54. Ortiz and his men rebelled at Ojitlan (Oax.), were swiftly dispersed, and compelled to spend the duration of the Madero revolution in the mountains; Ortiz reappears in no less straitened circumstances below, vol. 2 ch. 1.

20 Melesio Sánchez to Gobernación, 18 July 1911, AG legajo 898.

21 Cresencio Jiménez to Madero, 7 July 1911, AFM, r.20; Bolio, *Yucatán*, p. 50; Ochoa Campos, *Guerrero*, p. 284.

22 Ing. Joce to Luis Cabrera, 12 May 1911, AARD 16/2.

23 Glenn, Guanajuato, 16 May 1911, SD 812.00/1648, *Actuación*, p. 24; G. and G. Gaona Salazar to Madero, 10 Oct. 1912, in Fabela, DHRM, RRM, IV, pp. 149–50.

24 Alberto Terrazas to E. Creel, 22 Dec. 1910, STA (E. Creel), r.2; Benjamín Hill quoted by Aguilar, *La Revolución Sonorense*, p. 19; Gavira, *Actuación*, p. 35 on the problems facing urban man who sets off into the sierra.

25 Robles Domínguez to Gustavo Madero, 10 June 1911, AARD 7/106.

26 Carothers, Torreón, 22, 26 Nov.; G. McCall, West Mexican Mines Co., Guadalupe y Calvo, 26 Nov. 1910, SD 812.00/509, 533; /578.

27 Meyer, *Mexican Rebel*, pp. 13–8; Ramon Puente, *Pascual Orozco y la revuelta de Chihuahua* (Mexico, 1912), p. 23; Letcher, Chihuahua, 20 Mar. 1912, SD 812.00/3424. There is also some evidence that Orozco had Protestant leanings.

28 Puente, *Pascual Orozco*, p. 23; see also Beezley, *Insurgent Governor*, pp. 36, 48.

29 Ellsworth, C.P.D., 11, 24 Dec. 1910, SD 812.00/569, 594.

30 Bonthrone, Chihuahua, 2 Mar. 1911, FO 371/1147, 17472; Ellsworth, from San Antonio, 10 Mar. 1911, SD 812.00/951; Ross, *Madero*, p. 124; Lister, *Chihuahua*, p. 212.

31 Guzmán, *Memorias*, pp. 48–54; R. Valle, Parral, to José Maria Sánchez, 8 Oct. 1910, STA, box 28, on Villa's recent activities.

32 Guzmán, *Memorias*, pp. 46; Reed, *Insurgent Mexico*, pp. 53, 55; Urbina to Gobernación, 31 July 1911, AG legajo 898, refers to 300 *indios de infantería* out of a total force of 1,000 at his command by the summer of 1911.

33 Hamm, Durango, 20 May 1911, SD 812.00/2106; Cumberland, *Constitutionalist Years*, p. 274.

34 Alger, Mazatlan, 1 Apr.; Freeman, Durango, 23 Feb. 1911; SD 812.00/1249; /882.

35 Guzmán, *Memorias*, 52; F. Mateus to A. Terrazas, 7 Dec. 1910, STA, box 28.

36 Report of the manager of the Guadalupe Mine, Inde, in Hohler, Mexico City, 28 June 1911, FO 371/1148, 27072.

37 Alberto Terrazas to E. Creel, 22 Dec. 1910, STA (E. Creel), r.2. 'Socialist', needless to say, can be taken with a pinch of salt.

38 Quoted by Lefaivre, 14 Dec. 1910, AAE, Mex., Pol. Int., N.S. II; F. Mateus to A. Terrazas, 17 Dec. 1910, STA, box 28; and for similar evidence from the Mineral de Dolores, José Sánchez to A. Terrazas, 2 Dec. 1910, STA (E. Creel), r.2.

39 S. Ramírez to Madero, 21 Sept. 1911, AFM, r.19; Hohler, Mexico City, 13 Mar. 1911, FO 371/1146, 11453, where the trouble at Aviño is compared with the calm prevailing at the nearby Tominil mines.

40 Jesus Vega Bonilla to A. Terrazas, 30 Nov. 1910, STA, box 28.

41 Lefaivre (n. 38 above); Fuentes Mares, *Y México se refugió*, pp. 240–1.

42 Guzmán, *Memorias*, pp. 53–4; J. B. Tighe, quoted in the *El Paso Herald*, 28 Jan. 1911.

43 Ross, *Madero*, p. 132; Ellsworth, C.P.D., 24 Jan. 1911, SD 812.00/687.

44 By this time many 'prominent Mexican families' were also leaving for Mexico City and the same exodus was affecting Durango. See Leonard, Chihuahua, 1 Feb., Freeman, Durango, 20 Feb. 1911, SD 812.00/749, 853; Fuentes Mares, *Y México se refugió*, p. 243.

45 Vasconcelos, *Ulises criollo*, p. 258.

46 Hohler, Mexico City, 3 Apr. 1911, FO 371/1146, 14297.

47 Hohler, Mexico City, 1 Mar. 1911, FO 371/1146, 9734.

48 O'Hea, *Reminiscences*, p. 8; Martínez Alier, *Haciendas*, pp. 15, 48, 131ff.

49 O'Hea, *Reminiscences*, p. 8; Graham, Durango, 18 Feb., 19 Apr. 1911, FO 371/1146, 8191, /1147, 17946; T. Fairbairn to T. Conduit, 20 Feb. 1911, SD 812.00/862.

50 Freeman, Durango, 31 Mar. 1911, SD 812.00/1252.

51 *Ibid.*, 24 Feb., 19 Mar. 1911, SD 812.00/880, 1105.

52 O'Hea, *Reminiscences*, p. 8; Macías to Madero, 6 July 1911, AFM, r.19; Adrián Aguirre Benavides to Madero, 29 May 1911, AFM, r.18.

53 Aguirre Benavides to Madero, 29 May 1911, AFM, r.18.

54 J. Reina, Mapimí to Madero, 2 July 1911, AFM, r.20.

55 Carothers, Torreón, 8 Mar. 1911, Coen Durango, 23 Feb. 1912, SD 812.00/962, 3250; J. P. C., Tlahualilo to J. B. Potter, 13 Apr. 1911, FO 371/1147, 16690.

56 Vera Estañol, *Revolución mexicana*, p. 212; Reed, *Insurgent Mexico*, pp. 194, 200.

57 E. Brondo Whitt, *La division del Norte (1914) por un testigo presencial* (Mexico, 1940), p. 125.

58 E. K. Knotts, Guanacevi, 20 April 1911, SD 812.00/2091; manager's report in Hohler, Mexico City, 28 June 1911, FO 371/1148, 27072.

59 Cf. Meyer, *Mexican Rebel*, p. 9; see the comments of Governor Ahumada to the British vice-consul at Chihuahua, in Hohler, Mexico City, 23 Feb. 1911, FO 371/1146, 8519.

60 Cf. Bonney, San Luis, 18 Mar. (twice), Lespinasse, Frontera, 21 Mar. 1911, SD 812.00/998, 1071, 1175.

61 F. Mateus, Casas Grandes, to J. M. Sanchez, 7 Dec.; F. Porras to E. de la Garza, 11 Dec. 1910; STA, box 28; (Creel), r.2.

62 Lawrence, Topia, 2 Feb., Witherbee, Santa Cruz Mines, near Zapotes, 29 March 1911, SD 812.00/808, 1436; Urbina to Gobernación, 31 July 1911, AG legajo 898.

63 José Trinidad Cervantes to Madero, 4 July 1911, AG legajo 898; Holms, Guadalajara, 25 Mar. 1911, FO 371/1146, 13581.

64 Cf. Reina, *Rebeliones campesinas*; Meyer, *Problemas campesinos*.

65 Alger, Mazatlan, 21 Mar. 1911, SD 812.00/1112; Aguírre Benavides, *De Francisco I. Madero*, p. 28.

66 At San José del Sitio, for example, in Chihuahua, 'the greater part' of the population joined the attacking Maderistas: F. Porras to E. de la Garza, STA (E. Creel), r.2.

67 Hohler, Mexico City, 16 Feb. 1911, FO 371/1146, 8189.

68 Fuentes Mares, *Y México se refugió*, p. 241.

69 Ross, *Madero*, p. 131; Ellsworth, C.P.D., 24 Jan. (twice); Carothers, Torreón, 27 Feb.; Freeman, Durango, 20 Feb. 1911; SD 812.00/681, 687; /891; /853; Fuentes Mares, *Y México se refugió*, p. 240.

70 Leonard, Chihuahua, 4 Feb., 4, 6, Mar. 1911, SD 812.00/770, 871, 938.

71 *Ibid.*, 6 Mar., 27 Feb., 1911, SD 812.00/938, 847.

72 Freeman, Durango, 26 Feb., 10 Mar.; Hostetter, Hermosillo, 27 Jan. 1911; SD 812.00/877, 968; /764.

73 Wilson, Mexico City, 6 Feb. 1911, SD 812.00/739.

74 Edwards, Juárez, 23 Jan.; Freeman, Durango, 19 Mar. 1911; SD 812.00/686; /1105; A. Terrazas to E. Creel, 22 Dec. 1910, STA (E. Creel), r.2.

75 Fuentes Mares, *Y México se refugió*, pp. 244–5.

76 Letcher, Jiménez, 5 Mar.; Ellsworth, El Paso, 4 Feb. 1911; SD 812.00/918; /804.

77 Even Creel admitted that 'almost all the state of Chihuahua favours the revolution': Fuentes

Mares, *Y México se refugió*, p. 246. See also Carothers, Torreón, 27 Feb. 1911, SD 812.00/891.

78 Leonard, Chihuahua, 1, 4 Feb. 1911, D 812.00/693, 770; Hohler, Mexico City, 23 Feb. 1911, FO 371/1146, 8519.

79 Dearing, Mexico City, 28 Feb. 1911, SD 812.00/881; cf. Ernesto Madero to Banco Minero, 23 Feb. 1911, deploring the recent 'unfortunate' events, and their effect on business: STA (E. Creel), r.2.

80 Edwards, Juárez, 13 Mar.; Ellsworth, San Antonio, 7 Mar. 1911; SD 812.00/989, 924.

81 Guzmán, *Memorias*, pp. 53–4; Alberto Calzadíaz Barrera, *Hechos reales de la revolución mexicana* (Mexico, 1961), pp. 43–4.

82 Ross, *Madero*, p. 135.

83 *Ibid.*, pp. 125–7; Aguirre Benávides, *De Francisco I. Madero*, pp. 15–16.

84 Ross, *Madero*, p. 129; Berta Ulloa, 'Las relaciones mexicano-norteamericanas, 1910–11', *Historia Mexicana*, XV 1965–6, pp. 27–8; P. Edward Haley, *Revolution and Intervention: The Diplomacy of Taft and Wilson with Mexico, 1910–17* (MIT, 1970), pp. 21–2.

85 Braulio Hernández, quoted in Calvert, p. 76; Hanna, Monterrey, 28 Nov. 1913, SD 812.00/10301.

86 Katz, *Secret War*, pp. 21–7, on the oil question; cf. Knight, 'Nationalism', pp. 18–23.

87 Campos, 'Científicos', pp. 14–15, 34.

88 Taft, in 1909, put American investment in Mexico at two billion dollars, when it was about half that amount; Bryan, five years later, believed that British 'commercial interests' were greater than America's, when they were nearer two-thirds. These examples do not argue a close, concerned interest in Mexico's receipt of foreign capital. See Haley, *Revolution and Intervention*, p. 9; Spring-Rice, Washington, 7 Feb. 1914, FO 371/2025, 7144.

89 F. S. Dunn, *The Diplomatic Protection of Americans in Mexico* (New York, 1933), p. 315.

90 Ulloa, 'Relaciones', p. 27; Dunn, *Diplomatic Protection*, p. 1.

91 Karl M. Schmitt, *Mexico and the United States, 1821–1973: Conflict and Co-existence* (New York, 1974), p. 106.

92 Cockcroft, *Intellectual Precursors*, p. 53; Anderson, *Outcasts*, pp. 119–20; cf. Duhaine, Saltillo, 1 Aug. 1906, SD, microcopy M-300, who commented that 'foreigners in general and Americans in particular have no reason whatever to complain of the treatment they receive here in Mexico'; the Mexicans were 'particularly kind and courteous' and preferred foreign to Mexican employers.

93 Taft to Knox and vice versa, 10, 11 Oct. 1910, SD 812.00/358; note also Taft's comments to his wife, 17 Oct. 1909, quoted in Haley, *Revolution and Intervention*, p. 14. Lister, *Chihuahua*, p. 206 describes the meeting of the two presidents.

94 I have not canvassed every aspect of the question; for the Magdalena Bay issue, and supposed Mexican support for Santos Zelaya of Nicaragua (neither of which, I think, substantially affect the argument) see Calvert, pp. 28–9. Ultimately, of course, proponents of conspiracy theories can make their conspiracies so complex and devious as to defy falsification.

95 Bryce, Washington, 28 Mar. 1911, FO 371/1146, 12632; Wilson, Mexico City, 16 Nov. 1910, SD 812.00/447.

96 As the Secretary of State explained to the Mexican Ambassador more than once: Haley, *Revolution and Intervention*, pp. 21–2.

97 Haley, *Revolution and Intervention*, pp. 23–5; Ulloa, 'Relaciones', pp. 27–8.

98 Haley, *Revolution and Intervention*, p. 23.

99 Knight, 'Nationalism', pp. 18–22.

100 Calvert, *Mexican Revolution*, pp. 73–84 is the best account.

101 Agent's report enclosed in Attorney-General to Secretary of State, 2 May 1911, SD 812.00/1593.

102 Ross, *Madero*, p. 142.

103 Calvert, *Mexican Revolution*, pp. 82–3; Cumberland, *Genesis*, pp. 153–4; memo. of State Department solicitor, 8 May 1911 and other documents under SD 812.00/1593; Archbold to Knox, 15 May 1911, SD 812.00/1796.

104 Cumberland, *Genesis*, p. 129. As this shows, the US did not waive its neutrality laws for Madero's benefit.

105 Ross, *Madero*, pp. 135–6; Valadés, *Imaginación*, pp. 108–22.

106 Ross, *Madero*, pp. 146–7, pits 500 rebels against fewer defenders; the Federal commander, in Fabela, DHRM, RRM, I, pp. 270–80, claimed to have 500 (including 150 volunteers) against 800; José Garibaldi, Giuseppe's son, who was with Madero, reported that 300 Federals and 400 volunteers defended Casas Grandes: Letcher, Chihuahua, 29 Mar. 1911, SD 812.00/1222. Similar numerical problems arise with every military encounter; each side, it will be noted, inflates the number of the opposition.

107 Aguilar, *Revolución Sonorense*, pp. 162–3; the Federal commander at Casas Grandes dilated on these points: Fabela, DHRM, RRM, I, p. 280.

108 Letcher, 29 Mar. 1911, SD 812.00/1221.

109 Naval intelligence report, Veracruz, 14 Mar.; c/o USS Princeton, Salina Cruz, 21 Mar. 1911; SD 812.00/1162, 1219.

110 Haley, *Revolution and Intervention*, pp. 25–32.

111 Potential rebels would have seconded 'any other summons launched with a certain formality': *El Correo*, 8 Mar. 1911.

112 Vera Estañol, *Revolución Mexicana*, pp. 126–7.

113 Gavira, *Actuación*, p. 25.

114 Interview of Maria Isabel Souza with Simón Márquez Camarena, PHO 1/113, p. 28.

115 See pp. 270–2.

116 Though the geographical distinctions between north, centre and south have an obvious analytical validity, they are often drawn too sharply and crudely; other distinctions – between mountain and lowland, town and country, Indian and mestizo – must also be introduced, and these could cut across the north/centre/south trichotomy, creating thereby a more complex and variegated pattern within these regions, as within states.

117 The Chihuahua cases have already been mentioned; for Durango, Manuel Gamiz Olivas, *Historia de la Revolución en el Estado de Durango* (Mexico, 1963), p. 11.

118 Scott, *Moral Economy*, p. iv; Womack, *Zapata*, p. 61.

119 Womack, *Zapata*, p. 74.

120 *Ibid.*, pp. 5–7; Jesús Sotelo Inclán, *Raíz y razón de Zapata* (Mexico, 1943), p. 169.

121 Womack, *Zapata*, pp. 64–5.

122 *Ibid.*, pp. 75–6, 87.

123 *Ibid.*, p. 78 on events at Jojutla; cf. José Fernández Rojas, *De Porfirio Díaz a Victoriano Huerta, 1910–13* (Mexico, 1913), pp. 71, 88, 214–15.

124 Hohler, Mexico City, 28 Mar. 1911, FO 371/1146, 13581.

125 Hohler, Mexico City, 3 May 1911, FO 371/1147, 18521; Limantour, *Apuntes*, p. 273; *El País*, 26 Aug. 1911.

126 This is not to say that there was no 'pure' banditry during the Revolution; there was. See pp. 339, 354–5.

127 Womack, *Zapata*, p. 81.

128 'Only rarely (in the spring of 1911) did they recruit rebels among the gente de casa, who anyway preferred their bonded security': Womack, *Zapata*, pp. 87, 122; and Lamberto Marín to Clemente Jacques y Cia., 9 June 1911 AARD 17/131, concerning Axochiapam.

129 Womack, *Zapata*, p. 56.

130 Buve, 'Peasant movements', pp. 124–30.

131 *Ibid.*, p. 128.

132 Above, pp. 107–8.

133 Miller, Tampico, 23 Nov. 1910, SD 812.00/468.
134 British rancher, Valles, in Hohler, Mexico City, 15 Mar.; Wilson, Tampico, 21 Apr., 1911; FO 371/1146, 11451; /1147, 17946. It was the arrest of Leopoldo Lárraga at his ranch near Valles in December 1910 which spurred his brother, Manuel, towards a distinguished revolutionary career: Joaquín Meade, *Historia de Valles* (Mexico, 1970), p. 174.
135 Miller, Tampico, 8, 18, 30 Mar., 22 Apr. 1911, SD 812.00/950, 1106, 1150, 1530.
136 *Ibid.*, 6, 18 May 1911, SD 812.00/1651, 1845; Martínez Núñez, *San Luis Potosí*, p. 34.
137 *Ibid.*, pp. 32–3.
138 Bonney, San Luis, 4 May 1911, SD 812.00/1774. There were expectations that Papantla, to the south, another known centre of agrarian disaffection, would give trouble, as eventually it did: Miller, Tampico, 28 Mar.; Canada, Veracruz, 8 Apr. 1911; SD 812.00/1200; 1247.
139 Bonney, San Luis, 18 Mar., 4 May 1911, SD 812.00/1071, 1774.
140 *Ibid.*, 18 Mar., 17 Apr. 1911, SD 812.00/1071, 1750.
141 *Ibid.*, 18 Mar., 4 Apr., 1911, SD 812.00/998, 1291.
142 Cf. Guerra, 'La révolution méxicaine'.
143 Cockcroft, *Intellectual Precursors*, p. 4; Bonney, San Luis, 27 May 1911, SD 812.00/2030.
144 Aguilar, *Revolución Sonorense*, pp. 137–8, 142, 144.
145 *Ibid.*, pp. 164–5; 204–5. Calles was then busy with the latest of his many jobs: running the Hotel California, Guaymas.
146 *Ibid.*, pp. 133, 143; Hostetter, Hermosillo 9 Mar. 1911, SD812.00/984; manifesto of Rosario García, 4 Aug. 1911, SS, r.9.
147 Dye, Nogales, 18 Mar., 17, 21 May 1911, SD 812.00/1044, 1893, 1954.
148 Aguilar, *Revolución Sonorense*, pp. 143, 154, 163.
149 *Ibid.*, pp. 139–43, 155–6.
150 Hostetter, Hermosillo, 19 Mar. 1911, SD 812.00/1074.
151 Aguilar, *Revolución Sonorense*, p. 145.
152 Dye, Nogales, 4 Feb., McCarthy, Alamos, 5 Mar. 1911, SD 812.00/767, 984.
153 Medina Barrón to Cubillas, 20 Apr. 1911, in Aguilar, *Revolución Sonorense*, p. 170; H. Loomis, enclosed in Ellsworth, San Antonio, 12 Mar. 1911, SD 812.00/970.
154 McCarthy, Alamos, 5 Mar. and Hanna, Monterrey, 24 Feb. 1911, SD 812.00/984, 858, both make this distinction. Descriptions of the Sonoran rebels from McCarthy and *La Constitución* 13 Feb. 1911, quoted by Aguilar, *Revolución Sonorense*, p. 156.
155 Loomis, in Ellsworth, San Antonio, 12 Mar. 1911, SD 812.00/970 coins the phrase.
156 Aguilar, *Revolución Sonorense*, pp. 59–60.
157 *Ibid.*, pp. 165–7; Ellsworth, San Antonio, 12, 21, 22 Mar. 1911, SD 812.00/970, 1071, 1082.
158 Hostetter, Hermosillo, 3 June 1911, SD 812.00/2127; Aguilar, *Revolución Sonorense*, pp. 173–4; Robles Domínguez to Madero, 6 June 1911, AARD, 20/10.
159 Aguilar, *Revolución Sonorense*, pp. 183–4.
160 Gil, 'Mochis'.
161 Olea, *Sinaloa*, p. 40.
162 *Ibid.*, pp. 23–6, 31.
163 *Ibid.*, pp. 22–6; Womack, *Zapata*, p. 208; Alger, Mazatlán, 21 Mar., 2, 5 Apr. 1911, SD 812.00/1112, 1250, 1288.
164 Casasola, *Historia gráfica*, I, p. 282; Olea, *Sinaloa*, pp. 24–5; Gill, 'Mochis'.
165 See below, pp. 236–8.
166 Anon, report, n.d., in AARD 27/1.
167 Olea, *Sinaloa*, p. 84.
168 Cf. Schryer, *Rancheros of Pisaflores*.
169 Alger, Mazatlán, 30 Mar., 4 May 1911, SD 812.000/1216, 1820. It bears repeating that,

even while foreign consuls deplored mounting brigandage and anarchy, their nationals rarely suffered worse than petty extortions from the rebels: a British rancher, for example, held up by 'bandits' at Villa Unión (Sin.), successfully concealed the 150 pesos payroll he carried with him and surrendered only 5 pesos in small change; 'when asked for a drink he ... irritated them by producing a bottle of cold tea from his saddlebag, that being all he carried': Stait-Gardner, Mazatlán, 20 Apr 1911, FO 371/1147, 17946.

170 Enrique Aguirre to Gobernación, 22 July 1911, AG 898; Salida de G. G. Sanchez en campaña, 22 July 1911, same source, is a very detailed account.

171 Edwards, Juárez, 21 Mar. 1911, SD. 812.00/1063.

172 Casasola, *Historia gráfica*, I, p. 260; T. Fairbairn to W. Conduit, 20 Feb. 1911 SD 812.00/862; Salida de G. G. Sánchez en campaña, 22 July 1911, AG 898.

173 Gavira, *Actuación,* pp. 28–9; Thompson, Mérida, 19 Mar. 1911, SD 812.00/1260.

174 Lespinasse, Frontera, 2 Jan. 1911, SD 812.000/651; Colmenares Ríos to Robles Domínguez, 13 June 1911, AARD 25/218.

175 Freeman, Durango, 27 Feb. 1911, SD 812.00/895.

176 'I never told the [hacienda] employees and owners how many men I had, fearing they would ask questions and find out how badly organised I was'; Salida de G. G. Sanchez, 22 July 1911, AG 898.

177 Freeman, Durango, 16 Apr. 1911, SD 812.00/1453.

178 Cf. above, pp. 151, 165.

179 Dye, Nogales, 17 May 1911, SD 812.00/1893: Cabral and Alvarado in fact entered Cananea on 13 May at the head of 300 men: Aguilar, *Revolución Sonorense*, p. 176. Enrique Aguirre to Gobernación, 22 July 1911, AG 898, goes on to describe another 'buen golpe de audacia' at Pachuca; though similarly hyperbolic, it contains a core of truth, which can be corroborated.

180 Ellsworth, San Antonio, 7 Mar. 1911, SD 812.00/924.

181 Reed, *Insurgent Mexico*, pp. 75–6; Wilson, Mexico City, 19 Apr. 1911, SD 812.00/1460.

182 Wilson, Mexico City, 19 Apr. 1911, SD 812.00/1460; Thord-Grey, *Gringo Rebel*, pp. 275–361.

183 One individual joined the rebels at San Felipe in protest at 'the abuses which (Cipriano Espinosa, "Científico" ex-*jefe político*) committed in the town, during his administration': Rodrigo González to Madero, 9 Nov. 1911, AG, CRCFM.

184 Glenn, Guanajuato, 16 May 1911, SD 812.00/1948 for the Navarro revolt.

185 There were reckoned to be between 1,000 and 2,000 rebels in the Tonichi district of Sonora in February; but 'this includes quite a number who are local men who fought on the side of the revolutionists and then went back to their homes': Dye, Nogales, 4 Feb. 1911, SD 812.00/767. See also n. 66 above.

186 Aguirre to Gobernación, 22 July 1911, AG 898.

187 Ross, *Madero*, p. 162.

188 Womack, *Zapata*, p. 85.

189 Letcher, Chihuahua, 6 Apr. 1911; Ellsworth, C.P.D., 22 May 1912, SD 812.00/1318;/4307.

190 Cf. Romero Flores, *Michoacán*, p. 72.

191 Alger, Mazatlán, 21 Mar.; McCarthy, Alamos, 25 May 1911, SD 812.00/1112;/2056.

192 Goetter, Saltillo, 2 May 1911, SD 812.00/1678.

193 Rutherford, *Mexican Society*, p. 136, citing *El Diario*.

194 Edwards, Acapulco, 13 May 1911, SD 812.00/1947.

195 Tower, Mexico City, 31 Dec. 1910, FO 371/1149, 1574; Limantour, *Apuntes*, p. 257; Cumberland, *Genesis*, pp. 136, 149.

196 *El Correo*, 1 Mar. 1911, expressed its preference for 'Evolution' over 'Revolution', and argued that 'the principal cause which gave rise to the revolt (sc., the Creel–Terrazas

caciacazgo) . . . has fallen, never to rise again'; hence peace was opportune. *Ibid.*, 2 Mar., reports Ahumada's transfer of state funds from the (Creel–Terrazas) Banco Minero to the Treasury-General.
197 Ross, *Madero*, pp. 153–5; Limantour, *Apuntes*, p. 234.
198 Canada, Veracruz, 3 Apr.; Pangburn, Acapulco, 3 Apr.; Miller, Tampico, 5 Apr.; Alger, Mazatlán, 29 Mar. 1911, SD 812.00/1181, 1183, 1292, 1195.
199 Ross, *Madero*, p. 154.
200 *Ibid.*, pp. 155–8. Limantour offered certain changes in political personnel and an acceptance of the principle of 'No Re-election'; but not the removal of Díaz.
201 Edwards, Juárez, 13 May; Bonney, San Luis, 4 May 1911, SD 812.00/1765, 1774.
202 Ross, *Madero*, p. 163; Valadés, *Imaginación*, I, p. 162.
203 Valadés, *Imaginación*, p. 158; Sánchez Azcona, *Apuntes*, pp. 237–8.
204 Ross, *Madero*, p. 135; Sepúlveda Otaiza, p. 7. The leader in question, Luis García, was reckoned a Magonista; it is hard to assess how far Magonista–Maderista rivalry counted in this instance.
205 Sanchez Azcona, *Apuntes*, pp. 238–40.
206 Letcher, Chihuahua, 24 Apr. 1911, SD 812.00/1577. There were about 700 Federals facing 1,500–2,000 rebels.
207 Ross, *Madero*, pp. 164–5; Edwards, Juárez, 13 May 1911, SD 812.00/1846.
208 Cumberland, *Genesis*, p. 149.
209 Ross, *Madero*, p. 170; Fabela, DHRM, RRM, I, pp. 400–1. That Díaz would be replaced by de la Barra, then the new Foreign Minister, had been rumoured weeks before: *El Correo*, 27 Mar. 1911.
210 Lespinasse, Frontera, 7, 26 Apr., 11 May; Brickwood, Tapachula, 25 May 1911; SD 812.00/1242, 1489, 1721;/1944.
211 Lespinasse, Frontera, received 24 May; Edwards, Acapulco, 13 May; Alger, Mazatlán, 10 May 1911; SD 812.00/1924;/1947;/1869.
212 Pangburn, Acapulco, 6, 20, Mar. (twice), 11 Apr., 2 May; Edwards, Acapulco, 13 May 1911; SD 812.00/1237, 1425, 1426, 1452, 1575;/1947. For the Ometepec revolt, see below, p. 221–2.
213 Salgado to de la Barra, 24 July 1911, ALB, carpeta 3.
214 Womack, *Zapata*, pp. 82–3; Ochoa Campos, *Guerrero*, pp. 283–7; memo. de la situación política del estado de Morelos, 29 Dec. 1911, probably by Robles Domínguez, AARD 37/5; Jacobs, 'Aspects', pp. 122–7.
215 Womack, *Zapata*, pp. 85–6.
216 Chambers, Puebla, 18, 21 Apr., 12 May 1911, SD 812.00/1479, 1521, 1884; possibly this estimate included the Morelos forces. For further information, AARD expediente 19 *passim*.
217 Womack, *Zapata*, p. 81; for Veracruz, AARD expediente 25 *passim*; Gavira, *Actuación*, pp. 34–42; Tapia, *Mi participación*, pp. 21–35.
218 Ramírez, *Oaxaca*, p. 22; n.19 above.
219 Bonney, San Luis, 14 May 1911, SD 812.00/1847.
220 Voetter, Saltillo, 27 Mar., 21 Apr., 1, 14 May 1911, SD 812.00/1198, 1495, 1557, 1855; MacMillan, Saltillo, 17 Apr. 1911, FO 371/1147, 16692.
221 José G. Zuno, *Historia de la revolución en el estado de Jalisco* (Mexico, 1964), has a rather exiguous theme, certainly for 1910–11; see pp. 26–7, 58–9. Holms, Guadalajara, 17 Apr. 1911, FO 371/1147, 16692, bears out this picture of political discontent devoid of revolutionary potential: 'the state of Jalisco has been notably free from active manifestations of political discontent. Notwithstanding the passive attitude assumed by the people, there is no . . . doubt that their entire sympathies are with the revolutionary party'.
222 Freeman, Durango, 12 Apr. 1911, SD 812.00/1438.
223 Gamiz, *Durango*, p. 25.

224 Freeman, Durango, 19, 22 (twice) Apr. 1911, SD 812.00/1451, 1529, 1579.

225 Gamiz, *Durango*, p. 30; Freeman, Durango, 19 May 1911, SD 812.00/2087. Colonel Cortés repeatedly paraded his 170 men in different uniforms, creating the impression (it was hoped) of a garrison of 500.

226 Freeman, Durango, 5 May 1911, SD 812.00/2080.

227 *Ibid.*, 3 June 1911, SD 812.00/2106; Gamiz, *Durango*, p. 32.

228 Carothers, Torreón, 2 May 1911, SD 812.00/1588.

229 Events at Torreón are described by Carothers, Torreón, 22 May 1911, SD 812.00/1968 and Gamiz, pp. 25–7; the latter dwells on Castro's *sang-froid* but tastefully skips the bloody events of 15 May, for which see the useful account *Tulitas of Torreón: Reminiscences of Life in Mexico by Tulitas Jamieson, As Told to Evelyn Payne* (Texas Western Press, 1969), pp. 116–22.

230 J. P. C., Tlahualilo, 20 May 1911, SD 812.00/1998.

231 C. A. Heberlein, Torreón, 15 May 1911, SD 812.00/2026.

232 Details from Carothers and Heberlein (ns. 229, 231). Cf. Cumberland, 'Sonoran Chinese'.

233 Knight, 'Nationalism', pp. 310–12.

234 Salvador Benavides to Madero, 8 Nov. 1911, Fabela, DHRM, RRM, ii, p. 257.

235 Cf. Rutherford, *Mexican Society*, pp. 186–7.

236 The distinctions made here between 'political' and 'economic' riots may require brief clarification, both theoretical and empirical. In the first instance it should be clear that the terms are used in a common-sense way, differentiating political targets (e.g., officials) from economic (e.g., shopkeepers), but not implying some radical divorce between 'the political' and 'the economic'; in the second, it should be noted that economic riots could and did include political targets (though in a good many cases such targets managed to absent themselves more promptly than the economic victims; the *jefe* quit his office more readily and rapidly than the shopkeeper did his shop); hence political riots, as defined here, were specifically political, and did not involve wider upheaval, reprisals and looting.

237 Hobsbawm, *Primitive Rebels*, pp. 108–25; Rudé, *The Crowd*, pp. 237–57.

238 Cf. above pp. 132, 158–9.

239 Above, pp. 130–2.

240 Freeman, Durango, 5 May 1911, SD 812.00/2080.

241 Adrián Aguirre Benavides to Madero, 29 May 1911, AFM n. 18.

242 Bonifacio Soto to Robles Domínguez, 22 May 1911, AARD 11/2.

243 Below, pp. 237–8 explains the inverted commas.

244 Soto to Robles Domínguez, 2 June 1911, AARD 11/69.

245 Ciro Valenzuela to Gobernación, 26 May 1911, AARD 11/19.

246 *El Diario del Hogar*, 23 Mar. 1911; Fernando Lizardi to Carlos Robles Domínguez, 1 June 1911, AARD 11/53.

247 Above, pp. 132–3.

248 Rowe, Guanajuato, 23 May 1911, SD 812.00/2046.

249 The Maderista, 'pro-riot' accounts are: Rutino Zamora and Manuel Herrera to Robles Domínguez, 27, 30 May 1911, AARD 11/22, 11/43, and Herrera to Cosío Robelo, 26 May, AARD 6/54; for the 'anti-riot' point of view, see the petition of a hundred or so residents of San Miguel to Gobernación, 27 May 1911, AG 898.

250 Salida de G. G. Sánchez en campaña. 22 July 1911, AG 898.

251 Spanish Minister, Mexico City to Minister of War, 29 May 1911, AARD 6/102; C. Stanhope, San Luis, to B. Catling, 15 May 1911, FO 371/1148, 22111. The Maderista leader who connived at this sack, Nicolás Torres, was a particularly wild character who, within weeks, was caught and executed by fellow-Maderistas: *Diario del Hogar*, 29 May 1911, Bonney, San Luis, 23 May 1911, SD 812.00/1980.

252 Fernández (a British consular representative, though himself a Spaniard), Acapulco, 30

Apr.; Hohler, Mexico City, 11 May 1911, FO 371/1147, 20161; 20167; Chambers, Puebla, 8 May 1911, SD 812.00/1813.

253 Hohler, Mexico City, 17 May 1911, FO 371/1147, 20780, blames the miners; *El Diario del Hogar*, 23 May 1911, blames criminals released from the gaol (but does not indicate who released them); see also Aguirre to Gobernación, 22 July 1911, AG 898; E. Bordes Mangel to Madero, 16 June 1911, AFM r.20.

254 Manager, Cía Minera de los Reyes, to managing director, Mexico City, 31 May 1911, AARD 6/136.

255 A. Wedelen to H. Moran, 29 May 1911 and Carlos Robles Domínguez to Alfredo Robles Domínguez, 30 May 1911, AARD 6/103, 6/127.

256 *Jefe político*, Zitácuaro, to Governor Silva, 3 July 1911, AG 14, 'Relaciones con los Estados' (Mich.).

257 Marcos Méndez to Gobernación, 30 July 1911; Silva to Gobernación 25 July 1911; both in AG 14 (n.256 above).

258 Aguilar, *Revolución Sonorense*, p. 161.

259 Wiswall, Cananea, 14 May 1911, SD 812.00/1757; Aguilar, *Revolución Sonorense*, p. 173.

260 Hanna, Monterrey, 11 Aug.; Johnson, Matamoros, 2 June 1911; SD 812.00/2346, 2076.

261 Knight, 'La révolution mexicaine'.

262 Cf. Thompson, *Making of the English Working Class*, p. 68; Tillys, *Rebellious Century*, pp. 17–19.

263 There were, possibly, cases of revolutionary Luddism when 'peasant–artisan' forces from Tlaxcala controlled the textile region of Puebla; see vol. 2 ch. 2.

264 Miguel Zamora to Robles Domínguez, 25 May 1911, AARD 25/59; Francisco Cosío Robelo to Tapia, 26 May 1911, AARD 25/65; Voetter, Saltillo, 14 May 1911, SD 812.00/1855.

265 Navarro to Robles Domínguez, 1 June 1911, AARD 21/14, 16.

266 Hohler, Mexico City, 17 May 1911, FO 371/1147, 20780. In the capital, as in other towns of the centre and south, the Federal garrison had been depleted: Baron de Vaux to Quai d'Orsay, 11 May, AAE Mex. Pol. Int., N.S. II.

267 On the qualitative distinction between economic and political riots, see n.236 above.

268 Manuel Plata to Minister of War, 27 May 1911, AARD 21/2; Bonney, San Luis, 27 May 1911, SD 812.00/2030.

269 Voetter, Saltillo, 27 May, 1 June 1911, SD 812.00/2028, 2032.

270 Hohler, Mexico City, 24 May 1911, FO 371/1148, 21858.

271 Cumberland, *Genesis*, p. 150.

272 Holms, Guadalajara, 25 May 1911, FO 371/1148, 22770; McGill, Guadalajara, 24 May 1911, SD 812.00/2017; *El Diario del Hogar*, 26 May 1911, lists Cuesta Gallardo's abuses.

273 Information on the Tampico events derives from: Wilson, Tampico, 30 May 1911, FO 371/1148, 23457; Miller, Tampico, 25, 30 May, 1, 2, June 1911, SD 812.00/1989, 2050, 2062, 2110.

274 It must be assumed that gaols were such frequent targets – even in the more narrowly political riots – because they housed the most obvious victims of Porfirian authority, in particular political dissidents. It was not unknown for liberated prisoners (of the latter kind) to be installed at once in municipal office.

275 Below, pp. 401–9.

276 Below, pp. 241–2.

277 Limantour, *Apuntes*, pp. 266–7.

278 Wilson, Mexico City, 24, 31 May 1911, SD 812.00/1943, 2037; Ross, *Madero*, p. 171.

279 Cumberland, *Genesis*, p. 151.

280 'It seems as if Madero has started something he is unable to handle': Alger, Mazatlán, 30 Mar. 1911, SD 812.00/1216.

281 A dispute between Pablo Lavín and Juan Ramírez, conquerors of Lerdo, allowed the

Federals briefly to retake the town; the attack on Torreón, for which several thousand Maderistas were gathered under Castro's command, began when Benjamín Argumedo and his 300 men decided to storm the city, forcing Castro to commit all his men: a pattern reminiscent of the attack on Juárez. See Carothers, Torreón, 22 May 1911, SD 812.00/1968; Gamiz, *Durango*, p. 27.

282 Luis Cabrera in Silva Herzog, *La Cuestión de la Tierra*, II, p. 301.

283 Womack, *Zapata*, p. 87.

284 Freeman, Durango, 30 July 1911, SD 812.00/2265.

285 Lewis, *Tepoztlán*, p. 233.

286 Again, some of the victims were Spaniards. Womack, *Zapata*, p. 87; Vera Estañol, *Revolución mexicana*, p. 149.

287 A. Guzmán to Robles Domínguez, 31 May 1911, AARD 13/23. San Antonio Tochatlaco, however, does not seem to have been disrupted: in the first working week of June 1911, 89 employees worked an average of 6.3 days; a year before eighty-seven employees worked an almost identical average: AT, *libro de raya*.

288 M. Martínez to A. Torres Rivas, 23 May 1911, AARD 13/5.

289 They suffered only robbery and arbitrary arrests: C. Contreras memo., 23 May 1911, AARD 7/190.

290 Dolores Huerta to Robles Domínguez, 25 May 1911; A. del Pozo to same, 5 June 1911; AARD 24/2, 19/102.

291 S. Gómez to G. Madero, 24 Apr. 1912, Fabela, DHRM, RRM, III, pp. 341–2.

292 McGill, Guadalajara, 5 Aug. 1911, SD 812.00/2282.

293 R. Ibarrola to Governor Silva, 29 June 1911, AG 14, 'Relaciones con los Estados' (Mich.).

294 M. Delille to Gobernación and E. Michot to Delille, AG 14 (n.293 above).

295 J. Narvarte to prefect, Pátzcuaro, 29 Aug. 1911; I. Tovar to same, 30 Aug. 1911; AG 14 (n.293 above); for Cantabria's history, see pp. 104–5.

296 T. Ortiz to Governor Silva, 18 Oct. 1911, AG 14 (n.293 above).

297 Marcos Méndez to Gobernación, 30 July 1911, AG 14 (n.293 above).

298 M. Ruiz, *jefe político*, Tepic to Gobernación, 14 Mar., 4 Apr. 1911, and other documents in AG 17, 'Tepic 1910–11'; and above, p. 110.

299 By the end of April, Añorve led 1,000 men: Pangburn, Acapulco, 24 Apr. 1911, SD 812.00/1687. The basic source for this account is AARD 12/22, 29, 35, and 27/2-210.

300 I. López Moctezuma and eight signatories to de la Barra, 22 Sept. 1911 AARD 12/35 call Reyna 'an inkpot of bad law and bad faith'; a village lawyer/intellectual, in fact.

301 López Moctezuma (n.300 above); Vda de G. Median to Añorve, 12 May 1911, AARD 27/15.

302 López Moctezuma (n. 300 above); Vda de G. Medina to Añorve, 12 May 1911, AARD 27/15.

303 J. Baños to Añorve, 9 June 1911, AARD 27/73; cf. Atristain, *Notas*, pp. 16–26.

304 C. Díaz to Añorve, 9 June 1911, and Vda de Rodríguez to same, 8 June, AARD 27/68, 58.

305 P. García, to Añorve, 15 July 1911, AARD 27/210.

306 Proclamation of Añorve, 29 May 1911, AARD, 27/191.

307 See vol. 2 ch. 20.

308 Morelos has been mentioned; for Tepic, Fabela, DHRM, RRM, III, pp. 316–8.

309 William T. Sanders, 'Settlement Patterns', in *Handbook of Middle American Indians*, VI, p. 69.

310 Lespinasse, Frontera, 28 Jan., 8 Apr., 18 May 1911, SD 812.00/745, 1405, 2016; Leonardo Pasquel, *La generación liberal veracruzana* (Veracruz 1972), pp. 321–2.

311 B. Cluff, manager, Utah-Mexican Rubber Co., El Provo, 24 Dec. 1910, SD 812.00/651.

312 J. Ramírez Garrido *et al.*, Acta Levantada, 28 May 1911, AARD 22/7.

313 Magaña to Madero, 11 Nov. 1911, AG, CRCFM.

314 Lespinasse, Frontera, 28 Sept. 1910, SD 812.00/348; M. Candelas to Robles Domínguez, 7 June 1911, AARD 22/30. Maderismo had not been particularly strong in Tabasco in

1909–10; see Justo A. Santa Aña, 'Los precursores de la revolución en Tabasco', *Universal Gráfico*, 2 Apr. 1936; González Calzada, *Tabasco*, pp. 53–9.

315 Lespinasse, Frontera, 21 Mar. 1911, SD 812.00/1175; Madero to Pino Suárez, 1 Oct. 1911, AFM r.10.

316 US Naval Intelligence, Veracruz, 14 Mar. 1911, SD 812.00/1162.

317 Brickwood, Tapachula, 19 Mar. 1911, SD 812.00/1412; F. Pineda to Madero, 24 Aug. 1911, AFM r.19; Benjamin, 'Passages', pp. 111–14.

318 J. Martínez to Madero, 4 Aug. 1911, AFM r.21.

319 Above, pp. 71–2, 75.

320 Cumberland, *Genesis*, p. 111.

321 Bolio, *Yucatán*, pp. 44–51, 58; Reed, *Caste War*, pp. 247–8; Joseph, 'Revolution from without' (diss.), p. 109.

322 Bolio, *Yucatán*, p. 61.

323 *Ibid.*, pp. 58–9.

324 *Ibid.*, p. 60; McGoogan, Progreso, 11 Mar. 1911, SD 812.00/985.

325 McGoogan (n.324 above); Thompson, Mérida, 19 Mar. 1911, SD 812.00/1260; Bolio, pp. 61–2.

326 Genovese, *Roll, Jordan, Roll*, pp. 587–97; F. W. Knight, *Slave Society in Cuba during the Nineteenth Century* (Madison, 1970), pp. 81, 95.

327 Joseph, *Revolution From Without* (book), pp. 71, 84; Reed, *Caste War*, pp. 209, 248.

328 Bolio, *Yucatán*, pp. 62–3; Hohler, Mexico City, 28 Mar.; Pierce, Mérida, 1 May 1911; FO 371/1146, 13581;/1147, 20161; Young, Progreso, 24 Apr. 1912, SD 812.00/3778.

329 Brickwood, Tapachula, 19 Mar. 1911, SD 812.00/1412.

330 Wilson, Mexico City, 28 Aug. 1912, SD 812.00/4899: one of the American Ambassador's rare, apposite remarks. The other one appears on p. 252.

331 See above, pp. 165–6.

332 Madero to Evaristo Madero, 17 Sept. 1909, AFM r.9.

333 Evaristo Madero to Rafael Hernández, 18 July 1911, Fabela, DHRM, RRM, I, pp. 433–5 (Hernández, Francisco Madero's cousin, was one of the Maderistas in de la Barra's hybrid administration).

334 Madero, *La sucesion presidencial*, p. 296.

335 Womack, *Zapata*, p. 101; P. Illodi to Directorate of the Mexican Agricultural Society 12 Aug. 1911, AG 898; G. Hernández to Robles Domínguez, n.d., late May 1911, AARD 13/4; Secretary of War to Gobernación, 25 Jan. 1912, AG 898.

336 E.g., Ross, *Madero*, pp. 170–1; Womack, *Zapata*, pp. 90–1; Gilly, *Revolución interrumpida*, p. 47.

337 Aguirre, Benavides, *De Francisco I. Madero*, p. 21.

338 Minutes of meeting, 22 May 1911, AG 898.

339 Ross, *Madero*, pp. 135, 144; Valadés, *Imaginación*, I, p. 140; J. M. Arriola and T. Torres to SRE, 12, 14 May 1911, Fabela, DHRM, RRM, I, pp. 383, 387–8.

340 A. Lomeli, El Paso, to SRE 25 Nov.; A. Lozano, Los Angeles to same, 27 Nov. 1910, Fabela, DHRM, RRM, I, pp. 102–3, 106; though Porfirian (and later Huertista) consuls in the US, having little good news to report, maintained a willing suspension of disbelief when reports of revolutionary feuds and divisions were received.

341 Cockcroft, *Intellectual Precursors*, pp. 176–83; the quote from p. 177.

342 *Ibid.*, p. 177; Mexicali, incidentally, was not the capital of Baja California (sic), either North or South; the capital of Baja California Norte was Ensenada.

343 Valadés, *Imaginación*, I, pp. 112–13.

344 In the extensive papers of the Terrazas archive (STA, boxes 26–8), the only names of any real significance for 1910–11 are José de la Luz Soto (recipient of a letter from Ricardo Flores Magón, June 1905, Box 26), and Miguel and Juan Baca (Magonista contacts, under police surveillance); though it was Guillermo Baca who, as a Maderista, joined the

revolution in November 1910 and was killed two months later: see Almada, *Diccionario*, p. 55. As for Orozco, an individual who might have been Orozco (or someone else) was seen by a government spy at San Isidro station in October 1906 in the company of a friend reading an opposition newspaper: F. Antillon to E. Creel, 20 Oct. 1906, STA, box 26. Upon such tenuous foundations do authoritarian regimes and later radical historians combine to build records of pre-revolutionary subversion.

345 See below, pp. 293–5.

346 Names taken from the casualty list after the battle of Casas Grandes, in Letcher, Chihuahua, 1 June 1911, SD 812.00/2111; Lozoya, *Ejército*, p. 35, quoting Urquizo; M. Triana to Governor of Durango, 19 June 1911, AG 898. Heroic, historical names also tended to conceal a local and personalist origin: Trinidad Rodríguez's Cuauhtémoc Brigade, for example, came from Huejotitlán, west of Parral: Calzadíaz Barrera, *Hechos Reales*, pp. 179–80.

347 Reed, *Insurgent Mexico*, p. 81.

348 Martínez del Toro to SRE, 9 Dec. 1912, Fabela, DHRM, RRM, IV, p. 239; Womack, *Zapata*, p. 79.

349 See pp. 224, 264.

350 For example, Méndez vs. Valladares in Michoacán: see María y Campos, *Múgica*, p. 44; and such conflicts tended to become more not less common as time went by: see vol. 2 ch. 2.

351 Manifesto to the Mexican People, from Juárez, n.d., and Mexico City, 24 June 1911, Fabela, DHRM, RRM, I, pp. 416–7, 422–5.

352 Circular of Robles Domínguez, and same to Rojas, both 28 May 1911, AARD 6/80, 15/31.

353 See the list of Emilio Madero's officers (a remarkable concentration of revolutionary talent) in AFM r.19; and Pedro Sandoval to Gobernación, 26 July 1911, AG 898.

354 Robles Domínguez to del Pozo, 3 June; to Mendoza, 29 May; to López, 30 May; to Hernández 5 June; AARD 19/86; 19/57; 25/141; 13/35.

355 María y Campos, *Múgica*, pp. 43–5, which reproduces part of Múgica's report from AG 14 'Relaciones con los Estados' (Mich.); Olea, *Sinaloa*, pp. 34, 37–8.

356 María y Campos, *Múgica*, p. 45.

357 Almazán to Gobernación, 2 June 1911, AARD 17/97.

358 Madero to Carreón, 21 June 1911, AFM r.19; Peña y Reyes to Robles Domínguez, 29 May and latter to G. Berriozabal, 6 June 1911, AARD 19/54, 15/119; Womack, *Zapata*, p. 90.

359 D. Magaña to Gobernación, 29 Aug. 1911, AG 14 'Relaciones con los Estados' (Tab.).

360 The distinction between official and unofficial agrarian reform is developed below, pp. 417–23.

361 Márquez to Robles Domínguez, 29 May; Magaña to same, 27 May; Carbajal to same, 30 May 1911; AARD 19/50, 22/2, 25/142. Magaña's desired destination was San Juan Bautista (Villa Hermosa).

362 E. Espinosa to Gobernación, 25 May 1911, AARD 25/56.

363 Paredes to Robles Domínguez, 30 May 1911, AARD 25/134; Gayou to Madero, 12 June 1911, AFM, r.22.

364 Banderas to Madero, 11 July 1911, AG legajo 14, 'Relaciones con los Estados' (Sin.); and p. 269.

365 A. De la Peña y Reyes to Robles Domínguez, 29 May 1911, AARD 19/47.

366 D. Huerta to Robles Domínguez, 3 June, 27 May 1911, AARD 19/93, 24/6. 'Gente muy cerrada' was the phrase; cf. the 'provincial suspicion' of the Zapatistas, Womack, *Zapata*, p. 204.

367 *Ibid.*, p. 91.

368 Madero to Orozco, 5 July 1911, AFM r.18.

369 Marcos López Jiménez to Madero 24, 30 June 1911, AG 898. It is probable (though I have

been unable to confirm) that this was the same López Jiménez who later ran the Maderista Department of Labour; he was clearly one of the respectable and articulate civilians who made a belated conversion to 'armed' rebellion in the late spring.

370 References of this first kind are easy to find; this one, from D. Covarrubias to Robles Domínguez, 8 June 1911, AARD 21/17, was sent by a *bona fide* Maderista who had just spent three months in Belem gaol; the 'bandit' label was therefore more significant. On the whole problem of rebellion and banditry, see pp. 351–67.

371 See pp. 38–9, 196–7.

372 Ellsworth, C.P.D., 23 Jan. 1911, SD 812.00/676; Aguilar, *Revolución Sonorense*, pp. 22-3, 144, 146.

373 Freeman, Durango, 13 Mar. 1911, SD 812.00/1021.

374 Caldwell, San Dimas, 20 Apr. 1911, SD 812.00/1660.

375 Hanna, Monterrey, 18 May 1911, SD 812.00/1903.

376 Junta of the Independent Reformist Party, Linares, to Madero, 2 June 1911, AFM r.20.

377 Hanna, Monterrey, 18 May 1911, SD 812.00/1903; E. Bordes Mangel to Madero, 16 June 1911, AFM r.20.

378 Joce to Cabrera, 12 May 1911, AARD 16/2.

379 E. Tirado to E. Arenas, 1 June and Arenas to Gobernación, 12 June 1911, AG 898; *El Diario del Hogar* 29 May 1911; Abel Guzmán to Robles Domínguez 7 June and D. Bonilla to same, 27, 28 May 1911; AARD 19/108, 25, 34.

380 Municipal president, Cuetzalá to de la Barra, 31 May 1911, AARD 19/72.

381 E. Arenas to Gobernación, 12 June 1911, AG 898; H. Márquez to Robles Domínguez, 29 May 1911, AARD 19/49; Gavira, *Actuación*, pp. 41–4.

382 H. Márquez to Robles Domínguez 27 May 1911, AARD 26/85; Gavira, *Actuación*, pp. 41–4.

383 Cahuantzi to Arrioja, 27 May; to Robles Domínguez, 28 May; latter to Espinosa Caloca 29 May; Arrioja to Cosio Robelo 3 June (Arrioja's efforts to keep Zapatistas out of the state): AARD 24/12, 16, 21, 34.

384 *El Diario del Hogar*, 14 May 1911; Hohler, Mexico City, 17 May 1911, FO 371/1146, 20780.

385 Romero Flores, *Michoacán*, p. 54; Salvador Escalante to Madero 22 May 1911, AARD 16/6; manager, Michoacán Power Co., 16 May 1911, SD 812.00/1948.

386 Jean Meyer, *La Révolution Méxicaine* (Paris, 1973), p. 39; Falcón, 'Orígines Populares', pp. 198–9; Brading, 'Introduction', are all indicative of the recent, 'anti-populist' trend.

387 F. González Roa to Robles Domínguez, 7 June 1911, AARD 7/73.

388 Soto to Robles Domínguez, 22 May, 2 June 1911, AARD 11/2, 69; to Gobernación, 28 July 1911, AG 898.

389 Rowe, Guanajuato, 29 Apr. 1911, SD 812.00/1613.

390 González Roa (n.387 above); and see below, p. 260.

391 US Naval Intelligence, Veracruz, 13 Mar. 1911, SD 812.00/1162; cf. similar reports from Rowe, Guanajuato, 3 Apr., and Pangburn, Acapulco, 7 Apr. 1911, SD 812.00/1300, 1361.

392 Acta levantada dated between 6 and 18 May 1911, AARD 25/4, 6, 8, 9, 14, 17, 18.

393 Gavira, *Actuación*, p. 42, provides a list.

394 *Ibid.*, pp. 35–41; Ochoa to Cosio Robelo, 31 May 1911, AARD 24/147; acta levantada 1 June 1911 AARD 24/183, 185.

395 Chausson, Veracruz, 1 June 1911, Mex., Pol. Int., N.S.II.

396 Cf. Meyer, *Révolution Méxicaine*, pp. 38–9; Huntington, *Political Order*, p. 306; Rutherford, *Mexican Society*, pp. 26–7.

397 Escalante to Robles Domínguez, 26 May 1911, AARD 16/25. Contreras, to Madero, 25 May 1911, AFM r.20, reported installing new officials who were 'functioning perfectly' at Zamora, Jiquilpam, and Los Reyes.

398 Cf. above, pp. 179–81, 204–5, 235.
399 José Trinidad Cervantes to Madero, 4 July 1911, AG legajo 898; *El Diario del Hogar*, 6 Oct. 1910; petition from Jiquilpam to Gobernación, 26 June 1911, AG legajo 898; Ramírez, *Oaxaca*, p. 24.
400 Gavira, *Actuación*, p. 39.
401 C. Patraca to Robles Domínguez, 5 June 1911, AARD 10/27; León Medel y Alvarado, *Historia de San Andrés Tuxtla* (Mexico, 1963), p. 31; A. Landa to Robles Domínguez, 4 July 1911, AARD 13/63.
402 Salida de G. G. Sánchez en campaña, 12 July 1911, AG legajo 898.
403 Serratos to Robles Domínguez, 4 July 1911, AARD 13/63.
404 F. Mier to Robles Domínguez, 31 May 1911, AARD 15/42; Salida de G. G. Sánchez (n.402).
405 C. Patraca to Robles Domínguez, 5 June 1911, AARD 10/27; acta levantada, Chapulhuacán, 16 May 1911, and other documents, AG legajo 898.
406 M. Zamora to Robles Domínguez, 26 May 1911, AARD 25/59.
407 F. Mier to Robles Domínguez, 30 May 1911, AARD 15/40; E. Aguirre to Gobernación, 22 July 1911, AG legajo 898.
408 F. Mier (n.407); municipal president, Atlacomulco to Robles Domínguez, 1 June 1914, AARD 15/74.
409 F. Mier (n.407); Trinidad Cervantes (n.399).
410 Robles Domínguez to E. Ponce, 29 May, to T. Rojas, 29 May 1911, AARD 15/36, 37.
411 Governor of Yucatán to Madero, 16 June 1911, AFM r.20; Cepeda to Madero, 30 June 1911, AFM r.18.
412 Robles Domínguez to Navarro, 31 May 1911, AARD 21/13.
413 C. Guerrero to Robles Domínguez, 5 June; B. Cadena to same, 6 June; vecinos of San Juan Evangelista to same, 19 June 1911; AARD 11/89; 16/130; 26/2.
414 Robles Domínguez to Gobernación, 2 June; Tapia to Robles Domínguez 4 June; M. Caldelas to same, 7 June; AARD 7/23; 25/194; 22/30.
415 Acta levantada, 4 June 1911, AARD 15/144, 145, 147.
416 Miller, Tampico, 8 June 1911, SD 812.00/2125.
417 Robles Domínguez to Gobernación, 5 June 1911, AARD 15/110; petition of 200 vecinos Jilotepec, to Gobernación, July 1911, AG 898.
418 Miller, Tampico, 30 June; Hanna, Monterrey, 11 Aug; Ellsworth, C.P.D., 18 June 1911 SD 812.00/2200, 2346, 2159.
419 Aguilar to Robles Domínguez, 6 June 1911, AARD 7/81; Gavira, pp. 47, 52; M. Guzmán to Madero, 23 Dec., and J. Ceballos to same, 19 Dec. 1911, AG, CRCFM.
420 M. Gómez to Madero, 25 Nov. 1911, AG, CRCFM; Ramírez, *Oaxaca*, pp. 37–8.
421 The term 'populist' is not used with any esoteric theoretical connotations in mind; it refers to leaders whose power and authority derived from popular support, usually of a local, rural kind, and who were usually of lower-class origins themselves.
422 'It is a matter of common note here that a remarkable change has occurred in the matter of free speech, that people are bolder than ever before in expressing their convictions in public matters [and] fear of the Government's strong arm is lessening': Letcher, Chihuahua, 24 April 1911, SD 812.00/1577. This point will be followed up.
423 Cf., for example, Rutherford, *Mexican Society*, pp. 189, 236–7: 'at no stage was it a full-scale revolution; its numbers were very small and it was confined, until the very moment of success, to the northern frontier of Mexico'; 'there was no spontaneous mass uprising of the Mexican people ... the Revolution ... only achieved the significant proportions of a social conflagration three years after it started'.
424 J. Trinidad Cervantes to Madero, 4 July, and M. Triana to Governor Alonso y Patiño, 19 June 1911, AG 898.

425 Clearly, this comparison is based upon one fundamental dimension of the Mexican Revolution: the breakdown of the old socio-political order, brought about by an (uneasy) alliance between progressive politicans and the masses, especially the rural masses, and accompanied therefore by the politicisation of the peasantry; the same ingredients can be seen in the collapse of the liberal order in post First World War Italy, in the turbulent history of the Spanish Republic, and in the fall of the Goulart and Allende regimes. But whereas in these cases fascist, military or fascist-military forces triumphed at the expense of progressive politicians and politicised peasantry alike, the equivalent forces in Mexico (Huertismo) proved incapable of crushing the social revolution: an indication of the latter's strength, in particular when it assumed the character of a 'peasant war'. This dimension of the Revolution – weak or non-existent in the four comparative cases mentioned here – Eric Wolf rightly places alongside the 'peasant wars' which culminated in Communist regimes in Russia and China.

426 Rutherford, *Mexican Society*, pp. 140–1; Vera Estañol, *Revolución Mexicana*, p. 212; and for further discussion see vol. 2 ch. 3.

427 María Aguirre to Juan Baños, 9 June 1911, AARD 27/71.

428 A. Conde to Robles Domínguez, 10 June 1911, AARD 6/159.

429 R. Rangel to Gobernación, 14 Aug. 1911, AG 898. Azuela, a native of Lagos de Moreno, presents a vivid description of an urban riot in his novel *Los Caciques*.

430 Lombardo Toledano in James W. Wilkie and Edna Monzón de Wilkie, *México visto en el siglo XX: entrevistas de historia oral* (Mexico, 1969), p. 239. Later, the phenomenon became quite common.

431 T. Armedariz to Madero, 16 June 1911, AFM r.20.

432 A copy of the speech is enclosed with the petition of vecinos of San Miguel in AG 898; note the close parallel with Madero's June 1911 manifesto in Fabela, DHRM, RRM, I, pp. 422–5.

433 It should not be overlooked, though, that while the liberal reformers and the adherents of the old regime disagreed over *political* solutions, they usually shared a commitment to *economic* stability and development; hence there would have been broad agreement between the two camps on the need to discipline, moralise, and set the Mexican people to work. In this respect, Don Domingo's Maderista progressivism was not so removed from Científico thought and practice.

5 The Madero Regime: 1: The Revolution goes on

1 Alfonso Taracena, *La verdadera revolución mexicana, Primera Etapa,* Mexico, 1960, pp. 401–3; Madero to F. González Garza, 30 June 1911, Fabela, DHRM, RRM, I, p. 443; Fuentes Mares, *Y México se refugió*, p. 248.

2 Ross, *Madero*, pp. 174–5; Sánchez Azcona, *Apuntes*, pp. 285–6; Madero to Rosales, 22 Mar. 1912, Fabela, DHRM, RRM, III, p. 222.

3 Vicente T. Mendoza, *El corrido de la revolución mexicana*, Mexico, 1956, p. 45; Rutherford, pp. 28, 142.

4 Ross, *Madero*, p. 176; Ramón Beteta in Wilkie, *Mexico Visto*, p. 25. From now on, 'opposition' (as in 'opposition newspaper') denotes anti-Madero – and thus often Porfirian – opinion.

5 Rutherford, *Mexican Society*, pp. 142–3.

6 Baron de Vaux, Mexico City, 13 June 1911, AAE, Mex. Pol. Int., N.S.II, n. 55; Wilson, Mexico City, 13 June 1913, SD 812.00/2142.

7 Pedro Sandoval to E. Vázquez Gómez, 26 July 1911, AG 898; F. Mier and J. Cacho to A. Robles Domínguez, 31 May, 4 June, AARD 15/42, 25/191; see also Aguirre Benavides, *De Francisco I. Madero*, pp. 32–3.

8 Though Madero was a little coy about admitting this: see Madero to F. González Garza, 30 June 1911, Fabela, DHRM, RRM, I, p. 445.

9 J. B. Body to Cowdray, 18, 27 May 1911; Cowdray Papers, box A3; Gavira, *Actuación*, p. 24, Ross, *Madero*, p. 120.

10 Fabela DHRM, RRM, I, p. 416; Robles Domínguez to Madero, Oct. 1911, AARD 36/1; F. Cosio Robelo to Madero, 20 Oct. 1911; Fabela, DHRM, RRM, II, pp. 184–9.

11 Estrada to Madero, 26 June 1911, AFM r.20; *El Diario del Hogar*, 23 July 1911; Madero to de la Barra, 13 July 1911, ALB carpeta, 3, admits as much.

12 F. Cosio Robelo to Madero, 20 Oct. 1911, Fabela, DHRM, RRM, I, p. 188; Macías to Madero 6 July 1911, AFM, r.20; Maria y Campos, *Múgica*, pp. 46–7; 'Acuerdo de los principales jefes', July 1911, in Fabela, DHRM, RRM, I, pp. 428–9; Cumberland, *Genesis*, pp. 159–60.

13 Ross, *Madero*, p. 203; cf. Cumberland, *Genesis*, p. 153, n. 4: 'the sincerity of their revolutionary ideals may be seriously questioned, but there seems to be little doubt of their ambition'; Cumberland's view is more convincing.

14 Vázquez Gómez to Robles Domínguez, 8 June 1911, AARD 7/84; Ross, *Madero*, pp. 203–6; Fabela, DHRH, RRM, II, 15–16, 35; Casasola, *Historia gráfica*, I, p. 354.

15 Ross, *Madero*, pp. 206–9; Cumberland, *Genesis*, pp. 162–3. No-one dared challenge Madero for the presidency: as in 1909–10 conflict centred around the vice-presidency.

16 J. F. Villar to Robles Domínguez, 13 Aug. 1911, AARD 9/113; F. Martínez Olmaraz to Gobernación, AG 898.

17 S. Saucedo to Sánchez Azcona, 7 Aug. 1911; list of Tlaxcala clubs; E. Arenas to G. Madero, 24 Aug. 1911; anon., Guadalajara, 26 Aug., and J. A. Ruiz to Sánchez Azcona, 23 Aug. 1911; all AFM r.20; Martínez Olmaraz, n. 16 above.

18 S. Ramírez to Madero, 21 Sept. 1911, AFM r.19.

19 M. Vidal to G. Madero, 15 Aug. 1911; anon. correspondent, *Nueva Era*, to Sánchez Azcona, 25 Aug. 1911; AFM, r.20, 19.

20 Fabela, DHRM, RRM, II, pp. 130–1.

21 Cosío Villegas, *Vida política*, p. 629; Bonney, San Luis, 18 Nov. 1912, SD 812.00/5575; T. Martínez Plata to F. Pastor Artigas, 30 Aug. 1911, AARD 8/143.

22 Robles Domínguez to Pino Suárez, Oct. 1911, AARD 36/5.

23 Most clearly expressed in the abortive Plan de Tacubaya, 31 Oct. 1911: Fabela, DHRM, RRM, II, pp. 210–15; but also in provincial revolts in, for example, Oaxaca and Guanajuato: Ramírez, *Oaxaca*, p. 40; Glenn, Guanajuato, 18 Aug. 1912, SD 812.00/4713; the case of Chihuahua is discussed in detail below.

24 Valadés, *Imaginación*, II, p. 199; Ross, *Madero*, pp. 211–12.

25 Cumberland, *Genesis*, pp. 165–6.

26 Illegible delegate, Saltillo, to Sánchez Azcona, 15 Sept. 1911, AFM r.20; Casasola, *Historia gráfica*, I, p. 370; Reyes Manifesto, 4 Aug. 1911, Fabela, DHRM, RRM, II, pp. 29–32. Ross, *Madero*, p. 213, asserts that 'the Reyes candidacy ... attracted little support', which is untenable.

27 Alger, Mazatlán, 29 Mar. 1911, SD 812.00/1195.

28 Shanklin, Mexico City, 17 May 1911, SD 812.00/1950.

29 Miller, Tampico, 5 June, 20 July 1911, SD 812.00/2110, 2238: 'the lower classes', he added, 'are Maderistas'.

30 Consular replies collected under SD 812.00/2346.

31 Body to Cowdray, 3 June 1911, Cowdray Papers, box A3.

32 Miller, Tampico, 15 Aug. 1911 SD 812.00/2346; Maytorena to Madero, 5 Oct. 1911, AFM r.19 on Reyista overtures; see also Meyer, *Huerta*, pp. 26–8, 30. At Tapachula, the military band of the 14th Battalion turned out to play at Reyista functions: *Nueva Era* correspondent to Sánchez Azcona, 25 Aug. 1911, AFM r.19; and E. de los Ríos to Madero, 10 June 1911, AFM r.20 on Reyista 'outs' in Zacatecas.

33 Bonney, San Luis, 5 Aug.; Boyd, Cd del Carmen, 5 Sept.; Dye, Nogales, 15 Aug. 1911; SD 812.00/2346; 2402; 2307.

34 Lespinasse, Frontera, Aug. 1911, SD 812.00/2346.

35 *Nueva Era* correspondent to Sánchez Azcona, 25 Aug. 1911, AFM r.19.

36 Dearing, Mexico City, 4 Sept. 1911, SD 812.00/2324; Cumberland, *Genesis*, pp. 166–7.

37 Ross, *Madero*, pp. 223–4.

38 Wilson, Mexico City, 22 Sept. 1911, SD 812.00/2384. The original phrase is attributed (probably wrongly) to Bismarck; it is certainly more apposite in this context.

39 Berta Ulloa, *La revolución intervenida: relaciones diplomáticas entre México y Estados Unidos*, Mexico, 1971, pp. 19–21.

40 Niemeyer, *Reyes*, pp. 206–19.

41 Ross, *Madero*, pp. 214–15.

42 Hohler, Mexico City, 30 May 1911, FO 371/1148, 23276.

43 The Partido Católico Nacional was first formed in May 1911, but its national convention was not held until August: Alicia Olivera Sedano, *Aspectos del conflicto religioso de 1926 a 1929. Sus antecedentes y consecuencias*, Mexico, 1966, p. 46.

44 Madero to V. Martínez Cantú, 19 Nov. 1912, AFM r.11; Rutherford, *Mexican Society*, pp. 282–3; Olivera Sedano, *Aspectos*, p. 46.

45 Meyer, *Cristero Rebellion*, p. 10.

46 Barry Carr, 'Anti-Clericalism during the Mexican Revolution, 1910–30', University of Glasgow seminar paper, 1971.

47 Miller, Tampico, 15 Aug.; Parker, Mazatlán, 16 Aug.; McGill, Guadalajara, Aug. 1911; SD 812.00/2346; A. Manzanil to Madero, 2 Oct. 1911, AFM r.19.

48 P. Urbina Santibáñez to Angel Barrios, 6 June 1911, AARD 18/38; anon. to Madero, 19 Oct. 1911, AFM r.21; Governor Robles Gil to Madero, 18 Oct. 1911, Fabela, DHRM, RRM, II, pp. 174–5; J. M. Azios to Robles Domínguez, 6 June 1911, AARD 31/82.

49 Vera Estañol, *Revolución Mexicana*, p. 247.

50 Rutherford, *Mexican Society*, p. 285, citing *La Nación*, 22 June 1912.

51 Dearing, Mexico City, 2 Sept. 1911, SD 812.00/2335; and below, pp. 400–4.

52 Wilson, Mexico City, 6 Sept. 1911, SD 812.00/2348.

53 J. Cruz Torres to Madero, 5 Nov. 1911, AG, CRCFM.

54 Ross, *Madero*, pp. 215–6; Cumberland, *Genesis*, p. 170; Casasola, *Historian gráfica*, I, pp. 386–7.

55 Casasola, *Historia gráfica*, I, pp. 411–12.

56 Wilson, Mexico City, 2, 27 Oct. 1811, SD 812.00/2393, 2453; cf. Casasola, *Historia gráfica*, I, p. 386, which asserts that 95% of the inhabitants (sic) of the capital voted; and Pani, pp. 111–4, which describes the process.

57 See the reports from Cananea, Nogales, Torreón, Tampico, Nuevo Laredo, Saltillo and Chihuahua in Hanna, Monterrey, 1 Oct. 1911, SD 812.00/2388, 2389, 2390; Lespinasse, Frontera, 22 Oct. 1911, SD 812.00/2480; A. Zevada Baldenvro to Manuel Alegre, 2 Oct. 1911, AFM, r.9, on electoral abuses in Michoacán.

58 A. Oliveros to Madero, from San Pablo (Ags.), 1 Oct. 1911, AFM r.20; various reports in AARD 28/144.

59 Miller, Tampico, 6 Oct. 1911, SD 812.00/2418.

60 E.g., at Acapulco: Pangburn, 18 Aug. 1911, SD 812.00/2346.

61 Young, Progreso, 4 Sept.; Lawton, Oaxaca, Aug. 1911; SD 812.00/2402, 2346.

62 Voetter, Saltillo, 12 Aug., 1 Oct. 1911, SD 812.00/2346, 2390.

63 L. Warfield to C. Hilles, 11 Feb. 1912, SD 812.00/2953.

64 Ramírez, *Oaxaca*, pp. 22–4; Miller, Tampico, 20 July 1911, SD 812.00/2238; Gavira, *Actuación*, pp. 41–3.

65 Aguilar, *Revolución Sonorense*, pp. 177–8.

66 Hamm, Durango, 22 Apr. 1911 (twice), 5 May 1911, SD 812.00/1451, 1579, 2080;

anon. to Robles Domínguez, 27 May 1911, AARD 6/69; Voetter, Saltillo, 27 May (twice); Letcher, Chihuahua, 2 June 1911; SD 812.00/1966, 2028; 2024.

67 Aguilar, *Revolución Sonorense*, pp. 196–7.

68 B. Centeño and D. Magaña to Robles Domínguez, both 29 May 1911, AARD 19/35, 10/12; Lespinasse, Frontera, 18 June 1911, SD 812.00/2185; petition of 200 to Madero, 2 June 1911, AARD 7/10.

69 Anon. 'Memo. de los asuntos políticos del estado de México', 15 Aug. 1911, AARD 28/115.

70 P. Campos and vecinos to Robles Domínguez in latter to Gobernación, 5 June 1911, AARD 15/110; Bonifacio Ramírez and Trinidad Rojas to same, 24 June, 30 May 1911, AARD 15/144, 15/46.

71 B. Cadena to Robles Domínguez, 10 June 1911, AARD 15/130.

72 Petition of 200 vecinos, Jilotepec, to Gobernación, July 1911, AG 898.

73 Rowe, Guanajuato, 20 May 1911, SD 812.00/1987.

74 *Ibid.*, 27 Apr. 16, 20 May 1911, SD 812.00/1613, 1948, 1987.

75 F. González Roa to Robles Domínguez, 7 June 1911, AARD 7/73; J. Castelazo to Madero, 29 Nov. 1911, AG, CRCFM.

76 J. Castelazo to C. Robles Domínguez, 10 June 1911, AARD 10/99.

77 C. Navarro to state legislature, 30 July 1911, in *El Obrero* (León), 4 Aug. 1911, which appears in AFM r.18.

78 J. Castelazo to Robles Domínguez, 7 June 1911, AARD 10/91.

79 Madero to de la Barra, 25 July 1911, ALB carpeta 3.

80 Casasola, *Historia gráfica*, I, p. 354; Ellsworth, Cd Porfirio Díaz, 18 Oct. 1911, Glenn, Guanajuato, 19 Aug. 1912. SD 912.00/2432, 4713.

81 Glenn, Guanajuato, 9 Apr. 1912, SD 812.00/3648.

82 *Ibid.*, 12 Apr. 1912, SD 812.00/3695; cf. Hobsbawm, *Bandits*, pp. 50–1.

83 Félix Galván to Madero, 8 Apr. 1912, Fabela, DHRM, RRM, III, p. 294.

84 F. Cosio Robelo to Madero, 20 Oct. 1911, Fabela, DHRM, RRM, II, p. 188.

85 Womack, *Zapata*, p. 86.

86 Cf. the case of Chihuahua: pp. 297–300.

87 'Memo. de la situación política del Estado de Morelos', 29 Dec. 1911 (probably by Robles Domínguez), AARD 37/5.

88 M. Asunsulo to Robles Domínguez, 25 May 1811, AARD 17/23; Womack, *Zapata*, pp. 89, 92–3.

89 Zapata to Robles Domínguez, 28 May 1911, AARD 17/45.

90 Carreón to Robles Domínguez, 31 May, AARD 17/63; same to Madero, 18 Nov. 1911, AG, CRCFM; Association of Sugar and Alcohol Producers to Carreón, 12 June 1911, AARD 17/144; Womack, *Zapata*, p. 93.

91 Womack, *Zapata*, pp. 97–107; Rutherford, *Mexican Society*, p. 149, dates the 'Attila' legend from June 1911; it reached its apotheosis in H. H. Dunn's *The Crimson Jester, Zapata of Mexico*, New York, 1934.

92 As recounted by de la Barra to Hohler, 3 May 1911, FO 371/1147, 18521.

93 Womack, *Zapata*, p. 109. Huerta's career is considered in greater detail below.

94 Womack, *Zapata*, p. 119; for Huerta's rebuttal to the press, 20 Aug. 1911, Fabela, DHRM, RRM, II, pp. 62–3.

95 Rebel troops entering Jojutla and Puente de Ixtla were accused of sacking and burning shops, attacking and killing 'Científicos', 'Porfiristas' and 'Gachupines' and making inflammatory speeches: 'the people should be on top. Down with the haciendas and ranches. Death to the "Gachupines"': see Fabela, DHRM, RRM, II, pp. 66–7 and Womack, *Zapata*, p. 117, who, while absolving Zapata of direct responsibility, perhaps goes too far in playing down these events, which had many parallels elsewhere in Mexico.

96 *El País*, 25 Aug. 1911; Womack, *Zapata*, pp. 122, 394.

97 Lewis, *Tepoztlán*, p. 232 (though it is not entirely clear which Federal campaign is referred to here); Womack, *Zapata*, p. 122.

98 Womack, *Zapata*, pp. 124–6. Off the record Madero may have been more conciliatory.

99 This point is developed below, pp. 452, 465, and vol. 2 ch. 2.

100 For a list of governors as of June 1911 see Shanklin, Mexico City, 16 June 1911, SD 812.00/2166. Guadalupe González had been the only Anti-Re-electionist deputy elected, though not seated, in the 1910 elections: Sánchez Azcona, *Apuntes*, p. 91.

101 Terrazas to Creel, 22 Dec. 1910, STA (Creel) r.2, on 'platonic' – that is, city-based, non-belligerent – revolutionaries.

102 D. Magaña to Gobernación, 11 July 1911, AG 14, 'Relaciones con los Estados' (Tab.).

103 Ross, *Madero*, pp. 200–1; Casasola, *Historia gráfica*, I, p. 417; Díaz Lombardo, Urueta *et al.* to Madero, 15 May 1911, AARD 16/3.

104 Fabela, DHRM, RRM, I, p. 426.

105 Vera Estañol, *Revolución Mexicana*, p. 201; Womack, *Zapata*, pp. 106–7.

106 Aguirre Benavides, *De Francisco I. Madero*, p. 28.

107 See pp. 391–2, 451–4, 479.

108 The stream of requests to Elías de los Ríos and Sara Madero is evident in the Madero Archive; see also Robles Domínguez's correspondence, AARD 8/26 and expediente 45 *passim*; María y Campos, *Múgica*, p. 47, for the quotation.

109 Maximino Avila Camacho to Madero, 12 Apr., 4 May 1912; to Sánchez Azcona 26 May; to Madero 24 June 1912: Fabela, DHRM, RRM, III, pp. 300, 346, 408–9, 469; to Madero, 14 Aug., 27 Nov. 1912, *ibid.*, IV, pp. 80–1, 218–9. At least by the 1930s Maximino's persistence had won him the governorship of Puebla (which he exercised conservatively); and in the following decade his brother Manuel became President; Ronfeldt, *Atencingo*, p. 18ff.

110 E. de los Ríos to Serratos, 10 Dec. 1912; to E. Bordes Mangel, 27 June 1912, AFM r.10; Ross, p. 114; Madero to B. Viljoen, 22 June 1912, AFM r.10.

111 Madero to E. Hay, 15 Sept. 1912; E. de los Ríos to Hacienda, 12 Dec. 1912, AFM r.12, 11.

112 See pp. 394–7.

113 Peter Bachrach and Morton S. Baratz, *Power and Poverty: Theory and Practice* (New York, 1970), pp. 43–6.

114 Madero to G. Treviño, 28 July 1912, AFM r.12; Peniche to Gobernación, 22 July 1911, AG 898.

115 Madero to M. Escudero y Verdugo, 9 Dec. 1912, E. de los Ríos to Bonilla, 18 Dec. 1912, AFM r.11.

116 E. de los Ríos to R. Hernández, 5 July 1912, AFM r.10.

117 Womack, *Zapata*, pp. 88–9, 108–9.

118 Casasola, *Historia gráfica*, I, p. 487; *El País*, 18 Nov. 1910; A. Serratos to Cabrera, 7 Nov. 1912, AFM r.2.

119 *El Diario del Hogar*, 23 May 1911, gives the implausibly high figure of 5,000; Gruening, *Mexico and its Heritage*, p. 309, prefers 3,000; Hohler, Mexico City, 8 June 1911, FO 371/1148, 24749 agrees with Gruening as to Hernández's 'Indian' ancestry; Casasola, *Historia gráfica*, I, pp. 303, 322, 561, where 'humble family' origins are mentioned.

120 *El Diario del Hogar*, 23 May 1911 and, for a more critical account, Enrique Aguirre to Gobernación, 14 July 1911, AG 898; Casasola, *Historia gráfica*, I, p. 303.

121 Gruening, *Mexico and its Heritage*, p. 309; Fabela, DHRM, RRM, II, p. 82.

122 Enrique Aguirre to Gobernación, 14 July 1911, AG 898; E. Bordes Mangel to Madero, 16 June 1911, AFM r.20, which explains how these policies made Silva unpopular 'despite his recognised political affiliation', i.e., despite his known Maderista credentials.

123 Tomás Hernández to Madero, 26 Sept. 1911, AFM r.19.

124 Above, pp. 236–7.

125 Concerning Hernández and these local squabbles: G. Madero to Madero, 26 March 1912, F. Mariel to E. de los Ríos, 14 Jan. 1913, Fabela, DHRM, RRM, III, pp. 246–7, IV, p. 328; Casasola, *Historia gráfica*, I, p. 561.

126 J. D. Burke, Jalacingo, 25 Sept. 1912, SD 812.00/5209.

127 F. Contreras to J. Sánchez Azcona, 15 June 1911, AARD 19/130.

128 *El País*, 3, 6 June 1911; Cañete to Madero, 16 Nov. 1911, Fabela, DHRM, RRM, II, p. 274.

129 Hohler, Mexico City, 15 July, Turnbull, Puebla, 19 July 1911, FO 371/1148, 30080, 31147; Cumberland, *Genesis*, p. 161; Vera Estañol, *Revolución mexicana*, p. 211.

130 Turnbull, Puebla, 19 July 1911, FO 371/1148, 31147, on rebel assaults on the Mayorazgo and Anatlán factories and the hacienda El Gallinero, south of the city; and on the Covadonga textile mill to the north, where German subjects were killed.

131 F. Contreras to J. Sánchez Azcona, 15 June 1911, AARD 19/130.

132 Madero to de la Barra, 14 July, to Vázquez Gómez, 15 July 1911, ALB carpeta 3; Evaristo Madero to Rafael Hernández, 18 July 1911, Fabela, DHRM, RRM, I, pp. 433–4.

133 Rafael Hidalgo to Gobernación, 10 Aug. 1911, AG 898.

134 Pablo Torres to F. Cosio Robelo, 5 June, Miguel Silva to Robles Domínguez, 27 May 1911, AARD 16/74, 23; Romero Flores, *Michoacán*, pp. 56–7; María y Campos, *Múgica*, p. 46.

135 Ramírez, *Oaxaca*, p. 29; Peter V. N. Henderson, 'Un Gobernador Maderista: Benito Juárez Maza y la revolución en Oaxaca', *Historia Mexicana*, XXIV (1974–5), pp. 372–81.

136 R. García to A. Barrios, 1 Nov. 1911, AARD 18/7.

137 Ramírez, *Oaxaca*, pp. 32–40.

138 Womack, *Zapata*, p. 80, where he notes Almazán's 'impressive talent for hoax and skulduggery' (Almazán was, after all, a student politician); Almazán to Vázquez Gómez, 2 June 1911, AARD 17/97.

139 Fabela, DHRM, RRM, II, pp. 51–4, which makes it clear that Almazán effectively set up a press conference, complete with photographer (as the pages of Casasola show, he was a photogenic individual).

140 Madero to Almazán, 22 June 1912, AFM r.12.

141 Womack, *Zapata*, p. 122; Pangburn, Acapulco, 3, 11 Dec. 1911, SD 812.00/5633, 5685.

142 Falcón, 'Orígenes Populares', pp. 204–6.

143 A. Aguirre Benavides to J. Sánchez Azcona, 28 June 1911, AARD 21/28; F. Covarrubías to Madero, 11 July 1911, AFM r.20.

144 Martínez Núñez, *San Luis Potosí*, pp. 29–30; Bonney, San Luis, 5 Aug., 30 Sept. 1911, SD 812.00/2346, 2401.

145 J. D. Cockcroft, 'El maestro de primaría en la revolución mexicana', *Historia Mexicana*, XVI (1967), pp. 576–80; Martínez Núñez, *San Luis Potosí*, pp. 34–6; Bonney, San Luis, 20 March, 9 Apr. 1912, SD 812.00/3778, 3608.

146 Bonney, San Luis, 16 Oct. 1912, SD 812.00/5310.

147 *Ibid.*

148 Bonney, San Luis, 6 June 1912, SD 812.00/4193; P. A. de los Santos to Madero in Fabela, DHRM, RRM, III, pp. 489–93, IV, pp. 254–7; Madero to de los Santos, 7 Nov. 1912, to Cepeda, 29 Oct. 1912, AFM r.11.

149 Falcón, 'Orígenes Populares', where the family is said to have been 'in dispute with the big *hacendados* of the region'. Despite the attention of skilled historians like Falcón, Fowler and Ankerson, however, the local politics of the Huasteca remain something of a mystery.

150 Cf. Tillys, *Rebellious Century*, pp. 52, 262.

151 Chausson, Veracruz, 18 May 1911, AAE, Mex. Pol. Int., N.S. II, No. 40; Gavira, *Actuación*, pp. 42–4, 52; Nunn, Veracruz, 3 July 1911, FO 371/1148, 28120.

152 Ross, *Madero*, p. 229; Tapia, *Mi participación*, p. xv; Canada, Veracruz, 25 Jan. 1912,

SD 812.00/2722; Gavira, *Actuación*, pp. 5–42; Gavira to Robles Domínguez, 31 May 1911, AARD 25/156, 169.

153 Tapia, *Mi participación*, p. 36.

154 Gavira, *Actuación*, p. 58.

155 Gavira, *Actuación*, p. 53; Canada, Veracruz, 25 Jan. 1912, SD 812.00/2722.

156 E. Lobato to Madero, 24 Dec. 1911, AG, CRCFM.

157 Gavira, *Actuación*, pp. 58–63; Canada, Veracruz, 12 Mar. 1912, SD 812.00/3314; Madero to F. Lagos Cházaro, 1 Apr. 1912, Fabela, DHRM, RRM, III, pp. 282–3; Casasola, *Historia gráfica*, I, p. 488 shows a grisly display of Gavirista corpses. Gavira, *Actuación*, p. 60, comments on the disillusionment of many ex-Maderistas like himself; and at least one other prominent leader of the region, Francisco Bertrani, also rebelled and was later amnestied; Burke, Jalacingo, 25 Sept. 1912, SD 812.00/5209.

158 Gavira, *Actuación*, pp. 63–8; Vera Estañol, no friend of Gavira, concurs, *Revolución mexicana*, p. 244.

159 Gavira, *Actuación*, p. 70; Canada, Veracruz, 27 Dec. 1912, SD 812.00/5776; A. Pérez Rivera to Madero, 16 Dec. 1912, AFM r.21.

160 Madero to Pérez Rivera, 14 Dec. 1912, AFM r.11.

161 Olea, *Sinaloa*, pp. 34, 37.

162 Banderas to Madero, 11 July 1911, AG Relaciones con los Estados (Sin.); Olea, *Sinaloa*, pp. 34–5; Womack, *Zapata*, p. 208; Casasola, *Historia gráfica*, I, p. 489, II, p. 898.

163 Parker, Culiacán, 16 Aug. 1911, SD 812.00/2346.

164 Olea, *Sinaloa*, pp. 36–8; F. Guerrero to Madero, 8 Nov. 1911, AG, CRCFM. Bonilla's own account of the period, *El Régimen Maderista* (Mexico, 1922) is strangely silent about these events, in which the author was closely involved.

165 Ross, *Madero*, p. 179.

166 Olea, *Sinaloa*, p. 38.

167 Banderas to Madero, 10 Jan. 1912, Fabela, DHRM, RRM, IV, pp. 317–9; Casasola, *Historia gráfica*, I, pp. 489–90 conveys a similar impression.

168 Casasola, *Historia gráfica*, I, p. 272; Alger, Mazatlán, 4 June 1912, SD 812.00/4196.

169 Olea, *Sinaloa*, pp. 40–1; Alger, Mazatlán, 29 Mar. 1912, Admiral Caperton, US Navy, 7 May 1915, SD 812.00/3495, 15055.

170 Olea, *Sinaloa*, p. 42.

171 *Ibid.*; Alger, Mazatlán, 27 Mar., 7 Apr. 1912, SD 812.00/3477, 3620.

172 Olea, *Sinaloa*, pp. 44–5; Bates, Southern Pacific Railroad attorney in memo., 29 Apr. 1912, SD 812.00/3764. Chinese stores were again among the principal victims of the sack of Culiacan: Alger, Mazatlán, 6 May 1912, SD 812.00/3949.

173 Hamm, Durango, 9 May; Alger, Mazatlán, 13 June; Hostetter, Hermosillo, 28 Apr. 1912; SD 812.00/392; 4248; 3939. Vera Estañol, *Revolución mexicana*, p. 208, places Sinaloa alongside Morelos and the Durango sierra as major trouble spots late in 1911.

174 G. Jones, Hacienda de Quimiches, to C. Hagel, 7 Apr. 1912, SD 812.00/3711.

175 Olea, *Sinaloa*, pp. 23–5, 32, 40–2; Alberto Galán, prefect of Mazatlán, to Inspector General of Rurales, 1 May 1912, AG 898 and *passim* in that file; Hostetter, Hermosillo, 23 Mar. 1912, SD 812.00/3463; Womack, *Zapata*, p. 208.

176 W. Windham, Cía Agrícola de Quimiches, to G. Jones, July 1912, SD 812.00/4419; Sra F. B. de Caneda to Madero, 1 Oct. 1911, AG, CRCFM.

177 Chase, *Mexico*, p. 16.

178 Later, with the professionalisation of revolutionary armies, the link between the harvest and the campaign faded. We shall note, however, a perverse variant, in which mercenary 'revolutionary' forces displayed most activity precisely during the harvest season and its immediate aftermath, when it was easiest and most profitable to live off the land, and at the expense of the peasantry. By then the wheel had come full circle; the fish-in-water guerrilla had turned into a predatory shark.

179 Alger, Mazatlán, 20 June, 13 July 1912, SD 812.00/4256, 4467.
180 *Ibid.*, 14 Dec. 1912, SD 812.00/5742; Olea, *Sinaloa*, p. 47.
181 Olea, *Sinaloa*, pp. 44–5.
182 Alger, Mazatlán, 7 Apr. 1912, SD 812.00/3620; Windham to Jones (n.176).
183 See Lino Cárdenas to Inspector General of Rural Corps, 22 July 1912, AG 898, protesting against the dissolution of his 53rd Corps.
184 Alger, Mazatlán, 13 June 1912, SD 812.00/4248; Olea, *Sinaloa*, p. 45.
185 Brown, Mazatlán, 14 Sept. 1912, SD 812.00/5041; Olea, *Sinaloa*, p. 47.
186 The main group of *serranos* came from Tamazula, Copalquín and the northern Sinaloa/Durango marches, but others were active further south, at the junction of these states with Tepic. On *serrano* activities and incursions: Olea, *Sinaloa*, pp. 31–2, 41, 45, 67, 84; Casasola, *Historia gráfica*, I, p. 489; Hamm, Durango, 10, 13 Apr.; Alger, Mazatlán, 9 May; Brown, Mazatlán, 10 Aug. 1912; SD 812.00/3641, 3676; 3933; 4660.
187 Rouaix, *Diccionario*, pp. 25–6, 310–11; Madero to Lt. Col. José Domínguez, 7 Aug. 1912, AFM r.12.
188 Carothers, Torreón, 22 May 1911; Ellsworth, Cd. Porfirio Díaz, 16 Feb. 1912; SD 812.00/1968, 2832.
189 Rouaix, *Diccionario*, p. 26; *El Diario del Hogar*, 6 Oct. 1910; T. Cervantes to Madero, 4 July 1911, AG 898.
190 Alonso y Patiño to M. Triana, 20 June 1911, AG 898.
191 M. Viesca y Arispe (ex-mayor) to Madero, 2 July 1911, AFM r.20.
192 Dorador, *Mi prisión*, pp. 20–2.
193 Hamm, Durango, 16 Feb. 1912, SD 812.00/2925.
194 *Ibid.*, 7 June 1911, 20 Apr. 1912, SD 812.00/2130, 3758. As 1913 was to show such fears of urban unrest were not delusions.
195 Hamm, Durango, diary entry for 31 May 1911, SD 812.00/2106; Julio Madero to Madero, 12 Feb. 1912, Fabela, DHRM, RRM, III, p. 93.
196 Hamm, Durango, 30 July 1911, SD 812.00/2265.
197 *Ibid.*
198 Cummins, Gómez Palacio, in Hohler, Mexico City, 17 July 1911, FO 371/1148, 30407.
199 *Ibid.*
200 Emilio Madero to Madero, 15 June 1911, AFM r.19. It is clear in this, as in other cases, that the revolution served to stimulate Magonismo, rather than vice versa.
201 'Many of the old Maderista chiefs have become disgusted because the government set up by them has done nothing for them and . . . all or almost all are only awaiting an opportunity to revolt again with the banner of Zapata and to make his Plan of Ayala triumph'; Julio Madero, 12 Feb. 1912, Fabela, DHRM, RRM, III, pp. 93–4.
202 Graham, Durango, 17 Nov. 1911, FO 371/1149, 48729.
203 Emilio Madero to Madero, 22, 25 June 1911, AFM r.19.
204 'Situación de fuerzas de los Cuerpos, 1–30 dic., 1911', AG 873; Francisco Urquizo, *Páginas de la revolución* (Mexico, 1956), p. 13, adds the 26th Corps under Martín Triana, but gives no figures.
205 Col. Cruz Guerrero, the aged rural commander already encountered feathering his nest in Hidalgo just before the revolution, survived into 1911; cf. the Veracruzano rebel Rosendo Villa who, with his *gente*, wanted to police their home patch around Altotonga, but who felt insulted at being offered no more than NCO rank: Villa to Madero, 19 Aug. 1911, AFM r.20.
206 See below, p. 331, 458, and vol. 2 ch. 2.
207 Urzquizo, *Páginas*, pp. 13, 20; Inman to Harlan, 5 June 1911, SGIA, box 12 describes a visit of Ugalde and his men ('all of them big rough fellows . . . with piercing eyes [and] a determined set of the head'), who attended his church Memorial Day at Cd Porfirio Díaz, 'sitting with gun in hand while they ate ice cream'.

208 Hamm, Durango, 29 Feb. 1912, SD 812.00/3238.
209 Hamm, Durango, 21 Mar. 1912, SD 812.00/3421.
210 Hamm, Durango, 9 May 1912, SD 812.00/3927.
211 R. E. Adams, 18 Mar. 1912, SD 812.00/3421.
212 Hamm, Durango, 11 Nov. 1911, SD 812.00/2505 on Antuna.
213 'The greater part of the young ladies of the city [sic] took refuge in one of the cathedrals [sic] whence they were abducted by the rebels': Hamm, Durango, 12 Oct. 1912, SD 812.00/5277. Though such collective abductions did occur during the Revolution, they tended to come in the later rather than the earlier years; this story is probably more indicative of urban rumour than of rebel concupiscence. See also Hamm, Durango, 29 Mar. SD 812.00/3499.
214 Hamm, Durango, 1, 10 Oct. 1912, SD 812.00/5179, 5240.
215 See vol. 2 ch. 3.
216 Hamm, Durango, 24 Aug. 1912, SD 812.00/4783. The abused properties were the haciendas of Santa Clara and Sombreretillo, the latter being Contreras' and Cuencamé's hereditary foe: Casasola, *Historia gráfica*, 1, p. 484.
217 Hamm, Durango, 22 Feb., 18 Mar. 1912, SD 812.00/3368, 3371.
218 Hamm, Durango, 16 Mar. 1912, SD 812.00/3362.
219 Hamm, Durango, 5 July, 4 Apr. 1912, SD 812.00/4424, 3557.
220 Hamm, Durango, 22 Feb. 1912, SD 812.00/3300.
221 Hamm, Durango, 17 June 1912, SD 812.00/4280.
222 Hamm, Durango, 18 Mar. 1912, SD 812.00/3371. No details of the plan are given. Clearly, there was a potential contradiction in any plan promising both agrarian reform (in the Laguna) and the protection of foreign interests; but such emphases are significant, and quite consonant with the character of popular agrarismo.
223 J. Reina to Madero, 2 July 1911, AFM r.20.
224 Adrián Aguirre Benavides to Madero, 29 May 1911, AFM r.18.
225 Julio Madero to Madero, 12 Feb. 1912, Fabela, DHRM, RRM, III, p. 93, communicating the opinion of Enrique Adame Macías.
226 Hamm, Durango, 27 Oct. 1912, SD 812.00/5400. Argumedo's force by then included the *gente* of Sixto Ugalde, mentioned above.
227 Hamm, Durango, 20 July, 18 Mar. 1912, SD 812.00/4480, 3371.
228 Cummins, Gómez Palacio, in Hohler, Mexico City, 17 July 1911, FO 371/1148, 30407.
229 Hamm, Durango, 30 Nov. 1912, SD 812.00/5653. Juan Pérez was the property of the Moncada family, who had the reputation of treating their peons well, though this does not appear to have saved them; Curbelo owed vast estates in the Cuencamé region, El Saucillo being the largest. Several of the haciendas mentioned here had appropriated village lands but, with the exception of the Cuencamé/Sombreretillo conflict, specific agrarian antagonisms are hard to establish. See Paz, 'El Latifundismo'.
230 O'Hea, 1 Nov. 1912, in Hamm, Durango, 2 Nov. 1912, SD 812.00/5497.
231 Graham, Durango, 17 Nov. 1911, FO 371/1149, 48729.
232 Reed, *Insurgent Mexico*, pp. 67, 70, 76.
233 Hamm, Durango, 3, 9, 30 Dec. 1912, SD 812.00/5666, 5675, 5822. As the British representative in the Laguna had commented a year before: 'there is undeniably a strong feeling against the Spanish people here': Cummins, Gómez, in Hohler, Mexico City, 17 July 1911, FO 371/1148, 30407.
234 Hamm, Durango, 12 Nov. 1912, SD 812.00/5547; Gómez, *Reforma Agraria*, p. 27, refers to this process of converting sharecroppers into *de facto* proprietors. As for Campos himself, Rouaix, *Diccionario*, pp. 72 calls him an ex-hacienda administrador, O'Hea, *Reminiscences*, pp. 59–60, a ruined ranchero.
235 Hamm, Durango, 9 Oct. 1912, SD 812.00/5239.
236 Hamm, Durango, 23 Dec. 1912, SD 812.00/5785.

237 O'Hea, 1 Nov. 1912 in Hamm, Durango, 2 Nov. 1912 and Hamm, 17 Dec. 1912, SD 812.00/5497, 5760.
238 Carothers, Torreón, 16 Feb., Hamm, Durango, 22 Sept. 1912, SD 812.00/3371, 5120.
239 Hamm, Durango, 21 Nov. 1912, SD 812.00/5609, referring to rebel groups totalling 1,500 'nominally under the orders of Cheche Campos and which work in harmony with his plans when there is greater promise of plunder'; the same 9 Oct., 10 Dec. 1912, SD 812.00/5239, 5720, on boltholes; 10 Apr., 17 Dec. 1912, SD 812.00/3641, 5760 on Ortiz and his *sinverguencistas* – rebels without a cause.
240 Coercion and cash held the Federal Army together: while the first had not yet faltered, financial constraints were beginning to make their mark. In October 1912, 125 Federals, marching on Rodeo, stopped at San Juan del Río, 'refusing to advance further north until the state had settled their arrears of pay': Hamm, Durango, 27 Oct. 1912, SD 812.00/5400.
241 Hamm, Durango, 10 Apr. 1912, SD 812.00/3641.
242 Hamm, Durango, 1 June 1912, citing *El Heraldo*, and 2 Jan. 1913, SD 812.00/4240, 5848.
243 Cummins, Gómez Palacio, in Hohler, Mexico City, 17 July 1911, FO 371/1148, 30407.
244 Hamm, Durango, 24 Aug. 1912, SD 812.00/4785.
245 Hamm, Durango, 10 Dec. 1912, SD 812.00/5720.
246 T. Fairbairn, Tlahualilo, to J. B. Potter, 30 Dec. 1912, SD 812.00/5880.
247 Hamm, Durango, 14 Jan. 1913, SD 812.00/5930.
248 *Ibid.*
249 Edwards, Juárez, 19 May 1911, SD 812.00/1927, gives a total of 4,575, of which Orozco's 700 was the largest single contingent; it is possible that even this did not represent the high point of rebel strength in the state.
250 F. Porras to E. de la Garza, 11 Dec. 1910, STA (Creel), box 2 on the early extent of this political renovation; Colmenares Ríos to Robles Domínguez, 13 June 1911, AARD 25/218; *El Diario del Hogar*, 23 May 1911.
251 Rafael Mendizabal to Gobernación, 12 Aug. 1911, AG 'Relaciones con los Estados' (Mich.). AFM r.20, lists twenty Maderista clubs in Tlaxcala: ten were named after Juárez, eight after Hidalgo, seven after Orozco, and six after Madero himself.
252 Womack, *Zapata*, pp. 126–7, 402.
253 Beezley, *Insurgent Governor*, pp. 14–68; see also Letcher, Chihuahua, 2 June 1911, SD 812.00/2024; Valadés, *Imaginación*, II, pp. 22–5; Giuseppe Garibaldi, *Toast to Rebellion*, New York, 1935, p. 222; Casasola, *Historia gráfica*, I, p. 473.
254 Letcher, Chihuahua, 22 June 1911, SD 812.00/2179; S. Terrazas to M. Balbas, 1 July 1911, STA, box 83.
255 P. Sandoval to E. Vázquez Gómez, 26 July 1911, AG legajo 898.
256 Womack, *Zapata*, p. 91; Meyer, *Mexican Rebel*, p. 57.
257 Meyer, *Mexican Rebel*, pp. 58–9.
258 *Ibid.*, p. 40; S. Terrazas to M. Bolaños Cacho, 1 July 1911, STA, box 83.
259 Letcher, Chihuahua, 20 Aug. 1911, SD 812.00/2296; Beezley, *Insurgent Governor*, p. 82; cf. Cumberland, *Genesis*, p. 191. The 'over thirty' rule which confounded Orozco's gubernatorial candidacy similarly stymied Pedro de los Santos in San Luis: it acted as a useful constitutional alibi for thwarting the ambitions of young, popular, revolutionary leaders.
260 Letcher, Chihuahua, 8, 18 Aug. 1911, SD 812.00/2346, 2306.
261 Meyer, *Mexican Rebel*, pp. 42–3.
262 Cásasola, *Historia gráfica*, I, p. 388.
263 Meyer, *Mexican Rebel*, pp. 44–5; A. Huerta Vargas to Madero, 1 Nov. 1911, Fabela, DHRM, RRM, II, p. 231.
264 Beezley, *Insurgent Governor*, pp. 84–5.

265 Long, Parral, 7 Aug. 1911, SD 812.00/2346.

266 Meyer, *Mexican Rebel*, p. 46; Beezley, *Insurgent Governor*, p. 124.

267 Edwards, Juárez, 18 May 1911, SD 812.00/1927. Rojas, aged twenty-three, had revolted at Dolores in the Sierra Madre in December 1910; his renewed rebellion a year later came after an unsuccessful attempt to win political control of his pueblo: Almada, *Diccionario . . . chihuahuense*, pp. 466–7.

268 Letcher, Chihuahua, 2 Feb. 1912, SD 812.00/2725.

269 Edwards, Juárez, 1, 6 Feb. 1912, SD 812.00/2717, 2766; *El Paso Times*, 2 Feb. 1912.

270 Edwards, Juárez, 7 Feb.; Letcher, Chihuahua, 2 Feb. 1912; SD 812.00/2751, 2729.

271 Letcher, Chihuahua, 13 Feb. 1912, SD 812.00/2844.

272 *Ibid.*

273 *Ibid.*, Beezley, *Insurgent Governor*, pp. 126–7.

274 *Ibid.*, p. 129; Edwards, Juárez, 15, 20 Feb. 1912, SD 812.00/2800, 2839.

275 Long, Parral, 19 Feb. 1912, SD 812.00/2833.

276 Ross, *Madero*, pp. 256–7, 264–5; Letcher, Chihuahua, 2 Feb. 1912, SD 812.00/2729, refers to the Casas Grandes rebels as 'Zapatistas or Vazquistas', indicating not only his own uncertainty, but also the fluidity of such national labels.

277 Almada, *Diccionario . . . chihuahuense*, pp. 83, 476–7; F. Barcenas, *jefe político*, Juárez to Creel, 18 May 1909, STA (Creel) box 2.

278 A. Lomelí, Porfirian consul, El Paso, to S.R.E., 25 Nov. 1910, Fabela, DHRM, RRM, I, pp. 101–2; Aguilar, *Revolución Sonorense*, pp. 195, 207–9, on fears (greatly exaggerated as it turned out) of Magonista subversion in Sonora; Beezley, *Insurgent Governor*, p. 90, on Chihuahua.

279 Jesús Flores Magón to F. González Garza, 18 Oct, 1911, to Abraham González, 20 Jan. 1912, Fabela, DHRM, RRM, II, p. 176, III, p. 57.

280 Almada, *Diccionario . . . chihuahuense*, p. 249; Ellsworth, Cd Porfirio Díaz, 17 Feb. 1912, SD 812.00/2875, citing Salazar's Plan, in which the rebels' declaration that 'we . . . fully realise that we need the foreign capital, enterprising spirit, and friendly cooperation (*sc.* of the US) to accomplish the full development of the vast natural resources of our country', clearly goes beyond prudent diplomacy, and casts doubt on notions of Orozquista economic nationalism.

281 Almada, *Diccionario . . . chihuahuense*, p. 249; Ellsworth, Cd Porfirio Díaz, 8 Feb. 1912, SD 812.00/2785; E. J. Westrup, Saltillo, to S. G. Inman, 22 Feb. 1906, SGIA, box 11, on Hernández's Protestant affiliation.

282 Letcher, Chihuahua, 13, 15 Feb., 10 May 1912, SD 812.00/2844, 2894, 3930.

283 Letcher, Chihuahua, 13 Feb. 1912; W. Llewelyn to Attorney-General Wickersham, 16 Feb. 1912; SD 812.00/2844; 2873; Ross, *Madero*, p. 257.

284 Letcher, Chihuahua, 10 May 1912, SD 812.00/3930, calles Hernández 'an impracticable dreamer, a socialist . . . and an anarchist'; Llewelyn to Wickersham 16 Feb. 1912, SD 812.00/2873, contains press cuttings to the same effect, but the writer, who had recently met Hernández, concluded that 'he is not so much a dreamer as they say he is', a view which must command more respect.

285 Ellsworth, Cd Porfirio Díaz, 15 Feb.; Edwards, Juárez, 28 Feb., 3, 6, 9 13 Mar. 1912; SD 812.00/2828; 2956, 3013, 3145, 3133.

286 Letcher, Chihuahua, 4, 7 Mar. (twice) 1912, SD 812.00/3192, 3088, 3188. Though Orozco's confrontation marked his military commitment to the rebel cause, he had, the day before, made a verbal commitment, involving the spirits of Juárez and Cuauhtémoc, as protocol required: Meyer, *Mexican Rebel*, p. 60.

287 Letcher, Chihuahua, 7 Mar. 1912, SD 812.00/3188.

288 Orozco to Juan Sarabia, 25 Mar. 1912, AARD 42/no number.

289 Madero to González, 5 Nov., 1912; AFM r.11; cf. Madero to Huerta, 7 June 1912, Fabela, DHRM, RRM, III, pp. 444–5, where an individual merits recognition and reward

for being 'one of the few who (at the time of the Orozco revolt) remained loyal, at the risk of his life'; see also Puente, *Pascual Orozco*, p. 122.

290 Meyer, *Mexican Rebel*, pp. 62–4.
291 *Ibid.*, p. 62; Cockcroft, *Intellectual Precursors*, p. 211.
292 Cockcroft, *Intellectual Precursors*, p. 130, n.27.
293 Meyer, *Mexican Rebel*, p. 64.
294 Ellsworth, Cd Porfirio Díaz, 17 Feb. 1912, SD 812.00/2875.
295 Beezley, *Insurgent Governor*, pp. 124–5.
296 For the Plan of Tacubaya of March 1911, promising immediate agrarian reform and 'Justice . . . to all men', Cockcroft, *Intellectual Precursors*, pp. 187–8.
297 Lister, p. 230; Almada, *Diccionario . . . chihuahuense*, p. 249.
298 Madero to González, 5 Nov. 1912, AFM r.11; Zapata to Orozco, 6 May 1912, AARD 43/5, which questions only Orozco's acceptance of the old Porfiristas/Maderista legislatures; Francisco Bulnes, *La Prensa* 23 May 1912, which declares that 'Orozquismo is only Zapatismo sung to another tune, expressed in another idiom'.
299 Meyer, *Mexican Rebel*, pp. 61–2; Letcher, Chihuahua, 28 June 1912, SD 812.00/4357.
300 Ross, *Madero*, pp. 167–8; Letcher, Chihuahua, 20 Mar. 1912, SD 812.00/3424; Garibaldi, *Toast*, p. 226.
301 S. Terrazas to M. Balbas, 1 July 1912, STA, box 83.
302 Valadés, *Imaginación*, II, p. 238; Puente, *Pascual Orozco*, p. 82.
303 Ross, *Madero*, p. 168; Mancisidor, *Historia de la Revolución Mexicana*, p. 178; Meyer, *Mexican Rebel*, pp. 58–9. *El País*, 6 July 1911, alleges that Terracista agents sponsored fiestas throughout Chihuahua and 'when spirits are receptive, they recommend Orozco's candidacy for the governorship'.
304 Meyer, *Mexican Rebel*, pp. 52, 66, borrowing a phrase from Letcher, Chihuahua, 20 Mar. 1912, SD 812.00/3424.
305 Letcher, Chihuahua, 4 Mar. (twice), 20 Mar. 1912, SD 812.00/3045, 3192, 3424.
306 Letcher, Chihuahua, 10 May, 28 June 1912, SD 812.00/3930, 4357.
307 Letcher, Chihuahua, 2 Mar., 28 June 1912, SD 812.00/3146, 4357.
308 Knight, 'Intellectuals'.
309 Letcher, Chihuahua, 7, 31 Mar. 1912; Wilson, Mexico City, 26 Apr. 1912; SD 812.00/3188, 3525; 3732; Fuentas Mares, *Y Mexico se refugió*, pp. 250–1.
310 Ross, *Madero*, p. 259; Cumberland, *Genesis*, p. 195; Calvert, *Mexican Revolution*, pp. 107–8, whose statement that 'large numbers of US citizens were involved in the Orozco movement' cannot be substantiated; apart from one or two soldiers of fortune, Americans studiously avoided revolutionary participation and, in 1912, the great majority of them sympathised with Madero and the established government: Letcher, Chihuahua, 12, 31 Mar. 1912, SD 812.00/3268, 3525.
311 E. Creel to J. Creel, 31 Mar., 22 Apr. 1912, STA (Creel) r.1.
312 E. Creel to J. Creel, 29 Mar., 19 Apr. 1912, STA (Creel) r.1; Fuentes Mares, *Y México se refugió*, pp. 250–2.
313 Letcher, Chihuahua, 20 Mar. 1912, SD 812.00/3424.
314 Letcher, Chihuahua, 12 Mar. 1912, SD 812.00/3268.
315 'An Appeal for Justice', n.d., SD 812.00/3724; Letcher, Chihuahua, 10 May 1912, same file.
316 Fuentes Mares, *Y México se refugió*, p. 240.
317 Letcher, Chihuahua, 20 Feb., 20 Mar. 1912, SD 812.00/2931, 3424; to the second of which Letcher added: 'it is not hard to believe'.
318 Beezley, *Insurgent Governor*, pp. 80–1, 97–9, 103–13.
319 *Ibid.*, pp. 110–11; Letcher, Chihuahua, 20 Mar. 1912, SD 812.00/3424 and enclosed manifesto.
320 E. Creel to J. Creel, 31 July 1911, 29 Mar. 1912, STA (Creel) r.1

321 Aguilar, *Revolución Sonorense*, pp. 234–5.

322 See below, pp. 367, 400–4.

323 Valadés, *Imaginación*, II, pp. 236–9.

324 Beezley, *Insurgent Governor*, pp. 103–5, 108–9, 112–13, on González's 'Calvinism' and policies to educate, moralise and dry out the people of Chihuahua.

325 Knight, 'Peasant and Caudillo', pp. 44–56.

326 Emmanuel Le Roy Ladurie, 'The "Event" and the "Long Term" in Social History: the Case of the Chouan Uprising', in *The Territory of the Historian* (Hassocks, 1979), pp. 111–31.

327 Rutherford, *Mexican Society*, p. 122.

328 F. Braudel, *The Mediterranean and the Mediterranean World in the Age of Philip II*, London, 1972, pp. 20–1; and the same author's 'Histoire et Sociologie' in *Ecrits sur l'Histoire*, Paris, 1969, pp. 102–3.

329 Implicit in this argument is an assumption of the relative (and sometimes the very considerable) autonomy of the state: the revolutionary state shaped as well as mirrored social classes, and its protagonists displayed an allegiance to the state which could override class or other sectional allegiances.

330 Braudel, *Mediterranean*, p. 21.

331 Womack, *Zapata*, p. 242.

332 Meyer, *Mexican Rebel*, p. 61; Almada, *Revolución . . . chihuahua*, I, p. 240.

333 Reed, *Insurgent Mexico*, p. 57.

334 Eugenia Meyer *et all.*, *La vida con Villa en la Hacienda de Canutillo*, DEAS, no. 1, Mexico, 1974; Graham Greene, *The Lawless Roads*, London 1971 (first published 1939), pp. 53–60.

335 See vol. 2 ch. 1.

336 See above, pp. 11, 118, 122, 125.

337 Anton Blok, 'The Peasant and the Brigand: Social Banditry Reconsidered', *Comparative Studies in Society and History*, XIV (1972), pp. 494–503.

338 Jacobs, 'Rancheros', pp. 78, 83–4 (the quotation was taken from an earlier draft of the paper, and does not appear *verbatim* in the published version).

339 *Ibid.*, p. 84.

340 *Ibid.*, p. 89.

341 *Ibid.*, pp. 79, 88.

342 Jacobs, *Aspects*, pp. 154–70; Womack, *Zapata*, p. 133.

343 Jacobs, 'Rancheros', p. 86.

344 Madero to A. Figueroa, 24 Feb. 1912, Fabela, DHRM, RRM, III, p. 141.

345 A. Figueroa to Madero, 27 Feb. 1912, Fabela, DHRM, RRM, III, pp. 149–50, politely refusing to quit Guerrero, with plausible reasons.

346 Jacobs, 'Rancheros', p. 90.

347 Above, pp. 261–3.

348 Womack, *Zapata*, pp. 126–6, 393–4; Gilly, *Revolución interrumpida*, pp. 59–67.

349 Womack, *Zapata*, p. 393.

350 *Ibid.*, pp. 401–2 (articles 1, 4).

351 *Ibid.*, p. 401 (article 1).

352 *Ibid.*

353 *Ibid.*, pp. 402–3 (article 7).

354 In addition, Maderistas who remained loyal to Madero would be regarded as traitors rather than prisoners-of-war: *ibid.*, pp. 397, 403 (article 10).

355 *Ibid.*, p. 87.

356 Friedrich, *Agrarian Revolt*, p. 53.

357 That is, 'communal' in the Tillys' sense of the word: Tillys, *Rebellious Century*, pp. 50–2.

358 Above, pp. 7, 158–9.

359 Womack, *Zapata*, pp. 225, 314. Examples of *serrano* (including Villista) excesses will follow.

360 Womack, *Zapata*, p. 224.

361 Córdova, *Ideología*, pp. 154–5.

362 Knight, 'Intellectuals'.

363 Robert P. Millon, *Zapata: The Ideology of a Peasant Revolutionary*, New York, 1969, subjects Zapatismo to a fairly crude Marxist taxonomy; pp. 83–101 argue against Zapatista 'socialism' or 'anarchism'. The role of Zapata's (urban) intellectuals is considered in vol. 2, ch. 2.

364 Womack, *Zapata*, p. 399.

365 Meyer, *Cristero Rebellion*, p. 12; Casasola, *Historia gráfica*, I, p. 261; Reed, *Insurgent Mexico*, p. 194.

366 Barry Carr, 'The Casa del Obrero Mundial, Constitutionalism and the Pact of February 1915' in Elsa Cecilia Frost *et al.*, eds., *El trabajo y los trabajadores en la historia de México*, Mexico and Arizona, 1979, pp. 620–1.

367 Womack, *Zapata*, p. 342.

368 Millon, *Zapata*, pp. 63, 93 and *passim*.

369 See vol. 2 ch. 2.

370 Above, pp. 99–101.

371 Córdova, *Ideología*, p. 151; Womack, *Zapata*, p. 399.

372 Córdova, *Ideología*, p. 153; cf. Millon, *Zapata*, pp. 91–2, who (wrongly) seeks to attribute Zapatista localism to military constraints, rather than to political preference. The argument here distinguishes between, on the one hand, a form of traditional *patriotism* nurtured in nineteenth-century tradition, associated with Juarista liberalism and its struggle against the empire, and focussing on the *patria*; and, on the other, the more aggressive *nationalism* of the twentieth century, an ideology of state-building, which (unlike patriotism) displayed a close affinity with anti-clericalism and economic nationalism.

373 Wolf, *Peasant Wars*, pp. 294 (not that all Wolf's own examples can be legitimately brought under this heading: Cuba strains the reader's credulity).

374 M. Ardit, A. Balcells, N. Sales, *Historia dels Paisos Catalans* (Barcelona, 1980), pp. 281–2, notes the kinship.

375 I stress 'approached' – but then what ideology (liberal, socialist, communist) has yet achieved complete practical expression? On the Proudhonian ideal see Robert L. Hoffman, *Revolutionary Justice, The Social and Political Theory of P.-J. Proudhon*, Urbana, 1972, especially p. 289ff.; George Woodcock, *Pierre-Joseph Proudhon*, London, 1956, pp. 271, 273, 279, notes Proudhon's affinity with peasant beliefs in general and with 'Mexican agrarianism' in particular.

376 Córdova, *Ideología*, p. 154.

377 Huntington, *Political Order*, p. 264ff.; Skocpol, *States and Social Revolutions*, pp. 4–5 is similar.

378 See vol. 2 ch. 3.

379 Córdova, *Ideología*, p. 155, argues the triumph of Zapatista aims, though with a studied ambivalence; Robert E. Quirk, *The Mexican Revolution 1914–15*, New York, 1970, pp. 292–3, is even less ambivalent, and produces a classic exposition of the consensual revolution school: no losers (bar the 'troglodyte' Carranza); everyone a winner.

380 Quoted by E. H. Carr, *What is History?*, London, 1964, p. 126.

381 *Ibid.*, in which Carr draws a spurious analogy with cricket – spurious in that cricket possesses clear rules for determining 'success', while history does not; the criteria of historical significance (which is not the same as 'success') would vary according to period, problem and historian.

382 Skocpol, *States and Social Revolutions*, pp. 10–11.

383 Knight, 'Intellectuals'.
384 Cf. above, p. 161.
385 Huntington, *Political Order*, p. 266.
386 'Statolatry' is used to denote analyses which elevate the state to the highest level of explanation. Skocpol, *States and Social Revolutions*, and Goldfrank, 'Theories of Revolution', are general examples. Brading, 'Introduction', pp. 12–16, in his (partly legitimate) concern to strip Mexican agriculture of its 'feudal' aspect, and to stress the role of the *ranchero*, displays an excessive – and logically unnecessary – scepticism about the role of the revolutionary peasantry; Brading's influence is apparent in Jacobs, 'Aspects', *passim*. Cf. Hans Werner Tobler, 'Conclusion', in the same volume; Hobsbawm, 'Peasants and Politics', p. 10; Falcón, 'Los orígenes populares' all of which are similarly sceptical, not least as a result of Jean Meyer's persuasive influence.
387 A. Figueroa to Madero, 15 Dec. 1911, Fabela, DHRM, RRM, II, p. 414.
388 Womack, *Zapata*, p. 131.
389 *Ibid.*, pp. 132–3; J. Morales to Madero, 28 Oct. 1911; J. Rosendo to Governor Cañete, 20 Dec. 1911; Cañete to Madero, 1 Dec. 1911; all in AG, CRCFM.
390 Lendrum, Puebla, 30 Mar., 20 Apr., 10 Sept. 1912, SD 812.00/3554, 3757, 4955; Madero to J. Robles, 6 July 1912, AFM r.12.
391 R. Duarte to C. Westbrook, Apr. 1912; J. Platt, Zacualpán, Aug. 1912; SD 812.00/3846; 4792, 4885. Salgado is further discussed below.
392 Ramírez, *Oaxaca*, pp. 32, 35–6, 40, 114; Lawton, Oaxaca, 1, 8 Apr., 19 Sept. 1912, SD 812.00/3609, 3648, 5121; cf. Henderson, 'Un Gobernador Maderista', p. 384. Womack, *Zapata*, p. 275, notes Barrios' later participation in the Zapatista movement.
393 Womack, *Zapata*, p. 132, gives figures of 1,000 and 5,000 *rurales* for Morelos alone; the latter figure seems inflated. Cf. Platt, Zacualpán, Aug. 1912, SD 812.00/4885.
394 Womack, *Zapata*, p. 133; Lawton, Oaxaca, 28 Mar. 1912, SD 812.00/3554.
395 Womack, *Zapata*, pp. 142–3; James Platt, witnessing a Zapatista attack on Zacualpán led by Francisco Pacheco, commented on the rebels' sparing use of ammunition, adding 'they were nearly worn out though full of enthusiasm': SD 812.00/4792. For Cuernavaca: King, *Tempest*, pp. 76–8.
396 Report of Major F. Enciso, 23 Dec. 1911, AG 645.
397 Report of Lt. Col. Luis Medina Barrón, 27 Jan. 1912, AG 645.
398 Womack, *Zapata*, pp. 131, 137.
399 *Ibid.*, pp. 138–40; Madero to Governor Naranjo, 10 Apr. 1912, Fabela, DHRM, RRM, III, pp. 298–9.
400 Reports of Lt. Col. Luis Medina Barrón, 3, 30 Apr. 1912, AG 645.
401 King, *Tempest*, p. 78. Though Mrs King appears to have bowed to opinion in the twenty-five years between adventure and recollection: her published version of Zapatismo (1935) is a good deal more sympathetic than the contemporary version she despatched to the Foreign Office: see Hohler, Mexico City, 2 Nov. 1914, FO 371/2031, 76893.
402 Womack, *Zapata*, pp. 139–40, quoting *El País* and *El Diario*, Feb. 1912.
403 *Ibid.*, p. 140.
404 Report of Corp. Pedro Gazcón, 23 Feb. 1912, AG 645.
405 Womack, *Zapata*, p. 142, quoting Pablo Escandón; J. Platt, Zacualpán, Aug. 1912, SD 812.00/4792. The burning had taken place some four months earlier: Womack, *Zapata*, p. 143.
406 Womack, *Zapata*, p. 143; and, for the same process in Puebla, Lendrum, 7 May 1912, 812.00/3901.
407 Womack, *Zapata*, p. 144.
408 Hamm, Durango, 27, 29 Mar. 1912, SD 812.00/3403, 3499; Womack, *Zapata*, pp. 141, 143; Platt, Zacualpán, Aug. 1912, SD 812.00/4792 (by which time the Zapatistas' hopes of Orozquista cash were excessively optimistic); Haskell, Salina Cruz, 30

Apr. 1912, SD 812.00/3851 – note the similar ploy of Yucatecan rebels in 1911, using the name of Madero.

409 Lespinasse, Frontera, 28 Mar.; Lawton, Oaxaca, 1 May 1912, SD 812.00/3551; 3609.

410 E. Creel to J. Creel, 29 Mar. 1912, refers to 'public opinion which is Chihuahua is universally favourable to the revolution': STA (Creel) r.1; Letcher, Chihuahua, 13, 31 Mar.; Edwards Juárez, 31 Mar. 1912; SD 812.00/3213, 3523, 3326.

411 Ellsworth, Cd Porfirio Díaz, 23 Mar.; Letcher, Chihuahua, 8 Mar. 1912; SD 812.00/3398; 3297; Martínez del Toro, consul, Marfa, to consul El Paso, 9 Dec. 1912, Fabela, DHRM, RRM, IV, p. 239; Guzmán, *Memorias*, p. 116.

412 Letcher, Chihuahua, 20 Feb., 3 Mar. 1912, SD 812.00/2931, 3027 (though Letcher is not the most objective source where Villa is concerned); Meyer, *Mexican Rebel*, p. 68; Reed, *Insurgent Mexico*, p. 127; Guzmán, *Memorias*, p. 105.

413 As already recognised, 'regional' allegiances may in fact mask other, anterior, class, cultural, or political allegiances: the term is therefore only used in cases such as this where no anterior allegiance can be discerned, where, in other words, regionalism seems to act as a first mover, and cannot be disaggregated. Of course, further research might permit disaggregation.

414 *Jefe político*, Jiménez, to Governor José María Sánchez, 17 Oct. 1910, STA, box 28, reports that Miguel Baca's ranch near Parral was frequented by 'many suspect people of bad reputation, including an individual named Francisco Villa'; see also Ross, *Madero*, p. 124; C. Ruegosechea (?), El Paso, to S.R.E., 17 Nov. 1915, ARE legajo 810, 98-R-2, p. 283, on Juan Baca's 'ascendancy' over Villa.

415 I. Grimaldo, *Apuntes Para La Historia*, San Luis 1916, pp. 13–18 on the early career of Maclovio Herrera.

416 Letcher, Chihuahua, 18 Mar. 1912, SD 812.00/3297.

417 Letcher, Chihuahua, 31 Mar. 1912, SD 812.00/3523; Meyer, *Mexican Rebel*, p. 68. It was now that the Terrazas interests made their financial commitment to the revolt – apparently (according to evidence already cited) rather too willingly. Other enterprises, like the French Banco Nacional, were assessed more heavily.

418 Meyer, *Mexican Rebel*, p. 70; Garrett, Nuevo Laredo, 20 Apr.; Letcher, Chihuahua, 15 Mar. 1912; SD 812.00/3739; 3310. Such artillery, with its short range, could not stand up to its Federal counterpart: see anon, report, El Paso to S.R.E., 28 May 1912, Fabela, DHRM, RRM, III, p. 146.

419 Meyer, *Mexican Rebel*, p. 70; Ulloa, *Revolución intervenida*, pp. 33–4.

420 Cowdray used his business connections with Taft's Attorney-General Wickersham to advocate an arms embargo; here – as in 1913 – his chief concern was not the survival of any specific government of persons or policies, but that of the constituted (Mexico City) government, *tout court*. American interests generally followed a similar line. See Ryder to Cowdray, 11 Mar., Cowdray to Brice, 13 Mar. 1912, Cowdray Papers, box A/3; Calvert, *Mexican Revolution*, p. 109; and Meyer, *Mexican Rebel*, p. 79 on Orozco's emissaries to the US.

421 Cf. Letcher, Chihuahua, 26 Feb., 25 Apr. 1912, SD 812.00/3045, 3773; by the later date the rebels were showing 'bitter hostility' to the US.

422 Of course, for short term crises to stimulate nationalist outbursts there had to exist an underlying nationalist sentiment and a potential nationalist consituency. The important point is that these were not the product of imperialist economic penetration; they antedated such penetration, were the product of education (and other forms of cultural socialisation), and thus were particularly evident among the urban, educated, middle and upper classes. As such they correlated less with revolutionary commitment than with convervatism and Catholicism. See Knight, 'Nationalism', especially pp. 258–68.

423 Cumberland, *Genesis*, p. 195.

424 Casasola, *Historia gráfica*, I, pp. 456–9; cf. Valadés, *Imaginación*, II, p. 238.

425 Meyer, *Huerta*, p. 133; Pani, *Apuntes*, 134.
426 Casasola, *Historia gráfica*, I, p. 454; Ross, *Madero*, p. 262; Letcher, Chihuahua, 31 Mar. 1912, SD 812.00/3525. As a native of Nazas, Campa was advancing into old home territory when he encountered the Federals: Rouaix, *Diccionario*, p. 70.
427 Ross, *Madero*, p. 262.
428 Meyer, *Mexican Rebel*, p. 72. Censorship reached such proportions that in Saltillo the newsagents stopped selling (official) newspapers, 'claiming that there is no demand for them'; Holland, Saltillo, 26 Mar. 1912, SD 812.00/3448.
429 Holland, Saltillo, 29 Mar., 2 Apr. 1912, SD 812.00/3428, 3544.
430 Meyer, *Mexican Rebel*, p. 73; Valadés, *Imaginación*, II, p. 239; Casasola, *Historia gráfica*, I, p. 455 shows a convalescent General Blanquet, who recovered to play a prominent role in later years.
431 Garret, Nuevo Laredo, 2 Apr.; Letcher, Chihuahua, 7, 11 Apr.; Gill, Parral and Durango Railway, 8 Apr. 1912; SD 812.00/3467; 3533, 3677; 3706. One American, a mercenary caught fighting for Villa, was however shot: *Mexican Rebel*, p. 77.
432 Letcher, Chihuahua, 11 Apr. 1912, SD 812.00/3677.
433 Gill, Parral, 8 Apr. 1912, SD 812.00/3706.
434 Letcher, Chihuahua, 31 Mar. 1912, SD 812.00/3523.
435 Casasola, *Historia gráfica*, I, pp. 455, 475, 484; Meyer, *Huerta*, pp. 1–18 and *passim*.
436 William L. Sherman and Richard E. Greenleaf, *Victoriano Huerta: A Reappraisal*, Mexico, 1960, represents an attempt at rehabilitation, scarcely successful; it has been superseded by Meyer, *Huerta*, which (correctly if also, ultimately, unsuccessfully) tries to reinterpret Huerta's regime rather than his claims to personal salvation.
437 Meyer, *Huerta*, p. 7; Ochoa Campos, *Guerrero*, p. 276.
438 Meyer, *Huerta*, pp. 5, 10, 34.
439 *Ibid.*, p. 15.
440 Nemesio García Naranjo, *Memorias*, Monterrey, n.d., VII, p. 14.
441 Sherman and Greenleaf, *Huerta*, pp. 23–4.
442 Meyer, *Huerta*, pp. 22–7; Madero to Huerta, 31 Oct. 1911, Fabela, DHRM, RRM, II, p. 218.
443 Cumberland, *Genesis*, p. 196; Bonilla, *Régimen Maderista*, p. 13.
444 Meyer, *Huerta*, p. 35; Carothers, Torreón, 28 Apr. 1912, SD 812.00/3826: 'everyone is afraid of Villa here, as his record as a bandit is well known'. Carothers later became one of Villa's chief American sympathisers and apologists.
445 Carothers, Torreón, 28 Apr. 1912, SD 812.00/3826. Meticulous organisation had been a feature of Huerta's earlier campaign, for example in Yucatán: Meyer, *Huerta*, pp. 12–13.
446 The prediction was made by ex-Governor Cárdenas of Coahuila. See Holland, Saltillo, 2 Apr.; Letcher, 6 May 1912; SD 812.00/3544; 3884.
447 Ellsworth, Cd Porfirio Díaz, 3 Apr.; Holland, Saltillo, 17 Apr. 1912; SD 812.00/3527; 3692.
448 Holland, Saltillo, 3, 17 Apr. 1912, SD 812.00/3559, 3692.
449 Ellsworth, Cd Porfirio Díaz, 10 May; Holland, Saltillo, 3 May 1912; SD 812.00/3898, 3842; whose accounts differ slightly.
450 Cumberland, *Genesis*, p. 197.
451 Texas state senator James McNeal returned from Coahuila after ten days in April reporting the looting and burning of several estates, the property of 'wealthy land and cattle owners': Ellsworth, Cd Porfirio Díaz, 1 May 1912, SD 812.00/3807.
452 Ellsworth, Cd Porfirio Díaz, 18, 21 Mar. 1912, SD 812.00/3341, 3370; Madero to Carranza, 12 Jan. 1912, Fabela, DHRM, RRM, III, p. 36, and to A. González, 7 Feb. 1913, AFM r.12.
453 Ellsworth, Cd Porfirio Díaz, 18 Apr. 1912, SD 812.00/3696.
454 Hanna, Monterrey, 4 June 1912, SD 812.00/4173.

455 Holland, Saltillo, 19 Mar. 1912, SD 812.00/3364.

456 Urquizo, *Páginas*, pp. 11, 33.

457 Gruening, *Mexico and its Heritage*, p. 310.

458 Taracena, *Carranza*, p. 61; Casasola, *Historia gráfica*, I, pp. 472–3; Holland, Saltillo, 7 May 1912, SD 812.00/3836.

459 Meyer, *Mexican Rebel*, pp. 70–1; Aguilar, *Revolución Sonorense*, pp. 251, 238ff.; Letcher, Chihuahua, 13 Apr. 1912, SD 812.00/3587.

460 Cumberland, *Genesis*, p. 197; Edwards, Juárez, 4, 8 May; Letcher, Chihuahua, 10 May 1912; SD 812.00/3801, 3841; 3930.

461 Casasola, *Historia gráfica*, I, p. 474; Letcher, Chihuahua, 28 June 1912, SD 812.00/4357 gives 200 rebels killed; Meyer, *Mexican Rebel*, pp. 36–7 mentions 650 Orozquista casualties against about 100 Federal.

462 Letcher, Chihuahua, 19 June; Edwards, Juárez, received 28 June 1912; SD 812.00/4257; 4313.

463 Letcher, Chihuahua, 28 June 1912, SD 812.00/4357.

464 Letcher, Chihuahua, 29 Aug. 1912, SD 812.00/4823; Casasola, *Historia gráfica*, I, pp. 481–2.

465 Meyer, *Mexican Rebel*, pp. 40–1; Casasola, *Historia gráfica*, I, p. 483.

466 Letcher, Chihuahua, 28 June 1912, SD 812.00/4357.

467 See the comments of an Orozquista deserter in the anon. police report from El Paso, 28 May 1912, Fabela, DHRM, RRM, III, pp. 416–7; Letcher, Chihuahua, 30 June 1912, SD 812.00/4238.

468 Cf. Meyer, *Mexican Rebel*, p. 87; Edwards, Juárez, 11 July, 10 Sept.; L. Wood, War Dept., 3 Sept.; Collector of Customs, Eagle Pass, 6 Sept. 1912; SD 812.00/4404, 4844; 4767; 4813.

469 Holland, Saltillo, 11 Sept.; Ellsworth, Cd Porfirio Díaz, 21 Sept., 12 Oct. 1912; SD 812.00/4957; 5069, 5248.

470 Aguilar, *Revolución Sonorense*, pp. 190–4, 209–10, 216–8, 234.

471 *Ibid.*, p. 269; Hostetter, Hermosillo, 30 Mar.; Dye, Nogales, 22 Apr., 24 June, 16, 31 July; Bowman, Nogales, 11 Dec. 1912; SD 812.00/3512; 3742, 4326, 4433, 4566; 5500; Lister, *Chihuahua*, pp. 220–5 on the tribulations of the Mormons.

472 Hostetter, Hermosillo, 21 July, 15 Aug. 1912, SD 812.00/4496, 4723; Aguilar, *Revolución Sonorense*, p. 282.

473 Aguilar, *Revolución Sonorense*, pp. 281–4; Dye, Nogales, 31 July, 27 Aug. 1912, SD 812.00/4566, 4728; Alvaro Obregón, *Ocho mil kilómetros en campaña* (Mexico, 1966), p. 21.

474 Aguilar, *Revolución Sonorense*, pp. 241–5.

475 *Ibid.*, pp. 266–76. Obregón's origins are considered below, pp. 412–3, and vol. 2 ch. 1.

476 *Ibid.*, p. 254.

477 Hostetter, Hermosillo, 16 Sept. 1912, SD 812.00/5070.

478 Aguilar, *Revolución Sonorense*, p. 283. According to an American cattleman, the Orozquistas held a tract of land south-east of Nacozari, but they did so only by virtue of terrorising the people; hence they found few sympathisers in the region: Dye, Nogales, 18 Sept. 1912, SD 812.00/5058.

479 Aguilar, *Revolución Sonorense*, p. 285; Obregón, pp. 22–6.

480 Letcher, Chihuahua, 18 Nov. 1912, SD 812.00/5532; *New York Times*, 9 Dec. 1912, reporting that 'the remnants of Orozco's army are undoubtedly showing more evidence of concerted action': the point is taken up below, p. 467.

481 The total number of Federals, volunteers and *rurales* rose from 40,000 to 70,000 during the spring and summer of 1912: Cumberland, *Genesis*, p. 198. This theme – the militarisation of Mexico, and its implications for the Madero regime – is explored in the following chapter.

482 Letcher, Chihuahua, 16 Oct. 1912, SD 812.00/5324; Meyer, *Huerta*, p. 34.

483 Meyer, *Huerta*, p. 38ff.; Madero to A. González, 5 Aug. 1912, AFM r.12, urging that Huerta take steps to block off rebel boltholes in the sierra, indicates continued presidential impatience.

484 Meyer, *Huerta*, p. 39; Taracena, *Carranza*, p. 59.

485 Letcher, Chihuahua, 29 Aug. 1912, SD 812.00/4823.

486 Letcher, Chihuahua, 16 Oct. 1912, SD 812.00/5324.

487 Letcher, Chihuahua, 16 Oct. 1912, SD 812.00/5324; T. Aubert to Madero, 27 Jan. 1913, AFM r.22; R. Hernández to A. Guajardo (also an irregular commander), 9 Dec. 1912, AG legajo 889.

488 Obregón withdrew from military service with the rank of colonel in Dec. 1912; his civilian retirement proved brief. Obregón, *Ocho mil*, p. 26; Madero to A. González, 7 Feb. 1913, T. Aubert to Madero, 27 Jan. 1913, AFM rs.12, 22.

489 Letcher, Chihuahua, 15 Sept. 1912, SD 812.00/5056.

490 Cf. Meyer, *Huerta*, p. 43. Huerta's penchant for hawkish policies will be amply documented in vol. 2 ch. 1. It even survived into retirement: see the interview of Apr. 1915 in Oscar Strauss to Woodrow Wilson, 30 Apr. 1915, WWP, box 129.

491 Letcher, Chihuahua, 15 Sept. 1912, SD 812.00/5056. Note also Bonilla, *Régimen Maderista*, p. 18.

492 Bonilla, *Régimen Maderista*, p. 13, quoting García Peña's supposed admission.

493 *Ibid.*, p. 16, 18.

494 See below, pp. 484–5, 487–9.

495 Lespinasse, Frontera, 1 June; Schuyler, Mexico City, 5 June; Alger, Mazatlán, 1 June; Haskell, Salina Cruz, 22 June; SD 812.00/4106; 4126; 4175; 4336.

496 Womack, *Zapata*, p. 145. I have slightly changed the punctuation here.

497 Womack, *Zapata*, pp. 149–50.

498 *Ibid.*, p. 151.

499 *Ibid.*, pp. 146–7, 152.

500 *Ibid.*, p. 152. While depicting the conservative character of the new state legislature, Womack does not explain how it came to be elected, or why it represented such a shift in policy and personnel.

501 *Ibid.*, p. 154; and below, p. 468.

502 Cf. Cumberland, *Genesis*, ch. 9.

503 Calvert, *Mexican Revolution*, p. 103.

504 Tannenbaum, *Peace by Revolution*, p. 147.

505 Cumberland, *Genesis*, p. 186, referring to Angel Barrios' rebellion.

506 Heap, Guaymas, 3 May 1911, FO 371/1147, 18523; Hostetter, Hermosillo, 13, 31 May 1911, SD 812.00/1913, 2092; informe of Carlos Randall to Sonora state legislature, 1 Sept. 1911, SS r.9; Maytorena to Madero, 17 Sept. 1911, AFM r.18.

507 Fabila, *Los tribus Yaquis*, p. 100; Aguilar, *Revolución Sonorense*, pp. 183–5.

508 Hostetter, Hermosillo, 3 June 1911, SD 812.00/2127.

509 Aguilar, *Revolución Sonorense*, p. 248. Not that Madero had made any such promise.

510 Hostetter, Hermosillo, 3 June 1911, SD 812.00/2127; Aguilar, *Revolución Sonorense*, pp. 183–5, 195–6, 214–5.

511 Maytorena to Madero, 17 Sept. 1911, AFM r.18.

512 B. Viljoen to Madero, 22 Nov. 1911, Fabela, DHRM, RRM, II, p. 316; Aguilar, *Revolución Sonorense*, p. 248, on Sonoran perception of the Yaqui problem.

513 Hostetter, Hermosillo, 6 June, 14 Dec. 1911, 20 Jan. 1912, SD 812.00/2174, 2661, 2714.

514 Hostetter, Hermosillo, 23 Dec. 1911, 24 Feb., 30 Mar., 12 Apr. 1912, SD 812.00/2677, 3004, 3512, 3577.

515 Hostetter, Hermosillo, 13, 28 Apr., 24 May, 1 July 1912, SD 812.00/3660, 3839,

4010, 4380; anon. to G. Madero, from Hermosillo, 24 Nov. 1911, Fabela, DHRM, RRM, II, pp. 323–4.

516 Hostetter, Hermosillo, 24 Feb. 1912, SD 812.00/3004; Aguilar, *Revolución Sonorense*, p. 292; Col. Javier de la Moure to Madero, 13 Jan. 1913, AFM r.22.

517 Hostetter, Hermosillo, 11 May, 20 July 1912, SD 812.00/3936, 4495; Aguilar, *Revolución Sonorense*, p. 292 on the scope of the Yaqui rebellion.

518 Bowman, Nogales, 30 July, 8 Aug. 1912, SD 812.00/4568, 4615; Aguilar, *Revolución Sonorense*, pp. 250–1, 292–3.

519 Aguilar, *Revolución Sonorense*, p. 293.

520 C/o USS Vicksburg, Guaymas, 9 Sept. 1912, SD 812.00/4985.

521 Dye, Nogales, 18 Oct. 1912; Bowman, Nogales, 18 Jan. 1913; SD 812.00/5297; 5897. There was, of course, nothing new in this phenomenon of Yaqui participation in both rebel and government forces: cf. Fabila, *Los tribus Yaquis*, pp. 84, 87, 89.

522 Aguilar, *Revolución Sonorense*, pp. 254, 293–4, 309.

523 See below, pp. 417–23.

524 Madero to J. Lara, 4 July 1911, AFM r.20; Aguilar, *Revolución Sonorense*, p. 293; cf. Madero, pp. 187–98.

525 Friedrich, *Agrarian Revolt*, p. 1; cf. above, p. 112.

526 Aguilar, *Revolución Sonorense*, p. 248.

527 E. V. Anaya to Madero, 16 Oct. 1911, Fabela, DHRM, RRM, II, p. 168.

528 Anon., Hermosillo, to G. Madero 24 Nov. 1911, Fabela, DHRM, RRM, II, pp. 323–4; similar views were expressed by Anaya (n.527).

529 Informe of Maytorena to twenty-third Sonoran state legislature, Sept. 1912, SS r.9.

530 E. V. Anaya to Madero, 16 Oct. 1911, Fabela, DHRM, RRM, II, p. 168.

531 E. de los Ríos to R. Hernández, 5 July 1912, AFM r.10.

532 E. de los Ríos to L. Cervantes, Hermosillo, 30 Dec. 1912, AFM r.11. Possibly Madero's desire to conciliate was tactical as much as moral: Aguilar, *Revolución Sonorense*, p. 293.

533 Cf. Womack, *Zapata*, p. 186; Thord-Gray, *Gringo Rebel*, p. 216.

534 Fabela, DHRM, PRM, II, 67–8. Womack, *Zapata*, p. 117 points out that Jojutla was a place where 'Zapata had never had much responsibility', but he is perhaps a little too keen to exonerate his hero from implication in this and similar cases, which were to recur in Morelos later. On local bandits: Womack, *Zapata*, p. 152; and the Chalco case, I. Noriega to de la Barra, 26 Dec. 1911, ALB, carpeta 3.

535 Bonney, San Luis, 30 Apr. 1912, SD 812.00/3814; Meade, *Valles*, facing p. 12; O. Cabrera Ipiña, *San Luis Potosí*, San Luis, n.d., p. 88.

536 See above, p. 107–9.

537 Miller, Tampico, 19 Mar., 18 Apr.; Bonney, San Luis, 30 Apr. 1912; SD 812.00/3296, 3714; 3814.

538 Miller, Tampico, 29 Aug., 10 Sept., 11, 29 Dec. 1911, 8 Jan. 1912, SD 812.00/2315, 2359, 2632, 2681, 2691.

539 These represent three examples, taken from districts mentioned: Bonney, San Luis, 12 Mar.; Miller, Tampico, 23 Feb. 1912; SD 812.00/3303; 2870.

540 Miller, Tampico, 8, 16 Jan., 10 Feb., 18 Apr., 9 May 1912, SD 812.00/2691, 2705, 2816, 3714, 3855; W. Hanson, Osorio, 25 May 1911, SD 812.00/4122; Braulio Hernández, the Chihuahuan radical, denounced Alegre as a 'Científico': 'Appeal for Justice' in SD 812.00/3724.

541 Cf. pp. 262, 409–10.

542 Santos to Madero, June 1912, 24 Dec. 1912, Fabela, DHRM, RRM, III, pp. 489–93, IV, pp. 254–7; Meade, *Valles*, pp. 134, 160, 163, 170.

543 Bonney, San Luis, 20 Mar., 29 May 1912, SD 812.00/3378, 4119.

544 Miller, Tampico, 12 Mar. 1912, SD 812.00/3178; Madero to Governor Levi, 17 Aug. 1912, Fabela, DHRM, RRM, IV, p. 85.

545 Miller, Tampico, 23 Feb., 18 Apr. 1912, SD 812.00/2995, 3714; Madero to Lagos Cházaro, 29 Oct. 1912, Fabela, DHRM, RRM, IV, p. 187.
546 Cf. above, p. 113. The Chinese also figured as victims here.
547 Miller, Tampico, 15 June 1912, SD 812.00/4262; Fall Report, testimony of G. Blalock, pp. 979–87.
548 Miller, Tampico, 17 Feb. (where 'lands passing into the hands of Americans' are cited as factors stimulating hostility); Bonney, San Luis, 30 Apr. 1912, SD 812.00/2901, 3814.
549 Cf. above, p. 115.
550 Ankerson, 'Saturnino Cedillo', pp. 141–2.
551 Martínez Núñez, *San Luis Potosí*, pp. 34–5.
552 *Ibid.*, p. 36; Cockcroft, 'El Maestro de Primaria'.
553 Martínez Núñez, *San Luis Potosí*, pp. 36–7; Juan Barragán Rodríguez, *Historia del ejército y de la revolución constitucionalista* (2 vols., Mexico, 1966), I, pp. 163–4, is less than flattering; cf. A. Lozano to S.R.E., 16 Jan. 1913, Fabela, DHRM, RRM, IV, p. 343.
554 Bonney, San Luis, 20 Mar. 1912, SD 812.00/3378.
555 Miller, Tampico, 18 Apr.; Bonney, San Luis, 25 May 1912; SD 812.00/3714; 4119.
556 Miller, Tampico, 20 Mar.; Bonney, San Luis, 25 May 1912; SD 812.00/3378; 4119; the subsequent mortality of the Cedillo family, however, was frightening.
557 Bonney, San Luis, 21 June and n.d., received 2 Aug. 1912, SD 812.00/4319, 4549.
558 Jan Bazant, *Cinco haciendas mexicanas: tres siglos de vida rural en San Luis Potosí* (Mexico, 1975), pp. 181–5, 216, showing the bumper profits recorded by Ipiña's Hacienda San Diego between 1910 and 1913. The Hacienda San Antonio Tochatlaco (Hidalgo) also reached a peak of activity (measured by the size of the labour force) in 1912–13: AT.
559 Tannenbaum, *Peace by Revolution*, p. 192.
560 Bonney, San Luis, 18 Nov. 1912, SD 812.00/5575. Bonney, it should be mentioned, was one of the most perceptive and reliable of foreign observers of the Revolution.
561 Bonney, San Luis, 18 Nov. 1912, SD 812.00/5575; Bazant, *Cinco haciendas,* pp. 182–3.
562 Bazant, *Cinco haciendas*, p. 182.
563 Bonney, San Luis, 26 Sept. 1912, SD 812.00/5140. Conversely, it should be added, 'it is not believed that the miners and railroad men have furnished many recruits to the disorderly bands'.
564 Bonney, San Luis, 4 Dec. 1912, SD 812.00/5665 gives the details, though 20 Mar. 1912, SD 812.00/3378 makes it clear the events had taken place earlier.
565 Bonney, San Luis, 16 Oct. 1912, SD 812.00/5310.
566 *Ibid.*
567 Bonney, San Luis, 30 Mar., 13 Aug. 1912, SD 812.00/3497, 4661.
568 Miller, Tampico, 23 Feb.; Bonney, San Luis, 25 May 1912; SD 812.00/2995; 4119.
569 Bonney, San Luis, 12 Mar. 1912, SD 812.00/3303.
570 Bonney, San Luis, 16 Oct. 1912, SD 812.00/5310.
571 Waterbury, 'Non-revolutionary peasants', pp. 410–42.
572 Comerciantes of Huanchilla to Robles Domínguez, 1 June 1911, AARD 18/8; Lawton, Oaxaca, Sept. 1911, SD 812.00/2346.
573 Details of this story, which does not figure in Ramírez's history, from: Hohler, Mexico City, 18 July, 2 Aug., 17 Oct., 24 Nov. 1911, FO 371/1148, 30410,/1149, 32133, 42961, 49501; Hohler to Ernesto Madero, 3 Nov. 1911 FO 371/1149, 46233; Woodhouse to Hohler, 2 Oct. 1911, FO 371/1149, 41407.
574 Etla had been occupied by a large Maderista force under Gabriel Solís in June 1911: hence, it would seem, the installation of Maderista authorities: Ramírez, *Oaxaca*, p. 31.
575 Lawton, Oaxaca, 10 May 1912, SD 812.00/3961.
576 Lawton, Oaxaca, 2 May 1912, SD 812.00/3904. Again, it is the presence of a foreign landlord which brings the matter to light. But the appearance of a kind of xenophobic agrarianism is an illusion, determined by the character of the sources rather than by

objective conditions. Here, an American landlord suffered along with his Mexican counterparts; there were plenty of examples of Americans (and other foreigners) escaping the vengeance visited upon Mexican (and Spanish) *hacendados*. Furthermore, the foreigners who *did* incur agrarian resentment were often those who approximated most closely to 'traditional', Mexican patterns of land and labour exploitation. In Woodhouse's case, we should note, the dispute antedated his purchase of the estate.

577 Lawton, Oaxaca, 6 May 1912, SD 812.00/3935; Ramírez, *Oaxaca*, pp. 123–4. The lack of detail in both accounts makes any successful conflation of the two impossible.

578 Lawton, 13, 18 May 1912, SD 812.00/3978, 4035; Ramírez, *Oaxaca*, p. 124.

579 Schmieder, *Tzapotec and Mije*, pp. 25–6.

580 Governor Lugo to Madero, 22 Dec. 1911, Fabela, DHRM, RRM, II, pp. 442–3.

581 See vol. 2 ch. 2.

582 Edwards, Acapulco, 13 Apr.; R. Duarte to C. Westbrook, Apr. 1912; Pangburn, Acapulco, 5 Nov., 15 Nov., 3 Dec. 1912; SD 812.00/3588; 3846, 5559, 5584, 5633; Governor Lugo to Madero, 6 Dec. 1911, Fabela, DHRM, RRM, II, p. 338, on the government's rejection of Salgado's request to command *rurales* in his home district.

583 Edwards, Acapulco, 26 Sept. 1912, SD 812.00/5213; Womack, *Zapata*, pp. 171, 180, dates the 'official' inclusion of these Guerrero chiefs into the Zapatista camp as a year later, in 1913.

584 Pangburn, Acapulco, 19 Nov. 1912, SD 812.00/5538; Jacobs, 'Aspects', pp. 158–9.

585 Pangburn, Acapulco, 3, 9, 30 Nov. 1912, SD 812.00/5464, 5559, 5681.

586 Edwards, Acapulco, 26 Sept. 1912, SD 812.00/5213; cf. Fyfe, *The Real Mexico*, p. 89 for a similar description of the genesis of revolution.

587 José M. Ortiz (mine-owner) to Madero, 1 Dec. 1911; Lugo to Madero, 6 Dec. 1911; Fabela, DHRM, RRM, II, pp. 371–3, 388.

588 Ortiz and Lugo to Madero (n. 587).

589 Jacobs, 'Aspects', pp. 163–4.

590 R. Duarte to C. Westbrook, Apr. 1912 (which may exaggerate); I. Mathewson to J. Hallihan, 26 Feb. 1912; SD 812.00/3846; 3478.

591 J. Anderson, Pátzcuaro, 4 Sept. 1912, SD 812.00/4958.

592 Gobernación report enclosed in Hohler, Mexico City, 24 July 1911, FO 371/1149, 31148; S. Escalante to Robles Domínguez, 26 May 1911, AARD 16/25. Cf. also pp. 107, 220 above.

593 Zapata and his allies finalised their plans for rebellion at the Cuautla Lenten fair in March 1911; two years later, Gertrudis Sánchez and others plotted revolt at a Huetamo (Mich.) fiesta. Fairs and fiestas not only permitted groups of dissidents to gather despite official surveillance; they may also have provided some of the collective inspiration and solidarity (not to mention the Dutch courage) which such risky undertakings required. For European parallels, see Le Roy Ladurie, *Peasants of Languedoc*, pp. 194–6, Georges Lefebvre, *The Great Fear of 1789* (New York, 1973), pp. 27, 43.

594 Friederich, *Agrarian Revolt*, p. 50.

595 *Ibid.*, pp. 53–4.

596 Ralph L. Beals, *Cherán: A Sierra Tarascan Village* (New York, 1973), p. 12.

597 Friedrich, *Agrarian Revolt*, pp. 54–7.

598 Tannenbaum, *Peace By Revolution*, p. 193.

599 *Ibid.*, pp. 192–3.

600 C. Bernaldo de Quirós, *El bandolerismo en España y México* (Mexico, 1959), pp. 70, 89–93, 97–8, 100–1.

601 Hamm, Durango, 4, 10 Apr. 1912, SD 812.00/3667, 3641; L. Medina Barrón to Inspector General of Rurales, 22, 24 Mar., 3 Apr. 1912, AG 645; Ismael Romero to same, 3 Aug. 1912, AG 929, and, in the same file, reports from 53rd Cuerpo Rural, Tepic, likewise blurring together Zapatistas, Reyistas and bandits.

602 Hohler, Mexico City, 26 Mar. 1911, FO 371/1146, 13581; R. Cañete to Madero, 16 Nov. 1911, Fabela, DHRM, RRM, II p. 274.
603 Womack, *Zapata*, pp. 138, 166, 393–5.
604 Schuyler, Mexico City, 2 Jan. 1913, SD 812.00/5802.
605 Garret, Nuevo Laredo, 1 Mar.; Carothers, Torreón, 2 Mar. 1912; SD 812.00/3111; 3120.
606 Madero to Governor Patoni, 1 Nov., to Ernesto Madero, 28 Dec.; E. de los Ríos to Jaime Gurza, 20 Nov. 1912; AFM r.20.
607 Hobsbawm, *Primitive Rebels*, pp. 1–29; and the same author's *Bandits*, pp. 17–29.
608 Cf. Blok, 'The Peasant and the Brigand'; Linda Lewin, 'Social Banditry in Brazil', *Past and Present*, LXXXII (1979), pp. 116–46.
609 Vanderwood, *Disorder and Progress*, pp. xv–xviii, 14, 95–6.
610 Hobsbawm, *Bandits*, p. 24.
611 Richard Cobb, *The Police and the People: French Popular Protest 1789–1820* (Oxford, 1972), p. 93. Hobsbawm himself notes that 'Robin Hoodism' has been most evident during periods of social upheaval, such as 'the Revolutionary transformations and wars at the end of the 18th century'; and that social banditry and peasant revolution readily blend together: *Primitive Rebels*, p. 24, *Bandits*, pp. 27–9, 98–109.
612 C. Ceballos to J. Corona, 30 May 1911, AARD 14/13; B. Villaseñor to Madero, 12 June 1911, AFM r.20.
613 Presidente municipal, Totoloapán to Robles Domínguez, 5 June 1911, AARD 15/113.
614 Womack, *Zapata*, pp. 274–5, 279.
615 G. González Berriozabal to Robles Domínguez, 2 June 1911, AARD 15/89.
616 A. Figueroa to Madero, 21 Feb. 1912, Fabela, DHRM, RRM, III, pp. 123–4. Other examples of bona fide Maderistas (like Enrique Añorve) quelling 'banditry' have been given.
617 J. W. Nye, Utd. Sugar Co., 25 Mar.; Alger, Mazatlán, 13 June; Miller, Tampico, 18 Apr.; Bonney, San Luis, 30 Apr.; O. Westlund to W. Devereux, 2 July; Glenn, Guanajuato, 19 Aug. 1912; SD 812.00/3465; 4248; 3714; 3814; 4440; 4713.
618 See vol. 2 ch. 3.
619 Brading, *Haciendas and Ranchos*, pp. 13–18, 205–6.
620 Above, pp. 199–200, 259–61.
621 The Maderista rebels led 200, it was reckoned, as against the bandits' 800–1,000: Glenn, Guanajuato, 2 Apr. 1912, SD 812.00/3553.
622 *Ibid*. The Governor of the state of Mexico likewise distributed arms to officials and prominent persons, 'assuring them that "they would not have to fight against revolutionaries conscious and respectful of the good name of their banner"'; which prompted Madero to ask indignantly who these estimable rebels might be. See Madero to M. Medina Garduno, 4 Oct. 1912, AFM r.12
623 Glenn, Guanajuato, 9, 12 Apr., 25 May 1912, SD 812.00/3648, 3695, 4126; R. Hernández to Governor Lizardi, 4 Dec. 1912, AG 889.
624 Glenn, Guanajuato, 17 Sept.; Magill, Guadalajara, 18 Oct. 1912; SD 812.00/5084; 5369.
625 Glenn, Guanajuato, 2 Apr., 19 Aug., 17 Sept.; Bonney, San Luis, 16 Oct. 1912; SD 812.00/3553, 4713, 5084; 5310. Puruándiro, where a thousand bandits were said to be active in 1912, later became the heartland of José Inés Chávez García's rampaging.
626 F. Galván to Governor Lizardi, 24 Apr. 1912, Fabela, DHRM, RRM, III, pp. 328–9.
627 F. Galván to Lt. Gov., Guanajuato, 13 July 1912, Fabela, DHRM, RRM, IV, p. 27.
628 Glenn, Guanajuato, 12 Apr., 11 May 1912, SD 812.00/3553, 3961.
629 Glenn, Guanajuato, 11 May, 17 Sept. 1912, SD 812.00/3961, 5084.
630 Cf. of the Federal practice of displaying rebel corpses in prominent places, by way of discouragement. Glenn, Guanajuato, 29 Apr. 1912, SD 812.00/3852.

631 F. Galván to Lt. Gov., Guanajuato, 13 July 1912, Fabela, DHRM, RRM, IV, p. 27; Glenn, Guanajuato, 17 Sept. 1912, SD 812.00/5084.

632 See below, pp. vol. 2 ch. 3.

633 Glenn, Guanajuato, 12 Apr.; Schmutz, Aguascalientes, 1 Apr. 1912; SD 812.00/3695, 3540.

634 Vanderwood, *Disorder and Progress*, p. 94.

635 Glenn, Guanajuato, 12 Apr. 1912, SD 812.00/3695.

636 Glenn, Guanajuato, 2 Apr., 19 Aug. 1912, SD 812.00/3553, 4713.

637 Glenn, Guanajuato, 2, 17, 29 Apr. 1912, SD 812.00/3553, 3731, 3852.

638 Glenn, Guanajuato, 17 Apr., 5 May 1912, SD 812.00/3731, 3978.

639 Glenn, Guanajuato, 17 Sept. 1912, SD 812.00/5084.

640 Especially if the miners were thrown out of work, 'there would be a period of riot and anarchy in this town unparalleled'; Glenn, Guanajuato, 12 Apr. 1912, SD 812.00/3695.

641 Glenn, Guanajuato, 2, 12 Apr. 1912, SD 812.00/3553, 3695.

642 Alfonso Ortiz Ortiz, *Episodios de la revolucion en Moroleón* (Mexico, 1976), pp. 14–15.

643 F. Galván to Lt. Gov., Guanajuato, 13 July 1912, Fabela, DHRM, RRM, IV, p. 27.

644 *Ibid.*

645 Gavira, p. 35; cf. Che Guevara, *Reminiscences of the Cuban Revolutionary War*, (Harmondsworth, 1969), p. 63. Distinctions should also be made within the rural population: *serranos* (north and south) were often good shots and expert horsemen; hacienda peons, in contrast, were 'not accustomed to handling firearms' and hence contributed to the prodigal expenditure of ammunition (relative to hits) noted by observers of revolutionary battles: Bonney, San Luis, 16 Oct. 1912, SD 812.00/5310.

646 Glenn, Guanajuato, 13 Dec. 1912, SD 812.00/5729. The cost of repression is considered more generally in the next chapter.

647 AARD legajo 25 *passim*; Gavira, *Actuación*, pp. 35–41.

648 De Szyszlo, *Dix mille kilomètres*, pp. 20–42 is perhaps the best description.

649 Covarrubias, *Mexico South*, pp. 22, 24–9; Foster, *A Primitive Mexican Economy*, pp. 14–15, 109; Katz, 'Labor Conditions', pp. 19–22; Gonzalez Navarro, *Vida social*, p. 244; Bernaldo de Quirós, *Bandolerismo*, pp. 370–5; Falcón, *El Agrarismo*, p. 29; Fowler, *Agrarian Radicalism*, pp. 9–12. As these two latter studies make clear, the heartland of Veracruz agrarismo lay to the north; Acayucán and Los Tuxtlas enjoyed a separate agrarian and revolutionary history.

650 See the reports of Pedro Carbajal and Guadalupe Ochoa, the local rebel leaders, to Robles Domínguez, June 1911; and Colmenares Ríos to same, 13 June; AARD 25/180, 183, 185, 188, 192, 215, 218.

651 Gavira, *Actuación*, pp. 58–60; Buve, 'Peasant movements', p. 133; Burke, Jalacingo, 25 Sept. 1912, SD 812.00/5209 (Burke had married into local society and was well briefed on events).

652 Lawrence, Potrero, 23 Aug.; Pennington, Omealco, 20 Sept.; Burke, Jalacingo, 25 Sept.; Canada, Veracruz, 22 June, 23 Aug. 1912; SD 812.00/4779; 5191; 5209; 4273, 4779; De Szyszlo, *Dix milles kilomètres*, pp. 39, 80, sets the scene.

653 Canada, Veracruz, 22 July 1912, SD 812.00/4499.

654 Canada, Veracruz, 26 Mar., 12, 17 Apr., 23 Aug. 1912, SD 812.00/3387, 3583, 3631, 4779.

655 Harvey, Tezonapa, 2 Aug., Dennis, Tierra Blanca, 15 May, 1912, SD 812.00/4779.

656 Haskell, Salina Cruz, 30 Apr.; Church, Tatahuicapa, 31 May 1912; SD 812.00/3851, 4779.

657 Abrahams, Bella Vista, 20 Sept. 1912, SD 812.00/5191.

658 Church, Tatahuicapa, 31 May 1912, SD 812.00/4779.

659 Canada, Veracruz, 27 Apr. 1912, SD 812.00/3748 (though Consul Canada was somewhat given to jeremiads).

660 Canada, Veracruz, 16, 23 Aug. 1912, SD 812.00/4649, 4779; a lull in summer 1912 was attributed to the defeat of Orozco and the fact that amnestied bandits were, for the moment, 'playing safe and pretend[ing] to be on the side of the government'; Gould, San Gabriel, 22 Sept. 1912, SD 812.00/5191.

661 Dennis, Tierra Blanca, 20 Sept., Gould, San Gabriel, 22 Sept. 1912, SD 812.00/5191.

662 J. Mercader, municipal president, Oluta, to Robles Domínguez, 1 June 1911, AARD 25/185.

663 Harvey, Tezonapa, 2 Aug. 1912, SD 812.00/4779.

664 Haskell, Salina Cruz, 17 Apr. 1912, SD 812.00/3729.

665 Covarrubias, *Mexico South*, p. 29, 30–7.

666 Gould, San Gabriel, 22 Sept., Church, Tatahuicapa, 31 May 1912, SD 812.00/5191, 4779.

667 Sanders, 'Settlement patterns', pp. 68–9.

668 Forman, *Brazilian Peasantry*, pp. 222–5.

669 D. Magaña to Gobernación, 11 July 1911, to Madero 1 Jan. 1912; I. Cortes and J. Valenzuela to Gobernación, 23 Sept. 1911; AG 14.

670 Lespinasse, Frontera, 18 Mar., 8 June, 4 July 1912, 10 Jan. 1913, SD 812.00/3447, 4238, 4354, 5925; anon. 'Situación Política del Estado de Tabasco', Fabela, DHRM, RRM, IV, pp. 273, 275.

671 R. Hernández to Governor Mestre Ghigliazzi, 5 Dec. 1912, AG 889; Lespinasse, Frontera, 13 July 1912, SD 812.00/4417.

672 Lespinasse, Frontera, 8 June 1912, SD 812.00/4239.

673 'Very hostile feeling exists against the Governor who, it is said, has failed to carry out his inaugural pledges relative to the agrarian problems which confront Tabasco'; these pledges included one to 'protect the small farmer against the rapacity of the large landowners': Lespinasse, Frontera, 23 Feb., 23 Aug. 1912, SD 812.00/3233, 4856; see also same, 8 Apr., 16, 18 May, 31 July, 21 Sept., 18 Dec. 1912, 8 Feb. 1913, SD 812.00/3649, 4081, 3944, 4530, 5011, 5783, 6204.

674 Lespinasse, Frontera, 4, 13 July 1912, SD 812.00/4354, 4417.

675 Lespinasse, Frontera, 17, 18 July 1912, SD 812.00/4439, 4502.

676 Lespinasse, Frontera, 2 July (twice), 8 July 1912, SD 812.00/4346, 4378, 4469.

677 Governor Guillén to Madero, 20 July 1912, Fabela, DHRM, RRM, IV, p. 44.

678 Lespinasse, Frontera, 8 July 1912, SD 812.00/4469; anon. report, Fabela, DHRM, RRM, IV, pp. 273–5.

679 Cf. Vanderwood, *Disorder and Progress*; Edward I. Bell, *The Political Shame of Mexico*, New York, 1914, pp. 215–33 (a book which in other respects, e.g., when depicting the political and journalistic scene in Mexico City, can be useful).

680 Bell, *Political Shame*, p. 219.

681 D. Magaña to Madero, 1 Jan. 1912; J. Casasus to Gobernación, 6 Apr. 1912; AG 14.

682 Governor Guillén to Madero, 20 July 1912, Fabela, DHRM, RRM, IV, p. 44; Lespinasse, Frontera, 3 Nov. 1912, SD 812.00/5489. The delinquents in this case were Federals.

683 Governor Mestre Ghigliazzi to Madero, 18 May 1912, Fabela, DHRM, RRM, III, p. 395.

684 Anon. report, Fabela, DHRM, RRM, IV, pp. 274–5.

685 Tillys, *Rebellious Century*, p. 12.

686 Burke, Jalacingo, 25 Sept. 1912, SD 812.00/5209.

687 Gavira, *Actuación*, pp. 60–1; Flandrau, *Viva Mexico!*, pp. 63–7 on the paternalism of the coffee planters.

688 Spillard, El Naranjal, 20 Sept. 1912, SD 812.00/5191; and Seig, Chacaltianguis, 19 Sept., same reference.

689 Spillard, El Naranjal, 20 Sept. 1912, SD 812.00/5191.

690 Lespinasse, Frontera, 18 May 1911, 28 July, 8 Sept. 1912, SD 812.00/2016, 4599, 5019.

691 Cossio Silva in Cosío Villegas, *Vida económica*, pp. 45, 50–1, 53; María y Campos, *Múgica*, pp. 95–101.

692 Múgica to Carvanza, 27 June 1916, in María y Campos, *Múgica*, p. 99; González Navarro, *Vida social*, pp. 210, 222, 224.

693 Madero to Governor Mestre Ghigliazzi, 25 July 1912, AFM r.12; Benjamin, 'Passages', pp. 102–3, although here the supposed severity of the debt peonage practised by American planters is not really borne out by the evidence put forward.

694 Benjamin, 'Passages', pp. 127–30.

695 Young, Progreso, 21 Mar., 18 Apr., 5 June; Gracey, Progreso, 18 Sept.; Germon, Progreso, 20 Nov. 1912; SD 812.00/3444, 3750, 4239; 5111; 5670. *Mexican Year Book* 1914 gives exports from Progreso as 20.9m pesos, July 1911 to June 1912; 29.3m. 1912–13; imports for these years, 8.5m. and 11.2m. respectively.

696 Porsch, Tapachula, 15 Mar., 14 Sept.; Brickwood, Tapachula, 11 Oct. 1912; SD 812.00/3445, 5119; 5371.

697 Juan Lara to Madero, 1 June and reply, 4 July 1911, AFM r.20; J. G. Rebollo to Madero, 12 Oct. 1911; AFM r.21.

698 Flores, 'Vida rural', p. 478.

699 Benjamin, 'Passages', p. 128.

700 *Ibid.*, p. 128, quoting the US consul at Tapachula; and p. 130.

701 Flores, 'Vida rural', pp. 479–80; anon. report, Fabela, DHRM, RRM, IV, pp. 275–6.

702 Warman, *Y venimos a contradecir*, p. 114.

703 Jacobs, 'Aspects', pp. 99–107, and 'Rancheros', pp. 77–81, 88; Beezley, *Insurgent Governor*, pp. 13–16.

704 Cf. Waterbury, 'Non-revolutionary Peasants'.

705 Benjamin, 'Passages', p. 144.

706 Alexis De Tocqueville, *L'Ancien Régime* (Oxford, 1962), p. 18.

707 See vol. 2 ch. 2.

708 Womack, *Zapata*, p. 225.

709 Schmieder, *Tzapotec and Mije*, pp. 13, 23; Nahmad, *Los mixes*, pp. 39–40; Beals, *Mexican Maze*, pp. 15.

710 Kearney, *Winds of Ixtepeji*, pp. 28–9; cf. Le Roy Ladurie, 'The "Event"', pp. 128–9.

711 It was precisely the rapid, ubiquitous growth of the Porfirian state – coming, as it did, after decades of ineffectual central government – which made *serrano* rebellion (an ancient enough phenomenon) so general after 1910, and thus so crucial for the Revolution.

712 Municipal president, Atlacomulca to Robles Domínguez, 1 June 1911, AARD 15/74.

713 E. Martínez to Madero, 14 Aug. 1911, with enclosures, AFM r.19.

714 Lesher, Tapachula, 11 June 1912, SD 812.00/4282.

715 In the past Mazatán had supplied labourers (notably lightermen) for the port of San Benito; with the building of the Panamerican Railway in the 1900s, however, San Benito's trade slumped, and with it the local economy.

716 Benjamin, 'Passages', pp. 41–2.

717 *Ibid.*, p. 77–8.

718 *Ibid.*, p. 109.

719 *Ibid.*, pp. 111–17; L. Castellanos to Robles Domínguez, 31 May 1911, AARD 10/24; Brickwood, Tapachula, 19 Mar., Aug. 1911, SD 812.00/1911, 2346.

720 Benjamin, 'Passages', p. 114.

721 Brickwood, Tapachula, Aug. 1911, SD 812.00/2346; M. Franco to Madero, 12 Oct. 1911, Fabela, DHRM, RRM, II, pp. 152–7; Luis Espinosa, *Rastros de sangre. Historia de la revolución en Chiapas*, Mexico, 1912, pp. 15–23.

722 Benjamin, 'Passages', pp. 117–20; Franco to Madero, 12 Oct. 1911, Fabela, DHRM, RRM, II, pp. 152–7; Casasola, *Historia gráfica*, I, p. 260, which shows that Tuxtleco stories of 'giants and pygmies' were not entirely fictional.